D1087979

MUSIC IN
HARVARD LIBRARIES

MRT-GEN
SS

MUSIC IN
HARVARD LIBRARIES

A Catalogue of Early Printed
Music and Books on Music in
the Houghton Library and the
Eda Kuhn Loeb Music Library

By David A. Wood

Université d'Ottawa
BIBLIOTHÈQUES
LIBRARIES
University of Ottawa

Houghton Library of the Harvard College Library
Harvard University Department of Music
Distributed by Harvard University Press
Cambridge, Massachusetts
1980

MUSIC IN HARVARD LIBRARIES
Michael Ochs, Editor

Funding for the publication of this volume was provided
by the Harvard College Library, the Houghton Library,
and the Harvard University Department of Music

6/1 772.

Copyright © 1980 by the President and Fellows of Harvard College
All rights reserved
Printed in the United States of America
Designed by Mike Fender
Composed in 9 pt. Trump Mediaeval by Progressive Typographers
Printed by Halliday Lithograph Corporation on 70# Mohawk Superfine
Bound by Halliday Lithograph Corporation in Holliston Roxite Linen

Library of Congress Cataloging in Publication Data:

Wood, David A   1935–
    Music in Harvard libraries.

    Includes index.

    1. Music—Bibliography—Union lists. 2. Harvard University. Library.
Houghton Library. 3. Eda Kuhn Loeb Music Library. I. Harvard University. Library. Houghton Library. II. Eda Kuhn Loeb Music Library. III. Title.

ML136.C23H33   016.78   79-26164
ISBN 0-674-59125-9

ML
136
.C23
H33
1980

To my father and mother

CONTENTS

ILLUSTRATIONS

INTRODUCTION

The first appearance of music in the collections of the Harvard College Library can no longer be traced with certainty. A catalogue of holdings published in 1720 lists several collections of hymn texts; Isaac Watts' [*Divine and Moral*] *Songs for Children*, also a collection of texts intended to be sung, is listed in a 1725 supplement. Occasional references to music appear in reports of the Librarian in the latter part of the nineteenth century, and some important acquisitions date from that period. But Harvard's research collection of music is largely a creation of the present century. Its growth has been marked by the interest and generosity of alumni and friends. The personal collections of Evert Jansen Wendell, '1882, Richard Aldrich, '1885, Ralph Isham, '1889, Ernest Lewis Gay, '1897, George Benson Weston, '1897, and Harry Elkins Widener, '07, all donated or bequeathed to Harvard, form a substantial portion of the material described in this catalogue. An equally substantial portion was purchased with income from special funds endowed by Francis Boott, '1831, Walter W. Naumburg, '1889, Elkan Naumburg, William Inglis Morse, and Mrs. Ralph Otis Isham. The remainder has come to Harvard through the generosity of many others by gift, bequest, exchange, or purchase.

The Libraries

This catalogue brings together descriptions of early printed music materials administered by three units of the Harvard College Library: the Houghton Library, the Eda Kuhn Loeb Music Library, and the Harry Elkins Widener Memorial Library. The Widener Library houses very little music material, the bulk of its music collection having been transferred to the Eda Kuhn Loeb Music Library in 1956.

The Music Library's collection of rare materials is housed in the Merritt Room of the Isham Memorial Library. The Isham Library itself, established originally in Memorial Church to house organ music, soon broadened greatly its collecting scope and now serves as a special collections adjunct to the Music Library.

The Houghton Library maintains the rare books and manuscripts belonging to Harvard College. Included among the Houghton items are some now housed separately in the Theatre Collection, several items in the Widener Memorial Room, and some volumes on deposit from other Harvard libraries. Numbered among the latter are fifty-one titles that were transferred from the Isham Memorial Library.

The Catalogue

This catalogue was begun in the early 1960's, under the auspices of the Eda Kuhn Loeb Music Library, with a purely local aim: to provide users of the Music Library's card catalogue with brief entries for the Houghton Library's musical holdings. Soon it became evident that the early music collections of the two libraries were both larger and richer than anyone had realized. At this juncture, the decision was made to prepare a formal printed catalogue that would provide ready access to the contents of both collections to members of the Harvard community and to scholars and researchers at large.

The principal research for the catalogue in its new format occurred between mid-1964 and early 1967, at which time the manuscript was essentially complete and my connection with it entered a lengthy hiatus. During the following three years, the manuscript was subjected to proofreading, but finally work drew to a halt. For nearly eight years, the project lay in abeyance and prospects for its revival seemed remote. In September 1977, however, the manuscript was exhumed and the entire project revived. I was reunited with the manuscript and spent the summer of 1978 bringing the catalogue portion to completion. Typesetting, proofreading, and indexing occupied the greater part of 1979.

The catalogue describes the music and books on music, printed before 1801, which had been added to the Harvard collections by January 1967. It includes scores; sets of parts; part-books; song books with music; monographs, treatises and pamphlets on music; music periodicals; and dance manuals containing music. Excluded are song books and dance manuals without music; songs in single-sheet form; liturgical books, hymnals and psalters; and librettos. Early items in all these categories may be found in Harvard library collections. Descriptions of these materials, of the musical manuscripts, and of the early printed musical works acquired since January 1967 undoubtedly will find their way into future publications.

Bibliographical Method

Because of the circumstances under which this catalogue was compiled, final decisions on bibliographical method did not rest entirely in my hands. Certain practices of informal library cataloguing were admitted, compromising the more rigorous principles of traditional descriptive bibliography that I would have favored. For this reason, I am not prepared to recommend to other bibliographers all elements of the bibliographical method employed in this catalogue.

Arrangement

Items are arranged in one alphabetical sequence by Entry (see below). Within a given entry arrangement is alphabetical by title, omitting extraneous words. Successive editions of a single work (for example, Händel's *Acis and Galatea*) are sub-arranged by date of publication. In a few cases (for example, Abel and Corelli) sub-arrangement is by opus number.

Name Forms

With some exceptions, name forms follow those established by the Library of Congress. *Die Musik in Geschichte und Gegenwart* served as a second authority. Cross references are provided from variant forms of each name, as well as from different parts of compound names.

Entry

Musical compositions are entered by composer, other works by author, and all anonyma by title. Anthologies are entered according to common usage by title, by editor, or by publisher, with appropriate cross-references. As a general rule, anthologies published before 1650 will be found under the publisher's name. *Pastiches* appear under the name of the chief composer or compiler if known, otherwise under the title. For the sake of simplicity, all editions of *The Beggar's Opera* are entered under Pepusch and all editions of *Love in a Village* under Arne.

Title-Page Transcription

Title-pages are transcribed in quasi-facsimile. Details of the transcription process, which was devised to accommodate considerable variety in title-page and type-face design, are enumerated below:

1. All type-faces are transcribed in roman form;
2. If a word is composed entirely of capital letters, only the first letter is capitalized;
3. Literary quotations, advertisements, volume and price statements, Stationer's Company notices, publishers' numbers, and part-book statements are omitted with ellipsis;
4. Devices and decorations, and any mottos associated with them, are omitted without ellipsis;
5. Engravers' signatures on ornaments, borders, or illustrations are omitted without ellipsis;
6. Punctuation is copied exactly, except that ornamental double punctuation is transcribed as single punctuation, and an apostrophe employed as a diacritical accent is transcribed as the appropriate modern accent;
7. Roman capital and lower-case letters *u, v, vv, i,* and *j* are copied as they appear on the title-page;
8. The gothic capital *J* is transcribed in terms of modern usage;
9. All superscript letters are lowered, except the superscript *e* employed as an umlaut;
10. Line endings are designated by a vertical bar.

Date of Publication

The thematic indexes, publishers' catalogues, plate-number lists, and special studies cited in the Bibliography were used to assign conjectural dates of publication. When prints could not be dated by means of these more authoritative sources, dates assigned in the *British Union-Catalogue of Early Music* were accepted.

Format

Format statements for books are based on the principles expounded in Ronald B. McKerrow's *An Introduction to Bibliography for Literary Students.* McKerrow's axioms regarding chain-line direction and watermark placement were used to determine the format of scores, but in some cases overriding consideration was given to size and shape.

Collation

Collations are given in full, and the presence of illustrative matter, plates, and music is noted. Signature collations are given only in the absence of printed page or folio numbers. Misnumbered pages, leaves, or signatures are noted only if the error affects the total collation.

Notes

Supplementary information, provided in notes below the collation statement, includes plate number statements, language statements, comments on significant errors in imprint or collation, and bibliographical references. The colophon is transcribed if it serves as the source of the imprint statement or if it contains important additional information. Publishers' catalogues appearing in the Harvard copies are noted. The Harvard College Library unit responsible for the present administration of each item is indicated.

Illustrations

The dimensions given in the captions refer to the maximum height and width of the printed portion of the page or pages shown.

Bibliography

The bibliography is limited to works drawn upon in the preparation of this volume. The Devriès and Lesure study could not be utilized to the fullest extent because it appeared after the catalogue portion had reached the corrected page proof stage.

Index

The index contains all names appearing on title-pages or in supplementary notes, except names of dedicatees and names of composers and authors when they appear as entries in the catalogue. References are to item numbers.

Acknowledgments

It is a pleasure to record my gratitude to the Houghton Library, the Harvard University Department of Music, and the Harvard College Library for providing the funds to publish this book. Professor Nino Pirrotta, Librarian of the Eda Kuhn Loeb Music Library from 1956 until 1970, was a kind and generous mentor. Professor William H. Bond, Librarian of the Houghton Library, graciously provided me with office space and extended to me the considerable hospitality of his library. Members of the staff of the Houghton Library who were generous with advice and assistance include Carolyn Jakeman, Assistant Librarian for Reference; James E. Walsh, Keeper of Printed Books; Rodney G. Dennis, Curator of Manuscripts; Ruth Mortimer, Cataloguer in the Department of Printing and Graphic Arts; and Joseph McCarthy, Supervisor of the Stacks.

The finished manuscript was typed by Marte Shaw (who also was helpful in her subsequent capacity as Curator of the Houghton Library Reading Room) and Esther Hecht. Most of the typescript was proofread against the original title-pages by Professor Mary Rasmussen of the University of New Hampshire, with the assistance of Esther Hecht and Philip Gambone. John Lynch most capably typed the bibliography and index. Richard Rainville read the galley and page proofs. Susan Hayes of the Harvard University Press gave freely of her expertise in book production.

Professors John M. Ward, Christoph Wolff (Curator of the Isham Memorial Library), and Lowell Lindgren (now of the Massachusetts Institute of Technology) read major portions of the galley proofs and offered valuable suggestions and corrections. At the eleventh hour, Dr. Hans-Joachim Schulze of Leipzig reduced by one the number of more serious errors in the book.

Florence Lynch, Cataloguer in the Eda Kuhn Loeb Music Library, checked the alphabetization and confirmed the locations. Larry G. Mowers, Assistant Librarian of the Music Library and Keeper of the Isham Library, contributed wise and perceptive advice. Dr. Michael Ochs, Librarian of the Music Library and Lecturer on Music, who served as editor of this volume, was a constant source of expert technical and editorial counsel and an indefatigable collaborator.

I am grateful to Merle Boylan, Director of Libraries at the University of Washington, who assigned my reporting station to Cambridge for a period of one month during the final stages of the project, and to Woodley Chapman and Mary Hogan, who generously provided me with living quarters for the summer of 1978. Christoph Wolff, Rodney Dennis, and Michael Ochs have gained my enduring gratitude for their part in bringing about the completion and publication of this catalogue. My friends Woodley and Catherine Weeks Chapman, Masakata Kanazawa, and Larry Mowers were a special source of encouragement and support.

CATALOGUE

ABBREVIATIONS

2°	folio
4°	quarto
8°	octavo
12°	duodecimo
24°	vicesimo-quarto
BN	BIBLIOTHÈQUE NATIONALE, *Catalogue général* (*see* Bibliography for full description)
BMC	BRITISH MUSEUM, *XVth Century Books* (*see* Bibliography)
BMGC	BRITISH MUSEUM, *General Catalogue* (*see* Bibliography)
col(s).	column(s)
comp.	compiler
ded.	dedication
ed.	edition, editor
F.	FALCK, *W. F. Bach* (*see* Bibliography)
facs.	facsimile
fold.	folded
front.	frontispiece
G.	GÉRARD, *Boccherini* (*see* Bibliography)
GW	*Gesamtkatalog der Wiegendrucke* (*see* Bibliography)
H.	HOBOKEN, *Haydn* (*see* Bibliography)
illus.	illustration(s)
incl.	including
intro.	introduction
K.	KÖCHEL, *Verzeichnis* (*see* Bibliography)
ℓ.	leaf, leaves
MGG	*Die Musik in Geschichte und Gegenwart* (*see* Bibliography)
no(s).	number(s)
obl.	oblong
op.	opus
P.	POŠTOLKA, *Koželuh* (*see* Bibliography)
p.	page(s)
pl.	plate(s)
port.	portrait
pref.	preface
pt(s).	part(s)
publ.	publisher
ʳ[superscript]	recto
RISM	*Répertoire international des sources musicales* (*see* Bibliography)
ᵛ[superscript]	verso
vol(s).	volume(s)
W.	WOTQUENNE, *C. P. E. Bach* (*see* Bibliography)

CATALOGUE

A

1 AARON, PIETRO

Toscanello In Mvsica Di Messer | Piero Aron Fiorentino Del Or-|dine Hierosoli-mitano Et | Canonico In Rimini Nvo-|va-mente Stampato | Con Laggivnta | Da Lvi Fatta | Et Con Di-|ligen-|tia | Corretto. | . . . | Con Privilegio. [Venice, 1529]

2° a⁴, A–K⁴, L⁶, M–N⁴, O⁶, illus. (incl. port.), music
Colophon: Stampato in Vinegia per maestro Bernardino & maestro Matheo| de Vitali venitiani el di. v. Iulii mille cin-quecento .xxix.
Hirsch I, no. 4; RISM B VI, 97
HOUGHTON

2 AARON, PIETRO

Toscanello | in Musica di messer Piero Aron | Fiorentino del ordine Hiero|soli-mitano & Canonico | in Rimini. Nuoua|mente Stāpa|to con la | Gionta da lui fatta & con di-|ligentia corretto. | . . . [Venice, 1539]

2° A–I⁴, illus. (incl. port.), music
Colophon: Stampato in Vineggia per Marchio Sessa Nelli anni del | Signore M.D.XXXIX. a di XIX. Marzo.
MortimerI, no. 1; RISM B VI, 97–98
HOUGHTON

3 ABEL, KARL FRIEDRICH

Op. 1

Six | Overtures | in Eight Parts | For | Violins, French-horns, Hoboys, one Tenor | With a Thorough Bass for the | Harpsicord Or Violoncello | Compos'd by | C. F. Abel | Opera Prima | London, Printed for C and S Thompson No. 75 St Pauls Church Yard. | . . . [176–?]

2° 8 pts.: *hautboy primo, hautboy se-condo:* 1 ℓ., 6 p. each; *corno primo, corno secondo:* 1 ℓ., 4 p. each; *violino primo, violino secondo, viola, basso:* 1 ℓ., 12 p. each
RISM A I, no. A 54
HOUGHTON

4 ABEL, KARL FRIEDRICH

Op. 1

Six | Overtures, | Composed and Adapted | For The | Piano Forte | By | C. F. Abel. | London. | Printed for Harrison & Co. No. 18 Paternoster Row. [1798?]

8° Score: 1 ℓ., 5–40 p. (*The Piano-Forte Magazine,* vol. III, no. 8)
Plate nos. 44–45
RISM A I, no. A 57 (op. 1)
MUSIC LIBRARY

5 ABEL, KARL FRIEDRICH

Op. 2

Six | Sonatas | for the | Harpsichord | With Accompaniments for a | Violin or German Flute, | & | Violoncello. | Dedi-cated to the Right Honble., | The Earl of Buckinghamshire. | Composed by | C. F. Abel. | Opera. II. | London Printed and Sold by R. Bremner opposite Somerset | House in the Strand. | . . . [ca. 1765]

2° Score: 1 ℓ., 40 p.
RISM A I, no. A 107
MUSIC LIBRARY

6 ABEL, KARL FRIEDRICH

Op. 3

Six | Sonatas | For | Two Violins, or a German Flute | and Violin, with a Thor-ough Bass | for the | Harpsichord, | Dedi-cated | To the Right Honourable | The Earl of Aschburnham &c. | Composed by

| Charles Frederick Abel. | Opera III | London Printed for the Author and sold at his Lodgings, at the | Dial in Greek Street St. Ann's Soho. [ca. 1765]

2° 3 pts.: *violino primo:* 1 ℓ., 13 p.; *violino secondo, basso:* 1 ℓ., 11 p. each
RISM A I, no. A 109
MUSIC LIBRARY

7 ABEL, KARL FRIEDRICH

Op. 4

Six | Overtures | in Eight Parts | For | Two Violins, Two Hoboys, Two French Horns, one Tenor | with a Thorough Bass for the | Harpsichord Or Violoncello | Dedicated to | His Royal Highness the Duke of York | Composed by | Charles Frederick Abel. | Opera 4th. | London. | Printed and Sold by R: Bremner opposite | Somerset House Strand. | . . . [ca. 1785]

2° 8 pts.: *oboe primo, oboe secondo:* 1 ℓ., 6 p. each; *corno primo, corno secondo:* 1 ℓ., 4 p. each; *violino primo, violino secondo, viola, basso:* 1 ℓ., 13 p. each
RISM A I, no. A 61
HOUGHTON

8 ABEL, KARL FRIEDRICH

Op. 5

Six | Sonates | Pour le | Clavecin | Avec l'accompagnement | D'un Violon. or Flute Traversiere. et d'un Violoncelle. | Tres humblement dediées | A Sa Majeste | Charlotte | Reine de la Grande Bretagne | Composées par | Chas. Fredk. Abel. | Musicien de la Chambre | Sa Majeste la Reine de la | Grande Bretagne | Opera V. | London Printed for the Author and Sold by R. Bremner. | Opposite Somerset house in the Strand. | . . . [ca. 1780]

2° *Score:* 1 ℓ., 25 p.
RISM A I, no. A 120
MUSIC LIBRARY

9 ABEL, KARL FRIEDRICH

Op. 5

Six | Sonates | Pour le | Clavecin | avec l'accompagnement | D'un Violon ou Flute Traversiere et d'un Violoncelle |

Tres humblement dediées | A Sa Majeste | Charlotte | Reine de la Grande Bretagne. | Composées par | Chas. Fredk. Abel. | Musicien de la Chambre | de Sa Majeste la Reine de la | Grande Bretagne. | Oeuvre V. | London. Printed for the Author, and Sold by R: Bremner, in the Strand. | . . . [ca. 1780]

2° 1 pt.: *violino o flauto:* 1 ℓ., 6 p.
RISM A I, no. A 117
HOUGHTON

10 ABEL, KARL FRIEDRICH

Op. 5

Six Sonatas | For The | Piano Forte. | With | An Accompaniment for a Violin. | Composed, | And | Dedicated to the | Queen, | By | Charles Frederick Abel, | Musician to her Majesty. | London: | Printed for Harrison & Co. No. 18, Paternoster Row. [1797?]

8° *Score:* 1 ℓ., 44 p. (*The Piano-Forte Magazine,* vol. I, no. 3)
RISM A I, no. A 122 (op. 5)
MUSIC LIBRARY (2 copies)

11 ABEL, KARL FRIEDRICH

Op. 8

Six | Quartettes | à Deux | Violons, Alto Viola, | et | Violoncello. | Obligato. | par | Charles Frederick Abel. | Opera VIII. | Chez S. Markordt, Marchand de Musique, à la Salle d'Estampes au haut de l'escalier | de la Bourse, á Amsterdam. [ca. 1780?]

2° 4 pts.: *violino primo:* 1 ℓ., 13 p.; *violino secondo:* 1 ℓ., 16 p.; *viola, violoncello:* 1 ℓ., 13 p. each
RISM A I, no. A 94
MUSIC LIBRARY

12 ABEL, KARL FRIEDRICH

Op. 14

Six | Overtures, | in Eight Parts; | With A Thorough Base | for the | Harpsichord; | Composed by | C: F: Abel, | Opera XIV. | London. | Printed for the Author and Sold by R. Bremner. opposite Somerset House in the Strand. | . . . [1778?]

2° 8 pts.: *oboe primo, oboe secondo, corno primo, corno secondo:* 7 p. each; *violino primo, violino secondo, viola, basso:* 1 ℓ., 13 p. each
RISM A I, no. A 75
HOUGHTON

13 ABEL, KARL FRIEDRICH

Op. 15

Six | Quatuors | pour | Deux Violons, Alto, et Violoncello, | obligés | Dediés avec le plus profond Respect | â | Son Altesse Royale, Monseigneur | Le Prince De Prusse | &. &. &. | Composés par | Charles Fréderic Abel | Musicien de la Chambre de Sa Majesté | Le Reine De La Grande Bretagne. | London | Printed for the Author and Sold at his House, | No. 6 Duke Street, Portland Place. | [ca. 1780]

2° 4 pts.: *violino primo:* 1 ℓ., 16 p.; *violino secondo, viola, violoncello:* 1 ℓ., 13 p. each
RISM A I, no. A 102 (op. 15)
HOUGHTON

14 ABEL, KARL FRIEDRICH

Op. 18

Six | Sonates | Pour le | Clavecin ou Piano-Forte, | avec l'accompagnement d'un Violon, | Dediées très respectueusement | á Son Altesse Serenissime Madame | La Duchesse Douairiere de Saxe-Weimar, | et Composées par | Charles Frederic Abel | Musicien de la Chambre de Sa Majesté | La Reine De La Grande Bretagne. | Oeuvre XVIII . . . | Londres | Imprimées Chez S. A. & P. Thompson, | No. 75, St. Pauls Church Yard. [ca. 1785]

2° *Score:* 1 ℓ., 43 p.
RISM, A I, no. A 139
MUSIC LIBRARY

15 ABELL, JOHN

A | Choice Collection | Of | Italian Ayres, | For All Sorts Of | Voices, Violin, or Flute: | Printed in the English Cliff, and Sung to the Nobi-|lity and Gentry in the North of England; and at | both Theatres in London. | By Mr. John Abell. | London: | Printed by William Pearson, in

Red-Cross-Alley in | Jewen-street; and Sold by the Author at his House | in Piccadilly; and at Mr. Whites's Chocalate-House | in St. James's-street, 1703.

2° *Score:* 2 ℓ., 16 p.
RISM A I, no. A 145
HOUGHTON

16 ABELL, JOHN

A | Collction [*sic*] | Of | Songs, | In Several | Languages. | Compos'd by Mr. John Abell. | London: | Printed by William Pearson, in Red-Cross Alley in Jewin-|street, for the Author. 1701.

2° *Score:* 2 ℓ., 24 p.
Day, no. 192, first entry; RISM A I, no. A 143
HOUGHTON

17 ABINGDON, WILLOUGHBY BERTIE, 4TH EARL OF

Twenty-One | Vocal Pieces | For several Voices | with a | Piano Forte | Accompaniment. | Selected from various English Poets. | Also | Seven Sonnets | Extracted from the late | very Ingenious Specimens | of Oriental Poetry, | By I. D. Carlyle. | With a | Frontispiece | of a | Turkish Pauper, | well known in the Metropolis | Of London: | and the | Original Words of his Prayer. | The Gift Of The | Earl of Abingdon | To | Mr. Monzani, | Humbly Dedicated | (with Permission) | To | Lady Viscountess Gage. | [London] Publish'd. Octr 1st. 1797 by Mr. Monzani No. 5 Hamilton Street Piccadilly. . . .

obl. 2° *Score:* 2 ℓ., 31 p.
RISM A I, no. A 150
MUSIC LIBRARY

18 ADGATE, ANDREW

Rudiments | Of | Music. | By Andrew Adgate, P. U. A. | The Fourth Edition. | Philadelphia, | Printed and sold by John McCulloch; and also sold by the Author, at No. 59, North Front-street. | M.DCC.XCI. | . . .

obl. 8° 20 p., 1 ℓ., 24 p., illus., music
The second section, which contains

music for two to four voices, has a separate title-page: Philadelphia Harmony, | Or, | A Collection of Psalm Tunes, Hymns, and Anthems, | Selected by Andrew Adgate. | . . .

HOUGHTON

19 ADLUNG, JAKOB

M. Jacob Adlungs, | Der churfürstl. maynzis. Akademie nützlicher Wissenschaften allhier | ordentl. Mitgliedes, des evangel. Rathsgymnasii ordentl. Lehrers, | wie auch Organistens an der evang. Raths- und Predigerkirche, | Anleitung zu der | musikalischen | Gelahrtheit | theils | vor alle Gelehrte, | so das Band aller Wissenschaften einsehen; | theils | vor die Liebhaber der edlen Tonkunst | überhaupt; | theils und sonderlich | vor die, so das Clavier vorzüglich lieben; | theils | vor die Orgel- und Instrumentmacher. | Mit Kupfern und einer Vorrede | des | Hochedlen und Hochgelahrten Herrn, | Herrn Johann Ernst Bachs, | Sr. hochfürstl. Durchlaucht zu Sachsen-Weimar | und Eisenach würklichen Kapellmeisters. | Erfurt, | druckts und verlegts J. D. Jungnicol, Sen. 1758.

8° 30, 814, [34] p., illus., 8 fold. pl. (music)
Hirsch I, no. 8; RISM B VI, 67
MUSIC LIBRARY

20 ADLUNG, JAKOB

Musica Mechanica | Organoedi. | Das ist: | Gründlicher Unterricht | von | der Struktur, Gebrauch und Erhaltung, &c. | der Orgeln, Clavicymbel, Clavichordien | und | anderer Instrumente, | in so fern | einem Organisten von solchen Sachen etwas zu wissen nöhtig ist. | Vorgestellet von | M. Jakob Adlung, | weil. der Churfürstl. Maynzis. Akademie nützlicher Wissenschaften in Erfurt ordentl. Mitgliede, | des evangel. Rathsgymnasii ordentl. Lehrer, wie auch Organisten an der evang. | Raths- und Predigerkirche daselbst. | Aus | der hinterlassenen Handschrift des seel. Hrn. Verfassers in Ordnung gebracht, | mit einigen Anmerkungen und einer Vorrede versehen, | und zum Drucke befördert |

von | M. Johann Lorenz Albrecht. | kaiserl. gekrönten Dichter, Collegen der vierten Classe am Gymnasio, wie auch Cantor und Musikdirektor | bey der oberstädtischen Hauptkirche, Beatå Mariå Virginis, zu Mühlhausen in Thüringen, | und der hochlöbl. deutschen Gesellschaft zu Altdorf Ehrenmitgliede. | Nebst zwey Tabellen und vielen Figuren. | Berlin, | gedruckt und verlegt von Friedrich Wilhelm Birnstiel, königl. privil. Buchdrucker, | 1768.

4° 2 vols.: *vol. I:* 2 ℓ., 291 p., illus.; *vol. II:* 4 ℓ., XX, 185 [i. e. 187], [14] p., illus., 3 fold. pl., music
Nos. 71, 72 repeated in paging in vol. II
Gregory, p. 8; Hirsch I, no. 9; RISM B VI, 67
MUSIC LIBRARY

21 AGRICOLA, MARTIN

[Musica instru-|metalis deudsch | ynn welcher begrif-|fen ist, wie man | noch dem gesange auff mancherley | Pfeiffen lernen sol, Auch wie auff | die Orgel, Harffen, Lauten, Gei-|gen, vnd allerley Instrument vnd | Seytenspiel, noch der recht-|gegründten Tabelthur | sey abzusetzen. | Mart. Agricola. ⟨Wittenberg, 1529⟩]

8° lvi numb. ℓ., [7] p., illus., music
Colophon: Gedruckt zu Wittemberg | durch Georg. Rhaw. | M. D. XXIX.
Imperfect: title-page lacking; supplied in facsimile
Brown, no. 1529₁; Davidsson II, no. 1; Wolfenbüttel, no. 1010; RISM B VI, 70
HOUGHTON

AIDES, NICOLAS DES *See* Dezède, Nicolas

22 AIGUINO, ILLUMINATO

La Illvminata | De Tvtti I Tvoni Di | Canto Fermo, | Con Alcvni Bellissimi Secreti, | non d'altrui piu scritti, | Composta Per Il Reverendo Padre | Frate Illuminato Aiguino da Bressa, | dell' ordine Seraphico | d'Osseruanza. | Con Priuilegio dell' Illustrissima Signoria di Vene-

tia, | per anni XV. | In Venetia Per Anto-
nio | Gardano, MDLXII.

4° 58 numb. *ℓ.*, [4] p., music
Hirsch I, no. 17; RISM B VI, 74
HOUGHTON

23   AIGUINO, ILLUMINATO

Il Tesoro | Illvminato | Di Tvtti I Tvoni
| Di Canto Figvrato, | Con Alcvni Bellis-
simi Secreti, | non da altre più scritti: |
Nuouamente composto dal Reuerendo
Padre | Frate Illuminato Aijguino Bre-
sciano, | dell'ordine Serafico d'os-
seruanza. | Con Privilegio. | In Venetia,
Appresso Giouanni Varisco. | MDLXXXI.

4° 2 *ℓ.*, 88 numb. *ℓ.*, [8] p., pl. (port.),
music
Hirsch I, no. 18; RISM B VI, 74
HOUGHTON

24   [AIKIN, JOHN]

Essays | On | Song-Writing: | With A
Collection Of Such | English Songs | As
Are Most Eminent For | Poetical Merit. |
The Second Edition, | With Additions
And Corrections. | . . . | Warrington: |
Printed by William Eyres, | For | Joseph
Johnson, No. 72, St. Paul's Church-Yard,
London. | MDCCLXXIV.

8° xix, 286 p.
RISM B VI, 74
HOUGHTON

25

Airs | De Covr, | Et De | Differents |
Avthevrs. | A Paris, | Par Pierre Ballard,
Impri-|meur de la Musique du Roy,
demeu-|rant rüe S. Iean de Beauuais, à
l'en-|seigne du mont Parnasse. | [1615] |
Auec Priuilege de sa | Majesté.

8° 77 numb. *ℓ.*, [4] p.
Imperfect: date erased on title-page;
numbered leaves 36, 39−41 lacking
RISM B I, no. 1615[12]
HOUGHTON

26

II. Livre | D'Airs | De Covr, | Et De |
Differents | Avthevrs. | A Paris, | Par

Pierre Ballard, Impri-|meur de la Mu-
sique du Roy, demeu-|rant rüe S. Iean de
Beauuais, à l'en-|seigne du mont Par-
nasse. | 1617. | Auec Priuilege de sa | Ma-
jesté.

8° 63 numb. *ℓ.*, [2] p.
Imperfect: numbered leaves 50, 51, 59
lacking
RISM B I, no. 1617[9]
HOUGHTON

27

III. Livre | D'Airs | De Covr, | Et De |
Differents | Avthevrs. | A Paris, | Par
Pierre Ballard, Impri-|meur de la Mu-
sique du Roy, demeu-|rant rue S. Iean de
Beauuais, à l'en-|seigne du mont Par-
nasse. | 1619. | Auec Priuilege de sa | Ma-
jesté.

8° 63 numb. *ℓ.*, [2] p.
Imperfect: numbered leaf 48 lacking
RISM B I, no. 1619[10]
HOUGHTON

28

IIII. Livre | D'Airs | De Covr, | Et De |
Differents | Avthevrs. | A Paris, | Par
Pierre Ballard, Impri-|meur de la Mu-
sique du Roy, demeu-|rant rüe S. Iean de
Beauuais, à l'en-|seigne du mont Par-
nasse. | 1621. | Auec Priuilege de sa | Ma-
jesté.

8° 35 numb. *ℓ.*, [2] p.
RISM B I, no. 1621[12]
HOUGHTON

29

V. Livre. | D'Airs | De Covr, | Et De |
Differents | Avthevrs. | A Paris, | Par
Pierre Ballard, Impri-|meur de la Mu-
sique du Roy, demeu-|rant rüe S. Iean de
Beauuais, à l'en-|seigne du mont Par-
nasse. | 1623. | Auec Priuilege de sa | Ma-
jesté.

8° 51 numb. *ℓ.*, [2] p.
Imperfect: numbered leaves 18, 19, 46
lacking
RISM B I, no. 1623[5]
HOUGHTON

30

VI. Livre. | D'Airs | De Covr, | Et De | Differents | Avthevrs. | A Paris, | Par Pierre Ballard, Impri-|meur de la Mu-sique du Roy, demeu-|rant ruë S. Iean de Beauuais, à l'en-|seigne du mont Parnasse. | 1624. | Auec Priuilege de sa | Majesté.

8° 61 numb. ℓ., 2 ℓ.
RISM B I, no. 1624[10]
HOUGHTON

31

VII Livre. | D'Airs | De Covr, | Et De | Differents | Avthevrs. | A Paris, | Par Pierre Ballard, Impri-|meur de la Mu-sique du Roy, demeu-|rant rue S. Iean de Beauuais, à l'en-|seigne du mont Parnasse. | 1626. | Auec Priuilege de sa | Majesté.

8° 56 numb. ℓ., 2ℓ.
RISM B I, no. 1626[11]
HOUGHTON

32

VIII. Livre | D'Airs | De Covr, | Et De | Differents | Avthevrs. | A Paris, | Par Pierre Ballard, Impri-|meur de la Mu-sique du Roy, demeu-|rant ruë S. Iean de Beauuais, à l'en-|seigne du mont Parnasse. | 1628. | Auec Priuilege de sa | Majesté.

8° 51 numb. ℓ., [2] p.
Imperfect: numbered leaves 22, 30, 31 lacking
RISM B I, no. 1628[9]
HOUGHTON

ALAYRAC, NICOLAS D' *See* Dalayrac, Nicolas

33 ALBERTI, GIUSEPPE MATTEO

Alberti's | Concerto's | for three | Vio-lins | an Alto Viola and a | Through Bass | for the | Harpsicord | or | Bass Violin | Compos'd by | Giuseppe Matteo Alberti | Opera Prima | London Printed for I: Walsh Servt: in Ordinary to his Majesty | at the Harp and Hoboy in Catherine street in the Strand | . . . [ca. 1730]

2° 6 pts.: *violino di concertino:* 1 ℓ., 24 p.; *violino primo:* 1 ℓ., 17 p.; *violino se-condo:* 1 ℓ., 15 p.; *alto viola:* 1 ℓ., 11 p.; *organo e violoncello:* 1 ℓ., 12 p. (2 copies)
No. 344 on title-page
RISM A I, no. A 669; Walsh II, no. 16
MUSIC LIBRARY

34 ALBRECHTSBERGER, JOHANN GEORG

Johann Georg Albrechtsbergers, | K. K. Hoforganistens zu Wien | gründliche | Anweisung | zur | Composition; | mit | deutlichen und ausführlichen Exempeln, | zum Selbstunterrichte, | erläutert; | und mit | einem Anhange: | Von der Beschaf-fenheit und Anwendung aller jetzt übli-chen | musikalischen Instrumente. | Leipzig, | bey Johann Gottlob Immanuel Breitkopf, 1790.

4° 2 ℓ., 440 p., music
RISM B VI, 76–77
MUSIC LIBRARY

35 ALCOCK, JOHN, THE ELDER

Harmonia Festi, | or a Collection of | Canons; Cheerful & Serious Glees, & Catches: | for | Four & Five Voices, in Score, | never before Publish'd, | Com-posed by | John Alcock | Doctor in Music, & Senior Vicar Choral of the Ca-thedral at Lichfield. | . . . | Printed for the Author, & Sold by him at Lichfield Mr. Smart, Oxford Street, Mr. Skillern, | No. 17 St. Martins Lane, Charing Cross, Messrs. Thompson's St. Pauls Church Yd. Music Sellers London. | MDCCXCI | . . .

obl. 2° *Score:* 1 ℓ., iv p., 1 ℓ., 59 p.
Alcock's autograph signature (initials) on title-page
RISM A I, no. A 764
MUSIC LIBRARY

36 ALCOCK, JOHN, THE YOUNGER

Six | Canzonets | Or | Glees | in three Parts | Composed By | J: Alcock M. B. | . . . | London: Printed for Longman Lukey and Co. No. 26 Cheapside. [ca. 1770]

obl. 2° *Score:* 1 ℓ., 13 p.
RISM A I, no. A 786
MUSIC LIBRARY

37 [ALEMBERT, JEAN LEROND D']

Élémens | De | Musique, | Theorique Et
Pratique, | Suivant | Les Principes De M.
Rameau. | A Paris, | Chez {David l'aîné,
rue S. Jacques, à la Plume d'Or. | Le Bre-
ton, Imprimeur ordinaire du Roi, au | bas
de la rue de la Harpe. | Durand, rue S. Jac-
ques, à S. Landry, & au Griffon. |
M.DCCLII. | Avec Approbation Et Privi-
lege Du Roi.

8° xvj, 171, [2] p., illus., 10 fold. pl.
(music)
RISM B VI, 77
HOUGHTON

38 [ALEMBERT, JEAN LEROND D']

Élémens | De | Musique, | Théorique Et
Pratique, | Suivant | Les Principes De M.
Rameau. | A Paris, | Chez Charles-An-
toine Jombert, Imprimeur-|Libraire, rue
Dauphine. | A Lyon, | Chez Jean-Marie
Bruyset, Imprimeur-Libraire, | rue Mer-
ciers, au Soleil. | M.DCC.LIX. | Avec Ap-
probation Et Privilege Du Roi.

8° xvj, 3–171, [1] p., 1 ℓ., illus., 10 fold.
pl. (incl. music)
RISM B VI, 77
MUSIC LIBRARY

39 ALEMBERT, JEAN LEROND D'

Élémens | De | Musique | Théorique Et
Pratique, | Suivant | Les Principes De M.
Rameau, | Éclaircis, Développés Et Sim-
plifiés, | Par M. D'Alembert, de
l'Académie Françoise, des | Académies
Royales des Sciences de France, de
Prusse & | d'Angleterre, de l'Académie
royale des Belles-Lettres de | Suede, & de
l'Institut de Bologne. | Nouvelle Édition,
| Revue, corrigée & considérablement
augmentée. | A Lyon, | Chez Jean-
Marie Bruyset, Imprimr. Libraire. |
M.DCC.LXII. | Avec Approbation Et
Privilege Du Roi.

8° 1 ℓ., xxxvj, 236 p., 2 ℓ., illus., 10 pl.
(incl. music)
RISM B VI, 77–78
MUSIC LIBRARY

40 ALEMBERT, JEAN LEROND D'

Élémens | De | Musique | Théorique et
Pratique, | Suivant | Les Principes De M.
Rameau, | Éclaircis, Développés Et Sim-
plifiés, | Par M. D'Alembert, de
l'Académie Françoise, des | Académies
Royales des Sciences de France, de
Prusse & | d'Angleterre, de l'Académie
Royale des Belles-Lettres de | Suede, & de
l'Institut de Bologne. | Nouvelle Édition,
| Revue, corrigée & considérablement
augmentée. | A Lyon, | Chez Jean-
Marie Bruyset, Imprimr. Libraire. |
M.DCC.LXXII. | Avec Approbation Et
Privilege Du Roi.

8° 2 ℓ., xxxvj, 236 p., 2 ℓ., illus., 10
fold. pl. (incl. music)
RISM B VI, 78
MUSIC LIBRARY

41 ALEMBERT, JEAN LEROND D'

Élémens | De | Musique | Théorique Et
Pratique, | Suivant | Les Principes De M.
Rameau, | Éclaircis, Développés Et Sim-
plifiés, | Par M. D'Alembert, de
l'Académie Françoise, des | Académies
Royales des Sciences de France, de
Prusse & | d'Angleterre, de l'Académie
Royale des Belles-Lettres de | Suede, & de
l'Institut de Bologne. | Nouvelle Édition,
| Revue, corrigée & considérablement
augmentée. | A Lyon, | Chez Jean-Marie
Bruyset, Pere & Fils. | M.DCC.LXXIX. |
Avec Approbation Et Privilege Du Roi.

8° 2 ℓ., xxxvj, 236, [4] p., illus., 10 fold.
pl. (incl. music)
Hirsch I, no. 23; RISM B VI, 78
MUSIC LIBRARY

42 ALEMBERT, JEAN LEROND D'

Hrn. d'Alembert, | Mitglieds der
königl. preuss. Academie der Wissen-
schaften, und der königl. Academie | der
Wissenschaften zu Paris, | Systematische
Einleitung | in die | Musicalische Setz-
kunst, | nach | den Lehrsätzen des Herrn
Rameau. | Aus dem Französischen über-
setzt | und mit Anmerkungen vermehret
| von | Friedr. Wilh. Marpurg. | Leipzig,
1757. | bey Joh. Gottlob Jmmanuel Breit-
kopf.

4° 6 ℓ., 136 p., illus., music
Page 119: Anmerkungen des Ueber-
setzers, | über einige Oerter | der vorher-
gehenden d'Alembertischen Einleitung |
in die musicalische Setzkunst.
Hirsch I, no. 21; Wolfenbüttel, no.
1020; RISM B VI, 78
MUSIC LIBRARY

ALESSANDRO, CHARLES GUILLAUME *See*
Alexandre, Charles Guillaume

43 ALEXANDRE, CHARLES
GUILLAUME

Georget | Et | Georgette | Opera Comi-
que | En Un Acte. | Mis En Musique | Par
Mr. Aléxandre | Représenté sur le
Théatre de l'Opera Comique | A La Foire
St. Laurent, | Le 28. Juillet 1761. | . . . |
Gravez par Le Sr. Hue | A Paris | Chez Mr.
Huberty, Rue des deux Ecus, au Pigeon
blanc, | Et aux adresses ordinaires de Mu-
sique, | A Lÿon chez Mrs. Les Freres le
Goux Place des Cordelliés, | A Rouen
chez les Marchand de Musique. | Avec
Privilege Du Roy. [ca. 1766]

2° *Score:* 1 ℓ., 119 p.
On verso of preliminary leaf: Cata-
logue | des Oeuvres de Mr. Huberty . . .
(issued between dates of JohanssonF
facs. 27 and 28)
Imperfect: pages 115–119 lacking;
supplied in positive photostat
RISM A I, no. A 834
MUSIC LIBRARY

44 ALGAROTTI, FRANCESCO, CONTE

Essai | Sur | L'Opéra, | Traduit De L'Ita-
lien | Du Comte Algarotti; | Par M. ✱✱✱, |
A Pise; | & se trouve | A Paris, | Chez
Ruault, Libraire, rue de la Harpe, | près de
la rue Serpente. | MDCCLXXIII.

8° viij, 190 p.
Pages [107]–174: the author's *Énée a
Troye* and *Iphigénie en Aulide*
Pages [iii]–viij: Préface du Traducteur
RISM B VI, 80
HOUGHTON

45 ALGAROTTI, FRANCESCO, CONTE

An Essay On The Opera | Written In
Italian | By Count Algarotti | F. R. S

F. S. A | Etc. | London, Printed For L.
Davis And | C. Reymers. MDCCLXVII.

8° 4 ℓ., 192 p.
Pages 113–186: the author's *Aeneas in
Troy* and *Iphigenia in Aulis*
RISM B VI, 80
HOUGHTON, MUSIC LIBRARY

46 ALGAROTTI, FRANCESCO, CONTE

Saggio | Sopra | L'Opera In Musica. |
. . . [In Venezia | Per Giambatista Pas-
quali. | MDCCLVII. | Con Licenza De'
Superiori.]

12° In his *Opere varie*, vol. II, p. [277]–
364
Pages 307–364: the author's *Enea in
Troia* and *Iphigenie en Aulide*
Caption title; imprint supplied from
title-page
HOUGHTON

47 ALGAROTTI, FRANCESCO, CONTE

Saggio | Sopra | L'Opera | In Musica. |
. . . | Livorno M.DCC.LXIII. | Per Marco
Coltellini In Via Grande. | Con Approva-
zione.

8° 157 p.
Author's name in dedication (page [3])
Pages 89–157: the author's *Enea in
Troia* and *Iphigenie en Aulide*
RISM B VI, 80
HOUGHTON

ALINE, REINE DE GOLCONDE *See* Monsigny, Pierre Alexandre *Aline, reine de
Golconde*

48 ALLACCI, LEONE

Drammatvrgia | Di | Leone Allacci |
Diuisa | in | Sette Indici. | In Roma, Per il
Mascardi. 1666. | Con licenza de' Su-
periori.

12° 12 ℓ., 816 p.
RISM B VI, 81
HOUGHTON

49 ALLACCI, LEONE

Drammaturgia | Di | Lione Allacci | Ac-
cresciuta | E Continuata | Fino All'Anno

MDCCLV. | In Venezia | MDCCLV. | Presso Giambatista Pasquali. | Con Licenza De' Superiori.

> 4° 4 ℓ., 1016 [i. e. 1014] col.
> Numbers 301, 302 omitted
> Columns 837–946 [i. e. 835–944]: Supplemento.
> Two columns to the page
> RISM B VI, 81
> HOUGHTON

ALLCOCK, JOHN *See* Alcock, John

50

Almanach | Général | De Tous Les Spectacles | De Paris Et Des Provinces, | Pour L'Année 1791. | Contenant une notice exacte de tous les Spec-|tacles de la Capitale, depuis l'Opéra jusqu'aux | Cafés les plus célèbres, Les noms des Directeurs, | Acteurs, Musiciens, Employés; la critique im-|partiale de toutes les pièces jouées à Paris en | 1790; le nom des Auteurs et Compositeurs; | l'emplacement et la description des salles; le | prix des places; des anecdotes et des réflexions | relatives à tous les Spectacles en général, et à | chacun en particulier; un tableau philosophique | de l'utilité générale et particulière de chaque | théâtre, de leurs succès relatifs, des obstacles | qui peuvent s'opposer à leurs progrès, &c. et | généralement de tout ce qui contribue aux | progrès de l'art dramatique en France. | Ouvrage absolument nouveau dans ce genre, |nécessaire à tous ceux qui ont des relations avec | les théâtres; curieux pour tous les amateurs, | et utile à tous les étrangers. | Par Une Société De Gens De Lettres. |...| A Paris, | Chez Froullé, Libraire, quai des Augustins. | M.DCC.LXXXXI.

> 12° 314, [6] p.
> Imperfect: pages 169, 170 lacking
> Grand-Carteret, no. 1008
> WIDENER

51 ALSTED, JOHANN HEINRICH

Templvm Mvsicvm: | Or The | Musical Synopsis, | Of | The Learned and Famous | Johannes-Henricus-Alstedius, | Being | A Compendium of the Rudiments | both of the Mathematical and | Practical Part of | Musick: | Of which Subject not any Book is extant in our English | Tongue. | Faithfully translated out of Latin | By John Birchensha. Philomath. | ... | London, Printed by Will. Godbid for Peter Dring at the | Sun in the Poultrey next Dore to the Rose-Tavern. | 1664.

> 8° 7 ℓ., 93 [i. e. 94] p., front., illus., music
> Page 94 misnumbered 93
> Hirsch I, no. 24; RISM B VI, 82–83
> HOUGHTON

52

The | American | Musical Magazine. | Published in Monthly Numbers; | Intended to Contain, | A Great Variety of Approved Music; | Carefully Selected from the works of best American | and Foreign Masters. | ... | New-Haven: | Published & Sold by Amos Doolittle & Daniel Read. [1786–1787]

> 4° *Score: vol. I:* 48, [2] p.
> Twelve undated issues, published from May, 1786 through September, 1787; no more published
> RISM B II, 85
> HOUGHTON

53

The | American Musical Miscellany: | A | Collection | Of The Newest and Most Appoved [*sic*] | Songs, | Set To Music. | ... | Printed At Northampton, Massachusetts. | By Andrew Wright, | For Daniel Wright and Company. | Sold by them, and by S. Butler, in Northampton; by I. Thomas, | Jun. in Worcester; by F. Barker, in Greenfield: and by | the principal booksellers in Boston. 1798.

> 8° 300 p.
> RISM B II, 85
> HOUGHTON (3 copies)

54 AMIOT, JOSEPH MARIE

Mémoire | Sur La Musique | Des Chinois, | Tant Anciens Que Modernes, | Par M. Amiot, Missionnaire A Pekin; |

Avec des Notes, des Observations & une Table des Matieres, par | M. l'Abbé Roussier, Chanoine d'Ecouis, Correspondant de | l'Académie Royale des Inscriptions & Belles-Lettres; | Faisant Partie Du Tome Sixième Des Mémoires Concernant | Les Chinois. | A Paris, | Chez Nyon l'aîné, Libraire, rue du Jardinet, vis-à-vis la rue | Mignon, près de l'Imprimeur du Parlement. | M.DCC.LXXIX. | Avec Approbation, Et Privilege Du Roi.

4° 1 ℓ., 254 p., illus., 30 pl. (1 fold.) on 32 ℓ., music
RISM B VI, 85
MUSIC LIBRARY

55   AMNER, JOHN

Sacred | Hymnes | Of 3. 4. 5 and 6. parts | for Voyces & Vyols. | Newly Composed by | Iohn Amner | Bachelor of Musique, | Master of the Chori-|sters and Organist | of the Cathe-|drall Church | of Ely. | . . . | Printed at London by Edw: Allde, dwelling neere Christ-Church. | Cum Priuilegio Regali. | 1615.

4° 1 pt.: *bassvs:* [A]², B–D⁴, E², illus. (coat of arms)
RISM A I, no. A 946
HOUGHTON

56

The | Amphion | A | Collection of Favourite English Songs | Never before Publish'd | Set to Musick by Several | Eminent Masters. | Printed for and sold by Iohn Simpson | at the Bass Viol & Flute in Sweetings Alley | Opposite the East Door of the Royal Exchange | London | . . . [ca. 1745]

2° Score: 1 ℓ., 12 numb. ℓ.
MUSIC LIBRARY

AMYOT, JOSEPH MARIE   *See* Amiot, Joseph Marie

ANCIENT SONGS FROM THE TIME OF KING HENRY THE THIRD   *See* Ritson, Joseph, comp. *Ancient Songs from the Time of King Henry the Third*

57   ANDRÉ, JOHANN

Lenore. | Von | Gottfried August Bürger. | In Musik gesetzt | von | Johann André. | Zweyte, verbesserte Auflage. | Berlin, | bey Friedrich Maurer. 1782.

4° Score: 1 ℓ., 33 p.
RISM A I, no. A 1064
MUSIC LIBRARY

58   ANDRÉ, YVES MARIE

Essai | Sur | Le Beau, | Par Le P. André J . . . | Avec | Un Discours Préliminaire, | Et des Réfléxions sur le Goût. | Par M. Formey. | A Amsterdam, | Chez J. H. Schneider, Libraire. | M.DCC.LX.

12° 2 ℓ., cxxviij, [4], 199 [i. e. 195] p.
Pages 114–172: Le Beau Musical
Numbers 175–178 omitted in paging
RISM B VI, 86
WIDENER

ANECDOTES OF GEORGE FREDERICK HANDEL   *See* Coxe, William *Anecdotes of George Frederick Handel*

59   ANFOSSI, PASQUALE

L'Inconnue | Persécutée | Comédie-Opèra | en Trois Actes | Dédiée | A Madame La Duchesse | De Polignac | Gouvernante des Enfans de France. | Représentée pour la premiere fois, par l'Academie | Royale de Musique, le vendredi, 21, Sepbre. 1781, et remise au | Théatre le Dimanche, 12. mai, 1782. et le Dimanche, 14. Decbre. 1783. | La Musique | Del Signor Anfossi | . . . | A Paris | Chez {Le Portier du No 86, Rüe de Clery, près la rue Mont-martre. | De Roullede, Md. de Musique, rüe St Honoré près l'Oratoire, | Lawalle l'Ecuyer, Md. de Musique Cour du Commerce Fg. St. Germain, | Houbaut, Md. de Musique Place de la Comedie Italienne, | Et aux adresses ordinaires. | Imprimé par Basset. [1784?]

2° Score: 2 ℓ., 215 p.
RISM A I, no. A 1174
MUSIC LIBRARY

60   ANGLEBERT, JEAN HENRY D'

Pieces De Clavecin | Composées | Par J. Henry D'Anglebert, | Ordinaire De La

Musique De La Chambre Du Roy, | Avec La Maniere De Les Jover. | Diverses Chaconnes, Ouvertures, & autres Airs de Monsier De Lully | mis sur cet Instrument. | Quelques Fugues pour l'Orgue. | Et les Principes de l'Accompagnement. | A Paris, | Chez Christophe Ballard, seul Imprimeur du Roy pour la | Musique, ruë S. Jean de Beauvais, au Mont-Parnasse. | M.DCCIII. | Avec Privilege de Sa Majesté.

obl. 2° *Score:* 1 ℓ., b–f, 128 p., pl. (port.)
Pages 123–128: Principes de l'accompagnement
RISM A I, no. A 1223
HOUGHTON

ANICAN, FRANÇOIS ANDRÉ D' *See* Philidor, François André Danican, known as

ANTHOLOGIE FRANÇOISE, OU CHANSONS CHOISIES *See* Monnet, Jean, comp. *Anthologie françoise, ou Chansons choisies*

61 ANTONIOTTO, GIORGIO

L'Arte Armonica | Or | A Treatise on the Composition of | Musick, | In Three Books; | With an Introduction, on the History, and | Progress of Musick, from it's beginning to this Time, | Written in Italian by | Giorgio Antoniotto, | And | Translated into English. | . . . | London; | Printed by John Johnson in Cheapside. | 1760.

2° 2 vols.: *vol. I:* 4 ℓ., 109 p.; *vol. II:* 1 ℓ., 62 pl. on 31 ℓ. (incl. music)
Imperfect: title-page lacking in vol. II
Hirsch I, no. 29; RISM B VI, 91
MUSIC LIBRARY

APLIGNY, LE PILEUR D' *See* Le Pileur D'Apligny

APOLOGIE DE LA MUSIQUE ET DES MUSICIENS FRANÇOIS *See* Bonneval, René de *Apologie de la musique et des musiciens françois*

APOLOGIE DU GOÛT FRANÇOIS *See* Caux de Cappeval, N. de *Apologie du goût françois*

AQUIN, LOUIS CLAUDE D' *See* Daquin, Louis Claude

ARBEAU, THOINOT *See* Tabourot, Jehan

62 ARCADELT, JACOB

. . . | Chansons A Troys | Parties De M. Iaqves | Arcadet. | nouuellement Imprimé | en troys volumes. | A Paris. | 1573 | Par Adrian le Roy, & Robert Ballard. | Imprimeurs du Roy. | Auec priuilege de sa magesté pour dix ans.

obl. 8° 1 pt.: *svperivs:* 23 numb. ℓ.
Imperfect: numbered leaves 20, 21 lacking
LesureL, no. 169
HOUGHTON

63 ARISTOXENUS

Aristoxeni | Mvsici Antiqviss. | Harmonicorvm Elementorvm | Libri III. | Cl. Ptolemaei Harmonicorum, seu de Musica lib. III. | Aristotelis de obiecto Auditus fragmentum | ex Porphyrij commentarijs. | Omnia nunc primum latine conscripta & edita | ab Ant. Gogauino Grauiensi. | Cvm Privilegiis. | Venetijs, Apud Vincentium Valgrisium | MDLXII.

4° 165, [1] p., illus.
Davidsson II, no. 4; Hirsch I, no. 32; RISM B VI, 95; Wolfenbüttel, no. 1023
HOUGHTON

ARISTOXENUS JUNIOR, PSEUD. *See* Mattheson, Johann

64 [ARNAUD, FRANÇOIS]

Lettre | Sur | La Musique, | A Monsieur Le Comte | De Caylus, | Académicien Honoraire de l'Académie | Royale des Inscriptions & Belles-Let-|tres, & de celle de Peinture. | [Paris] M.DCC.LIV.

8° 1 ℓ., 36 p.
RISM B VI, 96
HOUGHTON

65 ARNE, MICHAEL

Cymon | A | Dramatic Romance | Perform'd at the | Theatre Royal in Drury

Lane | Compos'd by | Michael Arne . . . | London Printed by Longman and Broderip No. 26 Cheapside and No. 13 Hay Market | . . . [ca. 1785]

> obl. 2° *Vocal score:* 1 ℓ., 74 p.
> Page II [i. e. 1]: Musical Publications | Printed and sold by Longman & Broderip . . .
> RISM A I, no. A 1439
> MUSIC LIBRARY

66 ARNE, MICHAEL

.Cymon, | A | Dramatic Romance, | As Perform'd At The | Theatres Royal | Drury Lane | And | Covent Garden, | Composed By | Mr. M. Arne. | London. | Printed for Harrison & Co. No. 18, Paternoster Row. [1798?]

> 8° *Vocal score:* 1 ℓ., 5–94 p. (*The Piano-Forte Magazine,* vol. III, no. 7)
> Plate nos. 40–43
> RISM A I, no. A 1441
> MUSIC LIBRARY

67 ARNE, THOMAS AUGUSTINE

The | Overture, Songs &c. | in the Opera of | Achilles In Petticoats | as Performed at the | Theatre Royal in Covent Garden | Composed by Dr. Arne | . . . | London Printed for and Sold by Welcker in Gerrard Street St. Ann's Soho | . . . [1774]

> obl. 2° *Score:* 1 ℓ., 43 p.
> RISM A I, no. A 1576
> HOUGHTON

68 ARNE, THOMAS AUGUSTINE

The | Masque | Of | Alfred | Compos'd By | Mr: Arne. | London. Printed for I. Walsh in Catharine Street in the Strand. | . . . [1757]

> 2° *Score:* 1 ℓ., [1], 86 p.
> RISM A I, no. A 1578; Walsh II, no. 66
> MUSIC LIBRARY

69 ARNE, THOMAS AUGUSTINE

Alfred; | A Masque. | As it is performed at the | Theatres-Royal in Drury-Lane and Covent-Garden. | Composed by | Dr. Arne. | For the | Voice, Harpsichord, And

Violin. | London: | Printed for Harrison & Co. No. 18, Paternoster-Row. [ca. 1785]

> obl. 2° *Vocal score:* 44 p.
> Plate nos. 67–69, which are those of *The New Musical Magazine*
> RISM A I, no. A 1581
> MUSIC LIBRARY

70 [ARNE, THOMAS AUGUSTINE]

The | Airs | with all the Symphonies | in the Opera of | Artaxerxes | Correctly Transpos'd for the | German Flute Violin & Guittar | London | Printed for J: Johnson opposite Bow Church Cheapside . . . | [176–?]

> obl. 8° 1 ℓ., 36 p.
> RISM A I, no. A 1626
> MUSIC LIBRARY

71 ARNE, THOMAS AUGUSTINE

Artaxerxes, | A | Serious Opera. | As it is performed at the | Theatres Royal | Covent-Garden and Drury-Lane. | Composed by | Dr. Arne. | London: | Printed for the Proprietors & Sold by Harrison and Co. | No. 18, Paternoster Row. [1797?]

> 8° *Vocal score:* 1 ℓ., 5–93 p. (*The Piano-Forte Magazine,* vol. II, no. 9)
> RISM A I, no. A 1620
> MUSIC LIBRARY

ARNE, THOMAS AUGUSTINE The Beggar's Opera *See* Pepusch, John Christopher *The Beggar's Opera*

72 ARNE, THOMAS AUGUSTINE

The | Songs and Duetto, | In The | Blind Beggar of Bethnal Green; | As perform'd by Mr. Lowe, and Mrs. Clive, | at the Theatre-Royal, in Drury-Lane. | With The | Favourite Songs, Sung by Mr. Lowe, | In | The Merchant of Venice, | At the said Theatre. | To which will be added, | A Collection of New Songs and Ballads, | The Words carefully selected from the Best Poets. | Compos'd By | Thomas Augustine Arne. | N. B. All the Songs and Ballads, which | are not in proper Keys for the German Flute, are tran-|spos'd, with the Bass to them, at the End of the Book. | London: | Printed by William Smith, at the Musick Shop, in Middle-Row, near Holbourn-|Bars; and sold by the Author, at his House, (No. 17.) in Craven-Build-ings, | near Drury-Lane. | . . . [ca. 1742]

2° *Score:* 1 ℓ., 28 p.
RISM A I, no. A 2000
MUSIC LIBRARY

73   ARNE, THOMAS AUGUSTINE

Britannia | A | Masque | as it is Per-form'd at the | Theatre-Royal | In | Drury-Lane. | Compos'd by | Mr. Arne. | London. Printed for I. Walsh, in Catharine Street in the Strand. | . . . [1755]

2° *Short score:* 1 ℓ., 23 p.
RISM A I, no. A 1744; Walsh II, no. 69
MUSIC LIBRARY

74   ARNE, THOMAS AUGUSTINE

The | Musick | In The | Masque | Of | Comus. | Written by Milton. | As it is perform'd at the Theatre-Royal in Drury-Lane. | Composed by | Mr. Arne. | Opera Prima. | London Printed for & sold by J. Simpson in Sweetings Alley Royal Ex-change. | . . . [ca. 1750]

2° *Score:* 1 ℓ., 47 p.
RISM A I, no. A 1746
MUSIC LIBRARY

75   ARNE, THOMAS AUGUSTINE

Comus; | A Masque. | As it is per-formed at the | Theatres Royal in Drury Lane and Covent Garden. | Composed by | Dr. Arne, | for the | Voice, Harpsichord, And Violin. | London: | Printed for Harri-son & Co. No. 18, Paternoster Row. [ca. 1785]

obl. 2° *Vocal score:* 18 p.
RISM A I, no. A 1749
MUSIC LIBRARY

76   ARNE, THOMAS AUGUSTINE

Comus; | A Masque. | As it is per-formed at the | Theatres Royal | Drury Lane | And | Covent Garden. | Composed By | Dr. Arne. | London: | Printed for Har-rison & Co. No. 18. Paternoster Row. [1797?]

8° *Vocal score:* 1 ℓ., 5–43, [1] p. (*The Piano-Forte Magazine,* vol. III, no. 2)
RISM A I, no. A 1750
MUSIC LIBRARY

77   ARNE, THOMAS AUGUSTINE

Cymon And Iphigenia | A Cantata | Set by Dr. Arne and Sung by Mr. Lowe at Vauxhall Gardens. [London, 177–]

2° *Vocal score:* 4 p.
Imperfect: title-page lacking; caption title
MUSIC LIBRARY

78   [ARNE, THOMAS AUGUSTINE]

The | Airs with all the Symphonies | With the Compleat Overture in the | Comic Opera | of | Love in a Village | Cor-rectly Transposed for the | German-Flute, Hautboy or Violin | . . . | London | Printed for J. Johnson at the Harp and Crown opposite Bow Church Cheapside [17—]

obl. 8° 1 ℓ., [2]–37 p.
MUSIC LIBRARY

79   [ARNE, THOMAS AUGUSTINE]

Love In A Village. | A Comic Opera | As it is Perform'd at the Theatre Royal in | Covent-Garden. | The Musick by |

Handel	Howard	Geminiani	Paradies
Boyce	Baildon	Galuppi	Agus
Arne	Festing	Giardini	Abos

For the Harpsicord, Voice, German Flute, or Violin. | London. Printed for I. Walsh in Catharine Street in the Strand. | . . . [1762?]

obl. 2° *Vocal score:* 2 ℓ., 62 p.
RISM A I, no. A 1857; Walsh II, no. 969 (variant paging)
MUSIC LIBRARY

80   [ARNE, THOMAS AUGUSTINE]

Love In A Village. | A Comic Opera | As it is Perform'd at the | Theatre Royal | in | Covent Garden. | The Music by |

Handel	Baildon	Giardini
Boyce	Festing	Paradies
Arne	Geminiani	Agus
Howard	Galuppi	Abos

For the | Harpsichord, Voice, | German
Flute, | Violin, or Guittar | London,
Printed for J. Longman & Co. at the Harp
& Crown No. 26 Cheapside . . . [ca.
1769]

2° *Vocal score:* III, 2–50 p.
Page III: Musical Publications |
Printed and Sold by Longman & Bro-
derip . . .
RISM A I, no. A 1859
MUSIC LIBRARY

81   [ARNE, THOMAS AUGUSTINE]

Love in a Village, | A | Comic Opera, |
as it is performed at the | Theatre Royal
Covent Garden; | the Music by |

Abel,	Carey,	Handel,
Agus,	Festing,	Dr. Howard,
Dr. Arne,	Galuppi,	Oswald,
Baildon,	Geminiani,	Paradies,
Dr. Boyce,	Giardini,	Weldon &c.

for the | Harpsichord, . . . | Voice, Ger-
man Flute or Guitar | London | Printed by
Longman and Broderip No. 26 Cheapside
and No. 13 Hay Market. | Manufacturers
of Musical Instruments and Music Sellers to Their Majesties, the Prince of
Wales, and all the Royal Family. [ca.
1783]

obl. 2° *Vocal score:* 2 ℓ., 3–62 p.
RISM A I, no. A 1860; RISM B II, 226
HOUGHTON

82   [ARNE, THOMAS AUGUSTINE]

Love in a Village, | A | Comick Opera. |
As Performed at the | Theatres-Royal, |
Covent Garden, And Drury Lane. | The
Musick by |

Handel,	Baildon,	Giardini,
Boyce,	Festing,	Paradies,
Arne,	Geminiani,	Agus,
Howard,	Galuppi,	Abos, &c.

for the | Piano Forte, | Voice, German
Flute or Guitar. | London: | Printed for
Harrison & Co. No, 18, Paternoster Row.
[1797?]

8° *Vocal score:* 82 p. (*The Piano-Forte
Magazine,* vol. I [no. 9])
RISM B II, 227
MUSIC LIBRARY

83   ARNE, THOMAS AUGUSTINE

Lyric Harmony | Consisting Of | Eight-
een entire new Ballads | With | Colin and
Phaebe, in Score. | As perform'd at Vaux
Hall Gardens | by | Mrs: Arne and Mr:
Lowe. | Compos'd By | Thomas Augus-
tine Arne: | Opera Quarta | . . . | London
Printed for and sold by J. Simpson at the
Bass Viol and | Flute in Sweetings Alley
opposite the East Door of the Royal Ex-
change | . . . [1748]

2° *Score:* 1 ℓ., 31 p.
Privilege on verso of title-page
RISM A I, no. A 1992
HOUGHTON (2 copies, 2d imperfect)

—another copy
Verso of title-page blank; page 24 im-
posed upside down
HOUGHTON

84   ARNE, THOMAS AUGUSTINE

Lyric Harmony | Consisting Of | Eight-
een entire new Ballads | With | Colin and
Phaebe, in Score. | As perform'd at Vaux
Hall Gardens | by | Mrs: Arne and Mr:
Lowe. | Compos'd By | Thomas Augus-
tine Arne: | Opera Quarta | . . . | London.
Printed for I. Walsh in Catharine Street
Strand. [ca. 1764]

2° *Score:* 1 ℓ., 31 [i.e. 30] p.
John Simpson's name erased from im-
print and John Walsh's superimposed
Number 29 omitted in paging
HOUGHTON

85   ARNE, THOMAS AUGUSTINE

An | Ode | Upon dedicating a Building
to | Shakespeare | which was Erected by
the Subscription | of the | Noblemen &
Gentlemen | in the Neighbourhood of
Stratford upon Avon | The Music Com-
posed by | Dr. Arne | London, Printed &
Sold by John Johnston, at No 11, York
Street, Covent Garden . . . [1769?]

obl. 2° *Vocal score:* 1 ℓ., 27 p.
RISM A I, no. A 1888
MUSIC LIBRARY

86   ARNE, THOMAS AUGUSTINE

Thomas and Sally | A | Musical Enter-
tainment | Set for a | German Flute, | Vio-

lin, or Guitar. | Compos'd by | Dr. Arne |
. . . | London Printed for J. Johnson oppo-
site Bow Church Cheapside [176–?]

obl. 8° 17 p.
RISM A I, no. A 1928
MUSIC LIBRARY

87 ARNE, THOMAS AUGUSTINE

Thomas and Sally | or | The Sailor's Re-
turn, | A Dramatic Pastoral. | With the
Overture in Score, Songs, | Dialogues
Duettos and Dance-|-tunes, as perform'd
at the Theatre | Royal in Covent Garden |
By | Mr. Beard and Miss Brent, | Mr. Mat-
tocks, Mrs. Vernon, | and Chorus. | The
Music compos'd by | Doctr. Arne | Lon-
don. | Printed for I. Walsh in Catharine
Street in the Strand. | . . . [1765]

2° *Score:* 1 ℓ., 51 p.
RISM A I, no. A 1925; Walsh II, no. 88
MUSIC LIBRARY

88 ARNE, THOMAS AUGUSTINE

Thomas and Sally. | A Dramatic Pas-
toral | As Perform'd at the Theatre Royal
in Covent Garden | by |

Mr. Beard   Miss Brent and
Mr. Mattocks   Miss Poitier.

Compos'd by Dr: Arne. | For the Harpsi-
cord, Voice, German Flute, or Violin. |
. . . | London. Printed for I. Walsh in
Catharine Street in the Strand. |
. . . [1765]

obl. 2° *Vocal score:* 1 ℓ., 17 p.
RISM A I, no. A 1926; Walsh II, no. 89
MUSIC LIBRARY

89 ARNE, THOMAS AUGUSTINE

Vocal Melody. | Book II [i.e. I]. | An En-
tire New | Collection of | English Songs |
and a | Cantata | Compos'd by | Mr. Arne.
| Sung by Mr. Beard, Mr. Lowe, and Miss
Falkner, | at Vaux-Hall, Ranelagh, and
Marybon-Gardens. | London. Printed for
I. Walsh in Catharine Street in the
Strand. | . . . [1749]

2° *Score:* 1 ℓ., 20 p.
RISM A I, no. A 2008; Walsh II, no. 91
HOUGHTON

90 ARNE, THOMAS AUGUSTINE

Vocal Melody | Book III. | A Favourite
Collection of | Songs and Dialogues |
Sung at Marybon-Gardens | by Master
Arne and Miss Falkner. | and at Vaux-
Hall Gardens | by Miss Stevenson and
Mr. Lowe. | Compos'd By | Mr. Arne. |
London. Printed for I. Walsh, in Cath-
arine Street, in the Strand. | . . . [1751]

2° *Score:* 1 ℓ., 21 p.
RISM A I, no. A 2008; Walsh II, no. 93
HOUGHTON

ARNOBAT, CHARLES PIERRE COSTE D'
See Coste d'Arnobat, Charles Pierre

91 [ARNOLD, JOHN, COMP.]

. . . | Essex Harmony, | Being a Choice
| Collection | of the most Celebrated |
Songs, Catches, Canons, | Epigrams,
Canzonets, and Glees, | For | Two, Three,
Four, Five, and Nine Voices, | From the
Works of the | Most Eminent Masters. |
. . . | London. | Printed & Sold at Bland &
Wellers, Music Warehouse, 23, Oxford
Strt. [ca. 1795]

8° *Score:* 2 vols.: *vol. I:* 1 ℓ., 108, [2] p.;
vol. II: 1 ℓ., 110 p.
RISM A I, no. A 2190
MUSIC LIBRARY

92 ARNOLD, SAMUEL

The | Agreeable Surprize. | A | Comick
Opera. | In | Two Acts. | As Performed at |
The | Theatre Royal | In the | Hay-Mar-
ket. | Composed by | Dr. Arnold. |
London: | Printed for Harrison & Co. No,
78, Fleet Street. | . . . [1798?]

8° *Vocal score:* 40 p. (*The Piano-Forte
Magazine,* vol. I [no. 1])
RISM A I, no. A 2195
MUSIC LIBRARY

93 ARNOLD, SAMUEL

The | Castle of Andalusia. | A | Comic
Opera, | as performed at the Theatre
Royal, | Covent Garden. | Composed By, |
Dr Arnold | London: | Printed for Harri-

son, Cluse, & Co. No. 78, Fleet Street. [1799?]

8° *Vocal score:* 93 p. *(The Piano-Forte Magazine,* vol. VII, no. 10)
Plate nos. 108–112
RISM A I, no. A 2222
MUSIC LIBRARY

94   ARNOLD, SAMUEL

The Children in the Wood | A Comic Opera In Two Acts | for the | Piano-Forte, Harpsichord, Violin &c. | as Performed at the | Theatre Royal Haymarket, | the Music Composed by |

Op: 35.   Dr. Arnold.   Pr: 8s.

Organist & Composer to His Majesty. | London: | Printed by Longman & Broderip, No. 26, Cheapside & No. 13, Haymarket. | . . . [1793?]

obl. 2° *Vocal score:* 1 ℓ., 30 p.
RISM A I, no. A 2228
MUSIC LIBRARY

95   ARNOLD, SAMUEL

The | Overture, Songs, Duet, | Choruses, Comic-Tunes & Glee, | in the Speaking Pantomime of | Harlequin Teague, | or the | Giant's Causeway, | as Performed at the | Theatre Royal in the Hay Market | Composed by | Dr. Arnold. | Opera XIX. | . . . | London | Printed for S A & P. Thompson No. 75, St. Pauls Church Yard. [1782?]

2° *Vocal score:* 1 ℓ., 43 p.
RISM A I, no. A 2256
MUSIC LIBRARY

96   ARNOLD, SAMUEL

Inkle and Yarico | A Comick Opera | As Perform'd at the Theatre Royal in the Hay Market | The Words by George Colman Esqr. Junr. | The Musick Composed by | Dr. Arnold | Organist & Composer to his Majesty | Adapted For The Voice, Harpsichord, Piano Forte &c. | Opera XXXth. . . . | London Printed & Sold by Longman & Broderip, No. 26 Cheapside, & No. 13 Hay Market. [1787?]

obl. 2° *Vocal score:* 1 ℓ., 45 p.
RISM A I, no. A 2261
MUSIC LIBRARY

97   [ARNOLD, SAMUEL]

The | Maid Of The Mill | a | Comic Opera | Adapted for the | German-Flute or Hautboy | London. | Printed for R: Bremner, opposite Somerset House in the Strand. | . . . [ca. 1765]

obl. 8° 1 ℓ., 30 p.
MUSIC LIBRARY

98   [ARNOLD, SAMUEL]

The | Maid Of The Mill: | A | Comic Opera; | as performed at the | Theatre Royal, | Covent Garden. | London: | Printed for Harrison, Cluse, & Co. No. 78, Fleet Street. [1798?]

8° *Vocal score:* 99 p. *(The Piano-Forte Magazine,* vol. VI, no. 1)
Plate nos. 80–83
RISM A I, no. A 2288
MUSIC LIBRARY

99   ARNOLD, SAMUEL

Peeping Tom of Coventry; | A Comic Opera. | Now performing, with universal Applause, | At The | Theatre Royal in the Haymarket. | Composed by | Dr. Arnold, | Organist & Composer to his Majesty. | For The | Voice, Harpsichord, And Violin. | (Opera XXV.) | London: | Published for the Author, by Harrison & Co. No. 18, Paternoster Row. [1784?]

obl. 2° *Short score:* 1 ℓ., 40 p.
MUSIC LIBRARY

100   ARNOLD, SAMUEL

Peeping Tom | Of | Coventry, | A | Comick Opera | In | Two Acts. | As Performed at | The | Theatre Royal | In the | Hay Market. | Composed by | Dr. Arnold. | London | Printed for Harrison & Co. No. 18. Paternoster Row. | . . . [1797?]

8° *Vocal score:* 40 p., 1 ℓ. *(The Piano-Forte Magazine,* vol. II, no. 3)
MUSIC LIBRARY

101   ARNOLD, SAMUEL

The | Shipwreck | a Comic Opera, in two Acts, | as performed with universal applause | at the | Theatre Royal, Drury Lane | written by S. Arnold Junr. | the Music Composed by | Dr. Arnold, | Organist & Composer to His Majesty. | Op. 40. . . . | London, Printed by Longman & Broderip, No. 26 Cheapside & No. 13 Haymarket [1796?]

 obl. 2° *Short score:* 1 ℓ., 56 p.
 RISM A I, no. A 2327
 MUSIC LIBRARY

102   ARNOLD, SAMUEL

The | Son In Law | a favorite Comic Opera, in two Acts | as it is Performed at the | Theatre Royal in the Hay Market | the Music Composed by | Dr. Arnold | for the Voice & Harpsichord, or Violin. | Op. 14 . . . | London | Printed and Sold by J. Preston at his Music Warehouse No. 97 Strand. [after 1778]

 obl. 2° *Short score:* 1 ℓ., 30 p.
 RISM A I, no. A 2344
 MUSIC LIBRARY

103   ARNOLD, SAMUEL

The | Son In Law. | A | Comic Opera, | As Performed At The | Theatre Royal | In The | Haymarket. | Composed By, | Dr. Arnold. | London: | Printed for Harrison, Cluse, & Co. No, 78 Fleet Street. [1799?]

 8° *Vocal score:* 40 p., 1 ℓ. (*The Piano-Forte Magazine,* vol. VII, no. 9)
 Plate nos. 106–107
 RISM A I, no. A 2345
 MUSIC LIBRARY

104   ARNOLD, SAMUEL

A Collection of the | Favourite Songs | Sung at Vaux Hall | by Mrs. Pinto, Mrs. Weichsell and | Mr. Vernon | Composed by | Samuel Arnold. | London. Printed by Welcker in Gerrard Street, St. Ann's. Soho. | . . . [1767?]

 2° *Score:* 1 ℓ., 39 p.
 RISM A I, no. A 2411
 HOUGHTON

105   ARNOLD, SAMUEL

The | Spanish Barber, | A Comic Opera. | As Performed At The | Theatre Royal, |

In The | Haymarket. | Composed By, | Dr. Arnold. | London: | Printed for Harrison, Cluse, & Co. No. 78, Fleet Street. [1799?]

 8° *Vocal score:* 43 p. (*The Piano-Forte Magazine,* vol. VIII, no. 5)
 Plate nos. 122–123
 RISM A I, no. A 2353
 MUSIC LIBRARY

106   ARNOLD, SAMUEL

Summer Amusement | or an | Adventure At Margate, | A Comic Opera | as Performed at the | Theatre Royal In The Hay-Market, | The Music by | Dr. Arne, Giordani, Dibdin, | and | Dr. Arnold. | for the | Voice, Harpsichord, or Violin | . . . | London: Printed for S. A. & P. Thompson No: 75 St. Pauls Church Yard. [1779?]

 obl. 2° *Short score:* 1 ℓ., 41 p.
 RISM A I, no. A 1908
 MUSIC LIBRARY

107   ARNOLD, SAMUEL

The | Surrender Of Calais, | as performed with the utmost applause, | at the | Theatre Royal Haymarket, | written by | George Colman Esqr Junr. | the Music by | Dr. Arnold. | Organist & Composer to His Majesty. | Op. XXXIII. . . . | London | Printed & Sold by Preston & Son, at their Wholesale Warehouses, | No. 97 Strand. [1791?]

 obl. 2° *Short score:* 1 ℓ., 41 p.
 RISM A I, no. A 2372
 MUSIC LIBRARY

ARON, PIETRO   *See* Aaron, Pietro

ARSINOE, QUEEN OF CYPRUS   *See* Clayton, Thomas *Arsinoe*

108   ARTEAGA, ESTEBAN

Stephan Arteaga's | Mitglieds der Akademie der Wissenschaften und Künste | zu Padua | Geschichte | der italiänischen Oper | von | ihrem ersten Ursprung an bis auf gegen-|wärtige Zeiten. | . . . | Aus dem Italiänischen übersetzt und | mit Anmerkungen begleitet | von | Johann Nicolaus Forkel | Doctor der Philosophie und Musikdirector zu | Göttingen. | Leipzig | im Schwickertschen Verlage. 1789.

8° 2 vols.: *vol. I:* X, [2], 344 p., fold. pl., music; *vol. II:* VI, [3]–532 p.
Hirsch I, Historischer Anhang, no. 4; Wolfenbüttel, no. 1025; RISM B VI, 99
MUSIC LIBRARY

109 ARTEAGA, ESTEBAN

Le Rivoluzioni | Del | Teatro Musicale | Italiano | Dalla Sua Origine Fino Al Presente | Opera | Di Stefano Arteaga | Socio Dell'Accademia Delle Scienze, Arti, | E Belle Lettere Di Padova. | Seconda Edizione | Accresciuta, variata, e corretta dall'Autore | . . . | In Venezia MDCCLXXXV. | Nella Stamperia di Carlo Palese | Con Pubblica Approvazione.

8° 3 vols.: *vol. I:* xlii, 361, [1] p., music; *vol. II:* 334 p., 6 pl. on 3 *ℓ.* (music); *vol. III:* 394 p.
Hirsch I, Historischer Anhang, no. 3; RISM B VI, 98–99
MUSIC LIBRARY

110 ARTUSI, GIOVANNI MARIA

[Prima Parte | Dell'Arte | Del Contraponto | Nella Qvale Si Tratta Dell'Vtile | & vso delle Dissonanze. | Divisa In Dve Libri. | Da. Gio: Maria Artvsi Bolognese. | Nouamente Data in luce. | In Venetia, Appresso Giacomo Vincenti | MDLXXXVI.,]

2° 2 *ℓ.*, 46 p., 1 *ℓ.*, illus., music
Imperfect: title-page lacking, supplied in manuscript facsimile; main title-page lacking (see Wolfenbüttel, no. 1026)
RISM B VI, 99
MUSIC LIBRARY

111 ARTUSI, GIOVANNI MARIA

Seconda Parte | Dell'Arte | Del Contraponto | Nella Qvale Si Tratta Dell'Vtile | & vso delle Dissonanze. | Divisa In Dve | Libri | Da Gio: Maria Artvsi Bolognese. | Nouamente Data in luce. | In Venetia, Appresso Giacomo Vincenti. | MDLXXXIX.

2° 47 p., illus., music
RISM B VI, 99
MUSIC LIBRARY

112 ARTUSI, GIOVANNI MARIA

L'Artvsi | Ouero | Delle Imperfettioni | Della Moderna Mvsica | Ragionamenti dui. | Ne' quali si ragiona di molte cose vtili, & necessarie alli | Moderni Compositori. | Del R. P. D. Gio. Maria Artvsi | Da Bologna. | Canonico Regolare nella Congregatione del Saluatore. | Nouamente Stampato. | In Venetia, Appresso Giacomo Vincenti, 1600.

2° 8 *ℓ.*, 71 numb. *ℓ.*, illus., music
RISM B VI, 100; Wolfenbüttel, no. 1028
HOUGHTON

113 ARTUSI, GIOVANNI MARIA

Seconda Parte | Dell'Artvsi | Ouero | Delle Imperfettioni | Della Moderna | Mvsica, | Nelle quale si tratta de' molti abusi introdotti da i moderni | Scrittori, & Compositori. | Nuouamente Ristampata. | In Venetia, MDCIII. | Appresso Giacomo Vincenti.

2° 6 *ℓ.*, 56, 54 p., illus., music
Pages 1–54, second sequence: Considerationi | Mvsicali, | Del R. P. D. Gio. Maria Artvsi | . . .
Hirsch I, no. 36; RISM B VI, 100
HOUGHTON

114 ATTERBURY, LUFFMAN

A Collection of | Catches & Glees | for three and four | Voices | Composed by | L. Atterbury | Musician in Ordinary to | His Majesty | . . . | London Printed by C. and S. Thompson No. 75 St Pauls Church Yard | . . . [1777?]

obl. 2° *Score:* 3 *ℓ.*, 31 p.
RISM A I, no. A 2656
MUSIC LIBRARY

115 ATTERBURY, LUFFMAN

A Collection of | Twelve Glees, Rounds &c. | for Three, Four & Five Voices, | as Performed at the | Noblemen and Gentlemens | Catch Club, Glee Club &c. | Composed by | L. Atterbury. | Musician in Ordinary to His Majesty. | Inscribed (by Permission) to His Grace the Duke of Leeds. | Opa. 2nd. . . . | London,

Printed, for G. Goulding, No. 6, James Street, Covt, Gardn. [ca. 1790]

> obl. 2° *Score:* 2 *ℓ.*, 36 p.
> RISM A I, no. A 2657
> MUSIC LIBRARY

116 ATTWOOD, THOMAS

The | Adopted Child, | A Musical Drama in Two Acts, | As performed at the | Theatre Royal, Drury Lane, | Composed & Humbly Dedicated (by Permission) | To Her Royal Highness | The Princess of Wales, | by | Thos. Attwood. | . . . | London, Printed by Longman & Broderip, 26, Cheapside & 13, Haymarket. | . . . [1795?]

> obl. 2° *Vocal score:* 1 *ℓ.*, 31 p.
> Attwood's autograph signature on title-page
> RISM A I, no. A 2676
> MUSIC LIBRARY

117 ATTWOOD, THOMAS

The | Smugglers, | A Musical Drama in Two Acts, | As performed at the | Theatre Royal Drury Lane | Composed by | Thomas Attwood, | Music Master To | Her Royal Highness | The Princess of Wales. | . . . The Words by Saml. Birch Esqr. . . . | Barnes Sculpsit. | London, Printed for Longman & Broderip, No. 26 Cheapside & 13 Haymarket. [1796?]

> obl. 2° *Vocal score:* 1 *ℓ.*, 38 p.
> RISM A I, no. A 2727
> MUSIC LIBRARY

AUDINOT, NICOLAS MÉDARD Le Tonnelier *See* Gossec, François Joseph *Le Tonnelier*

118 AUFSCHNAITER, BENEDIKT ANTON

Memnon Sacer | Ab | Orientesole Animatus. | Seu | Vesperae | Solennissimae | A 4. Vocibus Concertantibus. 2. Violinis, & 2. Violis necessariis. 4. Rip. | pro pleno Choro. Violone, cum duplici Basso continuo. | NB. Ad Dixit Dominus, & Magnificat in Vesperis Solennissimis, 2. Clarinis | Concert: in Psalmis autem So-

lennioribus ad | Libitum. | Singulari Studio, & arte elaboratae | A | Benedicto Antonio | Aufschnaiter, | Eminentissimi Ac Celsissimi Principis, | Ac Domini Domini | Joannis Philippi | Sac. Rom. Ecclesiae Cardinalis, Episcopi & S. R. I. | Principis Passaviensis &c. &c. | Capellae Magistro. | Opus Quintum. | . . . | Augustae Vindelicorum, | Typis & sumptibus Andreae Maschenbauer, Reip. Aug. Typogr. | Anno M.D.CC.IX.

> 2° 10 pts.: *canto:* 1 *ℓ.*, 30 p.; *alto:* 1 *ℓ.*, 32 p.; *tenore:* 1 *ℓ.*, 29 p.; *basso:* 1 *ℓ.*, 26 p.; *violino I, violino II:* 1 *ℓ.*, 27 p. each; *viola I:* 1 *ℓ.*, 24 p.; *viola II:* 1 *ℓ.*, 25 p.; *violone:* 1 *ℓ.*, 30 p.; *basso continuo pro organo:* 3 *ℓ.*, 35 p.
> RISM A I, no. A 2856
> HOUGHTON

AVAUX, JEAN BAPTISTE D' *See* Davaux, Jean Baptiste

119 AVELLA, GIOVANNI D'

Regole | Di Mvsica, | Divise In Cinqve Trattati, | con le quali s'insegna il Canto Fermo, | e Figurato, per vere, e facili regole. | Il Modo Di Fare Il Contrapvnto. | Di comporre l'vno, e l'altro Canto. Di cantare | alcuni Canti difficili, e molte cose nuoue, | e curiose. | Composte | Dal Padre Fra Giovanni | D'Avella, | Predicatore De' Minori Osseruanti | della Prouincia di Terra di Lauoro. | In Roma, | Nella Stampa di Francesco Moneta. MDCLVII. | Con Licenza De' Svperiori.

> 2° 2 *ℓ.*, 167, [1] p., illus., music
> Hirsch I, no. 39; RISM B VI, 102
> HOUGHTON

LES AVEUX INDISCRETS *See* Monsigny, Pierre Alexandre *Les Aveux indiscrets*

120 AVISON, CHARLES

Six | Concertos | In Seven Parts | For | Four Violins, one Alto Viola, a Violoncello | and a Thorough Bass for the | Harpsichord | With general Rules for Playing Instrumental | Compositions in Parts, but more especially | Calculated for the Use of this Work. | Dedicated to | Mrs.

Ord | By | Charles Avison | Organist in Newcastle upon Tine. | Opera Terza. | London. | Printed for John Johnson in Cheapside. | MDCCLI.

2° 7 pts.: *violino primo concertino:* 2 *ℓ.*, vi p., 1 *ℓ.*, 16 p.; *violino secondo concertino, violino primo ripieno, violino secondo ripieno, alto viola:* 1 *ℓ.*, 13 p. each; *violoncello:* 1 *ℓ.*, 14 p.; *basso:* 1 *ℓ.*, 13 p.
RISM A I, no. A 2915
MUSIC LIBRARY

121   AVISON, CHARLES

Eight | Concertos | In Seven Parts | For | four Violins, one Alto-Viola, a Violoncello, | and a Thorough Bass for the | Harpsichord | Dedicated to | Lady Milbanke. | By | Charles Avison, | Organist in Newcastle upon Tyne | Opera Quarta. | London. | Printed for John Johnson at the Harp & Crown, Cheapside. | MDCCLV.

2° 7 pts.: *violino primo concertino:* 5 *ℓ.*, 29 p., front; *violino secondo concertino, violino primo ripieno:* 1 *ℓ.*, 21 p. each; *violino secondo ripieno:* 1 *ℓ.*, 17 p.; *alto viola:* 1 *ℓ.*, 16 p.; *violoncello:* 1 *ℓ.*, 25 p.; *basso ripieno:* 1 *ℓ.*, 17 p.
RISM A I, no. A 2917
MUSIC LIBRARY

122   AVISON, CHARLES

Twelve | Concertos | (Divided into two Sets) | For | Two Violins, One Alto-Viola, and a Violoncello. | This Work is also adapted to the Practice of the | Organ or Harpsichord alone | Or these to serve as an Accompanyment to the Parts | in Concert, which may be Reinforced at Pleasure. | Composed by | Charles Avison, | Organist in Newcastle upon Tyne | Opera Nona. | Set I. | MDCCLXVI. | London, Printed for the Author, and Sold by R. Johnson in | Cheapside . . .

2° 1 pt.: *organo:* 2 *ℓ.*, 4, 27 p.
Contents: Concertos 1–6
RISM A I, no. A 2929
HOUGHTON

123   AVISON, CHARLES

Twelve | Concertos | (Divided into two Sets) | For | Two Violins, One Alto-Viola,

and a Violoncello. | This Work is also adapted to the Practice of the | Organ or Harpsichord alone | Or these to serve as an Accompanyment to the Parts | in Concert, which may be Reinforced at Pleasure. | Composed by | Charles Avison, | Organist in Newcastle upon Tyne | Opera Nona. | Set 2d. | MDCCLXVI. | London, Printed for the Author, and Sold By R Bremner in | the Strand, . . .

2° 1 pt.: *organo:* 2 *ℓ.*, 29–54 p.
Contents: Concertos 7–12
RISM A I, no. A 2929
HOUGHTON

124   AVISON, CHARLES

An | Essay | On | Musical Expression. | By Charles Avison, | Organist in Newcastle. | . . . | London: | Printed for C. Davis, opposite Gray's-Inn-Gate, | In Holborn. MDCCLII.

12° 4 *ℓ.*, 138 p.
Hirsch I, no. 40; RISM B VI, 103
MUSIC LIBRARY

125   AVISON, CHARLES

An | Essay | On | Musical Expression. | By Charles Avison, | Organist in Newcastle. | The Second Edition, | With Alterations and Large Additions | To which is added, | A Letter to the Author, concerning | the Music of the Ancients, and some | Passages in Classic Writers, relating | to that Subject. | Likewise, | Mr. Avison's Reply to the Author of Remarks | on the Essay on Musical Expression. In a | Letter from Mr Avison, to his Friend in London. | London: | Printed for C. Davis, opposite Gray's-Inn-Gate, in | Holborn. MDCCLIII.

8° 6 *ℓ.*, 152, 43 p., 2 *ℓ.*, 53, [6] p., 4 fold. pl., music
Page [1]: Proposals | For | Publishing by Subscription, | Specimens | Of the various Stiles in | Musical Expression. | . . .
RISM B VI, 103
MUSIC LIBRARY

126   AVISON, CHARLES

An | Essay | On | Musical Expression. | By Charles Avison, | Organist in Newcastle. | With Alterations and Large Additions. | To which is added, | A Letter to the Author, | concerning the Music of the Ancients, | and some Passages in Classic Writers, | relating to that Subject. | Likewise, | Mr. Avison's Reply to the Author of | Remarks on the Essay on Musical Expression. | In a Letter from Mr. Avison, to his Friend in London. | The Third Edition. | London, | Printed for Lockyer Davis, in Holborn. | Printer to the Royal Society. | MDCCLXXV.

8° viii, 221 p., 4 fold. pl. (music)
RISM B VI, 103
MUSIC LIBRARY

127   AVISON, CHARLES

Six | Sonatas, | For the | Harpsichord, | With Accompanyments, | For two Violins, & a Violoncello, | Composed by | Charles Avison, | Organist in Newcastle upon Tyne. | Opera Settima. | London | Printed for R. Bremner, facing Somerset House, | in the Strand. [ca. 1765]

2° 3 pts.: *violino primo, violino secondo, basso:* 1 ℓ., 9 p. each
RISM A I, no. A 2924
HOUGHTON

B

BACFARC, VALENTIN *See* Bakfark, Bálint

128   BACH, CARL PHILIPP EMANUEL

Karl Wilhelm Rammlers | Auferstehung | und | Himmelfahrt Jesu, | in Musik gesetzt | von | Karl Philipp Emanuel Bach. | Leipzig, | im Breitkopfischen Verlage. | 1787.

2° Score: 1 ℓ., 184 p.
RISM A I, no. B 115
W. 240
HOUGHTON

129   BACH, CARL PHILIPP EMANUEL

Exempel | nebst achtzehn Probe-Stücken | in | Sechs Sonaten | zu | Carl Philipp Emanuel Bachs | Versuche über die wahre Art | das | Clavier | zu spielen | auf XXVI. Kupfer-Tafeln. [Berlin, 1753?]

2° Score: 1 ℓ., 20 p., 6 pl. on 4 ℓ.
RISM A I, no. B 146?
W. 63
HOUGHTON

130   BACH, CARL PHILIPP EMANUEL

Exempel | nebst achtzehn Probe-Stücken | in | Sechs Sonaten | zu | Carl Philipp Emanuel Bachs | Versuche | über die wahre Art | das Clavier zu spielen | auf XXVI. Kupfer-Tafeln. [Berlin, 1759?]

2° Score: 1 ℓ., 20 p., 6 pl. on 4 ℓ.
RISM A I, no. B 147?
W. 63
HOUGHTON

131   [BACH, CARL PHILIPP EMANUEL]

Die Israeliten in der Wüste. [Hamburg, 1775]

2° Score: 114 p.
Imperfect: title-leaf lacking; caption title
RISM A I, no. B 109?
W. 238
HOUGHTON

132   BACH, CARL PHILIPP EMANUEL

Sinfonia | A | II. Violini | Violetta | E | Basso | Composta | Da | Carlo Filip. Eman. Bach | Musico di Camera di S. M il Re di Prussia | alle spese della Vedova di Balth. Schmid in Norimberga | . . . [1759]

2° 4 pts.: *violino Imo., violino IIdo., violetta:* 1 numb. ℓ., 3 p. each; *basso:* 2 numb. ℓ.
Plate no. LII
Numbered leaves printed on one side only
Title supplied from *basso* part
RISM A I, no. B 54
W. 177
HOUGHTON

133   BACH, CARL PHILIPP EMANUEL

Sei Sonate | Per Il | Clavicembalo | Solo | All'Uso Delle Donne | Composte | Da | Carlo Filippo Emmanuele Bach | Maestro Di Capella In Hamburgo. | In Riga, |

Presso Giovani Federico Hartknoch. 1786.

> 2° *Score:* 36 p.
> W. 54
> MUSIC LIBRARY

134   BACH, CARL PHILIPP EMANUEL

C. P. E. Bachs, Nichelmanns und Håndels | Sonaten und Fugen | fürs Clavier. | Zweite Auflage. | Berlin, | bey Arnold Wever. 1774.

> obl. 4° *Score:* 2 ℓ ., 28 p.
> Contains C. P. E. Bach's Sonata W. 62, no. 8 and Fugue W. 119, no. 3; Nichelmann's *Sonate* (in A minor); Händel's *Zweystimmige Fuge*; Kirnberger's *Allegro*; and an anonymous minuet.
> RISM B II, 111
> MUSIC LIBRARY

135   BACH, CARL PHILIPP EMANUEL

Versuch | über die wahre Art | das Clavier zu spielen | mit Exempeln | und achtzehn Probe-Stücken in sechs Sonaten | erläutert | von | Carl Philipp Emanuel Bach, | Königl. Preuss. Cammer-Musikus. | Berlin, in Verlegung des Auctoris. | Gedruckt bey dem Königl. Hof-Buchdrucker Christian Friedrich Henning. | 1753.

> 4° 4 ℓ., 135 p.
> RISM B VI, 105
> HOUGHTON (2 copies)

136   BACH, CARL PHILIPP EMANUEL

Carl Philipp Emanuel Bachs | Versuch | über die wahre Art | das Clavier zu spielen | mit Exempeln | und achtzehn Probe-Stücken in sechs Sonaten | erläutert. | Erster Theil. | Zweite Auflage. | In Verlegung des Auctoris. | Berlin, 1759. | Gedruckt bey George Ludewig Winter.

> 4° 4 ℓ., 118 p.
> RISM A I, no. B 144; RISM B VI, 105
> HOUGHTON

137   BACH, CARL PHILIPP EMANUEL

Carl Philipp Emanuel Bachs | Versuch | über die wahre Art | das Clavier zu spielen | Zweyter Theil, | in welchem die

Lehre von dem Accompagnement | und der freyen Fantasie | abgehandelt wird. | Nebst einer Kupfertafel. | In Verlegung des Auctoris. | Berlin, 1762. | Gedruckt bey George Ludewig Winter.

> 4° 5 ℓ., 341, [1] p., pl., music
> RISM B VI, 106
> HOUGHTON (2 copies)

138   BACH, CARL PHILIPP EMANUEL

Carl Phillipp Emanuel Bachs | Versuch | über die wahre Art | das Clavier zu spielen | mit Exempeln | und achtzehn Probe-Stücken in sechs Sonaten | erläutert. | Erster[-Zweyter] Theil. | Zweyte Auflage. | Leipzig, | im Schwickertschen Verlage | 1780.

> 4° 2 vols.: *vol. I:* 4 ℓ., 118 p.; *vol. II:* 5 ℓ., 341, [1] p., fold. pl., music
> Vol. II has separate title-page: Carl Phillipp Emanuel Bachs | Versuch | über die wahre Art | das Clavier zu spielen | Zweyter Theil, | in welchem die Lehre von dem Accompagnement | und der freyen Fantasie | abgehandelt wird. | Nebst einer Kupfertafel. | Leipzig | . . . | 1780
> Date altered in manuscript to 1789 in both vols.
> Hirsch I, no. 44, 45; RISM B VI, 106
> HOUGHTON

139   BACH, JOHANN CHRISTIAN

A second Sett of | Six | Concertos | For the | Harpsichord | or | Piano Forte | With Accompanyments, | For two Violins & a Violoncello | Humbly Dedicated To Her Majesty | Charlotta | Queen of Great Britain &c. &c. &c. | By | John Christian Bach | Opera VII . . . | London | Printed by Welcker in Gerrard Street. St. Anns Soho. | . . . [ca. 1775]

> 2° 4 pts.: *harpsichord or piano forte:* 1 ℓ., 39 p.; *violino primo:* 1 ℓ., 15 p.; *violino secondo, violoncello:* 1 ℓ., 12 p. each
> RISM A I, no. B 281; Terry, p. 294
> HOUGHTON; MUSIC LIBRARY (keyboard pt. only)

140   BACH, JOHANN CHRISTIAN

A | Third Sett of Six | Concertos | for the | Harpsichord or Piano Forte, | With

132 C. P. E. Bach, *Sinfonia*, Nuremberg, 1759: basso part, leaf 2 (325 × 205 mm.)

Modus.

Dif.

Alt⁹

Téor

Bass⁹

Prauitas atro fimilis ueneno
Mentibus rectis inimica peftis
Proforet nobis nihil, effet &fi
Nulla Gehenna.

Lacus.

Durius immundo flagrum debetur afello
Et cano plagæ puero medicina putantur.

Modus.

Eft deus magni dominator orbis
Omnium prudens operum repenfor
Ille mercedem tribuit merenti
Aftra uel orcum

330 CHELIDONIUS, *Voluptatis cum virtute disceptatio*, Vienna, 1515: leaf c iv^r
(162 × 125 mm.)

Accompaniments for two | Violins and a Bass two Hautboys | and two French Horns ad Libitum | Humbly Dedicated to | Mrs. Pelham. | and Composed by | John Christian Bach | Music Master to | Her Majesty The | Queen Of Great Britain. Opera XIII. | London Printed and Sold by Iohn Welcker No. 9 Hay Market opposite the Opera House . . . [ca. 1777]

2° 1 pt.: *harpsichord or piano forte:* 1 ℓ., 56 p.
Cancel label at head of title reads: Sold by John Lee. | at the Corner of | Eustace Street in | Dame-Street. (No. 70)
RISM A I, no. B 282; Terry, p. 295
MUSIC LIBRARY

141   BACH, JOHANN CHRISTIAN

Bach's | Celebrated Concerto, | For The | Piano Forte | From Opera 13. | London, | Printed for Harrison & Co. No. 18, Paternoster Row. [1798?]

8° *Score:* 22 p. (*The Piano-Forte Magazine,* vol. III, no. 6)
RISM A I, no. B 296 (op. 13, no. 4); Terry, p. 296
MUSIC LIBRARY

142   BACH, JOHANN CHRISTIAN

Six | Favourite Overtures | in 8 Parts | For Violins, Hoboys, French Horns, | with a Bass for the | Harpsichord and Violoncello. | Compos'd by | Sigr. Bach. | London. Printed for I. Walsh in Catharine Street in ye Strand. | . . . [1763]

2° 8 pts.: *oboe primo, oboe secondo, corno primo, corno secondo:* 1 ℓ., 2–7 p. each; *fagotti:* 1 ℓ., 13 p.; *violino primo:* 1 ℓ., 15 p.; *violino secondo, viola:* 1 ℓ., 13 p. each
Contents: overtures to *Orione, La Calamità, Artaserse, Il Tutore e la Pupilla, La Cascina* and *Astarto*
RISM A I, no. B 248?; Terry, p. 274; Walsh II, no. 126
MUSIC LIBRARY

143   BACH, JOHANN CHRISTIAN

Six | Sonates | Pour Le | Clavecin | Ou Le Piano Forte | Composees Par | Jean Cretien Bach | Maitre de Musique de S. M. la Reine D'angleterre | Oeuvre V. |

Gravée par Mlle. Vendôme et le Sr. Moria | . . . | A Paris | Aux adresses ordinaires de Musique. Avec Privilege Du Roy | . . . [after 1786]

obl. 2° *Score:* 1 ℓ., 34 p.
Plate no. 124
Page [1]: Catalogue | De toutes sortes de Musique Vocale et Instrumental qui se vendent chez Mr. Huberty, | . . .
RISM A I, no. B 385; Terry, p. 339
HOUGHTON

144   BACH, JOHANN CHRISTIAN

Six Sonatas, | For The | Harpsichord Or Piano Forte; | With An | Accompagnament For A Violin. | Humbly Dedicated | To | The Right Honble Lady Mellbourne. | And Composed | By | John Cristian Bach, | Music Master To Her Majesty. | Opera X. | London Printed & Sold by Welcker in Gerrard Street Soho . . . Mango Sculp [1775?]

obl. 2° *Score:* 1 ℓ., 37 p.
RISM A I, no. B 333; Terry, p. 322–323
MUSIC LIBRARY

145   BACH, JOHANN CHRISTIAN

Six | Sonates | Pour le | Clavecin | Ou le Piano Forte | Composés par | Jean. Cretian. Bach | Maitre de Musique de .S. M. la Reine D'angleterre | Oeuvre XII | . . . | A. Paris | Chez le Sr Sieber rue St honore a l'hotel d'aligre pres la croix du trahoir | Et aux adresse Ordinaires A Lyon chez Mr Casteau | A. P. D. P Script par Md Sieber. [1775?]

obl. 2° *Score:* 1 ℓ., 35 p.
Page [1]: Catalogue | De Musique Appartenant á M. Sieber . . . ⟨A later state of JohanssonF facs. 105⟩
RISM A I, no. B 390 (op. 17); Terry, p. 342
MUSIC LIBRARY

146   BACH, JOHANN CHRISTIAN

Four | Sonatas | and two | Duetts | for the | Piano Forte | Or | Harpsicord | with Accompaniments | humbly Dedicated to the Right Honble. the | Countess of Abingdon | and Composed by | John Christian Bach, | Music Master to her Majesty & the Royal Family. | Opera XV.

| . . . | London Printed and Sold for the Proprietor by J Welcker Music-seller | to their Majesties and the Royal Family, No. 80 Hay Market | . . . [ca. 1780]

2° 2 pts.: *cembalo secondo:* 1 ℓ., 9 p.; *violoncello obligato:* 3 p.
RISM A I, no. B 344; Terry, p. 340
MUSIC LIBRARY

147   BACH, JOHANN CHRISTIAN

Six Sonatas | For The | Harpsichord Or Piano Forte | With An Accompanyment | For The | Violin Or German Flute, | Respectfully Dedicated | To The | Miss Greenland, | And Composed By | John Christian Bach. | Opera XVI. [London, Welcker, ca. 1780]

obl. 2° *Score:* 1 ℓ., 37 p.
RISM A I, no. B 353?; Terry, p. 339
MUSIC LIBRARY

148   BACH, JOHANN CHRISTIAN

Three | Sonatas | for the | Harpsichord | or | Piano Forte, | with an Accompanyment for | A Violin, | Composed by | I. C. Bach. | Op. XX. . . . | London | Printed for and Sold by William Campbell, | at his Music Shop No. 11, New Street, | Covent Garden. [1783?]

2° *Score:* 20 p.
RISM A I, no. B 366; Terry, p. 329
MUSIC LIBRARY

149   BACH, JOHANN CHRISTIAN

Six | Sonates. | pour | Deux Violons | et | Basso. | Composées | par | J: C: Bach. | Maitre de Musique | de S: M: la Reine | d'Angleterre. | A Amsterdam | chez J: Mol et Comp: | Marchands et Graveurs de Musique, | dans le Rosemareinsteeg. . . . | Pierre Mol, Graveur de Musique. [179–?]

2° 3 pts.: *violino primo, violino secondo:* 1 ℓ., 10 p. each; *basso:* 1 ℓ., 7 p.
RISM A I, no. B 330 (op. 4)
HOUGHTON

150   BACH, JOHANN CHRISTIAN

A Second Collection of | Favourite Songs | Sung at | Vaux Hall | By | Mrs. Pinto & Mrs. Weichsell | Composed by | John Christian Bach | London Printed by Welcker in Gerrard Street St. Ann's Soho. | . . . [1767?]

2° *Score:* 1 ℓ., 18 p.
RISM A I, no. B 188; Terry, p. 254–255
MUSIC LIBRARY

151   BACH, JOHANN CHRISTOPH FRIEDRICH

D. Balthasar Münters, | Pastors an der deutschen Petrikirche zu Kopenhagen, | Zweyte Sammlung | Geistlicher Lieder. | Mit Melodien | von | Johann Christian Friedrich Bach, | Hochreichsgräflich-Bückeburgischen Concertmeister. | Leipzig, | in der Dyckischen Buchhandlung. | 1774.

large obl. 4° *Score:* 2 ℓ., 50 p.
Colophon: Leipzig, gedruckt bey Bernhard Christoph Breitkopf und Sohn.
RISM A I, no. B 417
MUSIC LIBRARY

152   BACH, JOHANN SEBASTIAN

Dritter Theil | der | Clavier Übung | bestehend | in | verschiedenen Vorspielen | über die | Catechismus- und andere Gesaenge, | vor die Orgel: | Denen Liebhabern, und besonders denen Kennern | von dergleichen Arbeit, zur Gemüths Ergezung | Verfertiget von | Johann Sebastian Bach, | Koenigl. Pohlnischen, und Churfürstl. Saechs. | Hoff-Compositeur, Capellmeister, und | Directore Chori Musici in Leipzig. | [Leipzig] In Verlegung des Authoris. [1739]

obl. 2° *Score:* 1 ℓ., 77 p.
Hirsch III, no. 39; RISM A I, no. B 488
HOUGHTON

BACH, KARL PHILIPP EMANUEL *See* Bach, Carl Philipp Emanuel

153   BACH, WILHELM FRIEDEMANN

[Sei Sonate | per il Cembalo | dedicate | al Signore Illustrissimo | il Signore George Ernesto Stahl | Consigliere della corte | di Sua Maestá | il Ré di Prussia Elettore di Brandeburgo | e composte | da | Guiglielmo Friedemanno Bach. | In Verlag zu haben 1. bey dem Autore in Dresden, 2. bey dessen Herrn Vater | in Leipzig, und 3. dessen Bruder in Berlin ⟨1745⟩]

obl. 2° *Score:* 2 *ℓ.*, 16 p.
Imperfect: title-leaf and second preliminary leaf lacking; supplied in positive photostat
Contents: Sonata I; no more published
RISM A I, no. B 526
F. 3
HOUGHTON

154   BACH, WILHELM FRIEDEMANN

[Sonate | pour | Le Clavecin | dédiée | A | Son Excellence | Monseigneur de Kaiserling | Comte du St. Empire Ambassadeur et Conseiller | prive de S. A. L'Imperatrice de toutes | les Russies Chevalier de l'Argle blanc, | Membre de la Société des sciences à | Berlin, Seigneur de Gros et Klein | Blieden &c. &c. | composée | par | Guillaume Friedemann Bach. | In Verlag zu haben 1. bey dem Autore in Halle, 2. bey dessen Herrn | Vater in Leipzig, und 3. dessen Bruder in Berlin. ⟨1763⟩]

obl. 2° *Score:* [1], 6 p.
Reprint of 1748 ed.
Imperfect: title-page lacking. Title supplied in manuscript on card which accompanies the volume
RISM A I, no. B 525
F. 5
HOUGHTON

155   [BACHOFEN, JOHANN KASPAR]

Musicalisch-|Wochentlicher | Aussgaaben, | Dritter Theil. | . . . [Zurich, 1750]
4° 200, [12] p.
Contains music for three voices, in choirbook format
Fifty numbered and two unnumbered issues; pages [10]–[12] at end contain an index to all three *Theilen*
RISM A I, no. B 561
HOUGHTON

156   [BACILLY, BÉNIGNE DE]

Remarques curieuses | Sur | L'art de bien Chanter | Et particulierement | pour ce qui Regarde | Le Chant François | Par

le sieur B. D. B. | A Paris ruë des Petits Champs vis a | vis la Croix chez vn Chandelier | auec Priuilege du Roy 1668

12° 6 *ℓ.*, 428, [2] p.
Colophon: A Paris, | De l'Imprimerie de C. Blageart, ruë | S. Iacques, à la Cloche Rouge. 1668.
RISM B VI, 108
HOUGHTON

157   BAILDON, JOSEPH

The | Laurel. | A New Collection of | English Songs | Sung by Mr. Lowe and Miss Falkner | at | Marybon-Gardens. | Compos'd by | Mr. Joseph Baildon. | London. Printed for I. Walsh, in Catharine Street in the Strand. [1750, 1752]

2° *Score:* 2 vols.: [*vol. I*]: 1 *ℓ.*, 11 p.; *vol. II:* 1 *ℓ.*, 19 p.
RISM A I, no. B 647; Walsh II, no. 130–131
MUSIC LIBRARY (2 copies; 2d copy: vol. II only)

158   BAKFARK, BÁLINT, ED.

Intabvlatvra Valen-|tini Bacfarc Transilvani Coronensis. | Liber Primvs. | Lugduni apud Iacobum Modernum. | Cum priuilegio ad triennium. [1553]

obl. 4° A–K⁴
Privilege dated 18 Jan 1552
Brown, no. 1553₁; Pogue, no. 58; RISM B I, no. 1552³⁰
HOUGHTON

BALDASSARINO, DA BELGIOJOSO *See* Belgiojoso, Baldassarino da

159   BALLARD, CHRISTOPHE, COMP.

Brunetes | Ou | Petits Airs Tendres, | Avec Les Doubles | Et La Basse-Continue; | Mélées | De Chansons A Danser; | Recüeillies, et mises en ordre par | Christophe Ballard, | seul Imprimeur de Musique, et Noteur | de la Chapelle du Roy. | . . . | A Paris, | Ruë S. Jean de Beauvais, au Mont Parnasse. | M.DCC.III. [–M.DCC.XI] | Avec Privilege de Sa Majesté.

12° Score: 3 vols.: *vol. I:* 9 ℓ., 293, [1] p.; *vol. II:* 9 ℓ., 296 p.; *vol. III:* 8 ℓ., 311, [1] p.; front. in each vol.

Imprint date, vol. II: M.DCC.IV; vol. III: M.DCC.XI

RISM B II, 118

MUSIC LIBRARY

160　BALLARD, CHRISTOPHE, COMP.

Nouvelles | Parodies | Bachiques, | Mélées | De Vaudevilles | Ou | Rondes De Table. | Recueillies et mises en ordre par | Christophe Ballard, | seul Imprimeur de Musique et | Noteur de la Chapelle du Roy. | . . . | A Paris, | Ruë Saint Jean de Beauvais, au Mont-Parnasse. | M.DCC. [–M.D.CCII.] | Avec Privilege de Sa Majesté.

12° 3 vols.: vol. I: 3 ℓ., 276, [12] p.; *vol. II:* 3 ℓ., 264, [10] p., 1 ℓ.; *vol. III:* 5 ℓ., 244, [6] p., front. in each vol.

Imprint date, vol. III: M.D.CCII

RISM B II, 267–268

MUSIC LIBRARY

BALLARD, PIERRE, PUBL. Airs de cour　*See* Airs de cour

BALTASAR, DE BEAUJOYEAULX　*See* Belgiojoso, Baldassarino da

161

The | Banquet of Musick: | Or, | A Collection of the newest and best Songs | sung at Court, and at Publick Theatres. | With | A Thorow-Bass for the Theorbo-Lute, | Bass-Viol, Harpsichord, or Organ. | Composed by several of the Best Masters. | The Words by the Ingenious Wits of this Age. | The Second Book. | Licensed, | May 3. 1688. Rob. Midgley. | [London] In the Savoy: | Printed by E. Jones, for Henry Playford, at his Shop near the Temple Church, 1688.

2° Score: 2 ℓ., 44 p.

RISM B I, no. 1688[7]

HOUGHTON

BARÔZAI, GUI, PSEUD. *See* La Monnoye, Bernard de

162　BARTHÉLEMON, FRANÇOIS HIPPOLYTE

[Six Lessons | with a favourite Rondou in each for the | Forte Piano or Harpsichord | with an Accompanyment for a | Violin ad Libitum | composed and humbly dedicated to | Mr Otteley | by F. H. Barthelemon | Opera V ⟨London, Welcker, 1775?⟩]

obl. 2° Score: 54[+] p.

Imperfect: title-page and all after page 54 lacking; title supplied from manuscript title on page [1]

RISM A I, no. B 1121

MUSIC LIBRARY

163　BARTHOLIN, CASPAR

Casp. Bartholini | Thom. Fil. | De Tibiis | Veterum, | Et | Earum Antiquo Usu | Libri Tres. | Editio altera, figuris auctior. | Amstelaedami, | Apud Henr. Wetstenium, | CIↃ IↃC LXXIX.

*12° 10 ℓ., 415, [5] p., front., illus., 6 pl. (incl. port., 5 fold.)

Davidsson II, no. 8; RISM B VI, 120; Wolfenbüttel, no. 1033

MUSIC LIBRARY

164　BARTHOLOMAEUS ANGLICUS

[De musica. Lyon, 1480]

2° In his *De proprietatibus rerum,* ℓ. H5ʳ–H7ʳ

Colophon: . . . Impres-|sus per Nicolaum pistoris de Bensheym | et Marcum reinhardi de Argentina so|cios. Sub anno dñi Millesimoquadrin|gētesimooctogesimo. die vero Julij .xxix

Two columns to the page

GW, no. 3404; Hain-Copinger, no. 2500

HOUGHTON

165　BARTHOLOMAEUS ANGLICUS

[De musica. Strassburg, 1485]

2° In his *De proprietatibus rerum,* ℓ. T5ʳ–T7ᵛ

Colophon: . . . Impressus Argentine| Anno dñi M.cccc.lxxxv. Finitus in die san|cti Valentini.

Printed by Georg Husner

Two columns to the page
GW, no. 3410; Hain-Copinger, no. 2506
HOUGHTON

166 BARTHOLOMAEUS ANGLICUS

[De musica. Heidelberg, 1488]

2° In his *Proprietates rerum*, ℓ. DD5ʳ– DD7ᵛ
Colophon: Explicit liber de p[ro]prietatibus rerum | editus a fratre Bartholomeo anglico or|dinis fratrum minorum. Anno domini | Mcccclxxxviij. Kalēdras vero Junij. xij.
Printed by Heinrich Knoblochtzer?
Two columns to the page
GW, no. 3411; Hain-Copinger, no. 2507
HOUGHTON

167 BARTHOLOMAEUS ANGLICUS

[De musica. Strassburg, 1491]

2° In his *De proprietatibus rerum*, ℓ. R3ᵛ–R5ᵛ
Colophon: . . . Impressus Argentine Anno | dñi M.cccc.xcj. Finitus altera die post fe|stum sancti Laurentij martyris.
Printed by Georg Husner
Two columns to the page
GW, no. 3412; Hain-Copinger, no. 2509
HOUGHTON

168 BARTHOLOMAEUS ANGLICUS

[De musica. Nuremberg, 1492]

2° In his *De proprietatibus rerum*, ℓ. I6ᵛ–I7ᵛ
Colophon: . . . Impressus p[er] industriosum virū Athonium | koburger inclute Nurenberge ciuem. Anno | salutis gratie. M.ccccxcij. xx. die Junij.
GW, no. 3413; Hain-Copinger, no. 2510
HOUGHTON

169 [BARTHOLOMAEUS ANGLICUS]

[De musica. Toulouse, 1494]

2° In his *De proprietatibus rerum*, ℓ. pp3ʳ–pp3ᵛ

Colophon: . . . Emprimido en | la noble çibdad de tholosa por henrique meyer | d' alemaña a honor de dios & d' nuestra señora & | al prouecho de muchos rudos & ynorantes aca-|bo se enel año del señor de mil & quatro çientos | & nouenta quatro a diez & ocho del mes de setiē|bre
Two columns to the page
GW, no. 3424; Hain-Copinger, no. 2523
HOUGHTON

170 BARTHOLOMAEUS ANGLICUS

De musica [Westminster, ca. 1495]

2° In his *De proprietatibus rerum*, ℓ. nn3ᵛ–oo3ʳ
Text in English; printed by Wynkyn de Worde
Caption title
Two columns to the page
GW, no. 3414; Hain-Copinger, no. 2520
HOUGHTON

171 [BARTHOLOMAEUS ANGLICUS]

[De musica. Paris, 1510]

2° In his *Le proprietaire des choses*, ℓ. X4ᵛ–X6ʳ
Colophon: . . . Imprime nouuel-|lemēt a Paris Lan de grace mil cinq cēs & dix | le. xv. iour de Nouembre. Pour Jehan petit & | Michel lenoir libraires Jurez en luniuersite de | paris, demourās en la rue sainct Jaques.
Text in French; two columns to the page
HOUGHTON

172 BARTHOLOMAEUS ANGLICUS

[De musica. Nuremberg, 1519]

2° In his *De rerū proprietatibus*, ℓ. G6ᵛ–G8ʳ
Colophon: Opus de Proprietatibus rerum: editū a patre | Bartholomeo Anglico ordinis fratrū minorū: | studiosissime reuisum, correctum et emendatū: | ac per Fridericū Peypus ciuem Nurembergñ. | impressum: Expensis prouidi viri Joannis Ko|berger eiusdem ciuitat[us] in-

cole Feliciter explicit. | Anno salutis nr̄e.
M.ccccc.xix. Id. iij. Maij.
Two columns to the page
HOUGHTON

173 [BARTHOLOMAEUS ANGLICUS]

[De musica. Paris, 1525]

2° In his *Le proprietaire des choses*, *ℓ*.
X4ᵛ–X6ʳ
Colophon: . . . Nouuelle-|ment Im-
prime a Paris. Lan de grace mil cinq |
cens. xxv. le xx. iour de may par Phelippe
le | noir Relieur Jure en Luniuersite de
Paris de-|mourant en la grant rue sainct
Jaques a len-|seigne de la rose blanche
Couronnee.
Text in French; two columns to the
page
HOUGHTON

174 [BARTHOLOMAEUS ANGLICUS]

[⟨De musica⟩ . . . On les vend a Paris
au Cloust Bruneau a lenseigne de | lescu
de Bretaigne pour Pierre Gaudoul.
⟨1528⟩]

2° In his *Le proprietaire des choses*, *ℓ*.
X4ᵛ–X6ʳ
Colophon: . . . Nouuellement Im-
prime a paris. Lan de | grace mil cinq cēs.
xxviii. le. x. iour de may.
Text in French; two columns to the
page
Imprint supplied from title-page
HOUGHTON

175 [BARTHOLOMAEUS ANGLICUS]

[De musica. Paris, 1534]

2° In his *Le proprietaire des choses*, *ℓ*.
P3ᵛ–P4ᵛ
Colophon: . . . Nouuellmēt Imprime
a paris par Nicolas | couteau. Lan de
grace mil cinq cēs. xxxix. auāt | pasques
le. vii. de Januier.
Text in French; two columns to the
page
HOUGHTON

176 BARTHOLOMAEUS ANGLICUS

De Musica [London | Imprinted by
Thomas East, dwel-|ling by Paules
wharfe. ⟨1582⟩]

2° In *Batman vppon Bartholome, His
Booke De Proprietatibus Rerum*, numb.
ℓ. 419ᵛ [i. e. 421ᵛ]–426ʳ
Text in English
Caption title; imprint supplied from
title-page
Leaf 421 misnumbered 419
HOUGHTON

177 BARYPHONUS, HEINRICH

Henrici Baryphoni | VVernigerodano |
Cherusci | Pleiades | Musicae, | Qvae In
Certas Sectiones | distributae praecipuas
quaestiones Musicas | discutiunt, et
omnia, quae ad Theoriam per-|tinent, et
Melopoeiae plurimùm inserviunt | ex
veris fundamentis Mathematicis ex-
|structa, Theorematis septenis propo-
nunt, | exemplis illustrant, et coram judi-
cio ratio-|nis et sensus examinant, stu-
diosis non so-|lùm Musices, verûm
etiam Matheseos scitu | necessariae et
lectu jucundae. | Αναχεφαλαιωσιν | Le-
ctori versa pagina reprae-|sentat. | Hal-
berstadi, | Ex officinâ typographicâ Ja-
cobi-Ar-|noldi Cotenii, | Anno M.DC.XV.

8° 8 *ℓ*., 95, [1] p., illus.
RISM B VI, 121; Wolfenbüttel, no.
1039
HOUGHTON

BASILLY, BÉNIGNE DE *See* Bacilly,
Bénigne de

178 BASSANI, GIOVANNI BATTISTA

. . . | Suonate | A Due, Tre Instru-
menti, Col Basso | Continuo Per L'Or-
gano | Da Gio. Battista | Bassani | Maestro
di Capella dell'Illustrissima Accademia
della Morte di | Ferrara, & Accademico
Filarmonico. | Opera Qvinta. | In An-
versa, | Appresso Henrico Aertssens,
Stampatore di Musica all' | Insegna del
Monte Parnasso, 1691. | Con Privilegio.

2° 4 pts.: *violino primo, violino secondo:* 24 p. each; *violoncello, organo:*
20 p. each
RISM A I, no. B 1173
HOUGHTON

BASSILY, BÉNIGNE DE *See* Bacilly,
Bénigne de

179   BATES, WILLIAM

Pharnaces | An English Opera | Perform'd at the | Theatre Royal | in | Drury Lane | Composed by | William Bates | London Printed by Welcker in Gerrard Street St. Ann's Soho [1765?]

obl. 2° *Vocal score:* 1 ℓ., 71 p.
RISM A I, no. B 1249
MUSIC LIBRARY

180   BATESON, THOMAS

. . . | The first set of English | Madrigales: | to 3. 4. 5. and 6. | voices. | Newly composed by Thomas Bateson | practicioner in the Art of Musicke, and | Organist of the Cathedral Church | of Christ in the Citie of | Chester. | 1604. | In London | Printed By Thomas | Este.

4° 1 pt.: *altvs:* [A]², B–D⁴, E²
RISM A I, no. B 1277
HOUGHTON

181   BATHE, WILLIAM

A Briefe Intro-|duction to the skill of | Song: | Concerning the practise, set forth | by William Bathe | Gentleman. | In which work is set downe X. sundry wayes of 2. parts | in one vpon the plaine song. Also a Table newly ad-|ded of the comparisons of Cleues, how one followeth | another for the naming of Notes: with other neces-|sarie examples, to further the learner. | . . . | London | Printed by Thomas Este. [158–?]

8° A–C⁸, illus., fold. pl., music
Brown, no. 158?₂; RISM B VI, 122
HOUGHTON

BATISTIN   *See* Stuck, Johann Baptist, called Batistin

182   [BÂTON, CHARLES]

Examen | De La Lettre | De M. Rousseau, | Sur La Musique Françoise. | Dans lequel on expose le plan d'une bonne | Musique propre à notre langue. | Par M. B***. | [Paris] M.DCC.LIII.

8° 2 ℓ., 36p.
Eitner I, 375; RISM B VI, 123
HOUGHTON

BAUME LE BLANC, LOUIS CÉSAR DE LA, DUC DE LA VALLIÈRE   *See* La Vallière, Louis César de la Baume Le Blanc, duc de

183   BAYLEY, DANIEL

A New and Complete | Introduction | To The | Grounds and Rules of Music. | In Two Books. | I. Containing the Grounds and Rules | Of Music; or an Introduction to the | Art of Singing by Note, taken from | Thomas Walter, M. A. | II. Containing a new and correct Intro-|duction to the Grounds of Music, | rudimental and practical; from Wil-|liam Tans'ur's Royal Melody. | The whole being a Collection of a Variety of the Choicest Tunes from | the most approved Masters. | By Daniel Bayley, | Chorister of St. Paul's Church, Newbury-Port. | . . . | Printed for and sold by Daniel Bayley of Newbury-Port. M,DCC,LXIV.

obl. 8° 24 p., 24 [+] numb. ℓ.
Numbered leaves 1–24: musical examples and hymns for three voices, without texts
Numbered leaves printed on one side only
Imperfect: numbered leaf 16 torn, with loss of music; all after leaf 24 lacking
HOUGHTON

184   BAYLY, ANSELM

The | Alliance | Of | Musick, Poetry and Oratory. | Under The Head of Poetry | Is Considered | The Alliance And Nature Of The | Epic And Dramatic Poem, | As It Exists In The | Iliad, Aeneid And Paradise Lost. | By Anselm Bayly, LL.D. | Sub-Dean Of His Majesty's Chapels Royal. | London, | Printed for John Stockdale, Piccadilly, | 1789.

8° iv p., 1 ℓ., 384 p., illus.
RISM B VI, 126
HOUGHTON, WIDENER

185   BAYLY, ANSELM

A | Practical Treatise | On | Singing And Playing | With Just Expression and Real Elegance. | Being An | Essay | On | I. Grammar. | II. Pronunciation; or, The | Art of Just Speaking. | III. Singing—Its Graces— | Their Application.—On Ca-

|thedral Compositions. | By Anselm
Bayly, L. L. D. | Sub-Dean of his Maj-
esty's Chapel-Royal. | London: | Printed
for J. Ridley, in St. James's-street. |
M.DCC.LXXI.

8° v, [1], 16, 99 p., music
RISM B VI, 127
MUSIC LIBRARY

BEAUJOYEAULX, BALTASAR DE   *See* Belgiojoso, Baldassarino da

186   BEDFORD, ARTHUR

The | Great Abuse | Of | Musick. | In
Two Parts. | Containing | An Account of
the Use and Design of | Musick among
the Antient Jews, Greeks, | Romans, and
others; with their Concern | for, and Care
to prevent the Abuse thereof. | And Also |
An Account of the Immorality and Pro-
faneness, | which is occasioned by the
Corruption of | that most Noble Science
in the Present | Age. | By Arthur Bedford,
M. A. | Chaplain to His Grace Wriothesly
Duke of | Bedford, and Vicar of Temple in
the City | of Bristol. | London: | Printed
by J. H. [i. e. John Humphreys?] for
John Wyatt at the Rose in | St. Paul's
Church-yard. 1711.

8° 2 ℓ., 276 p., music
Pages [269]–276: A | Canon | Of | Four
Parts in One, | According to Mr. Purcell's
Rule | Of Fuging . . .
RISM B VI, 129
MUSIC LIBRARY

187   BEDFORD, ARTHUR

The | Temple Musick: | Or, An | Essay |
Concerning the Method of | Singing | The
| Psalms of David, | In The | Temple, | Be-
fore the Babylonish Captivity. | Wherein,
| The Musick of our Cathedrals is Vindi-
cated, and | supposed to be Conformable,
not only to that of | the Primitive Chris-
tians, but also to the Practice | of the
Church in all preceding Ages. | By Arthur
Bedford, | Chaplain to His Grace Wrioth-
esly Duke of Bedford; and | Vicar of Tem-
ple, in the City of Bristol. | . . . | London,
Printed and Sold by J. Mortlock, at the
Phoenix in | St. Paul's Church-Yard; J.

Walsh in Catherine street, near | the
Strand; and Anth. Piesly near St. Mary's
Church in | Oxford. 1706.

8° 8 ℓ., 253, [1] p., music
RISM B VI, 129–130; Walsh I, no. 208
MUSIC LIBRARY

THE BEGGAR'S OPERA   *See* Pepusch, John
Christopher *The Beggar's Opera*

THE BEGGAR'S OPERA, PART 2   *See* Polly

BÈGUE, NICOLAS ANTOINE LE   *See*
Lebègue, Nicolas Antoine

BEHAUPTUNG DER HIMMLISCHEN MUSIK
See Mattheson, Johann *Behauptung der
himmlischen Musik*

BELESTA, JEAN BAPTISTE MERCADIER DE
See Mercadier, Jean Baptiste

188   BELGIOJOSO, BALDASSARINO DA

Balet Comiqve | De La Royne, Faict |
Avx Nopces De Mon-|sieur le Duc de
Ioyeuse & | madamoyselle de Vau-|de-
mont sa soeur. | Par | Baltasar De Bea-
vioyevlx, | Valet De Chambre Dv | Roy,
& de la Royne sa mere. | A Paris, | Par
Adrian le Roy, Robert Ballard, & Mamert
| Patisson, Imprimeurs du Roy. |
M.D.LXXXII. | Avec Privilege.

4° 8 ℓ., 75 numb. ℓ., illus., music
Brown, no. 1582₃; Hirsch III, no. 629;
LesureL, no. 248
HOUGHTON (2 copies)

LA BELLE ARSÈNE   *See* Monsigny,
Pierre Alexandre *La Belle Arsène*

BEMERKUNGEN EINES REISENDEN ǓBER
DIE ZU BERLIN VOM SEPTEMBER 1787
BIS ENDE JANUAR 1788 GEGEBENE
ǑFFENTLICHE MUSIKEN . . . *See* Rei-
chardt, Johann Friedrich *Bemerkungen
eines Reisenden ǔber die zu Berlin vom
September 1787 bis Ende Januar 1788
gegebene ǒffentliche Musiken . . .*

189   [BEMETZRIEDER, ANTON]

Lecciones | De Clave, | Y Principios | De Harmonía. | Por D. Benito Bails, | Director de Matemáticas de la Real Academia de S. Fernando, | Individuo de las Reales Academias Española, de la Historia, | y de las Ciencias naturales y Artes de Barcelona. | Madrid. | Por D. Joachin Ibarra, Impresor de Cámara de S. M. | M.DCC.LXXV. | Con Privilegio De S. M.

4° 4 *ℓ*., VI, 291 p., illus., fold. pl., music
A free translation by Bails of Bemetzrieder's *Leçons de clavecin* (see MGG I, col. 1620)
RISM B VI, 112
MUSIC LIBRARY

190   BEMETZRIEDER, ANTON

Leçons | De Clavecin, | Et | Principes | D'Harmonie, | Par Mr Bemetzrieder. | A Paris, | Chez Bluet, Libraire, Pont Saint-Michel. | M.DCC.LXXI. | Avec Approbation, & Privilege du Roi.

4° viij, 362 p., 1 *ℓ*., illus., music
Hirsch I, no. 56; RISM B VI, 132
HOUGHTON

191   BEMETZRIEDER, ANTON

Music made Easy to every Capacity, | In A | Series Of Dialogues; | Being | Practical Lessons | For The | Harpsichord, | Laid Down In A New Method, | So as to render that Instrument so little difficult, that any Person, with common | Application, may play well; become a thorough Proficient in the Principles of | Harmony; and will compose Music, if they have a Genius for it, in less than a | Twelvemonth. | Written In French By | Monsieur Bemetzrieder, | Musick Master To the Queen Of France. | And published at Paris, (with a Preface) by the Celebrated | Monsieur Diderot, | The Whole Translated, and adapted to the Use of the English Student, | By Giffard Bernard, M. A. | Perused And Approved Of By | Doctor Boyce And Doctor Howard. | London: | Printed By R. Ayre and G. Moore, No. 5, Bridges-Street, Covent-Garden; | And Sold By W. Randall, Catharine-Street, Strand. | MDCCLXXVIII. | . . .

4° 1 *ℓ*., vi, [iii]–vi, iv, 249 [i. e. 253] p., illus., music
Two unnumbered pages after page [88]; two more after page 198
RISM B VI, 132
MUSIC LIBRARY

192   BEMETZRIEDER, ANTON

Nouvel Essai | Sur L'Harmonie, | Suite du Traité de Musique, | Dédié A Monseigneur | Le Duc De Chartres, | Prince Du Sang. | Par M. Bemetzrieder. | A Paris, | Chez L'Auteur, rue Neuve S. Roch, près celle des | Moineaux. | Et chez Onfroy, Libraire, Quai des Augustins, | au Lys d'or. | M.DCC.LXXIX. | Avec Approbation, & Privilege du Roi.

8° 286 p., illus.
Page 286: Approbation, dated 1780
Imperfect: twenty plates on ten folded leaves lacking (see Gregory, p. 29)
RISM B VI, 133
MUSIC LIBRARY

193   [BENDA, JIŘÍ ANTONÍN]

Ariadne Auf Naxos [Vienna, Artaria, 1779]

obl. 2° *Vocal score:* 1 *ℓ*., 34 p.
Imperfect: title-page lacking; caption title
RISM A I, no. B 1870
MUSIC LIBRARY

194   BENDA, JIŘÍ ANTONÍN

Klavierauszug | von | Romeo und Julie, | einer Oper in drey Akten. | In Musik gesetzt | von | Herrn Kapelldirektor Benda. | Leipzig, | im Verlage der Dykischen Buchhandlung. | 1778.

large obl. 4° *Vocal score:* 54 p., 1 *ℓ*.
Colophon: Leipzig, gedruckt bey Johann Gottlob Immanuel Breitkopf
RISM A I, no. B 1883
MUSIC LIBRARY

195   BENDA, JIŘÍ ANTONÍN

Sammlung | Vermischter Clavier-und Gesangstücke | für | Geübte und Ungeübte. | Dem | Hochwürdigsten Fürsten, Herrn Martin, | Abten zu St. Blasien &c.

&c. | gewidmet | von | Georg Benda. | Zweyter Theil. | Gotha, | beym Verfasser und in Commission bey C. W. Ettinger. 1781.

large obl. 4° *Score:* 2 ℓ., 36 p.
Contents: Sonata in a minor for keyboard instrument; "Jesus am Kreuze," aria for soprano, two violins, viola and continuo; Sonata in G major for violin and keyboard instrument; "Stolz auf Gott und sein Erbarmen lebe," aria for soprano, two flutes, two violins, viola and continuo; two sonatinas in F major for keyboard instrument
RISM A I, no. B 1899
MUSIC LIBRARY

196   BENDA, JIŘI ANTONÍN

Walder, | eine ernsthafte Operette in einem Acte, | des Herrn Gotters. | In Musik gesetzt | von | Georg Benda, | Herzoglich Sachsin-Gothaischen Capelldirector. | Clavierauszug, nebst Begleitung einiger Instrumente. | Gotha, | bey Carl Wilhelm Ettinger. | 1777.

large obl. 4° *Score:* 2 ℓ., 82 p.
Version for use by small amateur groups
Colophon: Leipzig, gedruckt bey Johann Gottlob Immanuel Breitkopf.
RISM A I, no. B 1886
MUSIC LIBRARY

197   BENNET, JOHN

Madrigalls | To | Fovre Voyces | Newly Pvblished | By | Iohn Bennet | His First Works. | At London | Printed in little Saint Hellens by William | Barley, the Assigne of Thomas Morley. | Cum Priuilegio. | M.D.XC.IX. | . . .

4° 4 pts.: *cantvs, altvs, tenor, bassvs:* A–C⁴ each
RISM A I, no. B 1952
HOUGHTON

198   BERCKELAERS, JOHANNES

Cantiones | Natalitiae | IV. Vocvm Et IV. | Instrvment. | Avctore | Ioanne Berckelaers. | . . . | Antverpiae, | Apud Haeredes Petri Phalesii, Typographi Musices. | M.DC.LXVII.

4° 2 pts.: *altvs, tenor:* 8 p. each
Texts in Dutch
RISM A I, no. B 1982
HOUGHTON

199   BERCKELAERS, JOHANNES

Cantiones | Natalitiae | Duabus, quatuor & quinquè tam Vocibus, | quàm Instrumentis decantandae. | Avctore | Ioanne Berckelaers | . . . | Liber Secundus. | Antverpiae, | Apud Haeredes Petri Phalesii, Typographi, | Musices, ad insigne Davidis Regis. | M.D.C.LXX.

4° 1 pt.: *altvs:* 16 p.
Texts in Dutch
RISM A I, no. B 1983
HOUGHTON

200   BERCKELAERS, JOHANNES

Cantiones | Natalitiae, | Duabus, & quatuor vocibus decantandae, | Cum Reprisis 4. 5. 6. voc. & Instr. | Necessariis. | Avctore | Ioanne Berckelaers | Caeco. | Opvs Tertivm. | . . . | Antverpiae, | Apud Lucam De Potter, Typographum Musices, in Lilio albo | M.DC.LXXIX.

4° 1 pt.: *bassvs praecentus:* 42, [1] p.
Texts in Dutch
RISM A I, no. B 1984
HOUGHTON

201   BERMUDO, JUAN

Comiença el libro llamado de|claraciõ de instumētos musicales dirigido al illustrissimo señor el se|ñor don Francisco de çuniga Conde de Miranda, señor delas ca|sas de auellaneda y baçá &c. cõpuisto por el muy reuerendo pa|dre fray Iuã Bermudo dela ordē delos menores: en el qual halla|rã todo lo que en musica dessearē, y cõtiene seys libros: segũ enla | pagina siguiēte se vera: examinado y aprouado por los egregios musicos Bernardino de figueroa, y Christoual de morales. 1555 | Con priuilegio.

2° 8 ℓ., cxlij numb. ℓ., illus., music
Colophon: . . . fuerõ impressos ē la villa de Os|suna por Iuan de Leõ impressor de libros dela insigne | Vniuersidad del Illustrissimo señor dõ Iuã Tellez | Giron cõde de Vrueña &c. Y acabarõse de

| imprimir a treze dias del mes de Iulio sien|do bispera de sanct Buenauentura | Año de .M.D.L.v.

Brown, no. 1555₁; RISM B VI, 140
HOUGHTON

202 BERTAUD, JEAN

Encomivm | trium Mariarum cū earundē cultus defensione aduersus | Lutheranos. Solenniq[ue] missa & officio canonico, in qui-|bus omnibus desideres nihil, emissum opera & industria | Ioānis Bertaudi Petragorici vtriusq[ue] iuris licentiati. Tur-|risq[ue] alb[a]e in ducatu Engolismēsi, alūni: auspiciis augustis|sim[a]e principis Ioann[a]e Aurelianensis, Gyueriensiū domi-|nae, ac Comitis du Barcq. | [Paris] Venundatur Iodoco Badio. & Galeoto a pratis. [1529]

4° a⁸, b⁴, c⁶, A⁸, e–k⁸, 1⁴, [2d]a–i⁸, k⁴, ℓ.⁶, illus., music
Colophon: . . . apud parrhisios palatio.
Imprint data from leaf ℓ.6ʳ
MortimerF, no. 54
HOUGHTON

BERTIE, WILLOUGHBY, 4TH EARL OF ABINGDON *See* Abingdon, Willoughby Bertie, 4th earl of

203 BERTON, HENRI MONTAN

Montano | Et | Stéphanie | Opera en trois Actes | Par | Le Cit. Jaure. | Mis en Musique | Par Le Cit. H. Berton | Membre du Conservatoire | Représenté pour la premiere fois | Sur le Théâtre de l'Opéra comique National | le 26. Germinal de l'an 7. | . . . | A Paris | chez Des Lauriers, Editeur de Musique, rue des Peres No. 14. | . . . | Beaublé Sculpt. [1799?]

2° *Score:* 2 ℓ., 266 p.
Plate no. 60
Preliminary leaf 2ᵛ: Catalogue | de Musique | du fond de Des Lauriers . . .
RISM A I, no. B 2273
MUSIC LIBRARY

204 BERTON, PIERRE MONTAN

Silvie | Opéra En Trois Actes | Avec un Prologue | Représenté devant leurs Majestés à Fontainebleau le 17 Octobre | 1765, et par l'Accadémie royale de Musique le 18. Novembre 1766. | Dédiée | A son Altesse Sérénissime Monseigneur | Le Prince De Conty | Par Mrs. | Berton Et Trial | Directeurs de l'Accadémie royale de Musique | Les Paroles sont de Mr Laujon | Sécrétaire des Commandemens de son A. S. Mgr. le Comte de Clermont | . . . | A Paris | Chez {M. Trial rue St. Nicaise à l'Accadémie royale de musique. | M. De la Chevardiere md. de musique du Roi, rue du Roule à la croix d'or | Et aux adresses ordinaires de musique. | A. P. D. R. | Le Prologue et le 1er. Acte Gravés par Ceron de l'Imprimerie de Bernard rue Guénéguad [ca. 1767]

2° *Score:* 1 ℓ., 332 p.
RISM A I, no. B 2363
MUSIC LIBRARY

205 BERTONI, FERDINANDO GASPARO

Six | Quartetto's | for | Two Violins, a Tenor, | and | Violoncello. | Respectfully Dedicated | to | William Beckford Esqr. | by | Ferdinando Bertoni | London. | Printed for the Author No. 8 Great Marybone | Street, where the work may be had, & also at | R. Bremner's Music Shop in ye Strand, & all | other Music | Shops. [1783?]

2° 4 pts.: *violino primo:* 1 ℓ., 17 p.; *violino secondo:* 17 p.; *viola, basso:* 15 p. each
Dedication dated 1783 in contemporary manuscript
RISM A I, no. B 2405
MUSIC LIBRARY

206 BERTRAND, ANTOINE DE

Premier Livre | Des Amovrs De | Pierre De Ronsard. | mis en musique à IIII. parties par Anth. Bertrand. | A Paris. | Par Adrian le Roy, & Robert Ballard. | Imprimeurs du Roy. | M.D.LXXXVII. | Auec priuilege de sa majesté pour dix ans. | . . .

obl. 4° 1 pt.; *contra:* 28 numb. ℓ.
LesureL, no. 289; RISM A I, no. B 2414; Thibault, no. 121
HOUGHTON

207   BERTRAND, ANTOINE DE

Second Livre | Des Amovrs De | Pierre
De Ronsard. | mis en musique à IIII. par-
ties par Anth. Bertrand. | A Paris. | Par
Adrian le Roy, & Robert Ballard. | Impri-
meurs du Roy. | M.D.LXXXVII. | Auec
priuilege de sa majesté pour dix ans. |
. . .

　　obl. 4° 1 pt.: *contra:* 24 numb. *ℓ.*
LesureL, no. 290; RISM A I, no. B
2416; Thibault, no. 122
HOUGHTON

208   BERTRAND, ANTOINE DE

Troisiesme Livre | De Chansons |
mises en musique à IIII. parties par An-
toine | Bertrand natif de fontanges en
Auuergne. | A Paris. | Par Adrian le Roy,
& Robert Ballard. | Imprimeurs du Roy. |
M.D.LXXXVII. | Auec priuilege de sa ma-
jesté pour dix ans. | . . .

　　obl. 4° 1 pt.: *contra:* 20 numb. *ℓ.*
LesureL, no. 291; RISM A I, no. B
2419; Thibault, no. 123
HOUGHTON

209   BÉTHISY, JEAN LAURENT DE

Exposition | De La Théorie | Et De La
Pratique | De | La Musique, | Suivant les
nouvelles découvertes. | Par M. De. Be-
thizy. | Seconde Édition, | Corrigée &
augmentée par l'Auteur. | A Paris, | Chez
F. G. Deschamps, Libraire, | rue S.
Jacques, aux Associés. | MDCC.LXIV. |
Avec Approbation, & Privilége du Roi.

　　8° xvj, 331, [4], 60 p., illus., music
Pages 1–60 at end: musical examples
Hirsch I, no. 66; RISM B VI, 145
MUSIC LIBRARY

210   BETTS, EDWARD

An | Introduction | To The | Skill of
Musick. | I. The Grounds and Principles
of Musick, according to | the Gamut;
after an easy Method, for Young Begin-
ners. | II. A Table shewing the Names,
Numbers, Measures and Propor-|tions, of
the Notes. | III. All the Cliffs in Use, and
how to find your Me. | IV. What Flats and
Sharps belongs to every Key now us'd. |

V. The different Movements of Time
that are now us'd. | VI. Of the Tying
Notes, and other Marks and Characters
us'd in | Musick. | VII. Several short
Tunes, by Way of Solfaing, and how to
run | a Division, for the Improvement of
Young Practitioners. | VIII. A Rule how
to make a Shake, upon the Whole and
Half | Note. | IX. Several Duo's by Way of
Solfaing; and a Canon Four in | One to a
Gloria Patria, by Dr. Blow. | X. Several
Chants in Four Parts, for Choir Musick. |
XI. A Rule how to Express the Words in a
soft easie Manner, | with excellant An-
thems, Compos'd by very famous | Au-
thors. | Anthems, Hymns and Psalm-
|Tunes, in several Parts. | By Edward
Betts, Organist of Manchester. | London:
| Printed by William Pearson, for the Au-
thor; | and Sold by William Clayton
Bookseller, and | Roger Adams Printer, in
Manchester. 1724.

　　8° 11 *ℓ.*, 105, [1] p., illus., music
Pages [1]–105: Anthems, in Two,
Three and Four Parts.
MUSIC LIBRARY

BEUF, JEAN LE   *See* Lebeuf, Jean

BEVERINGEN, ANDRÉ   *See* Pevernage,
André

BEVERNAGE, ANDRÉ   *See* Pevernage,
André

BEW, JOHN, PUBL. Vocal Music, or the
Songster's Companion   *See* Vocal
Music, or the Songster's Companion

211   [BIANCHI, FRANCESCO]

La Villanella Rapita | Ou | La Villa-
geoise | Enlevée | Opera Bonffon [*sic*] En
Trois Actes, | Représenté au théâtre de
Monsieur en 1789. | Musique Italienne
de Diférens Célébres | Compositeurs, |
Paroles Italienne Traduite en Françaises,
Par M. D.***. | . . . | A. Paris. | Chez le Sr
Sieber Musicien, rue St honore entre
celles des | Vielles Etuve et celle D'or-
leans chez l'Apothicaire No 92 et 85
[1792?]

2° *Score:* 1 *ℓ.*, 267 p.
Plate no. 1060
"chez l'Apothicaire" cancelled in imprint
Hirsch II, no. 63; RISM A I, no. B 2560
MUSIC LIBRARY

212　BIANCHINI, FRANCESCO

Francisci Blanchini | Veronensis | Utriusque Signaturae Referendarii, & Praelati Domestici, | De | Tribus Generibus | Instrumentorum | Musicae Veterum | Organicae | Dissertatio. | Romae, MDCCXLII. | Impensis Fausti Amidei Bibliopolae in via Cursus. | Ex Typographia Bernabò, & Lazzarini. | Svperiorvm Permissv.

4° XI, 58 p., 8 pl.
Hirsch I, no. 71; RISM B VI, 148
MUSIC LIBRARY, HOUGHTON

BICKEL, CONRAD　*See* Celtes, Conradus

213　BICKHAM, GEORGE,
　　　THE YOUNGER

The | Musical | Entertainer | Engrav'd | By George Bickham junr. | . . . | London Printed for & Sold by Geo: Bickham, at his House ye Corner of Bedford-Bury, New-Street, Covent Garden. [1737?]

2° *Score: vol. I:* 1 *ℓ.*, 4 numb. *ℓ.*, 4 p., 100 numb. *ℓ.*, illus.
The bass is unfigured in the first two bars of Carey's "Generous Love" (numb. *ℓ.* 88; see Schnapper I, 107)
Numbered leaves engraved on one side only
RISM B II, 245
HOUGHTON (3 copies; 2d & 3d imperfect)

214　BICKHAM, GEORGE,
　　　THE YOUNGER

Bickham's | Musical Entertainer. | . . . | [London] Printed for C. Corbett at Addison's head, Fleet Street. | . . . [1738?]

2° *Score: vol. II:* 3 *ℓ.*, 100 numb. *ℓ.*, illus.
"The Prudent Adviser" (numb. *ℓ.* 14) ascribed to Händel; no composer named

on numb. *ℓ.* 86 (see Schnapper I, 107)
Numbered leaves engraved on one side only
RISM B II, 245; Hirsch III, no. 650
HOUGHTON

215　BIELING, FRANZ IGNAZ

Aerarium Marianum, | Hoc Est: | Litaniae VI. | Non nimis Longae | Lauretanae | De B. Virgine Maria | Sine | Labe Concepta; | Cum Annexis | II. Te Deum Laudamus. | A | IV. Vocib. ordinariis, partim 2. Violinis, partim Unisono | necess. 2. Tubis vel Lituis ex diversis clavibus, partim ob-|ligat. partim ad placitum producendis, Principale & | Tympano pro libitu interdum adjunctis, cum | duplici Basso Continuo. | à | Francisco Ignatio Bieling, | Ducalis Ecclesiae Campidonensis Organaedâ. | Opus II. | . . . | Cum Licentia Superiorum. | Augustae Vindelicorum, | Typis & Sumptibus Joannis Jacobi Lotteri, MDCCXXXI.

2° 2 pts.: *violoncello, organo:* 2 *ℓ.*, 28 p. each
RISM A I, no. B 2624
HOUGHTON

BIZCARGUI, GONÇALO MARTÍNEZ DE
See Martínez de Bizcargui, Goncalo

216　BLAINVILLE, CHARLES HENRI

L'Esprit | De L'Art | Musical, | Ou | Réflexions | Sur La Musique, | Et Ses Différentes Parties | Par C. H. Blainville. | A Genêve. | M.DCC.LIV.

8° 2 *ℓ.*, 126, [2] p., front.
Hirsch I, no. 70; RISM B VI, 152
HOUGHTON

217　BLAISE, ADOLPHE

Annette et Lubin, | Comedie en un Acte en Vers, | Par Me. Favart. | Melée d'Ariettes et Vaudevilles dont les accompagnements sont de | Mr. Blaise. | . . . | Gravée par Chambon. | A Paris Chez Mr. De la Chevardiere, rue du Roule, à la Croix d'Or | aux Adresses ordinaires [1762]

2° *Score:* 2 *ℓ.*, 50 p.

Preliminary leaves 1ᵛ–2ʳ: Catalogue No. I[–II.] | De Musique Vocale [–Instrumentale] Apartenant a M De La Chevardiere . . .
RISM A I, no. B 2780
MUSIC LIBRARY

218   BLAISE, ADOLPHE

Isabelle | Et Gertrude | Ou | Les Sylphes Supposés | Comédie en un Acte | Par | M Favart | Mise en Musique | Par M. Blaise | Représentée à la Comedie Italienne | . . . | A Paris | Chez Mr. de la Chevardiere rue du roule à la croix d'or. Md. de musique du Roi et de la Famille royale. | A Lion | Mrs. les Freres le Goux, Place des Cordeliers. | Mr. Castaud vis à vis la Comedie. | A. P. D. R. [ca. 1774]

2° *Score:* 2 ℓ., 48 p.
Preliminary leaves 1ᵛ–2ʳ: Catalogue No. I.[–II.] | De Musique Vocale [–Instrumentale] Appartenant a M. De La Chevardiere . . .
Hirsch II, no. 69; RISM A I, no. B 2808
MUSIC LIBRARY

BLANC, LOUIS CÉSAR DE LA BAUME LE, DUC DE LA VALLIÈRE *See* La Vallière, Louis César de la Baume Le Blanc, duc de

BLANCHINUS, FRANCISCUS *See* Bianchini, Francesco

BLAND, ANNE, PUBL. One hundred Cantici or Catches for 3 and 4 Voices *See* One Hundred Cantici or Catches for 3 and 4 Voices

BLAND, JOHN, PUBL. A Collection of Catches Glees &c *See* A Collection of Catches Glees &c

219   BLAND, JOHN, COMP.

The | Ladies Collection, | Of | Catches, Glees, Canons, | Canzonets, Madrigals, &c. | Selected from the Works of the Most | Eminent Composers. | By John Bland. | Continued | And Sold by Rt. Birchall at his Musical Circulating Library | 133 New Bond Street. | . . . [ca. 1789]

2° *Score: vol. I:* 1 ℓ., 121, [1] p.
Incomplete: vols. II–VI lacking
RISM B II, 214
MUSIC LIBRARY

220   BLIESENER, JOHANN

Three | Quartettos | for two | Violins, a Tenor | And | Violoncello Obligato | Composed by | Jean Bliesener | Opera 2. . . . | London Printed by Longman and Broderip No. 26 Cheapside | and No. 13 Hay Market | . . . [ca. 1790]

2° 4 pts.: *violino primo, violino secondo:* 11 p. each; *viola, violoncello:* 7 p. each
Plate no. 687
RISM A I, no. B 2965
MUSIC LIBRARY

BLOND, GASPAR MICHEL LE   *See* Leblond, Gaspar Michel, called

221   BLOW, JOHN

Amphion Anglicus. | A | VVork | Of Many | Compositions, | For One, Two, Three and Four | Voices: | With several Accompagnements of | Instrumental Musick; | And | A Thorow-Bass to each Song: | Figur'd for an | Organ, Harpsichord, or Theorboe-Lute. | By Dr. John Blow. | London: | Printed by William Pearson, for the Author; and are to be Sold at his House in the | Broad-Sanctnary, [*sic*] over-against Westminster-Abby, and by Henry Playford, at his Shop | in the Temple-Change, Fleet-street. MDCC.

2° *Score:* 4 ℓ., viii, [2], 216 p., front. (port.)
First unnumbered page after page viii: Books lately Printed and Re-printed for Henry Playford . . .
Day, no. 183; RISM A I, no. B 2985
HOUGHTON (2 copies; 2d imperfect)

222   BLOW, JOHN

Three | Elegies | Upon The | Much Lamented Loss | Of Our | Late Most Gracious | Queen Mary. | The Words of the two First by Mr Herbert. | The latter out of the Oxford Verse; | And Sett to Musick by | Dr Blow and Mr Henry Purcell. | London, | Printed by J. Heptinstall, for Henry Playford, near the | Temple-Church; or at his House over-against | the Blew-Ball in Arundel-street, 1695.

2° *Score:* 18 p.
Page 18: Books Reprinted this Term.
Contents: "The Queen's epicedium" by Blow; "Latine redditum" and "O dive Custos Auriacae domus" by Purcell
RISM B I, no. 1695⁹
HOUGHTON

223   BLOW, JOHN

A Second | Musical Entertainment | Perform'd On | St. Cecilia's day. | November XXII. 1684. | The Words | By the late ingenious Mr. John Oldham, | Author of the Satyrs against the Jesuits, &c. | Set to Music in two, three, four, and five Parts, | by Dr. John Blow, Master of the Children, | and Organist of His Majesty's Chappel-Royal. | London, | Printed by John Playford, and are to be sold by John | Carr, at the Middle-Temple Gate, 1685.

4° *Score:* 4 ℓ., 71, [1] p.
Unnumbered page at end: Music Books sold by John Carr, at the | Middle-Temple Gate in Fleet-Street.
RISM A I, no. B 3004
HOUGHTON

224   BOCCHERINI, LUIGI

Sei | Quintetti | Per due Violini Alto et due Violoncelli | Concertanti. | Composti Dall Sigor. | Luigi Boccherini | Virtuoso di Camera et Compositor di Musica | Di | S. A. R. Don Luigi | Infante di Spagnia. | Opera XII. | Libro primo di Quintetti. | Mis au jour par M. Boyer | . . . | N. B. la partie du second Violoncelle se poura executer | sur l'Alto ou un Basson. | A Paris. | Chez Naderman, rue de la Loi, à la Clef d'or, | Passage du Caffé de foy. | A Lyon. | Aux adresses de musique. | A. P. D. R. [ca. 1797]

2° 5 pts.: *violino primo:* 1 ℓ., 24 p.; *violino secondo:* 24 p.; *viola:* 20 p.; *violoncello primo* and *IIo.:* 22 p. each
RISM A I, no. B 3156
G. 265–270
MUSIC LIBRARY

225   BOCCHERINI, LUIGI

Sei | Quintetti | Per due Violini Alto et due Violoncelli | Concertanti. | Composti dall. Sigor. | Luigi Boccherini | Virtuoso di Camera et Compositor di Musica | Di | S. A. R. Don Luigi | Infante di Spagnia | Opera XIII. | Libro secondo di Quintetti | Mis au jour par M. Boyer. | . . . | A Paris. | Chez Naderman, rue de la Loi, à la Clef d'Or, | Passage du Caffé de foy. | Chez Made. Le Menu, rue du Roulle, à la Clef d'Or. [ca. 1797]

2° 5 pts.: *violino primo:* 1 ℓ., 25 p.; *violino secondo:* 25 p.; *viola obligata, violoncello Io.* and *IIo.:* 21 p. each
A cancel label mounted at the foot of the title-page of the *violino primo* part reads: Sauzeau Marchand Lutier, Sur La Fosse, No. 68, | A Nantes, | . . .
RISM A I, no. B 3162
G. 271–276
MUSIC LIBRARY

226   BOCCHERINI, LUIGI

Sei | Quintette | Per due Violini Alto et due Violoncelli | Concertanti. | Composti Dall. Sigor. | Luigi Boccherini | Virtuoso di Camera et Compositor di Musica. | Di | S. A. R. Don Luigi | Infante di Spagnia. | Opera XX. | Libro terzo di Quintetti. | Mis au jour par M. Boyer | . . . | N. B. Les parties de Violoncelles sont facile pour l'execution, et la second | se poura executer sur l'Alto ou un Basson. | A Paris. | Chez Naderman, rue de la Loi, à la Clef d'Or, | Passage du Caffé de foy. | A Lyon. | Mr. Castaud vis-à-vis la Comedie. | en Province, chez tous les Marchands de musique. | A. P. D. R. [ca. 1797]

2° 5 pts.: *violino primo:* 1 ℓ., 25 p.; *violino secondo:* 20 p.; *viola:* 17 p.; *violoncello primo:* 18 p.; *violoncello IIo:* 16 p.
RISM A I, no. B 3171
G. 277–282
MUSIC LIBRARY

227   BOCCHERINI, LUIGI

Vingt-quatre Nouveaux | Quintetti | Pour deux Violons, | deux Violoncelles et Alto. | Par Luigi Boccherini. | La premiere partie de Violoncelle pourra etre remplacée par l'Alto Violoncelle. | Oeuvre

37. [1] Livraison . . . | Gravés par Richomme. | A Paris | Chez Jgnace Pleyel, Rue Neuve des Petits Champs, No 1286, vis-à-vis la Trésorerie Natile. | Propriété de l'Editeur . . . | L. Aubert scripsit. [1798]

2° 5 pts.: *violino Io:* 1 *ℓ.*, 15 p.; *violino 2o:* 15 p.; *viola:* 13 p.; *violoncello Io, violoncello 2o:* 11 p. each
Plate no. 101
A cancel label mounted at the foot of the title-page of the *violino Io* part reads: Sauzeau Marchand Lutier, Sur La Fosse, No. 68, | Nantes, . . .
RISM A I, no. B 3182
G. 358, 362, 364
MUSIC LIBRARY

228   BOCCHERINI, LUIGI

Vingt-quatre Nouveaux | Quintetti | Pour deux Violons, | deux Violoncelles et Alto. | Par Luigi Boccherini. | La premiere partie de Violoncelle pourra etre remplacée par l'Alto Violoncelle. | Oeuvre 37. [2.] Livraison . . . | Gravés par Richomme. | A Paris | Chez Jgnace Pleyel, Rue Neuve des Petits Champs, No 1286, vis-à-vis la Trésorerie Natile. | Propriété de l'Editeur . . . | L. Aubert scripsit. [1798]

2° 5 pts.: *violino Io:* 1 *ℓ.*, 19 p.; *violino 2o:* 13 p.; *viola:* 12 p.; *violoncello Io, violoncello 2o:* 11 p. each
Plate no. 102
Sauzeau's cancel label mounted at foot of title-page in *violino Io* part
RISM A I, no. B 3182
G. 356, 369, 368
MUSIC LIBRARY

229   BOCCHERINI, LUIGI

Vingt-quatre Nouveaux | Quintetti | Pour deux Violons, | deux Violoncelles et Alto. | Par Luigi Boccherini. | La premiere partie de Violoncelle pourra etre remplacée par l'Alto Violoncelle. | Oeuvre 37. [3.] Livraison . . . | Gravés par Richomme. | A Paris | Chez Jgnace Pleyel, Rue Neuve des Petits Champs, No 1286, vis-à-vis la Trésorerie Natile. | Propriété de l'Editeur . . . | L. Aubert scripsit. [1799]

2° 5 pts.: *violino Io:* 1 *ℓ.*, 19 p.; *violino 2o:* 13 p.; *viola:* 15 p.; *violoncello Io:* 17 p.; *violoncello 2o:* 11 p.
Plate no. 146
Sauzeau's cancel label mounted at foot of title-page in *violino Io* part
RISM A I, no. B 3182
G. 310, 308, 366
MUSIC LIBRARY

230   BOCCHERINI, LUIGI

Vingt-quatre Nouveaux | Quintetti | Pour deux Violons, | deux Violoncelles et Alto. | Par Luigi Boccherini. | La premiere partie de Violoncelle pourra etre remplacée par l'Alto Violoncelle. | Oeuvre 37. [4.] Livraison . . . | Gravés par Richomme. | A Paris | Chez Jgnace Pleyel, Rue Neuve des Petits Champs, No 1286, vis-à-vis la Trésorerie Natile. | Propriété de l'Editeur . . . | L. Aubert scripsit. [1799]

2° 5 pts.: *violino Io:* 1 *ℓ.*, 17 p.; *violino 2o:* 14 p.; *viola:* 12 p.; *violoncello Io:* 13 p.; *violoncello 2o:* 10 p.
Plate no. 147
Sauzeau's cancel label mounted at foot of title-page in *violino Io* part
RISM A I, no. 3182
G. 359, 365, 346
MUSIC LIBRARY

231   BOCCHERINI, LUIGI

Vingt-quatre Nouveaux | Quintetti | Pour deux Violons, | deux Violoncelles et Alto. | Par Luigi Boccherini. | La premiere partie de Violoncelle pourra etre remplacée par l'Alto Violoncelle. | Oeuvre 37. [5.] Livraison . . . | Gravés par Richomme. | A Paris | Chez Jgnace Pleyel, Rue Neuve des Petits Champs, no 1286, vis-à-vis la Trésorerie Natile. | Propriété de l'Editeur . . . | L. Aubert scripsit. [1799]

2° 5 pts.: *violino Io:* 1 *ℓ.*, 13 p.; *violino 2o, viola, violoncello Io, violoncello 2o:* 13 p. each
Plate no. 261
Sauzeau's cancel label mounted at foot of title-page in *violino Io* part
RISM A I, no. B 3182
G. 351, 307, 312
MUSIC LIBRARY

232 BOCCHERINI, LUIGI

Six | Sestetti | Concertanti | Per Due Violini Due Viola e | Due Violoncelli | Composte per S. A. Rle. Don Luigi | Infante di Spagna & . . . | Da Luigi Boccherini | Virtuoso di Camera e Compositore di S. A. Rle.*** | Opera XXIV. | . . . | A Paris | Chéz le Sr. Sieber. Musicien, rue St Honoré à l'hôtel D'Aligre Ancien | Grand Conseil ou l'on trouve plusieur nouveaux ouvrages de Musique, | A. P. D. R. [ca. 1779]

2° 6 pts.: *violino primo:* 1 *ℓ.,* 19 p.; *violino secondo:* 19 p.; *viola prima, viola seconda:* 17 p. each; *violoncello primo:* 14 p.; *violoncello secondo:* 13 p.
Page [1] in *violino primo* part: Catalogue | De Musique Vocale et Instrumentale Appartenant á M. Sieber, | . . . ⟨JohanssonF, facs. 110⟩
RISM A I, no. B 3204
G. 454–459
HOUGHTON

233 BOCCHERINI, LUIGI

Sei Sonate | Di | Cembalo | E | Violino Obbligato | Dedicate, | A Madama | Brillon De Jouy | Da | Luigi Boccherini | Di Lucca. | Gravée par Mme. La Ve. Leclair. | Opera Va. | Novamente Stampata a Spese di G. B. Venier. | . . . | Plusieurs de ces Pieces peuvent s'executer sur la Harpe. | A Paris | Chez M. Venier, Editeur de plusieurs Ouvrages de Musique, à l'Entrée | de la rue St. Thomas du Louvre vis a vis le Chateau d'Eau, | Et aux Adresses Ordinaires. | A Lyon | M. Castaud, Place de la Comedie. | Avec Privilege Du Roy. | Imprimée par Richomme [1771?]

2° 1 pt.: *cembalo:* 1 *ℓ.,* 42 p.
Page [1]: Catalogue | De Musique Instrumentale que Mr. Venier a fait graver . . . ⟨issued between dates of JohanssonF facs. 123 and 124⟩
RISM A I, no. B 3032
G. 25–30
HOUGHTON

234 BOETHIUS

Boetij de Musica . . . [Venice, 1492]

2° In his *Opera,* vol. [I], *ℓ.* dd2ʳ–ii3ʳ, illus.

Colophon: Venetijs Impressum Boetij opus p[er] Joãnem & Gre|goriũ de gregorijs fratres f[o]elici exitu ad finẽ vsq[ue] p[ro]ductũ | accuratissimeq[ue] emẽdatũ Anno humane restaurationis. | 1492. die. 18 Augusti. . . .
Caption title
Goff, no. B-767; GW, no. 4511; Hain, no. 3351; RISM B VI, 157–158
HOUGHTON (2 copies)

235 BOETHIUS

Boetij de Musica . . . [Venice, 1499]

2° In his *Opera,* numb. *ℓ.* 21ᵛ–53ᵛ, second sequence, illus.
Colophon: Venetiis. Impressum Boetii opus per Joannem & | Gregorium de gregoriis fratres felici exitu ad finẽ | vsq[ue] perductum accuratissimeq[ue] emendatum Anno | humane restaurationis. 1499. die. 8. Julii. . . .
Caption title
BMC V, 351; Goff, no. B-768; Hain, no. 3352; RISM B VI, 158
HOUGHTON

236 BOETHIUS

Anitii Manlii Se-|verini Boethi, De Mvsica [Basel, 1546]

2° In his *Opera,* p. 1063–1173, illus., music
Colophon: Basileae Per Henrichvm Petrvm | Mense Martio, Anno | M.D.XLVI.
Caption title
RISM B VI, 157
HOUGHTON

237 BOETHIUS

Anitii Manlii Se-|verini Boethii, De Mvsica [Basel, 1570]

2° In his *Opera,* p. 1371–1481, illus., music
Colophon: Basileae, | Ex Officina Henric Petrina | Mense Martio, Anno | MDLXX.
Caption title
RISM B VI, 157
HOUGHTON

LA BOHÉMIENNE *See* Rinaldo di Capua *La Bohémienne*

238   Boieldieu, François Adrien

Zoraime Et Zulnar | Opéra En Trois Actes | Du Cen. St. Just | Dédié | A Mehul Et Cherubini | Par | Boieldieu | Membre du Concervatoire de Musique de Paris. | Représenté pour la 1re. Fois, | Au Théâtre de L'Opéra Comique Nal. Rue Favart, | Le 21. Floreal An 6. | Gravé par Mme. Brunet | . . . | A La Muse Du Jour, | A Paris | Chez Cochet . . . [1799?]

2° *Score:* 1 ℓ., 257 p.
Imprint covered by cancel label reading: Chez Sieber, (Gendre de Le Duc,) au Magasin de Musique et d'Instruments, | Rue de la Loi (ci-devant Richelieu,) vis-a-vis la Fontaine Traversière, No. 1245; | A la Flute enchantée. A Paris.
MUSIC LIBRARY

Bonanni, Filippo   *See* Buonanni, Filippo

239   Bonini, Pietro Andrea

. . . | Il Primo Libro | De Madrigali | A Cinqve Voci | Di Pier' Andrea Bonini | Maestro della Musica del Duomo | di Ciuidal di Belluno. | In Venetia Appresso Angelo Gardano. | M.D.LXXXXI.

4° 1 pt.: *qvinto:* 1 ℓ., 20 [i. e. 21], [1] p.
Page 21 misnumbered 20
Imperfect: some pages torn, with loss of texts and music
RISM A I, no. B 3493; Vogel, no. 388
HOUGHTON

240   [Bonnet, Jacques, ed.]

Histoire | De | La Musique, | Et De Ses Effets, | Depuis son origine jusqu'à présent. | Dediée | A S. A. R. Monseigneur | Le Duc D'Orleans. | . . . | A Paris, | Chez {Jean Cochart, au Palais, dans | la grande Salle, au second Pillier. | Etienne Ganeau, rue S. Jacque, | vis à vis la Fontaine saint Severin, | aux Armes de Dombes. | Jacque Quillau, rue Galande, | aux Armes de l'Université. | MDCCXV. | Avec Approbation & Privilege du Roy.

12° 8 ℓ., 487, [1] p., illus.
Begun by Pierre Bonnet and his uncle Pierre Bourdelot; edited and published by

Jacques Bonnet (see MGG II, col. 116)
Hirsch I, Historiscner Anhang, no. 8; RISM B VI, 165
MUSIC LIBRARY

241   [Bonnet, Jacques]

Histoire | De | La Musique, | Et De Ses Effets, | Depuis son origine jusqu'à présent: | Et en quoi consiste sa beauté. | . . . | à Amsterdam, | Chez Jeanne Roger. [1722?]

12° 4 vols.: *vol. I:* 3 ℓ., 333, [1] p. illus.; *vol. II:* 1 ℓ., 175 p.; *vol. III:* 1 ℓ., 322 p.; *vol. IV:* 1 ℓ., 230 p.
Vols. II–IV: reprint of Jean Laurent Le Cerf de la Viéville's *Comparaison de la musique italienne et de la musique françoise*
RISM B VI, 165
MUSIC LIBRARY

242   Bonnet, Jacques

Histoire | Generale | De | La Danse, | Sacrée Et Prophane; | Ses progrès & ses révolutions, depuis | son origine jusqu'à présent. | Avec un Supplément de l'Histoire de | la Musique, & le Paralele de la | Peinture & de la Poesie. | Dédiée à S. A. R. Monseigneur le Duc | D'Orleans, petit-fils de France. | Par M. Bonnet, ancien Payeur des Gages | du Parlement. | A Paris, | Chez D'Houry fils, rue de la Harpe, devant la rue S. Severin, au St Esprit. | MDCCXXIII. | Avec Approbation & Privilege du Roy.

12° xl, 269, [3] p.
RISM B VI, 165–166
HOUGHTON

243   [Bonneval, René de]

Apologie | De La Musique | Et | Des Musiciens François, | Contre les assertions peu mélodieuses, peu | mesurées & mal fondées du Sieur Jean-|Jacques Rousseau, ci-devant Citoyen | de Genêve. [Paris, 1754]

8° 15 p.
Hirsch I, no. 82; RISM B VI, 166
HOUGHTON

244   BONONCINI, GIOVANNI

The Anthem | which was Performed | In King Henry the Seventh's Chapel | at the Funeral of | The most Noble & Victorious Prince, | Iohn, | Duke of Marlborough. | The Words | taken out of Holy Scripture. | And Set to Musick by | Mr: Bononcini. | London. Printed for & Sold by I. Walsh, Musick Prin-|ter & Instrument maker to his Majesty, at the Harp & Hoboy | in Catherine Street in the Strand. . . . [ca. 1738]

2° *Score:* 1 ℓ., 19 p.
No. 631 on title-page
RISM A I, no. B 3600; Walsh II, no. 189
HOUGHTON

245   [BONONCINI, GIOVANNI]

Songs | In The New | Opera, | Call'd | Camilla | as they are perform'd at the | Theatre Royall | [London] Sold by I: Walsh Musicall Instrument maker in Or-|-dinary to her Majesty, at the Golden Harpe and Ho-boy, | in Catherine-Street near Sommerset House in the Strand. [ca. 1709]

2° *Vocal score:* 51 ℓ.
Leaves printed on one side only
RISM A I, no. B 3537; Walsh I, no. 298
HOUGHTON

BORDE, JEAN BENJAMIN DE LA   *See* Laborde, Jean Benjamin de

BORGON DE SCELLERY, CHARLES EMMANUEL   *See* Borjon, Charles Emmanuel

246   [BORJON, CHARLES EMMANUEL]

Traité | De La | Mvsette, | Avec Vne Novvelle | Methode, | Pour apprendre de soy-mesme à joüer de cét Instrument | facilement, & en peu de temps. | A Lyon, | Chez Iean Girin, & Barthelemy Riviere, | ruë Merciere, à la Prudence. | M.DC.LXXII. | Avec Privilege Dv Roy.

2° 5 ℓ., 39, 19 p., front., illus., 3 pl., music
Pages 6–17, second sequence: dances (and doubles) in musette tablature, with separate version in staff-notation

One plate included in paging, second sequence
Hirsch I, no. 84; RISM B VI, 169
HOUGHTON

BORMANN, GOTTLOB WILHELM   *See* Burmann, Gottlob Wilhelm

BOURDELOT, JACQUES BONNET   *See* Bonnet, Jacques

247   BOUTMY, LAURENT FRANÇOIS, ARR.

Four | Italian | Overtures. | Arranged For The | Piano Forte. | By | L. Boutmy. | London: | Printed for Harrison, Cluse, & Co. No. 78, Fleet Street. [1799?]

8° *Score:* 29 p. (*The Piano-Forte Magazine,* vol. VII, no. 7)
Plate nos. 104–105
Contains arrangements of symphonies by Giuseppe Sarti, Giovanni Paisiello and Antonio Salieri
MUSIC LIBRARY

248   BOYCE, WILLIAM

Burial Service, | in the Key of (E) with the Lesser third, | (by the late) | Dr. Wm. Boyce. | . . . | Organist, Composer & Master of the Band of Music, to King George 2d. | & his present Majesty. [London, ca. 1800]

2° *Score:* 173–186 p. (No. 64 [of John Page's *Harmonia sacra*])
Plate nos. 22–24
Caption title. Imprint and series statement supplied from Schnapper I, 129
RISM A I, no. B 4048?
MUSIC LIBRARY

249   BOYCE, WILLIAM, COMP.

Cathedral Music: | Being | A Collection in Score | of the | Most Valuable and Useful Compositions | For That Service, | By The | Several English Masters | Of the last Two Hundred Years. | The Whole Selected and Carefully Revis'd | By the late Dr. William Boyce, | Organist and Composer to the Royal Chapels, and | Master of his Majesty's Band of Musicians. | . . . | London: | Printed for John Ashley, | M.DCC.LXXXVIII. | Second Edition.

2° *Score:* 3 vols.: *vol. I:* 4 ℓ., xi, [1], iii–
iv, vii–xii, 290 p., front. (port.); *vol. II:*
2 ℓ., vii–xii, 306 p.; *vol. III:* vi, ix–xii,
300 p.
Imperfect: pages 179, 180 lacking in
vol. III
RISM B II, 124
MUSIC LIBRARY

250   BOYCE, WILLIAM

The | Chaplet. | A | Musical Entertain-
ment. | As it is Perform'd at the Theatre-
Royal | in Drury-Lane. | Compos'd by |
Dr. Boyce. | London. Printed for I. Walsh,
in Catharine Street, in the Strand. |
. . . [1750?]

2° *Score:* 1 ℓ., 46 p.
The privilege covers a full page
RISM A I, no. B 4054; Walsh II, no.
236?
MUSIC LIBRARY

—another copy [ca. 1755?]
The privilege covers two-thirds of a
page
Walsh II, no. 237?
MUSIC LIBRARY

251   BOYCE, WILLIAM

Lyra Britannica: | Book I. | Being | A
Collection of | Songs, Duets, and Can-
tatas, | on | Various Subjects. | Compos'd
by | Mr. Boyce. | . . . | London. Printed for
and Sold by I. Walsh, in Catharine Street,
in ye Strand. | . . . [1747]

2° *Score:* 1 ℓ., 21 p.
RISM A I, no. B 4112; Walsh II, no. 239
HOUGHTON, MUSIC LIBRARY

252   BOYCE, WILLIAM

Lyra Britannica: | Book II. | Being | A
Collection of | Songs, Duets, and Can-
tatas, | on | Various Subjects. | Compos'd
by | Mr. Boyce. | . . . | London. Printed for
and Sold by I. Walsh, in Catharine Street,
in ye Strand. | . . . [1747]

2° *Score:* 2 ℓ., 22–33 p.
RISM A I, no. B 4112; Walsh II, no. 240
HOUGHTON, MUSIC LIBRARY

253   BOYCE, WILLIAM

Lyra Britannica | Book 3d. | A | Cantata
| And | English Songs | Set to Musick by |
Dr. Boyce. | in which is inserted the
Songs of Johnny & Jenny. | To make the
Wife kind, you Say you Love &c. | Sung
at Vaux-hall, and Ranelagh Gardens. |
London. Printed for and Sold by John
Walsh in Catharine Street in the Strand. |
. . . [1748]

2° *Score:* 1 ℓ., [34]–47 p.
RISM A I, no. B 4112; Walsh II, no. 241
HOUGHTON, MUSIC LIBRARY

254   BOYCE, WILLIAM

Numb: IV. | Lyra Britannica. | A Col-
lection of | English Songs | Compos'd By |
Dr. Boyce. | In which are inserted some
Songs in Lethe. | London. | Printed for I.
Walsh in Catharine Street in the Strand. |
. . . [1754]

2° *Score:* 1 ℓ., [48]–68 p.
RISM A I, no. B 4112; Walsh II, no. 242
MUSIC LIBRARY

255   BOYCE, WILLIAM

Numb: V. | Lyra Britannica. | A Collec-
tion of | English Songs | And Cantatas |
Compos'd By | Dr. Boyce. | London. |
Printed for I. Walsh in Catharine Street
in the Strand. | . . . [1756]

2° *Score:* 1 ℓ., [67]–87 p.
RISM A I, no. B 4112; Walsh II, no. 243
MUSIC LIBRARY

256   BOYCE, WILLIAM

Numb: V [i. e. VI] | Lyra Britannica. | A
Collection of | English Songs | And Can-
tatas | Compos'd By | Dr. Boyce. | London.
| Printed for I. Walsh in Catharine Street
in the Strand. | . . . [1759]

2° *Score:* 2 ℓ., 89–108 p.
RISM A I, no. B 4112; Walsh II, no. 244
MUSIC LIBRARY

257   BOYCE, WILLIAM

The | Shepherds Lottery. | A | Musical
Entertainment. | As it is Perform'd at

the Theatre-Royal | in Drury-Lane. | Compos'd by | Dr. Boyce. | London. Printed for I. Walsh in Catharine Street in ye Strand. | . . . [1751]

2° *Score:* 1 ℓ., 52 p.
RISM A I, no. B 4071; Walsh II, no. 246
MUSIC LIBRARY (2 copies)

258 BOYCE, WILLIAM

Solomon; | A Serenata. | Composed by | Dr. Boyce, | For The | Voice, Harpsichord, And Violin; | With the | Chorusses in Score. | London: | Printed for Harrison & Co. No 18, Paternoster-Row. [ca. 1787]

obl. 2° *Vocal score:* 48 p.
Plate nos. 64–66
RISM A I, no. B 4077
HOUGHTON

259 BOYCE, WILLIAM

Twelve | Sonatas | For | Two Violins; | With a Bass for the | Violoncello or Harpsicord. | By | William Boyce, | Composer to His Majesty. | London, Printed for the Author. & Sold by I. Walsh | Musick Printer and Instrument Maker to his Majesty in | Catharine Street in the Strand. . . . | MDCCXLVII

2° 3 pts.: *violino primo, violino secondo:* 1 ℓ., 34 p. each; *basso e violoncello:* 1 ℓ., 30 p.
RISM A I, no. B 4174; Walsh II, no. 249
MUSIC LIBRARY

260 BRAUN, JOHANN

Concerto | A | Violoncelle Principale | Accompagnée de | Deux Violons, Alto & Basse, | Deux Hautbois & Deux Cors de Chasse. | Très humblement Dediée | À Sa Majesté | Frederic Guillaume II, | Roi de Prusse &. | Par | Jean Braun, | Premier Violon de Sa Majesté | la Reine de Prusse. | Oeuvre IV. Libro I. [i. e. II] | Chés J. J. Hummel, | à Berlin avec Privilége du Roi, | à Amsterdam au grand Magazin de Musique | et aux Adresses ordinaires. | . . . [1791?]

2° 9 pts.: *violoncello principale:* 7 p.; *flauto primo, flauto secondo, corno primo, corno secondo:* 1 ℓ. each; *violino*

primo, violino secondo: 4 p. each; *viola, basso:* 3 p. each
Plate no. 696
No. 681 on title-page
Contains an extra *violino primo* part in contemporary manuscript
RISM A I, no. B 4276
HOUGHTON

261 BREITKOPF, BERNHARD THEODOR

Neue | Lieder | In | Melodien | Gesetzt | Von | Bernhard Theodor Breitkopf. | Leipzig, | Bey Bernhard Christoph Breitkopf Und Sohn. | 1770.

obl. 4° *Score:* 2 ℓ., 43 p.
Texts by Goethe
Hirsch III, no. 668; RISM A I, no. B 4310
HOUGHTON

262 BRIQUET, FIRM, PARIS

Epreuve | Des | Caracteres | De La Fonderie | De | Briquet. | A Paris, | Cloître Saint-Benoît. | M.DCC.LVII.

4° A–K⁴, L1–3, illus., 2 fold. pl., music
Leaves printed on one side only
HOUGHTON

263

The | British Musical Miscellany, | or, the | Delightful Grove: | Being a Collection of Celebrated | English, and Scotch Songs. | By the best Masters. | Set for the Violin, German | Flute, the Common Flute, | and Harpsicord. | . . . | Engraven in a fair Character, and | Carefully Corrected. | London. Printed for & Sold by I. Walsh, Musick Printer, | & Instrument maker to his Majesty, at the Harp & Hoboy, | in Catherine Street, in the Strand. . . . [1734–1735?]

4° *Score:* vols. I–IV: 1 ℓ., IV, 145 p. each, front. in *vols. I, III*
Numbers 514, 525, 542, 571 respectively on title pages
Incomplete: *vols. V, VI* lacking
RISM B II, 117; Walsh II, no. 259–262
HOUGHTON

264

. . . | The British Orpheus | A Collection of | Favourite English Songs | Never Before Publish'd | Compos'd By | Different Authors | London. Printed for I. Walsh in Catherine Street in the Strand | . . . [1742]

2° *Score: vol. II:* 1 ℓ., 13–24 numb. ℓ.
Numbered leaves printed on one side only
Incomplete: *vols. I, III, IV* lacking
Imperfect: numbered leaf 15 lacking
RISM B II, 117; Walsh II, no. 266
MUSIC LIBRARY

265   [BROCKLESBY, RICHARD]

Reflections | On Antient and Modern | Musick, | With The | Application to the Cure of Diseases. | To which is subjoined, | An Essay to solve the Question, wherein | consisted the Difference of antient Musick, | from that of modern Times. | . . . | London: | Printed for M. Cooper, at the Globe in Pater-|noster-Row. 1749.

8° 2 ℓ., 82 p., 1 ℓ.
RISM B VI, 178
HOUGHTON

266   BROSSARD, SÉBASTIEN DE

Dictionaire | De Musique, | Contenant Une Explication | Des Termes Grecs, Latins, Italiens & François | les plus usitez dans la Musique. | A l'occasion desquels on rapporte ce qu'il y a de | plus curieux & de plus necessaire à sçavoir; | Tant pour l'Histoire & la Theorie, que pour la Composition, & | la Pratique Ancienne & Moderne De la Musique Vocale, In-|strumentale, Plaine, Simple, Figurée &c. | Ensemble, | Une Table Alphabetique des Termes François qui sont dans le | corps de l'Ouvrage, sous les Titres Grecs, Latins & Italiens; | pour servir de Supplement. | Un Traité de la maniere de bien prononcer, sur tout en | chantant, les Termes Italiens, Latins & François. | Et un Catalogue de plus de 900. Auteurs, qui ont écrit sur la | Musique, en toutes sortes de Temps, de Pays & de Langues. | Par M. Sebastien De Brossard, cy-devant Prébende | Député &

Maître de Chapelle de l'Eglise Cathedrale de Stras-|bourg; Maintenant Grand Chapelain & Maître de Mu-|sique de l'Eglise Cathedrale de Meaux. | Troisieme Edition. | A Amsterdam, | Aux dépens d'Estienne Roger, Mar-|chand Libraire, chez qui l'on trouve un assor-|timent general de toute sorte de Musique. [1707 or 1708]

8° 388 p., illus., 2 fold. pl., music
Imperfect: pages 385, 386 lacking
LesureR, p. 61; RISM B VI, 180
MUSIC LIBRARY

267   [BROSSARD, SÉBASTIEN DE]

A | Musical Dictionary; | Being A | Collection | Of | Terms and Characters, | As well Ancient as Modern; | Including The | Historical, Theoretical, and Practical Parts | Of | Music: | As also, an Explanation of some Parts of the | Doctrine of the Antients; | Interspersed With | Remarks on their Method and Practice, and curious | Observations on the Phoenomena of | Sound | Mathematically considered, | As it's Relations and Proportions constitute Intervals, | And those again | Concords and Discords. | The whole carefully abstracted from the best Authors | in the Greek, Latin, Italian, French, and English Languages. | By James Grassineau, Gent. | . . . | London: Printed for J. Wilcox, at Virgil's Head-|opposite the New Church in the Strand. 1740

8° xii, 347, [1] p., illus., 4 pl., music
Translated from the French by James Grassineau
Imperfect: pages [i], [ii] lacking
RISM B VI, 375
MUSIC LIBRARY

BROWN, DANIEL, PUBL. The Newest Collection of the Choicest Songs *See* The Newest Collection of the Choicest Songs

268   BROWN, JOHN, THE ELDER

A | Dissertation | On The | Rise, Union, and Power, | The | Progressions, Separations, and Corruptions, | Of | Poetry and Music. | To which is prefixed, | The Cure of Saul, | A | Sacred Ode. | Written by Dr.

Brown. | . . . | London, | Printed for L. Davis and C. Reymers against Gray's-Inn, Holbourn. | Printers to the Royal Society. | MDCCLXIII.

4° 244 [i. e. 248], [2] p.
Page 248 misnumbered 244
Pages [5]–19: libretto of *The Cure Of Saul*
RISM B VI, 181
HOUGHTON, MUSIC LIBRARY

269   BROWN, JOHN, THE YOUNGER

Letters | On The | Italian Opera: | Address To | The Hon. Lord Monboddo. | By The Late | Mr. John Brown. | Second Edition. | London: | Sold by T. Cadell, Strand. | MDCCXCI.

8° xviii, 141 p., 1 *ℓ.*, illus.
RISM B VI, 182
MUSIC LIBRARY

BRUN, LOUIS SÉBASTIEN LE   *See* Lebrun, Louis Sébastien

270   BRUNI, ANTONIO BARTOLOMEO

Toberne | ou | Le Pecheur Suédois | Opera | en deux Actes | Paroles de Patras | Musique de | Bruni | Représentée sur le Théâtre de la rue Feydeau, le 11. | Frimaire, 4e. année de la Républ. Française. | . . . | A Paris | Chez les frères Gaveaux, Tiennent magazin de Musique, d'Instrumens, et Cordes de Naples. Font | des envois dans les Départemens et chez l'étranger. À la Nouveauté passage du Théâtre Feydeau No. II. | Gravé par Vanjxem. [1796?]

2° *Score:* 1 *ℓ.*, 229 p.
RISM A I, no. B 4723
MUSIC LIBRARY

271   BRYENNIUS, MANUEL

Μανουηλ Βρυεννιου | Αρμονιχα. | Manuelis Bryennii | Harmonica. | Ex Codd. Mss. nunc primum edita. [Oxford, 1699]

2° In John Wallis's *Operum mathematicorum*, vol. III, p. [357]–508, illus.
Parallel texts in Greek and Latin; two columns to the page

Half-title
RISM B VI, 876
HOUGHTON

272   BUNTING, EDWARD, COMP.

A | General Collection | of the | Ancient Irish Music, | Containing a variety of | Admired Airs | never before Published, and also | The Compositions of | Conolan and Carolan; | Collected from the Harpers &c in the different | Provinces of | Ireland, | and adapted for the | Piano-Forte, | with a Prefatory Introduction | . . . | By | Edward Bunting. | . . . | Dub: Publish'd by Hime at his Musical Circulating Library 34 College Green . . . [ca. 1798]

2° *Score: vol: I:* 1 *ℓ.*, iv, 36 p.
No more published
RISM B II, 76
HOUGHTON

273   BUONANNI, FILIPPO

Descrizione | Degl'Istromenti Armonici | D'Ogni Genere | Del Padre Bonanni | Seconda Edizione | Rivedvta, Corretta, Ed Accrescivta | Dall'Abbate Giacinto Cervti | Ornata Con CXL. Rami | Incisi D'Arnoldo Wanwesterout | In Roma MDCCLXXVI | Á Spese Di Venanzio Monaldini | Libraro Al Corso

4° XVI, xxiij, [1], 114 [i. e. 214], [2] p., 141 pl.
Title also in French
Page 214 misnumbered 114
RISM B VI, 161–162
MUSIC LIBRARY

274   BUONANNI, FILIPPO

Gabinetto | Armonico | Pieno d'Istromenti sonori | Indicati, E Spiegati | Dal Padre | Filippo Bonanni | Della Compagnìa di Giesù | Offerto | Al Santo Rè | David. | In Roma M.DCC.XXII. | Nella Stamperìa di Giorgio Placho, Intagliatore, e Gettatore | de' Caratterri a S. Marco. Con licenza de' Superiori.

4° 8 *ℓ.*, 170 p., 1 *ℓ.*, front. on 2 *ℓ.*, 139 pl. (1 double)
RISM B VI, 161
HOUGHTON

275   BUONANNI, FILIPPO

Gabinetto | Armonico | Pieno d'Instro-
menti sonori | Indicati, spiegati, e di
nuovo | corretti, ed accresciuti | Dal
Padre | Filippo Bonanni | Della Compa-
gnia Di Giesù | Offerti | Al Santo Ré |
David. | In Roma MDCCXXIII. | Nella
Stamperìa di Giorgio Placho Intagliatore,
e Gettatore | di Caratteri alla Piazza di S.
Marco. | Con Licenza De' Svperiori.

4° 8 ℓ., 177, [1] p., front., 149 pl. (1
fold.)
RISM B VI, 161
MUSIC LIBRARY

BUONONCINI, GIOVANNI   *See* Bononcini, Giovanni

276   BURGESS, HENRY, THE YOUNGER

Six | Concertos | for the | Harpsicord or
Organ | Compos'd by | Mr. Henry Burgess
Junr. | London. Printed for the Author. |
Sold by I. Walsh in Catharine Street in
the Strand. [1743]

2° *Score:* 1 ℓ., 38 p.
RISM A I, no. B 5015; Walsh II, no. 272
HOUGHTON

277   BURMANN, GOTTLOB WILHELM

Kleine Lieder | Für | Kleine Jünglinge. |
Text Und Musick | von | Gottlob Wil-
helm Burmann. | Berlin Und Königsberg,
| Bey G. I. Decker Und G. L. Hartung,
1777.

4° *Score:* 4 ℓ., 59, [1] p.
RISM A I, no. B 5032
MUSIC LIBRARY

278   BURNEY, CHARLES

Account | Of An | Infant Musician. |
By Charles Burney, | Doctor of Music,
F. R. S. | Read at the Royal Society,
Feb. 18, 1779. | London: | Printed by J.
Nichols (Successor to Mr. Bowyer). |
MDCCLXXIX.

4° 26 p., music
RISM B VI, 190
HOUGHTON (2 copies)

279   BURNEY, CHARLES

An | Account | Of The | Musical Per-
formances | In | Westminster-Abbey, |
And The | Pantheon, | May 26th, 27th,
29th; and June the 3d, and 5th, 1784. | In |
Commemoration | Of | Handel. | By
Charles Burney, Mus. D. F. R. S. | . . . |
London, | Printed for the Benefit of the
Musical Fund; and Sold by T. Payne and |
Son, at the Meuse-Gate; and G. Robin-
son, Pater-noster-Row. | MDCCLXXXV.

4° vii, [1], xvi, 8, 56 [i. e. 62], 139 [i. e.
145], [2] p., front., 7 pl., music
Nos. 19–24, fourth sequence, repeated
in paging; three unnumbered half-title
leaves in last number sequence
Hirsch I, Historischer Anhang., no. 14;
RISM B VI, 191
HOUGHTON (2 copies)

280   BURNEY, CHARLES

A | General History | Of | Music, | From
The | Earliest Ages to the Present Period.
| To which is prefixed, | A Dissertation |
On The | Music Of The Ancients. | By |
Charles Burney, Mus. D. F. R. S. | . . . |
London, | Printed for the Author: And
sold by T. Becket, Strand; J. Robson, |
New Bond-Street; and G. Robinson,
Paternoster-Row. | MDCCLXXVI.
[–MDCCLXXXIX.]

4° 4 vols.: *vol. I:* xx, [12], 522 [i. e. 544]
p., 1 ℓ., front (port.), 8 pl., (4 fold.), music;
vol. II: 2 ℓ., 597 p., 1 ℓ., front., illus., pl.,
music; *vol. III:* xi, 622 [i. e. 632], [12] p.,
front., music; *vol. IV:* 2 ℓ., 685, [15] p.,
front., music
Imprint, vol. II: . . . Printed for the
Author: And Sold by J. Robson, New
Bond-Street; and | G. Robinson, Pater-
noster-Row. | MDCCLXXXII; vol.
III: . . . | Printed for the Author: And
sold by Payne and Son, at the Mews-
Gate; Robson | and Clark, Bond-Street;
and G. G. J. and J. Robinson, Paternoster-
Row. | MDCCLXXXIX; imprint date, vol.
IV: MDCCLXXXIX
Numerous errors in paging
Hirsch I, Historischer Anhang, no. 16
(Hirsch copy of volume I is the second
edition); RISM B VI, 190–191
HOUGHTON

281 BURNEY, CHARLES

Memoirs | Of The | Life and Writings | Of The | Abate Metastasio. | In Which Are Incorporated, | Translations | Of His | Principal Letters. | By Charles Burney, Mus. D. F. R. S. | . . . | In Three Volumes. | . . . | London: | Printed For G. G. And J. Robinson, | Paternoster-Row. | M.DCC.XCVI.

8° 3 vols.: *vol. I:* xv, 407, [31] p., front. (port.), music; *vol. II:* 1 *ℓ.*, 420, [31] p.; *vol. III:* 1 *ℓ.*, 414, [25] p.
RISM B VI, 192
WIDENER

282 BURNEY, CHARLES

Dr. Karl Burney's | Nachricht | von | Georg Friedrich Händel's | Lebens-umständen | und | der ihm zu London im Mai und Jun. 1784 angestellten | Gedächtnissfeyer. | Aus dem Englischen übersetzt | von | Johann Joachim Eschenburg, | Professor in Braunschweig. | Mit Kupfern. | Berlin und Stettin, | bei Friedrich Nicolai, 1785.

4° 13 *ℓ.*, LII, 102 p., 1 *ℓ.*, front. (port.), pl., music
Hirsch I, Historischer Anhang, no. 15; RISM B VI, 192
MUSIC LIBRARY

283 BURNEY, CHARLES

The | Present State | Of | Music | In | France and Italy: | Or, | The Journal of a Tour through those | Countries, under-taken to collect Materials for | A General History Of Music. | By Charles Burney, Mus. D. | . . . | London, | Printed for T. Becket and Co. in the Strand. | MDCCLXXI.

8° vii, 396 p., 6 *ℓ.*, illus.
RISM B VI, 192
MUSIC LIBRARY

284 BURNEY, CHARLES

The | Present State | Of | Music | In | Germany, | The Netherlands, | And | United Provinces. | Or, | The Journal of a Tour through those | Countries, under-taken to collect Materials for | A General History of Music. | By Charles Burney, Mus. D. | In Two Volumes. | . . . | London, | Printed for T. Becket and Co. Strand; J. Robson, New Bond-|Street; and G. Robinson, Paternoster Row. 1773.

8° 2 vols.: *vol. I:* viii, 376 p., music; *vol. II:* vi, 352 p., illus., music
Hirsch I, Historischer Anhang, no. 13; RISM B VI, 192–193
MUSIC LIBRARY

285 BURNEY, CHARLES

The | Present State | Of | Music | In | Germany, | The Netherlands, | And | United Provinces. | Or, | The Journal of a Tour through those | Countries, under-taken to collect Materials for | A General History Of Music. | By Charles Burney, Mus. D. F. R. S. | In Two Volumes. | . . . | The Second Edition, Corrected. | London, | Printed for T. Becket, Strand; J. Robson, New Bond-|Street; and G. Robinson, Paternoster-Row. 1775.

8° 2 vols.: *vol. I:* viii, 380 p., music; *vol. II:* 2 *ℓ.*, 352 p., illus., music
RISM B VI, 193
MUSIC LIBRARY

286 BURNEY, CHARLES

Four | Sonatas or Duets | For two Performers on One | Piano Forte | Or | Harpsichord | Composed by | Chas. Burney Mus. D | . . . | London. | Printed for the Author and Sold by R. Bremner in the Strand, | and at all the Music Shops [pref. 1777]

obl. 2° *Score:* 2 *ℓ.*, 43 p.
RISM A I, no. B 5059
MUSIC LIBRARY

287 BURTON, JOHN

The Courtship, | The Chace, | And | Tit For Tat. | Three Favorite | Concertos, | For The | Piano Forte, | Composed By | Mr. Burton. | London: | Printed for Harrison & Co. No. 18, Paternoster Row. [1798?]

8° *Score:* 19 p. (*The Piano-Forte Maga-zine,* vol. III, no. 12)
Plate no. 49
RISM A I, no. B 5081
MUSIC LIBRARY

288   BURTON, JOHN

Ten | Sonatas | for the | Harpsichord, Organ, | Or | Piano Forte; | Compos'd by | John Burton, | Se vend a Paris avec Privi-lege du Roi. | London, Printed for the Au-thor, in Princes Street Cavendish Square. | . . . T. Bennett Sculp. 1766?]

obl. 4° *Score:* 2 ℓ., 55 p.
RISM A I, no. B 5076
HOUGHTON

289   BUSBY, THOMAS

Six | Sonatas, | For The | Piano Forte. | Composed By, | T. Busby. | London: | Printed for Harrison, Cluse, & Co. No. 78, Fleet Street. [1799?]

8° *Score:* 45 p. (*The Piano-Forte Maga-zine,* vol. VII, no. 5)
Plate nos. 100–101
RISM A I, no. B 5109
MUSIC LIBRARY

290   BUTLER, CHARLES

The | Principles | Of Musik, | In | Sing-ing And Setting: | VVith | The two-fold Use thereof, | [Ecclesiasticall and Civil.] | By | Charls Butler Magd. Master of Arts. | London, | Printed by John Haviland, for the Author: | 1636.

4° 8 ℓ., 135 p., illus., music
Brackets printed on title-page
Hirsch I, no. 96; RISM B VI, 194
HOUGHTON

291   BUTTSTETT, JOHANN HEINRICH

Ut, Mi, Sol, | Re, Fa, La, | Tota Musica | Et | Harmonia | Aeterna, | Oder | Neu-eröffnetes, altes, wahres, eintziges | und ewiges | Fundamentum Musices, | entge-gen gesetzt | Dem neu-eröffneten Or-chestre, | und in zweene Partes eingethei-let. | In welchen, und zwar im ersten Theile, des Herrn Authoris des Or-|chestre irrige Meynungen, in specie de Tonis seu Modis Musicis, | wiederleget, |

Im andern Theile aber das rechte Funda-mentum Musices gezeiget, | Solmisatio Gvidonica nicht allein defendiret, son-dern auch solcher | Nutzen bey Einführung eines Comitis gewiesen, dann auch behauptet | wird, dass man dereinst im Himmel, mit eben den Sonis, welche | hier in der Welt gebräuchlich, musiciren werde, | von | Johann Heinrich Buttstett, | Bey der Evangel. Prediger Haupt-Kirche Organ. | Erffurt, | Ge-druckt, bey Otto Friedr. Werthern, Adj. Universit. Buchdr. | zu finden in Leipzig, bey Johann Herbord Kloss. [1717]

4° 5 ℓ., 176 p., 1 ℓ., front., illus., 23 pl. (music)
Hirsch I, no. 97; RISM B VI, 194–195
HOUGHTON

292   BYRD, WILLIAM

. . . | Psalmes, Sonets, & songs of sadnes and | pietie, made into Musicke of fiue parts: whereof, | some of them going abroad among diuers, in vntrue coppies, | are heere truely corrected, and th'other being Songs | very rare & newly com-posed, are heere published, for the re-|creation of all such as delight in Musick: By William Byrd, | one of the Gent. of the Queenes Maiesties | honorable Chappell. | [London] Printed by Thomas East, the assigne of W. Byrd, | and are to be sold at the dwelling house of the said T. East, by | Paules wharfe. 1588. | Cum priuilegio Regiae Maiestatis.

4° 1 pt.: *svperivs:* [A]², B–F⁴, G²
Brown, no. 1588₂; RISM A I, no. B 5209
HOUGHTON

293   BYRD, WILLIAM

. . . | Psalmes, Sonets, & songs of sadnes and | pietie, made into Musicke of fiue parts: whereof, some | of them going abroad among diuers, in vntrue coppies, are | heere truely corrected, and th'other being Songs very rare | and newly com-posed, are heere published, for the recre-ation | of all such as delight in Musicke: By William Byrd one | of the Gent: of the Queenes Maiesties | Royall Chappell. | Printed at London by Thomas Este, | dwelling in Aldersgate streete, ouer | against the signe of the George. [1599?]

4° 1 pt.: *bassvs:* [A]², B–F⁴, G²
Imprint date supplied from Andrews,
p. 20
Brown, no. 159?₂; RISM A I, no. B 5210
HOUGHTON

294   BYRD, WILLIAM

. . . | Songs of sundrie natures, some of
| grauitie, and others of myrth, fit for all
compa-|nies and voyces. Lately made and
composed in-|to Musicke of 3. 4. 5. and 6.
parts: and pub-|lished for the delight of
all such as take plea-|sure in the exercise
of | that Art. | By VVilliam Byrd, one of
the Gentlemen | of the Queenes Maies-
ties honorable | Chappell. | Imprinted at
London by Thomas | East, the assigne of
William Byrd, and are to be | sold at the
house of the sayd T. East, being in | Al-
dersgate streete, at the signe of the |
blacke Horse. 1589. | Cum priuilegio Re-
giae Maiestatis.

4° 1 pt.: *sextvs:* [A]², B⁴, C²
Imprint date altered in manuscript to
1582; colophon dated 1589
Brown, no. 1589₂; RISM A I, no. B 5212
HOUGHTON

C

LE CADI DUPÉ *See* Monsigny, Pierre
Alexandre *Le Cadi dupé*

295   CAHUSAC, LOUIS DE

La Danse | Ancienne | Et | Moderne |
Ou | Traité Historique | De La Danse. |
Par M. De Cahusac, de l'Acadé-|mie
Royale des Sciences & Belles-|Lettres de
Prusse. | . . . | A La Haye, | Chez Jean
Neaulme. | M.DCC.LIV.

12° 3 vols.: *vol. I:* 1 ℓ., xxxij, [4], 168,
[16] p.; *vol. II:* 1 ℓ., 180, [16] p.; *vol. III:* 1
ℓ., 168, [12] p.
RISM B VI, 196
HOUGHTON

296   CALDARA, ANTONIO

Chorus Musarum | Divino Apollini |
Accinentium. | Sive | Sex Missae | Sele-
ctissimae | A | Quatuor Vocibus | Canto,
Alto, Tenore, Basso, 2. Violinis & Or-
gano Concertantibus, | 2. Clarinis, Tym-
pano, Violoncello, Pro Libitu. | Quarum
Quinque | Authore | Celeberrimo &
Praestantissimo Domino | Antonio Cal-
dara | Chori Musici in Aula Caroli VI.
glor. mem. | Imperatoris Rom. Vice-Di-
rectore | in Lucem prodierunt; | Una | Et
quidem in Ordine Tertia, eodem, cujus
Sumptibus totum | Opus editum est,
Compositore. | . . . | Sumptibus Joannis
Nicolai Hemmerlein, Reverendissimi &
Celsissimi Principis Bam-|bergensis Mu-
sici Cameralis & Aulici Seminariique
Auffseessiani Musices | Instructoris.
Bambergae Anno MDCCXLVIII.

2° 11 pts.: *canto:* 33 p.; *alto:* 29 p.; *tenore:* 28 p.; *basso:* 29 p.; *clarino I,
clarino II:* 13 p. each; *tympano:* 5 p.; *violino I. violino II:* 36 p. each; *organo*
[i. e. *violoncello?*]: 44 p.; *organo:* 2 ℓ.,
44 p.
Page 36 misnumbered 33 in *violino II*
part
Title supplied from *organo* part
RISM A I, no. C 53
HOUGHTON

CALDERÓN, MANUEL PÉREZ   *See* Pérez
Calderón, Manuel

297   CALL, LEONHARD VON

Serenade | pour la | Guitarre Flute &
Viola | composée | Par | L. de Call. | Op:
50. | . . . | A Bonn Chez N. Simrock.
[1798?]

2° 3 pts.: *flauto, viola:* 4 p. each; *guit-
tara:* 7 p.
Plate no. 58
Title supplied from *guittara* part
MUSIC LIBRARY

298   CALLCOTT, JOHN WALL

Autumn, | A Glee for three equal
Voices Set to Music & most respectfully
inscribed by permission to the most
Noble | The Marquess Of Blandford, | By
J. W. Callcott. Mus. Bac. Oxon. [London]
June, 4th. 1798. | . . .

obl. 2° *Score:* 4 p.

Caption title; place of publication supplied from Schnapper I, 150
MUSIC LIBRARY

299

Calliope | or | English Harmony | A | Collection | of the most Celebrated English and Scots Songs | Neatly Engrav'd and Embelish'd with Designs | adapted to the Subject of each Song taken from the | Compositions of the Best Masters in the most | Correct Manner with the thorough Bass and | Transpositions for the Flute (proper for all Teachers | Scholars and Lovers of Musick Printed on a fine | Paper on each side which renders the Undertaking more | compleat than anything of the kind ever Publish'd | . . . | London Engrav'd by Henry Roberts | Printed for & sold by John Simpson at the Bass Viol & Flute | in Sweetings Alley opposite the East Door of the Royal Ex-|change: Where may be had all sorts of Musical Instruments, | Musick Books &c. [1746?]

8° *Score:* 2 vols.: 3ℓ., 200 p., front., illus. each
RISM B II, 119
HOUGHTON

300

Calliope: | Or, The | Musical Miscellany. | A Select Collection | Of The Most Approved | English, Scots, And Irish Songs, | Set To Music. | London: | Printed for C. Elliot and T. Kay, | Opposite Somerset-Place, No 332, Strand; | And C. Elliot, Edinburgh. | M,DCC,LXXXVIII.

8° 1 ℓ., viii, 472 p.
RISM B II, 120
MUSIC LIBRARY

301   CAMBINI, GIUSEPPE MARIA
        GIOACCHINO

Six | Quatuors | Concertants | A deux Violons Alto et Basse | Composés | par | Mr Cambini | Oeuvre .3e. | . . . | A. Paris. | Chez le Sr. Sieber, Musicien, rue St. Honoré à l'hôtel D'Aligre | Ancien Grand Conseiil . . . | A. P. D. R [ca. 1779]

2° 4 pts.: *violino primo:* 1 ℓ., 13 p.; *violino secondo, alto viola, basso:* 13 p. each

Cancel label on title-page of *violino primo* part reads: Imported & Sold | by Longman & Broderip | (at their Music Warehouse) | No. 26 | Cheapside London. Page [1] in *violino primo* part: Catalogue | De Musique Vocale et Instrumentale Appartenant á M. Sieber, | . . . ⟨JohanssonF facs. 110⟩
RISM A I, no. C 403
MUSIC LIBRARY

302   CAMBINI, GIUSEPPE MARIA
        GIOACCHINO

Six | Quatuors | Concertants | A Deux Violons Alto et Basse | Composés par | Monsr. Cambini. | Oeuvre III. . . . | London. Printed & sold by Wm: Forster Violin & Violoncello | Maker to his Royal Highness the Duke of Cumberland | opposite the Church St. Martins Lane. [ca. 1780]

2° 4 pts.: *violino primo, violino secondo, viola, basso:* 1 ℓ., 13 p. each
RISM A I, no. C 404
MUSIC LIBRARY

CAMPANALOGIA   *See* Stedman, Fabian *Campanalogia*

303   CAMPBELL, JOSHUA

A Collection of | Favourite Tunes | With new Variations Adapted for the | Violin & German-Flute | With a Bass for the Violoncello and | Thorough-Bass For The Harpsichord | By Joshua Campbell | Corrected by P. Urbani. | Printed and Sold by Urbani & List[on] . . . Warehouse No. 10 Princes Street Ed[inburgh] | D. Smith Sc[ulpt.] | [ca. 1800]

obl. 8° *Score:* 2 ℓ., 81 p.
Imperfect: title-page cropped, with loss of part of imprint
HOUGHTON

CAMPION, CARLO ANTONIO   *See* Campioni, Carlo Antonio

304   CAMPION, THOMAS

The | Discription Of | A | Maske, | Presented before the Kinges Maiestie | at

White-Hall, on Twelfth Night | last, in honour of the Lord Hayes, and | his Bride, Daughter and Heire to the | Honourable the Lord Dennye, their | Marriage hauing been the same Day | at Court solemnized. | To this by occasion other small Poemes | are adioyned, | Inuented and set forth by Thomas | Campion Doctor of Phisicke. | London | Imprinted by Iohn Windet for Iohn Brovvn | and are to be solde at his shop in S. Dunstones | Churchyeard in Fleetstreet. 1607.

4° A–E⁴ (E4 blank), illus., music
Contains five songs by Campion, Lupo and Giles for one or two voices, lute and bass, in *Tafelmusik* format
RISM A I, no. C 624; RISM B I, no. 1607²⁷
HOUGHTON

305   CAMPIONI, CARLO ANTONIO

Six | Sonatas | For The | Harpsichord | Composed by Sigr: | Carlo Antonio Campioni. | London. | Printed and Sold, by R: Bremner, at the Harp and Hautboy, | opposite Somerset House, in the Strand. | . . . [1763?]

2° *Score:* 1 ℓ., 33 p.
Sonata 6 is with obligato violin
RISM A I, no. C 653 (op. 4b)
MUSIC LIBRARY

306   CAMPRA, ANDRÉ

Hesione, | Tragedie | Mise En Musique | Par Monsieur Campra; | Representée | Par L'Academie Royalle | De Musique | Le vingt-uniéme jour de Decembre 1700. | A Paris, | Chez Christophe Ballard, seul Imprimeur du Roy pour la Musique, | ruë S. Jean de Beauvais, au Mont-Parnasse. | M.DCC. | Avec Privilege de Sa Majesté.

obl. 4° *Score:* 4 ℓ., lviij, 259, [1] p.
RISM A I, no. C 730
MUSIC LIBRARY

307

. . . | Cantica Sacra: | Containing | Hymns and Anthems | For | Two Voices to the Organ, | both Latine and English. | Composed | By {Mr. Richard Dering. {Dr. Benjamin Rogers. | Dr. Christoph: Gib-

bons.} Mr. Matth: Locke, and Others. | The Second Sett. | London, Printed by W. Godbid, for John Playford, 1674.

2° 1 pt.: *bassvs:* 2 ℓ., 45, [1] p.
RISM B I, no. 1674²
HOUGHTON

308

CANTORINUS

Compēdium musices | confectū ad faciliorē instructio-|nē cantum choralē discentiū: | necnō ad ītroductionē hu-|ius libelli: q[uod] Cantorinus | intitulat[ur]: oīb[us] diuino | cultui deditis perutilis & | necessari[us]: vt in tabu-|la hic immediate | sequēti latius | apparet. | M.D.XXXVIII. | Venetijs. Sub signo | Agnus Dei.

8° 16 ℓ., 88 numb. ℓ., illus. (incl. device), music
Colophon: Finis Cantorini Romani: Anno | Salutis. 1538. Venetijs. Apud | Petrū Liechtenstein Colo-|niensem Hermanum.
Imperfect: numbered leaves 1–8 lacking
RISM B VI, 926
HOUGHTON

309

Cantorinus. | Ad eorum instructionem: qui cantum ad | chorum p[er]tinentem: breuiter & qm̃ facillime | discere concupiscunt: & non clericis mo-|do: sed omnibus etiam diuino cultui | deditis, perqm̃ utilis, & necessarius. | In quo facilis modus est additus | ad discendam manū: ac tonos | psalmorum: vt sequens | Tabula indicabit. | Nouissime castigatus, cui etiam | addite sunt Letanie. | Venetiis MDI. [i. e. MDL]

8° 8 ℓ., 104 numb. ℓ., illus., music
Colophon: Explicit Cantorinus ad commodum noui-|tiorum clericorū factus: nouissime | impressus & diligētissime reuisus. | In officina heredū Lucean|tonij Junte. Venetijs | Anno Salutis. 1550. | Mense Januario.
Imprint date altered in manuscript to MDL.
Wolfenbüttel, no. 1079
HOUGHTON

CANTUS; SONGS AND FANCIES TO THREE, FOUR OR FIVE PARTS *See* Songs and Fancies to Three, Four or Five Parts

CAPPEVAL, N. DE CAUX DE *See* Caux de Cappeval, N. de

CAPUA, RINALDO DI *See* Rinaldo di Capua

310 [CAREY, HENRY]

Faustina: | Or The | Roman Songstress, | A | Satyr, | On The | Luxury and Effeminacy | of the Age. |. . . | London: | Printed for J. Roberts, at the Oxford Arms, in | Warwick Lane. |. . . [1726]

4° 11 p.
An attack in verse directed against Faustina Bordoni Hasse
Foxon C42
HOUGHTON

311 CAREY, HENRY

The | Musical Century, | In | One Hundred English | Ballads, | On | Various Subjects and Occasions; | Adapted | To several Characters and Incidents in Human Life. | And Calculated | For Innocent Conversation, Mirth, and Instruction. | The | Words and Musick of the Whole Work, | By Henry Carey. |. . . | The Second Edition. | London: | Printed for the Author, and sold at the Musick-Shops, 1740. |. . .

2° *Score:* 2 vols.: *vol. I:* 6 ℓ., 54 numb. ℓ., front. (port.); *vol. II:* 5 ℓ., 55 numb. ℓ.
Mixed edition; vol. II is from the first edition
Frontispiece portrait trimmed and mounted; numbered leaves printed on one side only
RISM A I, no. C 1057
HOUGHTON

CARLIERI, CARLO MARIA, PUBL. Corona di sacre canzoni *See* Corona di sacre canzoni

CARLO DEL VIOLINO *See* Cesarini, Carlo Francesco

312 CAROSO, FABRITIO

Il Ballarino | Di M. Fabritio Caroso | Da Sermoneta, | Diuiso in due Trattati; | Nel primo de' quali si dimostra la diuersità de i nomi, che si danno à gli | atti, Et mouimenti, che interuengono ne i Balli: Et con molte Regole | si dichiara con quali creanze, Et in che modo debbano farsi. | Nel secondo s'insegnano diuerse sorti di Balli, & Balletti sì | all'uso d'Italia, come à quello di Francia, & Spagna. | Ornato di molte Figure. | Et con l'Intauolatura di Liuto, & il Soprano della Musica | nella sonata di ciascun Ballo. | Opera nuouamente mandata in luce. | Alla Serenma. Sigra. Bianca Cappello De Medici, | Gran Dvchessa Di Toscana. | Con Privilegio. | In Venetia, Appresso Francesco Ziletti. MDLXXXI.

4° 7 ℓ., 16 numb. ℓ., [8] p., 184 numb. ℓ., illus., pl. (port.), music
Numerous errors in paging and binding
Text of numbered leaves 109–112 printed alternately on recto and verso of eight leaves
Brown, no. 1581₁; Davidsson II, no. 18; Hirsch I, no. 100; MortimerI, no. 106; RISMA A I, no. C 1233; RISM B VI, 207
HOUGHTON

—another copy
Text of numbered leaves 109–112 printed normally on four leaves
Imperfect: unnumbered pages [1]–[8], numbered leaf 64 lacking; supplied in facsimile
HOUGHTON

313 CAROSO, FABRITIO

Nobiltà di Dame | Del Sr. Fabritio Caroso | Da Sermoneta, | Libro, altra volta, chiamato | Il Ballarino. | Nuouamente dal proprio Auttore corretto, | ampliato di nuoui Balli, di belle Regole, | & alla perfetta Theorica ridotto: | Con le Creanze necessarie à Caualieri, e Dame. | Aggiontoui il Basso, & il Soprano della Musica: | & con l'Intauolatura del Liuto à ciascun Ballo. | Ornato di vaghe & bellissime Figure in Rame. | Alli Sermi. Sigri. | Dvca, Et Dvchessa | di Parma, e di Piacenza, &c. | Con licenza de' Superiori, & Priuilegi. | In Venetia, Presso il Muschio, MDC | Ad instantia dell'Auttore.

4° 12 ℓ., 370, [6] p., illus. (incl. ports.), music
Revised and expanded edition of his *Il ballarino* (Brown, no. 1581₁)
Imprint date altered in manuscript to MDCV
Hirsch I, no. 101; RISM A I, no. C 1234; RISM B VI, 207
HOUGHTON

314   CAROSO, FABRITIO

Raccolta di varij Balli | Fatti In Occorrenze | Di Nozze, E Festini | Da Nobili Cavalieri, E Dame | di diuerse nationi. | Nuouamente ritrouati negli scritti | Del Sig. Fabritio Caroso | Da Sermoneta | Eccellente Maestro di ballare. | Data alle stampe da Gio. Dini, arricchita | di bellissime Figure in Rame. | Con aggiunta del Basso, e Soprano della musica, | & intauolatura di Liuto à ciascun ballo. | In Roma, | Appresso Guglielmo Facciotti. 1630. | Con licenza de' Superiori. | Ad instanza di Gio. Dini Libraro all'insegna | della Gatta in Nauona.

4° 10 ℓ., 370, [6] p., illus., pl., music
Reissue of his *Nobiltà di Dame*; illustrations and choreographies mismatched
Imperfect: pages 89, 90 lacking
RISM A I, no. C 1236; RISM B VI, 207
HOUGHTON

CARR, JOHN, PUBL. Comes amoris   *See* Comes amoris

315   CARTER, THOMAS

Canons, | Glees, and Catches, | For | Two, Three, and Four | Voices; | Composed, | and Dedicated to his Grace | The | Duke of Queensberry, | By | Thomas Carter. | London: | Printed for Harrison & Co. No. 18, Paternoster Row. | . . . [1797]

8° Score: 27 p., 1 ℓ. (*The Piano-Forte Magazine*, vol. I, no. 4)
MUSIC LIBRARY

CARTES, RENÉ DES   *See* Descartes, René

CASSANÉA DE MONDONVILLE, JEAN JOSEPH   *See* Mondonville, Jean Joseph Cassanéa de

CASTAGNÈRES, FRANÇOIS DE, ABBÉ DE CHÂTEAUNEUF   *See*   Châteauneuf, François de Castagnères, abbé de

316

The | Catch Club | or | Merry Companions | being | a Choice Collection of the most Diverting | Catches | for Three and Four Voices | Compos'd by | the late Mr. Henry Purcell Dr. Blow &c. | 1st part. . . . | London Printed for I: Walsh Servant to his Majesty at the Harp and Hoboy | in Catherine street in the Strand, . . . [ca. 1740]

obl. 4° 1 ℓ., 48 p.
Number 297 on title-page
John and Joseph Hare's names erased from imprint
RISM B II, 123; Walsh II, no. 340?
HOUGHTON

317

The Second Book of the | Catch Club | or | Merry Companions | being | a Choice Collection of the most Diverting | Catches | for Three and Four Voices | Compos'd by the late | Mr. Henry Purcell Dr. Blow &c. | 2d. part. . . . | London. Printed for and Sold by I. Walsh Musick Printer and Instru-|ment maker to his Majesty at the Harp & Hoboy in Catherine Street in the Strand. [ca. 1740]

obl. 4° 2 ℓ., 48 p.
Number 298 on title-page
John and Joseph Hare's names erased from imprint
RISM B II, 123; Walsh II, no. 340?
HOUGHTON

318

Catch that Catch can: | Or The | Musical Companion. | Containing | Catches and Rovnds for Three and Four Voyces. | To which is now added a Second Book | Containing | Dialogves, Glees, Ayres, & Ballads, &c. | Some for {Two | Three | Foure} Voyces. | London, Printed by W.

Godbid for J. Playford at his Shop in the Temple. 1667.

obl. 4° 6 ℓ., 88, [8], [89]–214 p.
Imperfect: some pages torn; pages 215 to 231 lacking
Day, no. 26, second entry; RISM B I, no. 1667[6]
HOUGHTON

319   [CAUX DE CAPPEVAL, N. DE]

Apologie | du | Goût François, | Relativement à L'Opéra: | Poeme, | Avec un Discours Apologétique, | & des Adieux aux Bouffons. | [Paris?] 1754 | . . .

8° 1 ℓ., 80 p.
Hirsch I, no. 109; RISM B VI, 213
HOUGHTON

CAVEIRAC, JEAN NOVI DE   *See* Novi de Caveirac, Jean

320   [CAZOTTE, JACQUES]

Observations | Sur | La Lettre | De | J. J. Rousseau, | Au sujet de la Musique Françoise. | . . . | [Paris] M.DCC.LIII.

8° 1 ℓ., 19 p.
Hirsch I, no. 111a
HOUGHTON

321   CELTES, CONRADUS

Ludus Diane in modum Comedie coram Maximili-|ano Rhomanorum Rege Kalendis Martijs & | Ludis saturnalibus in arce Linsiana danu-|bij actus: Clementissimo Rege & Regi|na ducibusq[ue] illustribus Medio|lani totaq[ue] Regia curia spe-|ctatoribus: p[er] Petrum | Bonomum Re-|gi: Cancel. | Joseph Grun-|pekium Reg. Secre. | Conradum Celten: Reg: | Poe. Vlseniū Phrisium: Vin|centium Longinum in hoc | Ludo Laurea dona-|tum foeliciter et | iucundissi-|me repre|senta|tus [Nuremberg, 1501]

4° [12] p., music
Play, with two short choruses for three and four voices
Colophon: Impressum Nuremberge ab Hieronymo Hŏlcelio Ciue Nu-|rem-

bergēsi Anno. M.ccccc. Et primo noui seculi Idib[us] Maijs
Hirsch III, no. 684
HOUGHTON

CELTIS, CONRAD   *See* Celtes, Conradus

CERF DE LA VIÉVILLE, JEAN LAURENT LE *See* Le Cerf de la Viéville, Jean Laurent

322   CERRETO, SCIPIONE

Scipione Cerreto | Napolitano, | Della Prattica Mvsica | Vocale, Et Strvmentale, | Opera Necessaria A Coloro, | che di Musica si dilettano. | Con Le Postillo Poste Dall'Avtore | à maggior dichiaratione d'alcune cose occor-|renti ne' discorsi. | In Napol | Appresso Gio: Iacomo Carlino, MDCI.

4° 4 ℓ., 335, [1] p., illus. (incl. port.), music
Hirsch I, no. 115; RISM B VI, 216
HOUGHTON

323   CESARINI, CARLO FRANCESCO

A | Concerto, | Composed For The | Piano Forte. | By | F. Cesarini. | London: | Printed for Harrison & Co. No. 78 Fleet Street. [1798?]

8° *Score:* 9 p. (*The Piano-Forte Magazine,* vol. IV, no. 6
Plate no. 58
RISM A I, no. C 1759
MUSIC LIBRARY

324   [CHABANON, MICHEL PAUL GUI DE]

De La Musique | Considérée En Elle-Même | Et Dans Ses Rapports | Avec | La Parole, Les Langues, La Poésie, | Et Le Théatre. | . . . | A Paris, | Chez Pissot, Libraire, Quai des Augustins. | M.DCC.LXXXV.

8° 2 ℓ., 459, [1] p., pl., music
Page 459: De l'Imprimerie de M. Lambert, rue de | la Harpe, près S. Côme. 1785.
RISM B VI, 217
MUSIC LIBRARY

325 CHALON, JOHN

The | Favourite Air, ["Tell Tale Eyes"] | In The | Barbier De Seville, | With Variations, For The | Piano Forte. | By, | J. Chalon. | London: | Printed for Harrison, Cluse, & Co. No. 78, Fleet Street. [1799?]

8° *Score:* 10 p. (*The Piano-Forte Magazine,* vol. VII, no. 1)
Plate no. 97
RISM A I, no. C 1784
MUSIC LIBRARY

326 CHAMPEIN, STANISLAS

La | Mélomanie | Opera Comique En Un Acte | en Vers mêlé d'Ariettes | Mis | en Musique | Par M. S. Champein. | Représenté pour la premiere fois sur | le Théâtre de l'Opera Comique National, | Le 23 Janvier 1781. | . . . | A Paris. | Chez Des Lauriers Md. de Papiers, rue St. Honoré à côté de celle des Prouvaires, | chez qui se trouve toutes sortes de Papiers à copier la Musique. [ca. 1781]

2° *Score:* 2 ℓ., 128 p.
Preliminary leaf 2ʳ: Catalogue | de Musique | du fond de Des Lauriers . . .
Hirsch II, no. 125; RISM A I, no. C 1815
MUSIC LIBRARY

327

Le | Chansonnier | François. | Ou | Recueil | De Chansons | Ariettes, Vaudevilles & autres | Couplets choisis. | I. [–XVI.] Recueil. | [Paris?] M.DCC.LX [–1762]

12° 16 vols.: *vol. I:* 4 ℓ., 232, 32 p.; *vol. II:* 6 ℓ., 227, 57 p.; *vol. III:* 5 ℓ., 230, 49 p.; *vol. IV:* 5 ℓ., 230, 57 p.; *vol. V:* 6 ℓ., 216, 52 p.; *vol. VI:* 6 ℓ., 240, 60 p.; *vol. VII:* 6 ℓ., 227, 52 p.; *vol. VIII:* 6 ℓ., 228, 48 p.; *vol. IX:* 4 ℓ., 244, 48 p.; *vol. X:* 1 ℓ., 233, [5], 50 p.; *vol. XI:* 6 ℓ., 216, 52 p.; *vol. XII:* 3 ℓ., 186, lx, 44 p.; *vol. XIII:* 4 ℓ., 240, 48 p.; *vol. XIV:* xij, 228, 64 p.; *vol. XV:* viij, 231, 56 p.; *vol. XVI:* ij, 221, [5] p.
The melodies appear in the last paginal sequence in each vol.; vol. XVI published without music

Imprint in vol. I only; altered in manuscript to M.DCC.LXXX. Advertisements in succeeding vols. indicate that vols. VII–XII were published in 1761, vols. XIII–XVI in 1762
RISM B II, 126
HOUGHTON

328

Chansons | Choisies, | Avec Les Airs Notés. | . . . | A Genève. | M.DCC.LXXXII.

24° 4 vols.: *vol. I:* 2 ℓ., xvj, 220, XXXIII p., front.; *vol. II:* 2 ℓ., 236 [i. e. 238], XXXII p.; *vol. III:* 2 ℓ., 240, XXIV p.; *vol. IV:* 2 ℓ., 339 [i. e. 239], XXVI p.
The melodies appear in the last paginal sequence in each vol.
Imprint date in vols. III and IV: M.DCC.LXXVII (in error?)
Numbers 229, 230 repeated in paging in vol. II; page 239 misnumbered 339 in vol. IV
RISM B II, 127
HOUGHTON

329 [CHÂTEAUNEUF, FRANÇOIS DE CASTAGNÈRES, ABBÉ DE]

Dialogue | Sur | La Musique | Des Anciens. | A Monsieur De *** | A Paris, | Chés Noel Pissot, à la Croix | d'Or, Quai des Augustins, à la | descente du Pont-Neuf. | M.DCC.XXV. | Avec Approbation & Privilege du Roi.

12° 4 ℓ., 126, [4] p., 1 ℓ., 7 pl. (1 fold.)
Hirsch I, no. 118; RISM B VI, 219
HOUGHTON

330 CHELIDONIUS, BENEDICTUS

Voluptatis cum Virtute disceptatio: | Carolo Burgūdiae duce Illustrissimo, Diuiq[ue] Caes. Maxaemi-|liani Nepote, litis diremptore aequissimo. Viennae Pan-|noniae corā Maria Hungaror[um] Regina designata, | Dominoq[ue] Matteo S. angeli diac. Cardinali | Reuerendissimo recitata. A Benedicto | Chelidonio Heroicis lusa uersibus. [Vienna, 1515]

4° A⁴, b–c⁶, illus. (coat of arms), music
Colophon: Impressum Viennae Pan-

noniae per Ioannem | Singrenium Ex-
pensis uero Leonardi | Alantse. quinto
Idus Iunii. | Anno. M.D.XV.

Play, with three short choruses

HOUGHTON

331   CHERUBINI, LUIGI

Démophoon | Tragédie Lyrique en
Trois Actes. | Représentée pour la pre-
miere fois par l'Académie Royale de Mu-
sique, | le Mardi 2 Décembre 1788. | Les
Paroles sont de M. Marmontel. | Mise en
Musique | Par | M. Cherubini | . . . |
Gravée par Huguet Musicien de la
Comédie Italienne. | A Paris | Chez le
Suisse de l'Hotel de Noailles No. 151. |
Et aux Adresses Ordinaires de Musique.
[1788?]

2° *Score:* 1 ℓ., 375 p.
Composer's autograph signature on
title-page
Imperfect: pages 373–375 lacking;
supplied in twentieth-century manu-
script
Hirsch II, no. 129
HOUGHTON

332   CHERUBINI, LUIGI

Les | Deux Journées | Opera En Trois
Actes | Par le Cen. Bouilly | Représenté
pour la premiere fois sur le Théâtre | de la
Rue Faydeau, le 26 Nivose an 8. | Mis En
Musique | Par le Cen. Chérubini | Dédié
Au Cen. Gossec | Membre de l'Institut
des Sciences et des Arts, l'un des Inspec-
teurs du Consre. de Musque. | . . . | A
Paris | A l'Harmonie Chez Gaveaux ainé,
Editeur Marchand de Musique et d'In-
strumens | Il tient Cordes de Naples et de
Piano, Papier règlé de tout format. | à
Paris rue St. Marc No. 10 entre l'hotel
Montmorency et le passege des Pan-
oramas. | Tous les exemplaires sont
signés Gaveaux ainé [ca. 1800?]

2° *Score:* 1 ℓ., 308 p.
Plate no. I
"Les Frères" erased from title-page and
"ainé" superimposed
Hirsch II, no. 132
HOUGHTON

333   CHERUBINI, LUIGI

Eliza | Ou | le Voyage aux Glaciers du
Mont St. Bernard | Opera En Deux Actes |
Par Saint Cyr | Mis En Musique Par
Cherubini | et Representé au Théatre de
la Rue Faydeau le 13. Décembre 1794 |
Gravé par la Citne. Le Roy. | . . . | A Paris
| A l'Imprimerie du Conservatoire, |
. . . [ca. 1794]

2° *Score:* 1 ℓ., 387 p.
Plate no. II
Imprint partially covered by cancel
labels
Hirsch II, no. 130
HOUGHTON

334   [CHERUBINI, LUIGI]

[Lodoïska. Paris, Naderman, ca. 1791]

2° *Score:* 410, 9 p.
Imperfect: title-page lacking
Hirsch II, no. 133
MUSIC LIBRARY

335   CHERUBINI, LUIGI

Lodoïska | Comédie Héroïque En Trois
Actes | Par le Cen. Fillette-Loraux | Re-
presentée pour la premiere fois sur le
Théâtre de la Rue Feydeau le 18 Juilte.
1791. | Mise En Musique | Par Le Cen.
Cherubini | . . . | Gravée par Huguet Mu-
sicien Pensionnaire de la Comédie Ita-
lienne | A Paris | Chez JH. Naderman,
Editeur, Luthier, Facteur de Harpe, et
autres | Instruments de Musique, Rue
d'Argenteuil, Butte St. Roch, à Apollon |
Et aux Adresses Ordinaires | l'Auteur
prévient que les Exemplaires sont signés
par l'Editeur, | Et les non signés seront
échangés en indiquant le Contrefacteur.
[1791?]

2° *Score:* 1 ℓ., 434 p.
Plate no. 695
HOUGHTON, MUSIC LIBRARY

336   [CHEVRIER, FRANÇOIS ANTOINE]
          SUPPOSED AUTHOR

La | Constitution | De | L'Opera. | A
Amsterdam. | MDCCXXXVII.

8° 31 p.
RISM B VI, 220
MUSIC LIBRARY

337   CHILCOT, THOMAS

Six | Suites of Lessons | of the | Harpsi-
cord or Spinet | Compos'd by Mr Thomas
Chilcot | Organist of Bath | London |
Printed and Sold by Wm Smith, at
Corellis Head, near St Clements Church
in ye Strand. | and by the Author, at his
House, in Barton Fields Bath, as also by
Mr: James Leake, | Bookseller in Bath.
[1734?]

  obl. 2° *Score:* 3 *ℓ.,* 52 p.
RISM A I, no. C 2055
HOUGHTON

338

Choice | Ayres & Songs | To Sing to the
| Theorbo-Lute or Bass-Viol, | Being |
Most of the Newest Ayres and Songs,
Sung at Covrt, | And at the Publick The-
atres. | Composed by several Gentlemen
of His Majesties Musick, and others. |
The Second Book. | London, | Printed by
Anne Godbid, and are Sold by John Play-
ford, at his | Shop near the Temple
Church, 1679.

  2° *Score:* 2 *ℓ.,* 67, [1] p.
Page [1]: Books Printed and Sold by
John Playford . . .
Day, no. 48; RISM B I, no. 1679⁷
HOUGHTON

339

Choice | Ayres and Songs | To Sing To
The | Theorbo-Lute, or Bass-Viol: | Being |
Most of the Newest Ayres and Songs
sung at Court, | And at the Publick The-
atres. | Composed by several Gentlemen
of His Majesty's Musick, and others. |
The Third Book. | London, | Printed by A.
Godbid and J. Playford Junior, and are
Sold by John Playford, at his Shop | near
the Temple Church; and John Carr, at
his Shop at the Middle Temple-Gate,
1681.

  2° *Score:* 2 *ℓ.,* 52 p.
Day, no. 55; RISM B I, no. 1681⁴
HOUGHTON

340

Choice | Ayres and Songs | To Sing To
The | Theorbo-Lute, or Bass-Viol: | Being |
Most of the Newest Ayres and Songs
sung at Court, | And at the Publick The-
atres. | Composed by several Gentlemen
of His Majesty's Musick, and others. |
The Fourth Book. | London, | Printed by
A. Godbid and J. Playford Junior, and are
Sold by John Playford, at his Shop | near
the Temple Church; and John Carr, at
his Shop at the Middle-Temple Gate,
1683.

  2° *Score:* 2 *ℓ.,* 87, [1] p.
Unnumbered page at end: Musick
Books printed for John Playford . . .
Day, no. 59; RISM B I, no. 1683⁵
HOUGHTON, MUSIC LIBRARY

341

Choice | Ayres and Songs | To Sing To
The | Theorbo-Lute, or Bass-Viol: | Being |
Most of the Newest Ayres and Songs
sung at Court, | And at the Publick The-
atres. | Composed by several Gentlemen
of His Majesty's Musick, and others. |
The Fifth Book. | London, | Printed by J.
Playford Junior, and are sold by John
Playford, at his Shop near | the Temple
Church; and John Carr, at his Shop at the
Middle-Temple Gate, 1684.

  2° *Score:* 2 *ℓ.,* 63, [1] p.
Page [1]: Musick Books printed for
John Playford . . .
Day, no. 68; RISM B I, no. 1684³
HOUGHTON

342

Choice | Ayres, Songs, & Dialogues |
To Sing to the | Theorbo-Lvte, or Bass-
Viol. | Being | Most of the Newest Ayres,
and Songs, Sung at Covrt, | And at the
Publick Theatres. | Composed by several
Gentlemen of His Majesties Musick, and
others. | The Second Edition Corrected
and Enlarged. | London, | Printed by W.
Godbid, and are to be sold by John Play-
ford, | near the Temple Church, 1675.

  2° *Score:* 2 *ℓ.,* 87, [1] p.
Unnumbered page at end: Books
Printed and Sold by John Playford . . .

Day, no. 40, first entry; RISM B I, no. 1675[7]

HOUGHTON

343

Choice | Ayres, Songs, & Dialogues | To Sing to the | Theorbo-Lvte, or Bass-Viol. | Being | Most of the Newest Ayres and Songs, Sung at Covrt, | And at the Publick Theatres. | Composed by Several Gentlemen of His Majesties Musick, and others. | Newly Re-printed with large Additions. | London, | Printed by William Godbid, and are Sold by John Playford | near the Temple Church, 1676.

2° *Score:* 2 ℓ., 95, [1] p.
Page [1]: Books Printed and Sold by John Playford . . .
Day, no. 42; RISM B I, no. 1676[3]

HOUGHTON

344

A Choice | Collection | Of | New Songs and Ballads. | The | Words made to several Pleasant Tunes, | By Mr. D'urfey. | With the Tunes Transpos'd for the Flvte. | London: | Printed by William Pearson, next door to the Hare and Feathers, in Alders-|gate-street, for Henry Playford, and Sold by him at his Shop in the Temple-|Change Fleet-street; and at all other Musick Shops in Town. 1699. | . . .

2° *Score:* 1 ℓ., 10 p.
Day, no. 170

HOUGHTON

345   [CHOQUEL, HENRI LOUIS]

La Musique | Rendue Sensible | Par La Méchanique, | Ou Nouveau Systeme pour apprendre | facilement la Musique soi-même; | Ouvrage utile & curieux approuvé par l'Académie | Royale des Sciences. | . . . | A Paris, | Chez {Ballard, seul Imprimeur du Roi pour la Musique & Noteur | de la Chapelle de Sa Majesté, rue S. Jean-de-Beauvais. | Duchesne, rue S. Jacques, au Temple du Goût. | Lambert, rue & à côté de la Comédie Françoise, au Parnasse. | l'Auteur, rue S. Honoré, Maison du Cloître, à la ville de

Gand. | Et aux Adresses ordinaires de Musique. | M.DCC.LIX. | Avec Approbation & Privilége du Roi.

8° 2 ℓ., xiv, 213, [4] p., illus., fold. pl., music
Pages 175–213: musical examples (texts and melodies) taken from operas and motets, with tempo indications based on the length of a pendulum
BN XXVIII, col. 894; RISM B VI, 222

HOUGHTON

346   CIAMPI, VINCENZO

Sonate | Per | Cembalo | Composte Da | Vincenzo Ciampi. | London. Printed for I. Walsh, in Catharine Street, in the Strand. | . . . [1751]

obl. 2° *Score:* 1 ℓ., 27 p.
Walsh II, no. 371

HOUGHTON

347   CIAMPI, VINCENZO

Six | Sonatas | for two | Violins | with a | Thorough Bass | for the | Harpsichord, | Composed by | Sigr. Vincenzo Ciampi | Opera Prima | Printed for J. Johnson facing Bow Church in Cheapside, London. | . . . [1751?]

2° 3 pts.; *violino primo, violino secondo:* 1 ℓ., 16 p. each; *violoncello:* 1 ℓ., 13 p.
RISM A I, no. C 2134

MUSIC LIBRARY

348   CIMAROSA, DOMENICO

L'Impresario in Angustie | Ou | Le Directeur | Dans L'Embarras, | Opera Bouffon en Deux Actes, | Représenté Sur le theatre de Monsieur | Musique Del Sgor Cimarosa. | Paroles Françaises Par Mr D*** | . . . | A, Paris, | Chez le Sr Sieber Musicien rue St honore entre celle des | Vielles Etuve et celle D'orleans chez l'Apothicaire No. 92. [1790]

2° *Score:* 1 ℓ., 214 p.
Plate no. 1051
Hirsch II, no. 135; RISM A I, no. C 2279

MUSIC LIBRARY

The SONG Tunes for the FLUTE.

Where Divine Gloriana,

Now the ground is hard Froze, and cawd Winter is come;

Books lately Printed for, *and Sold by*, Henry Playford *at his* Shop in the Temple-Change Fleet-ftreet.

W*It and Mirth: Or, Pills to purge Melancholy*, Being a Collection of the beft Old and New Ballads, and Songs, containing near 200, with the Tunes to each. Price 2 *s.* 6*d.* in Calf 3 *s.* Printed for *Henry Playford* at his Shop in the *Temple-Change.*

Orpheus Britannicus, being the Choiceft Songs of one ; two and three Voices, by the late Mr. *Henry Purcell* in Folio. Price Bound 18 *s.*

An Introduction to the Skill of Mufick, the Thirteenth Edition , to which is Added the whole Art of Compofition by the late Mr. *Henry Purcell.* Price bound 2 *s.*

The Dancing-Mafter, the 10th. Edition in two Parts, Price Bound 3 *s.*

Dr. *Blow's* Choice Collection of Leffons, for the *Harpfichord*, or *Spinnett*, Engraven. Price ftitcht 1 *s.* 6 *d.*

Mercurius Muficus : For *January*, and *February* being a Monthly Collection of New Teaching Songs, with the Tunes Tranfpos'd for the *Flute* at the end of the Book. Price Six-pence.

Apollos Banquet, being the eafieft and beft Inftructions for young beginners yet publifh'd, containing above a Hundred of the choiceft Tunes, for the *Violin*; The 7th. Edition. Price 1 *s.* 6 *d.*

The Divifion Violin in 2 Books, being all the beft Grounds and Divifions, the 4th. Edition ; Price of both 4 *s.* 6 *d.*

A Sheet of Cotches fett by the late Mr. *Henry Purcell.* Price 3 *d.*

A Sheet Engraven on Copper, being Directions for the Bafs *Viol.* Price. 6 *d.*

F I N I S.

344 *A Choice Collection of New Songs and Ballads,* London, 1699: page 10 (276 × 167 mm.)

PLAN

Des Figures de la Contredance

1	2	3
4	5	6
7	8	9
10	11	

DESCRIPTION

Des Figures de la Contredance

1. Le Rond ordinaire
2. Les 4 Hom. balancent devant leur Femme et forment la Croix
3. Les 4 Hom. avancent d'une Place à droite et se trouve en avant de la Fem. en dehors
4. Les 4 Fem. font de même et se trouvent vis à vis de leur Hommes
5. Les 4 Hom. vont en avant et ... 4 Femmes
6. Les 4 Hom. promenent les 2 mains de la Femme qu'ils a leur droite, les font tourner pour se mettre comme au commencement
7. Etant à leur place les 2 figures de côté se retrouvent des autres balancent et se trouvent sur 2 lignes
8. Etant sur 2 lignes, font un roulade sur 2, et tournent un tour pour se remettre sur 2 autres lignes
9. Les 4 du milieu vont en arrière pendant que les 2 Dames de côté font la Chaine pour regagner leur place
10. Contreparties de la précédente qui met tout les 3 à leur place
11. La Main

Ceux qui desireront faire un Recueil de l'Contredanse pourront trouver les Semaines en trouveia deux nouvelles, et très aisé à suivre.

479 DUBOIS, *La Dubois Allemande*, Paris, ca. 1769: pages [22]–[23] (both 155 × 82 mm.), showing "Les Plaisirs de l'inconstance; ou, L'Infidelle"

349 CIMAROSA, DOMENICO

Il Matrimonio Segreto, | Dramma Giocoso in due Atti | Ou | Le Mariage Secret | Opera Comique en deux Actes | Musique De Cimarosa | paroles françaises de Moline. | . . . | A Paris | Chez Imbault, Md. de Musique, au Mont d'Or Rue Honoré No. 200 entre la Rue | des Poulies et la Maison d'Aligre. | Et Péristile Du Théâtre De L'Opéra Comique Rue Favart, No. 461. | Gravé par L. Aubert. [ca. 1799]

2° *Score:* 3 ℓ., 492 p.
Plate no. 738
Preliminary leaves 1ᵛ–3ʳ: Catalogue | De Musique Vocale Et Instrumentale Mise Au Jour Par Imbault, | . . .
Hirsch II, no. 137; RISM A I, no. C 2304
MUSIC LIBRARY

—another copy
2° *Score:* 4 ℓ., 492 p.
Preliminary leaf 2ʳ: Répertoire; 3ʳ–4ᵛ: Catalogue . . .
HOUGHTON

350 CIRRI, GIOVANNI BATTISTA

Six | Duetts | For a | Violin and a Violoncello | Dedicated To | Sir Richard Phillipps Bart. | Composed by | Gianbattista Cirri | Musick Master to his Royal Highness | the Duke of Gloucester | Opera XII | London Printed by Welcker in Gerrard Street St. Ann's Soho | . . . [1770]

2° 2 pts.: *violino:* 2 ℓ., 13 p., front. (port.); *violoncello:* 1 ℓ., 13 p.
RISM A I, no. C 2525
HOUGHTON

CLAIR, JEAN MARIE LE *See* Leclair, Jean Marie

CLAIRAMBAULT, LOUIS NICOLAS *See* Clérambault, Louis Nicolas

351 [CLAYTON, THOMAS]

Songs | in the | Opera | Call'd | Arsinoe | Queen | of | Cyprus | London Printed for & Sould by I: Walsh Musicall Instru-

ment maker in Ordinary to her Majesty at the | Golden Harp & Ho-boy in Catherine-street, near Summerset-house in ye strand [1706]

2° *Score:* 2 ℓ., 49 numb. ℓ.
RISM A I, no. C 2642; Walsh I, no. 220
MUSIC LIBRARY

352 CLAYTON, THOMAS

Songs | in the New | Opera | Call'd | Rosamond | as they are perform'd at the | Theatre Royall | Compos'd | by | Mr. Tho. Clayton | London Printed for I. Walsh Servt. to Her Matie. at ye Harp & Hoboy in Katherine Streed [*sic*] | near Somerset House in ye Strand and P. Randall at ye Violin & Lute by Paulsgrave | head Court without Temple Barr [1707]

2° *Score:* 2 ℓ., 47 numb. ℓ.
RISM A I, no. C 2660; Walsh I, no. 247
HOUGHTON

353 CLEMENTI, MUZIO

Six | Sonatas, | For The | Piano Forte. | Composed By | Muzio Clementi. | London: | Printed for Harrison, Cluse, & Co. 78, Fleet Street. [1798?]

8° *Score:* 45 p. (*The Piano-Forte Magazine*, vol. VI, no. 3)
Plate nos. 86–87
Op. 1
MUSIC LIBRARY

354 CLEMENTI, MUZIO

Trois | Sonates | Pour le | Forte Piano | Ou | Le Clavecin. | Composèes par | Muzio Clementi. | Op. VIII. . . . | London. | Printed by Longman & Broderip, No. 26, Cheapside & No. 13 Hay Market. [178–?]

2° *Score:* 1 ℓ., 21 p.
RISM A I, no. C 2789
MUSIC LIBRARY

355 CLEMENTI, MUZIO

Two Sonatas | And | Two Capriccios | for the | Piano Forte, | Composed & Dedicated to | Miss Isabella Savery | by | Muzio Clementi. | Op. 34. . . . | London,

Printed for the Author, & | Sold by Gray, Bookseller, No. 8, Glasshouse Street, Piccadilly, | near Sackville Street. [ca. 1795]

2° *Score:* 1 ℓ., 37 p.
RISM A I, no. C 3002
MUSIC LIBRARY

356   CLEONIDES

. . . | Cleonidae harmonicum intro-|ductorium in-|terprete Georgio Valla Placentino. [Venice, 1497]

2° In a vol. entitled Hoc in uolumine haec opera continentur. | Cleonidae harmonicum introductorium . . . , ℓ. [–]2ʳ –[–]7ᵛ
Colophon: Impressum Venetiis per Simonem Papiensem dictum Biuila-quam | Anno ab incarnatione: M.CCCC.LXXXXVII. Die Tertio Augusti.
Caption title
BMC V, 522; Hain-Copinger, no. 5451; RISM B VI, 226; Stillwell, no. C-677
HOUGHTON

357   [CLEONIDES]

Ευκλειδου | Εἰσαγωγὴ Ἁρμονική. | Τοῦ αὐτοῦ κατατομὴ κανόνος. | Euclidis Rudimenta | Mvsices. | Eiusdem sectio regulae harmonicae. | E Regia bibliotheca desumpta, ac nùnc primùm | Graecè et Latinè excusa, | Ioanne Pena Regio Mathematico interprete. | Ad | Illvstrissimvm Principem Caro-|lvm Lotharingvm Cardinalem. | Parisiis, | Apud Andream Wechelum, sub Pegaso, in | vico Bellouaco: Anno Salutis, 1557. | Cvm Privilegio Regis.

4° 2 ℓ., 5–16, 1–10 numb. ℓ.
Separate texts in Greek and Latin
This work now attributed to Cleonides. The *Sectio regulae harmonicae,* better known as *Sectio canonis,* is attributed to Euclides
Davidsson II, no. 31; RISM B VI, 296; Wolfenbüttel, no. 1113
HOUGHTON

358   CLÉRAMBAULT, LOUIS NICOLAS

Cantates | Françoises | A I. Et. II. Voix. | Avec Simphonie, et sans Simphonie. | Composées | Par Mr. Clerambault | Organiste, et Maistre de Clavecin. | Partition In Folio. | Livre Premier. | . . . | À Paris. | Chés L'Auteur, Rüe pavée, prés Saint André des Arcs. | Le Sr. Foucault Marchand, Rüe St. Honoré, a la regle d'or. | Avec Privilége Du Roy. M.DCC.X | Gravé par Barlion.

2° *Score:* 1 ℓ., 104 p., 1 ℓ.
Contents: *L'Amour piqué par une abeille, Le jaloux, Orphée, Poliphême, Medée, L'Amour et Baccus*
RISM A I, no. C 3163; Wolfenbüttel, no. 62
MUSIC LIBRARY

359   CLÉRAMBAULT, LOUIS NICOLAS

Cantates Françoises | Mellées de Simphonies. | Dediées | A Son Altesse Electoralle | Monseigneur | Le Duc De Baviere. | Par Mr. Clerambault. | Livre IIe. | Se Vend À Paris. | Chez l'Autheur, rüe pavée prés St. André des Arts, et chez le Sr. Foucault | marchand, rüe St. Honoré, à la regle dor. . . . | Avec Privilége du Roi. | 1713

2° *Score:* 2 ℓ., 123, [1] p.
Contents: *Alphée et Arethuse; Leandre, et Hero; La musette; Pigmalion; Le triomphe de la Paix*
RISM A I, no. C 3168; Wolfenbüttel, no. 62
MUSIC LIBRARY

360   CLÉREAU, PIERRE

. . . | Les Odes De Pierre | De Ronsard, | mis en Musique | à troys parties, | par Pierre Clereau. | Imprimé en troys volumes. | A Paris. | 1575 | Par Adrian le Roy, & Robert Ballard. | Imprimeurs du Roy. | Auec priuilege de sa magesté pour dix ans.

obl. 8° 1 pt.: *svperivs I:* 32 numb. ℓ.
LesureL, no. 185; RISM A I, no. C 3193; Thibault, no. 68
HOUGHTON

CLÉREMBAULT, LOUIS NICOLAS   *See*
Clérambault, Louis Nicolas

361   COELHO, MANOEL RODRIGUES

Flores | De Mvsica: | Pera O Instrv-
mento De | Tecla, & Harpa. | Compostas
por o Padre Manoel Rodrigues Coelho,
Capellão | do seruiço de sua Magestade,
& tangedor de Te-|cla de sua Real Capella
de Lisboa, natural | da cidade de Eluas. |
Dedicado A S. C. R. Magesta-|de del Rey
Phelippe terceiro das Espanhas. | Com
licença do S. Officio da Inquisição, Or-
dinario & Paço. | Em Lisboa: | Na officina
de Pedro Craesbeeck. | Anno Dñi
M.DCXX.

2° *Score:* 6 ℓ., 233 numb. ℓ., [4] p.,
illus.
RISM A I, no. C 3262
HOUGHTON

362   COFERATI, MATTEO

Cantore | Addottrinato | In Tutte Le
Regole | Del Canto Corale; | Ovvero |
Modo facile, e breve per la pratica de' pre-
cetti più | necessarj del Canto Fermo, per
mantenere il | Coro alla medesima al-
tezza di voce, e di | ripigliarla dove resta
l'Organo. | Con l'Intonazione di molte
singolari cose, che | fra l'Anno si cantano.
| In Specie | Inni, Invitatorj con il lor
Salmo, e Offizio parvo | della B. Vergine,
e de' Morti, con tutte le Se-|guenze, e An-
tifone da cantarsi alla distri-|buzione
delle Candele, e Palme. | Terza Edizione
Ampliata. | Opera data in luce dal Molto
Rev. Sig. | Matteo Coferati | Sacerdote,
Cappellano, e Cantore della | Metropoli-
tana Fiorentina. | In Firenze per Michele
Nestenus, e Antonmaria | Borghigiani.
Con licenza de' Super. 1708. | Ad in-
stanza di Gio. Antonio Scaletti Librajo.

8° xvj, 391 p., illus., music
Imperfect: pages 15,16 lacking
RISM B VI, 228
MUSIC LIBRARY

363   COFERATI, MATTEO, COMP.

Corona | Di Sacre | Canzoni, | O | Lavde
| Spiritvali | di più divoti Autori | Nuova-
mente corrette, ed accresciute | In questa
seconda impressione | per opera di | Mat-
teo Coferati | Sacerdote Fiorentino. | In
Osseqvio | Della Venerabile Congrega-
zione | Di | Giesv̀ Salvadore | In Firenze,
Dagli Eredi di Francesco Onofri. 1689. |
Per Iacopo Carlieri, all'Insegna di S. Luigi
| Con Licenza, e Privilegìo di S. A. S.

12° 12 ℓ., 151 [i. e. 551], [20] p., illus.
Page 551 misnumbered 151
RISM B I, no. 1689²
MUSIC LIBRARY

364   COFERATI, MATTEO

Manuale | Degli | Invitatorj | Co' suoi
Salmi da cantarsi nell'Ore Canoniche |
per ciascheduna Festa, e Feria di tutto
l'An-|no: nell'Ufizio parvo della Beatis-
sima | Vergine, e de' Morti. | Coll'ag-
giunta delle Sequenze, e lor Canto, | e
Antifone da cantarsi alla distribuzione |
delle Candele, e delle Palme. | Opera Rac-
colta | Dal Molto Rev. Sig. Matteo Co-
ferati | Sacerdote, Cappellano, e Cantore |
della Metropolitana Fiorentina | Seconda
Edizione. | In Firenze, M.DCC.XVIII. |
Per Michele Nestenus. Con lic. de' Su-
periori. | Ad istanza di Sebastiano Sca-
letti.

8° viij, 200 p., music
Hirsch I, no. 129; RISM B VI, 229
MUSIC LIBRARY

365   COLASSE, PASCAL

Achille | Et Polixene, | Tragedie. | Mise
En Musique | Le premier Acte par Feu
Monsievr De Lvlly. | Le Prologue, & les
quatres autres Actes | Par Monsieur
Colasse, | Maistre de la Chapelle du
Roy. | Sur la Copie de Paris. | A Amster-
dam, | Par Antoine Pointel, dans le
Kalver-straet, vis à vis la Chapelle, au
Rosier. | Et Se Trouve, | Chez Henry
Desbordes, Marchand Libraire dans le
Kalver-straet | M.DC.LXXXVIII.

4° *Score:* 2 ℓ., xxxvj, 288 p.
RISM A I, no. C 3384
MUSIC LIBRARY

366 COLIN, PIERRE

Liber Octo | Missarvm, Qvarvm Prio-|res, quae numero sex sunt, quatuor uocum concentu com-|positae sunt: hisce postposita est una quinq[ue] uocum. | Postrema uerò in sex uoces est distincta. | Modvli, Qvos Mottetos | usitatiori nomine uulgus uocat, Totidem sunt, | Parthenica Cantica In Lav-|dem illibatae Virginis conscripta (quae notiori nomi-|ne, atq[ue] Musicis peculiari, Magnificat in-|scribuntur) octo sunt, singulaq[ue] pro-|prio Tono distin-|guuntur. | Quae omnia Petrus Colinius Musicae modulatio-|nis peritia conspecuus composuit. | Lvgdvni Iacobvs Mo-|dernus excudebat. | M.D.XLI.

2° 112 numb. *ℓ.*
In choirbook format
MortimerF, no. 144; Pogue, no. 33; RISM A I, no. C 3307
HOUGHTON

367

A Collection of | Catches | by the following Masters |

Dr. Arne	Dr. Boyce
Dr. Hayes	Dr. Nares
Sigr. Giardini	Mr. Baildon
Sigr. Marella	Mr. Berg
Mr. Savage	Mr. Howard
Mr. Battishill	Mr. Warren &c:

London Printed by Welcker in Gerrard Street St. Ann's Soho | . . . [ca. 1764]

obl. 4° 1 *ℓ.*, 40 p.
RISM B II, 62
HOUGHTON

368

A Collection of | Catches, Canons, Glees, Duettos &c. | Selected from the Works of the most eminent Composers | Antient & Modern | Edinburgh, | . . . | Printed for J. Sibbald & Co. and Sold at | their Circulating Library Parliament Square. | J. Johnson Sculpt. Edinr. [pref. 1780]

obl. 8° *Score: 4 vols.: vol. I: 4 ℓ., 112 p.; vol. II: 3 ℓ., 112 p.; vols. III, IV: 2 ℓ., 112 p. each*

Imprint, vols. II, IV: Edinburgh | Printed for J. Sibbald Parliament Square, and | Messrs. Corri & Sutherland Music | Sellers to Her Majesty. | J. Johnson Sculpt. Edinr.
RISM B II, 62–63
MUSIC LIBRARY

369

A | Collection | of | Catches Glees | &c &c | Selected from the Works | of the most | Eminent Composers | . . . | London | Printed by J. Bland No: 45 Holborn. | . . . [178–?]

2° 11 p.
RISM B II, 63
MUSIC LIBRARY

370

A | Collection | Of Favorite | & familiar Pieces, | Adapted For The | Piano Forte. | London: | Printed for Harrison, Cluse, & Co. No. 78 Fleet Street. [1799?]

8° *Score:* 18 p. (*The Piano-Forte Magazine*, vol. VII, no. 12)
Plate no. 113
MUSIC LIBRARY

A COLLECTION OF HIGHLAND VOCAL AIRS *See* McDonald, Patrick, comp. *A Collection of Highland Vocal Airs*

371

A | Collection | Of | Overtures and Symphonies. | By |

Vanhall	Bach of Berlin
Ditters	Stamitz and
Martini	Cimorosa

London: | Printed for Harrison & Co. No. 18, Paternoster Row. [1797?]

8° *Score:* 73 p. (*The Piano-Forte Magazine*, vol. II, no. 5)
RISM B II, 69
MUSIC LIBRARY

372

A Collection of | Songs and Ballads | Sung by | Mr. Lowe and Miss Stevenson |

at | Vaux Hall | London | Printed for Robert Thompson at the Bass Violin in Paul's Alley | St. Paul's Church-Yard. [before 1770]

 2° *Score:* 1 ℓ., 32 p.
 HOUGHTON

373

A Collection | of the most admired | Glees and Catches, | For three Four and five | Voices, | Selected from the Works of all the | Celebrated Authors | Dublin | Published by Anne Lee, Numbr. 2 | Dame street near the | Royal Exchange. | . . . [1780?]

 2° *Score: vol. II:* 2 ℓ., 44 p.
 RISM B II, 72
 MUSIC LIBRARY

COLLIER, JOEL, PSEUD. *See* Veal, George

374

Comes Amoris: | Or The | Companion of Love. | Being a Choice Collection | Of The Newest Songs now in Use. | With | Thorow-Bass to each Song for the Harpsichord, Theorbo, or Bass-Viol | The Second Book. | London, | Printed by Tho. Moore for John Carr at his Shop at the Middle Temple Gate, and | Sam Scott at his Shop in Bell-Yard near Temple-Barr. 1688.

 2° *Score:* 1 ℓ., 24, 4 p., 1 ℓ.
 Pages 1–4 at end: A Small Collection | Of The | Newest Catches | For 3 Voices.
 Colophon, page 2, second sequence: London, Printed for John Carr at the Middle Temple-Gate. 1687
 Colophon, page 4, second sequence: London, Printed for Sam. Scott next door to the Devil-Tavern by Temple-Bar. 1687.
 Unnumbered leaf at end: Mvsick Books sold by John Carr . . .
 Day, no. 98; RISM B I, no. 1688[8]
 HOUGHTON

375

Commemoration | Of | Handel. | First Performance. | London: | Printed by H.

Reynell, No. 21, Piccadilly, near the Hay-market. | MDCCLXXXIV. | . . .

 4° 22 p., illus. (port.)
 Program
 HOUGHTON (2 copies)

376

Commemoration | Of | Handel. | Fourth Performance. | London: | Printed by H. Reynell, No. 21, Piccadilly, near the Hay-market. | MDCCLXXXIV. | . . .

 4° 22 p., illus. (port.)
 Program
 HOUGHTON

COMPENDIUM MUSICES *See* Cantorinus

377

Compleat Instructions | For The | Guitar, | Containing the most modern directions with proper Examples for learners | to obtain a speedy proficiency Corrected by the most eminent Masters. | To which is added | A Collection of favourite Minuets Marches Songs &c. | Adapted purposely for that Instrument | . . . | London. | Printed by Longman and Broderip No: 26 Cheapside. | . . . [after 1776]

 obl. 4° 1 ℓ., 39 p., illus., music
 Imperfect: pages 27, 28 lacking
 HOUGHTON

378

The | Compleat Tutor | For the | Flute | Containing | The Best and Easiest Instructions | for Learners to Obtain a Proficiency. | To which is Added | A Choice Collection of the most Celebrated | Italian, English, and Scotch Tunes. | Curiously adapted to that Instrument. | Printed for & Sold by John Simpson | at the Bass Viol, & Flute, in Sweetings Alley, | opposite ye East Door of the Royal Exchange. | London | . . . [after 1765]

 8° 1 ℓ., 29, 2 p., front., illus., music
 Page 1 at end: A | Dictionary | Explaining Such Greek, Latin, Italian | and French Words as generally occur in | Musick

Page 2 at end: Musick to be had where this is Sold
Bound with 17 leaves of melodies for one and two flutes in nineteenth-century manuscript
Page 9 printed as folded plate
HOUGHTON

379 [CONTANT D'ORVILLE, ANDRÉ GUILLAUME]

Histoire | De | L'Opera Bouffon, | Contenant les jugemens de toutes les Piéces qui | ont paru depuis sa naissance jusqu'à ce jour. | Pour servir à l'Histoire des Théâtres de Paris. | . . . | A Amsterdam, | Et se trouve A Paris, | Chez Grangé, Libraire, Pont Notre-Dame; | au Cabinet Littéraire, près la Pompe. | M.DCC.LXVIII.

12° 2 vols.: *vol. I:* 4 ℓ., 266, [2] p.; *vol. II:* 2 ℓ., 214, [2] p.
RISM B VI, 234
HOUGHTON

LA CONSTITUTION DE L'OPÉRA *See* Chevrier, François Antoine, supposed author *La Constitution de l'opéra*

380

The | Contre Temps; | Or, | Rival Queans: | A | Small Farce. | As it was lately Acted, with great Applause, at | H[ei]d[egge]r's private Th[eat]re near the | H[a]y M[arke]t. | . . . | London: | Printed for A. Moore, near St. Paul's. 1727. | . . .

4° 16 p.
Satirical dramatic poem; the "cast" includes Faustina, Cuzzoni, Händel, Senesino and others
Foxon C400
HOUGHTON

381 CONVERÇAO, RAYMUNDO DA

Manval | De | Tvdo O Qve Se Canta Fora Do Choro, | conforme ao uzo dos Religiosos, & Religiosas | da sagrada ordem de Penitencia de nosso | Seraphico Padre Saõ Francisco | do Reyno de Portugal. | Pello | P. Fr. Raymvndo Da Converçam, | Religioso da mesma Ordem. | Contem As Ceremonias Do Altar, | & Choro, em todos os actos solemnes que oc-|correm em o descurso do

anno: conforme | o Breviario, Missal mais correctos. | Em Coimbra, | Com todas as licenças necessarias. | Na Officina de Rodrigo De Carvalho | Coutinho, Impressor da Vniversidade, | Anno de 1675.

4° 4 ℓ., 485, [5] p., illus., music
Hirsch IV, no. 1678; RISM B VI, 234
HOUGHTON

382

The | Convivial Songster, | Being A | Select Collection | Of The | Best Songs | In the English Language; | Humourous Satirical. Bachanalian. &c. &c. &c. | With | The Music prefixed to each Song. | London: | Printed for John Fielding, No. 23 Pater-noster Row. | . . . [1782]

12° 1 ℓ., xii, 371, [1] p., front.
Imprint date supplied from frontispiece
Imperfect: pages 107–110 lacking
RISM B II, 146
MUSIC LIBRARY

383 COOKE, BENJAMIN

Nine Glees | and | Two Duets, | (never before Printed) | Composed by the late | Dr. Benjamin Cooke. | Published from the original manuscripts by his Son, | Robert Cooke; | Organist of St. Martin's in the Fields. | Opera V. MDCCXCV. . . . | London, Printed by Longman & Broderip, and may be had of The Editor No. 47, Upper Titchfield Street.

obl. 2° *Score:* 1 ℓ., 5 p., 1 ℓ., 64 p.
RISM A I, no. C 3556
MUSIC LIBRARY

384 COPERARIO, JOHN

Songs of Mourning: | Bevvailing | The vntimely death of | Prince Henry. | VVorded by Tho. Campion. | And set forth to bee sung with one voyce | to the Lute, or Violl: | By John Coprario. | London: | Printed for Iohn Browne, and | are to be sould in S. dunstons | Churchyard. 1613.

2° *Score:* 2 ℓ., 7 numb. ℓ., 1 ℓ.
RISM A I, no. C 3617
HOUGHTON

385 CORELLI, ARCANGELO

Op. 1

Arcangelo Corelli | Opera Prima | XII | Sonatas | of three parts for two | Violins and a Bass | with | A Through Bass for ye Organ | Harpsicord or Arch Lute | Engrav'd from ye Score and | Carefully Corected by ye | best Italian Masters | . . . | London Printed for I. Walsh Servt. to his Matie. at ye Harp & Hoboy in Katherine Street near Somerset House in ye Strand | . . . [ca. 1730?]

2° 1 pt.: *violino secondo:* 1 ℓ., 13 p.
J. Hare's name erased from imprint, and no. 364 superimposed
Hirsch III, no. 160; RISM A I, no. C 3673; Walsh II, no. 412?
MUSIC LIBRARY

—another edition [ca. 1740?]
2° 3 pts.: *violino primo, violoncello, organo:* 1 ℓ., 24 p. each
The title-page and publisher's no. are the same as the above, but the music is printed from different plates
Walsh II, no. 413?
MUSIC LIBRARY

386 CORELLI, ARCANGELO

Op. 1

Sonate | a Tre | Due Violini e Violone Col Basso per L'Organo | Di | Arcangelo Corelli | Da Fusignano Detto Il Bolognese | Nouvelle Edition Trez Exactement Corrigee | Opera Prima | London. | Printed for and Sold by Benjamin Cooke, at the | Golden Harp in New-street, Covent Garden. | . . . [ca. 1735]

2° 4 pts.: *violino primo, violino secondo, violoncello, organo:* 1 ℓ., 25 p. each, front. (port.) in *violino primo* part
RISM A I, no. 3683
HOUGHTON

387 CORELLI, ARCANGELO

Op. 2

Sonate | a Tre | Due Violini e Violone Col Basso per L'Organo | Di | Arcangelo Corelli | Da Fusignano Detto Il Bolognese | Nouvelle Edition Trez Exactement Corrigee | Opera Secunda | London. | Printed for and Sold by Benjamin Cooke, at the | Golden Harp in New-street, Covent Garden | . . . [ca. 1735]

2° 4 pts.: *violino primo, violino secondo, violoncello, organo:* 1 ℓ., 12 p. each
RISM A I, no. C 3720
HOUGHTON

388 CORELLI, ARCANGELO

Op. 2

Arcangelo Corelli | Opera Secunda | XII | Sonatas | of three parts for | two Violins and a Bass | with | A Through Bass for ye. Organ | Harpsicord or Arch Lute | Engrav'd from ye Score and | Carefully Corected by ye. | best Italian Masters | . . . | London Printed for I Walsh Servt. to his Matie. at ye. Harp & Hoboy in Katherine Street near Somerset House in ye. Strand. | . . . [ca. 1740]

2° 2 pts.: *violino secondo, violone o cimbalo:* 1 ℓ., 13 p. each
Plate no. 2
No. 365 on title-page
Hirsch III, no. 160; RISM A I, no. C 3711; Walsh II, no 416?
MUSIC LIBRARY

—another edition
2° 2 pts.: *violino primo, violone o cimbalo:* 1 ℓ., 18 p. each
The title-page, plate no. and publisher's no. are the same as the above, but the music is printed from different plates
MUSIC LIBRARY

389 CORELLI, ARCANGELO

Op. 3

Sonate | a Tre | Due Violini e Violone Col Basso per L'Organo | Di | Arcangelo Corelli | Da Fusignano Detto Il Bolognese | Nouvelle Edition Trez Exactement Corrigee | Opera Terza | London. | Printed for and Sold by Benjamin Cooke, at the | Golden Harp in New-street, Covent Garden. | . . . [ca. 1735]

2° 4 pts.: *violino primo, violino secondo, violoncello, organo:* 1 ℓ., [1], 24 p. each
RISM A I, no. C 3750
HOUGHTON

390   CORELLI, ARCANGELO

Op. 3

Arcangelo Corelli Opera Terza | XII | Sonatas | of three parts for two | Violins and a Bass | with | A Through Bass for ye Organ | Harpsicord or Arch Lute | Engrav'd from ye Score and | Carefully Corected by ye | best Italian Masters | . . . | London Printed for I. Walsh Servt. to His Matie. at the Harp and Hoboy in Katherine Street near Somerset House in ye Strand | . . . [ca. 1740]

2° 1 pt.: *violino secondo:* 1 ℓ., 14 p.
Plate no. 3
No. 366 on title-page
Hirsch III, no. 160; RISM A I, no. C 3755; Walsh II, no. 420
MUSIC LIBRARY

—another edition
2° 3 pts.: *violino primo, violoncello, organo:* 1 ℓ., 25 p. each
The title-page, plate no. and publisher's no. are the same as the above, but the music is printed from different plates
MUSIC LIBRARY

391   CORELLI, ARCANGELO

Op. 4

Sonate | a Tre | Due Violini e Violone Col Basso per L'Organo | Di | Arcangelo Corelli | Da Fusignano Detto Il Bolognese | Nouvelle Edition Trez Exactement Corrigee | Opera Quarta | London. | Printed for and Sold by Benjamin Cooke, at the | Golden Harp in New-street, Covent Garden. | . . . [ca. 1735]

2° 4 pts.: *violino primo:* 1 ℓ., 14 p.; *violino secondo:* 1 ℓ., 11 p.; *violoncello, organo:* 1 ℓ., 14 p. each
Imperfect: title-page lacking in *violoncello* part
RISM A I, no. C 3784
HOUGHTON

392   CORELLI, ARCANGELO

Op. 4

Arcangelo Corelli | Opera Quarta | XII | Sonatas | of three parts for two | Violins and a Bass | with | A Through Bass for ye Organ | Harpsicord or Arch Lute | En-

grav'd from ye Score and | Carefully Corected by ye | best Italian Masters | . . . | London Printed for I Walsh Servt. to his Matie. at ye. Harp & Hoboy in Katherine Street near Somerset House in ye. Strand. | . . . [ca. 1740]

2° 2 pts.: *violino secondo, violone o cimbalo:* 1 ℓ., 13 p. each
Plate no. 4
No. 367 on title-page
Hirsch III, no. 160; RISM A I, no. C 3788; Walsh II, no. 424
MUSIC LIBRARY

—another edition
2° 2 pts.: *violino primo, violone o cimbalo:* 1 ℓ., 16 p. each
The title-page, plate no. and publisher's no. are the same as the above, but the music is printed from different plates
MUSIC LIBRARY

393   CORELLI, ARCANGELO

Op. 5

Sonate | a Violino e, Violono o Cimbalo | Da | Arcangelo Corelle | Da | Fusigano | Opera Qvinta | . . . | London. | Printed for and sold by Benjamin Cooke, at | the Golden Harp in New-street, Covent Garden. | . . . [ca. 1735]

4° *Score:* 1 ℓ., 69 p.
Parte seconda (Sonatas 7–12) has separate title-page: Preludi Allemande | Correnti Gigue Sarabande | Gavotte E Follia | . . .
Colophon: The Whole Engraven by T: Cross
RISM A I, no. C 3824
MUSIC LIBRARY

394   CORELLI, ARCANGELO

Op. 5

Opera Quinta | Del Signore | Arcangelo Corelli | Nuovamente Ristampata, | E Dedicata | All'Autore | Parte Prima | Da Ranieri Del Vivo | Incisore In Firenze L'Anno 1777

obl. 2° *Score:* [1], 46 p.
RISM A I, no. C 3834
MUSIC LIBRARY

395 CORELLI, ARCANGELO

Op. 6

Concerti Grossi | Con duoi Violini e Violoncello di Concertino obligati e duoi | altri Violini, Viola e Basso di Concerto Grosso ad arbitrio, | che si potranno radoppiare; | Dedicati All' | Altezza Serenissima Elettorale | Di | Giovanni Guglielmo | Principe Palatino Del Reno; Elettore e Arci-Marescialle | Del Sacro Romano Impero; Duca Di Baviera, Giuliers, | Cleves & Berghe; Principe Di Murs; Conte Di | Veldentz, Spanheim, Della Marca e | Ravenspurg; Signore Di | Ravenstein &c. &c. &c. | Da | Arcangelo Corelli Da Fusignano. | Opera Sesta. | . . . | A Amsterdam | Chez Estienne Roger, Marchand Libraire. | . . . | [ded. 1712]

2° 7 pts.: *violino primo del concertino:* 2 ℓ., 34 p.; *violino secondo del concertino:* 1 ℓ., 33 p.; *violoncello del concertino:* 1 ℓ., 34 p.; *violino primo del concerto grosso, violino secondo del concerto grosso, alto viola, basso del concerto grosso:* 1 ℓ., 27 p. each

No. 197 on each title-page

Parte secondo (Sonatas 9–12) has separate title-page in each part: Preludii, | Allemande, Correnti, Gighe, | Sarabande, Gavotte | e Minuetti. | . . .

Imperfect: frontispiece lacking (see Schnapper I, 216)

RISM A I, no. C 3844

MUSIC LIBRARY

396 CORELLI, ARCANGELO

Op. 6

Concerti Grossi | Con duoi Violini, e Violoncello di Concertino | obligati, e duoi altri Violini, Viola, e Basso di Concerto | Grosso, ad arbitrio, che si potranno radoppiare; | Da | Arcangelo Corelli da Fusignano | Opera Sesta. | XII | Great Concertos, or | Sonatas, | for two Violins and a Violincello: | or for two | Violins more, a Tenor, | and a Thorough-Bass: | which may be doubled at Pleasure. | being the Sixth and last work of | Arcangelo Corelli. | Note all the other Works of this Author may be had where this is sold. | London Printed for I: Walsh, Servant in Ordinary to his Majesty: at the |

Harp and Hoboy, in Katherine Street, in the Strand: and I: Hare, at the | Viol and Flute, in Cornhill, near the Royall Exchange. [1715]

2° 1 pt.: *violino secondo del concerto grosso:* 1 ℓ., 27 p.

RISM A I, no. C 3845; Walsh I, no. 466

HOUGHTON

397 [CORELLI, ARCANGELO]

Op. 6

[Concerti grossi, op. 6. London?, ca. 1725?]

2° 2 pts.: *flauto primo:* 34 p.; *flauto secondo:* 33 p.

Parte seconda (Concertos 9–12) has separate title-page in each part: Preludii | Allemande Gighe | Corrente Sarabande | Gavotte e Minuetti | . . .

Imperfect: title-page lacking in each part

MUSIC LIBRARY

398 CORELLI, ARCANGELO

Op. 6

Concerti Grossi | Con duoi Violini, e Violoncello di Concertino | obligati, e duoi altri Violini, Viola, e Basso di Concerto | Grosso, ad arbitrio, che si potranno radoppiare; | Da | Arcangelo Corelli da Fusignano | Opera Sesta. | XII | Great Concertos, or | Sonatas, | for two Violins and a Violincello: | or for two | Violins more, a Tenor, | and a Thorough-Bass: | which may be doubled at Pleasure. | being the Sixth and last work of | Arcangelo Corelli. | Note all the other Works of this Author may be had where this is sold. | London | Printed & Sold by Preston, at his Wholesale Warehouses, 97, Strand. [ca. 1790]

2° 1 pt.: *violoncello del concertino:* 1 ℓ., 31 p.

RISM A I, no. C 3851

HOUGHTON

399 CORELLI, ARCANGELO

Op. 6

The Score | of the Twelve Concertos | Compos'd by | Arcangelo Corelli. | For two Violins & a Violoncello, | with two Violins more, a Tenor & | Thorough Bass for Ripieno Parts, | which may be doubled at pleasure. | Dedicated to | Ralph Jenison of Walworth Hall | in the Bishoprick of Durham Esqr. | . . . | The Whole Carefully Corrected by several | most Eminent Masters, and revis'd by Dr. Pepusch. | Engrav'd with the utmost exactness by Tho: Cross. | London | Printed for and sold by John Johnson at the Harp and Crown | in Cheapside | . . . [ca. 1754]

2° *Score:* 2 ℓ., 139 p., front. (port.)
RISM A I, no. C 3853 (op. 6)
HOUGHTON

400   CORELLI, ARCANGELO

Op. 6, no. 8

Corelli's | Concerto. | Composed | For The | Celebration | Of The | Nativity. | London: | Printed for Harrison, Cluse, & Co. No. 78 Fleet Street. [1799?]

8° *Score:* 12 p. (*The Piano-Forte Magazine,* vol. VII, no. 2)
Plate no. 97
Arranged for keyboard instrument
MUSIC LIBRARY

401   CORFE, JOSEPH

Twelve Glees | For Three and Four Voices, | Dedicated (by Permission) to his Grace | The Duke of Leeds, | Composed from Ancient Scotch Melodies, | By Joseph Corfe, | Gentleman of His Majesty's Chapels Royal, & Organist of the Cathedral at Salisbury. | To be had at all the principal Music Shops in London &c. | 2d. Edition. | . . . [ca. 1795]

obl. 2° *Score:* 2 ℓ., 35 p.
RISM A I, no. C 3918
MUSIC LIBRARY

402   CORFE, JOSEPH

Nine | Vocal Trios | Arranged from | The most Favorite Airs and Duetts of | Purcell, Wise, Travers, Hayden & Harington. | By | Jos. Corfe | Gentleman of His Majestys Chapels Royal & Organist of the Cathedral Salisbury | . . . | Lon-

don | Printed by Broderip & Wilkinson No. 13 Haymarket | . . . [ca. 1800]

obl. 2° *Score:* 2 ℓ., 29 p.
RISM B II, 399
MUSIC LIBRARY

403

Corona | Di Sacre | Canzoni | O | Lavde | Spiritvali | Di Piv Divoti Avtori | Jn questa terza impressione | notabilmente accresciute di | materie, & arie nuove | Ad Vso | De Pij Trattenimenti | Delle | Conferenze. | In Firenze | Da Cesare Bindi. 1710. | Per il Carlieri, all'Insegna di S. Luigi | Con Licenza De' Svperiori.

12° xxiv, 768 p.
Imperfect: pages 743, 744 lacking
HOUGHTON

404   CORRETTE, MICHEL

Les Amusemens Du Parnasse | Methode | Courte et facile pour apprendre à toucher le Clavecin. | Avec Les Plus Jolis Airs A La Mode. | où les doigts sont chiffrés pour les Commençans. | Avec | Des Principes De Musique. | Livre Ier. | Par Mr. Corrette | . . . | A Paris, | Chez {l'Auteur, rue [erased] | Me. Boivin, rue St. Honoré à la Régle d'Or, | Mr. LeClerc, rue du Roule à la Croix d'or. | avec Privilege du Roy. | [1749?]

obl. 4° 1 ℓ., A–Z, Aa–Ak p., illus., music
RISM B II, 85–86; RISM B VI, 236
MUSIC LIBRARY

405   [COSTE, HILARION DE]

La Vie | Dv R. P. | Marin Mersenne | Theologien, | Philosophe Et Mathematicien | de l'Ordre des Peres Minimes. | Par F. H. D. C. Religieux du mesme | Ordre. | A Paris, | {Chez Sebastien Cramoisy, | Imprimeur ordin. du Roy, | & de la Reyne Regente, | Et | Gabriel Cramoisy. |} ruë S. | Iacques | aux Ci-|cognes. | M.DC.XLIX. | Avec Approbation.

8° 4 ℓ., 119 p., front. (port.)
Hirsch I, Historischer Anhang, no. 19
HOUGHTON

406 [Coste d'Arnobat,
Charles Pierre]

Doutes | D'Un | Pyrronien, | Proposés |
Amicalement | A J. J. Rousseau. | . . . |
[Paris] M.DCC.LIII.

8° 2 ℓ., 36 p.
Hirsch I, no. 134; RISM B VI, 239
HOUGHTON

407 Couperin, Armand Louis

Sonates En Trio | Pour le Clavecin,
Violon et Violon-celle. | Dédiées | à Ma-
dame la Duchesse | De Bethune. |
Composées | Par Mr. Couperin, | Orga-
niste de l'Eglise de Paris, et de Saint Ger-
vais &c. | Oeuvre III. | . . . | A Paris, |
Chés l'Auteur, attenant l'Eglise Saint
Gervais. | et aux adresses ordinaires de
Musique. | Avec Privilége Du Roi. | La-
bassée Sculp. De l'Imprimerie de Maillet.
[1770?]

obl. 2° 2 pts.: *clavecin:* 1 ℓ., 21 p.; *vio-
lino e basso:* 19 p.
RISM A I, no. C 4268
HOUGHTON

408 Couperin, François

L'Art | De toucher Le Clavecin, | Par |
Monsieur Couperin | Organish [*sic*] du
Roi, &c. | Dédié | A Sa Majesté. | . . . | A
Paris | Chés {L'Auteur, rüe de Poitou au
Marais | Le Sieur Foucaut rüe St. Honoré
à la Régle d'or, | proche la rüe des Bour-
donnois | Avec Privilége Du Roi. | 1717. |
gravé par Berey

2° 3 ℓ., 71, [2] p., music
Pages 52–65: eight preludes for harp-
sichord
RISM B VI, 240
HOUGHTON

409 Couperin, François

Pieces | De | Clavecin | Composées |
Par | Monsieur Couperin | Organiste de la
Chapelle du Roy, etc. | Et Gravées par du
Plessy. | Premier Livre. | . . . | A Paris |
Chés {L'Auteur vis-a-vis les Ecuries de
L'Hôtel de Toulouse | Le Sieur Le Clerc
Marchand rüe du Roûle à la Croix d'or. |
Le Sieur Boivin rüe St. Honoré, a la Régle

d'or. | 1713. [i. e. 1725?] | Avec Privilége
de sa Majesté | Gravé par Berey

2° *Score:* 3 ℓ., 78, [1] p.
Preliminary leaf 3ᵛ: Prix | des Ouvrages
de L'Auteur en 1725
Page 74–75: Explication des Agré-
mens, et des Signes
Hirsch III, no. 165; RISM A I, no. C
4284
HOUGHTON

410 Couperin, François

Second Livre de piéces | De | Clavecin |
Composé Par | Monsieur Couperin, | Or-
ganiste de la Chapelle du Roy; ordinaire |
de la Musique de la Chambre de sa Ma-
jesté; et | cy-devant Professeur-maître de
composition et | d'accompagnement de
feu Monseigneur Le | Dauphin Duc de
Bourgogne. | Gravé par Sr. du Plessy | . . .
| A Paris | Chés {L'Auteur vis-a-vis les
Ecuries de L'Hôtel de Toulouse, | Le
Sieur Boivin à la Régle d'or, rüe St.
Honoré vis a vis | la rüe des Bourdonnois.
| Et de puis peu, chés Le Sr. le Clerc Mar-
chand rüe du Roûle a la Croix d'or. | Avec
Privilége du Roy. | gravé par Berey
[1725?]

2° *Score:* 2 ℓ., 85, [1] p.
Preliminary leaf 2ᵛ: Prix | des Ouvrages
de l'Auteur en 1725
Hirsch III, no. 165; RISM A I, no. C
4292
HOUGHTON

411

Court-Ayres: | Or, | Pavins, Almains,
Corant's, and Sarabands, of two parts, |
Treble & Basse, for Viols or Violins. |
Which may be performed in Consort to
the Theorbo Lute, or Virginalls. | . . . |
London, Printed for John Playford, at his
Shop in the Temple, 1655.

obl. 8° 1 pt.: *basse:* 2 ℓ., 86 [i. e. 90] p.
Page 90 misnumbered 86
RISM B I, no. 1655⁵
HOUGHTON

412 [Coxe, William]

Anecdotes | Of | George Frederick Han-
del, | And | John Christopher Smith. |
With | Select Pieces Of Music, | Com-

posed | By J. C. Smith, | Never Before Published. | London: | Printed By W. Bulmer And Co. | Sold By Cadell and Davies, Strand; E. Harding, Pall-Mall; | Birchall, Music-Seller, Bond-Street; And | J. Eaton, Salisbury. | 1799.

4° 4 *ℓ.*, iv, 64, 34 p., front. (port.), illus. Pages 1–34 at end: music
RISM B VI, 241
HOUGHTON

413

The | Song and Duet | Sung by | Sigr. Delfini, Miss Field, & Miss Abrams, | in the Entertainment of the | Critic | As perform'd at the Theatre-Royal in Drury-Lane, | Published by Permission of the Managers. | . . . | London | Printed for S. A & P. Thompson, No. 75, St. Paul's Church Yard. [ca. 1790]

obl. 2° *Score:* 1 *ℓ.*, 7 p.
HOUGHTON

414   CROCE, GIOVANNI

. . . | Mvsica Sacra: | To | Sixe Voyces. | Composed in the Italian tongue | By | Giovanni Croce. | Newly Englished. | In London | Printed by Thomas Este, | the assigne of William Barley. | 1608.

4° 6 pts.: *cantvs, altvs, tenor, bassvs, qvintvs, sextvs:* 24 p. each
RISM A I, no. C 4486
HOUGHTON

415   CROFT, WILLIAM

Musica Sacra: | Or, | Select Anthems | In | Score, | Consisting of 2, 3, 4, 5, 6, 7 and 8 Parts: | To which is added, | The Burial-Service, as it is now occasionally | perform'd in Westminster-Abbey. | Compos'd by Dr. William Croft, Organist, Com-|poser, and Master of the Children of His Majesty's. | Chapel-Royal, and Organist of St. Peter's Westminster. | . . . | London, | Printed for and sold by John Walsh, Servant to His Majesty, at the Harp and | Hautboy in Catherine-street in the Strand; and John and Joseph Hare, at | the Viol and Flute in Cornhill, near the Royal-Exchange. [1724–1725]

2° *Score:* 2 vols.: *vol. I:* 3 *ℓ.*, 4 p., 1 *ℓ.*, 184 p.; *vol. II:* 2 *ℓ.*, 155 p.

John Hare's name omitted from imprint in vol. 2
Imperfect: frontispiece portrait lacking in vol. I (see Schnapper I, 240)
RISM A I, no. C 4505; Walsh II, no. 523
MUSIC LIBRARY

416   CROTCH, WILLIAM

Ode to Fancy | by | Dr. J. Warton. | Set to Music and performed as | an Exercise for | his Doctor's Degree, | and respectfully dedicated (by permission) to | Miss Mackworth, | by Wm. Crotch Mus. Doc. | Professor of Music & Organist of Christ Church, St. John's Chapel & the University Church, Oxford. | . . . | London: Printed (for the Author) by Broderip & Wilkinson, 13, Haymarket. [ca. 1800]

2° *Score:* 2 *ℓ.*, 102 p.
MUSIC LIBRARY

CUISSE, DE LA *See* La Cuisse, _____ De

417   CULLMAN, J. A.

Ludmille | Und | Heinrich Von Posen, | Eine Ballade | Von | I. I. Ihle. | In Musik Gesetzt | Und | Seiner Hochfürstlichen Durchlaucht | Dem Regierenden Fürsten Und Herrn | Friedrich Wilhelm | Von Nassau Weilburg | Unterthänigst Zugeeignet | Von | I. A. Cullmann. | Leipzig, | In Der Breitkopfischen Buchhandlung. [179–?]

obl. 2° *Score:* 1 *ℓ.*, 32 p.
RISM A I, no. C 4579
MUSIC LIBRARY

418   CURTIS, THOMAS

The Jessamine | A Collection of Six | New Songs, | Composed by | Mr. Thomas Curtis | Organist of St. Mildred's Bread Street | Set for the | Violin, German Flute, with a | Thorough Bass for the | Harpsicord or Organ. | London Printed & sold for the Author, by J. Cox at Simpson's Musick Shop in | Sweeting's Alley, opposite the East Door of the Royal Exchange. [ca. 1755]

2° *Score:* 3 *ℓ.*, 11 p.
RISM A I, no. C 4603
MUSIC LIBRARY

D

Da Gagliano, Marco   *See* Gagliano, Marco da

419   Dalayrac, Nicolas

Adolphe | Et | Clara | Ou | Les Deux Prisonniers, | Comédie En Un Acte Et En Prose | Paroles de B. J. Marsollier. | Représentée pour la premiere fois a Paris sur le Théâtre de l'Opera | Comique de la ruë favart, le 22 Pluviôse, An 7. | Musique de | N. Dalayrac, | Membre de l'Académie de Musique de Stockholm. | . . . | Gravée par Huguet, Musicien. | A Paris | Chez Pleyel Auteur et Editeur de Musique Rue Neuve des Petits Champs. | No. 1286. vis-à-vis la Trésorerie Nationale | . . . [1796]

2° *Score:* 1 ℓ., 120 p.
Plate no. 9
On verso of preliminary leaf: Catalogue | Des Ouvrages Gravés du C. Dalayrac | Qui se trouvent Chez Pleyel . . .
RISM A I, no. D 22
MUSIC LIBRARY

420   [Dalayrac, Nicolas]

L'Amant Statue | Comédie en un Acte | et en Prose | Représentée, pour la premiere fois, par les Comédiens Italiens Ordinaires du Roi, le Jeudi 4 Août 1785. | Dédiée | À Monsieur | Le Bailli De Crussol | Grand-croix de Malthe, Chevalier des Ordres du Roi, Maréchal de ses Camps et | Armées, Capitaine des Gardes du Corps de Monseigneur Comte d'Artois. | Mise en Musique | Par M. Dal*** | . . . | Gravé par Huguet Musicien de la Comédie Italienne | . . . | A Paris | Chez Le Duc successeur de M. De La Chevardier Ruë du Roule No. 6. | au Magasin de Musiques et d'Instruments, | et aux Adresses Ordinaires de Musique. [1785?]

2° *Score:* 1 ℓ., 89, [2] p.
Imprint partially covered by cancel label
Hirsch II, no. 150; RISM A I, no. D 66
MUSIC LIBRARY

421   [Dalayrac, Nicolas]

Azémia, | ou | Les Sauvages, | Comédie, en Trois Actes, | Représentée à Fontainebleau, devant leurs Majestés, le 17 Octobre 1786, | et à Paris, le 3 Mai 1787 par les Comédiens Italiens Ordinaires du Roi. | Mise en Musique | Par | M. Dal*** | . . . | Oeuvre VII. | Gravé par Huguet Musicien de la Comédie Italienne | A Paris Chez Le Duc Successeur et Proprietaire du fond de Mr. | de la Chevardiere Rue de Roule a la Croix d'Or No. 6. | au Magasin de Musique et d'Instruments. [ca. 1786]

2° *Score:* 1 ℓ., 211 p.
Hirsch II, no. 153; RISM A I, no. D 89
MUSIC LIBRARY

422   Dalayrac, Nicolas

Camille | Ou | Le Souterrain | Comédie En Trois Actes En Proses | Par Mr. Marsollier. | Représentée par les Comédiens Italiens | le Samedy 19 Mars 1791. | Mises En Musique | Par | M. D'Alayrac | . . . | Oeuvre [XII] | Gravée par Huguet Musicien Pensionnaire de la Comédie Italienne. | A Paris | Chez le Duc Md. de Musique et d'Instrumens, rue du Roule No. 6. [ca. 1791]

2° *Score:* 2 ℓ., 239 p.
Preliminary leaves 1^v–2^v: advertisements for music printed by Le Duc (JohanssonF facs. 76)
Hirsch II, no. 154; RISM A I, no. D 137 (without plate no.)
MUSIC LIBRARY

423   Dalayrac, Nicolas

Le Chateau | De | Montenero, | Comédie En Trois Actes Et En Prose. | Paroles du Cen. Hoffmann, | Représentée pour la premiere fois à Paris, sur le Théâtre de l'Opera | Comique de la rue Favart, le 24 Vendémaire, An 7. | Musique de | N. Dalayrac, | Membre de L'Académie de Musique de Stockholm | . . . | Gravée par Huguet, Musicien. | A Paris. | Chez l'Auteur, rue Helvétius, No. 591. | . . . [ca. 1798]

2° *Score:* 1 ℓ., 209 p.
On verso of preliminary leaf: Catalogue | Des Ouvrages Gravés du C. Da-

layrac, | Qui se trouvent Chez lui . . .
Hirsch II, no. 155 (without plate no.)
MUSIC LIBRARY

424   DALAYRAC, NICOLAS

Les Deux | Petits Savoyards | Comédie
en un Acte | Par M. Mars. . . . . Des
V. . . . . . [i. e. Marsollier des Vi-
vetières] | Représentée, pour la premiere
fois, par les Comédiens Italiens ordi-
naries du Roi, le | Mercredi 14 Janvier
1789 et a Versailles, devant leurs Ma-
jestés, le Vendredi suivant | Dédiée | A
Monsieur | De Sentelle | Commissaire
général de la Maison du Roi en suivante |
Par M. Dal*** | . . . | Oeuvre X. | Gravé
par Huguet Musicien de la Comédie Ita-
lienne. | A Paris Chez Pleyel, Auteur et
Editeur de Musique Rue Neuve des
Petits Champs | No. 1286. vis-à-vis la
Trésorerie Nationale. | . . . [1797]

2° *Score:* 1 ℓ., 133 p.
Plate no. 89
On verso of preliminary leaf: Cata-
logue | Des Ouvrages Gravés du C. Da-
layrac | Qui se trouvent Chez Pleyel . . .
RISM A I, no. D 165
MUSIC LIBRARY

425   [DALAYRAC, NICOLAS]

La Dot | Comédie en trois Actes et en
Prose | Par M. Desfontaines | Repré-
sentée, pour la prémiere fois, par les
Comédiens Italiens Ordinaires du Roi,
devant | leurs Majestés, à Fontaine-
bleau, le 8 Novembre 1785 et a Paris le
Lundi 21 du même Mois | Dédiée | À
Monseigneur Le Duc | De Fronsac | Pre-
mier Gentilhomme de la Chambre du
Roi | Lieutenant Géneral de ses Armées,
&c. | Mise en Musique | Par M. Dal*** |
. . . | Oeuvre IV. | Gravé par Huguet Mu-
sicien de la Comédie Italienne | A Paris
Chez Le Duc Successeur de M. de la Che-
vardiere Rue du Roule | No. 5. au Maga-
sin de Musique et d'Instruments. [ca.
1785]

2° *Score:* 1 ℓ., 199 p.
Hirsch II, no. 156; RISM A I, no. D 240
MUSIC LIBRARY

426   [DALAYRAC, NICOLAS]

Nina | ou | La Folle Par Amour |
Comédie en un Acte et en Prose | Repre-
sentée pour la Premiere fois par les
Comédiens Italiens Ordinaires | du Roy
le Lundi 15 Mai 1786. | Dédiée | À Mon-
seigneur | Comte D'Artois | Mise en Mu-
sique | Par M. Dal*** | . . . | Oeuvre V. |
Gravé par Huguet Musicien de la
Comédie Italienne. | A Paris Chez Le
Duc Successeur de Mr. De La Chevar-
diere Ruë du Roule à | la Croix d'Or au
Magasin de Musique et d'Instrumens
No. 6. [ca. 1786]

2° *Score:* 1 ℓ., 113 p.
Hirsch II, no. 168; RISM A I, no. D 432
MUSIC LIBRARY

427   [DALAYRAC, NICOLAS]

Nina, | or the | Love distracted Maid, |
Translated from the French | With all the
original Music, adapted for the | Voice
and Harpsichord | as acted at Paris and
London, with universal applause, | to
which are added two favorite Airs by |
Haydn and Gossec. | . . . | London,
Printed for G. Goulding No. 6, James
Street, Covent Garden . . . [1787?]

obl. 2° *Vocal score:* 1 ℓ., 61 p.
RISM A I, no. D 442
MUSIC LIBRARY

428   [DALAYRAC, NICOLAS]

Sargines | ou | L'Eleve De L'Amou[r] |
Comédie en Quatre Actes en Prose | Par
M. Monvel. | Représentée pour la pre-
miere fois par les Comédiens Italiens
ord[inaires] | du Roi le Mercredi 14 Mai
1788. | Mise en Musique | Par M. Dal*** |
Oeuvre IX. | . . . | Gravée par Huguet
Musicien de la Comédie Italienne. | A
Paris Chez Le Duc Successeur de Mr. De
La Chevardiere Rue du Roule | a la Croix
d'Or au grand Magazin de Musique et
d'Instruments No. 6. [1788?]

2° *Score:* 1 ℓ., 241 p.
Imperfect: title-page torn, with loss of
some letters
Dalayrac's autograph signature on
title-page
RISM A I, no. D 583
MUSIC LIBRARY

429 DALE, JOSEPH

Three | Favorite Duetts | for | Two Performers on One | Piano Forte | Or | Harpsichord; | Composed & humbly Dedicated to | The Miss Graham's | by | Joseph Dale. | Opera VII. . . . | London: | Printed & sold by the Author, at his Warehouses | No. 19. Cornhill, and No. 132. Oxford Street. [ca. 1785]

2° *Score:* 1 *ℓ.,* 17 p.
RISM A I, no. D 752
MUSIC LIBRARY

430 DALE, JOSEPH

Six | Sonatas | For The | Harpsichord | Piano Forte, And Organ. | Composed By | Joseph Dale. | Opera Primo. | London: | Printed and Sold by R. Falkener, No. 45. Salisbury-court, Fleet-street. | . . . [177–?]

2° *Score:* 1 *ℓ.,* 26 p.
RISM A I, no. D 746
MUSIC LIBRARY

D'ALEMBERT, JEAN LEROND *See* Alembert, Jean Lerond d'

DALEYRAC, NICOLAS *See* Dalayrac, Nicolas

DALLAIRAC, NICOLAS *See* Dalayrac, Nicolas

431 DANBY, JOHN

Danby's First Book | of | Catches, Canons and Glees, | For Three, Four & Five | Voices, | Dedicated (by Permission) to Chas. Butler Esqr. | London | Printed by J. Bland at his Music Warehouse, No. 45 Holborn: | . . . | Neele sculpt. 352 Strand. | . . . [ca. 1785]

obl 2° *Score:* 2 *ℓ.,* 60 p.
Imperfect: pages 59, 60 lacking
RISM A I, no. D 841
MUSIC LIBRARY

432 DANBY, JOHN

Danby's Second Book | of | Catches, Canons & Glees. | for three, four and five

| Voices, | Humbly Dedicated by Permission | to the | Right Honourable Lady Sarah Crespigny | Op. 3. . . . | London | Printed for the Author, No. 26. Henrietta Street Covent Garden | to be had at Bland's No. 45 Holborn, & all the Music Shops. | Neele sculpt. 352 Strand. | . . . [1789?]

obl. 2° *Score:* 2 *ℓ.,* 60 p.
RISM A I, no. D 842
MUSIC LIBRARY

433

The Dancing-Master: | Or, Directions for Dancing Country Dances, with the Tunes to each Dance for the Treble-Violin. | The Tenth Edition Corrected; with the Addition of several new Dances and Tunes never before Printed. | [London] Printed by J. Heptinstall, for Samuel Sprint at the Bell in Little-Britain, and H. Playford at his Shop in the Temple-Change, or | at his House in Arundel-street in the Strand, 1698.

obl. 12° 4 *ℓ.,* 215 [i. e. 214] p., music
Preliminary leaf 4ᵛ: Books printed for and sold by Henry Playford . . .
Number 197 omitted in paging
HOUGHTON

434

The Dancing-Master: | Or, Directions for Dancing Country Dances, with the Tunes to each Dance, for the Treble-Violin. | The Sixteenth Edition, containing 358 of the Choicest Old and New Tunes now used at Court, and other Publick Places. | The whole Work Revised and done on the New-Ty'd-Note, and much more correct than any former Editions. | London: Printed by W. Pearson, and sold by John Young, Musical-Instrument-Maker, at the Dolphin and Crown at the West [End of St. Paul's] | Church, 1716. . . .

obl. 12° 4 *ℓ.,* 358 p., music
Imperfect: title-page and preliminary leaf 3 torn, with loss of text
HOUGHTON

435

The Second Part of the Dancing Master: | Or, Directions for Dancing Country Dances, with the Tunes to each Dance for the Violin or Flute. | The Second Edition, with Additions. | [London] Printed for Henry Playford at his Shop in the Temple-Change over-against St. Dunstan's Church in Fleetstreet: 1698. | . . .

obl. 12° 2 ℓ., 48 [i. e. 60], 24 p., music
Pages 37–48 [i. e. 49–60]: An Additional Sheet to the Second Part of the Dancing-Master.
Pages 1–24 at end: Twenty four New Country Dances.
Numbers 25 to 36, first sequence, repeated in paging
Imperfect: pages 21, 22, final sequence, lacking
HOUGHTON

436

[The Second Part of the Dancing Master:] | Or, Directions for D[ancing Country Dances . . .] | The Second Edition, [. . .] | London: Printed by W. [Pearson and sold by John Young, Musical-Instrument-Maker, at the Dolphin and Crown at the West End of St. Paul's] | Church, 1714. . . .

obl. 12° 3 ℓ., [192+] p., music
Imperfect: title-page torn, with loss of text; all after page [192] lacking. Missing portions of title-page supplied conjecturally from the sixteenth edition of part 1 (1716); total number of pages inferred from index
HOUGHTON

D'ANGLEBERT, JEAN HENRY *See* Anglebert, Jean Henry d'

DANICAN, FRANÇOIS ANDRÉ *See* Philidor, François André Danican, known as

437   DANZI, FRANZ

Concerto | Pour | Violoncelle | Composé Par | François Danzi | No. I. . . . . |A Zuric Chez Jean George Naigueli. [179–?]

2° 11 pts.: *violoncello principale:* 1 ℓ., 9 p.; *flauto Io.:* 4 p.; *flauto 2o.:* 3 p.; *fagotto Io.:* 4 p.; *fagotto 2o.:* 3 p.; *corno Io., corno 2o.:* 1 p. each; *violino Io., violino 2o.:* 7 p. each; *alto viola, basso:* 5 p. each
Plate no. 7
RISM A I, no. D 987
MUSIC LIBRARY

438   DANZI, FRANZ

Sextuor | pour | Deux Violons | Deux Cors, Alto | & | Violoncelle | Composée | par F. Danzi. | Oeuvre 15. . . . | Munic chez Mac. Falter. [ca. 1798]

2° 6 pts.: *violino Imo.:* 1 ℓ., 8 p.; *violino IIdo., viola:* 6 p. each; *cornu Imo., cornu IIdo.:* 2 p. each; *violoncello:* 6 p.
RISM A I, no. D 998
HOUGHTON

D'APLIGNY, LE PILEUR *See* Le Pileur D'Apligny

439   DAQUIN, LOUIS CLAUDE

Ier. Livre | De | Pieces De Clavecin | Dedié | A. S. A. Mademoiselle | De Soubise | Composées | Par Mr. Daquin | Organiste de St. Paul, du Petit St. Antoine | Et des Cordeliers. | . . . | Gravées par L. Hue | A Paris {Chés [L'Auteur rue St. Antoine, Cour St. Pierre vis a vis | L'Hôtel de Sully. | La Veuve Boivin, rue St. Honoré à la Regle d'or. | Le Sr. Le Clerc, rue du Roule à la Croix d'or. | Avec Privilege Du Roy | 1735.

2° *Score:* 4 ℓ., 49, [1] p.
RISM A I, no. D 1046
HOUGHTON

D'ARNOBAT, CHARLES PIERRE COSTE *See* Coste d'Arnobat, Charles Pierre

DA SILVA, MANUEL NUNES *See* Nunes da Silva, Manuel

DA SILVA LEITE, ANTONIO *See* Silva Leite, Antonio da

440 DAVAUX, JEAN BAPTISTE

Six | Quartetto's | for two | Violins, a Tenor, | and | Violoncello | Composed by | R. Davaux | Opera IX. . . . | London. | Printed for Willm: Napier No. 474 Strand. [ca. 1780]

2° 4 pts.: *violino primo:* 1 ℓ., 14 p.; *violino secondo, viola, basso:* 1 ℓ., 13 p. each
   Plate no. 105
   RISM A I, no. D 1158
   MUSIC LIBRARY

441 DAVAUX, JEAN BAPTISTE

Six | Quatuors | D'Airs Connus | Mis en Variations et en dialogue, | Pour deux Violons un Alto | et un Violoncel. | Par Mr. Davaux | Oeuvre X. | Mis au jour par Mr. Bailleux. | . . . | A Paris. | Chez Mr. Bailleux Md. de Musique Ordinaire | du Roi et de la Famille Royale, | Rue St. Honoré à la Regle d'Or. | A. P. D. R. [1780]

2° 4 pts.: *violino primo:* 1 ℓ., 13 p.; *violino secondo, alto:* 13 p. each; *basso:* 11 p.
   Imprint in *violino primo* part partially covered by cancel label reading: Imported & Sold | by Longman & Broderip | (at their Music Warehouse) | No. 26 | Cheapside London.
   Page [1] in *violino primo* part: Catalogue, | De Musique Françoise et Italienne Vocale et Instrumentale, que Mr. Bailleux . . . à fait graver . . . ⟨issued between dates of JohanssonF facs. 7 and 8⟩
   RISM A I, no. D 1165
   MUSIC LIBRARY

D'AVELLA, GIOVANNI *See* Avella, Giovanni d'

DE ERUDITIONE MUSICA *See* Mattheson, Johann *De eruditione musica*

DE LA MUSIQUE CONSIDÉRÉE EN ELLEMÊME *See* Chabanon, Michel Paul Gui de *De la musique considérée en ellemême*

DE BELESTA, JEAN BAPTISTE MERCADIER *See* Mercadier, Jean Baptiste

DE BERTRAND, ANTOINE *See* Bertrand, Antoine de

DE BÉTHISY, JEAN LAURENT *See* Béthisy, Jean Laurent de

DE BROSSARD, SÉBASTIEN *See* Brossard, Sébastien de

DE CAHUSAC, LOUIS *See* Cahusac, Louis de

DE CAPPEVAL, N. DE CAUX *See* Caux de Cappeval, N. de

DE CASTAGNÈRES, FRANÇOIS, ABBÉ DE CHÂTEAUNEUF *See* Châteauneuf, François de Castagnères, abbé de

DE CAUX DE CAPPEVAL, N. *See* Caux de Cappeval, N. de

DE CAVEIRAC, JEAN NOVI *See* Novi de Caveirac, Jean

DE CHABANON, MICHEL PAUL GUI *See* Chabanon, Michel Paul Gui de

DE COSTE, HILARION *See* Coste, Hilarion de

DEGIARDINO, FELICE *See* Giardini, Felice

DE GOUY, JACQUES *See* Gouy, Jacques de

DE LA BAUME LE BLANC, LOUIS CÉSAR, DUC DE LA VALLIÈRE *See* La Vallière, Louis César de la Baume Le Blanc, duc de

DE LA BORDE, JEAN BENJAMIN *See* Laborde, Jean Benjamin de

DE LA CUISSE *See* La Cuisse, _____ De

DE LA MONNOYE, BERNARD *See* La Monnoye, Bernard de

DE LAMORLIÈRE, JACQUES ROCHETTE
See Lamorlière, Jacques Rochette de

DE LA RUE, PIERRE *See* La Rue, Pierre de

442 DeLATRE, CLAUDE PETIT JEAN

Sixiesme Livre Des | Chansons A Qvatre | Parties Composez Par Maistre | Iehan de Latre, Conuenables tant aux instrumentz | Comme à la Voix. | . . . | Imprimé à Louain par Pierre Phalese Libraire Iuré. L'an 1563. | Auecq Grace & Priuilege.

obl. 4° *svperivs:* A–D⁴
Leaf D4 missigned D3
Imperfect: leaves D2, D3 lacking
HOUGHTON

DE LA VIÉVILLE, JEAN LAURENT LE CERF
See Le Cerf de la Viéville, Jean Laurent

DE LÉRIS, ANTOINE *See* Léris, Antoine de

443

The Delightful | Pocket Companion. | For the | German Flute | Containing | A Choice Collection of the most Celebrated | Italian, English, and Scotch Tunes, | Curiously Adapted to that Instrument. | Printed for | & Sold by John Simpson | At the Bass-Viol, & Flute, in Sweetings-Alley, | opposite ye East Door of the Royal Exchange. | London. | . . . [ca. 1750]

8° 1 *ℓ.*, 36, 34, 36, 32 p., front.
Pages 33, 34, second sequence, printed as folded plates
Imperfect: contains only the first four of six books
RISM B II, 150–151
MUSIC LIBRARY

DE LIROU, JEAN FRANÇOIS ESPIC *See* Espic de Lirou, Jean François

DELLA MARIA, DOMENICO *See* Maria, Domenico della

DELLA VALLE, GUGLIELMO *See* Valle, Guglielmo della

DE MONDONVILLE, JEAN JOSEPH CASSANÉA *See* Mondonville, Jean Joseph Cassanéa de

DE MONSIGNY, PIERRE ALEXANDRE *See* Monsigny, Pierre Alexandre

DE MONTE, PHILIPPE *See* Monte, Philippe de

DE MONTÉCLAIR, MICHEL PINOLET *See* Montéclair, Michel Pinolet de

DE MORAND, PIERRE *See* Morand, Pierre de

444 [DÉMOTZ DE LA SALLE, ABBÉ]

Methode | De | Musique | Selon | Un Nouveau Système | Très-court, très-facile & très-sûr, | Approuvé Par Messieurs | de l'Academie Royale des Sciences, & | par les plus habiles Musiciens de Paris. | Dediée A La Reine. | Par M. *** Prêtre. | A Paris, | Chez Pierre Simon, Imprimeur du | Clergé de France & du Parlement, ruë | de la Harpe, à l'Hercule. | MDCC.XXVIII. | Avec Approbation Et Privilege Dv Roy.

8° 6 *ℓ.*, 3–216, [4] p., illus., music
RISM B VI, 258
MUSIC LIBRARY

DE NOINVILLE, JACQUES BERNARD DUREY *See* Durey de Noinville, Jacques Bernard

DE PAEP, ANDREAS *See* Papius, Andreas

DE PIIS, AUGUSTIN *See* Piis, Augustin

DES BALLETS ANCIENS ET MODERNES *See* Menestrier, Claude François *Des ballets anciens et modernes*

DES REPRESENTATIONS EN MUSIQUE AN-
CIENNES ET MODERNES *See* Menestrier,
Claude François *Des representations en
musique anciennes et modernes*

DESAIDES, NICOLAS *See* Dezède, Nicolas

DE SALINAS, FRANCISCO *See* Salinas,
Francisco de

DE SANTA MARÍA, TOMÁS *See* Tómas de
Santa María

445 [DESBOULMIERS, JEAN AUGUSTE
JULIEN, KNOWN AS]

Histoire | Du Théatre | De | L'Opéra
Comique. | . . . | A Paris, | Chez La-
combe, Librarie, Rue | Christine, près la
rue Dauphine. | M.DCC.LXIX. | Avec
Permission & Privilege.

12° 2 vols: *vol. I:* 1 ℓ., 497, [6] p.; *vol.
II:* 1 ℓ., 558, [2] p.
RISM B VI, 437
MUSIC LIBRARY

446 DESCARTES, RENÉ

Renatvs Des-Cartes | Excellent | Com-
pendium | Of | Musick: | With | Neces-
sary and Judicious | Animadversions |
Thereupon. | By a Person of Honovr. |
London, Printed by Thomas Harper, for
Humphrey Moseley, | and are to bee sold
at his Shop at the Signe of the | Princes
Armes in S. Pauls Church-Yard, and | by
Thomas Heath in Coven [*sic*] Garden.
1653.

4° 8 ℓ., 94 p. 1 ℓ., illus., music
Gregory, p. 73; RISM B VI, 262
HOUGHTON

447 DESCARTES, RENÉ

Renati | Des-Cartes | Musicae | Com-
pendium. | Trajecti Ad Rhenum, | Typis
Gisberti à Zijll, & Theodori ab Ackers-
dijck, | CIↃ IↃ CL.

4° 58 p., illus., music
Davidsson II, no. 24; Hirsch I, no. 143;
RISM B VI, 261; Wolfenbüttel, no. 1098a
HOUGHTON

448 DESCARTES, RENÉ

Renati | Des-Cartes | Musicae |
Compendium | Amstelodami, | Apud
Joannem Janssonium Juniorem. |
CIↃ IC CLVI

4° 2 ℓ., 34 p., illus., music
Davidsson II, no. 25; Hirsch I, no. 144;
RISM B VI, 262
HOUGHTON

DE SCELLERY, CHARLES EMMANUEL BOR-
JON *See* Borjon, Charles Emmanuel

LE DESERTEUR *See* Monsigny, Pierre
Alexandre *Le Deserteur*

449 DESPREZ, JOSQUIN

[Misse Josquin | Lōme arme. Sup.
voces musicales | La. sol. fa. re. mi. | Gau-
deamus. | Fortuna desperata. | Lōme
arme. Sexti toni. | . . . ⟨Venice, 1502⟩]

obl. 4° 1 pt.: *tenor:* D⁸, E⁶
Colophon: [Impressum Venetijs per
Octauianum Petrutiū Forosem-
p[ro]ni|ēsem die 27. setēbris anno 1502
Cum priuilegio inuictissimi Do|mini
Venetiarum q[ue] nullus possit cantum
Figuratum Impri|mere sub pena in ipso
priuilegio contenta]
Title and colophon supplied from mi-
crofilm copy of *superius* and *bassus* part-
books respectively in the Civico Museo
Bibliografico Musicale in Bologna
Imperfect: leaf E6 lacking
RISM A I, no. J 666; SartoriP, no. 4
HOUGHTON

450 DESPREZ, JOSQUIN

[Missarum Josquin | Liber Tertius |
Mater patris | Faysans regres | Ad fugam |
Di dadi | De beata virgine | Missa sine
nomĩe ⟨Fossombrone, 1514⟩]

obl. 4° 1 pt.: *tenor:* CcC¹²
Colophon: [Impressum Forosempronii
per Octauianum | Petrutium ciuem
Forosemproniensem. Anno | Domini.
MDXIIII. Die primo martii. . . .]
Title and colophon supplied from mi-
crofilm copy of *superius* and *bassus* part-

books respectively in the Civico Museo Bibliografico Musicale in Bologna
Imperfect: leaves CcC3, CcC10, CcC12 lacking
RISM A I, no. J 673; SartoriP, no. 48
HOUGHTON

451   DESTOUCHES, ANDRÉ CARDINAL

[Issé, | Pastorale Heroïqve, | Représentée | Devant Sa Majesté | à Trianon, le 17. Decembre 1697. | Par L'Academie Royale De Musique; | Mise En Musique | Par Monsieur Destouches, Sur-Intendant | de la Musique du Roy, & Inspecteur general | de son Academie de Musique. | Partition Generale. | A Paris, De L'Imprimerie | De Jean-Baptiste-Christophe Ballard, Seul Imprimeur du Roy | pour la Musique, & Noteur de la Chapelle de Sa Majesté. | M.DCC.XXIV. | Avec Privilege Dv Roy.]

2° *Score:* 8, 300 p.
Imperfect: title-page lacking; supplied in positive photostat
RISM A I, no. D 1832.
MUSIC LIBRARY

D'ÉTAPLES, JACQUES LE FÈVRE   *See* Le Fèvre, Jacques, d'Étaples

DE VAUCANSON, JACQUES   *See* Vaucanson, Jacques de

452   DEVIENNE, FRANÇOIS

Les Visitandines | Comédie En Deux Actes Et En Prose, | Par Mr. Picard | Représentée pour la premiere fois par les Comédiens du | Théâtre de la rue Feydeau le Samedi Sept Juillet 1792. | Mises En Musique | Et Dédiée | A Mr. Louis Maillard | Son beau Pere | Par Mr. F. Devienne | . . . | Gravée par Huguet, Musicien Pensionnaire de la Comédie Italienne. [Paris, Cousineau, ca. 1795]

2° *Score:* 1 ℓ., 152 p.
Imprint covered by cancel label reading: Chez Le Duc, au Magasin de Musique et d'Instruments à Paris. | Rue neuve des petits Champs No. 1286, vis à vis la Trésorerie | Et Rue du Roulle à la Croix d'Or No. 290. | . . .

Hirsch II, no. 201; RISM A I, no. D 1869
MUSIC LIBRARY

453   DEZÈDE, NICOLAS

Blaise | Et | Babet | Ou | La Suite Des Trois Fermiers | Comédie en deux Actes | Par M. Monvel. | Représentée pour la premiere fois à Versailles | devant leurs Majestés par les Comédiens Italiens Ord. du Roi, | le 4. Avril 1783, et à Paris le 30. juin suivant. | Mise en Musique | Par M. Dezède. | . . . | A Paris. | Ches Des Lauriers . . . [ca. 1783]

2° *Score:* 1 ℓ., 178 p.
On verso of preliminary leaf: Catalogue | de Musique | du fond de Des Lauriers . . .
Imprint partially covered by illegible cancel label
RISM A I, no. D 2150
MUSIC LIBRARY

454   [DEZÈDE, NICOLAS]

Julie | Comédie | En trois Actes | Par | M. Monvel | Représentée pour la 1ere. fois par les Comédiens Italiens | ordinaires du Roi le lundy 22, Septembre 1772, | Mis en Musique | Par | M. D. Z. | . . . | Gravée par le Sr. Huguet, Musicien de la Comédie italienne. | A Paris. | Chés {M. Houbaut, Rue Mauconseil près la Comédie | A Lion. | M. Castaud, Place des Cordelliers. | A. P. D. R. [1777?]

2° *Score:* 1 ℓ., 210 p.
Hirsch II, no. 207; RISM A I, no. D 2238
MUSIC LIBRARY

DIALOGUE SUR LA MUSIQUE DES ANCIENS   *See* Châteauneuf, François de Castagnères, abbé de *Dialogue sur la musique des anciens*

455   DIBDIN, CHARLES

A Collection of | Catches and Glees | For Two Three or Four | Voices | With accompanyments for | Guitars and Flutes | Composed by | Charles Dibdin | . . . | London, Printed and sold by Iohn Iohn-ston, near Exeter change, Strand. . . . [1772?]

obl. 2° *Score:* 1 ℓ., 13 p.
RISM A I, no. D 2896
MUSIC LIBRARY

456 [DIBDIN, CHARLES]

Lionel, And Clarissa; | Or, A | School For Fathers. | A Comic Opera; | as performed at the | Theatres Royal. | London: | Printed for Harrison, Cluse, & Co. No. 78, Fleet Street. [1799?]

8° *Vocal score:* 95 p., 1 ℓ. (*The Piano-Forte Magazine,* vol. VI, no. 6)
Plate nos. 92–96
MUSIC LIBRARY

457 DIBDIN, CHARLES

The | Musical Tour | Of | Mr. Dibdin; | In Which—Previous To His Embarkation For India—He Finished His Career As | A Public Character. | . . . | Sheffield: | Printed For The Author By J. Gales, And Sold By All The Booksellers Throughout The | Kingdom. | M,DCC,LXXXVIII.

4° 3ℓ., iv, 443 [i. e. 447] p.
Fifteen unnumbered leaves containing music interspersed
Nos. 335–338 repeated in paging
RISM B VI, 266
HOUGHTON (2 copies)

458 DIBDIN, CHARLES

[Ode in honor of the nuptials of Their Royal Highnesses the Prince and Princess of Wales, written and composed by Mr. Dibdin. London, Printed by the author, ⟨1795?⟩]

2° *Score:* 1 ℓ., 53 p.
Imperfect: title-page lacking
RISM A I, no. D 2946
MUSIC LIBRARY

459 DIBDIN, CHARLES

The | Padlock | A Comic Opera: | as it is Performed at the | Theatre-Royal | In | Drury-Lane. | The Words by the Author of the Maid of the Mill, &c. &c. | The Music by | Mr. Dibdin. | London: | Printed for the Author & Sold by J. John-

ston, at the | Music Shop near Northumberland-House | in the Strand. | W. Palmer sculpt. [1768?]

2° *Vocal score:* 2 ℓ., 41 p.
RISM A I, no. D 2557
MUSIC LIBRARY

460 DIBDIN, CHARLES

The | Padlock; | A | Comic Opera | Composed & Adapted For, The | Piano Forte; | By, | C. Dibdin. | London: | Printed for Harrison, Cluse, & Co. No. 78, Fleet Street. [1798?]

8° *Vocal score:* 64 p. (*The Piano-Forte Magazine,* vol. V, no. 6)
Plate nos. 76–78
RISM A I, no. D 2563
MUSIC LIBRARY

461 DIBDIN, CHARLES

The | Overture, Songs, Duettos, Chorusses, Dances, Comic-Tunes, &c. | in the New Speaking Pantomime called | The Touchstone, | as it is performing | with the Greatest Applause at the | Theatre Royal in Covent Garden; | Composed by | Charles Dibdin. | . . . | London: Printed for S. and A. Thompson, No. 75 St. Paul's Church Yard. [1779?]

obl. 2° *Vocal score:* 1 ℓ., 46 p.
RISM A I, no. D 2722
HOUGHTON

462 DIBDIN, CHARLES

The | Waterman | a | Comic Opera | of two Acts | As performed with Universal applause | at the Theatre Royal | Hay Market | Composed by | C. Dibdin | . . . | London | Printed for & Sold by John Johnston near Exeter Change Strand | And Longman Lukey and Co. No. 26 Cheapside. [1774?]

2° *Vocal score:* 1 ℓ., 25 p.
RISM A I, no. D 2826
MUSIC LIBRARY

DI CAPUA, RINALDO *See* Rinaldo di Capua

DI LASSO, ORLANDO *See* Lasso, Orlando di

DISCOURS AU VRAY DU BALLET *See* Durand, Estienne *Discours au vray du ballet*

463   [DITTERS VON DITTERSDORF, KARL]

. . . | Apotheker und Doktor | für das | Clavier. | . . . | . . . bei Schott in Mainz. . . . [178–?]

obl. 2° *Vocal score:* 109 [i. e. 143] p.
Plate no. 60
Each section has separate title-page, often excluded from paging; many numbers repeated in paging
RISM A I, no. D 3151
MUSIC LIBRARY

464   DITTERS VON DITTERSDORF, KARL

Praeclari Viri | Domini Ditters, Nobilis De Dittersdorff | XII. Ariae, | Seu | Offertoria | Selectissima. | Tum Ad Promovendum Cultum Divinum; | Tum Ad Honestam Animi Relaxationem | Latino Idiomate | Ex | Canticis Salomonis, Davidis Psalterio | Aliisque Sacris Fontibus Desumpto | Adornata; | Concinnentibus 4. Vocibus ordinariis. | 2. Violinis, una vel 2. Alto-Violis, & Organo oblig. | 2. Flautis vero, vel Obois, 2. Cornibus & Violoncello | non obligatis. | . . . | Augustae Vindelicorum, | Sumptibus Joannis Jacobi Lotter & Filii. | 1795.

2° 1 pt.: *organo:* 2 ℓ., 22 p.
Imperfect: pages 17, 18 lacking
RISM A I, no. D 3150
HOUGHTON

465   DITTERS VON DITTERSDORF, KARL

Hieronymus Knicker, | eine komische Oper in zwey Aufzügen | vom | Herrn von Dittersdorf. | Im Klavierauszuge | von | Siegfried Schmiedt. | Leipzig, | in der Breitkopfischen Buchhandlung. [ca. 1792]

2° *Vocal score:* 1 ℓ., 136 p.
RISM A I, no. D 3189
MUSIC LIBRARY

466   DITTERS VON DITTERSDORF, KARL

Troisieme Sinfonie | exprimant | la | Métamorphose D'Ovide | Actéon changè en Cerf | composêe | par | Mr. C: Ditters Noble de Dittersdorff | arrangée pour le Forte-piano, ou Clavecin | A Vienne Ches Hoffmeister [1788]

obl. 2° *Score:* 14 p.
Plate no. 175
RISM A I, no. D 3261
HOUGHTON

467   DIXON, WILLIAM, ED.

A Collection of | Glees and Rounds, | for three four and five Voices. | Composed by the Members of the | Harmonic Society of Cambridge | and publish'd by | William Dixon. | . . . | Cambridge, | Engrav'd and printed by the Editor, and may be had at his House, in | Trumpington Street, and of Messrs. Preston and Son No. 97 Strand London. [1796?]

obl. 2° *Score:* 3 ℓ., 73 p.
RISM B II, 66
MUSIC LIBRARY

468   DODWELL, HENRY

A | Treatise | Concerning the | Lawfulness | Of | Instrumental Musick | In | Holy Offices. | By Henry Dodwell, M. A. | To which is prefixed, a Preface in Vindi-|cation of Mr. Newte's Sermon, concerning | the Lawfulness and Use of Organs in the | Christian Church, &c. From the Exceptions | of an Anonymous Letter to a Friend in the | Country, concerning the Use of Instrumental | Musick in the Worship of God, &c. | The Second Edition, with large Additions. | London, | Printed for William Haws, at the Rose in Ludgate-|street, MDCC.

8° 1 ℓ., 84 p. 2 ℓ., 143, [1] p.
Unnumbered page at end: Books Printed for W. | Hawes, at the Rose in | Ludgate-street.
RISM B VI, 269
MUSIC LIBRARY

469   DOLES, JOHANN FRIEDRICH

Melodien | zu des | Herrn Prof. C. F. Gellerts | Geistlichen Oden und Liedern,

| die noch nicht mit Kirchenmelodien versehen sind, | vierstimmig, mit unter-gelegtem Texte | und fũrs Clavier mit be-ziffertem Basse | zur privat und ŏffentli-chen Andacht gesetzt | von | Johann Friedrich Doles, | Cantor und College an der St. Thomasschule, und Director der Musik an beyden Hauptkirchen zu Leip-zig. | Leipzig, | verlegts Johann Gottlob Immanuel Breitkopf, | 1758

2° *Score:* 2 ℓ., 38 p.
RISM A I, no. D 3347
MUSIC LIBRARY

470   DOLES, JOHANN FRIEDRICH

Sei | Sonate | Per Il | Clavicembalo Solo | Composte | Da | Giovani Federico Doles, | Dilettante. | In Riga, | Presso Gio-vani Federico Hartknoch. | 1773.

2° *Score:* 1 ℓ., 38 p.
Hirsch III, no. 179; RISM A I, no. D 3351
MUSIC LIBRARY

471   DONI, ANTONIO FRANCESCO

La Libraria | Del Doni | Fiorentino. | Nella Qvale Sono Scritti | tutti gl'Autori uulgari con cento | discorsi sopra quelli. | Tvtte Le Tradvttioni Fat-|te dall'altre lin-gue, nella nostra & vna ta-|uola general-mente come si costu|ma fra Librari. | Di Novo Ristampata, Cor|retta, & molte cose aggiunte | che mancauano. | Con Pri-vilegio. | In Vinegia Appresso Gabriel | Giolito De Ferrari | Et Fratelli. | MDL.

12° 72 numb. ℓ.
Numbered leaves 63ᵛ–67ʳ: La Mvsica Stam|pata Madrigali | mottetti, messe, & Canzoni.
HOUGHTON (2 copies)

472   DONI, ANTONIO FRANCESCO

La Libraria Del | Doni Fiorentino, | Di-visa In Tre Trattati. | Nel primo sono scritti, tutti gli autori Volgari, con cen-|to & piu discorsi, sopra di quelli. | Nel secondo, sono dati in luce tutti i Libri, che L'Auto-|re ha ueduti a penna, il nome de' componitori, dell'o-|pere, i titoli, & le materie. | Nel terzo, si legge l'inuention dell'Academie insieme | con i sopranomi, i motti, le imprese, & l'opere fatte | da

tutti gli Academici. | Libro necessario, & utile, a tutti coloro che della cogni-|tione della lingua hāno bisogno, & che uo-gliono di tut|ti gli autori, libri, & opere sapere scriuere, & ragionare. | Con Privi-legio. | In Vinegia Appresso Gabriel | Gio-lito De' Ferrari. | MDLVII.

8° 296 p. illus. (ports)
Pages 150–160: La Mvsica Stampata | Madrigali, Mottetti, | Messe, Et Canzoni.
HOUGHTON

473   DONI, ANTONIO FRANCESCO

La Libraria | Del Doni | Fiorentino; | Nella quale sono scritti tutti gli Autori | volgari, con cento discorsi | sopra quelli; | Tutte le tradottioni fatte dall'altre lin-gue, | nella nostra, & vna tauola generale, | come si costuma fra Librari. | Opera vtile a ciascuno che si diletta della lingua | volgare, & che desidera fornir vno stu-dio | di libri, composti in essa lingua; | Di nuouo ristampata, & aggiuntiui tutti i libri volgari | posti in luce da trenta anni in quà, & leuatone | fuori tutti gli Autori, & libri prohibiti. | In Vinegia, | Presso Al-tobello Salicato. MDLXXX.

12° 12 ℓ., 90 numb. ℓ.
Numbered leaves 81ʳ–85ᵛ: La Mvsica | Stampata, | Madrigali, mottetti, messe & canzoni.
Hirsch I, no. 147
HOUGHTON

474   DONI, GIOVANNI BATTISTA

Compendio | Del Trattato | De' Generi E De' Modi | Della Mvsica. | Di Gio. Bat-tista Doni. | Con Vn Discorso Sopra La Perfettione | de' Concenti. | Et vn Saggio à due Voci Mutationi di Genere, e di Tuono in tre | maniere d'Intauolatura: e d'vn principio di Madrigale del | Principe, ridotto nella medesima Intauolatura. | All'Eminentiss. e Reuerendiss. Sig. | Il Sig. Cardinal Barberino. | In Roma, Per Andrea Fei. MDCXXXV. Con licenza de' Superiori.

4° 20 ℓ., 171, [1] p., illus., fold. pl., music
Hirsch I, no. 148; RISM B VI, 272; Wol-fenbüttel, no. 1100
HOUGHTON

475   Doni, Giovanni Battista

Io: Baptistae | Doni | Patricii Florentini | De Praestantia | Musicae Veteris | Libri Tres | Totidem Dialogis comprehensi | In quibus vetus ac recens Musica, cum singulis earum | partibus, accurate inter se conferuntur. | Adiecto ad finem Onomastico selectorum vocabulorum, | ad hanc facultatem cum elegantia, & proprietate | tractandam, pertinentium. | Ad Eminentiss. Cardinalem | Mazarinvm | Florentiae | Typis Amatoris Massae Foroliuien. M.DC.XLVII. | Superiorum Permissu.

4° 4 ℓ., 266 [i. e. 166] p.
Pages 145–166 misnumbered 245–266
Hirsch I, no. 150; RISM B VI, 273; Wolfenbüttel, no. 1101
MUSIC LIBRARY

476   Doni, Giovanni Battista

Io. Baptistae Doni | Patrici Florentini | Lyra Barberina | Αμφιχορδος. | Accedvnt | Eivsdem Opera, Pleraqve Nondvm Edita, | Ad Veterem Mvsicam Illvstrandam Pertinentia | Ex Avtographis Collegit, Et In Lvcem Proferri Cvravit | Antonivs Franciscvs Gorivs | Basilic. Bapt. Flor. Olim Praep. | Distribvta In Tomos II. | Absolvta Vero Stvdio Et Opera | Io. Baptistae Passeri | Pisavrensis | Cvm Praetationibvs Eivsdem. | Florentiae Typis Caesareis | Anno M.D.CC.LXIII. | Praesidibvs Adnventibvs.

2° 2 vols.: *vol. I:* XII, 8 p., 1 ℓ., 9–424 p., front. (port.), illus., 8 pl. (6 fold.), music; *vol. II:* XII, 306 p., 1 ℓ., IV, 100 p., illus., music
Vol. II has separate title-page: De' Trattati Di Mvsica | Di Gio. Batista Doni | Patrizio Fiorentino | . . .
At end of vol. II: Appendice | A' Trattati Di Musica | Di Gio. Batista Doni. (1 ℓ., IV, 100 p.)
Hirsch I, no. 151; RISM B VI, 273; Wolfenbüttel, no. 1102
HOUGHTON

D'Orville, André Guillaume Contant   *See* Contant d'Orville, André Guillaume

Doutes d'un Pyrronien   *See* Coste d'Arnobat, Charles Pierre *Doutes d'un Pyrronien*

477   Dreyer, Johann Melchior

Joannis Melch. Dreyer | Principalis Ecclesiae Elvacensis | Organaedi | VI. | Missae Breves | Et Rurales | Ad | Modernum Genium. | A | Canto, Alto, Tenore, Basso, | 2. Violini, & Organo, | obligatis. | 2. Clarini, 2. Corni, & Violoncello, | ad libitum. | Opus II. | . . . | Augustae Vindelicorum, | Sumptibus Joh. Jacobi Lotter, & Filii. 1790.

2° 1 pt.: *organo:* 2 ℓ., 50 p.
RISM A I, no. D 3552
HOUGHTON

478   Dreyer, Johann Melchior

Joannis Melchioris Dreyer, | Eccl. Princip. Elvac. Musices Direct. | Et Organaedi | XII. | Tantum Ergo | A | Canto, Alto, Tenore, Basso, | 2. Violinis, | 2. Corni, vel 2. Clarini, | Tympani, | Organo & Violoncello. | Juxta indicem partim obligatis | partim ad libitum. | Opus IX. | . . . | Augustae Vindelicorum, | Sumptibus Joannis Jacobi Lotter & Filii. | 1794.

2° 1 pt.: *organo:* 2 ℓ., 7 p.
RISM A I, no. D 3559
HOUGHTON

479   Dubois

La | Dubois Allemande | Contredanse | Par Mr. Dubois De L'Opéra | Penssionnaire du Roy et de L'Acadé-|mie Royale de Musique. | . . . | A Paris. | Chez l'Auteur rue Mazarine à | l'ancienne Hôtel des Pompes, Quar-|tier du Faubourg St. Germain, | Et aux Adresses Ordinaires. [ca. 1769]

8° [52] p., illus., music
Contains instructions for performing various dances, interspersed with choreographic notation and melodies
RISM A I, no. D 3596
HOUGHTON

480   Dubois

Recueil | de | Six Menuets | et | Six Allemandes | Par | Mr. Dubois, | Danseur de l'Opera | . . . | Gravé par Mme. Annereau | A Paris | Chez l'Auteur rue Mazarine Faubourg | St. Germain a l'ancien Hotel des Pompes | Et aux Adresses ordinaires | P. Monroy Scripsit | [17—]

8° *Score:* 1 ℓ., 2–13 p.
For keyboard instrument
RISM A I, no. D 3593
HOUGHTON

DUFLITZ, JACQUES *See* Du Phly, Jacques

481 DUFORT, GIOVANNI BATTISTA

Trattato | Del | Ballo Nobile | Di | Giambatista | Dufort | Indirizzato | All'Eccellenza | Delle Signore Dame, E | De' Signori Cavalieri | Napoletani. | In Napoli MDCCXXVIII. | Nella Stamperia di Felice Mosca. | Con licenza de' Superiori.

8° 12 ℓ., 160 p., illus.
RISM B VI, 282
HOUGHTON

482 DU FOUILLOUX, JACQUES

Neuw Jag vnnd | Weydwerck Buch, | Das ist Ein | grundtliche beschreibung | Vom Anfang der Jagten, Auch vom Jåger, seinem Horn vnd | Stim̃, Hunden, Wie die zu allerley Wildpret abzurichten, zu Pfneischen, vnd vor | der Wůt vnd andern Zufållen zu bewahren. Item von der Hirsch, Schweins, Hasen, wilden Kůllen, | Fůchs, Dachs, Beeren, Luchs, Steinbocks, Gemsen vnd Wolffs Jagt, das ist, von allerley hohem vnd niderm, rotem | vnd schwartzem, auch Steinwildpret, vnd wie der Jåger durch gewisse Merckzeichen auff der Jagt, | dieselben erkennen, jagen, fangen vnd erlegen, auch Weydmånnisch von | jedem insonderheit reden sol. | Item vom Adelichen Weydwerck der Falcknerey, Beyssen | vnd Federspiel, auch wie die Falcken zu tragen, zu hauben, zu locken, åtzen, vnd | aauff den Raub anzubringen, vnd wie man allerley Feld vnd Wassergeflůgel, als Kra-|nich, Rephůner, Wachteln, Reyger, wilde Gåns, vnd Antvôgel, &c. Beys-|sen vnd fangen sol. | Dessgleichen vom Fisch, Krebs, Otter vnd Biber Fang, wie mans mit Ne-|tzen, Reusen, Angeln, Ka-

sten, Otter vnd Biberhunden, vnd allerley darzu | gehôriger Gelegenheit fahen sol. | Allen Fůrsten, Grauen, Herrn, Adelspersonen, vnd andern hohes vnd ni-|driges Stands, so diese Adeliche vbung dess Jag vnd Weydwercks lieb haben, zu sonderm | lust vnd gefallen, Durch raht vnd hilff etlicher dess Weydwercks erfahrne Personen, Auss allen hiebevor | aussgegangenen Frantzôsi-schen, Italienischen vnd Teutschen Jagbůchern, in diese Ordnung zusam-|men ge-|bracht. Auch durchauss mit schônen Figuren gezieret, dergleichen zu-|vor nie aussgangen. | Mit Rôm. Kays. Maiest. Freyheit nicht nachzu-drucken. | Gedruckt zu Franckfurt am Mayn bey Johañ Feyerabendt, | In verlegung Sigmundt Feyerabendts. | M.D.LXXXII.

2° 4 ℓ., 103, 73 numb. ℓ., illus., music
Contains hunting calls
The second section has separate title-page: Anderes Theil der | Adelichen Weydwerck, nem-|lich Falckenerey . . .
HOUGHTON

483 DU FOUILLOUX, JACQUES

La | Venerie de Iaques du | Foüilloux, Gentil-homme, Seigneur | dudit lieu, pays de Gastine, | en Poitou. | Dediee au Roy Tres-chrestien Charles, | neufiesme de ce nom. | Avec | Plusieurs Receptes & Remedes pour guerir les | Chiens de diuerses maladies. | Plvs | L'Adolescence de l'Autheur. | Auec Priuilege du Roy. | A Poitiers, | Par les de Marnefz, et Bouchetz, freres. [ca. 1566]

4° 4 ℓ., 295 p., illus., music
Contains hunting calls
Imperfect: pages 289, 290, 295 lacking; supplied in facsimile
HOUGHTON

484 DU FOUILLOUX, JACQUES

La | Venerie | De Iacqves | Dv Fovil-lovx, Seignevr | Dvdit Liev, Gentil-Homme Dv | pays de Gastine en Poictou. | Dediee Av Roy. | Et De Novveav Re-veve, Et | augmentée, outre les precedentes impressions. | A Paris, | En La Bov-tiqve De L'Angelier, | Chez Clavde Cramoisy, au premier pilier de la | grand'

Salle du Palais. | M.DC.XXIV. | Avec Privilege Dv Roy.

4° 4 ℓ., 124 numb. ℓ., [8] p., illus., music

Contains hunting calls

HOUGHTON

485 DUNI, EGIDIO ROMUALDO

Les | Deux Chasseurs | Et La Laitiere, | Comedie, | En Un Acte, | Par Mr. Anseaume. | Mis en Musique | Par | Mr. Duny | Pensionaire de S. A. R. Infant Don Philippe. | Représentée pour la premiere fois sur le Théâtre des Comediens Italiens | Ordinaires du Roy, Le 21 Juillet 1763. | . . . | Gravé par Le Sr. Hue. | A Paris | Chez {le Sr Sieber musicien rue St honoré à l'hôtel D'Aligre | Et aux adresses ordinaires de Musiques. | A Lyon chez le Sr. Castaud Md. de Musique Place de la Comedie. | . . . | Avec Privilege Du Roy [1775]

2° *Score:* 1 ℓ., 106 p.

Hirsch II, no. 217; RISM A I, no. D 3734

MUSIC LIBRARY

486 [DUNI, EGIDIO ROMUALDO]

Ninette | A | La Cour | Parodie de Bertholde à la Ville | Comedie en deux Actes, | melés d'Ariettes | Par | Mr. Favart. | Representée sur le Theatre de la Comedie Italiene | . . . | A Paris | Chez {Mr. de la Chevardiere, Editeur successeur de Mr. le Clerc, | ruë du Roule à la Croix d'Or. | Mr. Bayard, ruë St. Honoré à la Regle d'Or. | Melle. Castagnerie, ruë des Prouvaires à la musique royale. | Mr. de Lormel, ruë du Foin à l'Image Ste. Genevieve. | A Lyon | Mrs. les Freres Legoux, Place des Cordeliers. | Avec Privilege Du Roy. | Gravé par Melle. Vendome [ca. 1763]

2° *Score:* 1 ℓ., 73, 76 p.

On verso of preliminary leaf: Catalogue | de Musique Vocale et Instrumentale que M. De Lachevardiere Successeur de | M. Le Clerc . . . a fait graver . . . ⟨A later state of JohanssonF facs. 48⟩

Hirsch II, no. 222; RISM A I, no. D 3781

MUSIC LIBRARY

487 DUNI, EGIDIO ROMUALDO

[Les | Sabots | Piece En Un Acte | Par | M. Sedaine | Mis en Musique | Par | M. Duny | Pensionaire de S. A. R. l'Infant Don Ferdinant | Représentée pour la lre. fois sur le Théâtre des Comédiens Ital. ord. du Roi. | . . . | Gravée par le Sr. Dezauche. | A Paris | Chez {l'Auteur, rue du four S. Honoré, vis à vis la nouvelle halle | Faubourg St. Denis No 30. | Et aux Adresses ordinaires | A. Lion M. Castaud vis-à vis la Comedie | A. P. D. R. ⟨1768?⟩]

2° *Score:* 1 ℓ., 90 p.

Imperfect: title-page lacking; supplied in positive photostat

Hirsch II, no. 224; RISM A I, no. D 3795

MUSIC LIBRARY

488 DU PHLY, JACQUES

Pieces De | Clavecin | Dediées | A Monseigneur Le Duc | D'Ayen | Composées Par | Mr. Du Phly. | Gravées par Melle. Vandome. | . . . | A Paris | Chez {L'Auteur, rüe de la Verrerie à la porte Cochere vis-a-|-vis la rüe du Coq. | Madame Boivin, Marchande rüe St. Honoré à la Regle d'Or | Le Sieur Le Clerc, Marchand rüe du Roule à la Croix d'Or. | Avec Privilege Du Roy. [1744]

2° *Score:* 1 ℓ., 25 p.

RISM A I, no. D 3838

HOUGHTON

489 DU PHLY, JACQUES

Second Livre | De | Pieces De | Clavecin | Composées | Par | Mr. Du Phly. | Gravées par Melle. Vandôme | . . . | A Paris | Chez L'Auteur, rüe de la Verrerie à la porte Cochere. | vis-à vis la rüe du Coq. | Madame Boivin, Mde. rüe St. Honoré à la Regle d'Or. | Monsieur le Clerc, Md. rüe du Roule à la Croix d'Or | Mlle. Castagnerie, rüe des Prouvaires à la Musique Royal | Avec Privilege Du Roy. [1748]

2° *Score:* 2 ℓ., 29 p.

RISM A I, no. D 3839

HOUGHTON

490   DUPUIS, THOMAS SANDERS

Pieces | for the | Organ Or Harpsichord, | Principally intended for the use of Young Organists, | Composed and Humbly Dedicated to the | Honble. John Spencer, | By | Thos. Sanders Dupuis, Mus. Doc. | Organist & Composer to His Majesty. | Op. VIII. . . . | London: | Printed & Sold by Preston & Son, at their Wholesale Warehouses, 97 Strand. [1794?]

obl. 4° *Score:* 1 ℓ., 33 p.
Page [1]: New Musical Publications, | Engraved, Printed & Sold, | By Preston & Son . . .
HOUGHTON

491   [DURAND, ESTIENNE]

Discovrs | Av Vray Dv Ballet | Dansé Par Le Roy, | Le Dimanche XXIXe Iovr | De Ianvier. M.VIc.XVII. | Auec les desseins, tant des machines et apparences differentes, | que de tous les habits des Masques. | A Paris, | Par Pierre Ballard, Imprimeur de la Musique du Roy, demeurant | ruë sainct Iean de Beauuais, à l'enseigne du mont Parnasse. | 1617. | Auec Priuilege de sa Majesté.

4° 34 numb. ℓ., illus., music
HOUGHTON

492   [DUREY DE NOINVILLE, JACQUES BERNARD]

Histoire | Du Théatre | De L'Académie Royale | De Musique | En France, | Depuis son établissement jusqu'à présent. | Seconde Édition, | Corrigée & augmentée des Pieces qui ont été | représentées sur le Théatre de l'Opera par les | Musiciens Italiens, depuis le premier Août | 1752. jusqu'à leur départ en 1754. avec un | Extrait de ces Piéces & des Ecrits qui ont | paru à ce sujet. | . . . | A Paris, | Chez Duchesne, Libraire, rue S. Jacques, près la | Fontaine S. Benoît, au Temple du Goût. | M.DCC.LVII. | Avec Approbation & Privilége du Roi.

8° 2 vols: *vol. I:* 6, [8], 320 p., front., pl.; *vol. II:* 1 ℓ., 221, [6], 11 p.
Pages 1–11 at end of vol. II: Catalogue | De quelques Livres qui traitent de l'o-

pera, de la Musique & de la Danse, | & qui ont rapport à l'Histoire du | Théâtre de l'Opera.
Hirsch I, Historischer Anhang, no. 21; RISM B VI, 285
MUSIC LIBRARY

493   [DUREY DE NOINVILLE, JACQUES BERNARD]

Histoire | Du Théatre | De | L'Opera | En France. | Depuis L'Etablissement De | l'Académie Royale de Musique, | jusqu'à présent. | En Deux Parties. | . . . | A Paris, | Chez Joseph Barbou, rue S. Jacques, près la | Fontaine S. Benoît, aux Cigognes. | M.DCC.LIII. | Avec Approbation & Privilége du Roi.

8° 2 vols.: *vol. I:* 2 ℓ., 264 p.; *vol. II:* 3 ℓ., 221, [3] p.
RISM B VI, 285
HOUGHTON

494   D'URFEY, THOMAS

A New | Collection | Of | Songs | And | Poems. | By Thomas D'urfey, Gent. | London: | Printed for Josoph [*sic*] Hindmarsh, at the Black | Bull in Cornhill: 1683.

8° 1 ℓ., 89 p., 2 ℓ.
Unnumbered leaves at end: Books printed for, and sold by Joseph Hind-|marsh, at the Black Bull in Cornhill, | over against the Royal Exchange.
Day, no. 64
HOUGHTON

495   DUSSEK, JOHANN LADISLAUS

A Complete & exact delineation | of the Ceremony, from St. James's to St. Pauls; on Tuesday, the 19th. Decr. 1797. | on which day, their Majesties, together with both Houses of Parliament, went in | solemn Procession, to return thanks for the several Naval Victories obtained by the | British Fleet, over those of France, Spain, & Holland. The whole forming an | elegant Frontispiece to new Music; for the Piano Forte. composed expressly on | the occasion, by J. L. Dussek. to which is added, the form of the Church Service | with part of the Vocal Music, sung at that Celebrity. the March & Organ Piece, | by Mr. Attwood. the Sanctus by, Mr. Hudson. &c. &c. | . . . | [London] . . . Printed for Corri, Dussek, & 'Co. No. 28 Haymt. & 67 Dean Street Soho. | & Edgh [1798?]

2° *Score:* 21 p., front.
RISM A I, no. D 4602?
MUSIC LIBRARY

DU TILLET, ÉVRARD TITON *See* Titon du Tillet, Évrard

E

---

496   EASTCOTT, RICHARD

Sketches | Of The | Origin, Progress and Effects | Of | Music, | With An Account Of The | Ancient Bards and Minstrels. | Illustrated With Various | Historical Facts, Interesting Anecdotes, & Poetical Quotations. | By the Rev. Richard Eastcott, | Of Exeter. | . . . | Bath: Printed and sold by S. Hazard; | Sold likewise by Messrs. G. G. J. & J. Robinson, Paternoster-row; | Cadell, Strand, Dilly, Poultry, and Vernor and Hood, | Birchin-Lane, London; Messrs. Trewman, Woolmer, Sweet-|land, Grigg, Penny, Manning, and Hedgland, Exeter; | Mr. Collins, Salisbury; Mr. Hayden, and Richardson, | Plymouth; and all other Booksellers. | M,DCC,XCIII.

8° vii, [3], viii, iv p., 1ℓ., 277, [1] p.
RISM B VI, 287
MUSIC LIBRARY

497   EBDON, THOMAS

Six Glees, | for Three Voices. | To which is added an accompaniment for the | Harpsichord or Piano-Forte, | and the Melody adapted for a Single Voice. | Composed, | and most respectfully dedicated, to | The Hon. & Rt. Revd. The Lord Bishop of Durham, | By | Thomas Ebdon. | Op. III. Simpkins Sc. . . . | London. | Printed for the Author & Sold by Longman & Broderip, 26 Cheapside, & 13 Haymarket. | Prestons, 97 Strand, & Dale, 19 Cornhill. | . . . [ca. 1785]

obl. 2° *Score:* 3 ℓ., 37 p.
RISM A I, no. E 33
MUSIC LIBRARY

498   ECCLES, JOHN

. . . This Dialogue between Mrs. Willis and Mr. Wiltshire, and | The Two following Songs in the Musical Interlude for the Peace, | Performed at the Theatre in Little Lincolns-Inn-Fields. Set by Mr. John Eccles. [London, 1698?]

2° *Score:* [8] p. (Nos. 5–7 [of an unidentified collection of songs])
Colophon: London Printed for Henry Playford at his Shop in the Temple-Change, where | the other Numbers may be had . . .
Caption title
Day, no. 169
HOUGHTON

499   ECCLES, SOLOMON

A Musick-Lector: | Or, | The Art of Musick (that is so | much vindicated in Christendome) | Discoursed of, by ways of Dialogue | between three men of several Judg-|ments: | The one a Musician, and Master of that Art, | and zealous for the Church of England; who | calls Musick The gift of God. | The other a Baptist, who did affirm it to be | a decent and a harmless practice. | The other a Quaker (so called) being for-|merly of that Art, doth give his Judgment and | Sentence against it; but yet approves of the | Musick that pleaseth God. | Written by Solomon Eccles. | . . . | London, Printed in the Year, 1667.

4° 28 p.
RISM B VI, 289
HOUGHTON

500   EDELMANN, JOHANN FRIEDRICH

A | Celebrated | Overture | For The | Piano Forte. | Composed By | Edelman. | London. | Printed for Harrison & Co. No. 18. Paternoster Row. [1797]

8° *Score:* 1 ℓ., 10 p. (*The Piano-Forte Magazine* [vol. I, bound as no. 10])
Schnapper lists this issue as vol. II, no. 1., RISM A I as vol. II, no. 2
RISM A I, no. E 393 (op. 4)
MUSIC LIBRARY

501   EDELMANN, JOHANN FRIEDRICH

Four | Sonatas, | For The | Piano Forte. |
Composed By, | E. Edelmann. | Op: 11. |
London: | Printed for Harrison, Cluse, &
Co. No. 78, Fleet Street. [1799?]

8° *Score:* 55 p. (*The Piano-Forte Maga-
zine*, vol. IX, no. 5)
Plate nos. 137–139
RISM A I, no. E 423 (op. 9)
MUSIC LIBRARY

502   EDELMANN, JOHANN FRIEDRICH

IV Sonates | Pour Le Clavecin | Avec
accompagnement d'un Violon | ad Libi-
tum | Dediées | À Madame | D'Argenville
| Par Mr. Edelmann | Oeuvre V. | . . . | A
Paris |

Chez
A
A Lion
{ L'auteur rue du temple au coin
de la rue pastourelle. |
Me. le Menu rue du roule à la
clef d'or |
Me. Bérault rue de la comédie
françoise au dieu de l'harmonie |
Castaud place de la comédie
[1775]

2° 2 pts.: *clavecin:* 1 ℓ., 27 p.; *violino:*
8 p.
RISM A I, no. E 396
MUSIC LIBRARY

503   EDELMANN, JOHANN FRIEDRICH

III Sonates | Pour Le Clavecin | Avec
accompagnement d'un Violon | ad Libi-
tum. | Dediées | À Madame | De La Guil-
laummye | par Mr. Edelmann | Oeuvre
VI. | Gravées par G. Magnian. | . . . | A
Paris | Chez {L'auteur Chez M. D'argen-
ville rue Dutemple au coin de celle de
Pastourelle | Mme. LeMarchand rue Fro-
manteau et à l'Opera | A. P. D. R. [ca.
1777]

2° 2 pts.: *clavecin:* 1 ℓ., 21 p.; *violino:*
6 p.
MUSIC LIBRARY

504   [EGLI, JOHANN HEINRICH]

Fortsetzung | Auserlesener mora-
lischer Lieder, | von den | neusten und
besten Dichtern. | Zum Singen beym
Clavier. | Zürich, gedruckt bey David
Bůrgklj. 1780.

4° *Score:* 63, [1] p.
Contains songs by Johann Heinrich
Egli and Johann Jakob Walder
RISM A I, no. E 465
MUSIC LIBRARY

505   EICHNER, ERNST

Three | Sonatas | for the | Harpsichord |
or | Forte Piano | with Accompanyments
for a | Violin and Bass | ad Libitum | Com-
posed by | Ernesto Eichner. | . . . | Opera
3d. | London Printed and Sold by R.
Bremner opposite Somerset House in the
| Strand . . . [ca. 1775]

2° 2 pts.: *harpsichord or forte piano:* 19
p.; *violino:* 7 p.
Sonatas 1–3
RISM A I, no. E 545
MUSIC LIBRARY

506   EICHNER, ERNST

Three | Sonatas | for the | Harpsichord |
or | Forte Piano | with Accompanyments
for a | Violin and Bass | ad Libitum | Com-
posed by | Ernesto Eichner. | . . . | Opera
3d. | London Printed and Sold by R.
Bremner opposite Somerset House in the
| Strand . . . [ca. 1775]

2° 2 pts.: *harpsichord or forte piano:* 1
ℓ., 20–38 p.; *violino:* [1], 8–13 p.
Sonatas 4–6
RISM A I, no. E 546?
MUSIC LIBRARY

507   EICHNER, ERNST

Six | Sonates | Pour Le Clavecin Ou Le
Forte Piano | Avec accompagnement
d'un Violin | Et Violoncelle ad-Libitum |
Composée Par | Ernesto Eichner | Si de-
vant Maître des Concerts de Monsei-
gneur le Duc des deux Ponts | Oeuvre
VIII. | . . . | A Paris | Chez {Madame
Berault Marchande de Musique rue de la
Comédie | Francoise Faubourg St. Ger-
main au Dieu de l'Armonie. | Et aux
adresses ordinaires de Musique. | à Metz
chez Mr. Kar | A. P. D. R. [ca. 1772?]

2° 2 pts.: *clavecin ou forte piano:* 1 ℓ.,
35 p.; *violino:* 13 p.
On verso of preliminary leaf in *clave-
cin ou forte piano* part: Catalogue | Des

ouvrages qui se vendent chez Madame Berault | . . .

RISM A I, no. E 552

MUSIC LIBRARY

508 EICHNER, ERNST

Six | Sonates | Pour Le Clavecin | Ou Piano Forte | Avec accompagnement d'un Violon | Par | Ernesto Eichner | Ci devant Maitre des Concerts de S. A. S. Monseigneur le Duc des dex [*sic*] Ponts | Et présentement au Prince royale de Prusse | Oeuvre IX | . . . | A Paris | Chez {Madame Berault Mde. de Musique rue de la Comédie françoise | fauxbourg St. Germain au Dieu de l'Harmonie. | Et aux adresses ordinaires, | a Metz chez Mr. Kar. | A. P. D. R. [ca. 1773?]

2° 2 pts.: *clavecin:* 1 ℓ., 24 p.; *violino:* 7 p.

Page [1] in *clavecin* part: Catalogue | Des Ouvrages qui se vendent chez Madame Berault . . .

RISM A I, no. E 556

MUSIC LIBRARY

ÉLÉMENS DE MUSIQUE *See* Alembert, Jean Lerond d' *Élémens de musique*

ELLIOT, CHARLES, publ. Calliope, or The Musical Miscellany *See* Calliope, or The Musical Miscellany

509

An | Epistle | From | S[enesin]o, | To | A[nastasi]a R[obinso]n. | . . . | London: Printed in the Year 1724.

2° 1 ℓ., 3 p.

A satire in verse concerning a supposed love affair between Senesino and Anastasia Robinson

Foxon E378

HOUGHTON

510

An | Epistle | From | S[enesin]o, | To | A[nastasi]a R[obinso]n. | . . . | London: | Printed for M. Smith, near the Royal Ex-

change; and Sold | by the Booksellers of London and Westminster, 1724. | . . .

2° 1 ℓ., 3 p.

A satire in verse concerning a supposed love affair between Senesino and Anastasia Robinson

Foxon E377

HOUGHTON

511

An | Epistle | From | S[igno]r S[enesin]o | To | S[ignor]a F[austin]a. | . . . | London: | Printed for J. Roberts at the Oxford-Arms in Warwick-Lane. | MDCCXXVII. . . .

2° 8 p.

A satire in verse concerning a supposed love affair between Senesino and Faustina Bordoni

Foxon E379

HOUGHTON

512

An | Epistle | From the Platonick | Madam B[arb]ier, | To the Celebrated | Signor Car[est]ino. | . . . | London: | Printed for R. Smith in the Strand. | MDCCXXXIV.

2° 11 p.

A tribute to the singer Giovanni Carestino.

Foxon E381

HOUGHTON

513

An | Epistle | To | Mr. Handel, | Upon His | Operas | Of | Flavius and Julius Caesar. | . . . | London: | Printed for J. Roberts, near the Oxford Arms in Warwick-|Lane. 1724. . . .

2° 1 ℓ., 3 p.

In verse

Foxon E402

HOUGHTON

ERREURS SUR LA MUSIQUE DANS L'ENCY-CLOPEDIE *See* Rameau, Jean Philippe *Erreurs sur la musique dans l'Encyclopedie*

514 ESCH, LOUIS VON

La Colombe Retrouvée, | An Air for the | Piano Forte with or without Additional Keys, | Composed and Dedicated to | Miss C. H. | By | Louis von Esch. | . . . (Second Edition) . . . | London Printed by Broderip and Wilkinson No. 13 Haymarket. [ca. 1800]

2° *Score:* 3 p.
Caption title
HOUGHTON

515 ESPIC DE LIROU, JEAN FRANÇOIS

Explication | Du Système | De L'Harmonie, | Pour abréger l'Étude de la Composition, | & accorder la Pratique avec la Théorie; | Par le Chevalier De Lirou. | A Londres, | Et se trouve à Paris, | Chez Merigot, Libraire, quai des Augustins. | Bailly, Libraire, rue Saint-Honoré, à la barriere | des Sergens. | Bailleux, Marchand de Musique du Roi & de | la Famille Royale, rue S. Honoré, à la Regle d'or. | Boyer, Marchand de Musique, rue de Richelieu, | à la Clef d'or, à l'ancien Café de Foi. | Et chez les Libraires du Palais Royal. | M.DCC.LXXXV.

8° 2 ℓ., 239 p., illus., 7 pl. (incl. music)
RISM B VI, 506
MUSIC LIBRARY

516

An | Essay | Upon | The Sacred Use | Of | Organs, | In | Christian Assemblies. | Proving, That it was peculiar to the Jewish Church; is no | where enjoyned in the New Testament; nor received into | the Primitive Church: But first introduced by Pope Vita-|lian; And is therefore deservedly banished the most part | of Protestant Churches, and condemned by the Current of | Orthodox Divines. | And Answering the Arguments usually adduced by Papists and Formalists for | its Defence. | . . . | [London] Printed Anno MDCCXIII.

4° 44 p.
HOUGHTON

ESSAYS ON SONG-WRITING *See* Aikin, John *Essays on Song-Writing*

ESSEX HARMONY *See* Arnold, John comp. *Essex Harmony*

ÉTAPLES, JACQUES LE FÈVRE D' *See* Le Fèvre, Jacques, d'Étaples

517

Etat Actuel | De La Musique | Du Roi | Et | des Trois Spectacles | De Paris | A Paris | Chez Vente Libraire | Au bas de la Montagne de Ste. Genevieve | près les RR. PP. Carmes. | M.D.CCLXVII.

12° 9 ℓ., xij, 132 p.
Pages [117]–132: Catalogue | Des ouvrages les plus remarquables | qui ont paru au sujet des spectacles | & des théatres & jeux publics, tant | polémiques qu'historiques: auquel | on a joint une liste de la plupart des | Théatres imprimés, tant anciens que | modernes, dont le plus grand nom-|bre se trouve chez Vente, Libraire . . .
Grand-Carteret, no. 396
HOUGHTON

518

État Actuel | De La Musique | Du Roi | Et | des Trois Spectacles | De Paris. | A Paris. | Chez Vente, Libraire, | Au bas de la Montagne Ste. Genevieve, | M.D.CC.LXX.

12° 15 ℓ., 130, [2], xx, [4] p., front., 4 pl.
Pages [i]–xvij at end: Catalogue | Des ouvrages les plus remarquables | qui ont paru au sujet des spectacles & des théatres & jeux publics, tant | polémiques qu' historiques: auquel | on a joint une liste de la plupart des | théatres imprimés, tant anciens que | modernes, dont le plus grand nom-|bre se trouve chez Vente, Libraire . . .
HOUGHTON

519

État Actuel | De La Musique | Du Roi | Et | des Trois Spectacles | De Paris. | A Paris. | Chez Vente, Libraire, | Au bas de la Montagne Ste. Genevieve, | M.D.CC.LXXI.

12° 1 ℓ., iv, [12], 140, vj, [6] p., front., 4 pl.

Pages [i]–vj at end: Catalogue | De tous les Théatres imprimés, qui | se trouvent chez le même Libraire.
HOUGHTON

520

Etrennes | Chantante | Ou | Choix des plus Nouvelles, | Ariettes, Romances | Et Vaudevilles. | Avec Accompagnement | De Guittare. | Dediés | Aux Dames. | Pour l'Année | 1787. | Gravée par Coulubrier. | A Paris. | Se vend par Goujon fils Distributeur | D'Ariettes ruë du bout-du-monde au coin de | celle Montmartre chez l'Erboriste. | . . . [1787?]

8° *Score:* 128 ℓ.
Contains sixty *ariettes* numbered 6–65 in table of contents, most with imprint: au Palais Royal, Chez les Freres Savigny, Cour du Jardin près le Passage Richelieu ⟨capitalization varies⟩.
Bound in at the beginning are three *ariettes* excluded from the table of contents: "Du malheur auguste" [from *Oedipe à Colone*] . . . A Paris Chez Cousineau Pere et Fils, Luthiers rue des Poulies; Couplets Des Dettes . . . "On doit soixante mille franc . . ." [no imprint]; "La prise de tabac" du Comte d'Albert Par Mr. Gretry . . . Gravé par Huguet
RISM B II, 167
MUSIC LIBRARY

521

Étrennes | De | Polymnie; | Choix De Chansons, | Romances, Vaudevilles, &c., | Avec de la musique nouvelle, gravée à la fin | du Recueil, et des timbres d'airs connus, | sur lesquels la plupart des morceaux peuvent | aussi être chantés. | A Paris, | Au Bureau de la Petite Bibliotheque des Théatres, | rue des Moulins, butte Saint-Roch, no. 11. | Chez {Bélin, Libraire, rue Saint-Jacques, près Saint-|Yves; | Brunet, Libraire, rue de Marivaux, Place du | Théatre Italien, | Et tous les Marchands de Musique et de Nouveautés. | M.DCC.LXXXVII. | Avec Approbation et Privilége du Roi.

12° 2 ℓ., 230 p.
Texts only; lacks the melodies mentioned on the title-page

RISM B II, 168
MUSIC LIBRARY

522

Étrennes | De | Polymnie; | Choix De Chansons, | Romances, Vaudevilles, &c., | Avec de la musique nouvelle et des timbres | d'airs connus, sur lesquels la plupart des | morceaux peuvent aussi être chantés. | A Paris, | Chez {Bélin, Libraire, rue Saint-Jacques, près Saint-|Yves; | Brunet, Libraire, rue de Marivaux, Place du | Théatre Italien; | Desenne, Libraire, | Gattey, Libraire, | Petit, Libraire,} au Palais-Royal, | Et tous les Marchands de Musique et de Nouveautés. | M.DCC.LXXXVIII. | Avec Approbation et Privilége du Roi.

12° 8 ℓ., 308 p., music
RISM B II, 168
MUSIC LIBRARY

523

Étrennes | De | Polymnie; | Choix De Chansons, | Romances, Vaudevilles, &c., | Avec de la musique nouvelle et des timbres | d'airs connus, sur lesquels la plupart des | morceaux peuvent aussi être chantés. | A Paris, | Chez {Bélin, Libraire, rue Saint-Jacques, près Saint-|Yves; | Brunet, Libraire, rue de Marivaux, Place du | Théatre Italien; | Desenne, Libraire, | Gattey, Libraire, | Petit, Libraire,} au Palais-Royal; | Le Duc, Marchand de Musique, rue du Roule. | Et tous les Marchands de Musique et de Nouveautés. | M.DCC.LXXXIX. | Avec Approbation et Privilége du Roi.

12° 8 ℓ., 308 p., music
RISM B II, 168
MUSIC LIBRARY

524   EUCLIDES

Le | Liure de la Mu-|sique d'Euclide | traduit par P. Forcadel | lecteur du Roy es | Mathematiques. | A Paris, | Chez Charles Perier, au Bellerophon rue | S. Iehan de Beauuais. | 1566.

8° A–F⁴, illus.
RISM B VI, 296
HOUGHTON

525   EULER, LEONHARD

Tentamen | Novae Theoriae | Mvsicae | Ex | Certissimis | Harmoniae Principiis | Dilvcide Expositae. | Avctore | Leonhardo Evlero. | Petropoli, Ex Typographia Academiae Scientiarvm. | cIɔ Iɔ cc XXXIX.

4° 21, [1], 263 p., illus., 6 pl. (5 fold., incl. music)
Hirsch, I, no. 161; RISM B VI, 298; Wolfenbüttel, no. 1114
HOUGHTON

EXAMEN DE LA LETTRE DE M. ROUSSEAU *See* Bâton, Charles *Examen de la lettre de M. Rousseau*

THE EXCELLENT CHOICE   *See* Pepusch, John Christopher *The Beggar's Opera*

526   EXIMENO Y PUJADES, ANTONIO

Del Origen | Y Reglas De La Musica, | Con La Historia De Su Progreso, | Decadencia Y Restauracion. | Obra Escrita En Italiano | Por El Abate Don Antonio Eximeno. | Y Traducida Al Castellano | Por D. Francisco Antonio Gutierrez, | Capellan de S. M. y Maestro de Capilla del Real | Convento de Religiosas de la Encarnacion | de Madrid. | . . . | De Orden Superior. | Madrid, En La Imprenta Real, | Año De 1796.

8° 3 vols.: *vol. I:* 24, [8], 359 [i.e. 259], [1] p., illus., 4 fold. pl. (incl. music); *vol. II:* 4 ℓ., 255, [1] p., illus., 17 fold. pl.; *vol. III:* 4 ℓ., 258 p., 1 ℓ., illus., fold. pl. (music)
Page 259 misnumbered 359 in volume I
RISM B VI, 299
HOUGHTON

527   EXIMENO Y PUJADES, ANTONIO

Dell' Origine | E Delle Regole | Della Musica | Colla Storia Del Suo Progresso, | Decadenza, E Rinnovazione. | Opera | Di D. Antonio Eximeno | Fra I Pastoria Arcadi Aristosseno Mega Reo | Dedicata | All'Augusta Real Principessa | Maria Antonia Valburga | Di Baviera | Elettrice Vedova Di Sassonia | Fra Le Pastorelle Ar-

cadi | Ermelinda Talia. | In Roma MDCCLXXIV. | Nella Stamperia Di Michel' Angelo Barbiellini | Nel Palazzo Massimi. | Con Facoltà De' Svperiori.

4° 6 ℓ., 466 [i. e. 474] p., 1 ℓ., front. (port.), illus., 22 fold. pl. (music)
Nine unnumbered pages between pages 16 and 22; numbers 393–396 repeated in paging
Hirsch I, no. 162; RISM B VI, 299
HOUGHTON

F

FABER, JACOBUS, STAPULENSIS   *See* Le Fèvre, Jacques, d'Étaples

FABRICIUS, BERNHARD   *See* Schmid, Bernhard

FALKENER, ROBERT, PUBL. Harmonia Vera   *See* Harmonia Vera

528

Farinelli's | Celebrated Songs &c. | Collected from | Sigr. Hasse, Porpora, | Vinci, and | Veracini's Operas | Set for a | German Flute | Violin or Harpsicord | . . . | London. Printed for and Sold by I. Walsh, Musick Printer, & | Instrument maker to his Majesty at the Harp and Hoboy in | Catherine   Street   in   the   Strand . . . [1737]

2° *Score:* vol. I [pt. 1]: 1 ℓ., 25 p.
No. 602 on title-page
RISM B II, 171; Walsh II, no. 771
MUSIC LIBRARY

529   FASOLD, BENEDICT

Melos Marianum | Mariae | Matri Mirabili | Magistrae Musicorum | Modulatum | seu | XXIV. | Antiphonae Marianae | à 4. Voc. Ord. 2. Violinis, & | duplici Basso continuo | necessar. 2. Cornu ex diversis clavibus | ad libitum. | Stylo suavi ac moderno elaboratae | Auctore | R. P. Benedicto Fasold, | Ord. S.

Ben. Professo ad S. Michaëlem Arch-Angelum | p. t. Musices Directore Fultenbachii. | Opus I. | . . . | Augustae-Vindelicorum, | Sumptibus Joannis Jacobi Lotteri Haeredum. MDCCLIII.

   2° 1 pt.: *organo:* 3 ℓ., 20 p.
RISM A I, no. F 120
HOUGHTON

FAUSTINA, OR THE ROMAN SONGSTRESS
See Carey, Henry *Faustina, or The Roman Songstress*

530

   The Favorite | New Glees | Composed by | Dr. Cooke, Mr. Callcott, | Mr. Danby, and Mr. Webbe. | expressly for, & performed at | Messrs, Harrison & Knyvett's | Vocal Concert, 1792. | most respectfully dedicated to | The Subscribers. | . . . | London. | Printed for Messrs. Harrison & Knyvett, & to be had at their houses | in Percy Street Rathbone Place. Stratton Street Piccadilly, | and at Messrs. Longman & Broderip's in Cheapside & the Haymarket. | Simpkins Sc[ulpt] [1792?]

   obl. 2° *Score:* 2 ℓ., 62 p.
RISM B II, 173
MUSIC LIBRARY

531

   A Favourite | Collection, | Of | Familiar Rondos; | For The | Piano-Forte. | London: | Printed for Harrison, Cluse, & Co. No. 78, Fleet Street. [1799?]

   8° *Score:* 10 p. (*The Piano-Forte Magazine,* vol. VII, no. 4)
Plate no. 99
MUSIC LIBRARY

FELIX   *See* Monsigny, Pierre Alexandre *Felix*

532   FELTON, WILLIAM

   Six | Concerto's | for the | Organ or Harpsichord | With Instrumental Parts | Compos'd by | Mr. William Felton, | London. | Printed for John Johnson Musick

Seller at the Harp and | Crown in Cheapside [1744]

   2° 10 pts.: *organo:* 1 ℓ., 45 p.; *hautboy primo:* 9 p.; *hautboy secondo, violino primo, violino secondo, violino primo ripieno, violino secondo ripieno:* 1 ℓ., 9 p. each; *viola:* 9 p.; *violoncello:* 1 ℓ., 9 p.; *basso:* 9 p.
Imperfect: title-page, page 2 lacking in *viola* part; pages 3–6 lacking in *violoncello* part
RISM A I, no. F 217 (op. 1)
HOUGHTON

533   FELTON, WILLIAM

   Six | Concerto's | for the | Organ or Harpsichord | With Instrumental Parts | Composed by | Mr. Felton | Opera Seconda | London Printed for J. Johnson at the Harp & Crown in Cheapside | . . . [1747?]

   2° 10 pts: *organ:* 2 ℓ., 50 p.; *hautbois primo, hautbois secondo:* 11 p. each; *violino primo, violino secondo:* 1 ℓ., 13 p. each; *violino primo ripieno, violino secondo ripieno:* 13 p. each; *viola:* 6[+] p.; *violoncello, basso:* 1 ℓ., 13 p. each
Imperfect: all after page 6 lacking in *viola* part; pages 11–13 lacking in *violoncello* part
RISM A I, no. F 221
HOUGHTON

534   FELTON, WILLIAM

   Eight Suits | Of | Easy Lessons | For The | Harpsichord | By | Mr. Felton | Opera Terza | London Printed for John Johnson at the Harp and Crown | facing Bow Church in Cheapside, | . . . [1752?]

   2° *Score:* 1 ℓ., 48 p.
RISM A I, no. F 222
HOUGHTON

535   FERRARI, GIACOMO GOTIFREDO

   Trois | Trios | Concertants | Pour le | Piano Forte | Violino & Violoncello | Composés et Dediés | À | Mademoiselle Josephine de Jacobi | par | J. G. Ferrari | Op. XI . . . | . . . | London | Printed by

Longman and Broderip No. 26 Cheapside and No. 13 Haymarket. | Manufacturers of Musical Instruments in general, and Music Sellers to Their Majesties, | the Prince of Wales, the Dukes of York, Clarence, and all the Royal Family [ca. 1795]

2° *Short score:* 1 *ℓ.*, 35 p.
RISM A I, no. F 416
MUSIC LIBRARY

536 FESTING, MICHAEL CHRISTIAN

An | English Cantata | Call'd | Sylvia | And two English Songs | Set to Musick by | Michael Christian Festing | . . . | London Printed by William Smith in Middle Row Holbourn; and sold by the Author | at his House in Queen street near Golden Square; . . . [1744?]

2° *Score:* 10 *ℓ.*
RISM A I, no. F 646
MUSIC LIBRARY

537 FESTING, MICHAEL CHRISTIAN

Milton's May-Morning | And several other | English Songs | Set to Musick by | Michael Christian Festing | . . . | London Printed & sold for the Author by J. Simpson at the Bass | Viol & Flute in Sweeting's Alley opposite the East Door of ye R. Exchange | . . . [ca. 1748]

2° *Score:* 1 *ℓ.*, 13 p.
RISM A I, no. F 650
HOUGHTON

538 FEUILLET, RAOUL AUGER

The Art of | Dancing, | Demonstrated by | Characters | And | Figures; | Whereby | One may learn easily, and of One's | Self, all sorts of Dances, be-|ing a Work very useful to all | such as practise Dancing, especially | Masters. | Done from the French of Monsieur Feüillet, with many Alterations in | the Characters, and an Addition of the English Rigaudon, and | French Bretagne, | By P. Siris, Dancing-Master. | London, | Printed for the Author, and may be had of him, at his | House in Newport Street. MDCCVI.

4° 2 *ℓ.*, 52 p., 41 pl. on 28 *ℓ.* (incl. music)
RISM B VI, 314–315
HOUGHTON

539 FEUILLET, RAOUL AUGER

Orchesography | Or The | Art | Of | Dancing | By | Characters and Demonstrative Figures. | Wherein | The whole Art is explain'd; with compleat | Tables of all Steps us'd in Dancing, and Rules for | the Motions of the Arms, &c. | Whereby | Any Person (who understands Dancing) may of | himself learn all manner of Dances. | Being | An Exact and Just Translation from the | French of Monsieur Feuillet. | By John Weaver, Dancing Master. | The 2d. Edition | N: B: To this Edition is added the Rigadoon, the Louvre, & the | Brittagne, in Characters, with the Contents, or Index; the whole En-|-graven: and likewise may be had where these are sold, 20 Dances in Cha-|-racters by Mr. Isaac, in one Vol-|lume. | London, Printed for, & Sold by Ino. Walsh, Musick Printer, & Instrument Maker | to his Majesty, at the Harp, in Catherine Street in the Strand; | & Ino. Hare at the Viol, & Flute, in Cornhill, near the Royal Exchange. [1721?]

4° 3 *ℓ.*, 120 p., illus., music
Paging includes numbered leaf 45
Imperfect: pages 15, 16 lacking
RISM B VI, 315; Walsh II, no. 617?
HOUGHTON

—Another copy
No. 160 on title-page
John Hare's name and address erased from plate
Walsh II, no. 618
HOUGHTON

540 FEUILLET, RAOUL AUGER

Recüeil | De | Contredances | mises en Chorégraphie, | d'une maniére si aisée, que | toutes personnes peuvent | facilement les apprendre | sans le secours d'aucun | maître et même sans avoir | eu aucune connoissance de | la Chorégraphie. | Par Mr. Feüillet. | Maître et Compositeur de Dance. | . . . | A Paris | Chez l'Auteur Rüe de Bussi | Faubourg Saint Germain à la Cour | Imperiale prés la ruë des mauvais garçons | Avec Privilége du Roy. 1706.

> 12° 16 ℓ., 192 p., illus., music
> Hirşch I, no. 172
> HOUGHTON

FÈVRE, JACQUES LE, D'ÉTAPLES *See* Le Fèvre, Jacques, d'Étaples

FIELDING, JOHN, PUBL. The Convivial Songster *See* The Convivial Songster

FIELDING, JOHN, PUBL. The Vocal Enchantress *See* The Vocal Enchantress

FIELTZ, ANTON *See* Filtz, Anton

FILIDOR DER DORFERER, PSEUD. Die geharnschte Venus *See* Stieler, Kaspar von *Die geharnschte Venus*

541   FILTZ, ANTON

Six | Quartettos | for two | Violins | a | Tenor | and a | Violoncello | Obligato | Compos'd by | Antonio Filtz | . . . | London. Printed for C. and S. Thompson No. 75 St. Paul's Church Yard. | . . . [1770?]

> 2° 4 pts.: *violino primo, violino secondo, viola, violoncello:* 1 ℓ., 13 p.
> RISM A I, no. F 763
> MUSIC LIBRARY

542   FISCHER, JOHANN CHRISTIAN

A Favourite | Concerto | Adapted for the | Harpsicord | or | Piano Forte | Composed by | Giovanno Christiano Fischer. | . . . | London. Printed for and sold by the Author in Frith Street | the Corner of Compton Street Soho | By his Majesty's Royal Licence. [ca. 1770]

> 2° *Score:* 10 p.
> RISM A I, no. F 994
> HOUGHTON

543   FISCHER, JOHANN CHRISTIAN

A | Favourite | Concerto | for the | Harpsichord | Composed by | Gio: Christiano

Fischer | . . . | London | Printed by Welcker in Gerrard Street St. Ann's Soho | . . . [ca. 1768]

> 2° *Score:* 9 p.
> RISM A I, no. F 990
> MUSIC LIBRARY

544   FISHER, JOHN ABRAHAM

The Favorite | Cantata | of | Diana and Cupid | and a Collection of | Song's | Sung by | Mr: Vernon, Mrs: Weichsell, & Mr: Owenson, | at | Vaux Hall | 1770 | Compos'd by | A. Fisher . . . | London Printed by Welcker in Gerrard Street St. Ann's Soho. | . . . [1770?]

> 2° *Short score:* 1 ℓ., 15 p.
> RISM A I, no. F 1066
> MUSIC LIBRARY

FLITZ, JACQUES DU *See* Du Phly, Jacques

545   FODOR, ANTON

Three | Sonatas | for the | Piano-Forte | or | Harpsichord | Composed by | A: Fodor | Opera II. | . . . | London | Printed by Longman and Broderip No. 26 Cheapside and No. 13 Haymarket | Manufacturers of Musical Instruments in general, and Music Sellers to Their Majesties, | The Prince of Wales, The Dukes of York, Clarence, and all the Royal Family. [after 1782]

> 2° *Score:* 30 p.
> Plate no. 794
> RISM A I, no. F 1240
> MUSIC LIBRARY

546   FOGLIANO, LODOVICO

Mvsica Theo|rica | Ludouici Foliani Mutinensis: docte si-|mul ac dilucide pertractata: in qua | quãplures de harmonicis inter-|uallis: non prius tentatae: | continentur specu-|lationes. [Venice, 1529]

> 2° 1 ℓ., XLIII numb. ℓ., 1 ℓ., illus.
> Colophon: Venetiis per Io. Antonium & Fratres de Sabio. | Anno Domini MDXXIX. | Mense Iulii.
> Hirsch I, no. 176; RISM B VI, 320
> HOUGHTON

547   [FONTANELLI, ALFONSO]

. . . | Il Primo Libro | De Madrigali | Senza Nome. | A Cinqve Voci. | Tertia Impressione. | Stampa Del Gardano. | In Venetia MDCXVI. | Appresso Bartholomeo Magni.

4° 1 pt.: *tenore:* 20 p.
RISM A I, no. F 1480; Vogel, no. 1001 bis
HOUGHTON

548   [FONTANELLI, ALFONSO]

. . . | Secondo Libro | De Madrigali | Senza Nome. | A Cinqve Voci. | Nouamente Ristampati. | Stampa Del Gardano | In Venetia MDCXIX. | Appresso Bartolomeo Magni.

4° 1 pt.: *tenore:* 1 ℓ., 21, [1] p.
RISM A I, no. F 1483; Vogel, no. 1004
HOUGHTON

THE FOOL'S PREFERMENT   *See* Purcell, Henry *The Fool's Preferment*

FORBES, JOHN, PUBL. Cantus   *See* Songs and Fancies to Three, Four or Five Parts

FORD, ANN   *See* Thicknesse, Ann (Ford)

549   FORD, THOMAS

Mvsicke | Of | Svndrie | Kindes, | Set forth in two Bookes. | The First Whereof Are, | Aries for 4. Voices to the Lute, Orphorion, | or Basse-Viol, with a Dialogue for two | Voices, and two Basse Viols in parts, | tunde the Lute way. | The Second Are | Pauens, Galiards, Almaines, Toies, | Iigges, Thumpes and such like, for two | Basse-Viols, the Liera way, so made as the | greatest number may serue to play alone, very | easie to be performde. | Composed by Thomas Ford. | Imprinted at London by Iohn Windet at the Assignes | of William Barley and are to be sold by Iohn Brovvne | in Saint Dunstons churchyard in Fleetstreet 1607.

2° A–M²
In *Tafelmusik* format

Imperfect: F2 and G closely cropped, with loss of music
RISM A I, no. F 1503
HOUGHTON

550   FORKEL, JOHANN NIKOLAUS

Allgemeine | Litteratur der Musik | oder | Anleitung zur Kenntniss musikalischer Bücher, | welche von den ältesten bis auf neusten Zeiten bey den Griechen, | Römern und den meisten neuern europäischen Nationen sind geschrie-|ben worden. | Systematisch geordnet, | und nach Veranlassung mit Anmerkungen und Urtheilen begleitet | von | Johann Nicolaus Forkel. | Leipzig, | im Schwickertschen Verlage, 1792.

8° XXIV, 540 p.
RISM B VI, 323; Wolfenbüttel, no. 1132
HOUGHTON (2 copies)

551   [FORKEL, JOHANN NIKOLAUS, ED.]

Musikalischer | Almanach | für | Deutschland | auf das Jahr | 1783.[–1784, 1789.] | Leipzig, | im Schwickertschen Verlag[e]. [1783–1784, 1789]

3 v.
1783: 4 ℓ., 206 p., 1 ℓ; *1784;* VIII, 274 p., 2 ℓ., *1789:* XI, [1], 163 p.
Vol. for *1782* lacking
No more published
Unnumbered leaf at end of *1783:* Nachstehende Musikalien sind bey mir zu | haben . . .; similar advertisement at end of *1784*
RISM B VI, 323–324
HOUGHTON

552   FORKEL, JOHANN NIKOLAUS

Sechs | Clavier Sonaten, | Nebst Einer | Violin-Und Violoncellstimme, | Zur | Willkührlichen Begleitung Der Zwoten Und Vierten Sonate, | Von | Johann Nicolaus Forkel. | Zwote Sammlung. | Goettingen, Auf Kosten Des Verfassers. 1779. | Gedruckt Bey Johann Gottlob Jmmanuel Breitkopf In Leipzig.

obl. 2° Score and 2 pts: *Score:* 2 *ℓ.*,
47 p.; *violino, violoncello:* 4 p. each
Hirsch III, no. 203; RISM A I, no. F
1515

MUSIC LIBRARY

553   FORMÉ, NICOLAS

Mvsica Simplex | Qvatvor Vocvm. |
Avthore | Nicolao Formé, | Regiae Musi-
cae Praefecto. | . . . | Parisiis. | Ex Offi-
cina Petri Ballard, in Musicis Typographi
Regij: in | vico D. Ioannis Bellouacensis,
sub signo montis Parnassi. | 1638. | Cum
Priuilegio Regis.

4° 4 pts.: *svperivs, contra, tenor,
bassvs:* 2 *ℓ.*, 6 numb. *ℓ.* each

HOUGHTON

FORT, GIOVANNI BATTISTA DU   *See* Dufort, Giovanni Battista

FORTSETZUNG   AUSERLESENER   MORA-
LISCHER   LIEDER   *See* Egli, Johann
Heinrich *Fortsetzung auserlesener mora-
lischer Lieder*

FOUILLOUX, JACQUES DU   *See* Du Fouilloux, Jacques

554   FOURNIER, PIERRE SIMON

Traité | Historique Et Critique | Sur |
L'Origine Et Les Progrès | Des Caractéres
De Fonte | Pour l'impression de la Musi-
que, | Avec des Épreuves de nouveaux
Caractères de Musique, | Présentés Aux
Imprimeurs De France. | Par M. Fournier
Le Jeune. | A Berne, | Et se trouve A Paris,
| Chez Barbou, Imprimeur-Libraire, rue
& vis-à-vis | la Grille des Mathurins. |
M.DCC.LXV.

4° 47 p., 1 *ℓ.*, music
Pages [39]–47: Ariette, | Mise En Mu-
sique | Par | M. L'Abbé Dugué. | A Paris, |
des nouveaux Caractères. | De Fournier
Le Jeune. | M.DCC.LXV.
RISM B VI, 325–326

HOUGHTON

555   FRAENZL, FERDINAND

Trois Quatuors | Pour | Deux Violons,
Alto & Basse, | Composés et Dédiés. | A.
Sa Majesté | Le Roi De Naples | Par | F.
Fraenzl | Oeuvre Premier | Libro I | Chéz
J. J. Hummel | à Berlin avec Privilége du
Roi | à Amsterdam au Grand Magazin de
Musique | et aux Adresses Ordinaires. |
. . . [1793]

2° 4 pts.: *violino primo:* 13 p.; *violino
secondo, viola:* 11 p. each; *violoncello:* 1
ℓ., 8 p.
Plate no. 903
Quartets 1–3

HOUGHTON

556   FRAENZL, FERDINAND

Trois Quatuors | Pour | Deux Violons,
Alto & Basse, | Composés et Dédiés | A.
Sa Majesté | Le Roi De Naples | Par | F.
Fraenzl | Oeuvre Premier | Libro I [i. e. II]
| Chéz J. J. Hummel | à Berlin avec Pri-
vilége du Roi | à Amsterdam au Grand
Magazin de Musique | et aux Adresses
Ordinaires. | . . . [1793]

2° 4 pts.: *violino primo:* 1 *ℓ.*, [13]–25
p.; *violino secondo:* 1 *ℓ.*, [11]–23 p.;
viola: [9]–18 p.; *violoncello:* 1 *ℓ.*, [9]–
17 p.
Plate no. 904
No. 903 on title-page
Quartets 4–6

HOUGHTON

557   [FRÉRON, ÉLIE CATHERINE]

Lettres | Sur | La Musique | Françoise. |
En Réponse | A Celle De | Jean-Jacques
Rousseau. | A Géneve. | M.DCC.LIV.

8° 64 p.
RISM B VI, 329

HOUGHTON

558   FRESCOBALDI, GIROLAMO
       ALESSANDRO

Toccate D'Intavolatvra | Di Cimbalo
Et Organo | Partite Di Diverse Arie E[t]
Cor-|rente, Balletti, Ciac-|cone, Passa-
chagli. | Di | Girolamo Frescobaldi | Or-
ganista In S. Pietro Di Roma. | . . . |
Stampato L'Anno M.D.C.XXXVII | Per

Nicolo Borbone in Roma Con licenza de Superiori.

2° *Score:* 2 vols.: *vol. I:* 2 ℓ., 94 p., 1 ℓ.; *vol. II:* 2 ℓ., 86 p.; illus. (port.) in each vol.

Vol. II has separate title-page: Il Secondo Libro | Di Toccate, Canzone | Versi D'Hinni Magnificat | Gagliarde, Corrente | Et Altre Partite | D'Intavolatvra | Di Cimbalo Et Organo | Di Girolamo Frescobaldi | Organista | In S Pietro Di Roma | Con priuilegio. | In Roma con licenza de Superiori 1637 Da Nicoló Borbone.

Hirsch III, no. 205; RISM A I, no. F 1859, F 1867; SartoriB, no. 1637f

HOUGHTON

559 FRIES, JOHANN HENRICH HERMANN

Johann Henrich Hermann Fries | Abhandlung | vom sogenannten | Pfeifer-Gericht, | so in der Kaiserl. Freien Reichs-Stadt | Frankfurt am Main, | von uralten Zeiten her mit besondern und merk-|würdigen Feierlichkeiten aljårlich einmal | gehalten zu werden pflegt: | welcher | Eine kurze Nachricht | Vom wahren Ursprung | der beiden dasigen von Alters her | berůmten | Reichs-Messen | einverleibet; | samt einigen andern zufälligen Anmerkungen und | einem Sendschreiben des Hőchstberůmten | Freiherrn von Senkenberg, | Kaiserl. Reichs-Hofrahts, | an den Verfasser. | Frankfurt am Main, im Jahr 1752. | Zu finden bey Wolffg. Christ. Multz im Rőmer.

8° 7 ℓ., 16, 248, [8] p., front. (music)
RISM B VI, 334
HOUGHTON, WIDENER

560 FROSCH, JOHANN

Rervm | Mvsicarvm | Opvscvlvm Rarvm Ac In-|signe, totius eius negotii rationem mira in-|dustria & breuitate complectens, iam | recens publicatum. Ioan. | Froschio, | Autore, [Strassburg, 1535]

2° [−]⁶, A–D⁶, E⁴, F1–5, illus., music
Colophon: Argentorati Apvd Petrvm | Schoeffer & Mathiam Apiarium. Anno Salutis | M.D.XXXV.

Hirsch I, no. 183; RISM B VI, 336–337; Wolfenbüttel, no. 1137
HOUGHTON

561 FUX, JOHANN JOSEPH

Elisa | Festa Theatrale Per Musica; | Rappresentata nel Giardino dell'Imperiale Favorita | Per il felicissimo Giorno Natalizio | Della Sacra Cesarea e Cattolica Reale Maestà | Di | Elisabetta Cristina | Imperadrice Regnante, | per comando della Saca:, Cesa: e Catta: Real Maestà di | Carlo VI. | Imperador de' Romani sempre Augusto. | Poësia di Pietro Pariati Poëta di S. M. Cesa: e Catta: | Musica di Gio: Giuseppe Fux, Maestro di Capella. | A Amsterdam | Chez Jeanne Roger | . . . [ca. 1720]

4° *Score:* 3 ℓ., 420 p.
No. 482 on title-page
Hirsch II, no. 235; RISM A I, no. F 2108
HOUGHTON

562 FUX, JOHANN JOSEPH

Gradus | Ad | Parnassum, | Sive | Manuductio | Ad | Compositionem Musicae | Regularem, | Methodo novâ, ac certâ, nundum antè | tam exacto ordine in lucem edita: | Elaborata à | Joanne Josepho Fux, | Sacrae Caesareae, ac Regiae Ca-|tholicae Majestatis Caroli VI. Ro-|manorum Imperatoris | Supremo Chori Praefecto. | Viennae Austriae, | Typis Joannis Petri Van Ghelen, Sac. Caes. Regiaéque Catholicae Ma-|jestatis Aulae-Typographi, 1725.

2° 4 ℓ., 280 p., front., illus., music
Hirsch I, no. 185; RISM B VI, 340
HOUGHTON

563 FUX, JOHANN JOSEPH

Salita | Al | Parnasso, | Osia | Guida | Alla | Regolare Composizione Della Musica | Con nuovo, e certo Metodo non per anche in ordine sì esatto | data alle luce, e composta | Da Giovanni Giuseppe Fux | Principale Maestro Di Cappella | Della S. C. e R. C. Maestà | Di Carlo VI. | Imperatore De' Romani | Fedelmente trasportata dal Latino nell'Idioma Italiano | Dal Sacerdote Alessandro Manfredi | Citta-

dino Reggiano, E Professore Di Musica. |
In Carpi 1761. | Nella Stamperia Del
Pubblico Per Il Carmignani. | Con licenza
de' Superiori.

2° 5 ℓ., 140 [i. e. 240] p., front., illus.,
music
Page 240 misnumbered 140
Hirsch I, no. 187; RISM B VI, 340–341
MUSIC LIBRARY

G

564   GAFFURIO, FRANCHINO

Franchini Gafurii Laudensis Regii Mu-
sici publice | profitentis: Delubriq[ue]
Mediolanensis Phona|sci: de Harmonia
Musicorum In|strumentorum Opus. |
. . . [Milan, 1518]

2° 4 ℓ., C numb. ℓ., [4] p., illus., music
Colophon: Impressum Mediolani per |
Gotardum Pontanum Calco|graphum
die. xxvii. Nouem|bris. 1518. Authoris
Praefectu|rae Anno trigesimoquinto.
Leo|ne Decimo Pōtifice Maximo: | ac
Christianissimo Fancorum | Rege Fran-
cisco Duce Medio|lani. . . .
Hirsch I, no. 197; MortimerI, no. 204;
RISM B VI, 342; Wolfenbüttel, no. 1139
HOUGHTON (2 copies)

565   GAFFURIO, FRANCHINO

Musice utriusq[ue] cantus practi|ca ex-
cellentis Frāchini Ga|fori Laudensis
libris | quatuor modu|latissima. [Brescia,
1497]

2° [–]⁴, a–b⁸, c⁶, aa–kk⁸, ℓℓ⁶, illus.,
music
Colophon: Impressa Brixiae opera &
impensa Angeli Britannici: anno salutis
Millesimo quatrin-|gentesimo nonage-
simo septimo: nono Kalen̄: Octobris.
Imperfect: leaves a1, b3–b6, ℓℓ1, ℓℓ6
lacking
BMC VII, 979; Goff, no. G-4; Hain-Copinger, no. 7408; Hirsch I, no. 193; RISM
B VI, 342
HOUGHTON

566   GAFFURIO, FRANCHINO

Practica Mvsice Franchini Gafori Lavdensis. [Milan, 1496]

2° Γ⁴, a–b⁸, c⁶, aa–kk⁸, ℓℓ⁶ (ℓℓ6 blank),
illus., music
Colophon: . . . Impressa Mediolani
opera & Impensa Ioannis petri de Loma-
tio per Guillermum | Signerre Rothoma-
gensem anno salutis Milessimo quadrin-
gentessimo nonagessi-|mo sexto die
vltimo Septembris . . .
BMC VI, 789; Goff, no. G-3; Hain-Copinger, no. 7407; RISM B VI, 342
HOUGHTON

567   GAFFURIO, FRANCHINO

Theorica Mvsice Franchini Gafvri |
Lavdensis. [Milan, 1492]

2° [–]⁴, a⁸, b–i⁶, k⁸, illus., music
Colophon: Impressum mediolani per
Magistrum Philippum Man-|tegatium
dictum Cassanum opera & impensa Ma-
gistri | Ioannis Petri de lomatio anno sa-
lutis M.cccc.Lxxxxii. | die xv Decembris.
BMC VI, 785; Goff, no. G-6; Hain-Co-
pinger, no. 7406; Hirsch I, no. 191; RISM
B VI, 343
HOUGHTON

568   GAGLIANO, MARCO DA

. . . | Di Marco | Da Gagliano, | Il
Qvarto Libro | De Madrigali. | A Cinqve
Voci. | Nouamente Stampato. | In Vene-
tia. | Appresso Angelo Gardano. |
MDCVI.

4° 1 pt.: *tenore:* 1 ℓ., 20 p., 1 ℓ.
RISM A I, no. G 112; RISM B I, no.
1606¹¹; Vogel, no. 1581
HOUGHTON

569   GAGLIANO, MARCO DA

. . . | Il Qvinto Libro | De Madrigali | A
Cinqve Voci. | Di Marco Da Gagliano |
Nell'Accademia De Gl'Elevati | L'Affan-
nato. | Nouamente Stampato. | In Vene-
tia. | Appresso Angelo Gardano, & Fra-
telli. | MDCLVIII. [i. e. MDCVIII]

4° 1 pt.: *tenore:* 1 ℓ., 20 [i. e. 21], [1] p.
Page 21 misnumbered 20

RISM A I, no. G 114; Vogel, no. 1582
HOUGHTON

570   GAGLIANO, MARCO DA

. . . | Sesto Libro | De Madrigali | A
Cinqve Voci. | Di Marco Da Gagliano |
Maestro di Cappella del Serenissimo |
Gran Duca di Toscana. | Al Molto Illre.
Sigr. E Patron Mio Colendissimo | Il Si-
gnor Cosmo Del Sera. | Nouamente Ri-
stampati. | Stampa Del Gardano | In Ve-
netia, MDCXX. | Appresso Bartholomeo
Magni.

4° 1 pt.: *tenore:* 1 ℓ., 20 [i. e. 21], [1] p.
Page 21 misnumbered 20
RISM A I, no. G 117; RISM B I, no.
1620[17]; Vogel, no. 1584
HOUGHTON

571   GALEAZZI, FRANCESCO

Elementi | Teorico-Pratici | Di Musica |
Con Vn Saggio Sopra L'Arte | Di Suonare
Il Violino | Analizzata, | Ed A Dimostra-
bili Principj Ridotta, | Opera Utilissima |
a chiunque vuol applicare con profitto |
Alla Musica, | E Specialmente A' Princi-
pianti, | Dieettanti, [*sic*] E Professori Di
Violino | Di | Francesco Galeazzi | Tori-
nese | Compositore Di Mvsica, | E Pro-
fessore Di Violino | . . . | In Roma
MDCCXCI. | Nella Stamperia Pilucchi
Cracas | Con licenza de' Superiori.

8° *Vol. I:* 2 ℓ., 252 i.e [254] p., illus.,
music
Numbers 127, 128 repeated in paging
Incomplete: vol. II lacking
RISM B VI, 344
MUSIC LIBRARY

572   GALEOTTI, SALVATORE

Six | Sonatas | For two Violins, with a |
Thorough Bass | For the | Organ or Harp-
sichord, | Five by | Sigr. Salvatore Gal-
leotti | and one by | Sigr. Cristiano Gius-
seppe Lidardi. | London Printed for Peter
Wetcker [*sic*] at his Music Shop in Ger-
rard Street, St Ann's Soho | . . . [1762?]

2° 3 pts.: *violino primo:* 1 ℓ., 26 p.; *vio-
lino secondo:* 1 ℓ., 21 p.; *basso:* 1 ℓ., 17 p.
RISM A I, no. G 124
HOUGHTON

573   GALILEI, VINCENZO

Dialogo | Di Vincentio | Galilei Nobile
| Fiorentino | Della Mvsica Antica, | Et
Della   Moderna. | In   Fiorenza
M.D.LXXXI. | Appresso Giorgio Mare-
scoti.

2° 2 ℓ., 149, [10] p., illus., music
Hirsch I, no. 201; RISM B VI, 344; Wolf-
enbüttel, no. 1140
HOUGHTON

574   GALILEI, VINCENZO

Fronimo | Dialogo | Di Vincentio Gali-
lei | Nobile Fiorentino, | Sopra L'Arte Del
Bene Intavolare, | Et Rettamente Sonare
La Mvsica | Negli strumenti artificiali si
di corde come di fia-|to, & in Particulare
nel Liuto. | Nuouamente ristampato, Et
dall'Autore istesso arrichito, | Et ornato
di nouità di concetti, Et d'essempi. | In
Vineggia, | Appresso l'Herede di Giro-
lamo Scotto, | M.D.LXXXIIII.

2° 4 ℓ., 182 p., music
Brown, no. 1584[5]; RISM B VI, 345
HOUGHTON

GALLEOTTI, SALVATORE   *See* Galeotti,
Salvatore

575   [GALLIARD, JOHN ERNEST]

[Songs | in the | Opera | of | Calypso &
Telemachus | as they are Perform'd | at
the Queens Theatre. | Compos'd by | Mr
Galliard. | the Words by | Mr Hughes |
⟨London, 1712⟩]

2° *Score:* 1 ℓ., [1], 62 p.
Imperfect: title-page lacking; supplied
in manuscript
RISM A I, no. G 179; Walsh I, no. 426
HOUGHTON

576   GALLIARD, JOHN ERNEST

Six | English | Cantatas | After the | Ital-
ian manner | Compos'd by | Mr: Galliard.
| London Printed for J: Walsh Servant in
Ordinary to his Britanick Majesty, at ye
Harp & Hoboy in Katherine street, | near
Somerset House in ye Strand, & J: Hare
at ye Viol & Flute in Cornhill near the
Royall Exchange. [1716]

2° Score: 2 ℓ., 28 numb. ℓ.
Numbered leaves printed on one side
only
RISM A I, no. G 233; Walsh I, no. 495
HOUGHTON

577   GALLIARD, JOHN ERNEST

The Hymn | Of | Adam and Eve, | Out
of the Fifth Book of | Milton's Paradise-
Lost; | Set to Musick by | Mr. Galliard. |
[London] J. Pine inv: & Sculp: Printed for
I. Walsh [1745]

obl. *2° Score:* 1 ℓ., 30 p.
Hirsch III, no. 759; Walsh II, no. 660
HOUGHTON

578   GALLIARD, JOHN ERNEST

The | Morning Hymn, | taken from the
Fifth Book of | Milton's | Paradise Lost. |
Set to Music by the Late | John Ernest
Galliard. | The Overture, Accompany-
ments & Chorusses | added by | Benjamin
Cooke, | Organist of Westminster Abby. |
London | Printed by Welcker in Gerrard
Street St. Ann's Soho, | And may be had
at Mr. Cooke's in Dorset Court West-
minster. [ded. 1773]

2° Score: 2 ℓ., 70 p.
Cooke's autograph signature on page 1
RISM A I, no. G 231
HOUGHTON

579   GALLICULUS, JOHANN

Libellvs De | Compositione | Cantvs. |
Ioannis Gallicvli. | Vitebergae | apud
Georgium | Rhau. | Anno M.D.XLVI.

8° a⁸, B⁸, c⁴, music
Hirsch I, no. 203; RISM B VI, 346
HOUGHTON

GALLIOTTI, SALVATORE   *See* Galeotti,
Salvatore

580   GAMBLE JOHN

Ayres | And | Dialogues | (To be Sung to
the Theorbo-Lvte or | Base-Violl:) By |
John Gamble. | . . . | London, | Printed by
William Godbid, for the Author, | 1656.

2° Score: 5 ℓ., 78 [i. e. 82] p., 1 ℓ., front.
(port.)
Page 82 misnumbered 78
Day, no. 9; RISM A I, no. G 317
HOUGHTON

581   GANDO, NICOLAS

Observations | Sur Le | Traité | Histori-
que Et Critique | De Monsieur Fournier
Le Jeune, | Sur l'Origine Et les Progrès des
Caractères | de Fonte, pour l'impression
de la Musique. | Par MM. Gando, Pere Et
Fils. | A Berne, | Et se trouve à Paris |
Chez Moreau, Libraire-Imprimeur de la
Reine & de Mgr le Dauphin, | rue Ga-
lande. | M.DCC.LXVI.

4° 27, [1] p., 3 ℓ., music
Leaves 1–3 at end: Pseaume CL. | Petit
Motet, | Par M. l'Abbé Roussier. | A Paris,
| Des nouveaux Caractères de Gando &
Fils. | M.DCC.LXVI.
RISM B VI, 347
HOUGHTON

582   GARNIER, HONORÉ

Nouvelle | Methode | Pour l'accompa-
gnement du Claveçin | Et bon pour les
Personnes qui pincent de la Harpe |
Dédiée | A Monseigneur | Poncet De La
Riviere | Ancien Evêque de Troyes, Abbé
Commendataire de l'Abbaye | de Saint
Benigne de Dijon et de Charlieu. | Par Mr.
Garnier, | Cy-devant Accompagnateur du
Roy de Pologne, | Duc de Lorraine et de
Bar. | . . . | A Paris | Chez Mlle. Girard
Mde. de musique rue | de la Monoye à la
Nouveauté | Et aux Adresses Ordinaires |
Avec Privilege Du Roy. | Gravée Par Mlle
Girard [ca. 1775]

2° 1 ℓ., 27 p., music
On verso of preliminary leaf: Cata-
logue | De toutes sortes de Musique Vo-
cale et Instrumentale, que Melle. Girard,
Mde | de Musique, a fait graver . . .
MUSIC LIBRARY

583   GARTH, JOHN

Six | Sonata's | for the | Harpsichord |
Piano Forte, and Organ; | With Accom-
panyments for | two Violins, and a Vio-
loncello; | Composed by | John Garth, |

Opera Seconda. | London, | Printed for the Author, and Sold by R. Bremner, in the Strand; R. Johnson, in Cheapside; | T. Smith, in Piccadilly; and by T. Haxby, in York. | MDCCLXVIII.

2° 1 pt.: *violino primo:* 1 ℓ., 13 p.
RISM A I, no. G 434
HOUGHTON

584   GASPARINI, FRANCESCO

L'Armonico | Pratico | Al Cimbalo. | Regole, Osservazioni, ed Avvertimenti per ben | suonare il Basso, e accompagnare sopra il | Cimbalo, Spinetta, ed Organo | Di | Francesco Gasparini | Lucchese, | Fu Maestro di Coro del Pio Ospedale della Pietà | in Venezia, ed Accademico Filarmonico. | Terza Impressione. | In Venezia, MDCCXXIX. | Appresso Antonio Bortoli. | Con Licenza De' Superiori, E Privilegio.

4° 4 ℓ., 86, [2] p., illus., music
Unnumbered page [2] at end: Opere Stampate, e che si trovano presso Antonio Bortoli | . . .
Hirsch I, no. 208; RISM B VI, 350
MUSIC LIBRARY

585   GAVEAUX, PIERRE

Le Petit Matelot | Opera En Un Acte | Paroles de Pigault le Brun. | Dédié | à Mademoiselle Sophie Martell. | Par P. Gaveaux | Auteur de la Musique | Représenté pour la Premiere fois sur le Théatre de la Rue Faydeau | le 7. Janvier 1796. (vieux style.) | . . . | Gravé par la Citoyenne Le Roi. | A Paris. | A La Nouveauté chez les Freres Gaveaux, Magazin de Musique et d'Instruments, | tiennent Cordes de Naples, et font des envoies dans tous les Départments et chez Létranger, | Passage du Théâtre Faydeau. | Tous les Exemplaires seront signes Gaveaux. [ca. 1800?]

2° *Score:* 2 ℓ., 198 p.
RISM A I, no. G 669
MUSIC LIBRARY

DIE GEHARNSCHTE VENUS *See* Stieler, Kaspar von *Die geharnschte Venus*

586   GEHOT, JOSEPH

Six | Quartettos | for two | Violins, | A | Tenor and Bass, | Humbly Dedicated to | The Earl of Pembroke, | By | J: Gehot. | Opera Ima. | . . . | London Printed and Sold by Welcker No. 9 Hay Market opposite the Opera House | . . . [ca. 1775]

2° 4 pts.: *violino primo, violino secondo, viola, violoncello:* 1 ℓ., 13 p. each
RISM A I, no. G 820
MUSIC LIBRARY

587   GEISLER, BENEDICT

Concentus Novus | Suave Sonans | Pro | Ecclesia Dei | Sive | VI. Missae | â Canto, Alto, Tenore, Basso, 2 Violinis, & 2 Cornibus vel Lituis non obliga-|tis, ac Violoncello non obligato, & Organo. | Dedicatae | Reverendissimo | Perillustri Amplissimo | Domino Domino | Augustino | Ordinis Canonicorum Regularium S. Augustini In Inclyta & Celeberri-|ma Canonia vulgò Triffenstein In Franconia Ad SS: Apo-|stolos Petrum & Paulum. | Praeposito | Ac | Praelato Infulato | Domino Suo Perquam Gratioso. | Caeterisque Plurimum Reverendis Ac Religiosissimis DD: Capitularibus | Canonicis Regularibus. |

âb Authore
Opus   R. P. Benedicto Geisler   VIII.
ejusdem Canoniae Professo.

| . . . | Bambergae Sumptibus Joannis Jacobi Schnell Rvdmi & Celsissimi Principis Bambergensis | Musiei Cameralis & Aulici. 1749. | NB: in Missa 5tâ 2 Voces Tenore & Basso. non sunt obligatae.

2° 10 pts: *canto, alto:* A–F², G1 each; *tenore:* A–E², F1; *basso:* A–F²; *corno vel clarino I, corno vel clarino II:* A–C² each; *violino I:* A–I²; *violino II, violoncello:* A–H², I1 each; *organo:* [–]², A–H², I1
Title supplied from *organo* part
RISM A I, no. G 850
HOUGHTON

588   GEISLER, BENEDICT

Fluenta | Roris Nectarei | è | Petra Stillante Tertia Jam | Vice Promanantia, | Vesperas | Quatuor Musicales | à | Canto,

Alto, Tenore, Basso, | II. Violinis, | II. Cornibus ad Libitum, | Violoncello & Organo constantes | effundentia: | Quas | Ad Majorem Dei gloriam, Deiparaéque sine ma-|culâ Conceptae ac Sanctorum Apostolorum Petri & | Pauli honorem contextas ac elaboratas, | in lucem publicam edidit | R. P. Benedictus Geisler, | Ordinis Canonicorum Regularium S. Augustini in Trieffenstein | in Franconiâ Professus. | Opus III. | . . . | Augustae Vindelicorum, | Typis & Sumptibus Haeredum Joannis Jacobi Lotteri, MDCCXLII.

2° 1 pt.: *organo:* 4 ℓ., 54 p.
RISM A I, no. G 845
HOUGHTON

589   GEISLER, BENEDICT

Fons | De novo prae Gaudio saliens è Petra Stillante, Roris Nectarei Uberta-tem demonstrans | In | XVIII. Offertoria | Diffusus. | Genuino Cultûs Divini Promotori, Sincero B. V. Mariae Clienti, ac vero Sanctorum Veneratori | ad gustandum Propositus. | Reverendissimo, | Perillustri, Amplissimo | ac Perquam Gratioso Domino, | D. Gaudentio | Canonicorum Regularium | S. Augustini | In | Celeberrima Canonia | Ad S. S. Apostolos Petrum & Paulum | In | Trieffenstein | Praeposito Ac Praelato Jnfulato | Domino Suo Perquam Gratioso | Dedicatus | Ab | Auctore | R. P. Benedicto Geisler | Canonico Regulari In Trieffenstein Professo. | Opus IV. | Apud Joannem Jacobum Schnell Reverendissimi ac Celsissimi Principis & Episcopi Bambergensis & | Herbipolensis, &c &c Musicum Camaralem & Aulicum, qui Typum hunc Primo Operi VI Missarum | conformem accuravit, Exemplaria reperienda sunt. Bambergae Anno MDCCXXXXIII.

2° 1 pt: *organo:* [−]l−3, A−E²
RISM A I, no. G 846
HOUGHTON

590   GEISLER, BENEDICT

Opvs II. | Continens In Se | VI. Missas | In Qvibvs | De | Festo Solennivna, | Aliae Breviores. | à | Canto, Alto, Tenore, Basso, | II. Violinis | atqve | II. Cornibvs pro Libitv, | Violoncello | Cvm | Organo. |

In lucem publicam editum | à | R. D. Benedicto Geisler, | Canonico Regulari, ad Petram stillantem vulgò Trieffen-|stein in Franconiâ Professo. | . . . | Augustae Vindelicorum, | Typis & Sumptibus Haeredum Joannis Jacobi Lotteri, MDCCXLI.

2° 1 pt.: *canto:* 1 ℓ., 38 p.
RISM A I, no. G 844
HOUGHTON

591   GEISLER, BENEDICT

. . . | V. Missis | Brevibus | Et Duobus | Missis De Requiem | à 2. Vocibus 1. Violino & Organo necessariis, Te-|nore, Basso, Violino II. & 2. Clarinis ad libitum, | Accomodatum | ad captum incipientium | & | Musicam gustantium | Auctore | R. P. Benedicto Geisler, | Sacri & Apostolici Ordinis Canonicorum Regularium | S. Augustini Canonico & Capitulari, | in Trieffenstein in Franconiâ Professo. | Opus V. | . . . | Augustae Vindelicorum, | Typis & Sumptibus Haeredum Joannis Jacobi Lotteri, MDCCXLIV.

2° 1 pt.: *organo:* 2 ℓ., 30 p.
Imperfect: title-page torn, with loss of text
RISM A I, no. G 847
HOUGHTON

592   GEMINIANI, FRANCESCO

Geminiani's, | Celebrated Six Concertos, | as Perform'd by Mr. Cramer before their Majesties at the | Antient Concert | Tottenham Street, and at the | Hanover Square Concert, | Adapted for the | Harpsichord, Organ, or Piano-Forte. | . . . | London, Printed for G. Goulding, No. 6 James St. Covent Garden. | . . . [1798?]

2° *Score:* 1 ℓ., 31 p.
RISM A I, no. G 1464 (op. 2)
MUSIC LIBRARY

593   GEMINIANI, FRANCESCO

Concerti Grossi | Con Due Violini | Viola e Violoncello | di Concertino obligati, e Due altri Violini | e Basso di Concerto Grosso | Da | Francesco Geminiani |

Opera Terza. | . . . | London. Printed for I. Walsh, in Catherine Street, in the Strand. [ca. 1740?]

2° 7 pts.: *violino primo concertino:* 1 *ℓ.*, 19 p.; *violino secondo del concertino:* 1 *ℓ.*, 15 p.; *alto viola, violoncello del concertino:* 1 *ℓ.*, 13 p. each; *violino primo repo.:* 1 *ℓ.*, 15 p.; *violino secondo, basso ripieno:* 1 *ℓ.*, 13 p. each
　Hirsch III, no. 215; RISM A I, no. G 1467; Walsh II, no. 697?
MUSIC LIBRARY

594 GEMINIANI, FRANCESCO

Six | Concertos, | Composed By | F. Geminiani. | Opera Terza. | The Second Edition, | Revised, Corrected, and Enlarged, by the Author; | And now first Published in Score. | London: | Printed for the Author, by John Johnson, in Cheapside. | . . . [175–?]

2° Score: 1 *ℓ.*, 47 p.
RISM A I, no. G 1474
HOUGHTON

595 GEMINIANI, FRANCESCO

Concerti Grossi | a due Violini, due Viole e Violoncello obligati | con due altri Violini, e Basso di Ripieno | Composti e dedicati | All' Altezza Reale | Di Federico Prencipe Di Vallia | Da | Francesco Geminiani | Londra MDCCXLIII, | a spese dell' Autore | Questi Concerti sono composti dalle Sonate a Violino e Basso | dell Opera IV.

2° 8 pts.: *violino primo concertino:* 1 *ℓ.*, 20 p., front.; *violino secondo concertino:* 14 p.; *violino primo ripieno:* 12 p.; *violino secondo ripieno:* 11 p.; *alto viola prima:* 12 p.; *alto viola 2da.:* 10 p.; *violoncello:* 15 p.; *basso ripieno:* 10 p.
　Hirsch III, no. 216; RISM A I, no. G 1477
HOUGHTON

596 GERBER, ERNST LUDWIG

Historisch-Biographisches | Lexicon | der | Tonkünstler, | welches | Nachrichten | von dem | Leben und Werken | musikalischer Schriftsteller, | berühmter Componisten, | Sänger, Meister auf In-

strumenten, | Dilettanten, | Orgel- und Instrumentenmacher, | enthält; | zusammengetragen | von | Ernst Ludwig Gerber, | Fürstlich Schwarzburg-Sondershausischen Kammermusikus und Hof-Organisten | zu Sonderhausen. | . . . | Leipzig, | verlegts Johann Gottlob Immanuel Breitkopf, | 1790.[–1792.]

8° 2 vols.: *vol. I:* XIV, [2] p., 992 cols.; *vol. II:* 1 *ℓ.*, 860 cols., XVI, 86 p.
Two columns to the page
Hirsch I, Historischer Anhang, no. 26; RISM B VI, 357–358
MUSIC LIBRARY

597 GERBERT, MARTIN, FREIHERR VON HORNAU

De | Cantv | Et | Mvsica Sacra | A | Prima Ecclesiae Aetate | Vsqve Ad | Praesens Tempvs. | Avctore | Martino Gerberto | Monasterii Et Congr. S. Blasii In Silva Nigra Abbate | S. Q. R. I. P. | . . . | Svperiorvm Permissv. | [St. Blasien] Typis San-Blasianis MDCCLXXIV.

4° 2 vols.: *vol. I:* 10 *ℓ.*, 590 p., front., illus., 6 pl., music; *vol. II:* 6 *ℓ.*, 409, [29], 112 p., illus., 37 pl., music
Pages 1–112, third sequence, in vol. II: Missa In Coena Domini.
Hirsch I, no. 217; RISM B VI, 358; Wolfenbüttel, no. 1147
MUSIC LIBRARY

598

The | German Erata, | A | Celebrated Collection | Of | Airs. | By, | Haydn, Mozart, &c. | London: | Printed for Harrison, Cluse, & Co. No. 78, Fleet Street. [1799?]

8° Score: 27 p. (*The Piano-Forte Magazine,* vol. IX, no. 3)
Plate nos. 135–136
MUSIC LIBRARY

599 GESUALDO, CARLO, PRINCIPE DI VENOSA

. . . | Madrigali | Del Venosa | A Cinqve Voci. | Libro Primo | Tertia Impressione. | Stampa Del Gardano. | In Venetia MDCXVI. | Appresso Bartholomeo Magni.

4° 1 pt.: *tenore:* 20 p.
RISM A I, no. G 1724; Vogel, no. 1156
HOUGHTON

600   GESUALDO, CARLO,
           PRINCIPE DI VENOSA

. . . | Madrigali | Del Venosa | A Cin-
que Voci. | Libro Secondo. | Terza Im-
pressione. | Stampa Del Gardano | In Ve-
netia MDCXVII. | Appresso Bartholomeo
Magni.

4° 1 pt.: *tenore:* 20 p.
RISM A I, no. G 1729; Vogel, no. 1161
HOUGHTON

601   GESUALDO, CARLO,
           PRINCIPE DI VENOSA

. . . | Madrigali | A Cinqve | Voci. | Del
Venosa | Libro Terzo. | Nouamente Ri-
stampato. | Stampa Del Gardano | In Ve-
netia MDCXIX. | Appresso Bartholomeo
Magni.

4° 1 pt.: *tenore:* 18 [i. e. 20] p.
Numbers 15, 16 repeated in paging
RISM A I, no. G 1734; Vogel, no. 1167
HOUGHTON

602   GESUALDO, CARLO,
           PRINCIPE DI VENOSA

. . . | Madrigali | A Cinqve | Voci. | Del
Venosa. | Libro Qvarto. | Nouamente Ri-
stampato. | In Venetia. | Appresso Angelo
Gardano, & Fratelli. | MDCXI.

4° 1 pt.: *tenore:* 1 ℓ., 21, [1] p.
RISM A I, no. G 1737; Vogel, no. 1170
HOUGHTON

603   GESUALDO, CARLO,
           PRINCIPE DI VENOSA

. . . | Madrigali | A Cinqve Voci. | Libro
Qvinto. | Del Prencipe Di Venosa. | Dedi-
cati | Al Molto Illvstre Signor | Alfonso
Strozzi. | Con Privilegio. | Stampa del
Gardano. In Venetia MDCXIV.

4° 1 pt.: *tenore:* 23, [1] p.
Colophon: Stampa Del Gardano. | In
Venetia. MDCXIV. | Aere Bartholom[a]ei
Magni.
RISM A I, no. G 1740; Vogel, no. 1173
HOUGHTON

604   GESUALDO, CARLO,
           PRINCIPE DI VENOSA

Del | Prencipe | Di Venosa | Madrigali. |
A Cinque voci. | Libro Sesto | Noua-
mente Stampati. | . . . | Stampa Del Gar-
dano. | In Venetia MDCXVI. | Appresso
Bartholomeo Magni.

4° 1 pt.: *tenore:* 22 [i. e. 24] p.
Page 24 misnumbered 22
RISM A I, no. G 1742; Vogel, no. 1176
HOUGHTON

605   GIARDINI, FELICE

Six | Trios | for a | Violin Tenor | and |
Violoncello | Composed & Dedicated to |
Henry Dashwood Esqr. | by | Felice Giar-
dini | Opera XVII. . . . | London Printed
by Welcker in Gerrard Street St. Ann's
Soho. | . . . [1773?]

2° 3 pts.: *violino, viola, violoncello:* 1
ℓ., 13 p. each
RISM A I, no. G 1947
MUSIC LIBRARY

606   GIARDINI, FELICE

Six | Trios | for the | Guittar, Violin, |
and | Piano Forte; | or | Harp, Violin and
Violoncello, | By | F. Giardini. | humbly
Dedicated | To the Right Honourable the
| Countess Spencer. | Opera 18. . . . |
London | Printed for Wm. Napier, Corner
of Lancaster Court, Strand. [ca. 1775]

2° 3 pts.: *guitar or harp, violino, basso:*
13 p. each
Plate no. 50
RISM A I, no. G 1955
MUSIC LIBRARY

607   GIBBONS, ORLANDO

. . . | The | First Set | Of | Madrigals |
And Mottets | of 5. Parts: apt for | Viols
and Voyces. | Newly Composed | by Or-
lando Gibbons, Batche-|ler of Musicke,
and Organist of | his Maiesties Honour-
able Chappell | in Ordinarie. | London: |
Printed by Thomas Snodham, | the As-
signe of W. Barley. | 1612.

4° 1 pt.: *qvintvs,* A–C⁴
RISM A I, no. G 1994
HOUGHTON

608 GIORDANI, TOMMASO

Six | Concerto's | for the | Piano-Forte, or Harpsichord | Composed by | Sigr. Giordani. | Op: XIV. | Humbly dedicated | to the Honble. | Miss Bertie. | . . . | London; Printed for Longman and Broderip No. 26, Cheapside, | . . . [1776?]

2° 4 pts.: *piano-forte:* III, 2-45 p.; *violino primo, violino secondo:* 1 ℓ., 21 p. each; *violoncello:* 1 ℓ., 14 p.
Pages II-III of *piano-forte* part: Musical Publications | Printed and Sold by Longman & Broderip . . .
RISM A I, no. G 2256
MUSIC LIBRARY

609 GIORDANI, TOMMASO

Overture | To The | Elopement. | For The | Piano Forte. | Composed By, | Giordani. | London: | Printed for Harrison, Cluse, & Co. No. 78, Fleet Street. [1799?]

8° *Score:* 11 p. (*The Piano-Forte Magazine,* vol. VII, no. 8)
Plate no. 105
RISM A I, no. G 2104
MUSIC LIBRARY

610 GIORDANI, TOMMASO

Six | Sonatas, | For The | Piano Forte; | Composed By, | Sig. Giordani. | London: | Printed for Harrison, Cluse, & Co. No. 78, Fleet Street. [1798?]

8° *Score:* 41 p. (*The Piano-Forte Magazine,* vol. V, no. 5)
Plate nos. 74–75
RISM A I, no. G 2296 (op. 10)
MUSIC LIBRARY

611 GIORDANI, TOMMASO

Six | Sonatas, | for the | Piano Forte, | Composed By, | Sigr. Giordani. | Op. 24. | London: | Printed for Harrison, Cluse, & Co. No. 78, Fleet Street. [1798?]

8° *Score:* 47 p. (*The Piano-Forte Magazine,* vol. V, no. 2)
Plate nos. 68–69
RISM A I, no. G 2298
MUSIC LIBRARY

612 GIORDANI, TOMMASO

Six | Favourite Sonatas | For The | Piano Forte. | Composed By | Sigr. Giordani. | Opera 27. | London: | Printed for Harrison, Cluse, & Co. No. 78, Fleet Street. [1799?]

8° *Score:* 57 p. (*The Piano-Forte Magazine,* vol. VIII, no. 2)
Plate nos. 116–118
RISM A I, no. G 2303
MUSIC LIBRARY

613 GIOVANELLI, PIETRO, COMP.

. . . | Novi Thesavri | Mvsici | Liber Primvs | Qvo Selectissime | Planeq; nou[a]e, nec vnquam in lucē [a]edit[a]e | cantiones sacr[a]e (quas vulgo moteta vo-|cāt) cōtinētur octo, septem, sex, quinq; | ac quatuor vocum, a prestantissimis ac | huius aetatis, precipuis Symphoniacis | composit[a]e, qu[a]e in sacra Ecclesia catho-|lica, sūmis solemnibusq; festiui-tatibus, | canuntur, ad omnis generis in-strumēta | musica, accommodat[a]e: Petri Ioannelli | Bergomensis de Gan-dino, summo | studio ac labore collectae, eiusq; | expensis impressae. | Venetijs Apud Antoniū Gardanū. 1568 | Cvm Grat: Et Privil: | Sac: Ro: Cae: Ma: Et Ill: Senatus Venet:

4° 6 pts.: *cantvs:* [B]⁴, C–Y⁴ (Y4 blank); *altvs, tenor, bassvs:* [A]⁴, B–Y⁴ (Y4 blank) each; *qvintvs:* [A]⁴, B–L⁴, M⁸, N–S⁴; *sextvs:* [A]⁴, B–L⁴; illus. (incl. port.) in all part-books except *cantvs*
Imperfect: gathering C lacking in *qvintvs* part-book
RISM B I, no. 1568²
HOUGHTON

614 GIOVANELLI, PIETRO, COMP.

. . . | Novi Atqve | Catholici The-|savri Mvsici. | Liber Secvndvs | Qvo Selectis-sime | atq; planè nouae, neq; vnquā antea in lucē | editae cātiones sacrae, quas vulgò moteta | vocant, octo, sex quinque, quatuor vocù | compositae à prestantis-simis huius aetatis | Symphoniacis, con-tinentur: quae in sa-|cris catholicorū templis diebus Domi-|nicis canuntur, atq; & ad quae vis instru-|menta musica accommodatae sunt: Petri | Ioānelli de

Gandino Bergomēsis summo | studio ac labore collectae, eiusq; expensis | impressae. | Venetijs Apud Antonium Gardanum. | 1568

4° 6 pts.: *cantvs, altvs, tenor, bassvs:* Z⁴, AA–GG⁴ each; *quintvs:* T–Z⁴, AA⁴, BB1–2; *sextvs:* M–P⁴, Ql
Imperfect: leaf DD4 lacking in *altvs* part-book; gathering GG lacking in *tenor* part-book
RISM B I, no. 1568³
HOUGHTON

615 GIOVANELLI, PIETRO, COMP.

. . . | Novi Atqve | Catholici The-|savri Mvsici. | Liber Tertivs | Qvo Selectissime | planeq; nouae, nec vnquā antea in lucem | editae cātiones sacrae, quas vulgo moteta | vocant, octo, septē, sex, quinque, quatuor | vocum compositae à prestantissimis no-|stri temporis Symphoniacis, continen-|tur: quae in sacris catholicorum templis | festis sanctorum diebus cantantur, atq; | & ad quae vis instrumenta musica accom-|modatae sunt: Petri Ioānelli de Gandino | Bergomēsis summo studio ac labore | collectae, eiusq: expēsis impressae. | Venetijs Apud Antonium Gardanum. | 1568

4° 6 pts.: *cantvs, altvs, tenor, bassvs:* HH–TT⁴ each; *qvintvs:* BB3–4, CC–KK⁴, LL1–2; *sextvs:* Q2–4, R–S⁴
Qvintvs and *sextvs* part-books have different title-pages: . . . | Tertivs | De Sanctis | Svavissimis Harmoniis | ornatus, tantūdē vocibus & à modernis | Symphonistis, recenteriam Musi-|calibus flosculis decoratus & | de nouo perpolitus. | . . .
RISM B I, no. 1568⁴
HOUGHTON

616 GIOVANELLI, PIETRO, COMP.

. . . | Novi Atqve | Catholici The-|savri Mvsici. | Liber Qvartvs | Qvo Selectissime | atq; planè nouae, neq; vnquā antea in luce | editae moteta, quae in sacris catholicorū | templis cōmunia vocare solent, De San-|ctissima virgine Maria, Apostolis, Marti-|ribus, confessoribus & virginibus, tum e-|tiā laudes aliquot dei parae virginis, quas | Salue regina appel-

lant, octo, sex, quinq; | quatuor vocū continentur; compositae à | prestantissimis nostri temporis musicis, | & ad omnis generis instrumenta musica | accommodata; summo studio atq; labore | Petri Ioannelli de Gandino Bergomensis | collectae, eiusq; expensis impressae. | Venetijs Apud Antonium Gardanū. 1568

4° 6 pts.: *cantvs, altvs, tenor, bassvs:* VV–ZZ⁴, AAA–FFF⁴ each; *qvintvs:* LL3–4, MM–TT⁴, VV1; *sextvs:* T–Y⁴, Z1–3
RISM B I, no. 1568⁵
HOUGHTON

617 GIOVANELLI, PIETRO, COMP.

. . . | Liber Qvintvs | & vltimus, quo vari[a]e, tum sacr[a]e, tū alijs | etiā locis honestissimis competentes ac | congruis, plane nou[a]e, neq; vnquā ātea, a | quopiā in luce [a]edit[a]e harmoni[a]e cōprehē-|duntur, veluti selectissima qu[a]edā, in D. | Ferdinandi III:, (felicissima memoria) | C[a]esaris obitū Epitaphia: necnō Inuictissi|mi Romanorū Imperatoris Maximiliani | II: &c. Serenissimorumq; Principum, | Ferdinādi & Caroli Fratrū, Archid: Aust: | &c. ac quorundam etiam aliorum Illu-|strissimorū Principū atq;, heroū gene-|rosorū encomia: octo, six, quinq; quatu-|or vocū, a prestantissimis nostri seculi | musicis, composit[a]e, & ad omnis generis | instrumenta musica accōmodata; summo | studio atq; labore Petri Ioānelli de | Gandino Bergomensis, collec-|tae, eiusq; expēsis impressae. | Venetijs Apud Antoniū Gardanū. 1568

4° 6 pts.: *cantvs, altvs, tenor, bassvs:* GGG–OOO⁴ each; *qvintvs:* VV2–4, XX–ZZ⁴, AAA–FFF⁴; *sextvs:* Z4, AA–II⁴; illus. (incl. port.) in each part-book
RISM B I, no. 1568⁶
HOUGHTON

GIROWETZ, ADALBERT *See* Gyrowetz, Adalbert

618 GIULIANI, FRANCESCO

Six | Sonatas, | For The | Piano Forte, | Composed By | F. Giuliani. | Op. 6. | London: | Printed for Harrison, Cluse, & Co. No. 78, Fleet Street. [1798?]

8° *Score:* 64 p. (*The Piano-Forte Maga-zine,* vol. V, no. 4)
Plate nos. 71–73
RISM A I, no. G 2570
MUSIC LIBRARY

GLANVILLE, BARTHOLOMEW DE *See* Bartholomaeus Anglicus

619   GLAREANUS, HENRICUS

Glareani | Δωδεκαχορδον | . . . | Basi-leae [1547]

2° 10 ℓ., 470, [6] p. illus., music
Colophon: Basileae Per Henrichvm Petri | Mense Septembris Anno Post | Vir-ginis Partvm. | M.D.XLVII.
   Davidsson II, no. 39; Hirsch I, no. 226; RISM B VI, 366
HOUGHTON

620   GLUCK, CHRISTOPH WILLIBALD, RITTER VON

Alceste. | Tragedia. | Messa In Musica | Dal | Signore Cavagliere Cristoforo Gluck. | Dedicata | A Sua | Altezza Reale, | L'Arciduca | Pietro Leopoldo | Gran-Duca | Di | Toscana, Etc. Etc. Etc. | In Vienna, | Nella Stamparia Aulica Di | Giovanni Tomaso De Trattnern. | MDCCLXIX.

2° *Score:* 6 ℓ., 233 p.
Hirsch II, no. 261; HopkinsonG, no. 37A; RISM A I, no. G 2661
MUSIC LIBRARY

621   GOODWIN, WILLIAM

A Favorite | Lesson | for the | Harpsi-chord | or | Piano Forte | Composed By | William Goodwin | No. II [i.e. III] | . . . | London Printed for C. and S. Thompson No. 75 St. Paul's Church Yard [ca. 1775]

obl. 2° *Score:* 1 ℓ., 5 p.
RISM A I, no. G 3022
MUSIC LIBRARY

622   [GOSSEC, FRANÇOIS JOSEPH]

Le | Tonnelier | Opera Comique | En un Acte | Mis en Musique Par | Messieurs *** | Represente pour la premiere fois sur le Théatre des Comé-|diens Italiens Or-dinaires du Roy, le 16 Mars 1765. | . . . | Gravé par Gerardin | A Paris | Ches M. De la Chevardiere, Rue du Roule á la Croix d'Or. | Et aux Adresses ordinaires de Mu-sique. | Avec Privilege Du Roi. | Imprimé par Bern[ard] [ca. 1765]

2° *Score:* 1 ℓ., 99 p.
An arrangement by Gossec of an ear-lier setting by Nicolas Médard Audinot (see Schnapper II, 1015)
Hirsch II, no. 294; RISM A I, no. G 3072
MUSIC LIBRARY

623   [GOUDAR, SARA, SUPPOSED AUTHOR]

De | Venise | Rémarques | Sur | La Mu-sique & La Danse | Ou | Lettres De Mr. G . . . | À Milord Pembroke. | À Venise | Chez Charles Palese Imprimeur | MDCCLXXIII.

12° 3 ℓ., 3–136 p.
Two letters on opera and ballet in Italy Also attributed to Ange Goudar (see BN LXII, 803)
RISM, B VI, 372
HOUGHTON

624   GOUY, JACQUES DE

Airs | A Qvatre Parties, | Sur la Paraphrase des Pseaumes | De | Messire Antoine Godeav, | Evesqve De Grasse. | Composez par Iacqves De Goÿy, Cha-noine en l'Eglise | Cathedrale d'Ambrun, & diuisez en trois parties. | Premiere Par-tie. | . . . | A Paris, | Par Robert Ballard, seul Imprimeur du Roy | pour la Musi-que. | Et se vendent chez l'Autheur ruë de l'Arbre-sec, vis à vis | la Ville de Rome, & le grand Henry. | M.DCL. | Auec Priui-lege de sa Majesté.

obl. 8° 1 pt.: *dessvs:* 16 ℓ., 50 numb. ℓ., 6 ℓ., front.
Hirsch III, no. 773; RISM A I, no. G 3218
HOUGHTON

625   GOW, NIEL

A | Collection | of | Strathspey Reels | With a Bass | for the | Violoncello or

Harpsichord | Most humbly Dedicated to her Grace | The Dutchess of Athole | By Niel Gow at Dunkeld | Edinburgh Printed for the Author; to be had of N: Stewart | Corrie & Sutherland & R: Bremner Edinr. W: Napier | London & J: Aird Glasgow. & at the other Music | Shops in Town & Country | Butterworth Script. Johnson Sculpt. [ca. 1785]

> 2° *Score:* 2 ℓ., 36 p.
> RISM A I, no. G 3245?
> HOUGHTON

626   GRAAF, CHRISTIAN ERNST

Proeve | Over De | Natuur Der Harmonie | In De | Generaal Bas, | Benevens Een | Onderricht | Eener Korte En Regelmaatige | Becyffering | Door | C. E. Graaf, | Kapel-Meester van zyn Doorl: Hoogheid, den | Heere Prinse van Orange en Nassau, | enz. enz. enz. | In 'sGraavenhaage, | By Bernardus Wittelaer, Boek-|verkooper agter de Groote Kerk. | 1782.

> 8° 46 p., 11 pl. (incl. music)
> RISM B VI, 373
> MUSIC LIBRARY

627   GRABU, LEWIS

Albion and Albanius: | An | Opera. | Or, | Representation in Musick. | Set by Lewis Grabu, Esquire; | Master of His late Majesty's Musick. | Licensed, Ro. L'Estrange. | March 15. 168⅘. | London, | Printed for the Author, and are to be sold at the Door of the Royal Theater; and by | William Nott, Bookseller in the Pall-Mall; 1687.

> 2° *Score:* 2 ℓ., 320 p.
> RISM A I, no. G 3260
> HOUGHTON

GRAF, CHRISTIAN ERNST   *See* Graaf, Christian Ernst

628   GRAF, FRIEDRICH HARTMANN

Six | Grand | Quartettos | for | Two Violins a Tenor and | Violoncello Obligato | Compos'd by | Federico Graff | Chamber Musician to His S. H. the | Elector and Arch Bishop of | Treves | London | Printed

for & Sold by J. Betz No. 2 Rupert street | . . . [ca. 1780]

> 2° 4 pts.: *violino primo, violino secondo, viola, violoncello:* 1 ℓ., 13 p. each
> RISM A I, no. G 3361
> MUSIC LIBRARY

629   GRAUN, KARL HEINRICH,
         SUPPOSED COMPOSER

The | Battle Of Rosbach. | A Favourite | Sonata, | For The | Piano Forte, | Composed By | Sigr. Gzaun. [*sic*] | London, | Printed for Harrison & Co. No. 18 Paternoster Row. [1798?]

> 8° *Score:* 13 p. (*The Piano-Forte Magazine,* vol. III, no. 5)
> RISM A I, no. G 3573
> MUSIC LIBRARY

630   GRAUN, KARL HEINRICH

Te Deum | Laudamus, | Posto | In Musica | Dal | Sign. Carlo Enrico Graun, | Maestro Di Capella Di S. M. Il Ré Di Prussia. | In Lipsia | Presso, Giov. Gottl. Imman. Breitkopf. | 1757.

> 2° *Score:* 1 ℓ., 134 p., 1 ℓ.
> Hirsch IV, no. 749; RISM A I, no. G 3550
> MUSIC LIBRARY

631   GRAUN, KARL HEINRICH

Der | Tod Jesu, | eine Cantate, | in die Musik gesetzt | von | Herrn Carl Heinrich Graun, | Kŏnigl. Preuss. Capellmeister. | Leipzig, | gedruckt und verlegt von Johann Gottlob Immanuel Breitkopf. | 1760.

> 2° *Score:* 1 ℓ., 116 p.
> Hirsch IV, no. 750; RISM A I, no. G 3553
> HOUGHTON

632   GRAUN, KARL HEINRICH

Herrn | Carl Heinrich Grauns | ehemal. Kŏnigl. Preuss. Kapellmeist. | Passions-Cantate: | Der | Tod Jesu, | in einem Clavierauszuge | herausgegeben | von | Johann Adam Hiller | Herzogl. Curlăndischen Kapellmeister. | Breslau, | bey Gottlieb Lŏwe, 1785.

obl. 2° *Vocal score:* 3 ℓ., 74 p.
RISM A I, no. G 3554
MUSIC LIBRARY

GREBUS, LOUIS *See* Grabu, Lewis

633 GREENE, MAURICE

Spensers | Amoretti | Set | To Music |
By | Dr. Greene | [London] Printed for
Jno. Walsh in Catherine Street in the
Strand. [1739]

   obl. 2° *Score:* 2 ℓ., 47, [1] p.
Hirsch III, no. 782; RISM A I, no. G
3750; Walsh II, no. 743
MUSIC LIBRARY

634 GREENE, MAURICE

Forty | Select Anthems | In | Score, |
Composed | For 1, 2, 3, 4, 5, 6, 7, and 8
Voices. | By [Maurice Greene,] | Organist
and Composer to His Majesty's Chapels
Royal, &c. | . . . | London: | Printed for,
and Sold by [j. Walsh], Musick-printer
and Instrument-maker to His | Majesty,
in [Catherine]-street in the [Strand] |
[174–]

   2° *Score:* 2 vols.: *vol. I:* 1 ℓ., 138 p.; *vol.
II:* 2 ℓ., 155 p.
Imperfect: title-page and pages 1, 2,
lacking in vol. I; composer's name and
publisher's name and address erased
from title-page in vol. II; pages 107, 108
lacking, 153, 154, 155 torn in vol. II; title
supplied from vol. II
RISM A I, no. G 3736; Walsh II, no.
729?
MUSIC LIBRARY

635 GREENE, MAURICE

A | Cantata | And | Four English Songs |
Set to Musick by | Dr. Greene. | [Book I]
London. Printed for I. Walsh, in the
Strand. | . . . [1745]

   2° *Score:* 1 ℓ., 12 p.
The privilege is on page [1]; blank page
between pages 7 and 8
RISM A I, no. G 3747; Walsh II, no.
735
HOUGHTON (2 copies)

—another copy
The privilege is imposed on the verso
of the title-page; page 8 ("Anacreon's
Dream") is imposed between the privi-
lege page and page 2
HOUGHTON

636 GREENE, MAURICE

A | Cantata | And | Four English Songs |
Set to Musick by | Dr. Greene. | [Book
2d.] | London. Printed for I. Walsh, in
Catharine Street in the Strand. |
. . . [1746?]

   2° *Score:* 1 ℓ., 13 p.
"Book 2d." added to title-page in man-
uscript
RISM A I, no. G 3747; Walsh II, no.
735
HOUGHTON

637 GRESSET, JEAN BAPTISTE LOUIS

Discours | Sur | L'Harmonie. [A
Londres, | Chez Edouard Kelmarneck. |
M.DCC.LVIII.]

   12° In his *Oeuvres,* vol. II, p. [5]–74
Caption title; imprint supplied from
title-page
WIDENER

638 GRESSET, JEAN BAPTISTE LOUIS

Discours | Sur | L'Harmonie. [A
Londres, | Chez Edouard Kelmarneck. |
M.DCC.LXV.]

   12° In his *Oeuvres,* vol. II, p. [3]–64
Caption title; imprint supplied from
title-page
WIDENER

639 GRESSET, JEAN BAPTISTE LOUIS

Discours | Sur | L'Harmonie. [A Rouen,
| Chez J. Racine, Libraire, rue Ganterie. |
M.DCC.LXXXVIII. | Avec Permission.]

   12° In his *Oeuvres,* vol. II, p. 1–42
Caption title; imprint supplied from
title-page
WIDENER

640   GRÉTRY, ANDRÉ ERNEST
        MODESTE

Colinette A La Cour | Ou La | Double
Epreuve | Comédie Lyrique | en Trois
Actes | Representée pour la premiere fois
par l'Académie Royale de Musique | le
Mardy premier Janvier 1782. | Dediée À
Monsieur Le Comte | De Vaudreuil |
Maréchal des Camps et Armées du Roy,
Inspecteur Général | de ses Troupes;
Grand Fauconnier de France. | Mise En
Musique Par M. Gretry | Conseiller in-
time de S. A. S. Mgneur. le Prince de
Liege, Membre de l'Académie des | Phil-
armoniques, de Bologne en Italie, et as-
socié honoraire de la Socté. d'emulation
de Liege. | Oeuvre XIX. . . . | Gravée par
le Sr. Huguet Musicien de la Comédie
Italienne. | A Paris, Chez Mr. Houbaut,
rue Mauconseil, près la Comédie Ita-
lienne. | et aux adresses ordinaires. | A
Lyon Chez Mr. Castaud place de la
Comédie. | Avec Privilége Du Roy | Im-
primée par Basset [ca. 1782]

2° *Score:* 1 ℓ., 244 p.
Preliminary leaf 1ᵛ: Catalogue | De la
Musique de M. Gretry
Hirsch II, no. 321; RISM A I, no. G
4061
HOUGHTON

641   GRÉTRY, ANDRÉ ERNEST
        MODESTE

Oeuvre VIIe. | Zemire | Et Azor |
Comédie-Ballet | En Vers et en Quatre
Actes | Représentée devant sa Majesté à
Fontainebleau | le 9. novembre 1771, et à
la Comédie Italienne le | 16. Decembre
1771. | Par | M. Gretry | Pensionnaire du
Roi | Et de l'Académie des Philarmoni-
ques de Boulogne. | . . . | Gravée par J.
Dezauche. | A Paris Chés Houbaut rue
Mauconseil prés la Comedie Italienne, et
| chés qui l'on trouvera les Parties
gravées separement. | Imprimé par Basset
[ca. 1772]

2° *Score:* 1 ℓ., 216 p.
Preliminary leaf 1ᵛ: Catalogue | De la
Musique de M. Gretry
Hirsch II, no. 366; RISM A I, no. G
4497
HOUGHTON

642   [GRIMALDI, FRANCESCO
        ANTONIO]

Lettera | Sopra | La Musica | All'Eccel-
lentissimo Signore | Agostino Lomellini |
Già Doge Della Serenissima Repubblica |
Di Genova. [Naples, 1766]

8° LXIV p.
Colophon: Di Napoli il dì 17. di Feb-
braio del 1766.
RISM B VI, 379
MUSIC LIBRARY

GROBSTIMME, HEINRICH   *See* Baryphonus, Heinrich

643   GUÉNIN, MARIE ALEXANDRE

Trois | Simphonies | A Premier et Se-
cond Dessus, Alto, | Basse, deux Haut-
bois et deux Cors, | Composées Par | M.
A. Guenin | Oeuvre VI. | Deuxieme Livre
de Simphonies | On peut aussi les
Exécuter à Quatre Parties. | . . . | Gravées
par Richomme | A Paris | Chez l'Auteur
Rue St. Louis St. Honoré, No. 8. [1788?]

2° 8 pts.: *oboe primo, oboe secondo,
corno Imo., corno 2do.:* 7 p. each; *violino
primo:* 1 ℓ., 13 p.; *violino secondo, viola
Ima. et 2a.:* 12 p. each; *basso:* 10 p.
Plate no. 8
Guénin's autograph signature on page
[1] in *violino primo* part
Page [1] in *violino primo* part: Cata-
logue, | Des Ouvrages du Sr. Guenin, et
autres qui se vendent chez lui . . .
RISM A I, no. G 4833
HOUGHTON

644   GUGLIELMI, PIETRO
        ALESSANDRO

The | Four Favourite | Italian Over-
tures, | Of | Signior Gulielmi. | Viz. |

Il Viaggiotore   Il Carnovale de Venezia
Orlando   Il Desertore

| London. | Printed for Harrison & Co.
No. 18 Paternoster Row. [1797?]

8° *Score:* 25 p. (*The Piano-Forte Maga-
zine,* vol. II, no. 4)
For keyboard instrument
RISM A I, no. G 4987
MUSIC LIBRARY

Gui de Chabanon, Michel Paul *See* Chabanon, Michel Paul Gui de

645 [Guilford, Francis North, 1st Baron]

A | Philosophical | Essay | Of | Musick | Directed to a | Friend. | . . . | London, | Printed for John Martyn, Printer to the Royal | Society; at the Bell in Saint Paul's | Church-Yard, 1677.

4° 35 p., illus., 2 pl. (1 fold., incl. music)

RISM B VI, 621

HOUGHTON

646 Guillaume, Simon

Almanach Dansant | Ou | Positions Et Attitudes De | L'Allemande | Avec un Discours Préliminaire sur l'Origine | et l'Utilité de la Danse | Dédie Au Beau Sexe | Par Guillaume Maitre de Danse | Pour l'Année 1770. | . . . | A Paris | Chez | l'Auteur Ruë des Arcis maison | du Commissaire | Valade Libraire rue St. Jacques | vis a vis celle de la Parcheminerie | Et Chez Dufour Rue de la Vieille Draperie [1770]

8° 1 *ℓ.*, 16 p., 12 *ℓ*. of pl., [17]–31, [1] p., 6 *ℓ*. of pl. (music), 1 *ℓ*.

Pages [17]–31 and leaves 1–6 (2d sequence): Recueil | De Contredanses | Et Menuets | Nouveaux Et Choisis, | De la composition des Sieurs Sauton, Lahante, | Et autres, avec la Description des Figures, | Et | L'Explication Intelligible Des Mouvements | usités dans toutes les Contredanses, par le sieur | Guillaume, Maître de Danse. | A Paris, | Chez {Dufour, Libraire, rue de la Vieille Draperie. | Le Sieur Guillaume, Maître de Danse, rue des Arcis | maison du Commissaire. | M.DCC.LX. | Avec Approbation.

RISM A I, no. G 5065; RISM B VI, 386 (variant)

HOUGHTON

647 Gumpeltzhaimer, Adam

Compendium | Musicae | Latino-Germanicum | Studio & opera | Adami Gumpelzhaimeri | Trospergy, Boy. | Nunc Editione hac decima Tertia non | nusquam correctum & | auctum | Permissu Su-

periorum. | Augustae | Apud Iacobum Enderlin Bibliopolam | Anno MDCLXXXI.

4° 78 numb. *ℓ*., [4] p., illus. (incl. port.), music

A later edition of Brown, no. 1595₄

RISM B VI, 388

HOUGHTON

648 Gyrowetz, Adalbert

Six | Quatuors | Concertants | Pour deux Violons, Alto et Basse | Composés | Par | Adalberto Gyrowetz | 4e. Livre de Quatuors | [Iere] Partie . . . | A Paris Chez Jmbault Rue Honoré au Mont d'Or No. 627 | et 200 de la Section. [ca. 1795]

2° 4 pts.: *violino primo:* 1 *ℓ*., 13 p.; *violino secondo:* 13 p.; *viola:* 11 p.; *violoncello:* 12 p.

Plate no. 494

Contents: Quartets 1–3

MUSIC LIBRARY

649 Gyrowetz, Adalbert

Trois | Quatuors | Pour | Deux Violons Alto et Basse, | Composée Par | A. Girowetz. | Oeuvre 16 . . . | A Paris | Chéz Sieber, Musicien rue honore entre celle des Vieilles | Etuve et D'orleans. No. 85. [1796]

2° 4 pts.: *violino primo:* 1 *ℓ*., 16 p.; *violino secondo:* 15 p.; *viola:* 12 p.; *violoncello:* 13 p.

Plate no. 1422

Contents: Quartets 4–6

MUSIC LIBRARY

650 Gyrowetz, Adalbert

A Sonata | for the | Piano Forte | Or | Harpsichord | With Accompanyments for a | Violin and Violoncello | Compos'd by | Adalbert Gyrowetz. | . . . | London | Printed by Longman. Clementi & Co. 26 Cheapside. | Manufacturers of Musical Instruments and Music Sellers to | Their Majesties | His Royal Highness the Prince of Wales and all the Royal Family [ca. 1800]

2° 1 pt.: *piano forte or harpsichord:* 11, III [i. e. I] p.

Page III [i. e. I]: Musical Publications | Printed and sold by Longman, Clementi & Co. | . . .

MUSIC LIBRARY

H

651   [HÄNDEL, GEORG FRIEDRICH]

The | favourite | Songs | in the | Opera | call'd | Acis | and | Galatea | London Printed for & sold by I: Walsh Servt. to his Majesty at the | Harp & Hoboy in Catherine Street in the Strand: & Ino. & Ioseph Hare | at the Viol and Flute in Cornhill near the Royal Exchange [1722]

2° *Short score:* 2 ℓ., 36 numb. ℓ.
Numbered leaves printed on one side only
RISM A I, no. H 386; Smith, p. 81, no. 1
HOUGHTON

652   HÄNDEL, GEORG FRIEDRICH

The | Songs | and Symphony's | in the Masque of | Acis and Galatea | made and perform'd for his | Grace | the Duke of Chandos | Compos'd by | Mr: Handel | Fairly Engraven and | carefully corrected | London Printed for J: Walsh Servant in Ordinary to his Britanick Majesty, at ye Harp & Hoboy in Katherine Street | near Somerset House in ye Strand, & J: Hare at ye Viol & Flute in Cornhill near the Royall Exchange. [1725–1728]

2° *Short score:* 1 ℓ., 36 p.
RISM A I, no. H 387; Smith, p. 81–82, no. 2
HOUGHTON

653   [HÄNDEL, GEORG FRIEDRICH]

Acis and Galatea | for a | Flute | containing the | Songs and Symphonys | Curiously Transpos'd and fitted to the | Flute | in a Compleat manner | The whole fairly Engraven & carefully Corected | London Printed for & Sold by I: Walsh Servant to his Majesty at | the Harp & Hoboy in Catherine Street in ye Strand. . . . [173–?]

obl. 4° 2 ℓ., 29 numb. ℓ.
No. 32 on title-page
John and Joseph Hare's names erased from imprint

Numbered leaves printed on one side only
Apparently a later issue of Smith, p. 85–86, no. 19
RISM A I, no. H 392
HOUGHTON

654   HÄNDEL, GEORG FRIEDRICH

The | Songs | and Symphony's | in the Masque of | Acis and Galatea | made and perform'd for his | Grace | the Duke of Chandos | Compos'd by | Mr: Handel | with the | Additional Songs | . . . | London Printed for J: Walsh Servant in Ordinary to his Britanick Majesty, at ye Harp & Hoboy in Katherine street | near Somerset House in ye Strand, [ca. 1732]

2° *Short score:* 1 ℓ., [1], 38 p.
No: 287 on title-page
J. Hare's name erased from imprint
RISM A I, no. H 389; Smith, p. 82, no. 4
HOUGHTON

655   HÄNDEL, GEORG FRIEDRICH

Acis | And | Galatea | A Mask | As it was Originally Compos'd | with the | Overture, Recitativo's, Songs, | Duets & Choruses, | for Voices and Instruments. | Set to Musick by | Mr. Handel | London. Printed for I. Walsh, in Catharine Street, in the Strand. [1743]

2° *Score:* 2 ℓ., 89 p.
RISM A I, no. H 380; Smith, p. 82–83, no. 6
HOUGHTON

656   HÄNDEL, GEORG FRIEDRICH

Acis | And | Galatea | A Mask | As it was Originally Compos'd | with the | Overture, Recitativo's, Songs, | Duets & Choruses, | for Voices and Instruments. | Set to Musick by | Mr. Handel | London. Printed for W. Randall. Succesor to the late Mr. Walsh in Catharine Street, Strand. [1769]

2° *Score:* 2 ℓ., 89 p.
RISM A I, no. H 381; Smith, p. 83, no. 8
HOUGHTON, MUSIC LIBRARY

657   HÄNDEL, GEORG FRIEDRICH

Acis And Galatea, | A Masque. | Composed by | Mr. Handel, | For the | Voice, Harpsichord, And Violin. | London: | Printed for Harrison & Co. No. 18, Paternoster Row. [1784]

obl. 2° *Score:* 47 p.
Plate nos. (8)–(10), which are those of *The New Musical Magazine*
Bound as issued with the composer's *Ode on St. Cecilia's Day*
RISM A I, no. H 385; Smith, p. 84–85, no. 14
HOUGHTON

658   HÄNDEL, GEORG FRIEDRICH

Acis | And | Galatea | A Mask | As it was Originally Compos'd | with the | Overture, Recitativo's, Songs, | Duets & Choruses, | for Voices and Instruments. | Set to Musick by | Mr. Handel | London. Printed for H. Wright. Succesor to the late Mr. Walsh . in Catharine Street, Strand. [ca. 1785]

2° *Score:* 2 ℓ., 89 p.
Imperfect: page 89 lacking; supplied in three pages of twentieth-century manuscript
RISM A I, no. H 382; Smith, p. 83–84, no. 10
HOUGHTON

659   HÄNDEL, GEORG FRIEDRICH

. . . | The | Overture And Songs | In | Acis And Galatea, | A Masque. | For the | Voice, Harpsichord, and Violin. | Composed by | Mr. Handel. | London: | Printed for Harrison & Co. No. 18, Paternoster Row [1736]

obl. 2° *Score:* 27 p.
Plate nos. (6*)–(7*)
At head of title: Harrisons Edition, Corrected by Dr. Arnold.
RISM A I, no. H 391; Smith, p. 85, no. 16
HOUGHTON

660   HÄNDEL, GEORG FRIEDRICH

Acis And Galatea | A Serenata | Composed for the | Duke of Chandois | in the

Year 1720 | By | G. F. Handel. [London, 1788]

2° *Score:* 103 p.
Plate nos. 28–30, which are those of Arnold's Edition
RISM A I, no. H 1508; Smith, p. 85, no. 17
HOUGHTON

661   HÄNDEL, GEORG FRIEDRICH

The | Overture, Songs, | Duett, and Trio, | in Acis & Galatea, | a Masque. | Composed By, | G. F. Handel. | London: | Printed for Harrison, Cluse, & Co. 78, Fleet Street. [1799?]

8° *Vocal score:* 43 p., 1 ℓ. (*The Piano-Forte Magazine,* vol. VI, no. 4)
Plate nos. 88–89
Smith, p. 85, no. 18
MUSIC LIBRARY

662   HÄNDEL, GEORG FRIEDRICH

Admetus, | An | Opera, | Compos'd by | Mr. Handel. | Engrav'd, Printed and Sold by J. Cluer in Bow-Church-Yard, London. [1727]

4° *Score:* 3 ℓ., 127 p.
RISM A I, no. H 42; Smith, p. 5, no. 1
HOUGHTON

663   HÄNDEL, GEORG FRIEDRICH

Alexander Balus | An | Oratorio | In Score, | Composed by | Mr. Handel | . . . | London, Printed for H: Wright, (Successor to Mr. Walsh) | in Catharine Street in the Strand. | . . . [1787]

2° *Score:* 2 ℓ., 233 p.
Imperfect: lacks frontispiece and list of subscribers noted in Smith, p. 89, no. 3
RISM A I, no. H 450
MUSIC LIBRARY

664   HÄNDEL, GEORG FRIEDRICH

The | Favourite Songs | in | Alexander's | Feast | By Mr. Handel | . . . | London Printed for & Sould by I: Walsh—Musicall Instrument maker in Ordinary to His Majesty at the | Golden Harp & Hoboy in Catherine-street near Summerset-house in ye strand [1739]

2° Score: 1 *ℓ.,* [47] p.
Irregular paging: 1–11, [1] (blank), 32–36, [1] (blank), 50–53, 64–71, 101–104, 116–121, 128–134
RISM A I, no. H 1007; Smith, p. 90–91, no. 3
HOUGHTON

665 HÄNDEL, GEORG FRIEDRICH

Alexanders Feast, | An Ode | On | Saint Cecilia's Day, | The Words By Dryden, | The Musick Composed in the Year 1736. | By | G. F. Handel. [London, 1790]

2° Score: 141, [2] p.
Plate nos. 65–67, which are those of Arnold's Edition
RISM A I, no. H 1521; Smith, p. 93, no. 13
MUSIC LIBRARY

666 HÄNDEL, GEORG FRIEDRICH

L'Allegro, | Il Penseroso, | Ed | Il Moderato. | The Words taken from | Milton. | Set to Musick by | Mr. Handel. | London. Printed for I. Walsh in Catherine | Street in the Strand. | . . . [1741?]

2° Score: 1 *ℓ.,* 63 p.
Hirsch IV, no. 758; RISM A I, no. H 461; Smith, p. 94, no. 5
HOUGHTON

667 HÄNDEL, GEORG FRIEDRICH

Belshazzar. | An | Oratorio | In Score, | Composed by | Mr. Handel | . . . | London, Printed for Wright & Co. (Successors to Mr. Walsh) | in Catharine Street, in the Strand. | . . . [1784]

2° Score: 3 *ℓ.,* 232 p.
Imperfect: lacks frontispiece noted in Smith, p. 99, no. 5
RISM A I, no. H 516
MUSIC LIBRARY

668 HÄNDEL, GEORG FRIEDRICH

Six | Concertos | For the | Harpsicord or Organ | Compos'd by | Mr: Handel | These Six Concertos were Publish'd by Mr. Walsh from | my own Copy Corrected by my Self, and to Him only I |

have given my Right therein. | George Frideric Handel. | London. Printed for & Sold by I. Walsh, Musick Printer & Instru-|ment maker to his Majesty, at the Harp & Hoboy in Catherine Street | in the Strand. . . . [ca. 1739]

2° 1 pt.: Harpsicord or organ: 1 *ℓ.,* 48 p.
Hirsch III, no. 234; RISM A I, no. H 1212?; Smith, p. 225, no. 3 or 5
HOUGHTON

669 HÄNDEL, GEORG FRIEDRICH

A Second Set of | Six | Concertos | For the | Harpsicord or Organ | Compos'd by | Mr: Handel | London. Printed for H: Wright, in Catherine Street in the Strand | . . . [ca. 1785]

4° 1 pt.: Harpsicord or organ: 1 *ℓ.,* 61 p.
Plate no. 681
RISM A I, no. H 1231?; Smith, p. 229–230, no. 4
HOUGHTON

670 HÄNDEL, GEORG FRIEDRICH

A Third Set of | Six | Concertos | for the | Harpsicord or Organ | Compos'd By | Mr. Handel. | London. Printed for H. Wright Catharine Street in the Strand. | . . . [ca. 1785]

4° 1 pt.: Harpsicord or organ: 1 *ℓ.,* 51 p.
RISM A I, no. H 1237; Smith, p. 231–232, no. 5
HOUGHTON

671 HÄNDEL, GEORG FRIEDRICH

The | Coronation | Anthem, | Composed By | Handel. | London: | Printed for Harrison & Co. No. 78, Fleet Street. [ca. 1798]

8° Score: 9 p. (*The Piano-Forte Magazine,* vol. IV, no. 4)
Plate no. 57
For keyboard instrument
RISM A I, no. H 1167; Smith, p. 152, no. 13
MUSIC LIBRARY

HÄNDEL, GEORG FRIEDRICH Dettingen Te Deum *See* Händel, Georg Friedrich *Te Deum*

672   HÄNDEL, GEORG FRIEDRICH

The | Most Celebrated | Songs | in the | Oratorio | call'd | Queen Esther | To which is Prefixt | The Overture in Score | Compos'd by | Mr: Handel. | London. Printed for & Sold by I. Walsh Musick Printer & Instrument-ma-|ker to his Majesty at the Harp & Hoboy in Catherine Street in the Strand | . . . [ca. 1732]

2° *Score:* 1 ℓ., 30 p.
No. 288 on title-page; verso of page 17 blank (see Schnapper I, 434)
Page [1]: The following Musick Compos'd by Mr. Handel, which | may be had, where these are Sold.
RISM A I, no. H 537; Smith, p. 104, no. 2
HOUGHTON

—another copy
No. 288 on title-page; no blanks (see Schnapper I, 434)
Smith, p. 104, no. 3
HOUGHTON

673   HÄNDEL, GEORG FRIEDRICH

Floridant. | an | Opera | as it was Perform'd | at the | Kings Theatre | for the | Royal Academy | Compos'd by | Mr: Handel. | Publish'd by the Author. | London Printed and Sold by I: Walsh Servant to his | Majesty at the Harp and Hoboy in Catherine-Street in | the Strand, and Ino & Ioseph Hare at the Viol and Flute | in Cornhill near the Royal Exchange. [1722]

2° *Score:* 2 ℓ., 81 p.
Page 1 printed as numbered leaf, with table of contents, etc. on verso
RISM A I, no. H 147; Smith, p. 27, no. 1
HOUGHTON

674   HÄNDEL, GEORG FRIEDRICH

Six Fugues | Or | Voluntarys | for the | Organ | Or | Harpsicord | Compos'd by | G. F. Handel. | Troisieme Ovarage [sic]. | London. Printed for and Sold by I. Walsh, Musick Printer, and Instrument maker to his Majesty, | at the Harp and Ho-boy in Catherine Street in the Strand. . . . [ca. 1735]

obl. 2° *Score:* 1 ℓ., 23 p.
No. 543 on title-page
RISM A I, no. H 1475; Smith, p. 236, no. 1
HOUGHTON

675   HÄNDEL, GEORG FRIEDRICH

Israel in Egypt | A Sacred | Oratorio | In Score | Composed in the Year 1738 | By | G. F. Handel. [London, ca. 1791]

2° *Score:* 282, [2] p., front. (port.)
Plate nos. 92–98, which are those of Arnold's Edition
RISM A I, no. H 1537; Smith, p. 109, no. 4
MUSIC LIBRARY (2 copies)

676   HÄNDEL, GEORG FRIEDRICH

Judas Macchabaeus | an | Oratorio | Set to Musick by | Mr. Handel | London. Printed for I. Walsh, in Catharine Street, in the Strand. | . . . [ca. 1749]

2° *Score:* 3 ℓ., 72 p., numb. ℓ. 48
Preliminary leaf 2ʳ: Musick Compos'd by Mr Handel Printed for I. Walsh . . .
Hirsch IV, no. 772; RISM A I, no. H 636; Smith, p. 114, no. 3
HOUGHTON

677   HÄNDEL, GEORG FRIEDRICH

Eight | Grand Chorusses | From The | Oratorio | of | Judas Maccabaeus | Adapted for the | Organ or Harpsicord | . . . | London | Printed for J. Bland No. 45 Holborn | . . . [ca. 1790]

2° *Score:* 1 ℓ., 24 p.
RISM A I, no. H 650
HOUGHTON

678   HÄNDEL, GEORG FRIEDRICH

Julius Caesar: | An | Opera. | Compos'd by | G. Frederick Handel, | of London, Gent. | London, | Printed at Cluer's Print-ing-Office in Bow-Church-Yard, | and sold there, and by B. Creake at ye Bible in Jermyn-street, St. | James's. [1724]

8° *Score:* 3 ℓ., 118 p.
RISM A I, no. H 166; Smith, p. 30, no. 1
HOUGHTON

679   HÄNDEL, GEORG FRIEDRICH

Messiah | An | Oratorio | In Score | As it
was Originally Perform'd. | Composed by
| Mr. Handel | To which are added | His
additional Alterations. | London. Printed
by Messrs. Randall & Abell Successors
to | the late Mr. J. Walsh in Catharine
Street in the Strand | . . . [ca. 1768]

2° *Score:* 3 ℓ., 188, 35 p.
Pages 1–35 at end: appendix contain-
ing additional arias, recitatives, duets
and choruses
Imperfect: frontispiece portrait lacking
Hirsch IV, no. 774; RISM A I, no. H
718; Smith, p. 125–126, no. 4a
HOUGHTON

680   HÄNDEL, GEORG FRIEDRICH

The | Overture, | Songs, | And | Recita-
tives; | In The | Messiah: | A Sacred | Ora-
torio. | Composed By, | G. F. Handel |
London: | Printed for Harrison, Cluse, &
Co. No. 78, Fleet Street. [1798?]

8° *Vocal score:* 42 p. (*The Piano-Forte
Magazine,* vol. VI, no. 2)
Plate nos. 84–85
RISM A I, no. H 732; Smith, p. 123, no.
18
MUSIC LIBRARY

681   HÄNDEL, GEORG FRIEDRICH

The | Songs | in the Ode wrote by | Mr.
Dryden for | St. Cecilia's Day | Set by |
Mr. Handel. | London Printed for & sould
by I: Walsh Musicall Instrument maker
in Ordinary to His Majesty at the |
Golden Harp & Ho-boy in Catherine-street near Summerset-house in ye
strand [1739]

2° *Score:* 1 ℓ., 23 p.
RISM A I, no. H 1038; Smith, p. 131,
no. 1
MUSIC LIBRARY

682   HÄNDEL, GEORG FRIEDRICH

Dryden's Ode on St. Cecilia's Day. |
Composed by Mr. Handel. [London, Harrison & Co., 1784]

obl. 2° *Vocal score:* 25 p.
Plate nos. 10–11, which are those of
The New Musical Magazine
Caption title; bound as issued (with-
out title-page) with the composer's *Acis
and Galatea* (no. 657, above)
RISM A I, no. H 1040; Smith, p. 131–
132, no. 4
HOUGHTON

683   HÄNDEL, GEORG FRIEDRICH

Eight | Select | Overtures, | From | Ora-
torios | Of | Handel. | London: | Printed
for Harrison & Co. No. 78 Fleet Street.
[1798]

8° *Score:* 1 ℓ., 5–56 [+] p. (*The Piano-
Forte Magazine,* vol. IV, no. 3)
Plate nos. 54–56
For keyboard instrument
Imperfect: all after page 56 lacking
Contents: overtures to the *Occasional
Oratorio, Saul, Esther, Deborah, Time
and Truth, Solomon, Jephtha*
RISM A I, no. H 1316; Smith, p. 288,
no. 34
MUSIC LIBRARY

HÄNDEL, GEORG FRIEDRICH Queen
Esther *See* Händel, Georg Friedrich
Esther

684   HÄNDEL, GEORG FRIEDRICH

Il | Radamisto | Opera | Rappresentata
Nel Regio | Teatro D'Hay Market | Com-
posta Dal | Sigre, Georgio Fredrico Han-
del | London | Publisht by the Author. |
Printed and Sold by Richard Meares Mu-
sical-Instrument-Maker | and Musick-
Printer in St. Pauls Church yd. & by
Christopher Smith | at ye Hand & Mu-
sick-Book in Coventry-Street near ye
Hay-Market. | NB. Not to be sold any
where else in England. [1720]

2° *Score:* 2 ℓ., 121 p.
Unnumbered blank page following
page 81
RISM A I, no. H 258; Smith, p. 53,
no. 1
HOUGHTON

685   HÄNDEL, GEORG FRIEDRICH

Arie Aggiunte | di | Radamisto | Opera | Rapresentata Nel Regio | Teatro D'Hay Market | Composta Dal | Sigre, Georgio Fredrico Handel | London | Publisht by the Author. | Printed and Sold by Richard Meares Musical-Instrument-Maker | and Musick-Printer in St. Pauls Church yd. & by Christopher Smith | at ye Hand & Musick-Book in Coventry-Street near ye Hay-Market. | NB. Not to be sold any where else in England. [1721]

  2° *Score:* 1 ℓ., 38 p.
  RISM A I, no. H 261; Smith, p. 53, no. 2

HOUGHTON

686   HÄNDEL, GEORG FRIEDRICH

Arie | dell'Opera di | Rinaldo | Composta dal | Signor Hendel | Maestro di Capella di | Sua Altezza Elettorale | d'Hannover. | London Printed for J: Walsh Servant in Ordinary to her Britanick Majesty, at ye Harp & Hoboy in Katherine street | near Somerset House in ye Strand, & J: Hare at ye Viol & Flute in Cornhill near the Royall Exchange. [1711?]

  2° *Score:* 1 ℓ., 67 p.
  Lacks table of contents noted in Smith, p. 56–57, no. 3
  RISM A I, no. H 280; Walsh II, no. 389

HOUGHTON

687   HÄNDEL, GEORG FRIEDRICH

[Rodelinda]. | An | Opera, | Compos'd by Mr. Handel. | Engrav'd, Printed and Sold by J. Cluer in Bow-Church-Yard, London. [ca. 1728]

  2° *Score:* 2 ℓ., 108 p.
  Title partly in manuscript
  RISM A I, no. H 292; Smith, p. 61, no. 3

HOUGHTON

688   HÄNDEL, GEORG FRIEDRICH

Samson | An | Oratorio | The Words taken from | Milton | Set to Musick by | Mr. Handel | London Printed for I. Walsh in Catherine Street in the | Strand . . . [1743]

  2° *Score:* 3 ℓ., 2–8, 1–30 [i. e. 9–38], 39–91 p.
  Hirsch IV, no. 782; RISM A I, no. H 831; Smith, p. 135, no. 2

HOUGHTON

689   HÄNDEL, GEORG FRIEDRICH

. . . | The | Overture And Songs | In | Samson, | An Oratorio. | For the | Voice, Harpsichord, and Violin. | Composed by | Mr. Handel. | London: | Printed for Harrison & Co. No. 18, Paternoster Row. [1786]

  obl. 2° *Vocal score:* 41 p., 1 ℓ.
  Plate nos. 8–10, which are those of *The Songs of Handel,* vol. I
  At head of title: Harrisons Edition, Corrected by Dr. Arnold.
  RISM A I, no. H 835; Smith, p. 138, no. 13

HOUGHTON

690   HÄNDEL, GEORG FRIEDRICH

The | Most Celebrated | Songs | in the | Oratorio | Call'd | Saul | Compos'd by | Mr: Handel. | London. Printed for & Sold by I. Walsh Musick Printer & Instrument maker | to his Majesty at the Harp & Hoboy in Catherine Street in the Strand. . . . [ca. 1740]

  2° *Score:* 1 ℓ., 168–178, 20, 2–17 p.
  No. 545 on title-page
  Hirsch IV, no. 783; RISM A I, no. H 877; Smith, p. 139, no. 3

HOUGHTON

691   HÄNDEL, GEORG FRIEDRICH

Saul, | A Sacred Oratorio, | In Score | Composed in the Year, 1740. | By | G. F. Handel. [London, ca. 1792]

  2° *Score:* 252 p., 1 ℓ.
  Plate nos. 111–117, which are those of Arnold's Edition
  RISM A I, no. H 1542; Smith, p. 140, no. 9

MUSIC LIBRARY

692   [HÄNDEL, GEORG FRIEDRICH]

[A Second Set of Songs in Semele in Score ⟨London, 174–?⟩]

2° *Score:* 33–62 p.
Without title-page, as issued?; title from advertisement
Smith, p. 141, no. 1 or 2
HOUGHTON

693   HÄNDEL, GEORG FRIEDRICH

Solomon, | A Sacred Oratorio | In Score, | With all the additional Altera-tions, | Composed in the Year, 1749. | By | G. F. Handel. [London, ca. 1790]

2° *Score:* 344 p.
Plate nos. 85–92, which are those of Arnold's Edition
RISM A I, no. H 1536; Smith, p. 143, no. 5
MUSIC LIBRARY

694   HÄNDEL, GEORG FRIEDRICH

Solomon | an | Oratorio | Set to Musick by | Mr. Handel | London. Printed for I. Walsh, in Catharine Street, in the Strand. | of whom may be had, | The Works of Mr. Handel, Geminiani, Corelli, and all the most | Eminent Authors of Musick. [1749]

2° *Score:* 2 ℓ., 80 p.
Lacks privilege noted in Smith, p. 142, no. 1
RISM A I, no. H 923
HOUGHTON

695   HÄNDEL, GEORG FRIEDRICH

Six Sonatas | For | Two Violins, Two Hautboys, | Or | Two German Flutes, & a Violoncello | First Published at Amster-dam 1731 | Composed by | G. F. Handel. [London, 1789]

2° *Score:* 60 p., front. (port.)
Plate nos. 47–48, which are those of Arnold's Edition
RISM A I, no. H 1513 (op. 2); Smith, p. 245, no. 7
MUSIC LIBRARY

696   HÄNDEL, GEORG FRIEDRICH

Seven Sonatas | or | Trios | For | Two Violins or Two German Flutes | And a | Violoncello | Composed & Published in the Year 1739 | By | G. F. Handel. [Lon-don, 1789]

2° *Score:* 59 p.
Plate nos. 48–49, which are those of Arnold's Edition
RISM A I, no. H 1514 (op. 5); Smith, p. 247, no. 5
MUSIC LIBRARY

697   HÄNDEL, GEORG FRIEDRICH

Handel's Songs | Selected from His Or-atorios, | For The | Harpsicord, Voice, Hoboy, or | German Flute. | . . . | London. Printed for I. Walsh in Catharine Street in the Strand. | . . . [ca. 1755]

obl. 2° *Vocal score: vol. I:* 2 ℓ., 170 p.
Incomplete: vols. II–V lacking
RISM A I, no. H 1075; Smith, p. 197, no. 17
MUSIC LIBRARY

698   HÄNDEL, GEORG FRIEDRICH

Suites de Pieces | Pour le | Clavecin. | Composées par | G. F. Handel. | . . . | London | Printed, & Sold by John Walsh Musick Printer & Instrument Maker | to his Majesty at the Harp & Hoboy in Catherine street in the Strand. | . . . [ca. 1736]

obl. 2° *Score:* [*vol. I*]: 1 ℓ., [1], 94 p.
Vol. statement erased from title-page
No. 490 on title-page
RISM A I, no. H 1433; Smith, p. 250, no. 6
HOUGHTON

699   HÄNDEL, GEORG FRIEDRICH

Suites de Pieces | Pour le | Clavecin. | Composées par | G. F. Handel. | . . . | London | Printed, & Sold by John Walsh Musick Printer & Instrument Maker | to his Majesty at the Harp & Hoboy in Catherine street in the Strand. | . . . [ca. 1733] obl. 2° *Score: vol. II:* 1 ℓ., 83 p.

No. 490 on title-page

RISM A I, no. H 1438; Smith, p. 249, no. 5

HOUGHTON

700 HÄNDEL, GEORG FRIEDRICH

Te Deum | In Score | Composed for His Grace the | Duke of Chandos | (in the Year 1720) | By | G. F. Handel. | [London, 1788]

2° *Score:* 31 p.

Plate no. 20, which is that of Arnold's Edition

Smith, p. 159, last entry: "A modification of the Te Deum in B♭ major (Chandos), with fuller chorus and orchestra, but considerably shortened. Prepared for use at the Chapel Royal. It may have been first used in 1727 on the accession of George II."

RISM A I, no. H 1503

HOUGHTON

701 HÄNDEL, GEORG FRIEDRICH

Handel's | Grand Dettingen | Te Deum | In Score. | For Voices and Instruments. | as Perform'd at the | Cathedral-Church of St. Paul. | . . . | London. Printed for H. Wright Successor to the late | Mr. Walsh in Catharine Street in the Strand. | . . . [ca. 1790]

2° *Score:* 1 ℓ., 92 p.

Vol. IV in an untitled series

RISM A I, no. H 1189; Smith, p. 156, no. 4

MUSIC LIBRARY

702 HÄNDEL, GEORG FRIEDRICH, SUPPOSED COMPOSER

Twelve | Voluntaries and Fugues | for the | Organ or Harpsichord | with Rules for Tuning | by the celebrated | Mr. Handel | Book IV | . . . | London Printed by Longman and Broderip No. 26 Cheapside | Music Sellers to the Royal Family | . . . [after 1782]

obl. 2° *Score:* 1 ℓ., 35, III [i. e. I] p.

Page III [i. e. I]: Musical Publications | Printed and Sold by Longman & Broderip

at the | Apollo No. 26, Cheapside & No 13 Hay Market London

RISM A I, no. H 1485; Smith, p. 254, no. 4

HOUGHTON

703 HÄNDEL, GEORG FRIEDRICH

The Celebrated | Water Musick | in Seven Parts | viz. | Two French Horns | Two Violins or Hoboys | a Tenor | and a Thorough Bass for the | Harpsicord | or | Bass Violin | Compos'd by | Mr: Handel. | . . . | London. Printed for and Sold by I: Walsh Musick Printer & Instrument | maker to his Majesty at the Harp & Hoboy in Catherine Street in the Strand. | . . . [ca. 1733]

2° 1 pt.: *corno secondo:* 4 p.

No. 489 on title-page

RISM A I, no. H 1318; Smith, p. 255, no. 1?

HOUGHTON

704 HÄSSLER, JOHANN WILHELM

Sechs | Klavier-Solos | halb leicht halb schwer, | komponirt | und | Sr. Freiherrl. Exzellenz | dem Herrn Statthalter von Dalberg | in Erfurt | unterthänig zugeeignet | von | Johann Wilhelm Hässler, | Musikdirector des öffentlichen Konzerts und Organist bey der evangelischen Barfüsserkirche in Erfurt. | Leipzig, | im Schwickertschen Verlage. [ca. 1785]

obl. 2° *Score:* 38 p.

RISM A I, no. H 1659

MUSIC LIBRARY

705 HÄSSLER, JOHANN WILHELM

Clavier-und Singstücke | verschiedener Art, | componirt | und dem | Fräulein Caroline von Keller, | Hofdame bey der regierenden Fürstin zu Nassau-Weilburg, | gewidmet | von | Johann Wilhelm Hässler. | Erste Sammlung. | Erfurt, | auf Kosten des Verfassers. 1782.

obl 2° *Score:* 2 ℓ., 44, [2] p.

RISM A I, no. H 1577

MUSIC LIBRARY

706   HÄSSLER, JOHANN WILHELM

Klavier-und Singstücke | verschiedener
Art, | componirt | von | Johann Wilhelm
Hässler. | Zweite Sammlung. | Leipzig, |
im Schwickertschen Verlage. [1786?]

> obl. 2° *Score:* 1 ℓ., 58 p.
> RISM A I, no. H 1578
> MUSIC LIBRARY

707   HÄSSLER, JOHANN WILHELM

Acht und vierzig | kleine Orgelstücke, |
theils zu | Choral-Vorspielen | beim
öffentlichen Gottesdienst, | theils zur |
Privatübung | für angehende Orgelspieler
und Schulmeister auf dem Lande | be-
stimmt | und herausgegeben | von | Jo-
hann Wilhelm Hässler | Direktor des
öffentlichen Konzerts und Organist der
evangelischen | Barfüsserkirche in Er-
furth. | Leipzig, | in Commission der Breit-
kopfischen Buchhandlung. | [Intro. 1789]

> 4° *Score:* 6, [2], 64 p.
> RISM A I, no. H 1661
> MUSIC LIBRARY (2 copies)

708   HÄSSLER, JOHANN WILHELM

Sechs | leichte | Sonaten | fürs Clavier, |
componirt | und | der Frau Baronin | von
Richter gebohrnen von Pirchen | gewid-
met | von | Johann Wilhelm Hässler, | Or-
ganist an der Evangelischen Barfüs-
ser-Kirche in Erfurth. | Erfurth, | in Com-
mission der Keyserschen Buchhandlung.
1780.

> obl. 2° *Score:* 2 ℓ., 35 p.
> RISM A I, no. H 1658
> MUSIC LIBRARY

709   HÄUSLER, ERNST

Gedicht | Kenst du das Land wo die
Cytronen blühn? | aus Wilhelm Meisters
Lehr–Jahren | von | Goethe. | Jn Musik
gesezt und Zugeeignet | der Frau | Baro-
nesse Fanny von Arnstein | gebohrne von
Izig. | vom | Ernst Haeusler | . . . | Augs-
burg in der Gombartischen Musik Hand-
lung. [1799?]

> obl. 2° *Score:* 7 p.
> Plate no. 177

Imprint covered by cancel label read-
ing: Mainz in der Hofmusikhandlung
von B. Schotts Söhnen.
Imprint date from MGG V, col. 1305
RISM A I, no. H 1680
MUSIC LIBRARY

710   HAGUE, CHARLES, ED.

A | Second Collection, | Of | Glees,
Rounds, & Canons, | For two, three, four,
five & six Voices. | Composed by the
Members of the | Harmonic Society of
Cambridge. | and Publish'd by | Charles
Hague, Mus. Bac. Camb. | . . . | Cam-
bridge. | Engraved & printed by W.
Dixon, for the Editor, & may be had at
the Music Shops in Cambridge, | Long-
man & Broderips, No. 26, Cheapside,
No. 13, Haymarket, & of Mr. Preston,
No. 97, Strand, London. [1800?]

> obl. 2° *Score:* 3 ℓ., 73 p.
> RISM B II, 102
> MUSIC LIBRARY

711   HAIGH, THOMAS

Six | Easy Sonatas | for the | Harpsi-
chord or Piano Forte, | Four with an ac-
companyment for a Violin, | and Two for
a German Flute; | Composed & Dedi-
cated to | Mrs. James Barton, | by Thomas
Haigh. | Op: 3d. London, . . . | Printed
for & Sold by T. Cahusac, at his Music
Warehouse, No 196 Strand. | Sudlow
Sculp. 191, Strand. [ca. 1790]

> 2° *Score:* 1 ℓ., 27 p.
> RISM A I, no. H 1773
> MUSIC LIBRARY

HAL, JOHANN VAN   *See* Wanhal, Johann
Baptist

712   HALE, THOMAS

Social Harmony | Consisting of a Col-
lection of | Songs and Catches | In two,
three, four and five Parts, | From the
Works of the most eminent Masters | To
which are added | Several Choice Songs
on | Masonry | by Thomas Hale, of Dam-
hall Cheshire | [Liverpool?] 1763

> 4° *Score:* 1 ℓ., 18 p., 1 ℓ., 31 p., 1 ℓ., 138
> p., 1 ℓ., 42, 62 p.

Published in four sections, with supplement
RISM B II, 358
MUSIC LIBRARY

713 HAMM, BENEDICTUS

Debitae Gratitudinis | Census | Pro Sacris Pignoribus | Deo | Et | Patronis Suis Exhibitus | Hoc Est | Missae V. | Solemnes | Qvarvm | Ultima De Requiem | Stylo Acriori | Adornatae | à | IV. Vocibus, & II. Violinis Obligatis cum Organo | Nec non | Tubis ad placitum | Authore | P. Benedicto Hamm | Benedictino Schutterano. | . . . | Schvtterae In Brisgoia | Typis Abbatialibus per Franciscum Gerster, Anno MDCCXLIX.

2° 1 pt.: *organo:* [–]², ⊙A–⊙Y²
RISM A I, no. H 1921
HOUGHTON

HANDEL, GEORGE FRIDERIC *See* Händel, Georg Friedrich

HARCHADELT, JACOB *See* Arcadelt, Jacob

714

Harmonia Sacra; | Or, | Divine Hymns | And | Dialogues: | With | A thorow-Bass for the Theorbo-Lute, | Bass-Viol, Harpsichord, or Organ. | Composed by the Best Masters of the Last and Present Age. | The Words by several Learned and Pious Persons. | . . . | [London] In the Savoy: | Printed by Edward Jones, for Henry Playford, at his Shop near the Temple Church, | MDCLXXXVIII.

2° *Score:* 3 ℓ., 79, [1] p., front.
Unnumbered page at end: Mvsick Books sold by Henry Playford . . .
RISM B I, no. 1688[1]
HOUGHTON

715

Harmonia Sacra: | Or, | Divine Hymns | And | Dialogues. | With | A Thorow-Bass for the Theorbo-Lute, | Bass-Viol, Harpsichord, or Organ. | Composed by the Best Masters. | The Words by several Learned and Pious Persons. | The Second Book. | . . . | [London] In the Savoy: Printed by

Edward Jones, for Henry Playford at his Shop near the Temple Church, | and at his House over-against the Blue-Ball in Arundel-Street in the Strand: | Where also the First Book may be had. MDCXCIII.

2° *Score:* 3 ℓ., 74 [i. e. 80] p., front.
Pages 1–16 numbered as leaves 1–8; numbers 46, 47 omitted in paging
Preliminary leaf 3ᵛ: A Catalogue of Vocal and Instrumental Musick, most of which are newly | Reprinted for Henry Playford . . .
RISM B I, no. 1693[1]
HOUGHTON (2 copies)

716

Harmonia Sacra: | Or, | Divine Hymns | And | Dialogues; | With | A Through-Bass for the Theorbo-Lute, | Bass-Viol, Harpsichord, or Organ. | Composed by the Best Masters of the Last and Present Age. | The Words by several Learned and Pious Persons. | The first Book. The 2d. Edition very much Enlarged and Corrected; also four | Excellent Anthems of the late Mr. H. Purcell's never before Printed. | . . . | London: | Printed by William Pearson, for Henry Playford, at his Shop in Temple-Change Fleet-street, | or at his House in Arundel-street in the Strand; and John Sprint at the Bell in Little-|Britain, where the second Book is to be had. 1703.

2° *Score:* 3 ℓ., 130 p., front.
RISM B II, 196
HOUGHTON

717

Harmonia Vera: | Or, | Six | Of the most Celebrated | Cantatas | In the English Language. | Viz. | Martillo, | Thyrsis, | Neptune and Amymone,} By Mr. Haydon. | Alexis, By Dr. Pepusch. | A Song with a Symphony, | And | The Famous Trio in Acis and Galatea,} By Mr. Handel. | London: | Printed and Sold by R. Falkener, No 45. Salisbury-court, Fleet-street. | MDCCLXXI. | . . .

2° *Score:* 26 p.
RISM B II, 197
HOUGHTON

HARRISON, JAMES, PUBL. A Collection of Overtures and Symphonies *See* A Collection of Overtures and Symphonies

HARRISON, JAMES, PUBL. A Select Collection of New Favourite and Popular Songs *See* A Select Collection of New Favourite and Popular Songs

HARRISON, JAMES, PUBL. Six Favourite Songs *See* Six Favourite Songs

HARRISON AND CLUSE, PUBL. A Collection of Favorite & Familiar Pieces *See* A Collection of Favorite & Familiar Pieces

HARRISON AND CLUSE, PUBL. A Favourite Collection of Familiar Rondos *See* A Favourite Collection of Familiar Rondos

HARRISON AND CLUSE, PUBL. The German Erata *See* The German Erata

HARRISON AND CLUSE, PUBL. Six Sonatas for the Piano Forte *See* Six Sonatas for the Piano Forte

HARRISON AND CLUSE, PUBL. Three Celebrated English Overtures *See* Three Celebrated English Overtures

HARRISON AND KNYVETT, PUBL. The Favorite New Glees *See* The Favorite New Glees

718   HASSE, JOHANN ADOLPH

Six | Concertos | Set for the | Harpsicord or Organ | Compos'd by Signor | Giovanni Adolffo Hasse | London. Printed for I. Walsh, in Catherine Street, in the | Strand . . . [ca. 1743]

2° *Score:* 1 *ℓ.*, 42 p.
A reduction for keyboard instrument of Concertos 1–3, 5, 6, 8 from his Twelve concertos in six parts . . . op. 3 (see MGG V, col. 1778)
RISM A I, no. H 2292; Walsh II, no. 802 (op. 4)
HOUGHTON

719   HASSE, JOHANN ADOLPH

A | Favourite | Concerto, | Composed By | Hasse. | London. | Printed for the Proprietors & Sold by Harrison & Co. | No. 18, Paternoster Row. [1797?]

8° *Score:* 11 p. (*The Piano-Forte Magazine*, vol. II, no. 8)
RISM A I, no. H 2291
MUSIC LIBRARY

720   HASSE, JOHANN ADOLPH

The | Favourite Songs | in the | Opera | Call'd | Il Re Pastore | by Sig: Hasse | London. Printed for I. Walsh in Catharine Street in the Strand | . . . [17—]

2° *Score:* 1 *ℓ.*, 25–40 p.
Plate no. w*F 1
RISM A I, no. H 2262
MUSIC LIBRARY

721   HASSE, JOHANN ADOLPH

The Famous | Salve | Regina | Compos'd by | Sigr. Hasse. | London Printed for & Sould by I: Walsh Musicall Instrument maker in Ordinary to His Majesty at the | Golden Harp & Ho-boy in Catherine-street near Summerset-house in ye strand [1740?]

2° *Score:* 1 *ℓ.*, 14 p.
Hirsch IV, no. 791; RISM A I, no. H 2238; Walsh II, no. 817
MUSIC LIBRARY

722   HAWKINS, JOHN

A | General History | Of The | Science and Practice | Of | Music, | By | Sir John Hawkins. | . . . | London, | Printed for T. Payne and Son, at the Mews-Gate. | MDCCLXXVI.

4° 5 vols: *vol. I:* 5 *ℓ.*, lxxxiv, 465 p., front., illus., 5 pl., music; *vol. II:* 1 *ℓ.*, 544 p., illus. (incl. ports.), music; *vol. III:* 1 *ℓ.*, 535 p., illus. (incl. ports.), music; *vol. IV:* 1 *ℓ.*, 548 p., illus. (incl. ports.), music; *vol. V:* 1 *ℓ.*, 482, [58] p., illus. (incl. ports.), music
Hirsch I, Historischer Anhang, no. 30; RISM B VI, 399–400
MUSIC LIBRARY (2 copies)

723 HAYDN, JOSEPH

Dr Haydn's, | VI Original | Canzonettas, | for the Voice with | an Accompaniment, for the Piano-Forte | Dedicated to | Mrs. John Hunter. | . . . | [London] Printed for the Author, & Sold by him at No. 1, Bury Street, St. James's | at Messrs. Corri, Dussek & Co., Music Sellers to her Majesty, | No. 67, Dean Street, Soho, & Bridge Street, Edinburgh. [1794]

2° *Score:* 31 p.
RISM A I, no. H 2656
H. XXVIa, 25–30
MUSIC LIBRARY

724 HAYDN, JOSEPH

The | Celebrated | Overture, | La Chasse. | Composed By | Haydn, | Adapted For The | Piano Forte. | London: | Printed for Harrison & Co. No. 18, Paternoster Row. [1798?]

Score: 20 p. (*The Piano-Forte Magazine,* vol. IV, no. 2)
Plate no. 53
An arrangement of the Symphony H. I, 73
RISM A I, no. H 4288
MUSIC LIBRARY

725 HAYDN, JOSEPH

Eco | Per Quatro Violini, E Due Violoncelli | Da Eseguirsi In Due Camere | Cioè | Li due Violini e Violoncello della Prima Camera si situeranno ove stà la Conversazione, | e l'altri in altra Camera la più lontana, che si possa; avertendo però, che siano | situati in modo, che scambievolmente possano vedersi, per andare uniti. | Del Signor | Giuseppe Haydn | In Napoli | Appresso Luigi Marescalchi Editore Privilegiato da S. M. (D. G.) | Si vende nelle Librerie di Antonio Hermil vicino alla Concezione di Toledo, | da Giuseppe Maria Porcelli a S. Biagio de' Librari, e per tutte le Città principali d'Europa | agli adrezzi ordinarj, dove si vende la Musica Stampata [1793?]

2° 6 pts.: *prima camera: Violino primo:* 3 p.; *violino secondo:* 2 p.; *violoncello:* 1 p.; *seconda camera: Violino primo, violino secondo:* 2 p. each; *violoncello:* 1 p.

RISM A I, no. H 3332
H. II, 39
HOUGHTON

726 HAYDN, JOSEPH

A | Favourite Lesson | For the | Piano Forte. | Composed by | Haydn. | London: | Printed for Harrison & Co. No. 18, Paternoster Row. [1797?]

8° *Score:* 9 p. (*The Piano-Forte Magazine,* vol. I [no. 7])
RISM A I, no. H 3350
H. XIV, 4
MUSIC LIBRARY

727 HAYDN, JOSEPH

Trois | Quatuors | Pour | deux Violons, Viola et Violoncelle | composés par | J. Haydn. | Op: 17. | . . . | Mayence, chez B. Schott fils. [179–?]

2° 4 pts.: *violino primo:* 13 p.; *violino secondo, viola, violoncello:* 9 p. each
Plate no. 169
RISM A I, no. H 3463
H. III, 25–27
MUSIC LIBRARY

728 HAYDN, JOSEPH

Trois | Quatuors | Pour | deux Violons, Viola et Violoncelle | composés par | J. Haydn. | Op: 17. | . . . Liv: II . . . | Mayence, chez B. Schott fils. [179–?]

2° 4 pts.: *violino primo:* 15 p.; *violino secondo:* 11 p.; *viola, violoncello:* 9 p. each
Plate no. 185
RISM A I, no. H 3463
H. III, 28–30
MUSIC LIBRARY

729 HAYDN, JOSEPH

Die Schöpfung, | Ein Musikalisches Oratorium | von | Herrn Joseph Haydn | übersetzt für das Clavier | von | Sigmund Neukomm. | Wien, bey Artaria und Compagnie. | . . . [1800]

obl. 2° *Vocal score:* 1 ℓ., 219 p.
Plate no. 855
RISM A I, no. H 4639
H. XXI, 2
MUSIC LIBRARY

730   HAYDN, JOSEPH

Six | Grand | Sonatas | For The | Harpsichord | Composed by the Celebrated | Guiseppe [*sic*] Haydn | of Vienna | Op. XIII. . . . | London | Printed for an sold by. | Messrs. Birchall and Andrew's at Handel's Head, | No. 129 New Bond Street. | . . . [178–]

2° *Score:* 1 ℓ., 33 p.
Plate no. 10
RISM A I, no. H 3862
H. XVI, 21–26
MUSIC LIBRARY

731   HAYDN, JOSEPH

Six | Sonatas | for the | Forte Piano | Or | Harpsichord | Composed by | Giuseppe Haydn | Opera XIV. | . . . | London. | Printed by Longman & Broderip No: 26 Cheapside | Music Sellers to the Royal Family [178–?]

2° *Score:* 30 p.
RISM A I, no. H 3871
H. XVI, 27–32
MUSIC LIBRARY

732   HAYDN, JOSEPH

Six | Sonatas | for the | Forte Piano | or | Harpsichord, | with an Accompaniment | for a Violin, | Composed by | Giuseppe Haydn. | Opera XVII. | . . . | London | Printed by Longman & Broderip No. 26, Cheapside & No 13 Hay Market | . . . [after 1782]

2° *Score:* 41 p.
RISM A I, no. H 3896?
H. XVI, 35–39
MUSIC LIBRARY

733   HAYDN, JOSEPH

Seven | Sonatas | with an | Introduction and Finale | For | The Piano Forte Or | Harpsichord | Composed by | Sigr. Giuseppe Haydn | Op: 45 | . . . | London | Printed by Longman and Broderip No. 26 Cheapside and No. 13 Hay Market | Music Sellers and musical Instrument makers to His Royal Highness the Prince of Wales | . . . [1788?]

2° *Score:* 27 p.
RISM A I, no. H 4384
H. XX, 1
MUSIC LIBRARY

734   HAYDN, JOSEPH

Three | Sonatas | for the | Harpsichord | or | Piano-Forte, | with an Accompaniment for a | Violin and Violoncello; | Composed by | Guiseppe [*sic*] Haydn, | Maestro di Capella di S. A. il | Principe d'Esterhazy &c. &c. | Opera 43. London. . . . |Printed and Sold by Preston & Son, at their Warehouses, 97 Strand & Exeter Change. | . . . [178–?]

2° 1 pt.: *harpsichord or piano-forte:* 1 ℓ., 21 p.
RISM A I, no. H 3655
H. XV, 6–8
MUSIC LIBRARY

735   HAYDN, JOSEPH

Trois | Sonates | pour le Clavecin ou le Piano Forte | avec Accompagnement | d'un Violon et Violoncelle | Dediées | A Madame la Comtesse | Marianne De Witzay | Par Joseph Haydn | Oeuvre 45e. | 9e. Livre de Clavecin. | . . . | A Paris | Chez M. Boyer, Rue de Richelieu, à la Clef d'Or, | Passage du Caffé de foy. | Chez Made. Le Menu, Rue du Roulle, à la Clef d'Or. | Ecrit par Ribiere. [1786?]

2° 3 pts.: *clavecin ou piano forte:* 21 p.; *violino:* 7 p.; *violoncello:* 6 p.
RISM A I, no. H 3643
H. XV, 6–8
MUSIC LIBRARY

736   HAYDN, JOSEPH

Three | Sonatas | for the | Harpsichord | or | Piano-Forte, | with an Accompaniment for a | Violin and Violoncello; | Composed by | Guiseppe [*sic*] Haydn, | Maestro di Capella di S. A. il | Principe d'Esterhazy &c &c. | Opera 43. London. . . . | Printed by Messrs. Birchall & Andrews, at | Handel's Head, No. 129 New Bond Street. | . . . [1789]

2° 1 pt.: *harpsichord or piano-forte:* 1 ℓ., 21 p.

On verso of preliminary leaf and on page [1]: A Catalogue of | Vocal and Instrumental Music Printed for and sold by | Messrs. Birchall & Andrew's . . .
Imprint date from Hoboken, p. 688
RISM A I, no. H 3654
H. XV, 6–8
MUSIC LIBRARY

737   HAYDN, JOSEPH

Trois | Sonates | Pour | Clavecin où Forte-Piano | avec Accompagnement | de Violon et Basse | Composées | Par J. Haydn. | Oeuvre 56e. | . . . | A Paris | Chez M. Boyer, Rue de Richelieu, à la Clef d'Or, | Passage de l'ancien Caffé de foy. | Chez Made. Le Menu, Rue du Roulle, à la Clef d'Or. | Ecrit par Ribiere. [1789?]

2° 3 pts.: *clavecin ou forte-piano:* 2 ℓ., 35 p.; *violino:* 14 p.; *violoncello:* 10 p.
On recto and verso of preliminary leaf 2 and page [1] of *clavecin ou forte-piano* part: No. 1 [–3] | Catalogue des Ouvrages appartenans à Mr. Boyer . . . ⟨a later state of JohanssonF, facs. 99–101⟩
RISM A I, no. H 3676
H. XV, 11–13
MUSIC LIBRARY

738   HAYES, PHILIP, COMP.

Harmonica Wiccamica. | The Original Music in Score of the | Graces, | Jam Lucis, and Dulce Domum. | Also | A Song and Ode Composed for & Perform'd at the | Anniversary Meeting in London. | The whole collated, revised, & corrected, by | Phil. Hayes. Mus. Doc. | Professor of Music in the University of Oxford. | London. | Printed for the Editor, and to be had of him only in Oxford. | . . . [ded. 1780]

obl. 2° *Score:* 3 ℓ., 25 p.
RISM B II, 197
MUSIC LIBRARY

739   HECK, JOHANN CASPAR

The | Art Of Playing | Thorough Bass | With Correctness according to the true Principles | Of Composition | Fully explained by a great Variety of Examples |

In Various Stiles | To which is added by way of Suppliment | Six Lessons Of Accompaniment | For the Particular Practice & improvement of the Studious | The Whole being designed for the Use of such Young Composers | & Performers in general as are desirous of being well Grounded in the | Science Of Harmony | By | John Casper Heck | . . . | London. Printed & Sold by Iohn Welcker No. 9 Hay Market Opposite the Opera House where may | be had every article in the Musical way. | [ca. 1777]

2° 1 ℓ., 99 p., music
RISM B VI, 401
HOUGHTON

740   HEINICHEN, JOHANN DAVID

Der | General-Bass | in der | Composition, | Oder: | Neue und gründliche | Anweisung, | Wie | Ein Music-Liebender mit besonderm Vortheil, durch | die Principia der Composition, nicht allein den General-Bass | im Kirchen- Cammer- und Theatralischen Stylô vollkommen, & in altiori | Gradu erlernen; sondern auch zu gleicher Zeit in der Composition selbst, wichtige | Profectus machen kônne. | Nebst einer Einleitung | Oder | Musicalischen Raisonnement | von der Music überhaupt, und vielen besondern | Materien der heutigen Praxeos. | Herausgegeben | von | Johann David Heinichen, | Kônigl. Pohln. und Churfl. Sâchs. Capellmeister. | In Dressden bey dem Autore zu finden. 1728.

4° 8 ℓ., 960, [28] p., 3 pl., music
Colophon: Freyberg, | gedruckt bey Christoph Matthäi.
Hirsch I, no. 244; RISM B VI, 403
HOUGHTON, MUSIC LIBRARY

741   HELLENDAAL, PIETER

Two Glees for four Voices | With Full Accompanyments In Score | Composed and most humbly Dedicated | To The Right Honorable | The Earl of Sandwich | by his Lordships most humble & obedient Servant | Peter Hellendaal | . . . | . . . Cambridge . . . | Printed & Sold by the Author & Son Opposite Peter house College | And to be had at the Music Shops. | . . . [ca. 1785]

obl. 2° *Score:* 2 ℓ., 23 p.
Contents: "Spirit! once wand'ring thro' this dreary vale" and "Music has charms"
RISM A I, no. H 4992
MUSIC LIBRARY

742   HERMANN, JOHANN DAVID

Troisième | Concerto | Pour le Piano-Forte ou Clavecin | Avec Accompagnement de deux Violons, Alto et Basse | Cors et Flûtes ad Libitum. | Dédié | Aux Amateurs | Par | M. Hermann. | Oeuvre V. . . . | A Paris, | Chez Naderman . . . | [before 1792]

2° 1 pt.: *Piano-forte ou clavecin:* 1 ℓ., 19 p.
Plate no. 719
Imprint partially covered by cancel label reading: A Bordeaux, chez A. Fillastre et Neveu, | Fossés du Chapeau-Rouge, No. 2.
RISM A I, no. H 5136
MUSIC LIBRARY

743   HEWITT, JAMES

An Introduction to | Singing, | or the | Rudiments Of Music; | To which is added a Compleat Set of | Practical Lessons, | Together with a Collection of the best | and most useful Psalm Tunes, | In all their Parts, | And several Anthems, by | Eminent Masters. | By James Hewitt. | [London] Sold by the Author, | In Sermon Lane near Doctors Commons, Mr. Buckland in | Pater Noster Row, Mr. Ashfield in the Old Change, and by | Mr. Chamberlaine in Milk Street, Cheapside. | MDCCLXV. | J. Ellis Sculpt. Neville Court, Fetter Lane.

8° 1 ℓ., 23, iii, 104 p., illus., music
RISM B VI, 412
HOUGHTON

744   HILLER, JOHANN ADAM

Anweisung | zum | musikalisch-richti-gen | Gesange, | mit | hinlänglichen Exempeln | erläutert, | von | Johann Adam Hiller. | Leipzig, | bey Johann Friedrich Junius 1774.

4° 10 ℓ., 224 p., illus., music
Hirsch I, no. 247; RISM B VI, 413
MUSIC LIBRARY

745   HILLER, JOHANN ADAM

Anweisung | zum | musikalisch-zierli-chen | Gesange, | mit | hinlänglichen Exempeln | erläutert, | von | Johann Adam Hiller. | Leipzig, | bey Johann Friedrich Junius 1780.

4° 4 ℓ., XXX, [2], 152 p., music
Hirsch I, no. 248; RISM B VI, 413
MUSIC LIBRARY

746   HILLER, JOHANN ADAM

Die Jagd, | eine comische Oper in drey Acten, | in die Musik gesetzt | von | Johann Adam Hiller. | Zweyte Auflage. | Leipzig, | gedruckt bey Bernhard Christoph Breitkopf und Sohn. 1772.

obl. 4° *Vocal score:* 101, [1] p.
RISM A I, no. H 5259
MUSIC LIBRARY

747   HILLER, JOHANN ADAM

Lisuart und Dariolette, | eine comische Oper in drey Acten, | in Musick gesetzt | von | Johann Adam Hiller. | Zweyte und vermehrte Auflage. | Leipzig, | gedruckt, bey Bernhard Christoph Breitkopf und Sohn. 1769.

obl. 4° *Vocal score:* 105, [1] p.
RISM A I, no. H 5268
MUSIC LIBRARY

748   HILLER, JOHANN ADAM

Der lustige Schuster, | oder | Der Teufel ist los, | Zweyter Theil. | Eine comische Oper in drey Aufzügen, | herausgegeben von | Johann Adam Hiller. | Leipzig, bey Johann Friedrich Junius. 1771.

obl. 4° *Vocal score:* 2 ℓ., VIII, 97, [1] p.
Colophon: gedruckt bey Bernhard Christoph Breitkopf und Sohn.
RISM A I, no. H 5272
MUSIC LIBRARY

749   HILLER, JOHANN ADAM

Die verwandelten Weiber, | oder | Der Teufel ist los, | Erster Theil. | Eine comische Oper in drey Aufzůgen, | herausgegeben von | Johann Adam Hiller. | Leipzig, bey Johann Friedrich Junius. 1770.

obl. 4° *Vocal score:* 2 ℓ., VIII, 70 p., 1 ℓ. Colophon: Leipzig, gedruckt bey Bernhard Christoph Breitkopf und Sohn. RISM A I, no. H 5276
MUSIC LIBRARY

750   HIRSCHBERGER, ALBRICUS

Philomela | Cisterciensis | Ex | Valle Barnadina | Raittenhaslacensi | In | Orbem evolans, tàm in Urbe, quàm | Rure Dei Laudem ter tremulâ Voce | decantatura, | Id Est, | Opus | Tripartitum | Constans | Sex Missis, totidémque Offertoriis, | ac Concertis, adjuncto Te Deum, &c. | Authore | P. Alberico Hirschberger, Sac. & Exempti | Ord. Cisterciensis p. t. Culinario in Celeberrimo | Monasterio Raittenhaslacensi Professo. | . . . | Burghusii, | Typis, Joannis Jacobi Luzenberger, Caesarei Regiminis Typographi. | M.DCC.XLIII.

2° 10 pts.: *canto:* 55 p.; *alto:* 45 p.; *tenore, basso:* 41 p. each; *violino primo* (imperfect—torn with loss of music): 94 p.; *violino secundo:* 84 p.; *clarino primo obligato:* 31 p.; *tympano:* 10 p.; *basso continuo pro batutta vel violone:* 88 p.; *organo sive bass. contin.:* 3 ℓ., 88 p., front.

Title supplied from *organo sive bass. contin.* part-book
Incomplete: part for clarino II lacking
RISM A I, no. H 5645
HOUGHTON

HIRSUTUS, GEORG   *See* Rhaw, Georg

HISTOIRE DE LA MUSIQUE, ET DE SES EFFETS   *See* Bonnet, Jacques, ed. *Histoire de la musique, et de ses effets*

HISTOIRE DE L'OPÉRA BOUFFON   *See* Contant d'Orville, André Guillaume *Histoire de l'opéra bouffon*

HISTOIRE DU THÉÂTRE DE L'OPÉRA COMIQUE   *See* Desboulmiers, Jean Auguste Julien, known as *Histoire du théâtre de l'Opéra comique*

HISTOIRE DU THÉÂTRE DE L'OPÉRA DE L'ACADÉMIE ROYALE DE MUSIQUE   *See* Durey de Noinville, Jacques Bernard *Histoire du théâtre de l'opéra de l'Académie royale de musique*

HISTOIRE DU THÉÂTRE DE L'OPÉRA EN FRANCE   *See* Durey de Noinville, Jacques Bernard *Histoire du théâtre de l'opéra en France*

751

The | Hoboy Preceptor | Or | The Whole Art of Playing the | Hoboy, | Rendered easy to all Capacities. | Wherein ev'ry Instruction relative to that Instrument is elucidated | in the most clear & simple manner, & by which any One may without | the Assistance of a Master Learn to play with Taste & Judment [*sic*] in a short time | To which is added a valuable Selection of | Airs, Song-Tunes & Duetts, by | Mr. Fischer. | . . . | London. Printed & Sold by G. Astor, No. 79 Cornhill. | Manufacturer of Grand & Small Piano Fortes. And Military Musical Instrument Maker to his Majesty's Army. [ca. 1800?]

obl. 4° 1 ℓ., 34 p., illus., music
Page 34: A Dictionary | Explaining such Latin Italian and French words as generally occur in Music
HOUGHTON

752   HOCHREITER, JOSEPH BALTHASAR

Oliva | In | Domo Dei | Fructifera | id est | Modici Vespertinorum | Qva Dominicalium Qva Festivalium | Psalmorum Palmites | Quos | E Tenui Musices Suae Arboreto | Novissime Excerpens | In Amaenos Quatuor Et Vocum Et | Instrvmentorvm Concertantivm | Ripienorumque Manipulos Collicavit | ac | Honori | Reverendissimi Praenobilis Et | Amplissimi Domini Domini | Maximiliani, | Celeberrimi Ac Antiquissimi Monasterii | Lambacensis In Superiore Austria Abbatis Vigilantissi-|mi Sacrae Caesareae Majestatis Consi-liarii, Nec Non Statuum | Provincialium Supra Onasum Assessoris Dignissimi &c. &c. Domini | Domini Mecaenatis Gratiosissimi In Humillimum Devo-tionis | Suae Mnemosynon Appendit | Josephus Balthasarus Hochreiter | Organista Lambacensis. | . . . | Augustae Vindelicorum, | Sumptibus Danielis Walder, Bibliopol. MDCCVI.

2° 7 pts.: *canto concert:* 1 ℓ., 25–47 p.; *alto concert:* 1 ℓ., 27 p.; *tenore concert:* 1 ℓ., 28 p.; *basso concert:* 1 ℓ., 26 p.; *violino I:* 1 ℓ., 121–143 p.; *violino II:* 1 ℓ., 145–166 p.; *organo:* 2 ℓ., 29 p.
RISM A I, no. H 5666
HOUGHTON

753   HOCHREITER, JOSEPH BALTHASAR

Philomela Mariana, | Id est | Vesperae | de Beatissima Virgine Maria, | à | 4. Vocibus & 2. Violinis Concert: necessariis, | 2. Violis Concertantibus ad libitum, | 4. Ripienis pro pleno Choro, | Violone, cum Basso Continuo. | Singulari moderni Styli methodo elaborata | à Josepho Balthasaro | Hochreither, | Celeberrimi & Antiquissimi Monasterii Lambacensis | Organoedo. | Opus II. | . . . | Augustae-Vindelicorum, | Sumptibus Danielis Walderi, Bibliopol. | Typis Andreae Maschenbaueri. | Anno MDCCX.

2° 7 pts.: *canto concert.:* 1 ℓ., 20 p.; *alto concert., tenore concert.:* 1 ℓ., 19 p. each; *basso concert.:* 1 ℓ., 16 p.; *violino I:* 1 ℓ., 18 p.; *violino II:* 1 ℓ., 16 p.; *organo:* 2 ℓ., 21 p.
RISM A I, no. H 5667
HOUGHTON

754   HOLCOMBE, HENRY

Six Solos | For A | Violin and Thorough Bass | With some Pieces for the | German Flute and Harpsicord | Compos'd By | Henry Holcombe | Opera Prima | London Printed by Wm. Smith Musick Printer at the golden Bass in Middle Row Holbourne and | sold only by the Author at his House in Southampton Street Bloomsbury. [1745?]

obl. 2° *Score:* 2 ℓ., 30 p.
RISM A I, no. H 6282
HOUGHTON

HOLDENDAAL, PIETER   *See* Hellendaal, Pieter

755   HOLDER, WILLIAM

A | Treatise | Of The | Natural Grounds, and Principles | Of | Harmony. | By William Holder, D. D. Fellow of the Royal | Society, and late Sub-Dean of their Majesty's Chapel | Royal. | To which is Added, by way of Appendix: | Rules for Playing a Thorow-Bass; with Variety | of Proper Lessons, Fuges, and Examples to Explain the said | Rules. Also Directions for Tuning an Harpsichord or | Spinnet. | By the late Mr. Godfrey Keller. | With several new Examples, which before were wan-|ting, the better to explain some Passages in the for-|mer Impressions. | The whole being Revis'd, and Corrected from many | gross Mistakes committed in the first Publication of | these Rules. | London: | Printed by W. Pearson, over against Wright's Coffee-|House in Aldersgate-street; for J. Wilcox in Little Britain; | and T. Osborne in Gray's-Inn. 1731.

8° 3 ℓ., 206 [i. e. 202] p., illus., pl., music
Numbers 157, 158, 175–178 omitted, 141, 142 repeated in paging
RISM B VI, 420
MUSIC LIBRARY (2 copies)

HOLLANDALE, PIETER   *See* Hellendaal, Pieter

756   HOMILIUS, GOTTFRIED AUGUST

Die | Freude der Hirten über die Geburt Jesu, | nach der Poesie | des Herrn Buschmann, | componirt | von | Gottfried August Homilius, | Cantor und Musicdirector an der Kreuzkirche zu Dressden. | Frankfurth an der Oder, | bey Carl Gottlieb Straus. | 1777.

obl. 2° *Score:* 1 ℓ., 98 p.
RISM A I, no. H 6434
MUSIC LIBRARY

757 HONAUER, LEONTZI

Six | Sonates | pour le | Clavecin | Avec accompagnement | de | Violon | Composèes par | L: Honauer &c Schobert | A: Londres | Chez A: Hummel, in King Street | St. Anns Soho Facing Nassau Street [176–?]

2° 1 pt.: *violino:* 1 *ℓ.*, 10 p.
RISM A I, no. H 6448
HOUGHTON

758 HOOK, JAMES

A Collection of | New English Songs | Sung at | the New Theatre at Richmond | by Mr. Fawcett, Mr. Smith and | Miss Slack | and also a Song Sung at Ranelagh | by Mr. Fawcett | Composed by | James Hook | Opera Prima | . . . | London | Printed for C. and S. Thompson in St. Paul's Church Yard. [1765?]

2° *Score:* 1 *ℓ.*, 15 p.
RISM A I, no. H 6608
MUSIC LIBRARY

759 HOOK, JAMES

The | Hermit | Written by the late Celebrated Dr. Goldsmith, | Set to Music by | James Hook. | Adapted for | Two Violins, Voice & Harpsichord. | Opera XXIV . . . | London | Printed for S. A. & P. Thompson No. 75 St. Pauls Church Yard. [1782?]

2° *Score:* 1 *ℓ.*, 19 p.
RISM A I, no. H 6859
MUSIC LIBRARY

760 HOOK, JAMES

The | Hours Of Love, | Composed For The | Voice, | And | Piano Forte, | By, | Mr. Hook. | London: | Printed for Harrison, Cluse, & Co. No. 78, Fleet Street. [1799?]

8° *Score:* 15 p. (*The Piano-Forte Magazine,* vol. IX, no. 4)
Plate no. 136
RISM A I, no. H 6621
MUSIC LIBRARY

761 HOOK, JAMES

Six | Familiar Sonatas, | For The | Piano Forte, | Composed By | Ja. Hook. | London: | Printed for Harrison & Co. No. 78, Fleet Street. [1798?]

8° *Score:* 41 p. (*The Piano-Forte Magazine,* vol. II, no. 11)
Plate nos. 63–64
RISM A I, no. H 7379
MUSIC LIBRARY

762 HOOK, JAMES

The | Triumph of Beauty | A | Musical Entertainment | As performed with universal Applause | By | Mr. Incledon, Miss Leary, Mrs. Martyr, and | Mrs. Wrighten | At Vauxhall Gardens | Written by a Lady, and | Set to Music by | Mr: Hook | Opera 46 . . . | London | Printed by Longman and Broderip No. 26 Cheapside and No. 13 Hay Market | . . . [1786?]

2° *Vocal score:* 1 *ℓ.*, 13, IIII [i. e. I] p.
Page IIII [i. e. I]: Musical Publications, | Printed and Sold by Longman & Broderip, . . .
RISM A I, no. H 6518
MUSIC LIBRARY

HORNAU, MARTIN GERBERT, FREIHERR VON *See* Gerbert, Martin, Freiherr von Hornau

HORSFIELD, ROBERT, PUBL. Vocal Music, or The Songsters Companion *See* Vocal Music, or The Songsters Companion

763 HOWARD, SAMUEL

A | Cantata | And | English Songs | Set to Musick by | Mr. Howard. | London. Printed for I. Walsh, in Catharine Street, in the Strand. | . . . [1745]

2° *Score:* 1 *ℓ.*, 13 p.
RISM A I, no. H 7484; Walsh II, no. 844
HOUGHTON

764 HOYLE, JOHN

A | Complete Dictionary | Of | Music. | Containing | A Full And Clear Explana-

tion, | Divested Of Technical Phrases, |
Of all the Words and Terms, English,
Italian, &c. | made use of in that Science, |
Speculative, Practical, and Historical. |
The Whole | Compiled from the best An-
cient and Modern Authors, and | particu-
larly adapted to Scholars, as well as Profi-
cients. | By John Hoyle, Musician. |
London: | Printed for H. D. Symonds, Pa-
ternoster-Row; | J. Dale, At His Music-
Warehouses, No. 132, Oxford-|Street,
And At No. 19, Cornhill;—Miller, No. 5,
| Old Bond-Street;—And J. Sewell, Corn-
hill. | M,DCC,XCI. | . . .

8° iv, 160 p., illus.
RISM B VI, 425
MUSIC LIBRARY

765   HOYLE, JOHN

Dictionarium Musica, | Being A | Com-
plete Dictionary: | Or, | Treasury Of
Music. | Containing, | A full Explanation
of all the Words and Terms made | use of
in Music, both Speculative, Practical and
| Historical. | All The | Words and Terms
made use of by the Italians, | are also in-
serted. The whole Compiled from the |
best Antient and Modern Authors who
have wrote | on the Subject. | By John
Hoyle, Musician. | London: | Printed For
The Author, And Sold By | S. Crowder,
No. 12, Pater-Noster-Row, London; |
And J. Binns, Bookseller, In Leeds, York-
shire. | MDCCLXX.

8° 2 ℓ., 112 p., music
RISM B VI, 425
MUSIC LIBRARY

HUBER, JACOB, PUBL. Sammlung auserlesener geistlicher Lieder *See* Sammlung auserlesener geistlicher Lieder

HUDGEBUT, JOHN, PUBL. Thesaurus musicus *See* Thesaurus musicus

HÜLLER, JOHANN ADAM *See* Hiller, Johann Adam

HULKENROY, ISAAC VAN, PUBL. 't Ver-
maakelyk zang-prieel *See* 't Vermaake-
lyk zang-prieel

766   HUMPHRIES, J. S.

XII | Sonatas, | For Two Violins; | With
A Through Bass For The | Harpsichord. |
Composed by | J: S: Humphries. | Opera
Prima. | N. B. These Sonatas are proper to
be play'd with two German Flutes &c. |
. . . | London. Printed for, and Sold by I:
Walsh, Musick Printer, and | Instrument
maker to his Majesty, at the Harp and
Hoboy, in | Catherine Street, in the
Strand. [ca. 1736]

2° 3 pts.: *violino primo:* 1 ℓ., 20 p.; *violino secondo, basso continuo:* 1 ℓ., 15 p.
each
RISM A I, no. H 7925; Walsh II, no.
852
MUSIC LIBRARY

I

767   ILLUMINATO DA TORINO,
             FRATE

Canto | Ecclesiastico | Diviso In Quat-
tro Libri | Che Contengono | Ventiquat-
tro Messe | Colle Regole Generali di tal
Canto. | Il Primo composto di nove
Messe solenni; Il Secondo di nove Messe
festive; | Il Terzo di sei Messe a puro
Canto Gregoriano; Il quarto di chiara | è
breve notizia delle Regole generali
dell'istesso Canto. | Del Padre Fra | Illu-
minato Da Torino | Lettore, Predicatore,
Minor Rifformato di San Francesco Nella
Provincia | di San Tommaso Appostolo
in Piemonte. | Opera Dedicata | A Sua Ec-
cellenza Il Signore | Luigi Pisani | Cava-
liere, E Procurator | Meritissimo Di S.
Marco. | In Venezia, MDCCXXXIII. | Ap-
presso Antonio Bortoli. | In Mercería
all'Insegna dell'Educazione. | Con Li-
cenza De' Superiori, E Privilegio.

2° 4 ℓ., 110 p., illus., pl. (port.), music
RISM B VI, 428
MUSIC LIBRARY

IOANNELLUS, PETRUS *See* Giovanelli,
Pietro

768 ISAAC, _____

The | Union | a New Dance | Compos'd | by | Mr. Isaac | Perform'd at Court | on Her Majestie's | Birth day | Febr: ye 6th. | 1707. | and writt down in Characters by Iohn Weaver. | [London?, 1707?] H Hulsbergh Schulp

4° 15 *ℓ.,* illus., music
RISM A I, no. I 83
HOUGHTON

769 ISAAC, ELIAS

The | Black-Birds | A Cantata | Set to Music by | Mr. Isaac | Organist at Worcester. | . . . | [London] Printed for the Author by J. Johnson in Cheapside. [ca. 1765]

2° *Score:* 9 p.
Without title-page (as published?); caption title; imprint at foot of page 1
RISM A I, no. I 86
MUSIC LIBRARY

770 ISIDORUS, SAINT,
BISHOP OF SEVILLE

. . . De mvsica Et Eivs Nomine [Augsburg, 1472]

2° In his *Ethimologiarum, ℓ.* 43ᵛ–46ᵛ
Colophon: . . . Per. Gintherum zainer ex | Reutlingen progenitum. literis impressi ahenis. Anno | ab incarnatione domini. Millesimo Quadringentesimo | Septuagesimosecundo. Decimanona die. Mensis. nouebris.
Caption title
BMC II, 317; Hain, no. 9273
HOUGHTON

771 ISIDORUS, SAINT,
BISHOP OF SEVILLE

De Mvsica Et Eivs Nomine [Strassburg, ca. 1473]

2° In his *Etymologiarum, ℓ.* 22ʳ–23ʳ
Printed by Johann Mentelin
Caption title
Two columns to the page
BMC I, 57; Hain-Copinger, no. 9270
HOUGHTON

772 ISIDORUS, SAINT,
BISHOP OF SEVILLE

de musica & eius noīe. [Cologne, ca. 1480]

2° In his *ethimologia[rum], ℓ.* 14ʳ–15ʳ
Printed by Conrad Winters de Homborch
Caption title
Two columns to the page
Hain-Copinger, no. 9271
HOUGHTON

773 ISIDORUS, SAINT,
BISHOP OF SEVILLE

De musica & eius nomine. [Venice, 1493]

2° In his *ethimologiarum,* numb. *ℓ.* 11ᵛ–12ᵛ [i. e. 13ᵛ–14ᵛ]
Colophon: . . . Impressus Venetijs p[er] Bonetū loca-|tellum mandato & expensis Nobilis viri Octauiani Scoti | Ciuis Modoetiensis. MCCCCXCIII. | Tertio Idus Decembres. Cū dei summa laude.
Caption title
Two columns to the page
Numbers 7, 8 repeated in foliation
BMC V, 442; Hain, no. 9280; Goff, no. I-186
HOUGHTON

774 ISIDORUS, SAINT,
BISHOP OF SEVILLE

De musica & eius nomine. [Venice: Bonetus Locatellus, for Octavianus Scotus, after 1500]

2° In his *Etymologiarum opus, ℓ.* bb5ᵛ –bb6ᵛ
Two columns to the page
Caption title
HOUGHTON

775 ISIDORUS, SAINT,
BISHOP OF SEVILLE

De musica et eius nomine. [Paris, 1520]

2° In his *Praeclarissimum opus diui Isidori Hyspalensis, quod [a]ethimologiarum inscribitur, ℓ.* c4ʳ–c5ʳ

Colophon: Impressum Parrhisij sum-
ptibns [*sic*] Ioannis Petit. | Anno salutis
Miliesimo quingentesimovicesimo. | die
vero vicesimaquinta mensis Septembris.
Two columns to the page
Caption title
HOUGHTON

J

776   JACKSON, WILLIAM

Twelve Canzonets | for two Voices; |
composed by | William Jackson | of Ex-
eter. | Opera Nona. | London | Printed for
the Author, and sold at the Music-Shops.
[ca. 1770]

2° *Score:* 2 ℓ., 27 p.
Preliminary leaf 2ʳ: Lately published,
by the Author of these Pieces, . . .
RISM A I, no. J 116
HOUGHTON, MUSIC LIBRARY

777   JACKSON, WILLIAM

Twelve Canzonets, | For | Two Voices. |
Composed by | William Jackson, | Of | Ex-
eter. | London: | Printed for Harrison &
Co. No. 18, Paternoster Row. [1797]

8° *Score:* 39, [1] p. (*The Piano-Forte
Magazine,* vol. I, no. 2)
RISM A I, no. J 124 (op. 9)
MUSIC LIBRARY

778   JACKSON, WILLIAM

Twelve | Canzonetts, | Composed By, |
Wm. Jackson, | Of Exeter. | Opera 13. |
London: | Printed for Harrison, Cluse, &
Co. No. 78, Fleet Street [1799?]

8° *Score:* 53 p. (*The Piano-Forte Maga-
zine,* vol. VIII, no. 7)
Plate nos. 128–130
RISM A I, no. J 172
MUSIC LIBRARY

779   JACKSON, WILLIAM

An | Ode to Fancy | by Warton, | set to
Music by | William Jackson | of Exeter. |

Opera Ottava. | London; | Printed for the
Author, and sold at the Music Shops.
[1773?]

2° *Score:* 3 ℓ., 83 p.
Preliminary leaf 3ᵛ: Lately published
by the Author of these Pieces.
RISM A I, no. J 115
MUSIC LIBRARY

780   JACKSON, WILLIAM

Twelve | Favourite Songs, | Composed
By, | Mr Jackson, | Of | Exeter. | Opera 4. |
London: | Printed for Harrison, Cluse, &
Co. No. 78, Fleet Street. [1799?]

8° *Score:* 45 p. (*The Piano-Forte Maga-
zine,* vol. VIII, no. 1)
Plate nos. 114–115
RISM A I, no. J 100
MUSIC LIBRARY

781   JACOB, GUNTHER WENZEL

ACratIsMVs | Pro Honore DeI | EX
EsCIs Sonorae PIetatIs | PraeparatVs. |
Diverso Instrumentorum Musicorum |
aromate conditus | Atque | Omnibus &
Singulis | non minus devotè quàm
musicè | Sacro-Sanctam & individuam |
Trinitatem | colentibus | ad sumendum
ex eo liberè | devotissimè | propositus, |
Sev | Missae V. | Vivorum IV. Defun-
ctorum I. | consistentes | in Vocibus IV.
Instrumentis ùt in Indice. | Opus II. | . . .
| Authore P. Gunthero Jacob Ord. S. Be-
nedicti | Monasterri S. Nicolai Vetero-
Pragae Professo &c. | Pragae, | Apud Pau-
lum Lochner Bibliopolam Norimbergen-
sem. | Anno M.D.CC.XXV.

2° 10 pts.: *canto:* [−]1, A–M², a–b², cl;
alto: [−]1, A–K², Ll, a–b², cl; *tenore:*
[−]1, A–M², a–b², cl; *basso* [−]1, A–L²,
Ml, a–b², cl; *clarino I:* [−]1, A–B², Cl,
D², a²; *clarino II:* [−]1, A–C², a²; *violino
I:* [−]1, A–O², Pl, a–b², cl; *violino II:*
[−]1, A–N², a–b², cl; *alto:* [−]1, A–I², a–
b²; *organo:*)(⁶, A–R², a–c², [−]1
Imprint   date   in   *organo*   part:
M.D.CC.XXVI
RISM A I, no. J 201
HOUGHTON

782 JAENISCH, ――――

Eine Sonate | Für das Clavier | nebst einigen kleinen | Clavier- und Singstücken | von | Jaenisch. | Riga, gedruckt von Julius Conrad Daniel Müller. | In Commission bey Johann Friedrich Hartknoch. [ca. 1795]

2° *Score:* 1 ℓ., 16 p.
RISM A I, no. J 426
MUSIC LIBRARY

783 JAMARD, T.

Recherches | Sur La Théorie | De La Musique, | Par M. Jamard, | Chanoine Régulier de Ste. Géneviève, Prieur | de Rocquefort, Membre de l'Académie | des Sciences, Belles-Lettres & Arts de | Rouen. | . . . | A Paris, | Chez {Jombert, Libraire du Roi pour l'artillerie & le | génie, rue Dauphine. | Merigot pere & fils, Quai des Augustins. | A Rouen, | Chez Et. Vinc. Machuel, rue S. Lo, vis-à-vis le Palais. | M.DCC.LXIX. | Avec Approbation & Privilége du Roi.

8° 2 ℓ., xxvij, [1], 296, [4] p., illus., fold. pl.
Hirsch I, no. 257; RISM B VI, 432
HOUGHTON

784 JOHNSTON, THOMAS

To learn to sing, observe These Rules. | . . . | Engrav'd Printed & sold by Thomas Johnston Brattle street Boston 1755.

8° 16 numb. ℓ., music
Numbered leaves 2–16: hymns and psalms for three and four voices
Caption title; imprint at foot of numbered leaf 1
Numbered leaves printed on one side only
HOUGHTON (2 copies)

785 JOMMELLI, NICOLÒ

The | Favorite Periodical | Overture | and | Chaconne | Composed by | Sigr. Jomelli | adapted for the | Harpsichord | or | Piano Forte | by | W. Smethergell . . . | London: Printed for the Editor by Longman and Broderip No. 26 Cheapside, . . . [ca. 1780]

2° *Score:* 7 p.
RISM A I, no. J 601
MUSIC LIBRARY

JOSQUIN DESPREZ *See* Desprez, Josquin

786

. . . | Journal | Des Spectacles. [Paris] 1793

8° [491]–861 [i. e. 866] p.
Consists of numbers 62–108, published daily (irregular) from September 1 through October 18, 1793
Numbers 71–73 misnumbered 70–72, number 97 misnumbered 96
Colophon: De l'imprimerie de Crétot, rue des Bons-Enfans, no 12.
Numerous errors in paging; five extra unnumbered pages
Hatin, p. 589
HOUGHTON

787

. . . | Journal | Des Spectacles. [Paris] 1793

8° 8, [870]–885 p.
Consists of numbers 103, 104, [2d]104, dated October 11, 12, 21 respectively
Colophon: De l'Imprimerie de la Citoyenne Fonrouge, | Jardin de l'Egalité, No. 71.
WIDENER

JULIEN, JEAN AUGUSTE *See* Desboulmiers, Jean Auguste Julien, known as

788 JUST, JOHANN AUGUST

Just's | Favorite Concerto, | For The | Piano Forte. | London. | Printed for Harrison & Co. No. 18 Paternoster Row. [1798?]

8° *Score:* 1 ℓ., 5–16 p. (*The Piano-Forte Magazine,* vol. III, no. 11)
RISM A I, no. J 774 (op. 10)
MUSIC LIBRARY

789   JUST, JOHANN AUGUST

Six | Favourite Sonatas | For The | Piano Forte. | Composed By, | J. A. Just. | London: | Printed for Harrison, Cluse, & Co. No. 78, Fleet Street. [1799?]

8° *Score:* 51 p. (*The Piano-Forte Magazine,* vol. VIII, no. 3)
Plate nos. 119–121
RISM A I, no. J 782 (op. 13)
MUSIC LIBRARY

JUSTIFICATION   DE   LA   MUSIQUE
FRANÇOISE   *See* Morand, Pierre de *Justification de la musique françoise*

K

790   KAMMEL, ANTON

Six | Notturnos | for two | Violins and a Bass | Humbly Dedicated to | Lady Young of Delaford | By her Grateful | and most Obedient humble Servant | Antonio Kammell | Opera VI. . . . | London Printed by Welcker in Gerrard Street Soho, | . . . [ca. 1772]

2° 3 pts.: *violino primo, violino secondo, basso:* 1 ℓ., 13 p. each
RISM A I, no. K 109
HOUGHTON

791

Kann man nicht in zwey, oder drey Monaten | die Orgel | gut, und regelmässig schlagen lernen? | Mit Ja beantwortet, und dargethan | vermittelst einer Einleitung | zum Generalbasse. | Verfasst | für die Pflanzschule | des fürstlichen Reichsstiftes | St. Emmeram. | Landshut, mit Hagenschen Schriften 1789.

obl. 4° 223, [6] p., illus., 2 pl., music
Plates included in paging
RISM B VI, 672
MUSIC LIBRARY

792   KAYSER, ISFRID

Cantatae | Sacrae | Complectentes | Arias XVIII. | Cum | Recitativis, Et Alleluja | Plerisque Anni | Festivitati-|bus | Accommodatas | à | Voce Sola, | 2. Violinis, Alto Viola, | Et | Organo. | Authore | R. P. Isfrido Kayser, | Imperialis, Candidae, & Exemptae Canoniae Marchtallensis, | Sacri, & Canonici Ordinis Praemonstratensis Professo, p. t. Musices | Directore, & in Parochialibus Cooperatore. | . . . | Cum Licentia Superiorum. | Monachii & Augustae Vindelicorum, | Sumptibus Mathaei Rieger, Bibliop. [17—]

2° 5 pts.: *vox:* [–]², *A–*L²; *violino I:* [–]², (A)–(M)²; *violino II:* [–]², (Aa)–(Mm)²; *alto viola:* [–]², †A–†K²; *organo:* [–]²,)()(1, A–M², N1
RISM A I, no. K 210
HOUGHTON

793   KAYSER, ISFRID

VI. Missae | à | 4. Vocibus ordinariis, | Canto, Alto, | Tenore, Basso, | 2. Violinis necessariis, 2. Lituis, | vel Clarinis, cum Tympanis, | ex diversis Clavibus ad Libitum, | decorè tamen concurrentibus, | Cum | Duplici Basso continuo. | Methodô facilî, & modernâ elaboratae | à | R. P. Isfrido Kayser, | Imperialis, Celeberriamae, ac Exemptae Canoniae Marchtallensis, | Ordinis Praemonstratensis Canonico, & Capellae Magistro. | Opus II. | . . . | Cum Licentia Superiorum. | Augustae Vindelicorum, | Sumptibus Mathaei Rieger, Bibliopolae. | MDCCXLIII.

2° 10 pts.: *canto:* 1 ℓ., 44 p.; *alto, tenore, basso:* 1 ℓ., 42 p. each; *clarino I:* 1 ℓ., 22 p.; *clarino II:* 1 ℓ., 20 p.; *violino I:* 1 ℓ., 50 p.; *violino II:* 1 ℓ., 48 p.; *violoncello:* 1 ℓ., 54 p.; *organo:* 3 ℓ., 54 p.
RISM A I, no. K 211
HOUGHTON

794   KAYSER, ISFRID

XII. | Offertoria | Solemnia | De | Communi | Sanctorum, | â | IV. Vocibus, Canto, Alto, Te-|nore, Basso, II. Violinis necessariis, II. Li-|tuis ac Tymp. ex diversis Clavibus, | ad libitum concurrentibus, | & | Organo, | Authore | R. P. Isfrido Kayser, | Imperialis, Celeberr. ac exemptae Canoniae March-|tallensis, Ordinis Praemonstrat. Canonico &c. &c. | Opus V. | Pars Prima. | . . . | Cum Licentia Superiorum. | Augustae Vindelicorum, | Sumptibus Matthaei Rieger, Bibliopolae, 1748.

> 2° 1 pt.: *organo:* 4 ℓ., 44 p.
> RISM A I, no. K 214
> HOUGHTON

795   KAYSER, ISFRID

XII. | Offertoria | Solemnia Breviora | De | Communi | Sanctorum, | Una Cum | VIII. Benedictionibus | Pro Solemnitatibus | Augustissimi Altaris | Sacramenti, | â | IV. Vocibus, Canto, Alto, Tenore, Basso, | II. Violinis necessariis, II. Lituis, ac Tympano ex di-|versis Clavibus, ad Libitum concurrentibus, | & | Organo, | Authore | A. R. P. Isfrido Kayser, | Imperialis, Celeberr. ac Exemptae Canoniae Marchtallensis, | Ordinis Praemonstratensis, Canonico, &c. &c. | Opus VI. | Pars Secunda. | . . . | Cum Licentia, & Facultate Superiorum. | Augustae Vindelicorum, | Sumptibus Matthaei Rieger, Bibliopolae, 1750.

> 2° 1 pt.: *organo:* 4 ℓ., 38 p.
> RISM A I, no. K 215
> HOUGHTON

796   KAYSER, ISFRID

Psalmi | Longiores, & Breves | In | Vesperas | De | Dominica, B. V. M. | Apostolis &c. | & | Sabbatho, | Distributi, | Cum reliquis Psalmis, per Annum occurentibus, | ac | Antiphonis Marianis. | A | Quatuor Vocibus ordinariis | Canto, Alto, Tenore, Basso, | II. Violinis necessar. II. Lituis ac Tymp. | ex diversis Clavibus ad Libitum colludentibus, | Methodo facillima elaborati | â | R. P. Isfrido Kayser, | Imper. Celeberrimae, ac Exemptae Canoniae March-|tallensis Ordinis Praemonstratensis Canonico. | Opus III. | . . . | Cum Licentia Superiorum. | Augustae Vindelicorum, | Sumptibus Matthaei Rieger, Bibliopolae, | MDCCXLVI.

> 2° 1 pt.: *organo:* 4 ℓ., 43 p.
> RISM A I, no. K 212
> HOUGHTON

797   KAYSER, ISFRID

III. | Vesperae | cum | consuetis Antiphonis | de | Beatissima Virgine ac Gloriosissima | Dei Genitrice | Maria, | à | 4. Vocibûs, & Instrumentîs ordinariîs, nimirùm | Canto, Alto, Tenore, Basso, 2. Violinis necessariis, 2. Lituis, | ac Tympanis, ex diversis Tonis ad Libitum concurrentibûs, | Viola ad Antiphonas solùm obligata, | cum Organo. | Authore | Reverendo, ac Religioso Domino Patre | Isfrido Kayser, | Imperialis, Exemptae, ac Celeberrimae Canoniae Marchtallensis, Ordinis Praemonstratensis | Canonico Capitulari &c. &c. | . . . | Opus VII. | Cum Facultate Superiorum. | Augustae Vindelicorum, | Sumtibus Matthaei Rieger, Bibliopolae. | MDCCLIV.

> 2° 1 pt.: *canto:* 1 ℓ., 38 p.
> RISM A I, no. K 216
> HOUGHTON

798   KEEBLE, JOHN

The | Theory | Of | Harmonics: | Or, | An Illustration | Of The | Grecian Harmonica. | In Two Parts: | I. As it is maintained by Euclid, Aristoxenus, and | Bacchius Senior. | II. As it is established on the Doctrine of the Ratio: in which | are explained the Two Diagrams of Gaudentius, and | the Pythagorean Numbers in Nicomachus. | With Plates, an Introduction to each Part, and a | General Index. | By John Keeble, | Organist of St. George's-Church, Hanover-Square. | London: | Printed for the Author; | And sold by J. Walter, at Charing-Cross; | J. Robson, in Bond-Street; B. White, in Fleet-Street; J. Sewell, in Cornhill; | And by the Booksellers of Oxford and Cambridge. | M.DCC.LXXXXIV.

> 4° 3 ℓ., 204, xxiii [2] p., illus., 29 [i.e. 28] pl. on 20 ℓ.
> Plate 11 omitted
> RISM B VI, 442
> MUSIC LIBRARY

799   [KELLNER, DAVID]

Treulicher | Unterricht | im | General-Bass, | worinne | alle Weitläufftigkeit vermieden, und dennoch | gantz deutlich und umständlich allerhand sothane neu-erfundene Vor-|theile an die Hand gegeben werden, vermôge welcher einer in | kurtzer Zeit alles, was zu dieser Wissenschafft gehôret, sattsam | begreiffen kan. | Zum Nutzen, | Nicht allein derer, so sich im General-Bass ûben, son-|dern auch aller andern Instrumentisten und Vocalisten, welche | einen rechten Grund in der Music zu legen sich befleissigen, | herausgegeben | von | D. K. | Hamburg, | Zu finden im Kissnerischen Buchladen. 1732.

4° 2 *ℓ.*, 93, [5] p., illus., music
RISM B VI, 444
HOUGHTON

800 KELLY, MICHAEL

The Grand Dramatic Romance | of | Blue Beard | or | Female Curiosity, | As now performing at the Theatre-Royal | Drury Lane | with unbounded Applause, | the words by | George Coleman the Younger, Esqr. | the Music Composed, & Selected | by Michael Kelly. | . . . | Printed for Corri, Dussek, & Co. Music-sellers to the Royal Family: No. 28, Haymarket, & no. 67, Dean St. Soho; London. No. 8, South St. Andrew St. & No. 37, Bridge St. Edinburgh. [1798?]

obl. 2° *Vocal score:* 1 *ℓ.*, 74 p.
RISM A I, no. K 291
MUSIC LIBRARY

801 KELLY, MICHAEL

The | Castle Spectre | as now performing with unbounded applause | at the Theatre Royal Drury Lane. | The Words by G: M: Lewis Esqr. | The Music by | Michael Kelly. | . . . | London, Printed for & Sold by J. Dale, No. 19 Cornhill, & the corner of Holles Street, Oxford Street. | . . . [1798?]

obl. 2° *Score:* 1 *ℓ.*, 7 p.
RISM A I, no. K 319
MUSIC LIBRARY

802 KELLY, MICHAEL

A Friend In Need, | A Musical Entertainment, | as Perform'd at the Theatre Royal Drury Lane. | The Music Composed and Selected | By | Michael Kelly, |

The Words by Prince Hoare. | . . . | London. Printed for & Sold by I, Dale, No, 19. Cornhill & the corner of Holles Street, Oxford Street. [1797?]

2° *Vocal score:* 1 *ℓ.*, 35 p.
Page [1]: advertisement for music, presumably from the shop of Joseph Dale; caption identifying publisher cropped
RISM A I, no. K 329
MUSIC LIBRARY

803 KELLY, MICHAEL

The Music of | Pizarro, | A Play, | As now Performing at the | Theatre Royal Drury Lane, | with unbounded Applause, | The Music Composed & Selected | By | Michael Kelly. | . . . | [London] Published for Mr. Kelly, No. 9, | New Lisle Street, & to be had at | all the Music Shops. [1799?]

2° *Vocal score:* 1 *ℓ.*, 30 p.
RISM A I, no. K 348
MUSIC LIBRARY

804 KENT, JAMES

Twelve Anthems | Composed by | James Kent | Organist of the Cathedral | and | College | at | Winchester. | . . . | London: | Printed & sold by Preston and Son, | No, 97 Strand & Exeter Change. [179–?]

2° *Score:* 2 *ℓ.*, 100 p.
RISM A I, no. K 403
MUSIC LIBRARY

805 KENT, JAMES

A | Morning & Evening Service, | with | Eight Anthems, | Composed by the late | James Kent, | Organist of the Cathedral | and College at | Winchester. | . . . | Revised and arranged by | Joseph Corfe, | Gentleman of his Majesty's Chapels Royal, | and Organist of the Cathedral at Salisbury. | [London] Printed for the Editor, & to be had at the | principal Music Shops in Town & Country. | . . . [179–?]

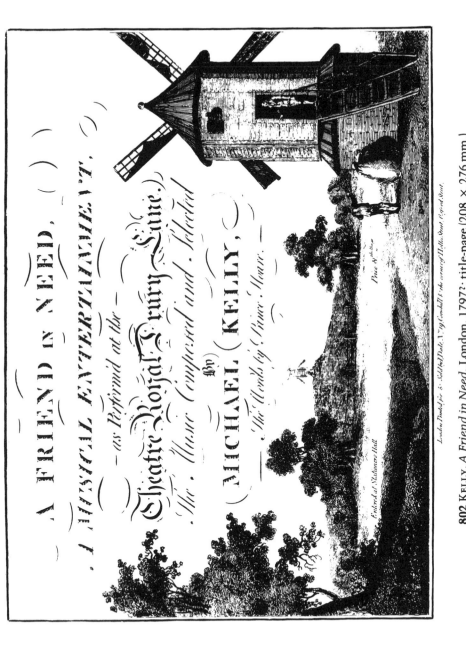

A FRIEND IN NEED.

A MUSICAL ENTERTAINMENT.

— as Performed at the —

Theatre Royal Drury Lane.

The Music Composed and Selected

By

MICHAEL KELLY,

The Words by Prince Hoare.

Entered at Stationers Hall

Price 8ˢ⁄₆ᵈ

London Printed for & Sold by I. Dale, N.º 19 Cornhill & the corner of Hollis Street Cavendish Street.

802 KELLY, *A Friend in Need*, London, 1797: title-page (208 × 276 mm.)

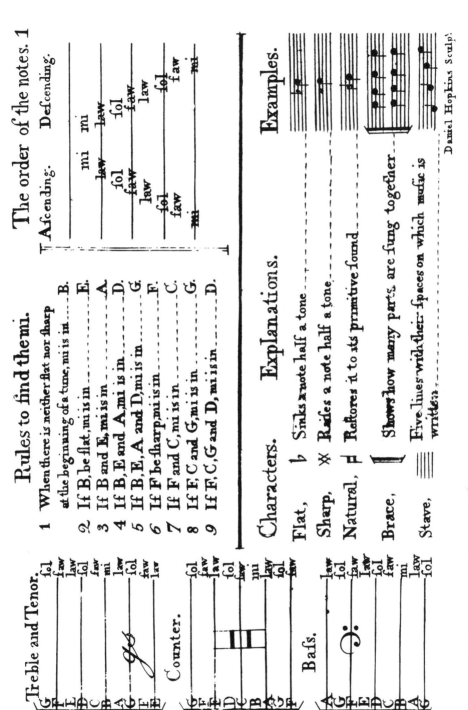

The order of the notes. 1

Ascending. **Descending.**

	mi	mi
	law	law
	fol	fol
	faw	faw
	law	law
	fol	fol
	faw	faw
	mi	mi

Rules to find them.

1 When there is neither flat nor sharp
at the beginning of a tune, mi is in .... B.

2 If B, be flat, mi is in .... E.

3 If B and E, mi is in .... A.

4 If B, E and A, mi is in .... D.

5 If B, E, A and D, mi is in .... G.

6 If F be sharp, mi is in .... F.

7 If F and C, mi is in .... C.

8 If F, C and G, mi is in .... G.

9 If F, C, G and D, mi is in .... D.

Explanations.

Characters.

Flat, ♭   Sinks a note half a tone.

Sharp, ✕   Raises a note half a tone.

Natural, ♮   Restores it to its primitive sound.

Brace,   Shows how many parts are sung together.

Stave, ≡   Five lines with their spaces on which music is written.

Treble and Tenor.

G	fol
F	faw
E	law
D	fol
C	faw
	mi
A	law
G	fol
F	faw
E	law

Counter.

G	fol
F	faw
D	law
	fol
B	faw
	mi
G	law
F	fol
E	law

Bass.

A	law
G	fol
F	faw
E	law
D	fol
C	faw
	mi
B	law
G	fol

Examples.

Daniel Hopkins Sculp!

856 Law, The Rudiments of Music, Cheshire, Conn., 1783: page 1, second sequence (113 × 181 mm.)

2° *Score:* 1 ℓ., 2, 121 p.
At foot of page 2, first sequence:
Printed By Thomas Collins, Harvey's
Buildings, Strand.
MUSIC LIBRARY

KERNBERG, JOHANN PHILIPP *See* Kirnberger, Johann Philipp

806   KING, WILLIAM

Poems | Of | Mr. Covvley | And Others.
| Composed into Songs and Ayres | with a
Thorough Basse to the Theorbo, | Harpsecon, or Base-violl; | By | William King Organist of New-Colledge | In the University of Oxon: | Oxford, | Imprinted By
William Hall, For the | Author 1668.

2° *Score:* 2 ℓ., 55 p.
Day, no. 27; RISM A I, no. K 626
HOUGHTON

807   KIRCHER, ATHANASIUS

Athanasii Kircheri | Fvldensis E Soc.
Iesv Presbyteri | Mvsvrgia | Vniversalis |
Sive | Ars Magna | Consoni Et Dissoni | In
X. Libros Digesta. | Quà Vniuersa Sonorum doctrina, & Philosophia, Musicaeque tam Theoricae, quam practicae |
scientia, summa varietate traditur; admirandae Consoni, & Dissoni in mundo,
adeòque | Vniuersà Naturà vires effectusque, vti noua, ita peregrina variorum speciminum | exhibitione ad singulares
vsus, tum in omni poenè facultate, tum
potissimùm | in Philologià, Mathematicà, Physicà, Mechanicà, Medicinà, Politicà, | Metaphysicà, Theologià, aperiuntur & demonstrantur. | . . . | Romae, Ex
Typographia Haeredum Francisci Corbelletti.   Anno Iubilaei.   MDCL. |
Svperiorvm Permissv.

2° 2 vols.: *vol. I:* 10 ℓ., 690 [i. e. 692] p.,
front., illus., 11 pl. (incl. port.), music;
vol. II: 1 ℓ., 462, [36] p., front., illus., 10
pl. (2 fold.), music
Imprint, *vol. II:* Romae, Typis Ludouici Grignani. Anno Iubilaei MDCL.
Numbers 575, 576 repeated in paging
in vol. I
Hirsch I, no. 266; RISM B VI, 449; Wolfenbüttel, no. 1190
HOUGHTON (2 copies)

808   KIRCHER, ATHANASIUS

Athanasii Kircheri | E Soc. Jesu. | Phonurgia | Nova | Sive | Conjugium Mechanico-physicum | Artis & Natvrae | Paranympha Phonosophia | Concinnatum; |
quâ | Vniversa Sonorvm Natvra, Proprietas, Vires | effectuúmq[ue] prodigiosorum Causae, novâ & multiplici experimentorum exhibitione enu-|cleantur;
Instrumentorum   Acusticorum,   Machinarúmq[ue] ad Naturae prototypon |
adaptandarum, tum ad sonos ad remotissima spatia propagandos, tum in abditis
domo-|rum recessibus per occultioris ingenii machinamenta clam [*sic*] palámve
sermo-|cinandi modus & ratio traditur,
tum denique in Bellorum tumul-|tibus
singularis hujusmodi Organorum Vsus,
& praxis | per novam Phonologiam describitur. | Campidonae | Per Rudolphum
Dreherr. Anno M.DC.LXXIII.

2° 21 ℓ., 229, [16] p., front., illus., 3 pl.
(incl. port.), music
Davidsson II, no. 50; Hirsch I, no. 267;
RISM B VI, 450; Wolfenbüttel, no. 1192
HOUGHTON

809   KIRMAIR, FRIEDRICH JOSEPH

Six Thêmes | tirés de divers opéras de |
Mozart | I. Klinget, Glöckchen, klinget;
Aus der Zauberflöte. | II. Liebstes Blondchen ach verzeihe; Aus Belmonte u.
Const: | III. Schnelle Füsse, rascher
Muth; Aus der Zauberflöte. | IV. Nie
werd ich diese Huld verkennen: Finale,
aus Belm. u. Const: | V. Drey Knäbchen,
jung, schön, hold und weise; Aus der
Zauberf: | VI. Wer ein Liebchen hat gefunden; Aus Belmonte u. Constanze. |
Variés pour le Forte Piano. | par Kirmair |
Maitre de Musique de LL. AA. RR. Madame la | Princesse Royale et Madame la
Princesse Epouse | de S. A. R. Monseigneur le Prince Louis de Prusse. | III Partie. | Chés J. J. Hummel, | à Berlin avec
Privilége du Roi, | à Amsterdam au grand
Magazin de Musique | et aux Adresses ordinaires. | . . . [1795–1797]

2° *Score:* 15 p.
Plate no. 859
RISM A I, no. K 673
HOUGHTON

810   Kirnberger, Johann Philipp

Gedanken | über die | verschiedenen
Lehrarten in der | Komposition | als Vor-
bereitung | zur Fugenkenntniss | von | J.
P. Kirnberger | . . . | Wien | Im Verlag der
k: k: priv: chemischen Druckerey am
Graben. | . . . [1793]

4° 31 p., music
No. 944 on title-page
Hirsch I, no 273
MUSIC LIBRARY

811   Kirnberger, Johann Philipp

Die Kunst | des reinen | Satzes in der
Musik | aus sicheren Grundsåtzen herge-
leitet und mit deutlichen | Beyspielen
erläutert | von | Joh. Phil. Kirnberger |
Ihrer Kŏnigl. Hoheit der Prinzessin Ama-
lia von Preussen Hof-Musicus. | Berlin, |
in Commission bey Christian Friedrich
Voss, 1771.

4° [vol. I]: 5 ℓ., 250, VI p., 3 ℓ., illus., 6
pl. on 3 ℓ., music
Incomplete: vol. II lacking
RISM B VI, 453; Wolfenbüttel, no.
1194
MUSIC LIBRARY

812   Kirnberger, Johann Philipp

Die Kunst | des reinen | Satzes in der
Musik | aus sicheren Grundsåtzen herge-
leitet und mit deutlichen | Beyspielen
erläutert | von | Joh. Phil. Kirnberger, |
Ihrer Kŏnigl. Hoheit der Prinzessin Ama-
lia von Preussen Hof-Musicus. | Berlin
und Kŏnigsberg, | bey G. J. Decker und G.
L. Hartung, 1774.[–1779.]

4° 2 vols.: [vol. I]: 5 ℓ., 250 p., 3 ℓ., VI
p., illus., 6 pl. on 3 ℓ., music; vol. II¹: 2 ℓ.,
153, [1] p., illus., music; vol. II²: 1 ℓ.,
232, [2] p., music; vol. II³: 2 ℓ., 188 p.,
music
Imprint date, vol. II¹: 1776; vol. II²:
1777; vol. II³: 1779
Hirsch I, no. 272; RISM B VI, 453
MUSIC LIBRARY

813   Kirnberger, Johann Philipp

Die wahren Grundsåtze | zum | Ge-
brauch der Harmonie, | darinn deutlich
gezeiget wird, | wie alle mŏglichen Ac-

corde aus dem Dreyklang und dem we-
sentlichen | Septimenaccord, und deren
dissonirenden Vorhålten, | herzuleiten
und zu erklåren sind, | als ein Zusatz | zu
der Kunst des reinen Satzes in der Musik,
| von | Johann Philipp Kirnberger, | Ihrer
Kŏnigl. Hoheit der Prinzessin Amalia
von Preussen Hofmusikus. | Berlin und
Kŏnigsberg, | bey G. J. Decker und G. L.
Hartung, 1773.

4° 115 [i. e. 113] p., music
Page 113 misnumbered 115
RISM B VI, 454
MUSIC LIBRARY

814   Klesatl, Remigius

XXIV. | Offertoria | Solennia | In | Festis
Domini, | B. Virginis Et Quo-|rumvis
Sanctorum, | Decantanda | â | Canto,
Alto, Tenore, Basso, | Violin. I. & II.
Clarino I. & II. | Tympano ac Organo. |
Auctoribus | P. Remigio Klesatl, | & | P.
Martino Gerbert, | Princip. Monast. &
Congreg. S. Blasii in Silva Nigra | Mona-
chis Benedictinis. | Opus I. | Pars I. | . . . |
Augustae Vindelicorum, | Sumptibus
Matthaei Rieger, Bibliopolae, |
MDCCXLVII.

2° 1 pt.: organo: 3 ℓ., 64 p.
HOUGHTON

815   Knapp, William

New | Church Melody: | Being A Set Of
| Anthems, Psalms, Hymns, &c. | On
Various Occasions. | In | Four Parts. |
With | A great Variety of other Anthems,
Psalms, Hymns, | &c. composed after a
Method entirely new, and never | printed
before. | By William Knapp, | Author of
the first Book of Psalm Tunes and An-
thems on various | Occasions. | With | An
Anthem on Psalm cxxvii. by one of the
greatest Masters in | Europe. Together
with four excellent Hymns, and an An-
them | for the Nativity. | I will give thee
Thanks in the great Congregation, I will
praise thee | among much People, Psalm
xxxv. 18. And all her Streets shall | say
Alleluia, Tobit xiii. 18. | To which is
added, | An Imploration to the King of
Kings. | Wrote by King Charles I. during
his Captivity in Carisbrook | Castle, in
the Isle of Wight, Anno Dom. 1648. | To-

gether with | An Anthem for the Martyr-
dom of that blessed Prince. | The Fourth
Edition | London: | Printed for R Baldwin,
and S. Crowder and Co. in Pater-noster-
Row; | the Author at Poole; B. Collins,
Bookseller, in Salisbury; and sold | by
most Booksellers in Great-Britain and
Ireland. . . . | MDCCLXI.

8° *Score:* v, [3], 193 p., front. (port.)
RISM A I, no. K 952
MUSIC LIBRARY

816 KNECHT, JUSTIN HEINRICH

XII. | Variations | Pour | Le Clavecin Ou
Pianoforte | Par | Justin Henry Knecht. | A
Leipsic, | Chez Engelhard Beniamin
Schwickert. [ca. 1785]

obl. 2° *Score:* 6 p.
RISM A I, no. K 963
MUSIC LIBRARY

817 KOBRICH, JOHANN JOSEPH
ANTON BERNHARD

Encomia | Mariano-|Lauretana | Seu | X.
Lytaniae | à | Quatuor Vocibus ordinariis,
| 2. Violinis & Organo | obligatis, | 2.
Clarinis vel Cornibus, & Violoncello | ad
libitum. | Typis Fulgatae | A | Joanne An-
tonio Kobrich, | Ecclesiae Parochialis
Landspergae Organaedo. | Opus XXIV. |
. . . | Augustae Vindelicorum, | Typis &
Sumptibus, Joannis Jacobi Lotteri, | 1762.

2° 2 pts.: *violino I:* 1 ℓ., 52 p.; *orga-
no:* 3 ℓ., 40 p.
RISM A I, no. K 1022
HOUGHTON

818 KOBRICH, JOHANN JOSEPH
ANTON BERNHARD

Joannis Antonii Kobrich | Ecclesiae
Parochialis Landspergensis | Organaedi |
Tres Missae | Solemnes | Cum | Tribus
Offertoriis | Ad Modulos Pastoritios | à |
Canto, Alto, Tenore, Basso, | Organo
cum duobus Violinis | obligat. | Alto-
Viola, 2. Clarinis, 2. Cornibus, | 2.
Flautis-Traversis, Violoncello | ad libi-
tum. | Opus XXV. | . . . | Augustae Vinde-
licorum, | Typis & Sumptibus, Joannis
Jacobi Lotteri, | 1762.

2° 1 pt.: *organo:* 1 ℓ., 30 p.
RISM A I, no. K 1023
HOUGHTON

819 KOBRICH, JOHANN JOSEPH
ANTON BERNHARD

Splendor | Vespertinus Quinque | Divi |
Joannis Nepomuceni | Martyris | Stellis
refulgens | seu | Vesperae Breves | ac | So-
lemnes Quinque Quinque praecipuis |
Ejusdem | Sancti Characteribus | Inscri-
ptae & consecratae | ac | à 4. Vocibus or-
dinariis, 2. Violinis, & Organo (teste In-
dice) | tum obligatis tum ad libitum,
Viola verò, 2. Clarinis, | vel Cornibus, ac
Tympano, semper ad libitum | decanta-
tae. | operâ | Joannis Antonii Kobrich, |
Ecclesiae Parochialis Landspergae Or-
ganaedi. | Opus XII. | . . . | Augustae-Vin-
delicorum, | Sumptibus Joannis Jacobi
Lotteri Haeredum. MDCCLIV.

2° 1 pt.: *canto:* 2 ℓ., 40 p.
RISM A I, no. K 1013
HOUGHTON

820 KOCŻWARA, FRANZ

The | Agreeable Surprize, | A Favorite |
Sonata, | For The | Piano Forte, | Com-
posed By | F. Kotzwara. | London | Printed
for Harrison & Co. No. 18 Paternoster
Row [1798?]

8° *Score:* 1 ℓ., 5–16 p. (*The Piano-Forte
Magazine,* vol. III, no. 10)
Plate nos. 47–48
RISM A I, no. K 1139
MUSIC LIBRARY

821 [KOCŻWARA, FRANZ]

The | Battle of Prague | A | Sonata | for
the | Piano Forte | Or | Harpsichord | with
Accompaniments for | A Violin, Bass &c.
| . . . | London | Printed by Longman and
Broderip No. 26 Cheapside and No. 13
Hay Market | Music Sellers and musical
Instrument makers to His Royal High-
ness the Prince of Wales [ca. 1793]

2° Score and 2 pts.: *score:* 1 ℓ., 8 p.; *vio-
lino, basso:* 3 p. each
The *basso* part includes a part for
drum
RISM A I, no. K 1091
MUSIC LIBRARY

822 [KOCŽWARA, FRANZ]

The | Battle | Of | Prague, | For The | Piano Forte. | London. | Printed for Harrison & Co. No. 18, Paternoster Row. [1798?]

8° *Score:* 17 p. (*The Piano-Forte Magazine,* vol. III, no. 4)
RISM A I, no. K 1127
MUSIC LIBRARY

823 KÖNIGSPERGER, MARIANUS

Chordae | Corda Tra-|hentes, | Seu | XII. Sonatae Concer-|tantes pro Missis So-|lemnibus, | A | Violino Principali, Violino Primo, Violi-|no Secundo, Alto Viola obligata, & | duplici Basso generali, | Adornatae | A | R. F. Mariano Königsperger, | Ord. S. P. Benedicti in exempto Monasterio Prüflin-|gensi Professo. | Opus IX. | . . . | Augustae Vindelicorum, | Sumptibus Philippi Ludovici Klaffschenckelii. | MDCCXLV.

2° 1 pt.: *violino I:* 1 ℓ., 42 p.
RISM A I, no. K 1249
HOUGHTON

824 KÖNIGSPERGER, MARIANUS

Mariale | Lauretanum, | Complectens | VI. Solemnes Lytanias | De | B. V. Maria. | 4. Vocibus obligatis, 2. Violi-|nis necessariis, Alto Viola, 2. Clarinis | vel Cornibus ad Libitum, ac duplici | Basso generali, | Confectum | A | R. F. Mariano Königsperger, | Ord. S. P. Benedicti in exempto Monasterio Prüf-|lingensi Professo. | Opus VII. | . . . | Augustae Vindelicorum, | Sumptibus Philippi Ludovici Klaffschenckelii. | MDCCXLIV.

2° 1 pt.: *organo:* 3 ℓ., 22 p.
RISM A I, no. K 1247
HOUGHTON

825 KOLBERER, CAJETAN

Partus Secundus, | Continens | Introitus | Breves, ac Faciles, | Secundum Claves Ordinarias, | In Tres Partes Divisos, | Per Totum Annum. | Dedicatus, & consecratus | Tribus Sacratissimis | Hostiis, | In Celeberrimo & Exempto Monasterio Montis Sancti Andex, Ordinis | S. Benedicti, Congregationis Bene-

dictino-Bavaricae SS. Angel. Custod. | Miraculis claris, | à | P. Cajetano Kolberer, ejusdem Ordinis ac | Monasterii Professo. | . . . | Cum Facultate Superiorum. | Augustae Vindelicorum, | Typis Andreae Maschenbaueri, | [Anno 1703]

2° 5 pts.: *canto:* [3], 80 p.; *alto:* [4], 80 p.; *tenore:* [3], 87 p.; *basso:* [3], 61 p.; *organo:* [3], 56 [+] p.
Imperfect: title-page lacking in *canto* part-book; title supplied from *alto* part-book; imprint cropped in *alto* part-book; all after page 56 lacking in *organo* part-book; numerous torn pages, with loss of text and music
RISM A I, no. K 1310
HOUGHTON

KOLOF, LORENZ CHRISTOPH MIZLER VON
See Mizler von Kolof, Lorenz Christoph

826 KOPP, MATTHAEUS ADAM

Promptuarium | Musico-Sacrum. | Continens | In Opere | Miscellaneo | II. Missas Vivorum: I. De Requiem. | II. Offertoria. | II. Litanias Lauretanas. | I. Te Deum Laudamus. I. Miserere. | II. Magnificat. | II. Salve Regina. I. Alma. I. Ave Regina. | I. Regina Coeli. | Opus Omni Tempori, Et Choro, | Auri Et Arti Accommodatum; | Constans | IV. Vocibus Canto, Alto, Tenore, Basso, II. Violinis, & Organo | necessariis, Tubis ac Lituis ex diversis clavibus, nec non Tympano | & Violoncello, pro libitu adhibendis, | Ut Ex Indice Patebit. | Authore | Mathia Adamo Kopp, | Organoedo Erdingensi, Bavaro. | . . . | Augustae Vindelicorum, | Typis & sumptibus Joannis Jacobi Lotteri, An. MDCCXXXVI.

2° 1 pt.: *canto:* 1 ℓ., 36 p.
RISM A I, no. K 1340
HOUGHTON

KOTŽWARA, FRANZ *See* Koczwara, Franz

827 KOŽELUH, LEOPOLD ANTONIN TOMÁŠ

Duo | Pour le Clavecin | Où | le Piano-Forte | Composé | Par | L. Kozeluch | Oeuvre IX. | . . . | No. 11. Du Journal De

Pieces De Clavecin | Par Differens Auteurs. | A Paris | Chez Mr. Boyer, Rue de Richelieu, à la Clef d'or, à l'ancien Caffé de foy. | Chez Made. Le Menu Rue du Roule a la Clef d'Or. | . . . [ca. 1785]

2° *Score:* 1 ℓ., 27 p.
Plate no. 206*
Imprint partially covered by cancel label reading: Chez Mercier, à la Musique Royale, Rue des Prouvaires | près la Rue St. Honoré, No. 33.
RISM A I, no. K 1654
P. XI, 2
MUSIC LIBRARY

828   Koželuh, Leopold Antonin Tomáš

Favourite | Overture, | Composed For The | Piano Forte, | And Dedicated To The | Emperor Of Germany; | By | L. Kozeluch. | London: | Printed for Harrison & Co. No. 18, Paternoster Row. [1798?]

8° *Score:* 8 p. (*The Piano-Forte Magazine,* vol. III, no. 14)
Plate no. 50
RISM A I, no. K 1800
P. III, 1
MUSIC LIBRARY

829   Koželuh, Leopold Antonin Tomáš

Trois | Sonates | Pour | le Clavecin où le Forte-Piano | Avec Accompagnement | de Violon et Violoncelle | Dediées | á son Altesse Serenissime Madame la Princesse | Tablonowska | Par L. Kozeluch. | Oeuvre 27e. | . . . | A Paris | Chez M. Boyer, Rue de Richelieu, à la Clef d'Or, | Passage du Caffé de foy. | Chez Made. Le Menu, Rue du Roulle, à la Clef d'Or. | Ecrit par Ribiere. [ca. 1789]

2° 3 pts.: *clavecin:* 1 ℓ., 35 p.; *violino:* 10 p.; *violoncello:* 1 ℓ., 8 p.
RISM A I, no. K 1523
P. IX, 13–15
MUSIC LIBRARY

830   Koželuh; Leopold Antonin Tomáš

Trois | Sonates | pour | Clavecin où Forte-Piano | Violon et Violoncelle |

Composées | par L: Kozeluch | Oeuvre 28e. | . . . | à Paris. | Chez M. Boyer, Rue de Richelieu, à la Clef d'Or, | Passage de l'ancien Caffé de foy. | Chez Made. Le Menu, Rue du Roulle, ä la Clef d'Or. | Ecrit par Ribiere. [ca. 1789]

2° 3 pts.: *clavecin:* 1 ℓ., 31 p.; *violino:* 1 ℓ., 8 p.; *violoncello:* 7 p.
RISM A I, no. K 1534
P. IX, 16–18
MUSIC LIBRARY

831   Koželuh, Leopold Antonin Tomáš

Three | Sonatas, | for the | Piano-Forte or Harpsichord | With Accompaniments | for the | Violin and Violoncello | Composed by | Mr. Leopold Kozeluch. | Op XXVIII. . . . | London | Printed by Longman and Broderip No. 26 Cheapside and No. 13 Hay Market | Music Sellers and musical Instrument makers to His Royal Highness the Princ [*sic*] of Wales. | . . . [ca. 1790]

2° Score and 2 pts.: *score:* 1 ℓ., 45 p.; *violino:* 1 ℓ., 13 p.; *violoncello:* 1 ℓ., 10 p.
RISM A I, no. K 1535
P. IX, 16–18
MUSIC LIBRARY

832   Kraus, Lambert

Passer | Solitarius In Tecto. | Id Est: | Octo Missae | A | 4. Vocibus ordinariis, Canto, Alto, Tenore, Basso, | 2. Violinis necessariis. 2. Flauttotraversiere, 2. Clarinis | cum Tympanis, 2. Cornibus, ex diversis clavibus | ad Libitum concurrentibus, cum duplici | Basso continuo | Suis Festis Et Tempori | Accommodatae, | Quarum sex priores Solemnitatibus majoribus, Septima Feriis Ro-|gationum, Octava Exequiis Defunctorum serviunt. | Opera | R. P. Lamberti Kraus, | Antiquissimi Monasterii Ord. Ss. P. Be-|nedicti Ad. S. Michaelem Archangelum In | Metten Professi, Ac p. t. Prioris Indigni. | Opus I. | . . . | Superiorum Permissu. | Avgvstae Vindelicorvm, | Sumptibus Matthaei Rieger, Bibliopolae. | Anno MDCCLXII.

2° 1 pt.: *organo:* 4 ℓ., 95 p.
Imperfect: pages 93, 94 lacking
HOUGHTON

833   KREUTZER, RODOLPHE

Lodoiska | Comedie en Trois Actes, en Prose | Paroles de Mr. de Jaure | Réprésentée pour la Premiere fois par les Comediens Italiens | Mise en Musique | Par | M. Kreutzer. | . . . | Gravé par Huguet Musicien Pensionnaire de la Comedie Italienne | A. Paris. | Chez Sieber . . . [1792]

2° *Score:* 1 ℓ., 198 p.
Plate no. 1222
Imprint partially covered by cancel label reading: Chez Jmbault rue Honoré au mont d'or. No. 266 de la section des Gardes-|-Françaises, entre la rue des Poulies et la maison d'Aligre. | Et Péristile du Théâtre de l'Opera Comique rue Favart No. 461.
RISM A I, no. K 2074
MUSIC LIBRARY

834   KREUTZER, RODOLPHE

Paùl Et Virginie | Comédie en Prose et en trois Actes, | Paroles de M∗∗∗ | Representée pour la premiere fois par les Comediens Italiens | le Samedy 15 Janvier 1791 | Mise en Musique | Par | M. Kreutzer | Musicien Ordinaire de la Musique des Italiens | . . . | Gravé par Huguet Musicien Pensionnaire de la Comedie Italienne | A Paris | Chez l'Auteur Rue Rochevuart No. 157 Fauxbourg [Montmartre] | Et aux | adresses Ordinaires. | A Lion Chez Garnier Md. de Musique et d'instrumens Place de la Comedie No. 18 [?] [1791?]

2° *Score:* 1 ℓ., 199 p.
Title-page worn and partly illegible
Hirsch II, no. 493; RISM A I, no. K 2144
MUSIC LIBRARY

KRITISCHE BRIEFE ÜBER DIE TONKUNST
See Marpurg, Friedrich Wilhelm, ed. *Kritische Briefe über die Tonkunst*

835   KUNZEN, FRIEDRICH LUDWIG
          AEMILIUS

Hemmeligheden. | Et Comisk Syngestykke i en Handling. | Sat i Musik og indrettet for Klaveret | af | F. L. A. Kunzen, |
Kongl. Kapelmester. | Kiobenhavn. | Trykt og forlagt af S. Sønnichsen, | Kongl. privil. Node- og Bogtrykker. [179–?]

obl. 2° *Vocal score:* 1 ℓ., 46 p.
Imprint covered by cancel label reading: Kjöbenhavn | hos C. C. Lose.
RISM A I, no. K 3029
MUSIC LIBRARY

L

LA BAUME LE BLANC, LOUIS CÉSAR DE, DUC DE LA VALLIÈRE *See* La Vallière, Louis César de la Baume Le Blanc, duc de

836   LABORDE, JEAN BAPTISTE DE

Le | Clavessin | Electrique; | Avec | Une Nouvelle Théorie | Du Méchanisme Et Des Phénomenes | De L'Électricité. | Par le R. P. Delaborde, de la | Compagnie de Jesus. | A Paris, | Chez H. L. Guerin & L. F. Delatour, | rue S. Jacques, à S. Thomas d'Aquin. | M.DCC.LXI. | Avec Approbation Et Privilege du Roi.

12° xij, 164 p., 2 ℓ., 2 fold. pl.
RISM B VI, 466
HOUGHTON

837   [LA BORDE,
          JEAN BENJAMIN DE]

Annette Et Lubin | Pastorale | Mise en Musique | Par | Monsieur D. L. B. . . . | . . . | Les parolles sont de M. Marmontel. | Gravée par Melle Vendome, chés Mr Moria. | A Paris | Chés Mr Moria Md de Musiques près la Comedie Françoise, | et aùx adresses ordinaires de Musique. | Avec Approbation. [176–?]

2° *Score:* 1 ℓ., 113 p.
Hirsch II, no. 494; RISM A I, no. L 62
MUSIC LIBRARY

838   LA BORDE,
          JEAN BENJAMIN DE

Choix | De Chansons | Mises En Musique | Par M. De La Borde, | Premier Valet-de-Chambre ordinaire du Roi, | Gouverneur du Louvre. | Ornées D'Estampes | Par J. M. Moreau, | Dédiées | A Madame La Dauphine | . . . | A Paris | Chez De Lormel, Imprimeur de l'Académie Royale | de Musique rue du Foin Saint Jacques, | M.DCC.LXXIII. | Avce [*sic*] Aprobation et Privilege du Roi | Gravées par Moria et Mlle. Vendôme.

8° *Score:* 4 vols.: *vol. I:* 154 p., 2 ℓ., 25 pl.; *vol. II:* 1 ℓ., 153 p., 25 pl.; *vol. III:* 1 ℓ., 150 p., 2 ℓ., 25 pl.; *vol. IV:* 1 ℓ., 150 p., 2 ℓ., 25 pl.
Plates included in pagination
RISM A I, no. L 100
HOUGHTON (3 copies; 3d copy: p. [145]–150 lacking in vol. 4)

839   LA CUISSE, _____ DE

Le | Répertoire | Des Bals | Ou | Theorie-Pratique Des Contredanses | décrites d'une maniere aisée avec | des Figures démonstratives pour | les pouvoir danser facilement, aux-|-quelles on a ajouté les Airs notés. | Par le Sr. De la Cuisse, Maitre de Danse. | 1762. | A Paris | chez Cailleau, Libraire, ruë St. Jaques, | près celle des Mathurins. | Melle. Castagnery, ruë des Prouvares. | avec Privilege du Roy

8° 28 p., 30 feuilles, illus., music
Each "feuille" consists of four pages, with the exception of numbers 6 and 12, which are folded plates
Hirsch I, no. 292; RISM B VI, 470
HOUGHTON

THE LADIES COLLECTION OF CATCHES, GLEES, CANONS, CANZONETS, MADRIGALS, &c *See* Bland, John, comp. *The Ladies Collection of Catches, Glees, Canons, Canzonets, Madrigals, &c.*

840   [LA MONNOYE, BERNARD DE]

Noei | Borguignon | De | Gui Barôzai. Cinqueime Edicion | Reveue, Et augmentée de lai | Nôte de l'Ar de chécun dé | Noei, Etc. | An Bregogne. | M.D.CC.XXXVIII.

12° 6 ℓ., 112, 24, 301, [1], xij p., music
Colophon: page 24, second sequence: De L'Imprimerie | De J-B-Christophe Ballard, | Seul Imprimeur du Roy pour la

Musique. | M.DCCXXXVII. | Avec Privilege du Roy.
Pages 1–289, third sequence: Glossaire | Alphabétique.
RISM A I, no. L 404
MUSIC LIBRARY, WIDENER

841   [LAMORLIÈRE, JACQUES ROCHETTE DE]

Lettre | D'Un Sage | A un Homme très respectable, et dont il a besoin. | . . . [Paris, 1754]

8° 1 ℓ., 18 p.
A reply to Jean Jacques Rousseau's *Lettre sur la musique françoise*
RISM B VI, 474
HOUGHTON

842   LAMPE, FRIEDRICH ADOLF

Friderici Adolfi | Lampe | De | Cymbalis | Vetervm | Libri Tres, | In quibus quaecunque ad eorum nomina, dif-|ferentiam, originem, historiam, ministros, | ritus pertinent, elucidantur. | Cum Figuris aeneis. | Trajecti Ad Rhenum, | Ex Bibliopolae Guilielmi a Poolsum, | MDCCIII.

12° 14 ℓ., 405, [43] p., front., 10 pl.
Hirsch I, no. 300; RISM B VI, 476
MUSIC LIBRARY

843   LAMPE, JOHN FREDERICK

British Melody; | Or, the | Musical Magazine. | Consisting | Of a large Variety of the most approv'd English and Scotch | Songs, Airs, &c the Words compos'd by the best Authors, | and Set to Musick by the Most Eminent Masters, in the | Execution whereof the Transposition necessary for the | German Flute (which is now a favourite Instrument) as well | as for ye Common Flute, is accurately & distinctly express'd | The Whole curiously Engrav'd on Threescore Folio | Copper Plates; All carefully revis'd and corrected, and One | fourth Part of them Set to Musick by | John Frederick Lampe | Author of ye Universally admir'd Musick to ye Burlesque | Opera, Entitled, The Dragon of Wantley. | And Each Plate | Beautifully Embellish'd with a New Head-Piece, Superior to, | and more fully expressive of the Proper Passions than | any Thing of the Like Nature hitherto extant, | London: | Printed for & Sold by ye Proprietor Benjn. Cole Engraver | at ye Corner of Kings-Head Court Holbourn, & at most Print Sellers, & Musick Shops, in Town & Country. | MDCCXXXIX |

2° *Score:* 3 ℓ., LX pl., illus.
Imperfect: plates XXI, XLVIII lacking
RISM B II, 117
HOUGHTON

844   LAMPE, JOHN FREDERICK

Songs and Duetto's | In The | Burlesque Opera, call'd, | The | Dragon of Wantley. | As perform'd at the | Theatre-Royal in Covent-Garden. | Composed and Carefully Corrected, | By Mr. John Frederick Lampe, | Author of the New Treatise of Thorough Bass. | London: | Printed for John Wilcox, against the New Church | in the Strand; where may be had the above Treatise of | Thorough Bass, and Sold at all the Musick-Shops in | Town and Country. | MDCCXXXVIII.

2° *Score:* 1 ℓ., LXI p.
RISM A I, no. L 453
MUSIC LIBRARY

845   LAMPE, JOHN FREDERICK

Songs and Duetto's | In The | Burlesque Opera, call'd, | Margery, Being a Sequel to the | Dragon of Wantley. | As performed at the | Theatre-Royal in Covent-Garden. | Composed and Carefully Corrected | By Mr John Frederick Lampe, | London: | Printed for, and sold by John Wilcox, against the New | Church in the Strand; (with or without the Dragon of | Wantley) and Sold also at all the Musick Shops in Town | and Country. | MDCCXXXIX. | . . .

2° *Score:* 1 ℓ., 101 p.
RISM A I, no. L 459
MUSIC LIBRARY

846   LAMPE, JOHN FREDERICK

Pyramus and Thisbe: | A | Mock-Opera. | The Words taken from Shakespeare. | as it is Perform'd at the | The-

atre-Royal | In | Covent-Garden. | Set to Musick by | Mr. I. F. Lampe. | London. Printed for I. Walsh, in Catharine Street, in the Strand. [ca. 1746]

2° *Score:* 1 ℓ., 39, [1] p.
RISM A I, no. L 460; Walsh II, no. 904
MUSIC LIBRARY

847   LANGLÉ, HONORÉ FRANÇOIS MARIE

Corisandre | Ou | Les Foux | Par Enchantement | Opera Ballet | Paroles, de . . . | Musique de H. F. M. Langlé, Bibliothècaire | du Conservatoire de Musique. | Dédié | A la Cne, La Chabeaussiere | . . . | A Paris | Chés Le Duc, Editeur de Musique et Md. d'Instruments, rue Neuve des Petits-|Champs vis-à-vis la Trésorerie No. 1286. près la rue Vivienne. | Et rue du Roulle a la Croix d'Or, No. 290. | [1799?]

2° *Score:* 1 ℓ., 329 p.
Plate no. 22
Hirsch II, no. 505; RISM A I, no. L 600
MUSIC LIBRARY

848   LA RUE, PIERRE DE

[Misse Petri de la Rue. | Beate virginis | Puer natus | Sexti. Ut fa | Lomme arme | Nūqua fue pena maior ⟨Venice, 1503⟩]

obl. 4° 1 pt.: *tenor:* Ccc¹⁰.
[Colophon: Imp[re]ssum Venetijs per Octauianum Petrutium forosemp[ro]-nien|sem 1503 die 31 Octobris. Cum priuilegio inuictissimi Dominij | Venetiarumq[ue] nullus possit cantum figuratum imprimere | sub pena in ipso priuilegio contenta.]
Title supplied from microfilm copy of *superius* part-book
Colophon supplied from microfilm copy of *bassus* part-book
RISM A I, no. L 718; SartoriP, no. 11
HOUGHTON

849   LASSO, ORLANDO DI

Selectissimae | Cantiones, Qvas Vvlgo | Motetas Vocant, Partim Omni-|no Novae, Partim Nvsqvam In Germania | excusae, Sex & pluribus vocibus compositae, per excellen-|tissimum Musicum |

Orlandum di Lassus. | Posteriori huic editioni accessère omnes Orlandi Motetae, quae in veteri nostro Thesauro Musico | impressae continebantur cum quibusdam aliis, ita ut ferè tertia parte opus hoc sit auctius. | Omnia denuò multò quàm antehac correctius edita. | . . . | Cum gratia & privilegio Imperiali. | Noribergae, | In officina typographica Catharinae Gerlachiae. | M.D.LXXXVII.

    obl. 4° 2 pts.: *qvinta vox:* Aa–Qq⁴, Rr²; *sexta vox:* AAa–RRr⁴
Unidentified piece in keyboard tablature (manuscript) on verso of leaf RRr⁴ in *sexta vox*
Davidsson I, no. 294; RISM A I, no. L 976
HOUGHTON

850   Lasso, Orlando di

Altera Pars | Selectissimarvm | Cantionvm, Qvas Vvlgo Mo-|tetas Vocant, Qvinqve Et Qva-|tvor Vocibvs Compositarvm Per | excellentissimum Musicum, | Orlandum di Lassus. | Aucta et restituta, ut suprà indicavimus. | . . . | Cum gratia & privilegio Imperiali. | Noribergae, | In officina typographica Catharinae Gerlachiae. | M.D.LXXXVII.

    obl. 4° 2 pts.: *altvs:* AA–SS⁴; *qvinta vox:* a–m⁴, n1–3
Davidsson I, no. 295; RISM A I, no. L 977
HOUGHTON

Lâtre, Claude Petit Jean de   *See* DeLâtre, Claude Petit Jean

851   [Laugier, Marc Antoine]

Apologie | De | La Musique | Françoise, | Contre M. Rousseau. | . . . | [Paris] M.DCC.LIV.

    8° 2 ℓ., 78 p.
Hirsch I, no. 306; RISM B VI, 484
HOUGHTON

Laurent de Béthisy, Jean   *See* Béthisy, Jean Laurent de

852   Laurentius von Schnüffis

Mirantisches | Flötlein. | Oder | Geistliche Schäfferey, | In welcher Christus, under dem | Namen Daphnis, die in dem Sünden-|Schlaff vertieffte Seel Clorinda zu einem | bessern Leben aufferweckt, und durch wunderliche | Weis, und Weeg zu grosser Heiligkeit | führet. | Durch | P. F. Laurentium | Von Schnüffis Vorder-Oesterrei-|chischer Provintz Capucinern, | und Predigern. | Mit Erlaubnuss der Obern: auch sonder-|barer Freyheit Ihro Röm. Käyserl. Majestät, | nicht nachzudrucken. | Gedruckt zu Costantz, | In der Fürstl. Bischöffl. Druckerey, | Bey David Hautt, Anno 1682. | In Verlegung Johann Jacob Mantelin Burgern, | und Handelsmann zu Lauffenburg.

    8° 8 ℓ., 315, [1] p., 1 ℓ., front., 30 pl., music
RISM A I, no. L 1098
HOUGHTON

853   [La Vallière, Louis César de La Baume Le Blanc, duc de]

Ballets, Opera, | Et Autres | Ouvrages Lyriques, | Par Ordre Chronologique | Depuis Leur Origine; | Avec | Une Table Alphabetique | Des | Ouvrages Et Des Auteurs. | A Paris, Quai des Augustins, | Chez Cl. J. Baptiste Bauche, Libraire, à l'Image | Sainte Genevieve & à St Jean dans le desert. | M.DCC.LX. | Avec Approbation Et Privilege Du Roi.

    8° 4 ℓ., 298 p., 1 ℓ.
RISM B VI, 486
HOUGHTON

854   Lavater, Johann Caspar

Sechszig | Lieder | nach dem Zürcherischen Catechismus. | Der | Petrinischen Jugend zugeeignet | Von | Johann Caspar Lavater, | Diakon am St. Peter. | Zürich, | Bey C. Füessli, Sohn im Niederdorf. | MDCCLXXX.

    8° 4 ℓ., 143, [1] p.
Pages 136–143: four musical settings for four voices, in choirbook format
HOUGHTON

La Viéville, Jean Laurent le Cerf de
See Le Cerf de la Viéville, Jean Laurent

855   Law, Andrew

[The] | Art Of Singing; | In Three Parts: | Viz. | I. The Musical Primer, | II. The Christian Harmony, | III. The Musical Magazine. | By Andrew Law, A. M. | Author of the Select Harmony, Rudiments of Music, Etc. | Published according to Act of Congress. | . . . | Cheshire; Connecticut: | M.DCC.XCIV.

obl. 8° 2 vols.: *vol. I:* 40 p., illus., music; *vol. II:* 64 p., music
Pages 24–40 in vol. I and 9–64 in vol. II: anthems, hymns and psalms for four voices
Imperfect: title-page in vol. I cropped, with loss of first word
Incomplete: vol. III lacking
RISM A I, no. L 1159
HOUGHTON

856   Law, Andrew

The | Rudiments of Music: | Or | A Short And Easy Treatise | On The | Rules of Psalmody. | To which are annexed, | A Number Of Plain Tunes And Chants. | By Andrew Law, A. M. | Author Of Select Harmony, | A Collection of plain Tunes for the Psalm Book, and a Collection of Hymn | Tunes, with their Hymns, lately published. | [Cheshire, Conn.] A. D. 1783.

obl. 8° 8, 4, 24 p., illus., music
Page 1, second sequence: Daniel Hopkins Sculpt.
RISM A I, no. L 1148; RISM B VI, 487
HOUGHTON (2 copies)

857   Law, Andrew

[Select Harmony. | Containing in a plain and concise manner, the | Rules Of Singing: Together with a Collection of Psalm Tunes, Hymns and Anthems | By Andrew Law, A. B. | J. Allen sculp. | ⟨New Haven, Conn., 1779)]

obl. 8° 1 ℓ., 8, 100 p., illus., music
Imperfect: title-page, pages 21, 22 lacking; title supplied in manuscript
RISM A I, no. L 1146
HOUGHTON

858   [Lawes, Henry]

Ayres | And | Dialogues, | For One, Two, and Three Voyces. | By | [Henry Lawes] | The First Booke. | London, | Printed by T. H. [i. e. Thomas Harper] for John Playford, and are to be sold at his Shop, in the Inner | Temple, near the Church door. 1653.

2° *Score:* 6 ℓ., 36, 28 p.
Portrait of Henry Lawes on title-page serves as composer statement
Page 28, second sequence: Musick Books Printed for John Playford . . .
Day, no. 5; RISM A I, no. L 1168
HOUGHTON

859   [Lawes, Henry]

The Second Book | Of | Ayres, | And | Dialogues, | For One, Two, and Three Voyces. | By | [Henry Lawes] | London, | Printed by T. H. [i. e. Thomas Harper] for Jo. Playford, and are to be sold at his shop in the Inner Temple. 1655.

2° *Score:* 6 ℓ., 48 [i. e. 56] p.
Portrait of Henry Lawes on title-page serves as composer statement
Eight unnumbered pages between pages 32 and 33
Page 48 [i. e. 56]: Musick Books lately Printed for John Playford . . .
Day, no. 8; RISM A I, no. L 1168
HOUGHTON

860   [Lawes, Henry]

Ayres, | And | Dialogues, | For One, Two, and Three Voyces. | By | [Henry Lawes] | The Third Book. | London, | Printed by W. Godbid for John Playford, at his Shop in the Inner Temple, | neer the Church dore. M.DC.LVIII.

2° *Score:* 3 ℓ., 48, [2] p.
Portrait of Henry Lawes on title-page serves as composer statement
Day, no. 11; RISM A I, no. L 1168
HOUGHTON

861   Lawes, Henry

Psalmody | For a Single Voice, | Being Twenty-Four Melodies for Private Devotion, | With a Base for Voice or Instrument; | First published with Mr. George Sandys's | "Paraphrase of the Psalms of David" in the year 1638. | By Henry Lawes, | Gentleman of his Majesty's Chapel Royal. | With a Variation of each Psalm Tune on the same Page, | By Matthew Camidge, | Lately one of the Children of the same Chapel Royal. | To which are prefixed, | Some Introductory Reasons for this Publication, | By W. Mason, M. A. | Precentor of York. | [York] Printed By W. Blanchard. | MDCCLXXXIX

4° *Score:* 4 ℓ., viii, 51 p.
RISM A I, no. L 1165
MUSIC LIBRARY

862   LAWES, HENRY

Choice Psalmes | Put Into | Musick, | For Three Voices. | The most of which may properly enough be sung | by any three, with a Thorough Base. | Compos'd by | Henry | and | William Lawes, Brothers; and Servants to | His Majestie. | With divers Elegies, set in Musick by sev'rall Friends, upon the | death of William Lawes. | And at the end of the Thorough Base are added nine Canons of | Three and Foure Voices, made by William Lawes. | London, | Printed by James Young, for Humphrey Moseley, at the Prince's Armes in | S. Pauls Church-yard, and for Richard Wodenothe, at the Star under | S. Peters Church in Corn-hill. 1648.

4° 2 pts.: *cantus primus:* A⁴, B–L⁴, [M1]; *cantus secundus:* A2–4, a², M–X⁴, illus. (port.) in each part-book
RISM A I, no. L 1164
HOUGHTON

—another copy: *cantus primus*
Issued without portrait
HOUGHTON

863   LEBÈGUE, NICOLAS ANTOINE

[Les | Pieces de Clauessin | Composées par N. A. Le Begue | Organiste de l'Eglise Sainct Mederic | Se vendent Chez le Sr. Baillon Maitre faiseur | de Clauessin Rüe Simon le Franc et Chez | l'Autheur dans la mesme Rüe | A Paris | Auec Priuilege du Roy | 1677]

obl. 4° *Score:* 1 ℓ., [1], 90 p., 1 ℓ.
Imperfect: title-page lacking; title supplied from microfilm of copy in the Bibliothèque nationale, Paris
RISM A I, no. L 1212
HOUGHTON

864   LEBEUF, JEAN

Traité | Historique Et Pratique | Sur Le Chant | Ecclesiastique. | Avec Le Directoire | qui en contient les principes & les régles, | suivant l'usage présent du Diocèse de Paris, | & autres. | Précedé d'une Nouvelle Methode, pour | l'enseigner, & l'apprendre facilement. | Par M. l'Abbé Lebeuf, Chanoine et Sous-Chantre | de l'Eglise Cathédrale d'Auxerre. | A Paris, | Chez {Cl. J. B. Herissant, Libraire-Imprimeur, | rue Neuve de notre Dame, aux trois Vertus. | Et | Jean Th. Herissant, Libraire, rue S. Jacques, | à S. Paul & à S. Hilaire. | M.DCC.XLI. | Avec Approbation et Privilége du Roy.

8° 4 ℓ., 290, [6] p., illus., music
Hirsch I, no. 308; RISM B VI, 488
HOUGHTON, MUSIC LIBRARY

LE BLANC, LOUIS CÉSAR DE LA BAUME, DUC DE LA VALLIÈRE *See* La Vallière, Louis César de la Baume Le Blanc, duc de

865   [LEBLOND, GASPAR MICHEL, ED.]

Mémoires | Pour Servir A L'Histoire | De La | Révolution | Opérée | Dans La Musique | Par M. Le Chevalier Gluck. | . . . | A Naples, | Et se trouve A Paris, | Chez Bailly, Libraire, rue Saint-Honoré, | à côté de la Barrière des Sergens. | M.DCC.LXXXI.

8° 2 ℓ., 491 p., front. (port.), illus.
Hirsch I, no. 310; RISM B VI, 489
MUSIC LIBRARY

866   LEBRUN, LOUIS SÉBASTIEN

Marcelin | Opera en un Acte et en prose, | Paroles de Bernard Valville, | Musique de Lebrun, Artiste du Théâtre Faydeau | Représenté sur le dit Théâtre le 2 Germinal an 8. | Dédié au Cen. Le Sueur |

Par Son Ami Lebrun | . . . | Propriété des Freres Gaveaux. . . . | A Paris | A La Nouveauté des [———. ⟨ca. 1800⟩]

2° *Score:* 1 ℓ., 88 p.
Colophon: Gravée par Vanixem
Imprint partially covered by cancel label reading: A Paris chez Augte. Le Duc Editeur et Marchand de Musique Rue de la Loi No. 267 | Près celle Faydeau. | . . .
MUSIC LIBRARY

LE CERF DE LA VIÉVILLE, JEAN LAURENT
Comparaison de la musique italienne et de la musique françoise *See* Bonnet, Jacques, ed. *Histoire de la musique, et de ses effets*

867   LECLAIR, JEAN MARIE

Premier Livre | De | Sonates | A Violon Seul avec | La Basse Continue | Composées | Par Mr. Leclair L'Ainé | Dediées | A Monsieur Bonnier | Tresorier General des Etats | de Languedoc. | Gravées par L. Hüe) Il y a quelqu'vnes de ces Sonates qui peuvent [se] jouer Sur la flute Traversiere | . . . | Se Vend A Paris | Chez {Le Sr. Boivin Marchand rue, | St. Honoré a la Regle d'or. | Avec Privilege du Roy 1723

2° *Score:* 2 ℓ., 81, [1] p.
Title-page rubbed
RISM A I, no. L 1306 (op. 1)
HOUGHTON

868   LECLAIR, JEAN MARIE

Second Livre | De | Sonates | Pour Le Violon Et Pour La Flute | Traversiere Avec La Basse Continue. | Composees | Par Mr. Leclair L'Ainé. | Dédiées | A Monsieur Bonnier | De La Mosson. | Marechal general des logis des Camps & Armées du Roi | Tresorier general des Etat de la Province du Languedoc. | Gravées Par Mlle. Louise Roussel. | . . . | Se vend A Paris, | Chez L'Auteur, rue St. Benoist du côté de l'Abeïs, Faubourg St. Germain. | Le Sr. Boivin Marchand Rue St. Honoré à la Règle D'or. | Le Sr. Leclerc Marchand Rue du Roule à la Croix D'or. | Avec Privilége du Roi. [ca. 1725]

2° *Score:* 1 ℓ., 85, [1] p.
RISM A I, no. L 1310 (op. 2)
HOUGHTON

869   LECLAIR, JEAN MARIE

Troisieme Livre | De | Sonates | A Violon Seul | Avec la Basse Continüe. | Composées | Par Mr. Leclair L'Ainé | Ordinaire de la Musique de la Chapelle | Et de la Chambre du Roy. | Gravées par Mme Leclair son Epouse. | Dediées | Au Roy. | Oeuvre V. | . . . | A Paris | Chez {L'auteur, rue St. Benoist proche la porte de l'Abaïe St. Germain. | La Ve. Boivin, rue St. honoré à la Régle D'or. | Le Sr. Leclerc, rue du Roule à la Croix D'or. | Avec Privilége du Roy. [ca. 1735]

2° *Score:* 1 ℓ., 82 p.
RISM A I, no. L 1320
HOUGHTON

870   LECLAIR, JEAN MARIE

Quatrieme Livre | De | Sonates | A Violon Seul | avec la Basse Continue. | Composées | Par Mr Le Clair L'Ainé | Gravées par Mme. LeClair son Epouse. | Dediées, | A son Altesse Royale | Madame La Princesse | D'Orange | Oeuvre IX. | . . . | A Paris, | Chez {L'auteur, ruë St. Benoist proche la porte de l'Abaïe St. Germain. | Mme. La Ve. Boivin, ruë St. Honoré à la Régle D'or. | Le Sr. Le clerc, ruë du Roule à la Croix D'or. | Avec Privilége du Roy [ca. 1745]

2° *Score:* 2 ℓ., 75, [1] p.
Imperfect: pages 21–24 lacking; supplied in manuscript
RISM A I, no. L 1327
HOUGHTON

871   LECLAIR, JEAN MARIE

Six | Sonatas | for two | Violins | with a Through Bass for the | Harpsicord or Violoncello | Compos'd by | Mr: Leclair | Op: IV. . . . | London. Printed for I. Walsh in Catharine Street in the Strand | . . . [1764]

2° 3 pts.: *violino primo:* 1 ℓ., 18 p.; *violino secondo:* 1 ℓ., 17 p.; *basso:* 1 ℓ., 15 p.
RISM A I, no. L 1319; Walsh II, no. 932
MUSIC LIBRARY

LEES, ANNE, PUBL. A Collection of the Most Admired Glees and Catches *See* A Collection of the Most Admired Glees and Catches

872 LE FÈVRE, JACQUES, D'ÉTAPLES

Jacobi Fabri Stapulensis Elementa Musicalia ad clarissimũ virũ | Nicolaum de haqueuille inquisitorium Presidẽtem. [Paris, 1496]

2° In a vol. entitled: In hoc opere contenta. | Arithmetica decem libris demonstrata | Musica libris demonstrata quattuor | Epitome ĩ libros arithmeticos diui Seuerini Boetij | Rithmimachie ludus q[ue] & pugna nũeror[um] appellat[ur] | . . ., *ℓ*. f 1ʳ–h6ᵛ
Colophon: . . . mandari ad studiorum vtilitatem Joannes | Higmanus, | et Volgangus Hopilius suis grauissimis laboribus & impensis Parhisij Anno salutis | domini: qui oĩa in numero atq[ue] harmonia formauit 1496 absolutũq[ue] reddiderunt eodem anno: die | vicesima secunda Julij suos labores vbicunq[ue] valebunt semper studiosis deuouentes. Et idem quoq[ue] | facit Dauid Lauxius Brytannus Edinburgensis: vbiq[ue] ex archetypo diligens operis recognitor.
Caption title
BMC VIII, 137; Goff, no. J-472; Hain, no. 9436; RISM B VI, 492
HOUGHTON

873 LE FÈVRE, JACQUES, D'ÉTAPLES

Jacobi Fabri Stapulensis elemẽta musicalia ad clarissimũ virũ Nicolaũ | de Haqueuille inquisitorium Presidentem. [Paris, 1514]

2° In a vol. entitled: In hoc opere contenta | Arithmetica decem libris | demonstrata. | Musica libris demõstrata | quatuor. | Epitome in libros Arith-|meticos diui Seuerini | Boetij. | Rithmimachie ludus qui | et pugna numerorũ ap-|pella-tur, | . . ., *ℓ*. f 1ʳ–h6ᵛ
Colophon: . . . mandari ad studiorum | vtilitatem Henricus Stephanus suo grauissimo labore et sumptu Parhisijs Anno salutis domini: | qui omnia in numero atq[ue] harmonia formauit 1514. absolutumq[ue] reddidit eodẽ anno: die septima | Septembris, suum laborem vbicunq[ue] valet semper studiosis deuouens.
Caption title
RISM B VI, 492
HOUGHTON (2 copies)

LEITE, ANTONIO DA SILVA *See* Silva Leite, Antonio da

874 LEMOYNE, JEAN BAPTISTE MOYNE, CALLED

Nephté, | Tragédie en Trois Actes, | Représentée pour la premiere fois, par l'Académie Royale de Musique, | le Mardi 15 Décembre 1789. | Mise en Musique | Et Dédiée A sa Majesté | Le Roi De Prusse | Par | M. Le Moyne | . . . | Gravée par Huguet Musicien de la Comedie Italienne. | . . . | A Paris Chez l'Auteur Rue Notre-Dame des Victoires No. 29. | Chez M. Korwer Facteur de Forte-Piano Rue Neuve St. Eustache No. 12. | et chez les Marchands de Musique. [179–?]

2° *Score*: 2 *ℓ*., 361 p.
Hirsch II, no. 509; RISM A I, no. L 1891
MUSIC LIBRARY

875 LEMOYNE, JEAN BAPTISTE MOYNE, CALLED

Phèdre | Tragédie en Trois Actes | Représentée devant leurs Majestés à Fontainebleau, le 26 Octobre 1786. | et à Paris sur le Théatre de l'Académie Royale de Musique | Le Mardi 21 Novembre de la même Année. | Mise en Musique | Et Dédiée A Madame | De Serilly | Par | M. Le Moyne | . . . | Gravée par Huguet Musicien de la Comédie Italienne | A Paris Chez Le Duc Successeur et Proprietaire du Fond de Mr. de la | Chevardiere Rue du Roule a la Croix d'Or No. 6 au Magazin de Musique | et d'Instruments. | Chez l'Auteur Rue Notre-Dame des Victoires No. 29. | Avec Privilege du Roi. [ca. 1789]

2° *Score*: 2 *ℓ*., 339 p.
RISM A I, no. L 1899
MUSIC LIBRARY

876 LEMOYNE, JEAN BAPTISTE MOYNE, CALLED

Les | Prétendus | Comédie Lirique | Représentée pour la premiere fois par l'Académie [Royale] de Musique | le Mardi 2 Juin 1789. | Mise en Musique | et Dediée A Madame | De La Ferté | Par | M.

Le Moyne | . . . | A Paris Chez l'Auteur . . . [1789?]

> 2° *Score:* 1 ℓ., 279 p.
> Imprint partially covered by illegible cancel label
> RISM A I, no. L 1915?

MUSIC LIBRARY

877   LENTZ, HEINRICH GERHARD VON

Trois | Sonates | Pour le Clavecin ou Forte Piano | avec Accompagnement | de Violon et Violoncelle | Par H. G. Lentz. | Oeuvre VIIIe. | . . . | Gravé par Van Jxem | A Paris | Chez JH. Naderman Editeur, Luthier, Facteur | de Harpe, Ordinaire du Service de la Reine, | Rue d'Argenteuil Bute St. Roch. | à Apollon. | Et aux adresses Ordinaires. [179–?]

> 2° Score and 2 pts.: *score:* 1 ℓ., 49 p.; *violino:* 13 p.; *violoncello:* 11 p.
> Page [1] in *score:* Catalogue, Des Ouvrages Appartenants à Mr. Naderman . . .
> RISM A I, no. L 1958

MUSIC LIBRARY

878   LE PILEUR D'APLIGNY

Traité | Sur | La Musique, | Et Sur Les Moyens | D'en Perfectionner L'Expression. | Par M. Le Pileur D'Apligny. | . . . | A Paris, | Chez Demonville, Imp.-Lib. rue S. Severin; | Saugrain & Compagnie, rue des Lombards; | L'Auteur, rue Saint-Victor, vis-à-vis | celle de Versailles. | M.DCC.LXXIX. | Avec Approbation, & Privilege du Roi.

> 8° viij, 174, [2] p.
> Hirsch I, no. 315; RISM B VI, 498

MUSIC LIBRARY

879   [LÉRIS, ANTOINE DE]

Dictionnaire | Portatif | Des Théatres, | Contenant | L'Origine Des Différens Théatres | De Paris; | Le nom de toutes les Piéces qui y ont été représentées | depuis leur établissement, & des Piéces jouées en | Province, ou qui ont simplement paru par la voie | de l'impression depuis plus de trois siécles; avec des | Anecdotes & des Remarques sur la

plûpart: | Le nom et les particularités intéressantes de la Vie des | Auteurs, Musiciens et Acteurs; avec le Catalogue | de leurs Ouvrages, et l'exposé de leurs talens: | Une Chronologie des Auteurs, des Musiciens & des | Opéra; | Avec une Chronologie des Piéces qui ont paru depuis vingt-cinq ans. | A Paris, | Chez C. A. Jombert, Imprimeur-Libraire du Roi en son | Artillerie, rue Dauphine, à l'Image Notre-Dame. | M.DCC.LIV. | Avec Approbation Et Privilège Du Roi.

> 8° xxxix, 557, [3] p.
> RISM B VI, 499

HOUGHTON

LEROND D'ALEMBERT, JEAN   *See* Alembert, Jean Lerond d'

880   LE ROY, ADRIAN, PUBL.

. . . | Chansonnettes Rimees | Mises En Mvsiqve | A Quatre parties. | A Paris. | Par Adrian le Roy, | & la Veufue. R. Ballard. | Imprimeurs du Roy: | Auec priuilége de sa Majesté | pour six ans. | 1594.

> 8° 1 pt.: *bassvs:* 40 numb. ℓ.
> LesureL, no. 309

HOUGHTON

881   LE ROY, ADRIAN, PUBL.

. . . | Premier Livre De | Chansons A Devx Parties | Compose de plusieurs autheurs | Imprimé en deux voulumes | A Paris. | M.D.LXXVIII. | Par Adrian le Roy, & Robert Ballard. | Imprimeurs du Roy. | Auec priuilege de sa magesté pour dix ans.

> obl. 8° 1 pt.: *svperivs:* 32 numb. ℓ.
> LesureL, no. 217; RISM B I, no. 1578[17]

HOUGHTON

882   LE ROY, ADRIAN, PUBL.

. . . | Second Livre De | Chansons A Trois Parties | Composé par plusieurs autheurs | Imprimé en Trois volumes. | A Paris. | M.D.LXXVIII. | Par Adrian le Roy, & Robert Ballard. | Imprimeurs du Roy. | Auec priuilege de sa magesté pour dix ans.

obl. 8° 1 pt.: *svperivs:* 24 numb. *ℓ.*
LesureL, no. 219; RISM B I, no. 1578[15]
HOUGHTON

883 LE SUEUR, JEAN FRANÇOIS

La Caverne | Drame Lyrique | en trois
Actes | Représenté pour la premiere fois
sur le Théâtre de la rue | Feydeau, le 16
Fevrier 1793 (vieux stil) l'an 1er. de la
République. | Paroles de Dercis | Musique
de Lesueur | Gravé par Huguet | . . . | A
Paris Chez JH. Naderman Editeur Lu-
thier Facteur de Harpe et autres Instru-
mens | de Musique Rue d'Argenteuil
Bute des Moulins à Apollon. [1793?]

2° *Score:* 1 *ℓ.*, 330 p.
Plate no. 3
RISM A I, no. L 2111
MUSIC LIBRARY

884 LE SUEUR, JEAN FRANÇOIS

Télémaque | Dans l'Isle de Calypso, |
ou le | Triomphe de la Sagesse. | Tragédie
Lyrique en trois Actes. | Représenté pour
la première fois sur le Théâtre Faydeau |
le 11 Mai 1796. (vieux Style) en Floréal
Année 4e. &c. | Paroles de P. Dercy. | Mu-
sique de Lesueur. | Inspecteur de l'ensei-
gnement du Conservatoire de Musique;
ci-devant | Maitre de Chapelle de la
Métropole de Paris, et de plusieurs | Aca-
demies de Belles Lettres, Sciences, et
Arts &c; Auteur de la | Musique de Paul
et Virginie (ou le Triomphe de la Vertu,)
et de celle de la | Caverne (ou le repentir)
Drames Lyriques Représentés au théatre
Faydeau | . . . | Gravé par Huguet Musi-
cien. | A Paris | Chez JH. Naderman Edi-
teur, Luthier, Facteur de Harpe et autres
Instruments, | Rue d'Argenteuil Butte
des Moulins à Apollon, et | Successeur
du Cen. Boyer Md. de Musique Rue de la
Loi à l'ancien Caffé de Foy. [1796?]

2° *Score:* 2 *ℓ.*, 400 p.
Plate no. 6
RISM A I, no. L 2149
MUSIC LIBRARY

LETTERA SOPRA LA MUSICA *See* Gri-
maldi, Francesco Antonio *Lettera sopra
la musica*

LETTRE D'UN VISIGOTH *See* Novi de Caveirac, Jean *Lettre d'un visigoth*

LETTRE SUR LA MUSIQUE *See* Arnaud,
François *Lettre sur la musique*

LETTRES SUR LA MUSIQUE FRANÇOISE *See*
Fréron, Élie Catherine *Lettres sur la musique françoise*

885 LEVERIDGE, RICHARD

A Collection | of | Songs, | With the
Musick, | by | Mr: Leveridge. | In Two
Volumes. | . . . | London | Engrav'd and
Printed for | the Author in Tavis-
tock-street, | Covent-Garden. 1727

8° *Score:* 2 vols.: [*vol. I*]: 1 *ℓ.*, 65 p.,
front.; [*vol. II*]: 1 *ℓ.*, 64 p.
RISM A I, no. L 2181
MUSIC LIBRARY

886 LÉVESQUE, ———, COMP.

Solfèges D'Italie | Avec la Basse
chiffrée, | Composés | Par Leo, Durante,
Scarlatti, Hasse, Porpora, Mazzoni, Caf-
faro, David Perez &c. | Dédiés A Messi-
gneurs | Les Premiers Gentils-Hommes |
De La Chambre Du Roi, | Et Recueillis
par les Srs. Levesque & Bêche, Ordinaires
de la Musique de Sa Majesté. |

[*col. 1:*]
A Paris
Chés le Sr. Cousineau
Md. Luthier Rue des Poulies
vis-à-vis le Louvre

[*col. 2:*]
Gravés par le Sr. Le Roy
. . .
Avec Privilége Du Roi

[*col. 3:*]
A Versailles
Chés les Editeurs
En Province
Aux Adresses Ordinaires

| Troisième Edition. [ca. 1780?]

obl. 2° 4 *ℓ.*, VI, 218, 68 p., illus., music
Prelíminary leaf 2ᵛ: Catalogue des
Oeuvres de Musique appartenants à Mr.
Cousineau Luthier | . . .
RISM B II, 360
MUSIC LIBRARY

LIBER DECEM MISSARUM *See* Moderne, Jacques, publ. *Liber decem missarum*

LIBER SELECTARUM CANTIONUM *See* Senfl, Ludwig, ed. *Liber selectarum cantionum*

887   LICHTENAUER, PAUL IGNAZ

Missae VI. | In | Honorem | Salvatoris | Nostri | Gloriam | Virginis, | Sancti Antonii, | Et | S. Nepomuceni. | à | IV. Vocibus, Canto, Alto, Tenore, Basso, | Variisque Instrumentis | Authore | Paulo Ignatio Liechtenauer, | Capellae Magistro, ac Organedo in Ecclesia Cathedrali | Osnabrugi. | Opus II. | . . . | Augustae Vindelicorum, | Typis & Sumptibus Haeredum Joannis Jacobi Lotteri MDCCXLI.

2° 1 pt.: *organo:* 1 ℓ., 48 p.
RISM A I, no. L 2340
HOUGHTON

888   LIDL, ANDREAS

Six | Quartettos | Three for two Violins, Tenor, & Violoncello, | and three for | Flute, Violin, Tenor, & Violoncello Obligato, | humbly Dedicated to | Thomas Fitzherbert, Esqr. | Compos'd By | A. Lidel. | Opera 2da. . . . | Printed & sold by Wm. Forster, Violin & Violoncello Maker | to His Royal Highness the Duke of Cumberland, | Corner of Dukes Court St, Martins Lane | London [178–?]

2° 4 pts.: *violino primo, violino secondo, viola, violoncello:* 1 ℓ., 12 p. each
Page [1] in *violino primo* part: A Catalogue of Music | Printed and Sold by Wm Forster . . .
RISM A I, no. L 2370
MUSIC LIBRARY

889   LIGNIVILLE, EUGENIO, MARCHE DI

Stabat Mater | à tre voci in Canone | Dedicato | À S. A. R. Pietro Leopoldo | Principe Reale D'Vngheria, E Di Boemia Arcidvca | D'Avstria Grandvca Di Toscana & & &. | Di | S. E. il Sigre Marche. di Ligniville Ciamberlano | delle LL. MM. GG., e RR. Direttore della | Musica

della Real Corte di Toscana. | [Florence?] Giuseppe Poggiali scolpi [1768?]

obl. 2° *Score:* [49] p.
RISM A I, no. L 2416
MUSIC LIBRARY

LINDEL, ANDREAS *See* Lidl, Andreas

890   LINLEY, THOMAS

Twelve | Ballads | Set to Music by | Thos. Linley | . . . | London Printed for Ab. Portal No. 163, opposite the New Church Strand. | . . . [ded. 1780]

obl 2° *Score:* 2 ℓ., 27 p.
RISM A I, no. L 2535
HOUGHTON

891   LINLEY, THOMAS

The | Camp | An Entertainment as performed at the | Theatre Royal in Drury Lane, | Composed by | Thomas Linley. | . . . | London | Printed for S & A Thompson No. 75 St. paul's Church Yard | . . . [1778]

obl 2° *Vocal score:* 2 ℓ., 27 p.
RISM A I, no. L 2447 (variant?)
HOUGHTON

892   [LINLEY, THOMAS]

The | Duenna | or | Double Elopement | a | Comic-Opera | As performed at the Theatre Royal in Covent Garden, | for the | Voice, Harpsichord, or Violin. | . . . | London, Printed for C. and S. Thompson, No: 75 St, Pauls Church Yard. [1775?]

obl. 2° *Short score:* 1 ℓ., 60 p.
RISM A I, no. L 2460
MUSIC LIBRARY

893   LINLEY, THOMAS

The | Duenna, | A | Comick Opera; | As Performed At The | Theatre Royal | Covent Garden. | Composed By | Mr. Linley. | London: | Printed for Harrison, Cluse, & Co. No. 78, Fleet Street. [1798?]

8° *Vocal score:* 66, [2] p. (*The Piano-Forte Magazine,* vol. V, no. 1)
Plate nos. 65–67
RISM A I, no. L 2465
MUSIC LIBRARY

894 LINLEY, THOMAS

Selima and Azor | A | Persian Tale | as Performed at the | Theatre Royal in Drury Lane, | Composed by | Thos. Linley, Senr. | . . . | London: Printed for C and S. Thompson No: 75, St. Pauls Church Yard. [1776]

    obl. 2° *Score:* 1 ℓ., 38 p.
RISM A I, no. L 2521
HOUGHTON

895 [LINLEY, THOMAS]

Tom Jones | A Comic Opera | as perform'd at the Theatre Royal in | Covent Garden | the Musick by the most celebrated Authors | the Words by | Joseph Reed | London Printed by Welcker in Gerrard Street St. Anns Soho | . . . [1769?]

    obl. 2° *Vocal score:* 1 ℓ., 6–29 p.
RISM B II, 390
MUSIC LIBRARY

LIONEL AND CLARISSA *See* Dibdin, Charles *Lionel and Clarissa*

896 LIPPIUS, JOHANNES

Philosophiae | Verae ac Sincerae | Synopticae | I. Praeparatio | per Musicam Diam: | II. Perfectio |

            Interior

Realis	Rationalis
per	per
Metaphysicam	Logicam

            Exterior

Realis	Rationalis
per	per
Ethicam	Rhetoricam

à Cl. et Doctiss. Viro | [?]n Joanne Lippio Ar-|gent. Als. Th. D. praelecta | Accessit in fine ejusdem Compendiolum | Oeconom[i]cae | Erfurti | Impensis Joannis Bischoffs Bibl. Erf. [1615]

    12°)(⁸, A–F¹², [2d]A–Z¹², a⁴, illus., fold. pl., music
Colophon: Erfurti | Typis Witteliani | M.DC.XV.
Title-page rubbed
RISM B VI, 505
MUSIC LIBRARY

LIROU, JEAN FRANÇOIS ESPIC DE *See* Espic de Lirou, Jean François

897 LISTENIUS, NICOLAUS

Mvsica | Nicolai Li-|stenii: | Ab Avctore Denvo Re-|cognita, multisq́[ue] nouis regulis | & exemplis adaucta. | Lipsiæ | Excvdebat Michael | Blvm. | Anno M.D.XLVII.

    8° A–F⁸, illus., music
RISM B VI, 507
HOUGHTON

898 LOCKE, MATTHEW

The | English Opera; | Or | The Vocal Musick | In | Psyche, | With The | Instrumental | Therein Intermix'd. | To which is Adjoyned | The Instrumental Musick | In The | Tempest. | By | Matthew Lock, Composer in Ordinary | to His Majesty, and Organist to the Queen. | . . . | London, | Printed by T. Ratcliff, and N. Thompson for the | Author, and are to be Sold by John Carr at his Shop at | the Middle Temple Gate in Fleet-street, MDCLXXV.

    4° *Score:* 4 ℓ., 72 [i. e. 76] p.
Pages 62–[76]: The Instrumental Musick used in the | Tempest
Page 76 misnumbered 72
Imperfect: pages 71, 72 [i. e. 75, 76] lacking; supplied in facsimile
RISM A I, no. L 2647
HOUGHTON

899 LOCKE, MATTHEW

The Original | Songs, Airs, & Chorusses, | Which were Introduced in the Tragedy of | Macbeth | in Score: Composed by | Matthew Locke, | Chapel Organist to Queen Catharine Consort to King Charles II | Revised & Corrected by | Dr. Boyce . . . | Dedicated to | David Garrick Esqr. | London Printed by Broderip & Wilkinson 13 Hay-market. [ca. 1800?]

    2° *Score:* 29 p.
RISM A I, no. L 2633
HOUGHTON

900 [Lockman, John]

Some | Reflexions | Concerning | Operas, Lyric Poetry, Music, &c. [London, 1740]

4° XXIV p.
Caption title
Extract from the preface to the libretto of the author's *Rosalinda*
RISM B VI, 512
MUSIC LIBRARY

901

Longman & Broderip's, | Select Collection | of the most Esteemed | Catches, Canons, Glees & Madrigals. | For Three Four & Five Voices. | By the most Eminent Composers Ancient & Modern | . . . | No. [3] . . . | London Printed by Longman & Broderip No. 26, Cheapside & No. 13 Hay Market. [1790?]

obl. 8° *Score:* 1 ℓ., [43]–61 p.
RISM B II, 225
MUSIC LIBRARY

902 Lorente, Andrés

El Porqve | De La Mvsica, | En Qve Se Contiene | Los Qvatro Artes De Ella, | Canto LLano, Canto De Organo, Contrapvnto, | Y Composicion, | Y En Cada Vno De Ellos | Nvevas Reglas, Razon Abreviada, En Vtiles | Preceptos, aun en las cosas mas dificiles, tocantes à la | Harmonia Musica, | Nvmerosos Exemplos, Con Clara Inteligencia, | en estilo breve, que al Maestro deleytan, y al Discipula ensenan, | cuya direccion se verà sucintamente anotada | antes del Prologo. | Dedicado | A Maria Santissima, Nvestra Abogada, Y Señora, | Concebida sin mancha de pecado Original, en el Primer | Instante de su Ser: | Maestra De Los Mejores Cantores, Qve En Esta | Mortal Vida se exercitaron en obras de Entendimiento, y Voz, auiendo dado con | ellas alabanças al Criador, y à nosotros disciplina para seguir su concento: à la | que es Reyna de los Musicos Celestiales, que libres de la fatiga humana, en | acordes Coros incessablemente proclamant, Sancta, Sancta, Sancta | Maria Dei genitrix, Mater, | & Virgo. | Por Sv Avtor, | El Maestro Andres Lorente, | Natvral De

La Villa De Anchvelo, | Arçobispado de Toledo, Graduado en la Facultad de Artes por la Vni-|uersidad de Alcalà, Comissario del Santo Oficio de la Inquisicion de To-|ledo, Racionero, y Organista de la Iglesia Magistral de S. Iusto, | y Pastor de la Villa de Alcalà | de Henares. | Con Licencia. | En Alcalà de Henares: En la Imprenta de Nicolàs de Xamares, | Mercader de Libros, Año de 1672.

4° 8 ℓ., 695 p., illus., music
RISM B VI, 516
MUSIC LIBRARY

Love in a Village *See* Arne, Thomas Augustine *Love in a Village*

903 Lully, Jean Baptiste

Armide, | Tragedie | Mise | En Musique, | Par Monsievr de Lvlly, Escvyer, Conseiller | Secretaire du Roy, Maison, Couronne de France et de ses Finances, | et Sur-Intendant de la Musique de Sa Majesté. | A Paris, | Par Christophe Ballard, seul Imprimeur du Roy pour la Musique, | ruë Saint Jean de Beauvais, au Mont-Parnasse. | Et Se Vend | A la Porte de l'Academie Royalle de Musique ruë Saint Honoré. | M.DC.LXXXVI. | Avec Privilege De Sa Majesté.

2° *Score:* 2 ℓ., lxij [i. e. lx], 271 p.
Page lx misnumbered lxij
Hirsch II, no. 530; RISM A I, no. L 2954
HOUGHTON

904 Lully, Jean Baptiste

Armide. | Tragedie. | Mise En Musique. | Par Feu Mr. De Lully Escer. Coner. | Secretaire du Roy, Maison Couronne | de France et de Ses Finances, et Sur-|Intendant de la Musique de Sa Majesté. | Seconde Edition. | Graveé par H. de Baussen. | A Paris. | A l'Entreé de la Porte de l'Academie Royale | de Musique au Palais Royal, rue | Saint Honoré | MDCCX. | Avec Privilege du Roy.

2° *Score:* 1 ℓ., 188 p., illus.
Hirsch II, no. 531; RISM A I, no. L 2955
HOUGHTON

905 LULLY, JEAN BAPTISTE

Atys, | Tragedie | Mise En Musique | Par Monsieur De Lully, Ecuyer-Con-seiller-|Secretaire du Roy, Maison, Couronne de France | & de ses Finances, & Sur-Intendant de la Musique | de Sa Majesté; | Representée Par L'Academie Royale | de Musique en l'Année 1676. | Seconde Edition. | Oeuvre VI. | De L'Im-primerie | De J-B-Christophe Ballard, Seul Imprimeur du Roy pour la Musique, | à Paris, rüe Saint Jean-de-Beauvais, au Mont-Parnasse. | M.DCCXX. | Avec Pri-vilege de Sa Majesté.

2° *Score:* 4, 225 p., illus.
RISM A I, no. L 2965
HOUGHTON

906 LULLY, JEAN BAPTISTE

Thesée | Tragedie | Mise | En Musique | Par Monsieur De Lvlly, | Sur-Intendant de la Musique du Roy. | A Paris, | Par Christophe Ballard, seul Imprimeur | du Roy pour la Musique, rüe S. Jean de Beau-vais | au Mont Parnasse. | Et Se Vend, | A la Porte de l'Academie Royale de Musi-que, rüe S. Honoré. | M.DC.LXXXVIII. | Avec Privilege De Sa Majesté.

2° *Score:* 3 ℓ., 372 [i. e. 364] p.
Numbers 217–224 omitted in paging
Davidsson I, no. 320; RISM A I, no. L 3037
HOUGHTON

907 LUSITANO, VICENTE

Introdvttione | Facilissima, Et Novis-sima, Di Canto | Fermo, Figvrato, Con-traponto | Semplice, Et Inconcerto, | Con Regole Generali Per Far Fvghe | Diffe-renti Sopra Il Canto Fermo, | A. II. III. Et IIII. Voci, Et Compositioni, | Proportioni, Generi. S. Diatonico, | Cromatico, Enar-monico, | Composta Per Vincentio Lvsi-tano. | In Venetia | Per Francesco Marco-lini. MDLVIII.

4° 26 numb. ℓ., illus., music
Title-page signed by Antonio Maria Abbatini
Hirsch I, no. 330; MortimerI, no. 530; RISM B VI, 521
HOUGHTON

LUSUS INGENII DE HARMONIA *See* Mizler von Kolof, Lorenz Christoph *Lusus in-genii de harmonia*

M

---

908 MCDONALD, PATRICK, COMP.

A | Collection | of | Highland Vocal Airs, | Never hitherto published. | To which are added a few of the most lively | Country Dances or Reels, | of the | North Highlands, & Western Isles: | And some Specimens of Bagpipe Music. | By | Pat-rick Mc.Donald | . . . | Minister of Kil-more in Argyleshire. | . . . | Edinburgh Printed for the publisher, and to be had at the Music Shops | of Corri and Suther-land Bridge Street, and N: Stewart Part. Square. [1784?]

2° *Score:* 2 ℓ., 22, 42 p.
RISM A I, no. M 15
HOUGHTON

909 MCDONALD, PATRICK, COMP.

A | Collection | of | Highland Vocal Airs, | Never hitherto published. | To which are added a few of the most lively | Country Dances or Reels, | of the | North Highland, & Western Isles: | And some Specimens of Bagpipe Music. | By | Pat-rick Mc. Donald | . . . | Edinr. Printed & Sold by J. Johnson Music Seller Lawn Market. [179–?]

2° *Score:* 2 ℓ., 43 p.
MUSIC LIBRARY

910 MACÉ, DENIS

Recveil | Des | Chansons | A Danser Et A Boire | De Denis Macé, | Maistre de Musique. | A Paris, | Par Robert Ballard, Impri-|meur du Roy pour la Musique, demeu-|rant rüe S. Iean de Beauuais, à l'en|seigne du mont Parnasse. | 1643. | Auec Priuilége de sa | Majesté.

8° 46 numb. ℓ., [2] p.
Davidsson I, no. 323; RISM A I, no. M 19
HOUGHTON

911   MACE, THOMAS

Musick's Monument; | Or, A | Remembrancer | Of the Best | Practical Musick, | Both Divine, and Civil, that has ever | been known, to have been in the World. | Divided into Three Parts. | The First Part, | Shews a Necessity of Singing Psalms Well, in Parochial Churches, | or not to Sing at all; Directing, how They may be Well Sung, Certainly; by | Two several Ways, or Means; with an Assurance of a Perpetual National-|Quire; and also shewing, How Cathedral Musick, may be much Improved, | and Refined. | The Second Part, | Treats of the Noble Lute, (the Best of Instruments) now made | Easie; and all Its Occult-Lock'd-up-Secrets Plainly laid Open, never before | Discovered; whereby It is now become so Familiarly Easie, as Any Instrument | of Worth, known in the World; Giving the True Reasons of Its Former | Difficulties; and Proving Its Present Facility, by Vndeniable Arguments; | Directing the most Ample Way, for the use of the Theorboe, from off the | Note, in Consort, &c. Shewing a General Way of Procuring Invention, and | Playing Voluntarily, upon the Lute, Viol, or any other Instrument; with | Two Pritty Devices; the One, shewing how to Translate Lessons, from | one Tuning, or Instrument, to Another; The other, an Indubitable Way, | to know the Best Tuning, upon any Instrument: Both done by Example. | In the Third Part, | The Generous Viol, in Its Rightest Vse, is Treated upon; with | some Curious Observations, never before Handled, concerning It, and | Musick in General. | By Tho. Mace, one of the Clerks of Trinity Colledge, in the | University of Cambridge. | London, | Printed by T. Ratcliffe, and N. Thompson, for the Author, and are to | be Sold by Himself, at His House in Cambridge, and by John Carr, | at His Shop at the Middle-Temple Gate in Fleetstreet, 1676.

2° 10 ℓ., 272 p., front. (port.), illus., music
Hirsch I, no. 334; RISM A I, no. M 20; RISM B VI, 523–524
HOUGHTON

—Another copy
2° 10 ℓ., 272 p., front. (port.), illus., 3 pl., music

In this copy three of the illustrations are printed as plates, and the pages for which they were intended are blank
HOUGHTON

912   McGIBBON, WILLIAM

A Collection | of | Scots Tunes | For the Violin or German Flute | And a Bass for the | Violoncello or Harpsichord | by | William Mc: Gibbon. | With some Additions by R: Bremner. | Books [1–4] . . . | London. | Printed and sold by Preston & Son at their Warehouses No. 97 Strand, and | Exeter Change. [1762?]

obl. 4° *Score:* 2 ℓ., 120 p.
RISM A I, no. M 28
MUSIC LIBRARY

913   MAGGI, GIROLAMO

Hieronymi Magii | De | Tintinnabvlis | Liber Postvmvs. | Franciscvs Sweertivs F. | Antuerp. | Notis illustrabat. | Hanoviae | Typis Wechelianis, apud Claudium | Marnium & heredes Ioannis Aubrii. | CIↃ IↃ CVIII.

8° 98, [14] p., illus.
RISM B VI, 525
HOUGHTON

914   MAGGI, GIROLAMO

Hieronymi Magii | Anglarensis | De | Tintinnabulis | Liber Postumus. | Franciscus Sweertius F. | Antverp. | Notis illustrabat. | Editio novissima aucta, emendata, et | figuris aeneis exornata. | Amstelodami, | Sumptibus Sebastiani Combi, | & joannis Lanou. | CIↃ IↃ CLXIV.

12° 15 ℓ., 151, [26] p., front., illus., 2 fold. pl.
RISM B VI, 525
HOUGHTON

915   MAGGI, GIROLAMO

Hieronymi Magii | Anglarensis | De | Tintinnabulis | Liber Postumus. | Franciscus Sweertius F. | Antverp. | Notis illustrabat. | Editio novissima aucta, emendata, et | figuris aeneis exornata. | Amstelodami, | Sumptibus Andreae Frissii. | CIC IↃ CLXIV.

12° 15 ℓ., 151, [26] p., front., illus., 2 fold. pl.
RISM B VI, 525
HOUGHTON

916   MAGNY, ———

Principes | De | Chorégraphie, | Suivis | D'un Traité de la Cadence, qui apprendra les tems & les | valeurs de chaque pas de la Danse, détaillés par carac-|teres, figures & signes démonstratifs. | Par M. Magny, Maître de Danse à Paris, aujourd'hui résident | à Senlis. | . . . | A Paris, | Chez {Duchesne, Libraire, rue Saint Jacques, près la | Fontaine Saint Benoît, au Temple du Goût; | Et | De La Chevardiere, rue du Roule, | à la Croix d'or. | M.DCC.LXV. | Avec Approbation, & Privilége du Roi.

8° 4 ℓ., 244 p., illus., music
Pages 139–239: dance tunes with choreographic notation
RISM B VI, 526
HOUGHTON

THE MAID OF THE MILL   *See* Arnold, Samuel *The Maid of the Mill*

917   [MAINWARING, JOHN]

Memoirs | Of The | Life | Of The Late | George Frederic Handel. | To which is added, | A Catalogue of his Works, | And | Observations upon them. | . . . | London: | Printed for R. and J. Dodsley, in Pall-Mall. | M.DCC.LX.

8° 2 ℓ., 208 p., front. (port.)
RISM B VI, 528
MUSIC LIBRARY

LE MAÎTRE EN DROIT   *See* Monsigny, Pierre Alexandre *Le Maître en droit*

918   MALCOLM, ALEXANDER

A | Treatise | Of | Mvsick, | Speculative, Practical, and Historical. | By Alexander Malcolm. | . . . | Edinburgh, | Printed for the Author. MDCCXXI.

8° v, [iii]–xxiv, 608 p., illus., 6 fold. pl.
Hirsch I, no. 339; RISM B VI, 530
HOUGHTON

919   MALCOLM, ALEXANDER

Malcolm's | Treatise | Of | Music, | Speculative, Practical, and Historical. | Corrected and Abridged | By an Eminent Musician. | . . . | London: | Printed for J. French, No. 47, Holborn. | M,DCC,LXXVI.

8° 1 ℓ., 104 p., illus.
RISM B VI, 531
MUSIC LIBRARY

920   MALPIED, N.

Traité | sur l'Art de la Danse. | Dedié | à Monsieur | Gardel L'Ainé, | Maître des Ballets, | de l'Academie Royale de Musique. | Seconde Édition | Augmentée d'une grande quantité des Pas tant anciens, | que modernes avec leurs Explications a chacun | Par | Mr. Malpied, Mtre. de Danse. | . . . | A Paris. | Chez M. Boüin, Md. de Musique, et de Cordes | d'Instruments, Rue St. Honoré, près St. Roch, | au Gagne-petit, No. 504. | . . . [ca. 1784?]

8° 2 ℓ., A–D, 166 p., illus., music
RISM B VI, 532
HOUGHTON

921   MANCINI, GIOVANNI BATTISTA

Riflessioni Pratiche | Sul Canto Figurato | Di | Giambattista Mancini | Maestro Di Canto Dell'Imperial Corte | Di Vienna | Accademico Filarmonico | Rivedute, corrette, ed aumentate. | Terza Edizione. | In Milano. MDCCLXXVII. | Appresso Giuseppe Galeazzi Regio Stampatore. | Con Approvazione.

8° 4 ℓ., 259, [2] p., A–D pl. (music)
RISM B VI, 532
MUSIC LIBRARY

922   MANFREDINI, VINCENZO

Regole Armoniche | O Sieno | Precetti Ragionati Per Apprendere I Principj Della Musica, | Il Portamento Della Mano, E L'Accompagnamento | Del Basso Sopra Gli Strumenti Da Tasto, | Come L'Organo, Il Cembalo ec. | Dedicate | A Sua Altezza Imperiale | Paul Petrovicz | Gran Duca Di Tutte Le Russie |

ec. ec. ec. | Da Vincenzo Manfredini | Già Maestro Di Cappella Di S. M. I. | Caterina II. | Felicemente Regnante. | In Venezia MDCCLXXV. | Appresso Guglielmo Zerletti | In Merceria all'Insegna della Scienza. | Con Licenza De' Superiori, E Privilegio.

4° xvi, 78 p., 1 *ℓ*., front. (port.), illus., 20 fold. pl., music
Folded plates 1–13 contain fourteen preludes for keyboard instrument
RISM B VI, 533
HOUGHTON

MANGEANT, JACQUES, PUBL. Recueil des plus beaux airs *See* Recueil des plus beaux airs

MANGEANT, JACQUES, PUBL. Recueil des plus belles chansons des comediens *See* Recueil des plus belles chansons des comediens

MANGEANT, JACQUES, PUBL. Le Recueil des plus belles chansons de dances de ce temps *See* Le Recueil des plus belles chansons de dances de ce temps

923   MARCELLO, BENEDETTO

Estro | Poetico-Armonico. | Parafrasi | Sopra li primi[–secondi] | Venticinque Salmi. | Poesia | di | Girolamo Ascanio Giustiniani, | Musica | di | Benedetto Marcello | Patrizj Veneti. | . . . | Venezia, | MDCCXXIV. [–MDCCXXVI.]

2° *Score:* 8 vols.: *vol. I:* 2 *ℓ*., 34, CXXX p., 1 *ℓ*.; *vol. II:* 2 *ℓ*., 22, CXLVIII p.; *vol. III:* 2 *ℓ*., VIII, 5–22, CXLI, [1] p.; *vol. IV:* 2 *ℓ*., VIII, 5–27, CXCVII, [1] p.; *vol. V:* 2 *ℓ*., 20, CXXXIII, [1] p.; *vol. VI:* 2 *ℓ*., 23, CXLVI p., 1 *ℓ*.; *vol. VII:* 2 *ℓ*., 28, CLXVIII p., 1 *ℓ*.; *vol. VIII:* 2 *ℓ*., VIII, 5–24, CLXXX, [2] p.; front. in each vol. except IV
Colophon in each vol. except II: Appresso Domenico Lovisa. | La Composizione de' caratteri musicali è diligente fatica | de Fortuniano Rosati.
Imprint date, vol. V: MDCCXXV; vols. VI–VIII: MDCCXXVI
RISM A I, no. M 423; RISM B VI, 534
MUSIC LIBRARY

924   MARCELLO, BENEDETTO

The | First Fifty Psalms. | Set to Music by | Benedetto Marcello, | Patrizio Veneto, | and adapted to the | English Version, | By | John Garth. | . . . | Engrav'd by Willm. Clark. | London | Printed for John Johnson, at the Harp & Crown, Cheapside | MDCCLVII.

2° *Score:* 8 vols.: *vol. I:* 3 *ℓ*., 2 p., 1 *ℓ*., [14], 130, [2] p.; *vol. II:* 3 *ℓ*., 2 p., 1 *ℓ*., 131, [2] p.; *vol. III:* 3 *ℓ*., 4, 2, 144, [2] p.; *vol. IV:* 3 *ℓ*., 2 p., 1 *ℓ*., 154, [2] p.; *vol. V:* 2 *ℓ*., 4 p., 1 *ℓ*., 123 p., 1 *ℓ*.; *vol. VI:* 2 *ℓ*., 4, [2], 127 p., 1 *ℓ*.; *vol. VII:* 2 *ℓ*., 4 p., 1 *ℓ*., 148, [2] p.; *vol. VIII:* 2 *ℓ*., 4 p., 1 *ℓ*., 150 p., 1 *ℓ*.
RISM A I, no. M 426
MUSIC LIBRARY

925   MARCELLO, BENEDETTO

Il | Teatro | Alla Moda | O Sia | Metodo sicuro, e facile per ben comporre, & eseguire | l'Opere Italiane in Musica all'uso moderno, | Nel quale | Si danno Avvertimenti utili, e necessarij à Poeti, Compositori | di Musica, Musici dell' uno, e dell'altro sesso, Impresarj, | Suonatori, Ingegneri, e Pittori di Scene, Parti buffe, | Sarti, Paggi, Comparse, Suggeritori, Copisti, | Protettori, e Madri di Virtuose, & altre | Persone appartenenti al Teatro. | Dedicato | Dall'Auttore Del Libro | Al Compositore Di Esso. | Stampato ne Borghi di Belisania per Aldiviva | Licante, all'Insegna dell'Orso in Peata. | Si vende nella Strada del Corallo alla | Porta del Palazzo d'Orlando. | E si ristamperà ogn'anno con nuova aggiunta. [ca. 1733]

8° 72 p.
Hirsch I, no. 344; RISM B VI, 535
MUSIC LIBRARY

926   MARENZIO, LUCA

. . . | Di Lvca Marenzio | Il Sesto Libro De Madrigali | A Cinqve Voci, | Nouamente posto in luce. | Con Privilegio. | In Venetia Appresso Angelo Gardano. | M.D.LXXXXIIII.

obl. 4° 1 pt.: *qvinto:* 1 *ℓ*., 20 [i. e. 21], [1] p.
Page 21 misnumbered 20

RISM A I, no. M 557; Vogel, no. 1629
HOUGHTON

927   MARENZIO, LUCA

. . . | Di Lvca | Marenzio | Il Nono Libro | De Madrigali | A Cinque Voci | Nouamente Ristampato. | In Venetia, | Appresso Alessandro Rauerij. M.D.CVIII.

4° 1 pt.: *basso:* 1 ℓ., 21, [1] p.
RISM A I, no. M 569; Vogel, no. 1641
HOUGHTON

928   MARENZIO, LUCA

Di Lvca Marenzio, | Mvsico Eccellentissimo. | Madrigali A Sei Voci, | In Vn Corpo Ridotti. | Nuouamente posti in luce, & con ogni | diligentia corretti. | Aggiunto vi di più vno Madrigale del istesso Authore à Dieci Voci. | . . . | In Anversa. | Appresso Pietro Phalesio & Giouanni Bellero. | M.D.XCIIII.

obl. 4° 2 pts.: *tenore:* 56 numb. ℓ.; *basso:* 55 numb. ℓ., 1 ℓ.
RISM A I, no. M 522; RISM B I, no. 1594¹⁴; Vogel, no. 1670
HOUGHTON

MARGARITA PHILOSOPHICA   *See* Reisch, Gregor *Margarita philosophica*

929   MARIA, DOMENICO DELLA

Le Prisonnier | Ou | La Ressemblance | Opera en un Acte | Paroles Du Cen. Duval | Musique du Cen. Domenico Della Maria | Eléve de Paësiello | . . . | A Paris | Chez l'Auteur, Rue Helvetius, No. 667. vis-à-vis celle des Orties | . . . [1798?]

2° *Score:* 1 ℓ., 146 p.
Imprint partially covered by cancel label reading: [Chez] Jmbault rue Honoré au mont d'or. No. 200 de la section des Gardes-|-Françaises, entre la rue des Poulies et la Maison d'Aligre.
RISM A I, no. D 1450
MUSIC LIBRARY

930   MARIA, DOMENICO DELLA

Le Vieux Chateau | ou | La Rencontre | Opera En Un Acte | Paroles du Cen.

Duval | Musique du Cen. Domenico Della Maria | Gravé par Favrot. | . . . | A Paris | Chez l'Auteur, Rue Helvetius, No. 667. vis-à-vis celle des Orties. | Propriété de l'Editeur—Enregistré [à] la Bibliothèque Nationale. [1798?]

2° *Score:* 1 ℓ., 188 p.
RISM A I, no. D 1486
MUSIC LIBRARY

931   MARPURG, FRIEDRICH WILHELM

Anfangsgründe | der Theoretischen Musik, | von | Friedrich Wilhelm Marpurg. | Leipzig, | bey Johann Gottlob Immanuel Breitkopf. | 1757.

4° 4 ℓ., 176 p., illus., music
Hirsch I, no. 356; RISM B VI, 540–541
MUSIC LIBRARY

932   MARPURG, FRIEDRICH WILHELM

Anleitung | zum | Clavierspielen, | der | schönern Ausübung | der heutigen Zeit gemäss | entworfen | von | Friedr. Wilh. Marpurg. | Nebst XVIII. Kupfertafeln. | Berlin, | bey A. Haude und J. C. Spener, | Königl. und der Academie der Wissenschaften privilegirten Buchhåndlern, | 1755.

4° 6 ℓ., 78, [6] p., 9 fold. pl. (music)
Hirsch I, no. 353; RISM B VI, 541
HOUGHTON

933   MARPURG, FRIEDRICH WILHELM

Herrn Georg Andreas Sorgens | Anleitung | zum | Generalbass | und zur | Composition. | Mit | Anmerkungen | von | Friedrich Wilhelm Marpurg. | Nebst vier Kupfertafeln. | . . . | Berlin, 1760. | Bey Gottlieb August Lange.

4° 6 ℓ., 152 p., illus., 4 pl. (music)
A commentary on Georg Andreas Sorge's *Compendium harmonicum*
Imperfect: pages 139–142 lacking; supplied in eight pages of manuscript. Plates lacking; supplied in positive photostat
Hirsch I, no. 359; RISM B VI, 792
MUSIC LIBRARY

934   [MARPURG, FRIEDRICH
WILHELM, ED.]

Des | critischen | Musicus | an der
Spree | erster Band. | Berlin, | zu finden
bey A. Haude und J. C. Spener, Königl.
und der | Academie der Wissenschaften
privil. Buchhåndler. | 1750.

4° 4 ℓ., 406 p., illus., 5 pl. (music)
Fifty issues published from March 4,
1749 to February 17, 1750; no more pub-
lished
Hirsch I, no. 349; RISM B VI, 542
MUSIC LIBRARY

935   MARPURG, FRIEDRICH
WILHELM

Historisch-Kritische | Beyträge | zur |
Aufnahme der Musik | von | Friedrich
Marpurg. | . . . | Berlin, | in Verlag
Joh. Schützens sel. Wittwe. | 1754.
[−1778]

8° 5 vols.
The collation of this set conforms to
the one described in Hirsch I, no. 352,
with the following exceptions: each vol.
contains a main title-leaf plus five extra
title-leaves interspersed; *vol. II:* nos. 182
−184 and 382−386 omitted in paging;
vol. IV: nos. 154−188 repeated in paging,
nos. 247−289 and 321−330 omitted; *vol.
V:* lacks one leaf of musical examples.
Publisher statement, *vol. II−V:* Verlegts Gottlieb August Lange.
RISM B VI, 543
HOUGHTON

936   [MARPURG, FRIEDRICH
WILHELM, ED.]

Kritische Briefe | über die | Tonkunst, |
mit kleinen | Clavierstücken und Sing-
oden | begleitet | von | einer musikali-
schen Gesellschaft in Berlin. | I. Band |
bestehend aus vier Theilen. | Berlin, | bey
Friedrich Wilhelm Birnstiel, privilegir-
tem Buchdrucker. 1760.

4° 5 ℓ., 506 [i. e. 508] p., 4 ℓ., illus.,
music
Fifty-four issues published weekly
from June 23, 1759 through September 6,
1760
Extra unnumbered leaves of music,
one each after pages [48], 56, two after

142; three extra unnumbered leaves containing title-pages for the "Zweyter" to
"Vierter Theil" after pages 126, 254 and
380 respectively; two extra unnumbered
pages between 65 and 66
Hirsch I, no. 360; RISM B VI, 543−544
HOUGHTON

937   MARPURG, FRIEDRICH
WILHELM

Kritische Einleitung | in | die Ge-
schichte und Lehrsätze | der alten und
neuen | Musik, | von Friedrich Wilhelm
Marpurg. | Nebst acht Kupfertabellen. |
Berlin, | bey Gottleib August Lange 1759.

4° 6 ℓ., 246, [8] p., front. (port.), illus., 8
pl.
Hirsch I, no. 358; RISM B VI, 544; Wolfenbüttel, no. 1221
MUSIC LIBRARY

938   MARPURG, FRIEDRICH
WILHELM

Die | Kunst | das Clavier zu spielen, |
Durch | den Verfasser | des critischen
Musicus an der Spree. | Berlin, | Bey
Haude und Spener, Königl. und der Aca-
demie der Wissenschafft | privilegirten
Buchhåndlern. | 1751.

4° 27 p., 4 pl. (music)
Hirsch I, no. 350; RISM B VI, 544
MUSIC LIBRARY (2 copies)

939   MARPURG, FRIEDRICH
WILHELM

Neue | Lieder | zum Singen | beym |
Clavier, | von | Friedrich Wilhelm Mar-
purg. | Berlin, | verlegts Gottlieb August
Lange. 1756.

obl. 4° *Score:* 3 ℓ., 58 p.
RISM A I, no. M 716
MUSIC LIBRARY

940   MARPURG, FRIEDRICH
WILHELM

Friedrich Wilhelm Marpurgs, | Königl.
Preuss. Kriegesraths, | Versuch | über die
musikalische | Temperatur, | nebst
einem | Anhang | über den Rameau- und
Kirnbergerschen | Grundbass, | und vier

Tabellen. | . . . | Breslau, | bey Johann Friedrich Korn, | 1776.

8° XIV p., 1 ℓ., 319, [1] p., illus., 4 pl. (music)
Hirsch I, no. 363; RISM B VI, 546
MUSIC LIBRARY

MARTIN, JOHANN PAUL AEGIDIUS *See* Martini, Jean Paul Égide

MARTIN, JOHANNES *See* Laurentius von Schnüffis

941 MARTÍNEZ DE BIZCARGUI, GONÇALO

Arte de canto lla-|no y contrapunto y can|to de organo cõ propor|ciones y modos breue-|mente cõpuesta: y nue-|uamête añadida | y glo-|sada por Gonçalo m[ar-]|tinez de Bizcargu[i en-]|dereçada al Jllustre y | muy. R. señor don Juã | rodri-guez de Fonseca. | Arçobispo de Rosano, | y obispo de Burgos mi | Señor. [Saragossa, 1550]

8° a–k⁸, ℓ1–3, illus., music
Colophon: Fue imprimida en çaragoça. Y es delas | que agora postreramente han estado | reuistas & algunas cosas ne-cessa|rias por el mismo Gonçalo | Mar-tinez de Bizcar-|gui añadidas. A-|cabose de im-|primir enel | año de | M.D.L.
Imperfect: title-page torn, with loss of some letters
RISM B VI, 550
HOUGHTON

942 MARTINI, GIOVANNI BATTISTA

Esemplare | O Sia | Saggio Fondamen-tale Pratico | Di Contrappunto | Sopra Il Canto Fermo | Dedicato all'Eminentis-simo, e Reverendissimo | Sig. Cardinale | Vincenzo Malvezzi | Arcivescovo di Bo-logna, Prencipe del S. R. I., | e Prodatario | Di N. S. Felicemente Regnante | Da F. Giambattista Martini Minor Conven-tuale | Accademico dell'Instituto delle Scienze, e Filarm. | . . . | In Bologna MDCCLXXIV. | Per Lelio dalla Volpe Im-pressore dell'Instituto delle Scienze. | Con licenza de' Superiori.

4° 2 vols.: *vol. I:* xxxii, 260 p., music; *vol. II:* xxxxviii, 328 p., fold. pl., music

Vol. II has separate title-page: Esem-plare | O Sia | Saggio Fondamentale Pra-tico | Di | Contrappunto Fugato | Dedi-cato | All'Illustrissimo, e Reverendis-simo Monsignore | Gennaro Adelelmo | Pignatelli | Arcivescovo Di Bari | Da F. Giambattista Martini Minor Conven-tuale | Accademico dell'Instituto delle Scienze, e Filarm. | . . . | In Bologna | Per Lelio dalla Volpe Impressore dell'Insti-tuto delle Scienze. | Con licenza de' Su-periori.
Hirsch I, no. 366; RISM B VI, 551–552
MUSIC LIBRARY

—another copy
Imprint date omitted from title-page of vol. I
HOUGHTON

943 MARTINI, GIOVANNI BATTISTA

Storia | Della Musica | Tomo Primo | Alla Sacra Reale Cattolica | Maestà | Maria Barbara | Infanta Di Portogallo, Re-gina | Delle Spagne ec. ec. ec. | Umiliato, e dedicato | Da Fr. Giambatista Martini De' Minori Conventuali | Accademico nell'Instituto delle Scienze, e Filar-monico. | In Bologna MDCCLVII. [–MDCCLXXXI.] | Per Lelio dalla Volpe Impressore dell'Instituto delle Scienze. | Con licenza de' Superiori.

4° 3 vols.: vol. I: XII, 507 p., illus., 9 pl., music; *vol. II:* xii, XX, 375 p., illus., 2 pl., music; *vol. III:* XX, 459 p., illus., 2 pl., music
Imprint date, vol. II: MDCCLXX; vol. III: MDCCLXXXI
RISM B VI, 552–553
HOUGHTON

—another copy
2° Large paper copy
MUSIC LIBRARY

MARTINI, GIUSEPPE *See* Sammartini, Giuseppe

944 MARTINI, JEAN PAUL ÉGIDE

Annette | Et | Lubin, | Opera Comique En Un Acte, | Remis en musique et Dédié | A Monseigneur | Comte D'Artois | Par | Mr. Martini | Sur-intendant de la Mu-

sique du Roi, Directeur de la Musique |
de Monseigneur Comte d'Artois, & Pen-
sionre. du Roi. | Représenté devant leurs
Majestés, par les Comédiens | Italiens
Ordinaires du Roi, le Vendredi 6. Fevrier
1789. | Paroles De M. Favart. | Gravé par
Huguet Musicien de la Comédie Ita-
lienne. | . . . | A Paris | Aux Adresses or-
dinaires de Musique. | A. P. D. R. [ca.
1789]

2° *Score:* 2 ℓ., 153 p.
Hirsch II, no. 872; RISM A I, no. M
1034
MUSIC LIBRARY

945   MARTINI, JEAN PAUL ÉGIDE

Le Droit | Du Seigneur | Comédie | En
trois Actes et en Prôse, | Dédiée | À Ma-
dame La Duchesse | De Fronsac. | Mise
en Musique | Par M. Martini. | Amateur |
Représentée pour la premiere fois devant
leurs Majestés à Fontainebleau | Le 17
Octobre 1783, par les Comédiens Ita-
liens ordinaires du Roy, | Et à Paris le 29
Decembre de la même Année. | . . . | A
Paris | Chez Brunet Libraire place du
Théâtre Italien, | Chez le Portier de Mr.
Lenormant d'Etioles Rue du Sentier No.
34, | Et aux Adresses ordinaires. |
. . . [1783]

2° *Score:* 2 ℓ., 200 p.
RISM A I, no. M 1045
MUSIC LIBRARY

946   MARTINI, JEAN PAUL ÉGIDE

Sapho | Tragédie en trois Actes et en
Vers | par la Citoyenne Pipelet | Mise en
Musique | par le Citoyen | Martini. |
Représentée, pour la prèmiere fois, sur le
Théâtre des amis de la Patrie, | rue de
Louvois le 22. Frimaire, l'an 3e. de la
République. (14 xbr. 1794. vieux stile) |
. . . | Gravé par le Cen. Lobry. | A Paris |
Chez l'Auteur rue du Sentier No. 34. | et
Chez les Marchands de Musique [1794?]

2° *Score:* 1 ℓ., 412 p.
RISM A I, no. M 1113
MUSIC LIBRARY

MARTINO, GIUSEPPE   *See* Sammartini,
Giuseppe

947   [MATTHESON, JOHANN]

Behauptung | der | Himmlischen
Musik | aus den Grůnden | der | Vernunft,
Kirchen-Lehre und | heiligen Schrift. |
. . . | Hamburg, | zu finden bey Christian
Herold. | 1747.

8° 4 ℓ., 144 p., illus.
Blank cancel label mounted over pub-
lisher statement on title-page
Hirsch I, no. 382; RISM B VI, 558
MUSIC LIBRARY

948   MATTHESON, JOHANN

Das | Beschützte | Orchestre, | oder des-
selben | Zweyte Erőffnung, | Worinn
| Nicht nur einem wůrckli-|chen ga-
lant-homme, der eben kein | Professions-
Verwandter, sondern auch man-|chem
Musico selbst die alleraufrichtigste und
deutlich-|ste Vorstellung musicalischer
Wissenschafften, wie sich | dieselbe vom
Schulstaub tůchtig gesäubert, eigentlich |
und wahrhafftig verhalten, ertheilet; al-
ler wiedrigen | Auslegung und gedun-
genen Aufbůrdung aber vőlliger | und
truckener Bescheid gegeben; so dann
endlich | des lange verbannet gewesenen
{Ut Mi Sol | Re Fa La | Todte (nicht tota)
Musica | Unter ansehnlicher Begleitung
der zwőlff Grie-|chischen Modorum, als
ehrbahrer Verwandten und Trauer-
|Leute, zu Grabe gebracht und mit einem
Monument, | zum ewigen Andencken,
beehret wird | von | Mattheson. | Ham-
burg, zu finden im Dom, im Schilleri-
schen | Buchladen, 1717.

12° 10 ℓ., 561, [1] p., front. on 2 ℓ., 7 pl.
(music)
Hirsch I, no. 368; RISM B VI, 558
HOUGHTON (2 copies)

949   MATTHESON, JOHANN

Mathesons | bewåhrte | Panacea, | als
eine Zugabe | zu seinem musikalischen |
Mithridat, | ůberaus heilsam | wider
die leidige Kachexie | irriger
Lehrer, schwermůthiger Veråchter | und
gottloser Schånder | der Tonkunst. | . . . |
Hamburg 1750.[–1751.]

8° 3 vols.: *vol. I:* 1 ℓ., 84 p., 1 ℓ.; *vol. II:*
119, [5] p.; *vol. III:* 15 ℓ., 207, [1] p.

Vol II has separate title-page: . . . |
Wahrer Begriff | des | Harmonischen |
Lebens. | . . . | Hamburg, | bey Johann
Adolph Martini, 1750.
Vol. III has separate title-page: Sieben |
Gespräche | der | Weisheit und Musik |
. . . | Hamburg, | bey Johann Adolph
Martini, 1751.
Hirsch I, no. 386–388; RISM B VI, 563
HOUGHTON

950   MATTHESON, JOHANN

Critica Musica. | d. i. | Grundrichtige |
Untersuch- | und | Beurtheilung, | Vieler,
theils vorgefassten, theils einfältigen |
Meinungen, Argumenten nnd [*sic*]
Einwürffe, so in | alten und neuen, ge-
druckten und ungedruckten, | Musica-
lischen Schrifften | zu finden. | Zur
müglichsten Ausräutung aller gro-
ben Irrthü-|mer, und zur Beförderung ei-
nes bessern Wachsthums der | reinen
harmonischen Wissenschafft, in ver-
schiedene | Theile abgefasset, | Und
Stück-weise heraus gegeben | Von | Mat-
theson. | . . . | Hamburg, im May. 1722.
[–1725.] | Auf Unkosten des Autoris.

4° 2 vols.: [*vol. I*]: 368 p., 1 ℓ., music;
vol. II: 8 ℓ., 380, [36] p.
Imprint, vol. II: Hamburg, gedruckt
und zu bekommen bey seel. Thomas von
| Wierings Erben, bey der Börse im
güldnen A, B, C. 1725.
Hirsch I, no. 371; RISM B VI, 558
HOUGHTON

951   MATTHESON, JOHANN

De | Eruditione | Musica, | Ad | Virum
plurimum Reverendum, Amplissimum |
atque Doctissimum, | Joannem Christo-
phorum | Krüsike, | Artium Magistrum &
Oratorem Sacrum apud | Hamburgenses
disertissimum, | Schediasma Epistoli-
cum | Joannis Matthesonii. | Accedunt
ejusdem literae | ad V. C. | Christo-
phorum Friedericum | Leisnerum | de
eodem argumento scriptae. | Hamburgi,
Apud Felgineri Viduam. 1732.

4° 16 p.
Colophon: Dabam e Musaeo, tertio
Non. Maji | A. R. S. CIↃ IↃ CCXXXII
RISM B VI, 559
HOUGHTON

952   MATTHESON, JOHANN

Exemplarische | Organisten-Probe | Im
Artikel | Vom | General-Bass. | Welche
mittelst 24. leichter, und eben so viel
etwas schwerer Exempel, | aus allen
Tonen, des Endes anzustellen ist, dass
einer, der | Diese 48. Prob-Stücke | Rein
trifft, und das darinn Enthaltene wohl
anbringt, sich vor | andern rühmen möge:
| Er sey ein Meister im accompagniren. |
Alles zum unentbehrlichen Unterricht
und Behuf, nicht nur einiger | Herren Or-
ganisten und Clavicymbalisten ex pro-
fesso, sondern | Aller Liebhaber der
Music, | Zuförderst derer, die der Haupt-
Wissenschafft des Claviers, des Ge-
|neral-Basses, und des geschickten,
manierlichen Accompagnements | flei-
sig obliegen, | Mit den nothwendigsten
Erläuterungen und Anmerckungen, bey
jedem Exempel, | und mit einer ausfüh-
lichen, zur Probe dienenden | Theore-
tischen Vorbereitung, | Uber verschiede-
ne musicalische Merckwürdigkeiten, |
versehen von | Mattheson. | . . . | Ham-
burg, im Schiller-und Kissnerischen
Buch-Laden, 1719

4° 8 ℓ., 128, 276 p., front. (port.), illus.,
fold. pl., music
Hirsch I, no. 369; RISM B VI, 559
HOUGHTON

953   MATTHESON, JOHANN

Das | Forschende | Orchestre, | oder
desselben | Dritte Eröffnung. | Darinn |
Sensvs Vindiciae | Et | Qvartae Bland-
itiae, | D. i. | Der beschirmte Sinnen-Rang
| Und der | Schmeichelnde Quarten-
Klang, | Allen unpartheyischen Syntech-
nitis | zum Nutzen und Nachdenken;
keinem Menschen | aber zum Nachtheil,
sana ratione & autoritate un-|tersuchet,
und vermuhtlich in ihr rechtes | Licht
gestellet werden | von | Joanne Matthe-
son, | Hoch-Fürstl. Schleswig-Hollstei-
nischem Capellmeister. | . . . | Hamburg,
bey Benjamin Schillers Wittwe, uud [*sic*]
| Joh. Christoph Kissner im Dom. 1721.

12° 23 ℓ., 789, [75] p., front., music
Hirsch I, no. 370; RISM B VI, 559
HOUGHTON

954 MATTHESON, JOHANN

Johann Matthesons | Grosse | General-Bass-Schule, | Oder: | Der exemplarischen | Organisten-Probe | Zweite, verbesserte und vermehrte Auflage, | Bestehend in | Dreien Classen, | Als: | In einer gründlichen Vorbereitung, | In 24. leichten Exempeln, | In 24. schwerern Prob-Stücken: | Solcher Gestalt eingerichtet, | Dass, wer die erste wol verstehet; und in den beiden andern Classen | alles rein trifft; so dann das darin enthaltene gut anzubringen weiss; derselbe | ein Meister im General-Bass heissen könne. | Hamburg, | Zu finden in Johann Christoph Kissners Buchladen. [1731]

4° 20 ℓ., 460 [i. e. 458] p., front. (port.), illus., 3 pl. (2 fold.), music
Numbers 199, 200 omitted in paging; folded plates included in paging
MUSIC LIBRARY

955 MATTHESON, JOHANN

Johann Matthesons | Grosse | General-Bass-Schule. | Oder: | Der exemplarischen | Organisten-Probe | Zweite, verbesserte und vermehrte Auflage, | Bestehend in | Dreien Classen, | Als: | In einer gründlichen Vorbereitung, | In 24. leichten Exempeln, | In 24. schwerern Prob-Stücken: | Solcher Gestalt eingerichtet, | Dass, wer die erste wol verstehet; und in den beiden andern Classen | alles rein trifft; so dann das darin enthaltene gut anzubringen weiss; derselbe | ein Meister im General-Bass heissen könne. | Hamburg, | Zu finden in Johann Christoph Kissners Buchladen. | 1731.
4° 21 ℓ., 484 p., illus., fold. pl., music
Hirsch I, no. 374; RISM B VI, 560
HOUGHTON

956 [MATTHESON, JOHANN, ED.]

Gültige | Zeugnisse | über die jüngste | Matthesonisch-Musicalische | Kern-Schrifft, | Als ein | Füglicher Anhang derselben, | zum Druck befördert | von | Aristoxen, dem jüngern. | . . . | Hamburg, 1738.

4° 15 p.
Hirsch I, no. 377; RISM B VI, 560
HOUGHTON

957 MATTHESON, JOHANN

Kern | Melodischer | Wissenschafft, | bestehend | in den auserlesensten | Haupt-und Grund-Lehren | der musicalischen | Setz-Kunst oder Composition, | als ein Vorläuffer des | Vollkommenen Capellmeisters, | ausgearbeitet von | Mattheson. | Hamburg, | Verlegts Christian Herold. | MDCCXXXVII.

4° 9 ℓ., 182, [8] p., music
Hirsch I, no. 376; RISM B VI, 561
HOUGHTON

958 MATTHESON, JOHANN

Johann Mattheson's, | Hoch-Fürstl. Schleswig-Hollsteinischen Capell-Meisters, und Königl. Gross-Britan-|nischen Gesandten-Secretars im Nieder-Sächsischen Kreise, | Kleine | General-Bass-Schule. | Worin | Nicht nur Lernende, sondern vornehmlich Lehrende, | Aus | Den allerersten Anfangs-Gründen des Clavier-Spielens, | überhaupt und besonders, | Durch | Verschiedene Classen u. Ordnungen der Accorde | Stuffen-weise, | Mittelst | Gewisser Lectionen oder stündlicher Aufgaben, | Zu | Mehrer Voll-kommenheit in dieser Wissenschafft, | Richtig, getreulich, und auf die deutlichste Lehr-Art, | kürtzlich angeführet werden. | . . . | Hamburg, bey Joh. Christoph Kissner. 1735.

4° 8 ℓ., 253, [13] p., illus., music
Added title-page has imprint date 1734
Hirsch I, no. 375; RISM B VI, 560–561
MUSIC LIBRARY (2 copies)

959 MATTHESON, JOHANN

Matthesons | Mithridat | wider | den Gift einer welschen | Satyre, | genannt: | La Mvsica. | . . . | Hamburg, MDCCXLIX. | Im Verlage des Verfassers, | und zu finden bey Carl Samuel Geissler.

8° 8 ℓ., LVI, 340, [20] p.
Hirsch I, no. 385; RISM B VI, 561
HOUGHTON

960 MATTHESON, JOHANN

Der Musicalische | Patriot, | Welcher seine gründliche | Betrachtungen, | über | Geist-und Weltl. Harmonien, | samt

dem, was durchgehends | davon abhån-
get, | In angenehmer Abwechselung | zu
solchem Ende mittheilet, | Dass | Gottes
Ehre, das gemeine Beste, | und eines
jeden Lesers besondere Erbauung | da-
durch befördert werde. | Ans Licht gestel-
let | Von | Mattheson. | Hamburg, im Jahr
1728.

4° 376 p., illus., music
Hirsch I, no. 373; RISM B VI, 562
HOUGHTON (imperfect: pages 289-296
lacking), MUSIC LIBRARY

961 MATTHESON, JOHANN

Das | Neu-Eröffnete | Orchestre, | Oder
| Universelle und gründliche | Anleitung,
| Wie ein Galant Homme ei-|nen voll-
kommnen Begriff von | der Hoheit und
Würde der edlen | Music | erlangen,
seinen Gout darnach formi-|ren, die Ter-
minos technicos verstehen | und ge-
schicklich von dieser vortreffli-|chen
Wissenschafft raisonni-|ren möge. |
Durch | J. Mattheson, Secr. | Mit bey-
gefügten Anmerckungen | Herrn Capell-
Meister Keisers. | Hamburg, bey Benja-
min Schillers Witt-|we im Thum 1713.

8° 7 *ℓ*., 338, [11] p., music
Hirsch I, no. 367; RISM B VI, 562−563;
Wolfenbüttel, no. 1227
HOUGHTON (2 copies), MUSIC LIBRARY
(imperfect: last page lacking)

962 MATTHESON, JOHANN

Der neue Göttingische | Aber | Viel
schlechter, als | Die alten Lacedämoni-
schen, | urtheilende | Ephorus, | wegen
der | Kirchen-Music | eines andern be-
lehret | Von | Io. Mattheson. | nebst des-
sen angehångtem, merkwürdigen | Lau-
ten-Memorial. |. . .| Hamburg, 1727. | In
Verlag des Verfassers, und zu bekommen
bey Joh. Christoph | Kissnern im Dom
daselbst, und zu Leipzig bey | Jacob Schu-
stern.

4° 2 *ℓ*., 124 p.
Hirsch I, no. 372; RISM B VI, 562
HOUGHTON

963 [MATTHESON, JOHANN]

Die neueste | Untersuchung | der |
Singspiele, | nebst beygefügter | musika-

lischen | Geschmacksprobe, | liefert hie-
mit | Aristoxenus, | der jüngere. |. . . |
Hamburg, | verlegts Christian Herold. |
1744.

8° 4 *ℓ*., 168 p.
Hirsch I, no. 380; RISM B VI, 563
MUSIC LIBRARY

964 [MATTHESON, JOHANN]

Aristoxeni | iunior. | Phthongologia
| systematica. | Versuch | einer systema-
tischen | Klang-Lehre | wider | die irrigen
Begriffe | von diesem geistigen Wesen,
| von dessen Geschlechten, | Ton-Arten,
Dreyklången, | und auch | vom mathema-
tischen Musikanten, | nebst einer | Vor-
Erinnerung | wegen der behaupteten him-
lischen Musik. |. . . | Hamburg, | in
Commission bey Joh. Adolph Martini.
1748.

8° 167 p., illus.
Hirsch I, no. 384; RISM B VI, 557
MUSIC LIBRARY

965 MATTHESON, JOHANN

Pieces De Clavecin | en Deux Volumes
| Consistant des | Ouvertures, Preludes,
Fugues, Allemandes, | Courentes, Sara-
bandes, Gigues, et Aires. | Composées |
par | J. Mattheson, | Secr. | 1714. | London
Printed for I. D. Fletcher. and Sold at
most Musick Shops. |. . . [1714]

2° *Score:* 2 vols., paged continuously:
[*vol. I*]: 5 *ℓ*., 3−24 p.; [*vol. II*]: 26−47 p.
RISM A I, no. M 1397
HOUGHTON

966 MATTHESON, JOHANN

Matthesonii | Plvs Vltra, | ein |
Stückwerk | von neuer und mancherley
Art. |. . . | Hamburg, verlegts Johann
Adolph Martini. | 1754.[−1756]

8° 4 vols., paged continuously: *vol. I:*
134 p., 2 fold. pl. (music); *vol. II:* [135]−
382, [16] p.; *vol. III:* [383]−606 p.; *vol.
IV:* [607]−786, [12] p., 4 fold. pl. (music)
Imprint date, vols. II, III: 1755; im-
print, vol. IV: Hamburg verlegts Conrad
König, 1756.
Hirsch I, no. 392: RISM B VI, 564
HOUGHTON

967　　MATTHESON, JOHANN

Der | Vollkommene | Capellmeister |
Das ist | Gründliche Anzeige | aller der-
jenigen Sachen, | die einer wissen,
können, und vollkommen inne haben
muss, | der einer Capelle | mit Ehren und
Nutzen vorstehen will: | Zum Versuch
entworffen | von | Mattheson. | Hamburg,
| Verlegts Christian Herold, 1739.

2° 28, [4], 484, [20] p., illus., music
Page [20] at end: Neues Verzeichniss |
bisheriger Matthesonischer Werke.
Hirsch I, no. 378; RISM B VI, 564
MUSIC LIBRARY

968　　MAYER, JOHANN BAPTIST

Twelve | Songs | Six English & Six Ital-
ian, | with an Accompaniment for the |
Harp Or Piano Forte, | Composed &
Humbly Dedicated by Permission, | To |
Her Royal Highness the | Dutchess Of
York, | by | John Baptist Mayer. | Op.
9. . . . | [London] Printed for the Author
by Wm. Napier, Musician in Ordinary to
His Majesty, . . . | Lisle Street, Leicester
Square, & also may be had at the Au-
thor's, No. 52 Titchfield Str[eet,] | Ox-
ford Road, & at the Music Shops. [ca.
1799]

2° *Score:* [*vol. II*]: 1 ℓ., 11–33 p.
Songs no. 6–12
Imperfect: title-page torn, with loss of
some words
RISM A I, no. M 1473
MUSIC LIBRARY

969　　MAYR, JOHANN SIMON

Twelve | Venetian Ballads. | Composed
& Arranged for the | Voice and Piano
Forte | By | The Celebrated S. Mayer, | and
Dedicated by Permission to | Her Royal
Highness the Duchess of York, | By Her
most Dutiful most Devoted & very
Humble Sert. | Cathne. Salvini. | . . . |
London. Printed & Sold at L. Lavenu's
Music Warehouse, No. 23, Duke St. St.
James's, | at Madam Salvini's, No. 17
Cronn Street Westmtr, & at all the Prin-
cipal Music Shops | in Town & Country.
[1797?]

obl. 2° *Score:* 1 ℓ., 17 p.
MUSIC LIBRARY

McDONALD, PATRICK　*See as if spelled*
MacDonald, Patrick

McGIBBON, WILLIAM　*See as if spelled*
MacGibbon, William

970　　MÉHUL, ÉTIENNE NICOLAS

Euphrosine | ou | Le Tyran Corrigé |
Comédie en Trois Actes et en Vers | Par
F. Hoffman. | Représentée pour la pre-
miere fois par les Comédiens Italiens | le
Samedi 4 Septembre 1790. | Mise en Mu-
sique | Par. E. Méhul | Et Dédiée | A Sa
Mere | . . . | A Paris Chez les Cens.
Cousineau Pere et Fils Luthiere, à la
Manufac-|ture de Harpe et de Piano-forte
rue de Thionville No. 1840. | et aux
Adresses ordinaires de Musique. [ca.
1795?]

2° *Score:* 1 ℓ., 242 p.
Plate no. 239
RISM A I, no. M 1810
MUSIC LIBRARY

971　　MÉHUL, ÉTIENNE NICOLAS

Euphrosine | ou | Le Tyran Corrigé |
Comédie en Trois Actes et en Vers | Par
F. Hoffman. | Représentée pour la pre-
miere fois par les Comédiens Italiens | le
Samedi 4 Septembre 1790. | Mise en Mu-
sique | Par. E. Méhul | Et Dédiée | A Sa
Mere | . . . | A Paris Chez les Cens.
Cousineau Pere et Fils Luthiere, à la
Manufac-|ture de Harpe et de Piano-forte
rue de Thionville No. 1840. | et aux
Adresses ordinaires de Musique [ca.
1800?]

2° *Score:* 1 ℓ., 242 p.
Plate no. 239
Cancel label mounted over imprint: A
La Muse Du Jour | Chez Cochet, Au Ma-
gasin de Musique et d'Instrumens Rue
Vivienne, | No. 40, vis-à-vis l'Hôtel des
Etrangers. | Tient Abonnement de Parti-
tions
HOUGHTON

972　　MÉHUL, ÉTIENNE NICOLAS

Stratonice. | Comédie Héroïque en un
Acte et en Vers, | Par Mr. Hoffman, |
Représentée pour la premiere fois par les

Comédiens | Italiens Ordinaires du Roi, le Jeudy 3 May 1792. | Mise en Musique. | Par | Mr. Méhul. | . . . | Les Parties se vendent séparement . . . | Gravée par Huguet, Musicien, Pensionnaire de la Comédie Italienne. | A Paris | Chez Mrs. Cousineau, Pere et Fils, Rue Dauphine, Hôtel de Mouy, No. 110 | Et aux Adresses Ordinaires de Musique [1792?]

2° *Score:* 1 ℓ., 127 p.
RISM A I, no. M 2033
HOUGHTON

973 MEIBOM, MARCUS, ED.

Antiqvae | Mvsicae | Avctores | Septem. | Graece Et Latine. | Marcvs Meibomivs | Restituit ac Notis explicavit. | . . . Amstelodami, | Apud Ludovicum Elzevirium, | CI ƆIƆC LII.

4° 2 vols.: *vol I:* 26 ℓ., 132 p., 2 ℓ., 68 p., 2 ℓ., 60, 8, 80 p., 2 ℓ., 40 p., 2 ℓ., 36 p., illus., 5 fold. pl., music; *vol. II:* 4 ℓ., 363 p., illus.
Parallel columns in Greek and Latin
Contents. vol. I: Aristoxeni Harmonicorvm Elementorvm Libri III. Evclidis [i. e. Cleonidae] Introdvctio Harmonica. Nicomachi Geraseni, Pythagorici, Harmonices Manvale. Alypii Introdvctio Mvsica. Gavdentii, Philosophi, Harmonica, Introdvctio. Bacchii Senioris Introdvctio Artis Mvsicae. vol. II: Aristidis Qvintiliani De Mvsica Libri III. Martiani Capellae De Mvsica Liber IX
Davidsson II, no. 64; Hirsch I, no. 394; RISM B VI, 568
HOUGHTON

974

Melody—The Soul of Music: | An | Essay | Towards The | Improvement | Of The | Musical Art: | With An Appendix, | Containing Account Of An Invention. | . . . | Glasgow, | Printed In The Courier Office. | 1798.

8° 82 p.
HOUGHTON

975 [MENESTRIER, CLAUDE FRANÇOIS]

Des | Ballets | Anciens | Et Modernes | Selon Les Regles | Du Theatre. | A Paris, | Chez René Guignard, rüe Saint | Jacques, au grand saint Basile. | M.DC.LXXXII. | Avec Privilege du Roi.

12° 28 ℓ., 232 [i. e. 323], [5] p.
Page 323 misnumbered 232
RISM B VI, 569
HOUGHTON

976 [MENESTRIER, CLAUDE FRANÇOIS]

Des | Representations | En Musique | Anciennes | Et Modernes. | A Paris, | Chez René Guignard, rüe Saint | Jacques, au grand saint Basile. | M.DC.LXXXI. | Avec Privilege du Roy.

12° 12 ℓ., 333, [3] p.
RISM B VI, 570
HOUGHTON

977 MERCADIER, JEAN BAPTISTE

Nouveau | Système | De | Musique | Théorique Et Pratique, | Par M. Mercadier De Belesta. | . . . | A Paris, | Chez Valade, Libraire & Bibliothécaire | de Monseigneur le Garde des Sceaux, rue | Saint-Jacques, vis-à-vis celle des Mathurins. | M.DCC.LXXVI. | Avec Approbation & Privilège du Roi.

8° lxxij, 304, [4] p., front. (port.), illus., 8 fold. pl. (music)
Colophon: De l'Imprimerie de R. Heirisson, Imprimeur | du Roi.
RISM B VI, 571
HOUGHTON

978 MERCHI, GIACOMO

Recueil D'Airs | Avec Accompagnement de Guitarre, | Dedié | A Monsieur Foucault | Ecuyer. | Par | Mr. Merchi. VIe. Livre De Guitarre. | Oeuvre VIIIe. Gravé par Madme. Oger. | . . . | A Paris

Chez L'Auteur, ruë St. Thomas du Lou-
vre, du côté du Chateau d'eau | chez le
1er. Menuisier, le second Escalier après la
Cour au 1er. | Et aux adresses ordinaires
de Musique. | Avec Privilege Du Roy.
[1762?]

    2° *Score:* 1 ℓ., 31 p.
    RISM A I, no. M 2288
    MUSIC LIBRARY

979   MERCHI, GIACOMO

    Choix D'Ariettes | Avec | Accompa-
gnement de Guitarre, | Par | Mr. Merchi. |
Xe. Livre De Guitarre | Oeuvre XIIIe. |
. . . | A Paris | Chez L'Auteur, ruë St.
Thomas du Louvre du côté du Chateau-|
-d'Eau, chez un Menuisier le 2d. Escalier
après la Cour. | Et aux adresses ordinaires
de Musique. | Avec Privilege Du Roy.
[176–?]

    2° *Score:* 1 ℓ., 15 p.
    RISM A I, no. M 2291
    MUSIC LIBRARY

980   MERCHI, GIACOMO

    La Guitarre | De Bonne Humeur | Ou |
Recueil de Vaudevilles Badins, | Avec ac-
compagnement de Guitarre | Par | Mr.
Merchi. | VIIe. Livre De Guitarre |
Oeuvre Xe. | . . . | A Paris | Chez L'Au-
teur, ruë du Rempart St. Honoré près des
Quinze-|-vingt chez un Tapissier. | Et aux
adresses ordinaires de Musique. | Avec
Privilege Du Roy. | [ca. 1760]

    2° *Score:* 1 ℓ., [25] p., front.
    Imperfect: page 25 lacking
    RISM A I, no. M 2289
    MUSIC LIBRARY

981

    Mercurius Musicus: | Or, The |
Monthly Collection | Of New Teaching |
Songs, | (For the Year, 1700.) | Compos'd
for, and Sung at the Theatres, | and other
Publick Places. | With | An addition of
Two Part Songs; and a Thorough | Bass to
each Song, for the Harpsichord, Spinett, |
or Bass-Viol. | Such Tunes as are not in
the Compass of the Flvte, are Trans-
|pos'd at the End of the Book. | For Jan-

uary and February. [–November and
December.] | . . . | London: | Printed
by W. Pearson, in Red-Cross-Alley in
Jewin-street, for D. Browne, | at the Black-
Swan and Bible without Temple-Bar,
and Henry Play-|ford, at his Shop in the
Temple-Change Fleet-street; or at his
House in | Arundel-street in the Strand,
. . . | . . . and at | most Booksellers
and Musick-Shops in Town. 1700. | . . .

    2° *Score:* 84 p.
    Seven issues, published from Jan-
uary/February through November/De-
cember
    Imprint, November/December issue:
. . . Sold by John Nut, near Stationes-
Hall [*sic*] . . .
    Day, no. 186
    HOUGHTON

982

    Mercurius Musicus: | Or, The |
Monthly Collection | Of New Teaching |
Songs, | Being | The single Songs in the
New Opera, call'd | (The Mad Lover) at
the Theatre in Little Lincoln's-Inn |
Fields. Compos'd by Mr. John Eccles
Master of His | Majesty's Musick. | With |
A Thorough Bass to each Song, for the
Harp-|sichord, Spinett, or Bass-Viol. |
Such Tunes as are not in the Compass of
the Flvte, are Trans-|pos'd at the End of
the Book. | For January and February.
[–September, October, November, and
December.] | . . . | London: | Printed
by W. Pearson, in Red-Cross-Alley in
Jewin-street, for Henry Play-|ford, at his
Shop in the Temple-Change Fleet-street;
. . . | . . . Sold by John Nutt, near
Stationers-Hall, and at most | Book-sel-
lers and Musick-Shops in Town. 1701.

    2° *Score:* 1 ℓ., 60 p.
    Five issues, published from
January/February through September–
December
    Day, no. 193
    HOUGHTON

983

    For January,[–October] 1702. . . . |
Mercurius Musicus.

    2° *Score:* B–G², [2d]G², H²

Imperfect? contains eight issues, numbered 1–7, 10, 11, published from January through October

Colophon, leaves C2ᵛ, D2ᵛ: London, Printed for Henry Playford, and Sold by him at his Shop in the Temple-Change, Fleet-street; and | Mr. John Hare, at the Golden Viol in St. Paul's Church-Yard, and at his Shop, in Freeman's-Yard in Cornhill.

Colophon, leaves F2ᵛ, G2ᵛ, [2d]G2ᵛ, H2ᵛ: London: Printed by William Pearson, for Henry Playford . . .

Caption title

Day, no. 199

HOUGHTON

984 MERCY, LOUIS

VI Sonate | A Fagoto ò Violoncello, | col' Basso Continuo; | da | Luidgi Merci | di natione Jnglesa | Opera Terza | London | Printed for the Author & Sold by Samll Weaver | at the Violin & Hautboy on London Bridge & John Johnson | at the Harpe & Crown near Wood street in Cheapside [ca. 1735]

obl. 2° *Score:* 1 ℓ., 15 p.

Imperfect: pages 14, 15 lacking

RISM A I, no. M 2313

HOUGHTON

MERLOTTI, CLAUDIO *See* Merulo, Claudio, da Correggio

985

The | Merry Musician; | Or, A | Cure for the Spleen: | Being | A Collection of the most | diverting Songs and pleasant Ballads, | set to Musick; adapted to every Taste and | Humour. | Together with a curious Compound of | State Pills, to allay the Malady of Male-|contents. | . . . | London, Printed by H. Meere, for J. Walsh | (Servant in ordinary to his Majesty) in Catherine-street | in the Strand, J. Hare at the Viol in Cornhill, A. Bettes-|worth in Pater-Noster-Row, and J. Brown without Temple-|Bar. 1716. . . .

12° *vol. I:* 6 ℓ., 336 p.

Imperfect: numerous pages lacking

Incomplete: vols. II-IV lacking

RISM B II, 232–233; Walsh I, no. 485

MUSIC LIBRARY

986

The | Merry-Musician; | Or, A | Cure for the Spleen. | Being | A Collection of the most di-|verting Songs and pleasant Ballads, set | to Musick; adapted to every Taste and | Humour. | Together with a curious Compound of State-|Pills, to allay the Malady of Male-|Contents. | . . . | The Second Edition. | London, Printed for J Walsh, Servant in Ordinary | to his Majesty, at the Harp and Hautboy in Katherine-|Street in the Strand, and J. Hare, at the Viol and Haut-|boy in Cornhil, near the Royal-Exchange, 1730. | . . .

12° *vol. I:* 6 ℓ., 336 p.

Imperfect: pages 59–62 lacking

RISM B II, 233; Walsh II, no. 1016

MUSIC LIBRARY

987

The | Merry Musician; | Or, A | Cure for the Spleen: | Being | A Collection of the | most diverting Songs & pleasant | Ballads set to Musick; adapted | to every Taste and Humour. | . . . | London. Printed for and sold by I: Walsh | in Catherine Street in the Strand. | Ios: Hare in Cornhill, and I: Young | in St. Paul's Church-yard. | . . . [1728?]

12° [*vol. II*]: 1 ℓ., IV, 180 p., front.

RISM B II, 233; Walsh II, no. 1018

HOUGHTON

988 MERSENNE, MARIN

Harmonicorvm | Libri XII | in Qvibvs Agitvr | De Sonorvm Natvra, | Cavsis, Et Effectibvs: De Consonantiis, | Dissonantiis, Rationibus, Generibus, Modis, Cantibus, Com-|positione, orbisque totius Harmonicis Instrumentis. | Authore F. M. Mersenno Minimo. | Ad Illustr. V. Henricvm Lvdovicvm Habertvm | De Montmor. | . . . | Editio Avcta. | Lvtetiae Parisiorvm, | Sumptibus Gvillelmi Bavdry, vià Iacobeâ, | prope Collegium Plessaeum. | M.DC.XLVIII. | Cum Priuilegio Regis Christianiss. et Approbatione Superiorum.

2° 8 ℓ., 184 [i. e. 172], 168 p., illus., music

Numbers 126–131, 154–159, first sequence, omitted in paging

Davidsson II, no. 67; RISM B VI, 572–573

HOUGHTON

989   MERSENNE, MARIN

Harmonie | Vniverselle, | Contenant La Theorie | Et La Pratiqve | De La Mvsiqve, | Où est traité de la Nature des Sons, & des Mouuemens, des Consonances, | des Dissonances, des Genres, des Modes, de la Composition, de la | Voix, des Chants, & de toutes sortes d'Instrumens | Harmoniques. | Par F. Marin Mersenne de l'Ordre des Minimes. | A Paris, | Chez Sebastien Cramoisy, Imprimeur ordinaire du Roy, | ruë S. Iacques, aux Cicognes. | M.DC.XXXVI. | Auec Priuilege du Roy, et Approbation des Docteurs.

1 vol. (various pagings), illus., 3 pl., music

This copy conforms to the one described in Hirsch I, no. 404, with the following exceptions: the mounted portrait of Mersenne on preliminary leaf 3 is lacking; two leaves containing the letter to Pascal and the preface to the reader in book 5 are lacking; book 5 contains a numbered leaf 323

The second part has a separate title-page with imprint: A Paris, | Par Pierre Ballard, Imprimeur de la Musique du Roy, demeurant ruë | S. Iean de Beauuais, à l'enseigne du Mont Parnasse. | M.DC.XXXVII. | . . .

Contemporary manuscript on title-page of 1st copy: Pour le Convent des freres [?] Minimes de dezise, donné l'an 1637.

Davidsson II, no. 66; Hirsch I, no. 404; RISM B VI, 573

HOUGHTON (2 copies, 2d incomplete)

990   [MERSENNE, MARIN]

Les | Prelvdes | De L'Harmonie | Vniverselle, | Ov | Qvestions Cvrievses. | Vtiles aux Predicateurs, aux Theologiens, | aux Astrologues, aux Medecins, | & aux Philosophes. | Composees par le L. P. M. M. | A Paris, | Chez Henry Gvenon, ruë S. Iacques, | prés les Iaco-

bins, à l'image S. Bernard. | M.DC.XXXIV. | Avec Privilege Et Approbation.

8° 7 ℓ., 224 p., illus.

Hirsch I, no. 402; RISM B VI, 573

HOUGHTON

991   MERSENNE, MARIN

F. Marini | Mersenni | Ordinis Minimorvm | S. Francisci De Pavla. | Qvaestiones Celeberrimae | In Genesim, Cvm Accvrata | Textvs Explicatione. | In Hoc Volvmine Athei, Et Deistae Impvgnantvr, | et expugnantur, et Vvlgata editio ab haereticorum calumnijs vindicatur. | Graecorum, & Hebraeorum Musica instauratur. | Francisci Georgii Veneti | Cabalistica Dogmata Fvsè Refellvntvr, | Qvae Passim In Illivs Problematibvs Habentvr. | Opvs Theologis, Philosophis, Medicis, | Iurisconsultis, Mathematicis, Musicis verò, et Catoptricis praesertim vtile. | Cum Indice quadruplici, videlicet locorum Scripturae Sacrae, quae in toto libro explicantur, | Concionatorio, Quaestionum, & rerum, quae passim agitantur. | Lvtetiae Parisiorvm, | Sumptibus Sebastiani Cramoisy, viâ Iacobaeâ sub Ciconijs. | M.DC.XXIII. | Cum Priuilegio Regis Christianissimi, et Doctorum Approbatione.

2° 12 ℓ., 1916 cols., [36] p. illus., music

Two columns to the page

Number 1637 designates a numbered leaf; numbers 1646, 1647, 1652–1662, 1689–1712 designate pages

Hirsch I, no. 398; RISM B VI, 573–574; Wolfenbüttel, no. 1231

HOUGHTON

992   [MERSENNE, MARIN]

Qvestions | Harmoniqves. | Dans lesquelles sont contenuës plu-|sieurs choses remarquables pour | la Physique, pour la Morale, | & pour les autres sciences. | A Paris | Chez Iaqves Villery, ruë Clopin | à l'Escu de France, & au coin de la ruë | Dauphine aux trois Perruques. | M.DC.XXXIIII. | Avec Privilege Dv Roy.

8° 4 ℓ., 276 p.

Hirsch I, no. 403; RISM B VI, 574

HOUGHTON

993   MERULO, CLAUDIO,
    DA CORREGGIO

[Toccate | D'Intavolatura | D'Organo Di Claudio | Merulo Da Correggio | organista del Serenisso. | Sig. Duca di Parma | et Piacenza Ec. | Nuovamente da lui date in luce, et | con ogni diligenza corrette. | Libro Primo. | In Roma appresso Simone Verovio | MD.XCVIII. | Con licenza de Superiori.]

2° *Score:* 43 p.
Imperfect: title-page lacking; title supplied from Brown, no. 1598₉
RISM A I, no. M 2376; SartoriB, no. 1598ᵦ
HOUGHTON

MÉTHODE DE MUSIQUE SELON UN NOUVEAU SYSTÈME   *See* Démotz de la Salle, abbé *Méthode de musique selon un nouveau systême*

MIDAS, A COMIC OPERA   *See* O'Hara, Kane *Midas, a Comic Opera*

994   MILLER, EDWARD

Elements | of | Thorough Bass | And | Composition, | In which the Rules of Accompaniment for the | Harpsichord or Piano-Forte | are rendered amusing by the Introduction of Eight Italian | Eight French & Twelve English Songs collected from the Works | of eminent Composers Antient & Modern. | With Proper Lessons For Practice | written by way of conversation between the Master & his Pupil for the | Use of such performers as are unacquainted with the principles of Harmony | Most humbly Dedicated to the Right Honourable | Lord Viscount Gallway | Knight of the Bath; | By | Edward Miller Mus: D. | Opera Quinta. . . . | London Printed & Sold by Longman & Broderip No. 26 Cheapside No. 13 Hay Market, & by the Author at Doncaster. [pref. 1787]

2° 8, 88p., illus., music
RISM B VI, 583
MUSIC LIBRARY

995   MILLER, EDWARD

Six Sonatas | For The | Harpsichord; | with | An Accompaniment | to three of them, for a | Violin, Or German Flute. | Composed by | Edward Miller, | Organist at Doncaster | London Printed by Welcker in Gerrard Street, St. Ann's, Soho | . . . [ca. 1765]

2° *Score:* 1 ℓ., 4, 31 p.
Colophon: Engraved by Sarah Phillips
Pages 1–4, first sequence: A Catalogue of Vocal and Instrumental Music Printed for and | Sold by Peter Welcker . . .
RISM A I, no. M 2785
MUSIC LIBRARY

996   MILLER, EDWARD

Thoughts | On The Present Performance Of | Psalmody | In The Established Church Of England. | Addressed To | The Clergy. | By Edward Miller, Mus. Doct. Cantab. | London: | Printed for W. Miller, Old Bond-Street: | Bookseller To His Royal Highness | The Duke of Clarence. | 1791.

8° 2 ℓ., 40 p.
RISM B VI, 584
MUSIC LIBRARY

997   [MIZLER VON KOLOF,
    LORENZ CHRISTOPH]

Lusus Ingenii | De Harmonia | Augustissimi Atque Potentissimi | Imperatoris | Caroli VI. | Cum Foederatis. | Ope Signorum Musicorum Illustrata, | Anno clɔlɔccxxxv. Mense Februario. | Onoldi apud Rönagelium.

4° [8] p., music
Musical examples in manuscript on printed staff
HOUGHTON

998   MODERNE, JACQUES, PUBL.

Liber Decem | Missarvm, À Praecla|ris Et Maximi Nominis Mv|sicis contextus: nuperrimè adiunctis duabus | Missis nunquam hactenus in lucem | emissis, auctior redditus, | & accuratè casti|gatus. | Missarum autem nomina & Autores subsequentis | paginae breuis Index con-

998 MODERNE (PUBL.), *Liber decem missarum*, Lyons, 1540: folios 22ᵛ

and 23ʳ (both 296 × 195 mm.), showing section of Mass by F. de Layolle

gruo ordine | commonstrat. | Iacobvs Mo-
dernvs À | Pinguento excudebat Lugduni,
| Anno publicae salutis | M.D.XL.

2° 2 ℓ., 113 [i. e. 114] numb. ℓ., illus.
Number 53 repeated in foliation
MortimerF, no. 379; Pogue, no. 22;
RISM B I, no. 1540[1]
HOUGHTON

999   MOLINI, _____

The | Fife Hunt, | A Favourite | Scotch
Air. | with Variations, for the | Piano
Forte. | Composed By, | Sigr. Molini. |
London | Printed for Harrison, Cluse, &
Co. No. 78, Fleet Street. [1799?]

8° *Score:* 8 p. (*The Piano-Forte Maga-
zine,* vol. VIII, no. 4)
Plate no. 121
RISM A I, no. M 2945
MUSIC LIBRARY

1000   MOLINI, _____

Of Noble Race Was | Shenkin. | A Cele-
brated | Welch Air, | With Variations For
The | Piano Forte. | Composed By, | Sigr.
Molini | London: | Printed for Harrison,
Cluse, & Co. No. 78, Fleet Street. [1799?]

8° *Score:* 6 p. (*The Piano-Forte Maga-
zine,* vol. VII, no. 11)
Plate no.112
RISM A I, no. M 2944
MUSIC LIBRARY

1001   MOLLER, JOHN CHRISTOPHER

Meddley with the most favorite Airs
and Variations, Composed by I. C.
Moller | . . . | Printed and sold at G. Wil-
ligs. Musical Magazin No. 165 Market
Street Philad. [179–?]

2° *Score:* 2–6 p.
Caption title and imprint from head
and foot of page 2
For keyboard instrument
RISM A I, no. M 2971
MUSIC LIBRARY

1002   MONDONVILLE, JEAN
            JOSEPH CASSANÉA DE

Daphnis | Et | Alcimadure | Pastorale |
Languedocienne | Dediée | A Madame La

Dauphine | Représentée à Fontainebleau |
Devant Leurs Majestés | Les 29 Octobre,
4 Novembre 1754. Et par L'Académie |
Royale de Musique Le 5. Janvier 1755. |
Les Paroles et la Musique sont de | Mr.
Mondonville | Maître de Musique de La
Chapelle du Roy. | Oeuvre IXe. | . . . |
Gravé par Le Sr. Hue | A Paris | Chez
{L'Auteur, Rüe des Vieux Augustins | Le
Sr. Bayard, Md. Rüe St. Honoré à la Regle
d'Or. | Le Sr. Vernadé, Md. Rüe du Roule
à la Croix d'Or. | Avec Privilege Du Roy. |
Imprimé par Montoulay. [1755?]

2° *Score:* 2 ℓ., 197 p., 1 ℓ.
Hirsch II, no. 602; RISM A I, no. M
3009
MUSIC LIBRARY

1003   MONDONVILLE, JEAN
            JOSEPH CASSANÉA DE

Pieces | De Clavecin | Avec Voix ou
Violon | Dediées | A Son Excellence |
Monseigneur | L'Evesque de Rennes | Par
Mr. Mondonville | Maître de Musique de
la Chapelle du Roy. | Oeuvre Ve. |
. . . Avec Privilege Du Roy. | . . . |
. . . A Paris {Chez l'Auteur rüe des |
Vieux Augustins | Et Chez {Madame Boi-
vin Mde rüe St. Honoré à la Regle
d'Or. . . . | Monsieur le Clerc Md. rüe du
Roule à la Croix d'Or. [1748]

2° *Score:* 2 ℓ., 19 p.
RISM A I, no. M 3027
HOUGHTON

1004   [MONNET, JEAN, COMP.]

Anthologie | Françoise, | Ou | Chan-
sons Choisies, | Depuis le 13e Siécle
jusqu'à   présent. | . . . | [Paris?]
M.DCC.LXV.

8° 3 vols.: *vol. I:* 7, [1], 64, 318 p., front.
(port.), 2 pl.; *vol. II:* 1 ℓ., 317 p.; *vol. III:* 2
ℓ., 320 p., front.
Pages [1]–64, first sequence, in vol. I:
Memoire | Historique | Sur La Chanson
En Général, | Et En Particulier | Sur La
Chanson Françoise, | Par M. Meusnier
De Querlon.
Imperfect: frontispiece lacking in vol.
II
RISM B II, 92
MUSIC LIBRARY

1005 MONNET, JEAN

Supplement | Au | Roman Comique, | Ou | Mémoires | Pour Servir A La Vie | De | Jean Monnet, | Ci-devant Directeur de l'Opéra-Comique | à Paris, de l'Opéra de Lyon & d'une | Comédie Françoise à Londres. | Ecrits par lui-même. | . . . | A Londres, | M.DCC.LXXII.

12° 2 vols.: *vol. I:* 4 *ℓ.*, 200 p., 2 *ℓ.*, front. (port.); *vol. II:* 288 p., 4 *ℓ.*

RISM B VI, 591

HOUGHTON

MONNOYE, BERNARD DE LA *See* La Monnoye, Bernard de

1006 [MONSIGNY, PIERRE ALEXANDRE]

Aline, | Reine De Golconde, | Ballet-Héroïque | En Trois Actes, | Par Mr. *** | Représentée pour la premiere fois, par L'Académie | Royale de Musique, Le Mardy 15 Avril 1766. | . . . | A Paris. | Chez {Claude Hérissant, Libraire Imprimeur, Rue | Neuve N. Dame, aux trois Vertus. | Et aux adresses ordinaires de Musique. | Avec Privilege Du Roy. | Gravé par Le Sr. Hue. [1766?]

2° *Score:* 1 *ℓ.*, 320 p.

RISM A I, no. M 3100

MUSIC LIBRARY

1007 [MONSIGNY, PIERRE ALEXANDRE]

Les | Aveux | Jndiscrets | Intermede | Par Mr. *** | Represente pour la premiere fois à | L'Opera Comique Le 7. Fevrier 1759. | . . . | Gravé par Le Sr. Hue. | A Paris | Aux Adresses Ordinaires. | Avec Approbation et privilege | Du Roy. | Imprimé par Monthulay. [1759?]

2° *Score:* 1 *ℓ.*, 99 p.

RISM A I, no. M 3105

HOUGHTON, MUSIC LIBRARY

1008 [MONSIGNY, PIERRE ALEXANDRE]

La | Belle Arsène | Comedie Féerie | En Quatre Actes | Par Mr. [*sic*] | Representée

devant Sa Majesté, a fontaineblaux | Le 6 Novenbre. [*sic*] 1773. Et a Paris le 14 Aoust 1775 | Et une Seconde fois devant leurs Majestés. le 4 Nbr. 1775 | . . . | A Paris | Chez {Le Sr. Houbaut Editeur, Musieien [*sic*] Copiste des Menus plaisies | du Roi. Et de la Comedie Italienne Et Md. de Musique | Rüe Mauconseil. | Et aux adresses Ordinaires | A Lion Le Sr. Casteau | Gravée par Mad: Vendôme Et Mlle. Sa fille rüe St. Honoré au coin de la rüe | chants fleuri | A. P. D. R Imprimé par Richome L'ainé [ca. 1775]

2° *Score:* 1 *ℓ.*, 109 p.

On verso of preliminary leaf: Catalogue, | Des Oeuvres de Musique que le Sr. Houbaut . . . à fait Graver . . .

Hirsch II, no. 607; RISM A I, no. M 3110

MUSIC LIBRARY

1009 [MONSIGNY, PIERRE ALEXANDRE]

Le Cadi | Dupé | Opera Bouffon | En un Acte | Representé sur le Théatre de l'Opera Comique | Mis en Musique | Par Mr. *** | . . . | A Paris | Chez {Mr. De La Chevardiere rue du Roule à la Croix d'Or. | Et aux Adresses Ordinaires. | A Lyon | Mrs. Les Freres Le Goux Place des Cordeliers. | Avec Privilége Du Roy. | Gravé | par P. L. | Charpentier | 1761.

2° *Score:* 1 *ℓ.*, 53 p.

On verso of preliminary leaf: Catalogue | De toutes sortes de Musique Vocale et Instrumentale que M De La Chevardiere . . . | . . . à fait graver . . . ⟨a later state of JohanssonF facs. 53⟩

Hirsch II, no. 608; RISM A I, no. M 3159

MUSIC LIBRARY

1010 [MONSIGNY, PIERRE ALEXANDRE]

Le Deserteur | Drame En Trois Actes, | Dédié | A Son Altesse Sérénissime | Monseigneur | Le Duc D'Orleans | Premier Prince Du Sang, | Represent é par les Comediens Italiens | ordinaires du Roi le 6 Mars 1769. | Gravé par Mlle. Vendôme et le Sr. Moria | . . . | A Paris | Chez {Claude Hérissant Libraire Imprimeur Rue neuve | Notre Dame aux trois Vertus | Et aux adresses ordinaires de Musique | Avec Privilege Du Roi. [1769?]

2° *Score:* 2 ℓ., 267 p.
Hirsch II, no. 609; RISM A I, no. M 3167

MUSIC LIBRARY

1011 [MONSIGNY, PIERRE ALEXANDRE]

Partition | De | Felix | Ou | L'Enfant Trouvé | Comedie en trois Actes | En Vers, et en Prose; | Représentée pour la premiere fois | sur le Théâtre de l'Opera comique Nationale | le 21 8bre. 1781. | Mise en Musique | Par M. M*** | . . . | A Paris | Chez Des Lauriers Md. de Papier rue St. Honoré | à côté de celle des Prouvaires. | [ca. 1785?]

2° *Score:* 1 ℓ., 210 p.
Plate no. 33
RISM A I, no. M 3237

MUSIC LIBRARY

1012 [MONSIGNY, PIERRE ALEXANDRE]

Partition | de | Felix | Ou | L'Enfant Trouvé | Comedie en trois Actes | En Vers, et en Prose; | Représentée devant leurs Majestés à Fontainebleau le 10 Novembre | Et par les Comediens Italiens ordinaires du Roy, le 24 Novembre 1777 | Et une Seconde fois devant leurs Majestés le 12 Octobre 1781. | Mise en Musique | Par M. M*** | . . . | A Paris | Chez Mr. Bailleux Md. de Musique ordinaire du Roy, | Et de la famille Royale; | A la Regle d'Or, Rue St. Honoré pres celle de la Lingerie | Gravée par Maignan | A. P. D. R. [1786?]

2° *Score:* 2 ℓ., 210 p.
On recto and verso of preliminary leaf 2: Catalogue No. I.[–II.] | De Musique Vocale [–Instrumentale] appartenant à Mr. Bailleux . . . ⟨JohanssonF facs. 11–12⟩
RISM A I, no. M 3236

MUSIC LIBRARY

1013 [MONSIGNY, PIERRE ALEXANDRE]

Le | Maitre | En Droit. | Opera Bouffon | En Deux Actes | Mis En Musique | Par | Monsieur *** | . . . | Gravé par Le Sr. Hue. | A Paris | Chez Le Sr. Hue Graveur Rue St. Honoré attenant le Palais Royale vis-|-a-vis Le Caffé du Sr. Dupuis Chez Mr. Martin Grennetier au Second. | Et aux adresses ordinaires. | Avec approbation Et Privilege | Du Roy. | Imprimé par Monthulay. [ca. 1760]

2° *Score:* 1 ℓ., 117 p.
Hirsch II, no. 612; RISM A I, no. M 3259

MUSIC LIBRARY

1014 [MONSIGNY, PIERRE ALEXANDRE]

[Rose | et | Colas. | Comedie | En un acte | Représentée pour la première fois par les | Comédiens Italiens Ordinaire du Roi le Jeudy | 8 Mars 1764. | Par M*** ⟨Paris, Hérissant? 1764?⟩]

2° *Score:* 1 ℓ., 154 p.
Imperfect: title-page and first 10 pages lacking; supplied in nineteenth-century manuscript
RISM A I, no. M 3272?

MUSIC LIBRARY

1015 [MONSIGNY, PIERRE ALEXANDRE]

Ariettes | Détachées | De Rose Et Colas | Comedie | En Un Acte | Par Mr. *** | Les paroles sont de Mr. Sedaine. | Gravées par Le Sr. Hue. | . . . | A Paris | Chez {Claude Hérissant Libre. Imprimeur | Rue neuve N. Dame aux trois Vertus. | Et aux Adresses ordinaires des Mds. | de Musique. | La Partition ainsi que le Poëme se | trouvera aux mêmes Adresses. | Avec Approbation et Privilege du Roy. [1764?]

8° 1 ℓ., 14 p.
RISM A I, no. M 3283

HOUGHTON

1016 [MONSIGNY, PIERRE ALEXANDRE]

Le Roy | Et Le Fermier | Comedie En Trois Actes. | Representée pour la première fois par les Comédiens | Italiens ordinaires du Roy le lundy 22 Novbre. 1762. | Par M. *** | . . . | Gravé par Le Sr. Hue. | A Paris | Chés Claude Herissant Imprimeur Libraire. | rue neuve Notre-dame, à la Croix D'or. | Et aux adresses ordinaires des | Marchands de Musique. | avec approbation Et Privilége | Du Roy. [1762?]

2° *Score:* 1 ℓ., 187 p.
Hirsch II, no. 615; RISM A I, no. M 3289
MUSIC LIBRARY

1017   MONTE, PHILIPPE DE

. . . | Di Filippo Di Monte | Maestro Di Capella | Della S. C. Maestà Dell'Impera-tore | Rodolfo Secondo. | Il Terzo Libro delli Madrigali, a cinque voci. | Con vno à sette nel fine. | Novamente Ristampati. | In Vineggia, Appresso l'Herede di Giro-lamo Scotto. | M.D.LXXXI

4° 1 pt.: *basso:* 1 ℓ., 22 [i. e. 20] p., 1 ℓ.
Numbers 5, 6 omitted in paging
RISM A I, no. M 3354; Vogel, no. 758
HOUGHTON

1018   MONTE, PHILIPPE DE

. . . | Il Sestodecimo Libro | De Madri-gali A Cinqve Voci | Di Filippo Di Monte | Maestro di Capella della Sacra Cesarea Maestà | Dell'Imperatore Rodolfo Se-condo. | Nouamente Composto, & dato in luce. | In Venetia Appresso Angelo Gardano. | M.D.LXXXXIII.

obl. 4° 1 pt.: *qvinto:* 1 ℓ., 29, [1] p.
RISM A I, no. M 3386; Vogel, no. 777
HOUGHTON

1019   MONTÉCLAIR, MICHEL PINOLET DE

Les | Festes | De L'Eté, | Ballet En Mvsiqve, | Par Monsieur Monteclair, de l'Academie | Royale de Musique; | Représenté Pour La Prémière Fois, | par la même Academie, le Vendredy douziéme Juin 1716. | Et remis au Théatre, avec une Entrée ajoûtée, le 29. Septembre suivant. | Nouvelle Edition. | De L'Imprimerie | De J-B-Christophe Ballard, seul Impri-meur du Roy pour la Musique, | à Paris,

ruë Saint Jean de Beauvais, au Mont-Par-nasse. | M.DCCXVI. | Avec Privilege de Sa Majesté.

2° *Score:* 2 ℓ., 166, [2] p.
On page [2] at end: Memoire des Oeuvres de Monsieur Monteclair.
Montéclair's autograph signature on page 166
RISM A I, no. M 3393
HOUGHTON

1020   MONTÉCLAIR, MICHEL PINOLET DE

Jephté. | Tragedie | tirée de l'Ecriture Sainte. | Representée pour la premiere fois, | par l'Accademie Royale de Mu-sique, | le Jeudy 28. fevrier 1732. | Mise en Musique, | Par Monsieur Montéclair. | Partition generalle in folio, Gravée. | A Paris. | Chez le Sr. Boivin Marchand, rüe St. Honoré | A le Regle d'Or. | . . . [ca. 1732]

obl. 2° *Score:* 1 ℓ., 249, [2] p.
Page [2] at end: Catalogue des Ouvrages de Mr. Montéclair.
RISM A I, no. M 3395
MUSIC LIBRARY

1021

The | Whole Volume | Compleat In-tituled | The Monthly Masks of | Vocal Musick Containing | all the Choisest Songs by | the Best Masters made for | the Play-houses Publick Consorts | and other Occasions for the | Year 170[3] with a Through Bass | to Each Song and most | of them with in | the Composs of | the Flute | . . . | London Printed for & sould by I: Walsh Musicall Instrument maker in Or-dinary to her Majesty at the | Golden Harp & Ho-boy in Catherine-street near Summerset-house in ye strand [1702–1703]

2° *Score:* 71 ℓ.
Twelve issues, published from No-vember, 1702 through October, 1703
Special issue for February: The | Songs | and Symphonys | Perform'd before Her | Majesty at her Palace | of St. Jame's on her Birth Day. 1703 | Composed by Mr: Eccles | Master of Her Majestys | Musick | . . .

John Hare's name erased from imprint
RISM B II, 240–241; Walsh I, no. 103
(variant)
HOUGHTON

1022

The | Whole Volume | Compleat In-
tituled | The Monthly Masks of | Vocal
Musick Containing | all the Choisest
Songs by | the Best Masters made for | the
Play-houses Publick Consorts | and other
Occasions for the | Year 170[4] with a
Through Bass | to Each Song and most | of
them with in | the Composs of | the Flute
| . . . | London Printed for & sould by I:
Walsh Musicall Instrument maker in Or-
dinary to her Majesty at the | Golden
Harp & Ho-boy in Catherine-street near
Summerset-house in ye strand [1703–
1704]

2° *Score: 67 ℓ.*
Twelve issues, published from No-
vember, 1703 through October, 1704
John Hare's name erased from imprint
RISM B II, 240-241; Walsh I, no. 160
HOUGHTON

1023

The | Whole Volume | Compleat In-
tituled | The Monthly Masks of | Vocal
Musick Containing | all the Choisest
Songs by | the Best Masters made for | the
Play-houses Publick Consorts | and other
Occasions for the | Year 1703 [i. e. 1705]
with a Through Bass | to Each Song and
most | of them with in | the Composs of |
the Flute | . . . | London Printed for &
sould by I: Walsh Musicall Instrument
maker in Ordinary to her Majesty at
the | Golden Harp & Ho-boy in Cathe-
rine-street near Summerset-house in ye
strand [1704–1705]

2° *Score: 64 ℓ.*
Twelve issues, published from No-
vember, 1704 through October, 1705
John Hare's name erased from imprint
Leaf 2ʳ: Books of Instrumental and
Vocal Musick Printed in ye Year 1705 for
I Walsh
RISM B II, 240-241; Walsh I, no. 188
HOUGHTON

1024

The | Whole Volume | Compleat In-
tituled | The Monthly Masks of | Vocal
Musick Containing | all the Choisest
Songs by | the Best Masters made for | the
Play-houses Publick Consorts | and other
Occasions for the | Year 1706 with a
Through Bass | to Each Song and most | of
them with in | the Composs of | the Flute
| . . . | London Printed for & sould by I:
Walsh Musicall Instrument maker in Or-
dinary to her Majesty at the | Golden
Harp & Ho-boy in Catherine-street near
Summerset-house in ye strand [1705–
1706]

2° *Score: 63 ℓ.*
Twelve issues, published from No-
vember, 1705 through October, 1706
John Hare's name erased from imprint
Leaf 2ʳ: Books of Instrumental and
Vocal Musick Printed in ye Year 1706 for
I. Walsh
RISM B II, 240-241; Walsh I, no. 223
HOUGHTON

1025

The | Whole Volume | Compleat In-
tituled | The Monthly Masks of | Vocal
Musick Containing | all the Choisest
Songs by | the Best Masters made for | the
Play-houses Publick Consorts | and other
Occasions for the | Year 170[7] with a
Through Bass | to Each Song and most | of
them with in | the Composs of | the Flute
| . . . | London Printed for & sould by I:
Walsh Musicall Instrument maker in Or-
dinary to her Majesty at the | Golden
Harp & Ho-boy in Catherine-street near
Summerset-house in ye strand [1706–
1707]

2° *Score: 62 ℓ.*
Twelve issues, published from No-
vember, 1706 through October, 1707
John Hare's name erased from imprint
Leaf 2ʳ: Books of Instrumental and
Vocal Musick Printed in ye Year 1707 for
I. Walsh
RISM B II, 240-241; Walsh I, no. 258
HOUGHTON

1026 [MORAND, PIERRE DE]

Justification | De La | Musique Fran-
çoise. | Contre la Querelle qui lui a été

faite | par un Allemand & un Allobroge. | Adressée par elle-même au Coin de la Reine | le jour qu'avec Titon & l'Aurore | elle s'est remise en possession de son | Théâtre. | . . . | A La Haye. | M.DCC.LIV.

8° 1 *ℓ*., viij, 55 p.
Hirsch I, no. 415; RISM B VI, 595
HOUGHTON

1027 MOREAU, JEAN BAPTISTE

Choeurs | De La | Tragedie | D'Esther, | Avec La Musique, | Composée par J. B. Moreav, Maistre de | Musique du Roy. | A Paris, | Chez {Denys Thierry, ruë saint Jacques. | Claude Barbin, au Palais. | Et | Christophle [*sic*] Ballard, ruë S. Jean de Beauvais. | M.DC.LXXIX. | Avec Privilege Du Roy.

4° *Score:* 4 *ℓ*., 99 p., illus.
Inserted at end is a leaf in eighteenth-century manuscript containing music and words of a stanza omitted from page 64
RISM A I, no. M 3622
HOUGHTON

1028 MORLEY, THOMAS

. . . | Of | Thomas Morley | The First Books Of | Balletts | To | Five Voyces. | In London | By Thomas Este. | CIↃ.IↃ.XC.V.

4° 4 pts.: *cantvs, altvs, bassvs, qvintvs:* [A]², B–D⁴, E² each
Imperfect: leaves B4, C3 in *altvs* part-book repaired, with lost text and music supplied in manuscript
RISM A I, no. M 3697
HOUGHTON

1029 MORLEY, THOMAS

Six | Canzonets | For two | Voices | Composed by | Thomas Morley B. M. | And first Publish'd by Him Anno Dom. | 1599. . . . | London Printed by Welcker in Gerrard Street St. Anns Soho. [ca. 1770]

obl. 4° *Score:* 1 *ℓ*., 17 p.
RISM A I, no. M 3703
MUSIC LIBRARY

1030 MORLEY, THOMAS

Canzonets. | Or | Little Short | Songs To Three | Voyces: | Pvblished | By | Thomas Morley, | Bacheler of Musicke, and one | of the Gent. of her Maiesties Royall | Chappel. | Now Newly Im-printed | with some Songs added by the | Avthor. | 1606. | In London | Printed By Thomas Este, | the assigne of William Barley. | . . .

4° 3 pts.: *cantvs, altvs, bassvs:* [A]², B–E⁴, F² each
RISM A I, no. M 3693
HOUGHTON

1031 MORLEY, THOMAS, COMP.

. . . | Madrigales | The Triumphes of Oriana, | to 5. and 6. voices: com-|posed by diuers seuerall | aucthors. | Newly published by Thomas Morley, | Batcheler of Musick, and one of | the gentlemen of hir | Maiesties honorable | Chappell. | 1601. | In London | Printed by Thomas Este, | the assigne of Thomas Morley. | Cum priuilegio Regiae Maiestatis.

4° 6 pts.: *cantvs, altvs, tenor, bassvs, qvintvs:* [A]², B–D⁴, E² each; *sextvs:* [A]², B⁴, C²
RISM B I, no. 1601¹⁶
HOUGHTON

1032 MORLEY, THOMAS

A | Plaine And | Easie Introdvcti-|on To Practicall | Mvsicke, | Set downe in forme of a dialogue: | Deuided into three partes, | The first teacheth to sing with all | things necessary for the knowledge of | pricktsong. | The second treateth of des-cante | and to sing two parts in one vpon a plainsong or | ground, with other things necessary | for a descanter. | The third and last part entreateth of com|position of three, foure, fiue or more parts with | many profitable rules to that effect. | With new songs of, 2. 3. 4. and. 5 parts. | By Thomas Morley, Batcheler of musick, & | one of the gent. of hir Maiesties Royall Chappell. | Imprinted at London by Peter Short dwelling on | Breedstreet hill at the signe of the Starre. 1597.

2° 3 *ℓ*., 183, [35] p., illus., music
Hirsch I, no. 416; RISM B VI, 598
HOUGHTON

1033   MORLEY, THOMAS

A | Plaine And | Easie Introdvcti-|on To Practicall | Mvsicke, | Set downe in forme of a dialogue: | Diuided into three parts. | The first teacheth to sing, with | all things necessarie for the knowledge | of pricktsong. | The second treateth of descante, and to | sing two parts in one vpon a plainsong or ground, with | other things necessarie for a descanter. | The third and last part entreateth of com-|position of three, foure, fiue or more parts, with | many profitable rules to that effect. | With new songs of, 2. 3. 4. and 5. parts. | By Thomas Morley, Batcheler of Musicke, and | one of the gent. of her Maiesties Royall Chappell. | Imprinted at London by Humfrey Lownes, dwel-|ling on Bredstreet hill at the signe of the Star. 1608.

2° 3 ℓ., 183, [35] p., illus., music
Hirsch I, no 417; RISM B VI, 598; Wolfenbüttel, no. 1236
HOUGHTON

1034   MORLEY, THOMAS

A Plain and Easy | Introduction to Practical Music, | Set down in Form of a Dialogue, | Divided into Three Parts, | The First Teacheth to Sing, | The Second Treateth of Descant, | The Third Treateth of Composition, | By Thomas Morley | Batchelor of Music. | As Printed in the year 1597. | Now reprinted for William Randall Successor to | the late Mr. J Walsh in Catherine Street, in the | Strand, London. | MDCCLXXI. | J. Caldwall Sculp. . . .

4° 5 ℓ., iv, 257, [1] p., 1 ℓ., 29 p., illus., music
Pages 1–29 at end: open score arrangement of the music printed in *Tafelmusik* format on pages 212–222 and 254–257
Hirsch I, no. 418; RISM B VI, 598
HOUGHTON, MUSIC LIBRARY

MORLEY, THOMAS, COMP. The Triumphes of Oriana *See* Morley, Thomas, comp. *Madrigales: The Triumphes of Oriana*

MORLIÈRE, JACQUES ROCHETTE DE LA *See* Lamorlière, Jacques Rochette de

1035   MOTTA, DOMENICO

Six Duetts, | for | Two Voices, | with a | Thorough Bass; | Composed and humbly Dedicated | to the | Right Honorable Lady Clive; | by | Dominico Motta | . . . | London: | Printed & sold for the Author, at Mr. Ganer's, Piano Forte | Manufactory No. 47, Broad Street Soho. [ca. 1790]

obl. 2° *Score:* 1 ℓ., 17 p.
RISM A I, no. M 3827
MUSIC LIBRARY

1036   MOTTA, DOMENICO

Six | Songs | with an Accompanyment for the | Harp Forte Piano or Harpsichord, | Composed & Humbly dedicated | To The Honble. | Miss Egerton | By | Sigr Domenico Motta. | . . . | London. | Printed for R. Birchall No. 133 New Bond Street. [after 1789]

obl. 8° *Score:* 27 p.
MUSIC LIBRARY

1037   MOURET, JEAN JOSEPH

Le Triomphe | Des Sens, | Ballet Hèroique, | mis en musique | Par Mr. Mouret. | Ordinaire de la Musique du Roy. | Representé pour la premiere Fois, par | L'accademie Royale de Musique le 29e. May. 1732. | . . . | Se Vend A Paris, | Chez {L'auteur rüe Ste Anne, proche le Carrefour des 4. cheminées. | Le Sr. Boivin, rüe St. honoré à la Régle D'or. | Le Sr. Le clerc, rüe du Roule à la Croix D'or. [1732?]

obl. 4° *Score:* 2 ℓ., 3, [1], 315, [1] p.
Unnumbered page after page 3, first sequence: Memoire | Des Oeuvres de Mr. Mouret.
RISM A I, no. M 3980
MUSIC LIBRARY

MOYNE, JEAN BAPTISTE *See* Lemoyne, Jean Baptiste Moyne, called

1038   MOZART, LEOPOLD

Versuch | einer gründlichen | Violinschule, | entworfen | und mit 4. Kupfertafeln sammt einer Tabelle | versehen | von | Leopold Mozart | Hochfürstl. Salzburgischen Cammermusikus. | In Verlag des Verfassers. | Augspurg, | gedruckt bey Johann Jacob Lotter, 1756.

4° 8 ℓ., 264, [8] p., 1 ℓ., front. (port.), illus., 4 pl. (1 fold.), music
Hirsch I, no. 419; RISM B VI, 600
HOUGHTON (2 copies)

1039 MOZART, LEOPOLD

Leopold Mozarts | Hochfürstl. Salzburgischen Vice-Capellmeisters | gründliche | Violinschule, | mit | vier Kupfertafeln | und | einer Tabelle. | Zweyte vermehrte Auflage. | Auf Kosten des Verfassers. | Augsburg, | gedruckt bey Johann Jacob Lotter, 1769.

4° 8 ℓ., 268, [8] p., front. (port.), illus., 4 pl. (1 fold.), music
RISM B VI, 601
HOUGHTON

1040 MOZART, WOLFGANG AMADEUS

A | Favourite Air | Adapted With | Variations | By | W. A. Mozart. | London. | Printed for Harrison & Co. No. 18, Paternoster Row. [1797?]

8° *Score:* 14 p. (*The Piano-Forte Magazine,* vol. III, no. 1)
K. 573
MUSIC LIBRARY

1041 MOZART, WOLFGANG AMADEUS

La | Clemenza di Tito | Opera seria di W. A. Mozart | in due atti | aggiustata per il Cembalo. | Titus der Grossmüthige, | eine ernsthafte Oper in zwey Akten, | von | W. A. Mozart. | Im Klavierauszuge | von | Siegfried Schmiedt. | Leipzig, | in der Breitkopfischen Musikhandlung. [ca. 1795]

obl. 2° *Vocal score:* 1 ℓ., 110 p.
Imperfect: frontispiece, pages 7–10 lacking
Hirsch IV, no. 212; RISM A I, no. M 5097
K. 621
MUSIC LIBRARY

1042 MOZART, WOLFGANG AMADEUS

Grand Concert | pour | Le Clavecin ou Forte-Piano | avec l'accompagnement des deux Violons, Alto, | et Basse, deux Hautbois, et deux Cors | composé par | W. A. Mozart. | Oeuvre IV. Livre [1.] | Publié a Vienne chez Artaria Comp. | . . . | C. P. S. C. M. [1783]

obl. 2° 1 pt.: *cembalo:* 25 p.
Plate no. 41
Hirsch IV, no. 66; RISM A I, no. M 5798
K. 385p (414)
MUSIC LIBRARY

1043 MOZART, WOLFGANG AMADEUS

Grand Concert | pour | Le Clavecin ou Forte-Piano | avec l'accompagnement des deux Violons, Alto, | et Basse, deux Hautbois, et deux Cors | composé par | W. A. Mozart | Oeuvre IV. Livre [2.] | Publié a Vienne chez Artaria Comp. | . . . | . . . C.P.S.C.M. . . . [1784]

obl. 2° 1 pt.: *cembalo:* 22 p.
Plate no. 42
Hirsch IV, no. 65; RISM A I, no. M 5793
K. 387a (413)
MUSIC LIBRARY

1044 MOZART, WOLFGANG AMADEUS

[Dom Juan, oder Der steinerne Gast . . . Bonn, Simrock ⟨1797⟩]

obl. 2° *Vocal score:* 205, [1] p.
Plate no. 42
Unnumbered page at end: Verzeichniss. | Der Operetten, welche in Partitur oder mit ausgeschriebenen Sing und Instrumentstimmen bey N. Simrock in Bonn im billigsten Preiss zu haben sind . . .
Imperfect: title-page, page [2] lacking; title supplied in manuscript
Hirsch IV, no. 130; RISM A I, no. M 4505
K. 527
MUSIC LIBRARY

1045   MOZART, WOLFGANG
          AMADEUS

Fuga | per | 2 Cembali | Di W: A: Mo-
zart | all attuale Servizio di Sua | Maesta
I: è R: | a Vienna presso Hoffmeister
[1788]

2° 2 pts.: *cembalo I, cembalo II:* 6 p.
each
Plate no. 144
Hirsch IV, no. 71; RISM A I, no. M
6653
K. 426
HOUGHTON

1046   MOZART, WOLFGANG
          AMADEUS

Idomeneo | Rè Di Creta. | Opera seria |
In Tre Atti, | Musica | Di. W. A. Mozart. |
Idomeneus | König von Creta. | eine
ernsthafte Oper | in drey Aufzügen, | von |
W. A. Mozart. | Bei N. Simrock in Bonn. |
. . . [1797]

obl. 2° *Vocal score:* 1 ℓ., 183 p.
Plate no. 51
Hirsch IV, no. 39; RISM A I, no. M
4192
K. 366
MUSIC LIBRARY

1047   MOZART, WOLFGANG
          AMADEUS

Jdomeneo | Rè Di Creta | Opera Seria in
3. Atti | Del Sign. W. A. Mozart | aggiu-
stata per il Piano Forte | Dj Gjov. Wenzel.
| Leipzig beÿ Schmidt und Rau. | Joh.
Berka sc. Praga. [1797?]

obl. 2° *Vocal score:* 1 ℓ., 182 p.
Hirsch IV, no. 41; RISM A I, no. M
4189
K. 366
MUSIC LIBRARY

1048   MOZART, WOLFGANG
          AMADEUS

Marche Des | Marriages Samnites, | Et |
L'Air De Julié, | With | Variations | By |
W. A. Mozart. | London. | Printed for Har-
rison & Co. No. 18 Paternoster Row.
[1798?]

8° *Score:* 1 ℓ., 5–30 p. (*The Piano-Forte
Magazine*, vol. III, no. 9)
Plate nos. 46–47
K. 374c (352) and K. 315d (264), Anh. B
RISM A I, no. M 7011
MUSIC LIBRARY

1049   MOZART, WOLFGANG
          AMADEUS

Le Nozze De Figaro. | Die Hochzeit
Des Figaro. | Eine Comische Oper in 4.
Aufzügen. | In Musick gesetzt | von | W.
A. Mozart. | Ins Deutsche übersetzt | vom
| Baron v. Knigge. | Und fürs Clavier ein-
gerichtet | von | C. G. Neefe. | bei |
Nicolaus Simrock | . . . Zu Bonn.
. . . [1796]

obl. 2° *Vocal score:* 228 p., 2 ℓ.
Plate no. 28
On recto of second leaf at end: Ver-
zeichniss. | Der Operetten, welche in Par-
titur oder mit ausgeschriebenen Sing und
Instrumentstimmen bey N. Simrock in
Bonn im billigsten Preiss zu haben
sind . . .
Hirsch IV, no. 99; RISM A I, no. M
4343
K. 492
MUSIC LIBRARY

1050   MOZART, WOLFGANG
          AMADEUS

Sonate | Pour le | Forte-piano, ou Cla-
vecin | Composé par | Mr. W. A. Mozart |
au Service de sa Majesté I. et R. | à Vienne
chez Hoffmeister. [ca. 1788]

2° *Score:* 21 p.
Plate no. 142
RISM A I, no. M 6848
K. 533 and K. 494
HOUGHTON

1051   MÜNSTER, JOSEPH JOACHIM
          BENEDICT

Epithalamium | Mysticum, | Das ist: |
Der andächtigen Seel, | Oder | in Gott
verliebten Braut | Geistliches | Hochzeit-
Lied, | Bestehend | in LX. solenn- und an-
muthig teutschen Arien, | Nach neuester
Art, auf die vornehmste Fest unsers
Herrn, der Mutter | Gottes, unterschied-

2

Allegro

142

1050 Mozart, *Sonate pour le forte-piano, ou clavecin*, Vienna, ca. 1788: page 2 (213 × 290 mm.)

Iusti ciaq3 dedit gentes frenare superbas.

CHEROICA BELLICA.

Heroica bellicaq3 harmonia é qua utimur in illis carminib.decantandis:quæ bellica facta deorũ hominũq3 describunt:cuius numeri sũt tales.

Bella p hermati os plusq̃ ciui li a campos

Iusq3 datũ sceleri canimus populũq3 potenté

In su a uictrici conuersũ uiscera dextra.

1060 NEGRI, *Brevis grammatica*, Venice, 1480: leaf 7 vi[v] (122 × 89 mm.); lines and initial decorations in manuscript

lichen Heiligen, vornehmsten Ordens-Stifftern, sonderbahren | Festen, auch andern Zeiten, als Kirchweyh, Primiz, jåhrliche Dancksagung, | um ein schönes Wetter, auch fruchtbahren Regen, die liebe Feld-Fruchten | vollkommen einerndten zu können, auch 6. sonderbahr de B. V. Maria | allezeit zu gebrauchen, dann endlich 3. vor die | Abgestorbne, | Von einer Vocal-Stimm, oder Solo, 2. Violinis obligatis, Cla-|rini cum Tymp. vel Cornua venat. verò, ubi apponuntur, par-|tim oblig. partim ad libitum sunto, prout Index do-|cebit, cum Organo & Violoncello. | Allen Gott liebenden, und durch die Music die Ehre desselben beförde-|renden Seelen zu tröstlicher Vergnügung sowohl in die Reimen verfasst, | als auch musicaliter mit sonderbahrem Fleiss componirt | von Josepho Joachimo Benedicto Münster, | J. C. Not. Pub. und Regente Chori in der Chur-Fürstlichen Grånitz-Stadt | Reichenhall in Ober-Bayrn. | Opus III. | . . . | Augspurg, | Gedruckt und verlegt von Johann Jacob Lotters seel. Erben, 1740.

2° 8 pts.: *vox cantans*: 2 *ℓ.*, 60 p.; *clarino vel cornu I*: 2 *ℓ.*, 27, [1] p.; *clarino vel cornu II*: 2 *ℓ.*, 22 p.; *violino I*: 2 *ℓ.*, 47 p.; *violino II*: 2 *ℓ.*, 43 p.; *violoncello*: 2 *ℓ.*, 51 p.; *tympano*: 2 *ℓ.*, 8 p.; *organo*: 4 *ℓ.*, 51 p.
RISM A I, no. M 8114
HOUGHTON

1052 MUFFAT, GOTTLIEB

Componimenti Musicali per il Cembalo | Di Theofilo Muffat | Organista di Corte e Camera | Di Sua Sacra, Cesarea, Cattolica, e Real Maestà | Carlo VI Imperadore | Di Sua Maestà L'Imperadrice Amalia Vedova | E Maestro di Cembalo D'Ambidue | Le Serenissime Arci-Duchesse Regnanti, | E Parimente | Di Sua Altezza Reale Duca di Lorena | E Gran Duca di Toscana. | Scolpit in rame et fatti Stampare | Da Giovanni Christiano Leopold Intagliatore in Augusta. | Con Gratia e Privileggio di sua Sacra Cesarea | Cattolica e Real | Maesta. [1727]

obl. 2° *Score*: 4 *ℓ.*, 105 p., 2 *ℓ.*
RISM A I, no. M 8134?
HOUGHTON

1053

The | Muses Delight. | An Accurate | Collection | Of | English and Italian | Songs, Cantatas and Duetts, | Set to Music for the | Harpsichord, Violin, German-Flute, &c. | With | Instructions | For The | Voice, Violin, Harpsichord or Spinnet, | German-Flute, Common-Flute, Hautboy, | French-Horn, Bassoon and Bass-Violin: | Also, | A Compleat Musical Dictionary, | And several Hundred | English, Irish and Scots Songs, | Without the Music. | Liverpool: | Printed, Published and Sold by John Sadler, in Harrington-street. | M,DCC,LIV.

8° 4 *ℓ.*, 323, [5] p., front., illus., fold. pl., music
Pages [1]–44: The | Complete Tutor, Etc.; pages [233]–254: A Musical Dictionary. | . . .; pages [255]–323: A Choice | Collection | Of | Favourite Songs, | Without The | Music.
Four unnumbered pages after pages 12, 44
RISM B II, 243
HOUGHTON

MUSICA TRANSALPINA *See* Yonge, Nicholas, comp. *Musica transalpina*

THE MUSICAL ENTERTAINER *See* Bickham, George, the younger *The Musical Entertainer*

THE MUSICAL MISCELLANY; A SELECT COLLECTION *See* Smith, Alexander comp. *The Musical Miscellany; a Select Collection*

1054

The Musical | Miscellany; | Being a Collection of | Choice Songs, | Set to the Violin and Flute, | By the most Eminent Masters. | . . . | London: | Printed by and for John Watts, at the Printing-|Office in Wild-Court near Lincoln's-Inn Fields. | MDCCXXIX.

8° *vol. I*: 7 *ℓ.*, 179 p.; *vol. II*: 5 *ℓ.*, 175 p., front. in each vol.
RISM B II, 247
HOUGHTON, MUSIC LIBRARY

1055

The Musical | Miscellany; | Being a Collection of | Choice Songs, | And | Lyrick Poems: | With the Basses to each Tune, and | Transpos'd for the Flute. | By the most Eminent Masters. | . . . | London: | Printed by and for John Watts, at the Printing-|Office in Wild-Court near Lincoln's-Inn Fields. | MDCCXXX. [–MDCCXXXI.]

8° *vol. III:* 7 *ℓ.*, 200 p.; *vol. IV:* 5 *ℓ.*, 204 p.; *vols. V, VI:* 7 *ℓ.*, 208 p. each; front. in each vol.
Imprint date, vols. V, VI: MDCCXXXI
Preliminary leaves 6ʳ–7ᵛ in vol. VI: Books Printed for J. Watts, | and Sold by the Booksellers both of | Town and Country.
RISM B II, 247
HOUGHTON, MUSIC LIBRARY

MUSICAL TRAVELS THROUGH ENGLAND *See* Veal, George *Musical Travels Through England*

MUSICALISCH-WOCHENTLICHER AUSS-GAABEN *See* Bachofen, Johann Kaspar *Musicalisch-wochentlicher Aussgaaben*

MUSICK'S DELIGHT ON THE CITHREN *See* Playford, John, comp. *Musick's Delight on the Cithren*

1056

Musicks Hand-maid: | New Lessons and Instrvctions | For The | Virginals or Harpsychord. | London, Printed for J. Playford, and are sold at his Shop near the Temple-Church. 1678.

obl. 4° 4 *ℓ.*, [72] p., illus., music
Preliminary leaf 4ᵛ: Musick Books lately Printed and Sold by John Playford.
RISM B I, no. 1678⁶
HOUGHTON

MUSIKALISCH-WOCHENTLICHER AUSS-GAABEN *See* Bachofen, Johann Kaspar *Musicalisch-wochentlicher Aussgaaben*

MUSIKALISCHER ALMANACH *See* Forkel, Johann Nikolaus, ed. *Musikalischer Almanach*

LA MUSIQUE RENDUE SENSIBLE PAR LA MÉCHANIQUE *See* Choquel, Henri Louis *La Musique rendue sensible par la méchanique*

N

NAPIER, WILLIAM, PUBL. A Selection of the Most Favourite Scots-Songs *See* A Selection of the Most Favourite Scots-Songs

1057   NARES, JAMES

Eight Setts | Of | Lessons | For The | Harpsichord, | Composed by | Mr. James Nares | Organist Of York-Minster. | London | Printed for the Author by J. Johnson in Cheapside. | MDCCXLVII.

obl. 2° *Score:* 3 *ℓ.*, 45 p.
RISM A I, no. N 62
MUSIC LIBRARY

1058   NASSARRE, PABLO

Fragmentos | Musicos, | Repartidos | En Qvatro Tratados. | En Que Se Hallan Reglas | generales, y muy necessarias para Canto Llano, | Canto de Organo, Contrapunto, y | Composicion. | Compuestos | Por Fr. Pablo Nassarre, Religioso | de la Regular Observancia de N. Serafico I. S. Francisco, | y Organista en su Real Convento de la Ciudad de Za-|rogoça. Y aora nuevamente añadido el vltimo tratado | por el mismo Autor; y juntamente exemplificados con | los Caractères Musicos de que careccìa. | Sacalos A Luz, Y Los Dedica | Al Excelentissimo Señor Don Manuel de Silva y | Mendoza, D. Joseph de Torres, Organista Princi-|pal de la Real Capilla de su Magestad. | Con Privilegio, En Madrid: | En su Imprenta de Musica. Año de 1700

4° 8 *ℓ.*, 288 p., music
Hirsch I, no. 427; RISM B VI, 610; Wolfenbüttel, no. 1239
MUSIC LIBRARY

1059   NEGRI, CESARE

Nvove | Inventioni | Di Balli, | Opera Vaghissima. | Di Cesare Negri Milanese | Detto Il Trombone, | Famoso, & eccellente Professore di Ballare. | Nella quale si danno i giusti modi del ben portar la vita, & di accommodarsi con ogni | leggiadria di mouimento Alle Creanze, Et Gratie D'Amore. | Conueneuoli à tutti i Cavalieri, & Dame, Per ogni sorte di Ballo, | Balletto, & Brando d'Italia, di Spagna, & di Francia. | Con figure bellissime in Rame, & Regole della Musica, & Intauolatura, | quali si richieggono al Suono, & al Canto. | Divisa In Tre Trattati. | Al Potentissimo, & Catholico | Filippo Terzo Rè Di Spagna. | Con Privilegio. | In Milano, Appresso Girolamo Bordone. M.DCIIII. | Con Licenza De' Svperiori.

2° 3 ℓ., 296 [i. e. 300], [4] p., illus., pl. (port.), music
Numbers 211–214 repeated in paging
Hirsch I, no. 429; RISM A I, no. N 359; RISM B VI, 611; Wolfenbüttel, no. 1240
HOUGHTON

1060   NEGRI, FRANCESCO

breuis grāmatica [Venice, 1480]

4° a–i⁸, k⁸⁺¹, l–s⁸, [2d]s⁸, t–z⁸, 9⁸, ⊅⁸, ℞⁸, aa–cc⁸, dd⁶, music
Colophon: Santritter helbronna genitus de gente ioannes | Lucilius: prompsit grammata docta nigri. | Herbipolisq[ue] satus: socio sudore: lacunis. | Hoc uenetis francus fert theodorus opus. | Anno Salvtis. M.CCCC.LXXX. XII. | Cal. April. Impressū ē hoc op[us] Venetiis | . . .
Title supplied from leaf a3ʳ
BMC V, 281–282 (IA.20923); Goff N-226; Hain-Copinger 11858
HOUGHTON

1061   NENNA, POMPONIO

. . . | Di Pomponio | Nenna Da Bari | Cavalier Di Cesare | Il Primo Libro | De Madrigali à Cinque voci. | Nouamente dati in luce. | Stampa Del Gardano | In Venetia MDCXVII. | Appresso Bartholomeo Magni.

4° 1 pt.: *tenore:* 23, [1] p.
RISM A I, no. N 383; RISM B I, no. 1617¹⁸; Vogel, no. 2019
HOUGHTON

1062   NENNA, POMPONIO

. . . | Di Pomponio | Nenna | Cavalier Di Cesare | Il Qvarto Libro | De Madrigali à Cinque voci. | Terza Impressione. | Stampa Del Gardano | In Venetia MDCXVII. | Appresso Bartholomeo Magni.

4° 1 pt.: *tenore:* 20 p.
RISM A I, no. N 385; Vogel, no. 2021
HOUGHTON

1063   NENNA, POMPONIO

. . . | Di Pomponio | Nenna. | Cavalier Di Cesare. | Madrígali A Cinque voci. | Qvinto Libro. | Nouamente Stampati. | In Venetia. | Appresso l'Herede di Angelo Gardano. | MDCXII.

4° 1 pt.: *tenore:* 1 ℓ., 20 p., 1 ℓ.
RISM A I, no. N 387; Vogel, no. 2022 bis
HOUGHTON

1064   NENNA, POMPONIO

. . . | Di Pomponio | Nenna | Cavalier Di Cesare | Il Sesto Libro | De Madrigali à cinque voci. | Quarta Impressione. | Stampa Del Gardano. | In Venetia. MDCXVIII. | Appresso Bartholomeo Magni.

4° 1 pt.: *tenore:* 1 ℓ., 21, [1] p.
RISM A I, no. N 391; Vogel, no. 2026
HOUGHTON

1065   NENNA, POMPONIO

. . . | Di Pomponio | Nenna | Cavalier Di Cesare | Il Settimo Libro | De Madrigali à Cinque Voci. | Quarta Impressione. | Stampa Del Gardano. | In Venetia MDCXXIV. | Appresso Bartholomeo Magni.

4° 1 pt.: *tenore:* 3 numb. ℓ., 4–19, [1] p.
RISM A I, no. N 396; Vogel, no. 2031
HOUGHTON

1066   NENNA, POMPONIO

. . . | Di | Pomponio Nenna | Cavalier | Di Cesare. | L'Ottavo Libro | De Madri-gali | A Cinqve | Nouamente con molta diligenza dati in luce | Da | Ferdinando Archilei | Dottor Di Legge. | In Roma, Ap-presso Gio. Battista Robletti. 1618. | Con Licenza De' Svperiori.

4° 1 pt.: *tenore:* 1 ℓ., 19, [1] p.
RISM A I, no. N 397; RISM B I, no. 1618[11]; Vogel, no. 2032
HOUGHTON

DIE NEUESTE UNTERSUCHUNG DER SING-SPIELE *See* Mattheson, Johann *Die neueste Untersuchung der Singspiele*

1067

The | New Merry Companion, | Or | Complete Modern Songster: | Being a Se-lect Collection | of the most Celebrated Songs, lately Sung at the | Theatres, Vauxhall, Ranelagh, &c. | Few of which ever were Printed in any Book of Songs. | Also | A Collection of the most esteem'd | Catches and Glees. | Set to Musick. | London: | Printed for John Wheble, No. 24 Pater Noster Row. [ca. 1775]

12° 1 ℓ., ix, 264, 24 p.
Imperfect: pages 71, 72 lacking
RISM B II, 258
MUSIC LIBRARY

1068

The | New Merry Companion | Or | Vocal Remembrancer; | being a | Select Collection | Of the most celebrated Songs lately sung at the | Theatres, Vaux-hall, Ranelagh &c | Few of which have ever been printed in any | Similar Publi-cation | To which are added the most fa-vorite | Catches and Glees, set to Music | The second Edition wth. considerable ad-ditions. | London | Printed for Wallis & Stonehouse Ludgate Street | J. Bew Pater Noster Row | W. Davenhill Cornhill & | Longman Lukey & Broderip Cheapside. [ca. 1776]

12° 1 ℓ., viii, 278, 24 p.
RISM B II, 259
MUSIC LIBRARY

NEWBERY, JOHN, PUBL. Universal har-mony *See* Universal harmony

1069

The | Newest Collection | Of The Choicest | Songs, | As they are Sung | At Covrt, | Theatre, | Mvsick-Schools, Balls, &c. | With | Musical Notes. | Lon-don, Printed by T. Haly, for D. Brown, at the Black | Swan and Bible without Tem-ple-Bar, and T. Benskin, | in St. Brides Church-Yard, Fleet-Street; 1683.

8° 72 [i. e. 64], [16] p.
Nos. 9–16 omitted in paging
HOUGHTON (2 copies, 2d imperfect: pages [9]–[12] lacking)

1070   NICOLAI, VALENTIN

Six | Sonatas, | For The | Piano Forte, | Composed By | V. Niccolai. | London: | Printed for Harrison & Co. No. 78, Fleet Street. [1798?]

8° *Score:* 59 p. (*The Piano-Forte Maga-zine,* vol. IV, no. 10)
Plate nos. 60–62
RISM A I, no. N 621 (op. 3)
MUSIC LIBRARY

1071   NICOLAI, VALENTIN

Six | Sonatas | for the | Harpsichord | or | Piano Forte, | with a | Violin Accompany-ment Obligate: | Composed and Humbly Dedicated | to the | Rt. Honble. Lady Vis-countess Gallway, | by | Valentino Nico-lai. | Op: V. | London. . . . | Printed by Longman and Broderip No. 26 Cheapside | and No. 13 Hay Market | . . . [1784?]

2° 2 pts.: *harpsichord or piano forte:* 1 ℓ., 35 p.; *violin:* 1 ℓ., 13 p.
RISM A I, no. N 638
MUSIC LIBRARY

1072   NICOLAI, VALENTIN

Six | Sonatas, | for the | Piano Forte | or | Harpsichord | with an Accompaniment for a | Violin | Composed by | Valentino Niccolai. | . . . | Op. XI. . . . | . . . | Lon-don | Printed by Longmand [*sic*] Broderip No. 26 Cheapside and No. 13 Hay Mar-ket | Music Sellers and musical Instrument makers, to | His Royal Highness the Prince of Wales. | . . . [1791?]

2° 2 pts.: *piano forte or harpsichord:* 1 ℓ., 31 p.; *violino:* 1 ℓ., 8 p.
RISM A I, no. N 647
MUSIC LIBRARY

NIGER, FRANCISCUS *See* Negri, Francesco

NIGRI, FRANCISCUS *See* Negri, Francesco

1073 NIVERS, GUILLAUME GABRIEL

Dissertation | Sur | Le Chant Gregorien. | Dediée Av Roy. | Par le Sr Nivers, Organiste de la Chapelle | du Roy, & Maistre de la Musique | de la Reyne. | . . . | A Paris, | Aux dépens de l'Autheur. | M.DC.LXXXIII. | Avec Approbation & Privilege du Roy.

8° 8 ℓ., 215, [1] p., illus., music
Colophon: . . . | Ex Typographia Christophori Ballard, unici | Regiae Musicae Typographi.
RISM B VI, 619
MUSIC LIBRARY

1074 NIVERS, GUILLAUME GABRIEL

Methode | Certaine | Pour Apprendre | Le Plein-Chant | De L'Eglise. | Dressée par le Sieur Nivers, Compositeur | en Musique & Organiste de | la Chapelle du Roy. | A Paris, | Chez Christophe Ballard, seul Imprimeur | du Roy pour la Musique, ruë Saint Jean | de Beauvais, au Mont-Parnasse. | M.DCC.XI. | Avec Privilege Dv Roy.

8° 47, [1] p., illus., music
RISM B VI, 619
MUSIC LIBRARY

1075 NIVERS, GUILLAUME GABRIEL

[Traité | De La Composition | De Mvsiqve. | Par le Sr Nivers, Me Compositeur | en Musique, Et organiste de l'Eglise | S. Sulpice de Paris. | A Paris, | Chez

l'Autheur proche S. Sulpice. | Et Robert Ballard, seul Imprimeur | du Roy pour la Musique, ruë S. Iean | de Beauvais, au Mont Parnasse. | M. DC. LXVII. | Avec Privilege Dv Roy.]

8° [61] p., illus., music
Imperfect: title-page, page 61 lacking; supplied in late seventeenth-century manuscript
Title supplied from Davidsson II, no. 69
RISM B VI, 620
HOUGHTON

1076 NIVERS, GUILLAUME GABRIEL

Traitté De La | Composition | De Musique. | Par le Sr. de Nivers, | Me. Compositeur en Musique & Organiste | de l'Eglise St. Sulpice de Paris; | Et traduit en Flamand par E. Roger. | Tractaat Van De | Saamenstellinge | Der Sangkunst | Door M. De Nivers Mr. Saamstelder in de | de Zangkunst en Orgelspeelder van de St. Sul-|pice Kerk tot Parys. | En in Duyts overgeset door E. Roger. | A Amsterdam, | Chez J. L. de Lorme & E. Roger, | Marchands Libraires sur le Rokin. | M.D.C.LXXXXVII.

8° 112, 10 p., illus., 4 pl. (music), music
Pages 1–10 at end: Voorbeelden van de Enkelde Vlugt . . .
Parallel text in French and Dutch, two columns to the page
RISM B VI, 620
HOUGHTON

THE NOBLE ART OF VENERIE OR HUNTING *See* Turberville, George *The Noble Art of Venerie or Hunting*

NOINVILLE, JACQUES BERNARD DUREY DE *See* Durey de Noinville, Jacques Bernard

NORTH, FRANCIS, 1ST BARON OF GUILFORD *See* Guilford, Francis North, 1st baron

1077 NOVERRE, JEAN GEORGES

Lettres | Sur | La Danse, | Et Sur | Les Ballets, | Par M. Noverre, | Maître des

Ballets de Son Altesse Sérénissime | Monseigneur le Duc de Wurtemberg, et | ci-devant des Théâtres de Paris, Lyon, | Marseille, Londres, et | A Stutgard, | Et se vend A Lyon, | Chez Aimé Delaroche, Imprimeur-Libraire | du Gouvernement & de la Ville, aux Halles | de la Grenette. | M.D.CC.LX.

8° 2 ℓ., 484 p.
Hirsch I, no. 436; RISM B VI, 622–623
HOUGHTON

1078   NOVERRE, JEAN GEORGES

Lettres | Sur La | Danse, | Et Sur Les | Ballets, | Par M. Noverre, | Maître des Ballets de Son Altesse Sérénissime | Monseigneur le Duc de Würtemberg, & | ci-devant | des Théâtres de Paris, Lyon, | Marseille, Londres, &c. | A Vienne, | Chez, Jean-Thomas De Trattnern, | Libraire Et Imprimeur De La Cour. | 1767.

12° 2 ℓ., 444 p.
Hirsch I, no. 437; RISM B VI, 623
HOUGHTON

1079   [NOVI DE CAVEIRAC, JEAN]

Lettre | D'Un | Visigoth, | A M. Freron, | Sur | Sa Dispute Harmonique | Avec M. Rousseau. | . . . | A Septimaniopolis, [i. e. Paris] | M.DCC.LIV.

8° 20 p.
Hirsch I, no. 440; RISM B VI, 623
HOUGHTON

NOVI THESAURI MUSICI   *See* Giovanelli, Pietro, comp. *Novi thesauri musici*

1080   NUNES DA SILVA, MANUEL

Arte | Minima, | Que Com Semibreve Prolaçam | tratta em tempo breve, os modos da Maxima, & | Longa sciencia da Musica, | Offerecida | A Sacratissima Virgem Maria | Senhora Nossa, debaixo da Invocaçaõ da | Quietaçam, | Cuja Imagem Esta Em A Santa | Sé desta Cidade, | Por Seu Author | O P. Manoel Nunes Da Sylva, | Mestre Cathedratico do Collegio de S. Catharina do Illustrissimo | Senhor Arcebispo, & do Coro da Paroquial Igreja de Santa | Maria Magdalena, na qual foi

baptizado. | Lisboa. | Na Officina de Joam Galram. | M.DC.LXXXV. | Com todas as licenças necessarias, & Privilegio Real.

4° 6 ℓ., 44, 52, 136 p., front., illus., pl., music
RISM B VI, 814; Wolfenbüttel, no. 1244
HOUGHTON

O

OBSERVATIONS ON THE CORRESPONDENCE BETWEEN POETRY AND MUSIC   *See* Webb, Daniel *Observations on the Correspondence Between Poetry and Music*

OBSERVATIONS SUR LA LETTRE DE J. J. ROUSSEAU   *See* Cazotte, Jacques *Observations sur la lettre de J. J. Rousseau*

1081

Odes and Dialogues. Book I. [London?, ca. 1699]

2° *Score:* 4 p.
Running title; fragment
Day, no. 175
HOUGHTON

1082   [O'HARA, KANE]

Midas | A Comic Opera | As it is Perform'd at the Theatre Royal | In Covent-Garden. | For the Harpsicord, Voice, German Flute, Violin, or Guitar. | London. Printed for I. Walsh in Catharine Street in the Strand. | . . . [1764?]

obl. 2° *Vocal score:* 39 p.
Originally issued in separate parts; pages numbered 8, 10–23, 27–30, 32–36, [53]–67 at head; 1–39 at foot
MUSIC LIBRARY

1083   OLEY, JOHANN CHRISTOPH

Variirte | Chorále | für die | Orgel, | von | Johann Christoph Oley. | Quedlinburg, | bey Christoph August Reussner. 1773. [–1776.]

2° *Score:* 2 vols., paged continuously: [*vol. I*]: 24 p.; *vol. II:* [25]–80 p.
Imprint date, vol. II: 1776
Incomplete: vols. III, IV lacking
RISM A I, no. O 27
MUSIC LIBRARY

1084

One Hundred | Cantici or Catches | for 3 and 4 Voices | Selected from the Works of the best | Italian Masters. | . . . | London: | Printed for A: Bland No. 23, Oxford Street. [ca. 1790]

obl. 8° *Score:* 2 ℓ., 57 p.
RISM B II, 121
MUSIC LIBRARY

OPUS AUREUM *See* Wollick, Nicolaus *Opus aureum*

ORCHESOGRAPHIE *See* Tabourot, Jehan *Orchesographie*

1085 ORNITHOPARCHUS, ANDREAS

Andreae | Ornithoparchi Meyningensis | de arte cantandi micrologus, libris | quatuor digestus, omnibus musicae | studiosis non tam utilis quam | necessarius. | Coloniae apud Heronem Alopecium | Anno. M.D.XXIIII.

obl. 4° A–L⁶, illus., music
RISM B VI, 627
HOUGHTON

ORVILLE, ANDRÉ GUILLAUME CONTANT D' *See* Contant d'Orville, André Guillaume

P

PAEP, ANDRIES DE *See* Papius, Andreas

1086 PAER, FERDINANDO

Camilla | eine Oper in drei Acten | mit deutsch-und italienischem Texte | von | F. Paer. | Clavierauszug von Cannabich. | . . . | Bonn bei N. Simrock | . . . [1799]

obl. 2° *Vocal score:* 189 p.
Plate no. 94
MUSIC LIBRARY

1087 PAISIELLO, GIOVANNI

Twelve | Capriccios and Rondos | For The | Piano Forte or Harpsichord | with an | Accompanyment | For The | Violin | Composed for the | Grand Dutchess of all the Russians, | By | Sigr: G. Paisiello. | . . . | London | Printed by Longman and Broderip No. 26 Cheapside and No. 13 Hay Market | Music Sellers and musical Instrument makers to | His Royal Highness the Prince of Wales | . . . [ca. 1790]

2° 1 pt.: *piano forte:* 27 p.
Imprint partially covered by cancel label reading: Chez Imbault marchand de musique au mont d'or rue st honoré entre l'hôtel d'aligre | et la rue des Poulies No. 627.
RISM A I, no. P 634
MUSIC LIBRARY

1088 PAISIELLO, GIOVANNI

L'Infante | De Zamora | Opéra Comique en Trois Actes | De | Paisiello | Parodie | Sous la Musique de la Fracatana [*sic*] | Par | Framery. | . . . | A Paris | Chez Leduc, au Magasin de Musique et d'Jnstruments, Rue Neuve des Petits Champs, | vis-a-vis la Trésorerie, No. 1286 | et Rue du Roule à la Croix d'Or No. 290 | Ecrit par Billet [ca. 1798]

2° *Score:* 1 ℓ., 308 p.
Plate no. 79 A
RISM A I, no. P 271
MUSIC LIBRARY

1089 PAISIELLO, GIOVANNI

Le Marquis Tulipano | Ou | Le Mariage | Jnattendu | Opera Bouffon en Deux Actes | Représénte Sur le théatre de Monsieur | Musique De Mr Paisiello | Paroles Par M * * * [i. e. Gourbillon] | . . . | A. Paris. | Chez le Sr Sieber Musicien rue St honore entre celles des Vielles | Etuve et celles D'orleans chez l'Apothicaire No 92 [ca. 1790]

2° *Score:* 1 ℓ., 163 p.
Cancel label mounted beneath imprint

reads: À Bordeaux, Chez les Freres Fil-
liatre Md. d'Estampes et de Musique, à la
Bource.
RISM A I, no. P 365
MUSIC LIBRARY

1090   PAISIELLO, GIOVANNI

Nina | oder | Wahnsinn aus Liebe |
Musik von Paisiello | mit Deutsch-und
Italienischem Text | Für das Clavier mit
begleitung einer Violine gesetzt | und
Unterthänigst gewidmet der | Durch-
lauchtigsten Regirenden Frau Herzoginn
| Von Zweybrücken | Von Carl Fränzl.
| . . . in Mannheim. bey I. M.
Götz . . . [ca. 1791]

obl. 2° *Vocal score:* 2 vols., paged con-
tinuously: [*vol. I*]: 75 p.; [*vol. II*]: 1 ℓ.,
76–163 p.
Plate no. 308
RISM A I, no. P 397
MUSIC LIBRARY

**1091   PALESTRINA, GIOVANNI
        PIERLUIGI DA**

. . . | Ioannis Petraloysii | Praenestini |
Sacrosanctae Basilicae Vaticanae Cappel-
lae Magistri. | Hymni Totivs Anni, | Se-
cundum S. Romanae Ecclesiae consuetu-
dinem, quattuor | quinque, & sex vocibus
concinendi | Necnon Hymni Reli-
gionvm. | Nvnc Denvo Impressi. | Vene-
tiis, | Apud Haeredem Hieronymi Scoti. |
MDLXXXX.

4° 4 pts.: *altus, tenor:* 70, [2] p. each;
bassvs: 48[+] p.; *qvintvs:* 15, [1] p.
Page 9 misnumbered 17 in *bassvs* part-
book (numerous other errors in paging)
Imperfect: title-page, pages 2, 7, 8,
all after 48 lacking in *bassvs* part-book
RISM A I, no. P 739
HOUGHTON

**1092   PALESTRINA, GIOVANNI
        PIERLUIGI DA**

. . . | Di Giovanni Petraloysio | Da Pa-
lestina | Il Secondo Libro De Madrigali |
A Qvatro Voci. | Nouamente posto in
luce. | Con Privileggio. | In Vinegia
Apresso l'Herede di Girolamo Scotto. |
MDLXXXVI.

4° 2 pts.: *alto, tenore:* 23 [i. e. 27], [1] p.
each
Page 27 misnumbered 23 in each part-
book
RISM A I, no. P 763; Vogel, no. 2099
HOUGHTON

**1093   PALESTRINA, GIOVANNI
        PIERLUIGI DA**

. . . | Ioannis Petraloysii | Praenestini |
Sacrosanctae Basilicae Vaticanae Cappel-
lae Magistri: | Missarum cum Quatuor
Quinque, Et Sex vocibus. | Liber Qvintvs.
| Nvnc Denvo Impressvs. | Aeterna
Christi munera. Nigra sum A 5. | Iam
Christus astra ascenderat. Sicut lilium
inter spinas. A 5. | Panis quem ego dabo.
Nasce la gioia mia. A 6. | Iste confessor.
Missa sine nomine. A 6. | Venetiis, |
Apud Haeredem Hieronymi Scoti. |
MDXCI.

4° 4 pts.: *altvs, tenor, bassvs:* 64 p.
each; *qvintvs:* 43 p.
Imperfect: pages 41, 42, 47, 48 lacking
in *bassvs* part-book
Davidsson I, no. 378; RISM A I, no. P
671
HOUGHTON

**1094   PALESTRINA, GIOVANNI
        PIERLUIGI DA**

. . . | Ioannis | Petraloysii | Praenestini
| Motectorvm Qvinqve Vocibvs | Liber
Qvartvs | Nunc recens in lucem aeditus. |
Venetijs, Apud Iacobum Vincentium. |
MDLXXXVIII.

4° 3 pts.: *altvs, tenor, qvintvs:* 1 ℓ., 29,
[1] p. each
RISM A I, no. P 719
HOUGHTON

**1095   PALESTRINA, GIOVANNI
        PIERLUIGI DA**

. . . | Ioan. Petraloysii | Praenestini, |
Motettorum Quinque vocibus. | Liber
Qvintvs. | Nvnc Denvo In Lvcem Ae-
ditvs. | Venetiis, | Apud Haeredem
Hieronymi Scoti. MDLXXVXIII. [i. e.
MDLXXXVIII]

4° 4 pts.: *altvs, tenor, bassvs, qvintvs:*
31, [1] p. each

Imperfect: all before page 27 and all after page 30 lacking in *bassvs* part-book
RISM A I, no. P 729
HOUGHTON

1096 PALESTRINA, GIOVANNI
PIERLUIGI DA

. . . | Ioannis Petraloysii | Praenestini, | Motettorum, quae partim quinis, partim senis, partim | octonis vocibus concinantur. | Liber Secvndvs. | Nunc denuò in lucem editus. | Cvm Privileggio. | Venetiis, Apud H[a]eredem Hieronymi Scoti. MDLXXXVIII.

4° 4 pts.: *altvs:* 52 p.; *tenor, qvintvs:* 48 p. each; *sextvs:* 25 [i. e. 27], [1] p.
Page 27 misnumbered 25 in *sextvs* part-book
RISM A I, no. P 709; RISM B I, no. 1588[9]
HOUGHTON

1097 PALESTRINA, GIOVANNI
PIERLUIGI DA

. . . | Liber Secvndvs | Ioan: Petri Aloysii | Praenestini | Motectorvm Qvae | Partim Qvinis, | Partim Senis, partim Octonis | Vocibus concinuntur. | Venetijs Apud Angelum Gardanum. | M.D.LXXXXIIII.

4° 1 pt.: *qvintvs:* 48 p.
Davidsson I, no. 379; RISM A I, no. P 710; RISM B I, no. 1594[1]
HOUGHTON

1098 PALESTRINA, GIOVANNI
PIERLUIGI DA

. . . | Iohannis Petraloysii | Praenestini | Motettorum quae partim Quinis, partim senis, | partim octonis vocibus concinantur, | Liber Tertivs | Nunc denuo in lucem aeditus. | Cvm Privilegio. | M.D.LXXXI | Venetiis, Apud Haeredem Hieronymi Scoti.

4° 4 pts.: *altvs, tenor:* 51, [1] p. each; *qvintvs:* 47 p., 1 *ℓ.; sextvs:* 23, [1] p.
Davidsson I, no. 376; RISM A I, no. P 712
HOUGHTON

1099 PALLAVICINO, BENEDETTO

. . . | Di Benedetto | Pallavicino | Il Settimo Libro | De Madrigali à Cinque voci. | Nouamente Ristampato. | In Venetia, Appresso Ricciardo Amadino. | MDCXI.

4° 1 pt.: *basso:* [1], 21 [i.e. 22], [1] p.
No. 2 repeated in paging
RISM A I, no. P 798; Vogel, no. 2128
HOUGHTON

PAMMELIA; MUSICKES MISCELLANIE *See* Ravenscroft, Thomas, comp. *Pammelia*

1100 PANERAI, VINCENZIO

Sei Ariette | Con Basso Continuo | Per iniziare i Dilettanti a cantare e accompagnarsi da Loro medesimi | Dedicate | Alla Molto Illustre ed Onorata Donzella La Sigra. | Giovanna Madioni | Dilettante | Dall'Abe. Vincenzjo Paneraj | Professore di Cimbalo e d'Organo, Maestro di Musica e di Cappella Fiorentino. | . . . | Si trovano in Firenze unitamente ai Principj di Musica, Solfeggj, Suonate, Concerti ec. | presso Rinaldo Bonini Librajo in Piazza del Duomo. [17—]

obl. 2° *Score:* [1], 9 p.
RISM A I, no. P 835
MUSIC LIBRARY

1101 PAOLUCCI, GIUSEPPE

Arte Pratica | Di Contrappunto | Dimostrata Con Esempj | Di Varj Autori | E Con Osservazioni | Di Fr. Giuseppe Paolucci | Minor Conventuale. | . . . | In Venezia, | MDCCLXV. | Per Antonio De Castro, | In Merceria Alla Costanza. | Con Licenza De' Superiori, E Privilegio

4° *vol. I:* xv, [1], 269, [5] p., music
Includes extended musical examples from the vocal works of O. di Lasso, G. A. Perti, C. M. Clari, G. P. da Palestrina, A. Caldara, B. Marcello, G. Bernabei, L. Vittori, G. P. Colonna, C. Porta and M. Asola.
Incomplete: vols. II, III lacking
RISM B VI, 635
MUSIC LIBRARY

1102 PAPIUS, ANDREAS

And. Papii | Gandensis | De | Conso-nantiis, | Sev | Pro Diatessaron | Libri Dvo. | Antverpiae, | Ex officina Christophori Plantini, | Architypographi Regij. | M.D.LXXXI.

8° 208, [22] p., 1 ℓ., music
Pages [1]–[22] at end: musical examples for two to three voices
Davidsson II, no. 71; RISM B VI, 635; Wolfenbüttel, no. 1248
HOUGHTON

1103 PARADEISER, MARIAN, SUPPOSED COMPOSER

Six | Quartettos | for | Two Violins | Tenor and Violoncello, | Composed by | Sigr. Paradeise | of Vienna | London Printed for William Forster | Violin, Violoncello, Tenor & Bow maker; also Music seller to their | Royal Highnesses, the Prince of Wales, & Duke of Cumberland, | Opposite the Church St. Martins Lane. | . . . [before 1785]

2° 4 pts.: *violino primo:* 18 p.; *violino secondo:* 15 p.; *viola, basso:* 13 p. each
Plate no. 38
RISM A I, no. P 886
MUSIC LIBRARY

1104 PARADIES, PIETRO DOMENICO

Paradiés' | Celebrated Concerto. | For The | Piano Forte. | London: | Printed for Harrison & Co. No. 18, Paternoster Row. [1798?]

8° *Score:* 14 p. (*The Piano-Forte Magazine,* vol. III, no. 13)
Plate no. 50
RISM A I, no. P 892
MUSIC LIBRARY

1105 PARADIES, PIETRO DOMENICO

A | Favourite | Minuet, | With | Variations, | Composed By | Dominico Paradies. | London | Printed for the Proprietors, & Sold by Harrison & Co. | No. 18, Paternoster Row. [1797?]

8° *Score:* 9 p. (*The Piano-Forte Magazine,* vol. II, no. 7)
RISM A I, no. P 903
MUSIC LIBRARY

1106 PARADIES, PIETRO DOMENICO

Sonate | di | Gravicembalo | dedicate | A Sua Altezza Reale | La Principessa Augusta | da | Pier Domenico Paradies | Napolitano. | London. | Printed for the Author by | John Johnson, | at the Harp & Crown in Cheapside | . . . [1754?]

2° *Score:* 3 ℓ., 47 p.
RISM A I, no. P 893
HOUGHTON

1107 PARENT, FRANÇOIS NICOLAS

Recueil | D'Hymnes Philosophiques, | Civiques Et Moraux, | Augmenté de la note en plain-chant, | d'après la musique des meilleurs auteurs, | pour faciliter, sur-tout dans les cam-|pagnes, la célébration des Fêtes répu-|blicaines, | Par Le Citoyen Parent. | . . . | A Paris. | Chez Chemin, Pont Michel, no. 21, au coin | de la rue Louis. | An VII. [i. e. 1798/99]

12° 1 ℓ., x, XII, 156, 80, [4] p.
Colophon: De l'Imprimerie de Belin, Imprimeur-Libraire, | rue Jacques, no. 22.
Imperfect: pages I–IV lacking
RISM B II, 338
MUSIC LIBRARY

1108 PARRAN, ANTOINE

Traité | De La | Mvsiqve | Theoriqve | Et Pratiqve. | Contenant Les Preceptes | de la Composition. | Par le R. P. Antoine Parran, | de la Compagnie de Jesvs. | A Paris, | Par Robert Ballard, seul Imprimeur du Roy pour | la Musique, demeurant ruë S. Iean de Beauuais, | à l'enseigne du Mont Parnasse. | 1646. | Auec Priuilege de sa Majesté.

4° 4 ℓ., 143, [1] p., illus., fold. pl., music
RISM B VI, 637
HOUGHTON

1109   PARSONS, WILLIAM

Six | English Ballads | With an Accompaniment | For the | Harp Or Piano-Forte, | Dedicated (by Permission) to | Her Royal Highness | Princess Mary, | Composed by | Willm. Parsons Mus: D. Oxon. | Master of His Majestys Band of Musicians. | . . . | [London] To be had at the Music-Shops. [ca. 1790]

2° *Score:* 1 ℓ., 21 p.
RISM A I, no. P 954
MUSIC LIBRARY

1110   PASQUALI, NICOLÒ

The | Art Of Fingering | The | Harpsichord. | Illustrated with Examples in Notes. | To which is added, | An approved Method of Tuning that Instrument. | By Nicolo Pasquali. | Edinburgh: Printed for Rob. Bremner, the Assigney of Sig. Pasquali, and sold at his Music-Shop. | . . . [ca. 1765]

obl. 2° vii, 28 p., 15 pl. on 8 ℓ. (music)
RISM B VI, 638
HOUGHTON

1111   PASQUALI, NICOLÒ

Thorough-Bass | Made Easy: | Or, | Practical Rules for finding & applying its Various Chords with Little Trouble; | Together with | Variety of Examples in Notes, shewing the manner of accompanying | Concertos, Solos, Songs, and Recitatives: | By | Nicolo Pasquali. | . . . | Edinburgh: Printed and Sold by Robt: Bremner, the Assigney of Sig: Pasquali, at his Music-Shop | . . . [1757]

obl. 2° 2 ℓ., 48 p., 29 pl. on 15 ℓ. (music)
RISM B VI, 638
HOUGHTON

1112   PECCI, TOMASO

. . . | Del Signor | Tomaso | Pecci. | Madrigali A Cinqve Voci. | Quarta Impressione. | Stampa Del Gardano | In Venetia MDCXVI. | Appresso Bartholomeo Magni.

4° 1 pt.: *tenore:* 1 ℓ, 21, [1] p.
RISM A I, no. P 1108; RISM B I, no. 1616¹⁶; Vogel, no. 2160
HOUGHTON

1113   PECCI, TOMASO

. . . | Del Signor | Tomaso Pecci | Madrigali A Cinque Voci. | Libro Secondo. | Terza impressione. | Stampa Del Gardano | In Venetia MDCXVII. | Appresso Bartholomeo Magni.

4° 1 pt.: *tenore:* 20 p.
RISM A I, no. P 1117; Vogel, no. 2163
HOUGHTON

1114   PELLEGRINI, FERDINANDO

Six | Sonatas | For the | Harpsichord | with an Accompaniment for a | Violin | Composed by | Sigr: F: Pellegrino. | Opera 4th. | London. | Printed for R: Bremner, in the Strand. and A: Hummel, in King Street St. Ann's Soho. | . . . [1763?]

2° *Score:* 1 ℓ., 33 p.
RISM A I, no. P 1159
MUSIC LIBRARY

1115   PENNA, LORENZO

Li Primi Albori | Mvsicali | Per li Principianti della Musica Figurata; | Distinti In Trè Libri | Dal Primo spuntano li Principij del Canto Figvrato; | Dal Secondo spiccano le Regole del Contrapvnto; | Dal Terzo appariscono li Fondamenti per suonare l'Organo | ò Clavicembalo sopra la Parte; | Del Padre Frà | Lorenzo Penna | Da Bologna | Carmelitano della Cong. di Mantoua, Maestro di S. Teologia, Dottore | Colleg. frà gli Accademici Filaschisi, Filarmonici, e Risoluti, | l'Indefesso. Quinta Impresione. | In Bologna, per Pier-maria Monti. 1696. Con licenza de' Superiori. | Si vendono da Marino Siluani, al'Insegna del Violino, con Priuileggio.

4° 199 p., illus., pl. (port.), music
Plate included in paging; additional slip hinged to page 138
Hirsch I, no. 454; RISM B VI, 643
MUSIC LIBRARY

1116   [PEPUSCH, JOHN CHRISTOPHER]

The | Tunes | To The | Songs | In The | Beggar's | Opera | Transpos'd for the

Flute. | Containing Sixty Nine Airs. | London: | Printed for John Watts, at the Printing-Office | in Wild-Court, near Lincoln's-Inn-Fields. | MDCCXXVIII. . . .

8° 2 ℓ., 25 p., 1 ℓ.
HOUGHTON

1117   [PEPUSCH, JOHN CHRISTOPHER]

The | Songs and Dialogues, | Duets and Trios, | in the | Beggar's | Opera | as they are perform'd at the | Theatre in Lincolns Inn Fields. | The Songs Transpos'd for the | Flute. | Those that are not in ye compass | of ye Flute are at the end of the Book. | also the Original Songs may be had | where these are sold. | [London] Printed for I: Walsh and I: Hare | and sold at the Musick-shops | . . . [1729]

8° 1 ℓ., 60, [4] p.
Walsh II, no. 148
HOUGHTON

1118   PEPUSCH, JOHN CHRISTOPHER

The | Excellent Choice | Being | A Collection of the most favourite | Old Song Tunes | in the Beggars Opera | Set for 3 Voices in the manner of Catches. | Or | for two German Flutes and a Bass. | By Dr. Pepusch and the most Eminent English Masters. | London. Printed for I. Walsh in Catharine Street in the Strand. | . . . [1755]

obl. 2° Score: 1 ℓ., 31 p.
RISM B II, 170; Walsh II, no. 1184
HOUGHTON

1119   [PEPUSCH, JOHN CHRISTOPHER]

The Airs in the | Beggars Opera | For the | Guittar | German Flute or Violin | As Perform'd at the Theatres. | London Printed for J. Johnson facing Bow Church Cheapside . . . [ca. 1762]

obl. 8° 1 ℓ., 20 p., front.
HOUGHTON

1120   [PEPUSCH, JOHN CHRISTOPHER]

The Airs in the | Beggars Opera | For the | Violin | or | German Flute | As Perform'd at the Theatres. | London, Printed for Thompson & Sons in St, Pauls Church Yard, . . . [ca. 1763]

obl. 4° 1 ℓ., 20 p.
HOUGHTON (2 copies)

1121   PEPUSCH, JOHN CHRISTOPHER

The | Songs | Of The | Beggar's Opera, | Adapted To The | Harpsichord, Violin, or German Flute. | With the Overture in Score, | As Composed by Dr. Pepusch. | Engraved on Copper Plates. | London, | Printed for R. Tonson: | And Sold by T. Lowndes, in Fleet-street; and W. Bathoe, | in the Strand. | . . . | Where may be had, . . . | The same Opera, Transposed for the Common Flute. | [ca. 1765]

4° Vocal score: 1 ℓ., 46 p.
HOUGHTON

1122   [PEPUSCH, JOHN CHRISTOPHER]

The | Beggars Opera | as it is Perform'd at both Theatres | with the Additional Alterations by | Dr: Arne | for the Voice Harpsichord and Violin | the Basses entirely New. | . . . | London. Printed for T. Straight & Skillern, in St. Martins Lane, next the Strand. | . . . [ca. 1775]

obl. 2° Vocal score: 1 ℓ., 29 p
RISM A I, no. A 1740
HOUGHTON

1123   [PEPUSCH, JOHN CHRISTOPHER]

The | Beggar's Opera, | as it is Perform'd at both | Theatres, | with the Additional Alterations by | Dr. Arne, | For The | Voice, Harpsichord & Violin. | The Basses entirely New. . . . | London Printed & Sold by Preston, at his Wholesale Warehouses, 97 Strand. | . . . [after 1778]

obl. 2° Vocal score: 1 ℓ., 29 p.
HOUGHTON

1124 [PEPUSCH, JOHN CHRISTOPHER]

The | Beggar's Opera, | as it is Perform'd at both | Theatres, | with the Additional Alterations by | Dr. Arne, | For The | Voice, Harpsichord & Violin. | The Basses entirely New. . . . | London. Printed for T. Skillern No. 17 St. Martins Lane next the Strand. | . . . [ca. 1780]

obl. 2° *Vocal Score:* 1 ℓ., 29 p.
HOUGHTON

1125 PEPUSCH, JOHN CHRISTOPHER

The | Beggars Opera, | As it is performed at the | Theatres Royal in Drury Lane, and Covent Garden. | Composed by | Dr. Pepusch, | For the | Voice, Harpsichord, and Violin. | London: | Printed for Harrison & Co. No. 18, Paternoster Row. [178–?]

obl. 2° *Vocal score:* 26 p.
HOUGHTON

1126 PEPUSCH, JOHN CHRISTOPHER

The | Beggars Opera, | As it is performed at the | Theatres Royal in Drury Lane, and Covent Garden. | Composed by | Dr. Pepusch, | For the | Voice, Harpsichord, and Violin. | London: | Printed for Harrison & Co. No. 18, Paternoster Row. [1784?]

obl. 2° *Vocal score:* 26 p.
Plate nos. 17–18, which are those of *The New Musical Magazine* (see Schnapper II, 768)
RISM A I, no. P 1205
HOUGHTON (2 copies)

1127 [PEPUSCH, JOHN CHRISTOPHER]

The | Beggar's Opera | As it is performed at both | Theatres | with the Additional Alterations, and new Basses by | Doctor Arne | for the | Voice, Harpsichord and Violin. | . . . | London Printed by Longman and Broderip No. 26 Cheap-side and No. 13 Hay Market | Manufacturers of Musical Instruments, and Music Sellers to Their Majesties, His Royal Highness the Prince of Wales | and all the Royal Family [ca. 1790]

obl. 2° *Vocal score:* 1 ℓ., 29, II [i. e. I] p.
Page II [i. e. I]: Musical Publications | Printed and Sold by Longman & Broderip at the | Apollo No. 26 Cheapside & No. 13 Hay market London
HOUGHTON

1128 PEPUSCH, JOHN CHRISTOPHER

Six | English | Cantatas | Humbly Inscrib'd | To the most Noble the | Marchioness of Kent | Compos'd by | Mr J: C Pepusch | London Printed for J: Walsh Servant in Ordinary to his Britanick Majesty, at ye Harp & Hoboy in Katherine street | near Somerset House in ye Strand, & J: Hare at ye Viol & Flute in Cornhill near the Royall Exchange. [1720]

2° *Score:* 1 ℓ., 31 p.
RISM A I, no. P 1241; Walsh I, no. 582
HOUGHTON, MUSIC LIBRARY

1129 PEPUSCH, JOHN CHRISTOPHER

Six | English Cantatas | for one Voice | Four for a Flute | and two with a Trumpet | and other Instruments | Compos'd by | J: C: Pepusch | Book ye Second | London Printed for J: Walsh Servant in Ordinary to his Britanick Majesty, at ye Harp & Hoboy in Katherine street | near Somerset House in ye Strand, & J: Hare at ye Viol & Flute in Cornhill near the Royall Exchange. [ca. 1730]

2° *Score:* 2 ℓ., 46 p.
RISM A I, no. P 1244; Walsh II, no. 1179
HOUGHTON, MUSIC LIBRARY

PEPUSCH, JOHN CHRISTOPHER The Excellent Choice *See* Pepusch, John Christopher *The Beggar's Opera*

1130   [PEPUSCH, JOHN
            CHRISTOPHER]

Songs | In the New | Opera | Of | Tho-
miris, | Queen of Scythia. | Collected out
of the Works of the most | Celebrated
Italian Authors, viz. | Scarlait, [*sic*] Bo-
nonchini, Albinoni, &c. | As they are Per-
form'd at the Theatre Royal. | Fairly In-
grav'd on Copper-Plates, and more | Cor-
rect then the former Edition. | Note:
These Songs are Printed so, that their |
Symphonies may be Plaid with them. |
London: | Printed for John Cullen, at the
Buck between the Two Temple-|Gates,
Fleet-street. [1707?]

2° *Vocal score:* 1 ℓ ., 51 numb. ℓ.
RISM A I, no. P 1226; RISM B II, 372
MUSIC LIBRARY

1131   PEREZ, DAVIDE

Mattutino de' Morti, | Composto | per
comando di Sua Maestà Fedelissima |
Don Giuseppe Io. | Dal | Sigr. David Perez
| Maestro di Capella dell istessa M. F. |
Maestro di Camera delle loro Altezze
Reali La Principessa | del Brasile, ed In-
fante di Portogallo. | . . . | Londra. |
Presso Roberto Bremner nello Strand, |
. . . | Ashby sculpt. Russel Court. |
[1774?]

2° *Score:* 3 ℓ., 156 p., 1 ℓ., front. (port.)
On recto of unnumbered leaf at end: A
Catalogue of Vocal .& Instrumental
Music, Printed & Sold by R.
Bremner . . .
RISM A I, no. P 1324
MUSIC LIBRARY

1132   PÉREZ CALDERÓN, MANUEL

Explicacion | De Solo El Canto-Llano, |
Que Para Instruccion De Los Novicios |
De La Provincia De Castilla | Del Real Y
Military Orden | De N. Señora De La
Merced, | Redencion De Cautivos, | Com-
puso | El P. Fr. Manuel Perez Calderon,
Maestro de Novicios | en el Convento de
Madrid. | A que añade las Cuerdas de
Alamire, Gsolreut, Ffaut, | y la que parti-
cularmente usa la Santa Iglesia de Tole-
|do, llamada por eso Cuerda Toledana. |
Contiene asimismo todas las Antifonas,
Lamentaciones, y Res-|ponsorios de los

tres dias de Tinieblas. | Todo lo que para
utilidad comun ha dispuesto, y da á | luz
el P. Fr. Isidro Lopez, Religioso del
mismo | Convento: | Y Lo Dedica | Al M.
R. P. M. Fr. Juan Ramirez de Orozco, Pro-
vincial | de dicha Provincia. | Madrid.
MDCCLXXIX. | Por D. Joachin Ibarra,
Impresor de Cámara de S. M. | Con las Li-
cencias necesarias. | Se ballará en la Por-
teria de la Merced Calzada.

4° 1 ℓ., V, [1], 189 p., illus., music
RISM B VI, 644
MUSIC LIBRARY

1133   PERGOLESI, GIOVANNI
            BATTISTA

Eight Lessons | For the | Harpsicord, |
Compos'd | By the Celebrated | Gio:
Batta. Pergolese. | Author of the Stabat
Mater. . . . | London, Printed and sold by
Longman, Lukey, and Co. No. 26 Cheapside, where may be had lately Publish'd
Justs Lessons | Opa. 1st., . . . [1771]

obl. 2° *Score:* 1 ℓ., 37 p.
RISM A I, no. P 1429
HOUGHTON

1134   PERGOLESI, GIOVANNI
            BATTISTA

La Serva Padrona | Intermezzo. | Del
Sigr. Giõ. Batta. Pergolese. | Rappresen-
tato in Pariggi nell' Autunno 1752. | A
Paris | Chez Le Clerc Md. rue St. Honoré,
entre la rue des Prouvaires et la rue Du-
four à Sainte Cecile. | Et aux Adresses Or-
dinaires | . . . Avec Privilége du Roi. |
. . . [ca. 1759]

obl. 2° *Score:* 2 ℓ., 68 p.
RISM A I, no. P 1394
MUSIC LIBRARY

1135   PERGOLESI, GIOVANNI
            BATTISTA

Stabat Mater, | del | Sigr. Giovanni Bat-
tista Pergolesi. | . . . | London, | Printed
& Sold by Robt. Birchall, | at his Musical
Circulating Library, No. 133, New Bond
Street. [ca. 1800]

2° *Score:* 43 p.
RISM A I, no. P 1349
HOUGHTON

1136 PESCETTI, GIOVANNI
BATTISTA

Sonate Per Gravicembalo | Nuova-
mente Composte | e in segno d'osse-
quiosa Gratitudine | dedicate | all
Illustrissima Signora | Grazia Boyle |
Degnissima ed unica Figlia | Dell'Eccel-
lentissimo Lord Viceconte Shanon | dal
suo | Umilissimo et obligatissimo Serve |
Giovambattista Pescetti [London, 1739?]

large obl. 4° *Score:* 1 ℓ., 59 p.
Pages 53–59: Ariette nell'Opere del
Sigr. Pescetti
HOUGHTON, MUSIC LIBRARY

1137 PETRI, JOHANN SAMUEL

Anleitung | zur | praktischen Musik |
von | Johann Samuel Petri. | Leipzig, | ver-
legt von Johann Gottlob Immanuel Breit-
kopf. | 1782.

4° 8 ℓ., 484 p., 1 ℓ., illus., music
Four unnumbered pages inserted be-
tween 482 and 483
Hirsch I, no. 458; RISM B VI, 647
MUSIC LIBRARY

1138 PEVERNAGE, ANDRÉ

Chansons | D'Andre Pevernage | Tant
Spiritvelles | Qve Prophanes | A Cincq
Parties | Nouuellement recueillies, &
reduites en vn liure. | . . . | En Anuers,
De l'Imprimerie de Pierre Phalese. |
M.DCVI.

obl. 4° 1 pt.: *svperivs:* 1 ℓ., 61, [1] p.
RISM A I, no. P 1676
HOUGHTON

1139 PHALÈSE, PIERRE, PUBL.

[Premier livre des chansons a quatre
parties. Louvain, ca. 1560]

obl. 4° 1 pt.: *svperivs:* 1 ℓ., xxx p.
A later edition of RISM B I, no. 1558[10]
Imperfect: title-page, pages i–viii lack-
ing
HOUGHTON

1140 PHALÈSE, PIERRE, PUBL.

Second Livre Des | Chansons A Qvatre
| Parties Novvellement Compo-|sez &
Mises en Musicque, Conuenables tant
aux instrumentz | Comme a la Voix. |
. . . | Imprime a Louain par Pierre Pha-
lese Libraire Iure Lan. D.M.LXI. [i. e.
MDLXI?] | Auecq Grace & Priuilege.

obl. 4° 1 pt.: *svperivs:* 1 ℓ., xxx p.
A later edition of RISM B I, no. 1559[7]
HOUGHTON

1141 PHALÈSE, PIERRE, PUBL.

Tiers Livre Des | Chansons A Qvatre |
Partie Novvellement Compo-|sez &
Mises en Musicque, Conuenables tant
aux instru-|mentz Comme à la Voix. |
. . . | Imprimé à Louain par Pierre Pha-
lese Libraire Iuré. L'an 1563. | Auecq
Grace & Priuilege.

obl. 4° 1 pt.: *svperivs:* 1 ℓ., xxx p.
A later edition of RISM B I, no. 1554[24]
HOUGHTON

1142 PHALÈSE, PIERRE, PUBL.

Qvatriesme Livre Des | Chansons A
Qvatre | Parties Novvellement Com-
|posees & mises en Musique, conue-
nables tant aux | Instruments comme à la
Voix. | . . . | A Lovain. | Par Pierre Pha-
lese Imprimeur & Libraire Iuré. L'an.
1564. | Auecq Grace & Priuilege.

obl. 4° 1 pt.: *svperivs:* 1 ℓ., 31
[i. e. 30] p.
Page 30 misnumbered 31
A later edition of RISM B I, no. 1555[20]
HOUGHTON

1143 PHALÈSE, PIERRE, PUBL.

[Cinquiesme livre des chansons a
quatre parties. Louvain, 156–?]

obl. 4° 1 pt.: *svperivs:* 1 ℓ., xxx p.
Imperfect: title-page, pages 5, 6 lacking
A later edition of RISM B I, no. 1555[21]
HOUGHTON

1144 PHILIDOR, FRANÇOIS ANDRÉ
DANICAN, KNOWN AS

Blaise | Le Savetier | Opera Bouffon |
Dedié | A Monsieur | Le Marquis de
Marigny | Mis en Musique | Par A. D.
Philidor | Oeuvre Ier. | Les paroles par Mr.

S. * * *. [i. e. M. J. Sedaine] | . . . | a Paris
chez {Mrs. De la Chévardiere et Huberti
Successeurs | de Mr. le Clerc rue du
Roule à la Croix d'Or, | Et aux adresses
ordinaires de Musique.} | Gravé par
Melle. Vendôme. | Imprimé par Tour-
nelle. [1760]

   obl. 2° *Score:* 1 ℓ., 104 p.
   On verso of title-page: Catalogue | de
Musique Vocale et Instrumentale que M.
De Lachevardiere Sucesseur de | M. Le
Clerc . . . a fait graver . . . ⟨An earlier
state of JohanssonF facs. 45⟩
   Hirsch II, no. 720; RISM A I, no. P
1800
   MUSIC LIBRARY

1145   PHILIDOR, FRANÇOIS ANDRÉ
         DANICAN, KNOWN AS

   Le Bucheron, | Ou | Les Trois Souhaits.
| Comedie | En un Acte Mêlées
d'Ariettes. | Représentée à Versailles de-
vant leurs Majestés, | le mardi 15 Mars
1763. par les Comediens Italiens | ordi-
naires du Roy. | Dédiée | A Monseigneur |
Le Dauphin. | La Musique par | A. D. Phi-
lidor. | Les Paroles de Mrs. G . . . [i. e. J. F.
Guichard] et C . . . [i. e. Castet] | . . . | A
Paris, | Chez {Mr. De la Chevardiere rue
du Roule a la Croix d'Or | Et aux
Adresses Ordinaires de Musique | Avec
Privilege Du Roy. Imprime par Montulay
[1765]

   2° *Score:* 2 ℓ., 80 p.
   On recto of preliminary leaf 2: Cata-
logue | de Musique Vocale et Instrumen-
tale que M. De Lachevardiere Successeur
de | M. Le Clerc . . . a fait graver
. . . ⟨A later state of JohanssonF facs.
49⟩
   Hirsch II, no. 721; RISM A I, no. 1812
   MUSIC LIBRARY

1146   PHILIDOR, FRANÇOIS ANDRÉ
         DANICAN, KNOWN AS

   Le Jardinier | Et son Seigneur. | Opera
Bouffon | En Un Acte | Representé sur le
Théatre de l'Opera Comique | Mis en
Musique | Par | M. A. D. Philidor | . . . | A
Paris | Chez {M. de la Chevardiere md. de
musique du Roi rue du Roule à la Croix
d'or | A Lion | Mrs les Freres le Goux

Place des Cordeliers. | M. Castaud vis a
vis la Comedie. | Avec privilege du Roi.
[1768]

   2° *Score:* 1 ℓ., 53 p.
   On verso of title-page: Catalogue | De
toutes sortes de Musique Vocale et Instrumentale que M. De La Chevardiere
Successeur de M. le Clerc | . . . à fait
graver . . . ⟨JohanssonF facs. 53⟩
   RISM A I, no. P 1847
   MUSIC LIBRARY

1147   PHILIDOR, FRANÇOIS ANDRÉ
         DANICAN, KNOWN AS

   Le Maréchal | Ferrant | Opera Comi-
que. | En Deux Actes. | Represénté sur le
Théatre de l'Opera Comique | Et de la
Comédie Italienne. | Mis En Musique |
Par | A. D. Philidor. | Les Paroles sont de
Mr. Quetant. | . . . | A Paris | Chez {Mr.
De La Chevardiere rue du Roule à la
Croix d'Or. | Et aux Adresses Ordinaires.
| A Lyon. | Mrs. Les Freres Le Goux Place
des Cordeliers. | Avec Privilége Du Roi.
[1762]

   2° *Score:* 1 ℓ., 72 p.
   On verso of title-page: Catalogue | de
Musique Vocale et Instrumentale que M.
De Lachevardiere Successeur de | M. Le
Clerc . . . a fait graver . . . ⟨A later
state of JohnssonF facs. 47⟩
   Hirsch II, no. 725; RISM A I, no. P
1854
   MUSIC LIBRARY

1148   PHILIDOR, FRANÇOIS ANDRÉ
         DANICAN, KNOWN AS

   Le Sorcier | Comedie Lyrique | En Deux
Actes | Par Mr. Poinsinet. | Mis en Mu-
sique | Par | A. D. Philidor. | Representée
pour la Premiere fois Par les Comediens
Jtaliens or-|-dinaire du Roy, Le Lundy 2.
Janvier 1764. Et a Versailles devant |
Leurs Majestés Le Mercredy 21. Mars de
la même année. | . . . | Gravé par Le Sr.
Hue | . . . | A Paris | Chez {Mr. Le Clerc,
rue St. Honoré près la Rue Des Prouvairs
à Ste. Cécile. | Mr. De La Chevardiere,
rue du Roule à la Croix d'Or. | Mr. Le
Menu, rue du Roule à la Croix d'Or. |
Mlle. Castagnery, rue des Prouvairs à la
Musique Royale. | Avec Approbation Et

Privilege du Roy. | Imprimé par Monthulay. [1765]

2° *Score:* 1 ℓ., 162 p.
RISM A I, no. P 1889
MUSIC LIBRARY

1149   PHILIDOR, FRANÇOIS ANDRÉ DANICAN, KNOWN AS

Tom Jones | Comedie Lyrique | En Trois Actes. | Représentée par les Comediens Italiens du Roy, pour la premre. fois | Le 27 fevrier 1765. Et remise avec des changements Le 30. Janvier 1766. | Dediée | A S. A. S. Monseigneur | Le Duc Regnant Des Deux Ponts | Prince Palatin du Rhin, Duc de Baviere &c, &c. | Mis en Musique | Par A. D. Philidor. | Les Paroles de Mr. Poinsinet. | . . . | Gravé par Le Sr. Hue | A Paris | Chez Le Duc, Successeur de Mr. la Chevardiere, Rue du Roule, à la Croix d'Or, | au Magazin de Musique, et d'Instruments, | No. 6 [1786?]

2° *Score:* 1 ℓ., 172 p.
Plate no. 3 A
RISM A I, no. P 1910
MUSIC LIBRARY

1150   PHILIPS, PETER

Di Pietro Philippi | Inglese | Organista Delli Sereniss. | Prencipi Alberto Et Isabela | Archidvchi D'Avstria &c. | Il Primo Libro | De Madrigali A Sei Voci | Nuouamente Ristampati & Corretti. | . . . | In Anversa | Appresso Pietro Phalesio M.DCIV.

obl. 4° 2 pts.: *basso, sesto:* 1 ℓ., 25, [1] p. each
RISM A I, no. P 1992; Vogel, no. 2210
HOUGHTON

1151   PHILIPS, PETER

Di Pietro Philippi | Inglese | Organista Delli Sereniss. | Prencipi Alberto Et Isabella | Archidvchi D'Avstria &c. | Il Secondo Libro | De Madrigali A Sei Voci | Nouamente Composto & dato in luce. | . . . | In Anversa. | Appresso Pietro Phalesio MDCIII.

obl. 4° 2 pts.: *basso, sesto:* 1 ℓ., [1], 32, [1] p. each
RISM A I, no. P 1997; Vogel, no. 2211
HOUGHTON

1152   PHILO ARMONICA, PSEUD.

Ten | Pieces | for the | Organ | adapted for the use of the | Church | By | Philo Armonica | . . . | London | Printed and Sold for the Author by Longman and Broderip No. 26 Cheapside [ca. 1785]

obl. 2° *Score:* III, 2–53 p.
Page III: Musical Publications | Printed and sold by Longman & Broderip . . .
RISM A I, no. P 2009
MUSIC LIBRARY

1153

La Philomele | Seraphiqve, | Partie Premiere, | ou elle chante les devots et ardans | Souspirs De L'Ame Penitente | qui s'achemine à la vraie perfection. | . . . | A Tournay, | De l'Imprimerie d'Adrien Qvinqve, | M.D.C.XXXII. | Auec grace et priuilege.

8° 63 ℓ., 276, [12] p.
"Cantiques spirituels" and "airs mondains" for treble and bass voices; parts on facing pages
Imperfect: frontispiece lacking (see Brunet IV, col. 617)
RISM B I, no. 1632³
MUSIC LIBRARY

1154

La Philomele | Seraphiqve | Partie Seconde: | Où elle chante en forme de Meditation | La Christiade | Specialement les Mysteres de la | Passion. | La Mariade | Auec les Mysteres du Rosaire. | Et | Les Cantiques de plusieurs | Saincts. | A Tovrnay, | De l'Imprimerie d'Adrien Qvinqve. | M.D.C.XXXII. | Auec grace & Priuilege.

8° 386, [14] p.
"Cantiques spirituels" and "airs mondains" for treble and bass voices; parts on facing pages
RISM B I, no. 1632⁴
MUSIC LIBRARY

A Philosophical Essay of Musick *See* Guilford, Francis North, 1st baron *A Philosophical Essay of Musick*

Phly, Jacques du *See* Du Phly, Jacques

1155 Piccinni, Niccolò

Atys | Tragédie Lyrique | en Trois Actes | Représentée pour la première fois par l'Académie | Royale de Musique, le Mardi 22 Février 1780. | Paroles de Quinault | Musique de M. Piccinni. | Gravé et Corrigé par Huguet Musicien de la Comédie Italienne | en 1781. | . . . | A Paris | Chez {le Suisse de l'Hotel de Noailles rue Saint Honoré. | De la Chevardiere, rue du Roule. | A Lyon chez Castaud. | Et aux adresses ordinaires. | Avec Privilége Du Roi. | Imprimé par Basset [1781?]

2° *Score:* 1 ℓ., 332 p.
RISM A I, no. P 2051
HOUGHTON

1156 Piccinni, Niccolò

La | Buona Figliuola | A | Comic Opera | Composed by Nicolo Piccini. | Adapted for the | German Flute Or Violin | by R: Bremner. | . . . | London. | Sold at his Music Shop Opposite | Somerset House in the | Strand. [17—]

obl. 8° 1 ℓ., 27 p.
Page 1: A Catalogue of Music for German Flutes & Violins
RISM A I, no. P 2069
MUSIC LIBRARY

1157 Piccinni, Niccolò

La Buona | Figliuola | Opera Boufon En III. Actes | Traduit de l'Italien | Dédiée | A Monseigneur le Maréchal | Duc De Richelieu | Musique De M. Piccini | Arrangée par | M. Baccelli | Représenté pour la prèmiere fois par les Comédiens Ital. | ordinaires du Roi le 10. Juin 1771. | . . . | Gravée par le Sr. Huguet musicien de la Comedie Italienne. | A Paris Ches M. Houbaut md. de musique près la Comedie Ital. | Et aux Adresses ordinaires.| de l'Imprimerie de Bernard rue S[—] [ca. 1771]

2° Score and 2 pts.: *score:* 1 ℓ., 150 p.; *oboe:* 8 p.; *corni:* 7 p.
Printer's address illegible
RISM A I, no. P 2066
MUSIC LIBRARY

1158 Piccinni, Niccolò

Diane | et | Endimion | Opéra en trois Actes | Représenté pour la Premiere fois, par l'Academie-Royale | de Musique, le Mardi 7 Septembre 1784. | Mis en Musique | Par | M. Piccini. | . . . | Gravé par Huguet Musicien de la Comédie Italienne | à l'Hôtel de Noailles chez le Suisses | A Paris, Chez l'Auteur, Place Vendome No. 17, | et aux Adresses Ordinaires de Musique. | [ca. 1784]

2° *Score:* [1], 230 p.
Hirsch II, no. 732; RISM A I, no. P 2097
HOUGHTON

1159 Piccinni, Niccolò

Didon | Tragédie Lyrique | en trois Actes | Representée à Fontainebleau devant leurs Majestés | le 16. Octobre 1783. | Et pour la premiere fois sur le Théatre de l'Académie Royale de Musique | Le Lundy 1er. Décembre de la même Année. | Dediée | A La Reine | Mise en Musique | Par M. Piccini | . . . | Gravée par Huguet Musicien de la Comédie Italienne. | A Paris Rue St. Honoré, Chez le Suisse de l'Hotel de Noailles. | Et aux adresses ordinaires de Musique | A Lyon chez Castaud place de la Comédie. | A. P. D. R. | Imprimé par Basset | [ca. 1783]

2° *Score:* 2 ℓ., 307 p.
Cancel label at foot of title-page reads: A Paris chez Leduc, rue Traversiere Saint-Honoré, au Magazin de Musique . . .
RISM A I, no. P 2101
MUSIC LIBRARY

—another copy
Without cancel label
On leaf 2ᵛ: Catalogue | De la Musique de M. Piccinni. | . . . | A Paris. | Chez le Suisse de l'Hotel de Noaille Rue St. Honore No. 151. | . . .
MUSIC LIBRARY

1160   PICCINNI, NICCOLÒ

Iphigénie | En Tauride | Tragédie Lirique | en quatre Actes | Representée pour la 1ere. fois par l'Académie Royale | de Musique le mardi 23. Janv. 1781. | Mise en Musique | Par M. Piccini | . . . | A Paris | Chez Des Lauriers Md. de Papier rue St. Honoré à côté | de celle des Prouvaires. [1781?]

2° *Score:* 1 *ℓ.*, 264 p.
RISM A I, no. P 2152? (without Leduc label or plate no.)
MUSIC LIBRARY

1161   PICCINNI, NICCOLÒ

Roland | Opera | En Trois Actes | Représenté pour la premiere fois par l'Académie royale | de Musique le mardi 27 Janvier 1778. | Mis en Musique | Et Dédié | A | La Reine | Par | M. Piccini | . . . | Gravé par J. Dezauche. | A Paris | Ches {l'Auteur rue St. Honoré vis à vis l'Hotel de Noailles chés le notaire. | M. De la Chevardiere rue du Roule à la Croix d'Or. | M. d'Enouville receveur de la Lotterie rue de Vannes à la nouvelle Halle. | Et aux Adresses ordinaires. | Avec Privilège du Roi. Imprimé par Basset [ca. 1778]

2° *Score:* 2 *ℓ.*, 466 p.
Hirsch II, no. 739; RISM A I, no. P 2162
MUSIC LIBRARY

1162   PICERLI, SILVERIO

Specchio Secondo | Di Mvsica, | Nel Qvale Si Vede Chiaro Il Vero, | E Facil Modo Di Comporre Di Canto | Figurato, e Fermo, di fare con nuoue Regole ogni sorte | di Contrapnnti [*sic*], e Canoni, di fomar li Toni di tutt'i | generi di Musica reale, e finta, con le loro caden-|ze à proprij luoghi, e di porre in prattica quan-|to si vuole, e può desiderare di detti Canto | figurato, e fermo. | Composto | Dal M. R. P. F. Silverio Picerli Rietino | Theologo dell'Ordine di Minori Osseruanti Riformati. | In Napoli. | Appresso Matteo Nucci. M.DC.XXXI. Con licenza de' Superiori.

4° 3 *ℓ.*, 196 [i. e. 192] p., 4 *ℓ.*, illus., music

Numbers 177, 180, 186, 187 omitted in paging
RISM B VI, 652; Wolfenbüttel, no. 1251
HOUGHTON

PICKEL, CONRAD   *See* Celtes, Conradus

1163   PIELTAIN, DIEUDONNÉ PASCAL

Six | Quartettos | for | Two Violins, a Tenor | and | Violoncello. | Composed by | D. Pieltain. | Op. 2d. . . . | London. | Printed for Willm. Napier, Music Seller to their Majesties, | No. 474. Strand. [178–?]

2° 2 pts.: *violino primo, violino secondo:* 1 *ℓ.*, 15 p. each; *viola:* 13 p.; *violoncello:* 15 p.
RISM A I, no. P 2324
MUSIC LIBRARY

PIERLUIGI, GIOVANNI, DA PALESTRINA
See Palestrina, Giovanni Pierluigi da

PIGNOLET DE MONTÉCLAIR, MICHEL   *See* Montéclair, Michel Pinolet de

1164   PIIS, AUGUSTIN

Chansons | Nouvelles | De M. De Piis, Écuyer, | Secrétaire-Interprète de Mgr Comte D'Artois; | Dédiées | A Monseigneur Comte D'Artois, | Et ornées de douze jolies Estampes gravées par | M. Gaucher, d'après les Dessins de | M. Le Barbier. | . . . | A Paris, | Chez Defer De Maisonneuve, | Libraire, rue du Foin St.-Jacques. [1785?]

16° 2 *ℓ.*, 4, 48, [4], 21 p., 12 pl.
RISM B II, 128
HOUGHTON

PILEUR D'APLIGNY, LE   *See* Le Pileur D'Apligny

PINOLET DE MONTÉCLAIR, MICHEL   *See* Montéclair, Michel Pinolet de

1165   PINZGER, ROMANUS

Laus Dei | Jucunda | Et | Sonora, | Sex Breviorum So-|lemnium Tamen Missarum | Modulatione Expressa. | Cum Vocibus Ordinariis | Canto, Alto, Tenore, Basso, | II. Violinis Et Organo Obligatis, | Clarinis Vero Et Tympano Ad | Libitum, | Et Iteratis Laboribus | Publicae lucis facta | A | R. P. Romano Pinzger, Ord. S. P. | Bened. in celeberrimo & antiquissimo Monasterio | Seonensi ad S. Lambertum in Bavaria Superiore Professo. | Opus II. | . . . | Cum Facultate Superiorum. | Augustae Vindelicorum. | Sumptibus Matthaei Rieger, Bibliopolae. 1750.

2° 1 pt.: *organo:* 3 ℓ., 38 p.
RISM A I, no. P 2409
HOUGHTON

PIPEGROP, HEINRICH *See* Baryphonus, Heinrich

1166   PIRLINGER, JOSEPH

Six | Quatuors | Concertants | Pour Deux Violons Alto Et Basse | Composés | Par | Mr Pirlinger | . . . | A. Paris | Chez Imbault Rue et vis-à-vis le Clôitre St honoré Maison du Chandellier | A. P. D. R. [1786?]

2° 4 pts.: *violino primo:* 1 ℓ., 21 p.; *violino secondo:* 14 p.; *alto, basso:* 13 p. each
RISM A I, no. P 2436
MUSIC LIBRARY

1167   PLANELLI, ANTONIO

Dell' | Opera | In Musica | Trattato | Del Cavaliere | Antonio Planelli | Dell'Ordine | Gerosolimitano. | Napoli | Nella Stamperia Di Donato Campo. | MDCCLXXII. | Con Licenza de' Superiori.

8° 15, [4], 272 p.
RISM B VI, 657
MUSIC LIBRARY

PLAYFORD, HENRY, PUBL. The Banquet of Musick *See* The Banquet of Musick

PLAYFORD, HENRY, PUBL. A Choice Collection of New Songs and Ballads *See* A Choice Collection of New Songs and Ballads

PLAYFORD, HENRY, PUBL. Harmonia sacra *See* Harmonia sacra

PLAYFORD, HENRY, PUBL. The Theater of Music *See* The Theater of Music

PLAYFORD, HENRY, PUBL. Two Divine Hymns *See* Two Divine Hymns

1168   [PLAYFORD, JOHN]

A | Breefe | Introduction | to the Skill | of | Musick | for | Song & Violl | by | J P | London Printed | 1654 | Sould by | Jo: Playford | at his shop | in the Inner | Temple

8° 2 ℓ., 34 p., 1 ℓ., illus., music
Page 34: Musick Books lately Printed for John Playford . . .
RISM B VI, 657
HOUGHTON

1169   [PLAYFORD, JOHN]

An | Introduction | To the Skill of | Mvsick. | In two Books. | First, a brief & plain Introduction to Musick, | both for singing, and for playing on the Violl. | By J. P. | Second, The Art of Setting or Composing of | Musick in Parts, by a most familiar and easie | Rule of Counterpoint. Formerly published | by Dr Tho. Campion: but now re-|printed with large Annotations, By | Mr. Christoph. Sympson, | and other Additions. | London, Printed for John Playford, & are sold at his | shop in the Inner Temple, 1655.

8° 5 ℓ., 56 p., 1 ℓ., [14], 48 p., front. (port.), illus., music
Page 56, first sequence: Music BOOKS lately Printed for John Playford . . .
Day, no. 7; RISM B VI, 657
HOUGHTON

1170   PLAYFORD, JOHN

A Breif | Introduction | To the Skill of | Musick: | For | Song and Viol. | In two Books. | First Book contains the Grounds

1168 PLAYFORD, *A Breefe Introduction to the Skill of Musick*, London, 1654: title-page (132 × 71 mm.)

AN INTRODUCTION

To the Skill of *MUSICK.*

In two Books.

First, a brief & plain *Introduction* to *Musick,* both for *singing,* and for *playing on the Viol.* By *J. P.*

Second, The Art of *Setting* or *Composing* of *Musick* in *Parts,* by a most familiar and easie Rule of *Counterpoint.* Formerly published by Dr THO. CAMPION : but now reprinted with large Annotations . By Mr. CHRISTOPH. SYMPSON, and other Additions.

London, Printed for *John Playford,* & are fold at his fhop in the Inner Temple. 1655.

1169 PLAYFORD, *An Introduction to the Skill of Musick*, London, 1655: title-page (143 × 82 mm.)

1481 TARTINI, *Sonata a violino solo col basso*, Paris, 1748: page 15 (269 × 197 mm.)

and Rules of | Musick for Song. | Second Book, Directions for the Playing on the | Viol de Gambo, [*sic*] and also on the Treble-Violin. | By J. Playford, Philo-Musico. | London, Printed by W. Godbid, for John Playford, | at his Shop in the Inner-Temple, neer the | Church dore. M.DC.LVIII.

8° 4 ℓ., 76 [i. e. 80] p., illus., music
Page 80 misnumbered 76
RISM B VI, 657
HOUGHTON

1171   [PLAYFORD, JOHN]

A Brief | Introduction | To the Skill of | Musick. | In two Books. | The first contains the Ground and | Rules of Mvsick. | The second, Instructions for the Viol, | and also for the Treble-Violin. | The Third Edition Enlarged. | To which is added a Third Book, entituled, The Art of Descant, | or Composing Musick in Parts, By Dr. Tho. Campion. | With Annotations thereon by Mr. Chr. Simpson. | London, Printed by W. Godbid for John Playford, | at his Shop in the Inner Temple, 1660.

8° 4 ℓ., 136 p., front. (port.). illus., music
Day, no. 15; RISM B VI, 657
HOUGHTON

1172   PLAYFORD, JOHN

A Brief | Introduction | To the Skill of | Musick. | In two Books. | The First contains the Grounds and | Rules of Mvsick. | The Second, Instructions for the Viol | and also for the Treble-Violin. | By John Playford, Philo-Musicae. | To which is added a Third Book, entituled, The Art of Setting, | or Composing Musick in Parts, By Dr. Tho. Campion. | Wi[t]h Annotations thereon by Mr. Chr. Simpson. | London, Printed for J. Playford and are sold at his | Shop in the Temple in Fleetstreet. 1662.

8° 4 ℓ., 136 p., front. (port.), illus., music
Book 3 has separate title-page with imprint date 1661
Day, no. 17; RISM B VI, 658
HOUGHTON

1173   [PLAYFORD, JOHN]

A Brief | Introduction | To the Skill of | Musick. | In two Books. | The First containes the General | Grounds and Rules of Mvsick. | The Second, Instructions for the Viol | and also for the Treble-Violin. | To which is added The Art of Descant, or Composing | Musick in Parts, By Dr. Thomas Campion. | With Annotations thereon by Mr. Chr. Simpson. | The Fourth Edition much Enlarged. | London, Printed by William Godbid for John Playford, and are | to be sold by Zach. Watkins, at their Shop in the Temple | near the Church-Dore. 1664.

8° 9 ℓ., 109, [5], 45, [1] p., front. (port.), illus., music
Pages 45[–46] at end: A catalogue of Musick Books lately | Printed and to be sold by J. Playford and Z. Watkins . . .
Day, no. 21, first entry; RISM B VI, 658
HOUGHTON

—another copy
Edition statement omitted from title-page
Day, no. 21, second entry
HOUGHTON

1174   PLAYFORD, JOHN

A Brief | Introduction | To The Skill Of | Musick: | In Three Books. | The First: | The Grounds and Rules of Mvsick, | according to the Gam-ut and other | Principles thereof. | The Second: | Instructions for the Bass-Viol, and also | for the Treble-Violin: | VVith | Lessons for Beginners. | By John Playford Philo-Musicae. | The Third: | The Art of Descant, or Composing Musick | in Parts. By Dr. Tho. Campion. | With Annotations thereon by Mr. C. Simpson. | London, Printed by William Godbid for John Playford, | and are to be sold at his Shop in the Temple. 1666.

8° 9 ℓ., 151, [1] p., front. (port.), illus., music
Book 3 has separate title-page with imprint date 1667
Unnumbered page at end: A Catalogue of Musick Books lately | Printed and to be sold by J. Playford at his | Shop in the Temple.

Day, no. 22; RISM B VI, 658

HOUGHTON

1175 PLAYFORD, JOHN

A Brief | Introduction | To The Skill Of | Musick: | In Three Books. | The First: | The Grounds and Rules of Mvsick, | according to the Gam-ut and other | Principles thereof. | The Second: | Instructions for the Bass-Viol, and also | for the Treble-Violin: | VVith | Lessons for Beginners. | By John Playford Philo-Musicae. | The Third: | The Art of Descant, or Composing Musick | in Parts. By Dr. Tho. Campion. | With Annotations thereon by Mr. C. Simpson. | London, Printed by William Godbid for John Playford, | and are to be sold at his Shop in the Temple. 1667.

8° 9 ℓ., 151, [1] p., front. (port.), illus., music

Unnumbered page at end: A Catalogue of Musick Books lately | Printed and to be sold by J. Playford at his | Shop in the Temple.

Day, no. 25; RISM B VI, 658

HOUGHTON

1176 PLAYFORD, JOHN

A Brief | Introduction | To The Skill Of | Musick: | In Three Books. | The First: | The Grounds and Rules of Mvsick, | according to the Gam-vt and other | Principles thereof. | The Second: | Instructions for the Bass-Viol, and also | for the Treble-Violin: | With | Lessons for Beginners. | By John Playford, Philo-Musicae. | The Third: | The Art of Descant, or Composing Musick | in Parts. By Dr. Tho. Campion. | With Annotations thereon, by Mr. Chr. Simpson. | London, Printed by William Godbid for John Playford, | and are to be Sold at his Shop in the Temple. 1670.

8° 9 ℓ., 134 p. front. (port.), illus., music

Book 3 has separate title-page with imprint date 1669

Day, no. 32; RISM B VI, 658

HOUGHTON

1177 PLAYFORD, JOHN

An | Introduction | To The Skill Of | Musick. | In Two Books. | The First: | The Grounds and Rules of Mvsick, | according to the Gam-vt, and other | Principles thereof. | The Second: | Instructions & Lessons for the Bass-Viol: | And | Instructions & Lessons for the Treble-Violin. | By John Playford. | To which is added, | The Art of Descant, | or Composing Mvsick in Parts. | By Dr. Tho. Campion. | With Annotations thereon, by Mr. Chr. Simpson. | The Sixt [*sic*] Edition Corrected and Enlarged. | London, Printed by W. Godbid for J. Playford at his | Shop in the Temple near the Church. 1672.

8° 7 ℓ., 117 [i. e. 113], [1] p., [1] ℓ., 41 [i. e. 43], [1] p. front. (port.), illus., music

The Art of Descant has separate title-page with imprint date 1671

Numbers 112–115, first sequence, omitted in paging; numbers 10, 11, second sequence, repeated in paging

Imperfect: some pages torn, with loss of text

Unnumbered page at end: Musical Books Printed for and Sold by J. Playford.

Day, no. 33; RISM B VI, 658

HOUGHTON

PLAYFORD, JOHN

An | Introduction | To The Skill Of | Musick. | In Two Books. | The First: | The Grounds and Rules of Mvsick, | according to the Gam-vt, and other | Principles thereof. | The Second: | Instructions & Lessons for the Bass-Viol: | And | Instruments [*sic*] & Lessons for the Treble-Violin. | By John Playford. | To which is added, | The Art of Descant, | or Composing Musick in Parts. | By Dr. Tho. Campion. | With Annotations thereon, by Mr. Chr. Simpson. | The Seventh Edition, Corrected and Enlarged. | London, Printed by W. Godbid, for J. Playford at his | Shop in the Temple near the Church. 1674.

8° 7 ℓ., 121, [3], 42, 10 p., front. (port.), illus., music

Pages 1–10 at end: The Order of Performing The Divine Service

Day, no. 38; RISM B VI, 658

HOUGHTON

1179 PLAYFORD, JOHN

An | Introduction | To The | Skill of Musick, | In Two Books. | The First Contains | The Grounds and Rules of Music, according | to the Gam-ut, and other Principles thereof. | The Second, | Instructions and Lessons | both for the Basse-Viol and Treble-Violin. | By John Playford. | To which is added, | The Art of Descant, or Composing | of Musick in Parts, by Dr. Tho. Campion; with | Annotations thereon by Mr. Chr. Simpson. | Also | The Order of Singing Divine Service in Cathedrals. | The Eighth Edition carefully Corrected. | London, Printed by A. G. [i. e. Anne Godbid] and J. P. [i. e. John Playford the younger] for John Playford, | at his Shop in the Temple near the Church. 1679.

8° 7 *ℓ.*, 119, [3], 34, 7, [1] p., front. (port.), illus., music
Pages 1–7 at end: The Order of Performing The Divine Service
Day, no. 49; RISM B VI, 658
HOUGHTON

1180 PLAYFORD, JOHN

An | Introduction | To The | Skill of Musick, | In Three Books. | The First Contains | The Grounds and Rules of Musick, | according to the Gam-ut, and other | Principles thereof. | The Second, | Instrvctions and Lessons | both for the Bass-Viol and Treble-Violin. | The Third, | The Art of Descant, or Composing of | Musick in Parts, in a more Plain and Easie | Method than any heretofore Published. | The Tenth Edition, Corrected and Enlarged. | By John Playford. | London, Printed by A. G. [i. e. Anne Godbid] and J. P. [i. e. John Playford the younger] for John Playford, | at his Shop in the Temple near the Church. 1683.

8° 7 *ℓ.*, 116, [2], 47, [3] p., front. (port.), illus., music
Day, no. 63; RISM B VI, 658
HOUGHTON

1181 PLAYFORD, JOHN

An | Introduction | To The | Skill of Musick, | In Three Books. | The First

Contains | The Grounds and Rules of Musick, | according to the Gam-ut, and other | Principles thereof. | The Second, | Instrvctions and Lessons both | for the Bass-Viol and Treble-Violin. | The Third, | The Art of Descant, or Composing | of Musick in Parts, in a more Plain and Easie | Method than any heretofore Published. | By John Playford. | The Eleventh Edition, Corrected and Enlarged. | London, Printed by Charles Peregrine, for Henry | Playford, at his Shop near the Temple Church, 1687.

8° 9 *ℓ.*, 116, [2], 51, [3] p., front. (port.), illus., music
Three unnumbered pages at end: Music Books sold by Henry Playford, | . .
Day, no. 91; RISM B VI, 658
MUSIC LIBRARY

1182 PLAYFORD, JOHN

An | Introduction | To The | Skill of Musick, | In Three Books. | The First Contains | The Grounds and Rules of Musick, | according to the Gam-ut, and other | Principles thereof. | The Second, | Instructions and Lessons both | for the Bass-Viol and Treble-Violin. | The Third, | The Art of Descant, or Composing | Musick in Parts: In a more Plain and Easie | Method than any heretofore Published. | By John Playford. | The Twelfth Edition. | Corrected and Amended by Mr. Henry Purcell. | [London] In the Savoy, Printed by E. Jones, for Henry | Playford at his Shop near the Temple Church. 1694.

8° 9 *ℓ.*, 144 p., front. (port.), illus., music
RISM B VI, 659
HOUGHTON

1183 PLAYFORD, JOHN

An | Introduction | To The | Skill of Musick: | In Three Books. | By John Playford. | Containing, | I. The Grounds and Principles of Musick | according to the Gamut; being newly Written, | and made more Easie for Young Practitioners, | according to the Method now in Practice, | by an Eminent Master in that Science. | II. Instructions and Lessons for the Treble, Tenor, | and Bass-Viols; and also for the Treble-Violin. | III. The Art of Descant, or Composing Musick | in Parts; made very Plain and Easie by the | late Mr. Henry Purcell. | The Thirteenth Edition. | [London] In the Savoy, Printed by E. Jones, for Henry Playford, | and sold by him at his Shop in the Temple Change, over-|against St. Dunstan's Church in Fleet-Street; 1697.

8° 2 ℓ., ix, [1], 134, [2] p., front. (port.), illus., music
RISM B VI, 659
HOUGHTON

1184   PLAYFORD, JOHN

An | Introduction | To The | Skill of Musick: | In Three Books: | By John Playford. | Containing | I. The Grounds and Principles of Musick, | according to the Gamut: In the most Ea-|sie Method, for Young Practitioners. | II. Instructions and Lessons for the Treble, | Tenor and Bass-Viols; and also for the | Treble-Violin. | III. The Art of Descant, or Composing Musick | in Parts: Made very Plain and Easie by the | late Mr. Henry Purcell. | The Fourteenth Edition. | Corrected and Enlarged. | London: printed by William Pearson, at the Hare and Feathers in Aldersgate-street, for Henry Playford, at his | Shop in the Temple-Change, Fleet-street. 1700.

8° 9 ℓ., 180 [i. e. 170], [2] p., front. (port.), illus., music
Numbers 81–90 omitted in paging
Pages [1]–[2] at end: Musick-Books, and Others, lately Printed and Re-|printed with large Additions, for H. Playford . . .
Day, no. 185; RISM B VI, 659
HOUGHTON

1185   PLAYFORD, JOHN

An | Introduction | To The | Skill of Musick: | In Three Books: | By John Playford. | Containing | I. The Grounds and Principles of Musick, | according to the Gamut: In the most Ea-|sie Method, for Young Practitioners. | II. Instructions and Lessons for the Treble, | Tenor and Bass-Viols; and also for the | Treble-Violin. |

III. The Art of Descant, or Composing Musick | in Parts: Made very Plain and Easie by the | late Mr. Henry Purcell. | The Fifteenth Edition. | Corrected, and done on the New Ty'd-Note. | London: | Printed by W. Pearson, for Henry Playford, at his Shop in | the Temple-Change, Fleet-street; and John Sprint at the | Bell in Little-Britain. 1703.

8° 9 ℓ., 180 [i. e. 170] p., front. (port.), illus., music
Numbers 81–90 omitted in paging
Day, no. 206; Hirsch I, no. 463; RISM B VI, 659
HOUGHTON

1186   PLAYFORD, JOHN

An | Introduction | To The | Skill of Musick: | In Three Books: | By John Playford. | Containing | I. The Grounds and Principles of Musick, | according to the Gamut: In the most Easie | Method, for Young Practitioners. | II. Instructions and Lessons for the Treble, | Tenor, and Bass-Viols; and also for the Treble | Violin. | III. The Art of Descant, or Composing Musick | in Parts: Made very Plain and Easie by the | late Mr. Henry Purcell. | The Sixteenth Edition. | Corrected, and done on the New Ty'd-Note. | London: Printed by William Pearson, for John Sprint | at the Bell in Little-Britain. 1713.

8° 9 ℓ., 170 p., front. (port.), illus., music
Day, no. 226; RISM B VI, 659
HOUGHTON

1187   PLAYFORD, JOHN

An | Introduction | To The | Skill of Musick: | In Three Books: | By John Playford. | Containing | I. The Grounds and Principles of Musick, | according to the Gamut: In the most Easie | Method, for Young Practitioners. | II. Instructions and Lessons for the Treble, | Tenor, and Bass-Viols; and also for the Treble-|Violin. | III. The Art of Descant, or Composing Musick | in Parts: Made very Plain and Easie by the | late Mr. Henry Purcell. | The Seventeenth Edition. | Corrected, and done on the New-Ty'd Note. | London: Printed by William Pearson, for

John and | Ben. Sprint at the Bell in Lit-tle-Britain. 1718.

8° 9 ℓ., 170 p., 1 ℓ., front. (port.), illus., music
Day, no. 230; RISM B VI, 659
HOUGHTON

1188   PLAYFORD, JOHN

An | Introduction | To The | Skill of Musick: | In Three Books: | By John Play-ford. | Containing | I. The Grounds and Principles of Musick, | according to the Gamut: In the most Easy | Method, for Young Practitioners. [*sic*] | II. Instructions and Lessons for the Treble, | Tenor, and Bass-Viols; and also for the Treble-|Vio-lin. | III. The Art of Descant, or Compos-ing Musick | in Parts: Made very Plain and Easy by the | late Mr. Henry Purcell. | The Eighteenth Edition. | Corrected, and done on the New-Ty'd Note. | London: Printed by William Pearson, for John and | Benj. Sprint at the Bell in Little-Britain. 1724.

8° 9 ℓ., 170, [2] p., front. (port.), illus., music
Book 3 has separate title-page with im-print date 1723
Day, no. 247; RISM B VI, 659
HOUGHTON

1189   PLAYFORD, JOHN

An | Introduction | To The | Skill of Musick: | In Three Books: | By John Play-ford. | Containing | I. The Grounds and Principles of Musick, | according to the Gamut: In the most Easy | Method, for Young Practitioners. | II. Instructions and Lessons for the Treble | Tenor, and Bass-Viols; and also for the Tre-|ble-Violin. | III. The Art of Descant, or Composing Musick | in Parts: Made very Plain and Easy by | the late Mr. Henry Purcell. | The Nineteenth Edition. | Corrected, and done on the New-Ty'd Note. | London: Printed by William Pearson, for Benja-min | Sprint at the Bell in Little-Britain. MDCCXXX.

8° 9 ℓ., 170, [2] p., front. (port.), illus., music

Two unnumbered pages at end: Books Printed for, and Sold by Ben-|jamin Sprint.
Day, no. 252; RISM B VI, 659
MUSIC LIBRARY

PLAYFORD, JOHN, PUBL. Cantica sacra
See Cantica sacra

PLAYFORD, JOHN, PUBL. Catch That Catch Can   *See* Catch That Catch Can

PLAYFORD, JOHN, PUBL. Choice Ayres, Songs, & Dialogues *See* Choice Ayres, Songs, & Dialogues

PLAYFORD, JOHN, PUBL. Court-Ayres *See* Court-Ayres

PLAYFORD, JOHN The Dancing Master *See* The Dancing Master

1190   PLAYFORD, JOHN, COMP.

[The] | Musical Companion, | In Two Books. | The First Book containing Catches and Rovnds for Three Voyces. | The Second Book containing Dialogves, Glees, Ayres and | Songs for Two, Three and Four Voyces. | Collected and Pub-lished by John Playford Practitioner in Mvsick. | London, Printed by W. Godbid for John Playford, at his Shop in the Tem-ple near the Church, 1673.

obl. 4° 4 ℓ., 223 [i. e. 227], [1], 8 p.
Predominantly in *Tafelmusik* format
Part 2 has separate title-page with im-print date 1672
Four additional pages numbered 113–116 inserted after page 112
Pages 1–8 at end: An Additional Sheet to the Book entituled, The Musical Com-panion.
Unnumbered page after page [227]: Mvsick-Books Printed and are to be Sold by John Playford.
Title-page cropped, with loss of text
Day, no. 36, fourth entry; RISM B I, no. 1673[4]
HOUGHTON

1191   PLAYFORD, JOHN, COMP.

Musick's Delight | On The | Cithren, | Restored and Refined to a more Easie and Pleasant | Manner of Playing than formerly; And set forth with | Lessons Al a [*sic*] Mode, being the Choicest of our late new Ayres, | Corants, Sarabands, Tunes, and Jiggs. | To which is added several New Songs and Ayres to Sing to the Cithren. | By John Playford Philo-Musicae. | London, Printed by W. G. [i. e. William Godbid] and are sold by J. Playford at his Shop in the Temple. 1666.

> obl. 8° [A]⁸, B–G⁸, front., illus., music
> Leaves B1ʳ–G8ʳ: cittern tablature
> Frontispiece included in signatures
> Leaf G8ᵛ: Musick Books sold by John Playford . . .
> Day, no. 24; RISM B I, no 1666⁴
> HOUGHTON

PLAYFORD, JOHN, PUBL. Musicks Hand-Maid *See* Musicks Hand-Maid

PLAYFORD, JOHN, PUBL. The Pleasant Musical Companion *See* The Pleasant Musical Companion

1192   PLAYFORD, JOHN

Psalms & Hymns | In Solemn Musick | Of Fovre Parts | On the Common Tunes to the Psalms in Metre: | Used in Parish-Chvrches. | Also Six Hymns for One Voyce to the Organ. | . . . | By John Playford. | London, Printed by W. Godbid for J. Playford, at his Shop in the Inner-Temple. 1671.

> 2° 6 ℓ., 97 [i. e. 93], [3] p.
> Numbers 13–16 omitted in paging
> HOUGHTON

1193

The Second Book of the | Pleasant Musical Companion: | Being | A New Collection of Select Catches, Songs, and | Glees, for Two and Three Voices. | The Second Edition, Corrected and much Enlarged. | London, Printed for John Playford near the Temple Church, or at his

House | over against the Blue-Ball in Arundel-Street, 1686.

> obl. 4° [A] 1–3, B–M⁴
> Imperfect: gathering K lacking
> Day, no. 85; RISM B I, no. 1686⁴
> HOUGHTON

1194   PLEYEL, IGNAZ JOSEPH

A | Select Collection | Of | Favourite | Airs And Rondos | For The | Piano Forte. | Composed by | I. Pleyel. | London: | Printed for Harrison & Co. No: 18, Paternoster Row. [1797]

> 8° Score: 17 p. (*The Piano-Forte Magazine*, vol. I, no. 6)
> Benton, no. (6538); RISM A I, no. P 4880
> MUSIC LIBRARY

1195   PLEYEL, IGNAZ JOSEPH

Pleyel's | celebrated | Concertante | as Performed with the greatest applause | at the Pantheon and Hanover Square | Concerts | adapted for the | Piano-Forte or Harpsichord, | with an Accompaniment for a | Violin and Violoncello | By | J: B: Cramer. | . . . | London | Printed by Longman & Broderip No 26 Cheapside & no 13 Hay Market | Music Sellers and musical Instrument makers to His Royal Highness the Prince of Wales | . . . [1790?]

> 2° Score: 1 ℓ., 24 p.
> Benton, no. (1224); RISM A I, no. P 3833
> B. 111
> MUSIC LIBRARY

1196   PLEYEL, IGNAZ JOSEPH

A | Celebrated | Concertante | For The | Piano Forte. | Composed By | I. Pleyel. | London. | Printed for Harrison & Co. No. 18. Paternoster Row. [1797?]

> 8° Score: 1 ℓ., 12 p. (*The Piano-Forte Magazine*, vol. II, no. 1)
> Benton, no. (1264); RISM A I, no. P 4833
> B. 111
> MUSIC LIBRARY

1197 PLEYEL, IGNAZ JOSEPH

XII. Nouveaux | Quatuors | dédiés | A Sa Majesté | Le Roi De Prusse | composés par | Ignace Pleyel | [1e.] Livraison. | . . . | A Paris. | Chez Imbault Md. de Musique au Mont d'or, rue St. honore, entre | l'hotel d'Aligre et la rue des Poulies, No. 627. | Et à Strasbourg, chez Mr. J. Reinhard Storck Md. de Musique | et d'Instrumens, près le Pont du Corbeau. [between 1787 and 1794]

2° 4 pts.: *violino primo:* 1 ℓ., 13 p.; *violino secondo, alto, basso:* 10 p. each
Plate no. 85
Page [1] in *violino primo* part: Catalogue | de Musique vocale & instrumentale | Mise au jour par Imbault . . . ⟨A later state of JohanssonF facs. 36⟩
Benton, no. (3245); RISM A I, no. P 3200
B. 331–333
MUSIC LIBRARY

1198 PLEYEL, IGNAZ JOSEPH

Douze Nouveaux | Quatuors | dédiés | A Sa Majesté | Le Roi De Prusse | Composés par | Ignace Pleyel. | [2e.] Livraison | . . . | A Paris, | Chez Imbault. Md. de Musique au Mont d'or rue St. Honoré, entre | l'hôtel d'Aligre et la rue des Poulies. No. 627. [ca. 1790]

2° 4 pts.: *violino primo:* 1 ℓ., 13 p.; *violino secondo:* 13 p.; *alto, basso:* 11 p. each
Plate no. 88
Page [1] in *violino primo* part: Catalogue | de Musique vocale & instrumentale | Mise au jour par Imbault . . . ⟨A later state of JohanssonF facs. 36⟩
Benton, no. (3250); RISM A I, no. P 3227
B. 334–336
MUSIC LIBRARY

1199 PLEYEL, IGNAZ JOSEPH

Douze Nouveaux | Quatuors | dédiés | A Sa Majesté | Le Roi De Prusse | Composés par | Ignace Pleyel. | [3e.] Livraison | . . . | A Paris, | Chez Imbault, Md. de Musique au Mont d'or rue St. Honoré, entre | l'hôtel d'Aligre et la rue des Poulies. No. 627. [1787–1794]

2° 4 pts.: *violino primo:* 1 ℓ., 13 p.; *violino secondo, alto basso:* 12 p. each
Plate no. 91
Page [1] in *violino primo* part: Catalogue | de Musique vocale & instrumentale | Mise au jour par Imbault ⟨A later state of JohanssonF facs. 36⟩
Benton, no. (3257); RISM A I, no. P 3251
B. 337–339
MUSIC LIBRARY

1200 PLEYEL, IGNAZ JOSEPH

Douze Nouveaux | Quatuors | dédiés | A Sa Majesté | Le Roi De Prusse | Composés par | Ignace Pleyel. | [4e.] Livraison | . . . | A Paris, | Chez Imbault, Md. de Musique au Mont d'or rue St. Honoré, entre | l'hôtel d'Aligre et la rue des Poulies. No. 627. [1787]

2° 4 pts.: *violino primo:* 1 ℓ., 13 p.; *violino secondo, alto:* 12 p. each; *basso:* 10 p.
Plate no. 93
Page [1] in *violino primo* part: Catalogue | de Musique Vocale & Instrumentale mise au jour par Imbault . . . ⟨JohanssonF facs. 37⟩
Benton, no. (3262); RISM A I, no. P 3274
B. 340–342
MUSIC LIBRARY

1201 PLEYEL, IGNAZ JOSEPH

Six | Quatuors | Concertans | pour deux Violons | Alto et Basse. | Composés par | I: Pleyel. | oeuvre I | à | Mannheim Munich | et Dusseldorff | chez le Sr. Götz Marchand et Editeur de Musique. | . . . | A. P. [ca. 1788]

2° 4 pts.: *violino primo:* 1 ℓ., 24 p.; *violino secondo, viola:* 24 p. each; *basso:* 19 p.
Plate no. 186
Benton, no. (3402); RISM A I, no. P 3297
B. 346–351
MUSIC LIBRARY

1202 PLEYEL, IGNAZ JOSEPH

Trois | Quatuors | de | Mr. Jgnace Pleyel | arrangeae | Pour Clavecin ou Piano-

Forte | avec accompagnemens de Violon et Basse | par | Mr. Lachnitt. | [4th.] Suitte | . . . | London. | Printed by Longman Et Broderip. No. 26 Cheapside & No. 13, Haymarket. | Music-Sellers & Musical Instrument Makers to His Royal Highness the Prince of Wales. | . . . [1789]

2° 3 pts.: *clavecin ou piano-forte:* 1 ℓ., 37 p.; *violino:* 1 ℓ., 9 p.; *basso:* 1 ℓ., 7 p.
Benton, no. (4739); RISM A I, no. P 3920 (variant)
MUSIC LIBRARY

1203 PLEYEL, IGNAZ JOSEPH

Trois | Quatuors | de | Mr. Jgnace Pleyel | arrangeae | Pour Clavecin ou Piano-Forte | avec accompagnemens de Violon et Basse | par | Mr. Lachnitt. | [5th.] Suitte | . . . | London. | Printed by Longman Et Broderip No. 26 Cheapside & No. 13, Haymarket. | Music-Sellers & Musical Instrument Makers to His Royal Highness the Prince of Wales. | . . . [1789]

2° 3 pts.: *Clavecin ou piano-forte:* 1 ℓ., 25 p.; *violino:* 2 ℓ. (1 blank), 11 p.; *basso:* 1 ℓ., 7 p.
Benton, no. (4740); RISM A I, no. P 3871 (variant)
MUSIC LIBRARY

1204 PLEYEL, IGNAZ JOSEPH

Trois | Quintetti | Concertans | pour deux Violons deux Alto | et Violoncelle | Composés | par Jgnace Pleyel | Oeuvre [5] | [1r.] Livre de Quintetti. | . . . | A Paris | Chez Naderman, Rue de la Loi, à la Clef d'or, | Passage de l'ancien Caffé de foy. | Chez Made. Le Menu, Rue du Roulle, à la Clef d'or. | Ecrit par Ribiere. [1796?]

2° 5 pts.: *violino primo:* 1 ℓ., 13 p.; *violino secondo:* 13 p.; *viola prima, viola seconda, basso:* 11 p. each
Benton, no. (2505), with Boyer's name and address erased from the title-page and Naderman's superimposed; opus no. supplied from Benton
B. 271–273
MUSIC LIBRARY

1205 PLEYEL, IGNAZ JOSEPH

Trois | Quintetti | Concertans | Pour deux Violons deux Alto | et Violoncelle |

Composés | Par J. Pleyel | Oeuvre [5] | [2e] Livre de Quintetti. | . . . | A Paris | Chez JH. Naderman, Editeur, Luthier, Facteur de Harpe, et autres Instrumens, | Rue d'Argenteuil, Butte des Moulins, à Apollon, et | Successeur de Boyer, Md. de Musique, Rue de la Loi, à l'ancien Caffé de foy. | Ecrit par Ribiere [1796]

2° 5 pts.: *violino primo:* 1 ℓ., 13 p.; *violino secondo, viola prima, viola seconda:* 13 p. each; *basso:* 9 p.
Opus no. supplied from Benton
Benton, no. (2549); RISM A I, no. P 3051
B. 274–276
MUSIC LIBRARY

1206 PLEYEL, IGNAZ JOSEPH

Trois | Quintetti | Concertans | Pour deux Violons deux Alto | et Violoncelle | Composés | Par J. Pleyel | Oeuvre [?] | [3e.] Livre de Quintetti. | . . . | A Paris | Chez JH. Naderman, Editeur, Luthier Facteur de Harpe, et autres Instrumens, | Rue d'Argenteuil, Butte des Moulins, à Apollon, et | Successeur de Boyer, Md. de Musique, Rue de la Loi, à l'ancien Caffé de foy. | Ecrit par Ribiere | . . . [1796]

2° 5 pts.: *violino primo:* 1 ℓ., 13 p.; *violino secondo:* 13 p.; *viola prima:* 1 ℓ., 12 p.; *viola seconda, basso:* 12 p. each
Plate no. 506
No. 1061 on title-page
Stamp at foot of title-page: Chez Sauzeau Luthier Â Nantes
Benton, no. (2578); RISM A I, no. P 3069
B. 277–279
MUSIC LIBRARY

1207 PLEYEL, IGNAZ JOSEPH

Trois | Quintetti | Concertans | Pour deux Violons deux Alto | et Violoncelle | Composés | Par J. Pleyel | Oeuvre [?] | [4] Livre de Quintetti. | . . . | A Paris | Chez JH. Naderman, Editeur, Luthier Facteur de Harpe, et autres Instrumens, | Rue d'Argenteuil, Butte des Moulins, à Apollon, et | Successeur de Boyer, Md. de Musique, Rue de la Loi, à l'ancien Caffé de foy. | Ecrit par Ribiere | . . . [1796]

2° 5 pts.: *violino primo:* 1 *ℓ.,* 15 p.; *violino secondo:* 16 p.; *viola prima:* 13 p.; *viola seconda:* 12 p.; *violoncello:* 15 p.

No. 1061 on title-page

Stamp at foot of title-page: Chez Sauzeau Luthier Â Nantes

Benton, no. (2625); RISM A I, no. P 3091

B. 111, 215, 201A

MUSIC LIBRARY

1208 PLEYEL, IGNAZ JOSEPH

Sextuor | A | Deux Violons, deux Violes, | Violoncelle & Basse | Composé | Par | Mr. J. Pleyel | . . . | A Paris | Chez Jmbault Rue S. Honoré près l'Hôtel d'Aligre au Mont d'Or No. 627. [1793]

2° 1 pt.: *violoncello:* 1 *ℓ.,* 3 p.

Plate no. 333

Benton, no. (2204); RISM A I, no. P 3020

B. 261

HOUGHTON

1209 PLEYEL, IGNAZ JOSEPH

Sestetto | Concertants | A Deux Violons Deux Alto | Violoncelle et Basse | Composés Par | Jgna. Pleyel, | Oeuvre [?] | . . . | A. Paris, | Chez le Sr. Sieber, Musicien rue St honoré entre celle des Vielles | Etuve et celle D'orleans chez l'Apothicaire No. 92. [1791]

2° 6 pts.: *violino primo:* 1 *ℓ.,* 5 p.; *violino secondo:* 5 p.; *viola prima, viola seconda, violoncello, basso:* 3 p. each

Plate no. 1189

Benton, no. (2207); RISM A I, no. P 3023

B. 261

HOUGHTON

1210 PLEYEL, IGNAZ JOSEPH

Six Sonatas | For The | Piano Forte or Harpsichord; | With an Accompaniment for a | Flute or Violin, and Violoncello: | Composed, and Dedicated (by Permission) to | Her Majesty | The Queen of Great Britain; | By Ignace Pleyel. | London, Printed by Longman & Broderip, No. 26. Cheapside and No. 13 Hay-|-Market, Music Sellers & Musical Instrument

Makers to His Royal | Highness the Prince of Wales; . . . [1788?]

2° Score and 2 pts.: *score:* III, 2–101 p.; *flauto, violoncello:* 1 *ℓ.,* 25 p. each

Page III in *score:* Musical Publications | Printed and Sold by Longman & Broderip . . .

Benton, no. (4363); RISM A I, no. P 3602

B. 431–436

MUSIC LIBRARY

1211 PLEYEL, IGNAZ JOSEPH

Three | Sonatas, | for the | Piano-Forte or Harpsichord; | with Accompaniments | For A | Violin and Violoncello. | Composed, and | Humbly Dedicated | To | Madame de Marclésy | By | Jgnace Pleyel. | . . . | Op. XXI[II] . . . | London. Printed by Longman & Broderip, No. 26 Cheapside, and No. 13 Haymarket: | . . . [1791]

2° 3 pts.: *piano-forte or harpsichord:* 1 *ℓ.,* 44 p.; *violino:* 1 *ℓ.,* 15 p.; *violoncello:* 1 *ℓ.,* 14 p.

Opus no. completed in manuscript

Benton, no. (4474) (variant); RISM A I, no. P 3699

B. 440–442

MUSIC LIBRARY

1212 PLEYEL, IGNAZ JOSEPH

Fourteen | Favorite Sonatinas, | for the | Piano Forte or Harpsichord | With an Accompaniment | for a Violin ad Libitum | Composed by | Jgnace Pleyel. | Book I. . . . | London | Printed by Longman and Broderip No. 26 Cheapside and No. 13 Hay Market | Music Sellers and musical Instrument makers to His Royal Highness the Prince of Wales | . . . [ca. 1790]

2° 2 pts.: *Piano forte or harpsichord:* III, 2–29 p.; *violino:* 1 *ℓ.,* 11 p.

Page III in *piano forte or harpsichord* pt.: Musical Publications | Printed and Sold by Longman & Broderip . . .

Benton, no. (5993); RISM A I, no. P 4592

MUSIC LIBRARY

1213 PLEYEL, IGNAZ JOSEPH

Twelve | Easy & Favorite | Sonatinas | for the | Piano-Forte or Harpsichord | with an Accompaniment | for the | Violin | ad Libitum | Composed by | Jgnace Pleyel | Book IId. . . . | London | Printed by Longman and Broderip No. 26 Cheapside and No. 13 Hay Market | Music Sellers and musical Instrument makers to His Royal Highness the Prince of Wales. [ca. 1790]

2° 2 pts.: *Piano-forte or harpsichord:* 1 *ℓ.,* 30 p.; *violino:* 1 *ℓ.,* 10 p.
Benton, no. (5994); RISM A I, no. P 4685
MUSIC LIBRARY

1214 PÖGL, PEREGRINUS

Sacrificium | Deo | Vespertinum | Sive | Quatuor Vesperae | Duae Solennes de Dominica & B. V. M. | Minus Solennes de Apostolis, | Brevissimae de Dominica, | Una cum | Psalmis per Annum occurrentibus. | Authore | P. Peregrino Poegl | Ord. S. Benedicti ad B. V. M. assumptam, & S. Martinum | in Neustatt ad Moenum Professo. | Opus III. [Bamberg, Johann Jakob Schnell, 1747]

2° 9 pts.: *alto:* A–G², H1; *tenore:* A–H²; *basso:* A–I²; *clarino vel cornu I, clarino vel cornu II:* A–C² each; *violino I, violino II, violoncello:* A–K² each; *organo:* [–]1, A–K²
Title supplied from *organo* part-book
Gathering G missigned H in *alto* part-book
Incomplete: *canto* part-book lacking
RISM A I, no. P 4966
HOUGHTON

1215

The | Tunes | to the | Songs | in | Polly an Opera | Being | the Second Part of the | Beggar's Opera | Transpos'd for the | Flute | Done from the Original | Songs; which Songs may | be had where these are Sold | London | Printed and sold at the | Musick-shops . . . | [John Walsh and Joseph Hare, 1729]

8° 1 *ℓ.,* 36 p.
Walsh II, no. 1216
HOUGHTON

1216

Polly; | An Opera. | Being | The Second Part of the Beggar's Opera. | For the | Voice, Harpsichord, And Violin. | London: | Printed for Harrison & Co. No. 18, Paternoster Row. [1784]

obl. 2° *Vocal score:* 24 p., 1 *ℓ.*
Plate nos. 18–19, which are those of *The New Musical Magazine* (see Schnapper II, 801)
RISM B II, 291
HOUGHTON (2 copies)

1217

Polymnia: | Or, The | Charms of Musick. | Being An | Ode, | Sacred To | Harmony; | Occasion'd by Mr. Handel's | Oratorio, and the Harmonia Sacra, | Perform'd at Whitehall, by the Gentlemen of | the Chappel-Royal. | Dedicated to Mr. Handel. | . . . | By a Gentleman of Cambridge. | London: | Printed for T. Game, at the Bible, facing the East-End of the New | Church in the Strand; and D. Gardner, in New Turnstile, High-|Holborn. MDCCXXXIII.

2° 2 *ℓ.,* 4 p.
In verse
Foxon, P720
HOUGHTON

1218 PONZIO, PIETRO

Dialogo | Del R. M. Don Pietro | Pontio Parmigiano | Ove Si Tratta Della Theo|rica è Prattica di Musica, | Et anco si mostra la diuersità | de Contraponti, Et | Canoni | In Parma | Appresso Erasmo Viotti | MDXCV | . . .

4° 3 *ℓ.,* 152 p., illus., pl., music
Hirsch I, no. 467; RISM B VI, 663; Wolfenbüttel, no. 1252
HOUGHTON

1219 PORPHYRIUS

Πορφυριον | Εἰζ Τα | Αρμονικα Πτολε-μαιον | Υπομνημα. | Porphyrii | In | Harmonica Ptolemaei | Commentarius. | Nunc primum ex Codd. Mss. (Graece et Latine) editus. [Oxford, 1699]

2° In John Wallis's *Operum mathematicorum,* vol. III, p. [183]–355, illus.

Parallel texts in Greek and Latin; two columns to the page
Half-title
RISM B VI, 876
HOUGHTON

1220   PRAETORIUS, MICHAEL

Syntagma Musicum | ex | Veterum | Et | Recentiorum | Ecclesiasticorum autorum lectione, | Polyhistorûm consignatione, | Variarum linguarum notatione, | Hodierni seculi usurpatione, | ipsius denique | Musicae artis observatione: | In | Cantorum, Organistarum, Organo-|poeorum, caeterorumq́; Musicam scientiam aman-|tium & tractantium gratiam collectum; | Et | Secundùm hunc generalem Indicem | toti Operi praefixum, | In | Quatuor Tomos Distributum, | à | Michaële Praetorio Creutzbergensi, Caeno-|bii Ringelheimensis Priori, & in aula Brun-|svicensi Chori Musici Magistro. | Anno | IVDICIVM pIos non terreat: nam | MIHI aDIVtor ChrIstVs. [Wittenberg, 1615–1619]

4° 3 vols.: [*vol. I*]: 12 ℓ.. 459 p., 16 ℓ., illus.; *vol. II*: 14 ℓ., 236 p., 2 fold. pl., 1 ℓ., 42 pl. (3 fold.) on 21 ℓ., 2 ℓ., illus., music; *vol. III:* 8 ℓ., 260 p., illus., music
Title and imprint vary: vol. II: . . . De | Organographia. . . . Gedruckt zu Wolffenbüttel, bey Elias Holwein Fürstl. Brauns. Buch-|trucker und Formschneider daselbst. In Verlegung des Autoris. | Anno Christi. M.DC.XIX.; vol. II [part 2]: Theatrum | Instrumentorum . . . Wolffenbüttel, Im Jahr 1620; imprint, vol. III: Gedruckt zu Wolffenbüttel, bey Elias Holwein, F. Br. Buchdr. vnd Forms. | daselbst. In Verlegung des Autoris. Im Jahr, 1619.
Numerous errors in paging
Vol. IV never published
Davidsson II, no. 74; Hirsch I, no. 468; RISM B VI, 666; Wolfenbüttel, no. 1258
HOUGHTON

LES PRELUDES DE L'HARMONIE UNIVERSELLE *See* Mersenne, Marin *Les Preludes de l'Harmonie universelle*

PREZ, JOSQUIN DES *See* Deprez, Josquin

PRIXNER, SEBASTIAN Kann man nicht in zwey oder drey Monaten *See* Kann man nicht in zwey oder drey Monaten

1221

The Professional | Collection of Glees, | for | Three, Four, and Five Voices; | Composed by | the following Authors, | Callcott, Cooke, Danby, | Hindle, Stevens & Webbe. | . . . | London | Printed for the Authors, & Sold by | Longman & Broderip, No. 26, Cheapside, & No. 13, Haymarket, | Manufacturers of Musical Instruments, & Music Sellers, to | Their Majesties, His Royal Highness the Prince of Wales, & all the Royal Family. [1791?]

obl. 2° *Score:* III [i. e. III], [1], 54 p.
Page IIII [i. e. III]: Musical Publications, | Printed and Sold by Longman & Broderip . . .
RISM B II, 292–293
MUSIC LIBRARY

1222   PTOLEMAEUS, CLAUDIUS

Κλαυδιον Πτολεμαιου | Αρμονικων | Βιβλια Γ'. | Claudii Ptolemaei | Harmonicorum | Libri Tres. | Ex Codd. Mss. Vndecim, nunc primum Graece editus. | Johannes Wallie, Ss. Th. D. Geometriae Professor Savilianus | Oxoniae, Regiae Societatis Londini Sodalis, Regiaeque Majestati à Sacris; | Recensuit, Edidit, Versione & Notis illustravit, & Auctarium adjecit. | Oxonii, | E Theatro Sheldoniano, An. Dom. 1682.

4° 10 ℓ., 328 p. front. (port.), illus., music
Parallel texts in Greek and Latin; two columns to the page
Pages 281–328: Appendix | De Veterum Harmonica ad Hodiernam comparata.
Davidsson II, no. 78; RISM B VI, 674
MUSIC LIBRARY

1223   PTOLEMAEUS, CLAUDIUS

Κλαυδιον Πτολεμαιου | Αρμονικων | Βιβλια Γ'. | Claudii Ptolemaei | Harmonicorum | Libri Tres. [Oxford, 1699]

2° In John Wallis's *Operum mathematicorum*, vol. III, p. [9]–[24], 1–182, illus., music

Parallel texts in Greek and Latin; two columns to the page
Half-title
RISM B VI, 674
HOUGHTON

1224 PUGNANI, GAETANO

Sei | Sonate | à | Violino è Basso | Dedicate | Alla Sacra Real Maesta | Di | Carlo Emanuele | Re Di Sardegna &. &. &. | Da | G. Pugnani. | Opera III | London Printed for R. Bremner, at the Harp & Hautboy, Opposite Somerset-House in the Strand. | . . . [ca. 1780]

2° *Score:* 1 ℓ., 25 p.
RISM A I, no. P 5611
MUSIC LIBRARY

PUIS, THOMAS SANDERS DU   *See* Dupuis, Thomas Sanders

PUJADES, ANTONIO EXIMENO Y   *See* Eximeno y Pujades, Antonio

1225 PURCELL, DANIEL

The Ivdgment Of Paris | A | Pastoral | Composed for the | Music-Prize | by | Mr: D: Purcell | . . . | London Printed for I. Walsh Servt to Her Matie. at the Harp and Hoboy in Katherine Street near Somerset House. in ye Strand [1702]

2° *Score:* 2 ℓ., 82 p.
Day, no. 198; Hirsch II, no. 749; RISM A I, no. P 5721; Walsh I, no. 89
HOUGHTON

1226 PURCELL, DANIEL

A | Collection | of new | Songs | With a Through Bass to each | Song for the Harpsicord. Compos'd by | Mr: Daniel Purcel. Perform'd in the Revis'd-|-Comedy call'd the Pilgrim, being the last | Writeings of Mr: Dryden. 1700. | London | Sould by I: Walsh Musicall Instrument maker in Ordinary | to his Majesty, at the Golden Harpe and Hoboy in Cathe-|-rine Street, near Summerset House in the Strand [1700]

2° *Score:* 5 ℓ.
Day, no. 184; RISM A I, no. P 5747; Walsh I, no. 30
HOUGHTON

1227 PURCELL, DANIEL

The Single | Songs | In | The New Opera, | Call'd | The World in the Moon. | Sett by Mr. Daniel Purcell, and Mr. Clark. | London, | Printed by J. Heptinstall, for Henry Playford at his Shop in the Temple-|Change Fleetstreet, where also may be had a General Catalogue of all | the Musick-Books for this Thirty Years last past down to this pre-|sent time. 1697. | . . .

2° *Vocal score:* 1 ℓ., 8 p.
Imperfect: pages 1–4 lacking
Day, no. 158; RISM A I, no. P 5766
HOUGHTON

1228 PURCELL, HENRY

The | Songs | In | Amphitryon, | With The | Musick. | Composed by Mr. Henry Pvrcell. | London, | Printed by J. Heptinstall for Jacob Tonson at the Judge's-Head | in Chancery-Lane. MDCXC.

4° *Vocal score:* 1 ℓ., 13 p.
Day, no. 104; RISM A I, no. P 5826; Zimmerman, no. 1690a
HOUGHTON

1229 PURCELL, HENRY

A | Collection | Of | Ayres, | Compos'd | For the Theatre, and upon other Occasions. | By the late Mr. Henry Purcell. | . . . | London, | Printed by J. Heptinstall, for Frances Purcell, Executrix of the Author; | And are to be sold by B. Aylmer at the Three Pigeons against | the Royal Exchange, W. Henchman in Westminster-Hall, and Henry | Playford at his Shop in the Temple-Change, Fleetstreet. 1697.

2° 4 pts.: *violino primo:* 2 ℓ., 48 p.; *violino secundo:* 1 ℓ., 48 p.; *tennor, bassus:* 1 ℓ., 40 p. each
RISM A I, no. P 5977; Zimmerman, no. 1697a
HOUGHTON

1230 PURCELL, HENRY

The Songs in the Tragedy of Bonduca. | Set by Mr. Henry Purcell. [London, Henry Playford, 1695?]

2° 3, [1] p.
Caption title; perhaps as published
Unnumbered page at end: Excellent Musick-Books lately Printed for and Sold by Henry | Playford . . .
Day, no. 138; Zimmerman, no. 1695n
HOUGHTON

PURCELL, HENRY Celebrate this Festival *See* Purcell, Henry *Ode on the Queen's Birthday*

PURCELL, HENRY Dioclesian *See* Purcell, Henry *The Prophetess*

1231 [PURCELL, HENRY]

[The | Songs | To | The New Play | Of | Don Quixote. | As they are Sung at | The Queen's Theatre | In | Dorset Garden. | Part the First. | Sett by the most Eminent Masters of the Age. | All Written by Mr. D'urfey. | . . . | London, | Printed by J. Heptinstall for Samuel Briscoe, at the corner of | Charles-street, Covent-Garden. 1694. | . . . .]

2° *Score:* 3 ℓ., 42 p.
Imperfect: title-page lacking; supplied from Day, no. 127, second entry; title-page in positive photostat from a different issue inserted
RISM A I, no. P 5854; Zimmerman, no. 1694o
HOUGHTON

1232 PURCELL, HENRY

New | Songs | In The | Third Part | Of The | Comical History | Of | Don Quixote. | Written by Mr. D'Urfey. | And Sung at the | Theatre Royal. | With other New Songs by Mr. D'Vrfey. | Being the last Piece set to Musick by the late Famous | Mr. Henry Purcell: And by Mr. Courtiville, Mr. Akeroyd, and | other Eminent Masters of the Age. | Engrav'd on Copper-Plates. | London, | Printed for Samuel Briscoe, at the Corner-shop of Charles-street, in Russel-street, | Covent-Garden, 1696. | . . .

2° *Vocal score:* 18 ℓ.
RISM A I, no. P 5855; Zimmerman, no. 1696i
HOUGHTON

1233 [PURCELL, HENRY]

New | Songs | Sung In | The Fool's Preferment, | Or, The | Three Dukes of Dunstable. | [London] In the Savoy: | Printed by E. Jones, for Jos. Knight and Fran. Saunders, | at the Blue Anchor in the Lower-Walk of the | New Exchange in the Strand, 1688.

4° *Vocal score:* 16 p.
Day, no. 99; RISM A I, no. P 5824; Zimmerman, no. 1688a
HOUGHTON

1234 PURCELL, HENRY

Harmonia Sacra | or | Select Anthems | In Score | for one, two, and three Voices. | Compos'd by the late | Mr. Henry Purcell. | London. Printed for I. Walsh, in Catherine Street, | in the Strand. [ca. 1730]

2° *Score:* 1 ℓ., 34 p.
RISM A I, no. P 5811; Walsh II, no. 1245; Zimmerman, no. 1730c
HOUGHTON

1235 PURCELL, HENRY

The | Songs | In The | Indian Queen: | As it is now Compos'd into an | Opera. | By Mr. Henry Purcell, | Composer in Ordinary to his Majesty. | And one of the Organists of his Majesty's Chapel-Royal. | London, | Printed by J. Heptinstall; and are to be Sold by John May, at his Shop under | St. Dunstan's Church: And for John Hudgbutt at Tho. Dring's, Bookseller, at the | Harrow at Clifford's-lane-end in Fleetstreet. 1695.

2° *Vocal score:* 1 ℓ., 14 p.
Page 14: Books Printed for, and Sold by John Hudgebutt.
Day, no. 137; RISM A I, no. P 5887; Zimmerman, no. 1695m
HOUGHTON

1236 [PURCELL, HENRY]

The | Indian | Queen | [London, Benjamin Goodison, ca. 1790]

2° *Score:* 1 ℓ., [53] p.
Imperfect: all after page 34 lacking
RISM A I, no. P 5885; Zimmerman, no. ?1790b (630)
MUSIC LIBRARY

1237 PURCELL, HENRY

The | Iovial Companions | or | Merry Club | being | A Choice Collection of the Newest | and most | Diverting Catches | for | three & four Voices | Together with | the most Celebrated | Catches | Compos'd by the | late Mr. Henr. Purcell & Dr. Blow | all fairly Engraven & Carefully Corrected | London. Printed for and sold by I: Walsh Musick Printer and Instrument-maker | [to] his Majesty at the Harp & Hoboy in Catherine Street in the Strand. [1709?]

2° 2 ℓ., 22 numb. ℓ., front.
Second imprint on cancel label: Sold by Iohn Barret Musical Instrument Maker at | the Harp and Crown in Coventry Street near Piccadilly
Interleaved copy
Walsh I, no. 303; Zimmerman, no. 1709e
HOUGHTON

1238 PURCELL, HENRY

The | Songs Airs Duets & | Chorusses | in the Masque of | King Arthur, | As perform'd at the Theatre Royal in | Drury Lane | Compos'd by | Purcel & Dr. Arne. | [London] Printed & Sold by John Johnston at No. 11. York Street, Covent Garden, | . . . [ca. 1770]

2° *Score:* 1 ℓ., IV, 81 p.
Paging includes numbered leaves 29, 30, 49; extra title-pages inserted after numbered leaves 29, 49
Cancel label mounted on each title-page reads: Bought of Benjamin Rhames at | the Sun on the Upper Blind Quay, | . . .
RISM A I, no. P 5894; Zimmerman, no. 1770d
HOUGHTON

1239 [PURCELL, HENRY]

A | Musical Entertainment | Perform'd | On November XXII. 1683. | It Being The | Festival of St. Cecilia, a great Patroness of Music; | Whose | Memory is Annually honour'd by a public Feast | made on that Day by the Masters and Lovers of | Music, as well in England as in Foreign Parts. | London, | Printed by J. Playford Junior, and are to be sold by John Playford near the | Temple Church, and John Carr at the Middle-Temple Gate, 1684.

4° *Score:* 2 ℓ., 40 p.
Text incipit: Welcome to all the pleasures
Zimmerman, no. 1684a
HOUGHTON

1240 [PURCELL, HENRY]

Ode | on the Queen's Birthday. | [London, Benjamin Goodison, ca. 1790]

2° *Score:* 16 [+] p.
In his *Odes and Choral Songs* [no. 3] (see Schnapper II, 860)
Caption-title
Text incipit: Celebrate this festival
Imperfect: all after page 16 lacking
RISM A I, no. P 5997; Zimmerman, no. ?1790b (321)
MUSIC LIBRARY

1241 PURCELL, HENRY

Orpheus Britannicus. | A | Collection | Of All | The Choicest Songs | For | One, Two, and Three Voices, | Compos'd | By Mr. Henry Purcell. | Together, | With such Symphonies for Violins or Flutes, | As were by Him design'd for any of them: | And | A Through-Bass to each Song; | Figur'd for the Organ, Harpsichord, or Theorbo-Lute. | All which are placed in their several Keys according to the | Order of the Gamut. | London, | Printed by J. Heptinstall, for Henry Playford, in the Temple-Change, | in Fleet-street, MDCXCVIII.

2° *Score:* 1 ℓ., vi, [2], 248 p., front. (port.)
Second unnumbered page after page vi: Books Printed for and Sold by Henry Playford . . .

Day, no. 166; RISM A I, no. P 5979; Zimmerman, no. 1698d
HOUGHTON

1242 PURCELL, HENRY

Orpheus Britannicus. | A | Collection | Of | The Choicest Songs, | For | One, Two, and Three Voices. | Compos'd | By Mr. Henry Purcell. | Together, | With such Symphonies for Violins or Flutes, | As were by Him design'd for any of them: | And | A Through-Bass to each Song. | Figur'd for the Organ, Harpsichord, or Theorbo-Lute. | The Second Book, which renders the First Compleat. | . . . | London: | Printed by William Pearson, for Henry Playford, at His Shop in the | Temple-Change, Fleet-street. 1702.

2° *Score:* 2 ℓ., ii. [2], 176 [i. e. 174] p.
Numbers 33, 34 omitted in paging
Page after page ii: Books lately Printed, and Re-printed, for Henry Playford . . .
Day, no. 200; RISM A I, no. P 5983; Zimmerman, no. 1702d
HOUGHTON (2 copies)

1243 PURCELL, HENRY

Orpheus Britannicus. | A | Collection | Of All | The Choicest Songs. | For | One, Two, and Three Voices, | Compos'd | By Mr. Henry Purcell. | Together, | With such Symphonies for Violins or Flutes, | As were by Him design'd for any of them: | And | A Through-Bass to each Song; | Figur'd for the Organ, Harpsichord, or Theorbo-Lute. | The Second Edition with Large Additions; and placed in their seve-|ral Keys according to the Order of the Gamvt. | London: | Printed by William Pearson, and Sold by John Young, at the Dolphin | and Crown in St. Paul's Church-Yard. MDCCVI.

2° *Score:* 1 ℓ., vi, [2], 286 [i. e. 288] p., front. (port.)
Supplementary leaf numbered 189–190 inserted after page 284
Page after page vi: A Catalogue of Books sold by John Cullen . . .
Day, no. 210; RISM A I, no. P 5980; Zimmerman, no. 1706a
HOUGHTON (2 copies, 2d imperfect)

—another copy
Large paper copy
HOUGHTON

1244 PURCELL, HENRY

Orpheus Britannicus. | A | Collection | Of All | The Choicest Songs | For | One, Two, and Three Voices, | Compos'd | By Mr. Henry Purcell. | Together, | With such Symphonies for Violins or Flutes, | As were by Him design'd for any of them: | And | A Through-Bass to each Song; | Figur'd for the Organ, Harpsichord, or Theorbo-Lute. | The Second Edition with Large Additions; and placed in their seve-|ral Keys according to the Order of the Gamvt. | London: | Printed by William Pearson, and Sold by John Cullen, at the Buck be-|tween the Two Temple-Gates in Fleet-street. MDCCVI.

2° *Score:* 1 ℓ., vi, [2], 286 [i. e. 288] p., front. (port.)
Supplementary leaf numbered 189–190 inserted after page 188
Page after page vi: A Catalogue of Books sold by John Cullen . . .
Day, no. 210, second entry; RISM A I, no. P 5981; Zimmerman, no. 1706b
HOUGHTON

1245 PURCELL, HENRY

Orpheus Britannicus. | A | Collection | Of | The Choicest Songs, | For | One, Two, and Three Voices, | Compos'd | By Mr. Henry Purcell. | Together. | With such Symphonies for Violins or Flutes, | As were by Him design'd for any of them: | And | A Through-Bass to each Song. | Figur'd for the Organ, Harpsicord, or Theorbo-Lute. | The Second Book, which renders the First Compleat. | The Second Edition with Additions. | . . . | London: | Printed by William Pearson, for S. H. Sold by J. Young, at the Dolphin and Crown in | St. Paul's Church-Yard, J. Cullen, at the Buck just thro' Temple-Bar. 1711

2° *Score:* 2 ℓ., ii, 204 [i. e. 202] p.
Numbers 33, 34 omitted in paging
Large paper copy
Day, no. 220; RISM A I, no. P 5984; Zimmerman, no. 1711b
HOUGHTON

1246   PURCELL, HENRY

Orpheus Britannicus. | A | Collection | Of | The choicest Songs | For | One, Two, and Three Voices, | Compos'd | By Mr. Henry Purcell. | Together, | With such Symphonies for Violins or Flutes, | As were by him design'd for any of them: | And | A Through-Bass to each Song. | Figur'd for the Organ, Harpsicord, or Theorbo-Lute. | The Second Book, which renders the First Compleat. | The Second Edition with large Additions. | . . . | London: | Printed by William Pearson, For S. H. and Sold by John Young, at the | Dolphin and Crown, in St. Paul's Church-Yard. MDCCXII.

2° *Score:* 2 ℓ., ii, 204 [i. e. 202] p.
Numbers 33, 34 omitted in paging
Day, no. 221; RISM A I, no. P 5985;
Zimmerman, no. 1712a
HOUGHTON

1247   PURCELL, HENRY

The | Vocal and Instrumental | Musick | Of The | Prophetess, | Or The | History | Of | Dioclesian. | Composed | By Henry Purcell, Organist of Their Majesties | Chappel, and of St. Peters Westminster. | London, | Printed by J. Heptinstall, for the Author, and are to be | Sold by John Carr, at his Shop at the Middle-|Temple Gate near Temple-Barr. MDCXCI.

2° *Score:* 2 ℓ., 173 p.
Day, no. 111; RISM A I, no. P 5927;
Zimmerman, no. 1691f
HOUGHTON

1248   PURCELL, HENRY

Ten | Sonata's | In | Four Parts. | Compos'd by the | Late Mr. Henry Purcell. | London, | Printed by J. Heptinstall, for Frances Purcell, Executrix of the Author; | And are to be sold by B. Aylmer at the Three Pigeons against | the Royal Exchange, W. Henchman in Westminster-Hall, and Henry | Playford at his Shop in the Temple-Change, Fleetstreet. 1697.

2° 4 pts.: *violino primo:* 2 ℓ., 21 p.; *violino secundo, bassus, through bass for the harpsichord or organ:* 21 p. each

RISM A I, no. P 6085; Zimmerman, no. 1697d
HOUGHTON

1249   PURCELL, HENRY

The | Music | In The | Tempest. | Composed By | Mr. Henry Purcell. | [London] Printed for Messrs. Longman and Broderip, and Sold at their | Music-Shops, in Cheapside and the Hay-Market. | . . . [ca. 1790]

2° *Score:* 1 ℓ., 50 p.
RISM A I, no. P 5948
MUSIC LIBRARY

PURCELL, HENRY Welcome to all the Pleasures *See* Purcell, Henry *A Musical Entertainment*

1250   [PURE, MICHEL DE]

Idée | Des | Spectacles | Anciens | Et | Novveavx. | Des | Anciens {Cirques. | Amphitheatres. | Theatres. | Naumachies. | Triomphes. | Novveavx. | Comedie. | Bal. | Mascarades. | Carosels. | Courses de Bagues | & de Testes. | Des Ioustes. | Exercises & Reveuës | Militaires. | Feux d'Artifices. | Entrées des Rois & des | Reynes. | Par M. M. D. P. | A Paris, | Chez Michel Brunet, à l'entrée de la | grand' Salle du Palais, du costé de S. Barthe-|lemy, au Loüis d'Or. | Avec Privilege du Roy. [1668]

12° 3 ℓ., 318 [i. e. 316], [10] p.
Colophon: Achevé d'imprimer pour la premiere fois, | le vingt-cinquiéme May. 1668.
Nos. 238, 239 omitted in paging
RISM B VI, 675
HOUGHTON

Q

1251   QUANTZ, JOHANN JOACHIM

Johann Joachim Quantzens, | Königl. Preussischen Kammermusikus, | Versuch einer Anweisung | die | Flöte traversiere | zu spielen; | mit verschiedenen, |

zur Beförderung des guten Geschmackes | in der praktischen Musik | dienlichen Anmerkungen | begleitet, | und mit Exempeln erläutert. | Nebst XXIV. Kupfertafeln. | Berlin, | bey Johann Friedrich Voss. 1752.

4° 7 *ℓ.*, 334, [20] p., 1 *ℓ.*, 24 pl. on 12 *ℓ.*
Imperfect: last leaf and all plates lacking; supplied in positive photostat
RISM B VI, 677
MUSIC LIBRARY

1252 QUANTZ, JOHANN JOACHIM

Johann Joachim Quantzens, | Königl. Preussischen Kammermusikus, | Versuch einer Anweisung | die | Flöte traversiere | zu spielen; | mit verschiedenen, | zur Beförderung des guten Geschmackes | in der praktischen Musik | dienlichen Anmerkungen | begleitet, | und mit Exempeln erläutert. | Nebst XXIV. Kupfertafeln. | Dritte Auflage. | Breslau, 1789. | bey Johann Friedrich Korn dem ältern, | im Buchladen nächst dem K. Ober- Zoll- und Accisamte auf dem grossen Ringe.

4° 8 *ℓ.*, 334, [18] p., 24 pl. on 12 *ℓ.* (music)
RISM B VI, 676–677
MUSIC LIBRARY

QUESTIONS HARMONIQUES *See* Mersenne, Marin *Questions harmoniques*

R

1253 RAISON, ANDRÉ

Livre D'Orgue | Contenant Cinq Messes Svffisantes | Pour Tous les Tons de l'Eglise | ou Qvinze Magnificats pour ceux qui n'ont pas | besoin de Messe auec des Eleuations toutes particulieres. | Ensuite des Benedictus: Et vne Offerte en action de | Grace pour l'heureuse Conualescence Dv Roy. En | Laquelle se peut aussi toucher sur Le Clauecin. | Le tout au naturel et facile auec Les plus beaux mouuemens et les plus belles | varietez du temps tant aux Musiques vocales

qu'Instrumentales et le Chiffre à bien | des Endroits pour bien passer les Interualles et les agrèmens, et bien placer les doits, | auec des jnstructions tres vtiles po. ceux qui n'ont point de Me. et qui veule se perfectiõner Eux mèmes | Composé par André Raison | Organiste de La Royalle Abbaye de Saincte Geneuiefue du mont de Paris. | Auec Priuilege du Roy. | [Paris] Chez L'Autheur Rüe et ancienne porte de St. Jacques vis a vis le petit Marché [1688]

obl. 4° *Score:* 4 *ℓ.*, 118, [1] p.
Paging includes numbered leaves 23, 46, 69, 90, 113
RISM A I, no. R 108
HOUGHTON

1254 RAMEAU, JEAN PHILIPPE

Code | De | Musique Pratique, | Ou | Méthode | Pour apprendre la Musique, même à des aveugles, pour former la | voix & l'oreille, pour la position de la main avec une méchanique | des doigts sur le Clavecin & l'Orgue, pour l'Accompagnement | sur tous les Instrumens qui en sont susceptibles, & pour le Prélude: | Avec de Nouvelles Réflexions sur le Principe sonore. | Par M. Rameau. | A Paris, | De L'Imprimerie Royale. | M.DCCLX.

4° 1 *ℓ.*, xx, 237, 33 p., front., illus., music
Pages 1–33 at end: Exemples Du Code De Musique Pratique | Musique.
Hirsch I, no. 490; RISM B VI, 682
HOUGHTON

1255 RAMEAU, JEAN PHILIPPE

Démonstration | Du Principe | De L'Harmonie, | Servant de base à tout l'Art Musical | théorique & pratique. | Approuvée par Messieurs de l'Acadé-|mie Royale des Sciences, & dédiée | à Monseigneur le Comte d'Argen-|son, Ministre & Sécrétaire d'Etat. | Par Monsieur Rameau. | A Paris, | Chez {Durand, rue Saint Jacques, au Griffon. | Pissot, Quay des Augustins, à la Sagesse. | M.DCC.L. | Avec Approbation Et Privilege Du Roy

8° 2 *ℓ.*, xxiij, 112, xlvij p., illus., 5 fold. pl.

Hirsch I, no. 487; RISM B VI, 682
HOUGHTON

1256   [RAMEAU, JEAN PHILIPPE]

Erreurs | Sur | La Musique | Dans | L'En-cyclopedie. | A Paris, | Chez Sebastien Jorry, Quai des | Augustins, près le Pont S. Michel, | aux Cigognes. | M.DCC.LV. [–1756] | Avec Approbation & Privilége du Roi.

8° 124 [i.e. 128] p.
Nos. 109–112 repeated in paging
RISM B VI, 683
HOUGHTON

1257   RAMEAU, JEAN PHILIPPE

Generation | Harmonique, | Ou | Traité De Musique | Theorique | Et Pratique. | Par M. Rameau. | A Paris, | Chez Prault fils, Quay de Conty, vis-à-vis | la descente du Pont-Neuf, à la Charité. | M.DCC.XXXVII. | Avec Approbation & Privilege du Roy.

8° 8 ℓ., 201 [i. e. 227], [17] p., illus., 12 pl. (incl. music)
Colophon: De l'Imprimerie de Charles Osmont.
Page 227 misnumbered 201
Imperfect: xlvij pages lacking (see Gregory, p. 224)
Hirsch I, no. 486; RISM B VI, 683
MUSIC LIBRARY

1258   RAMEAU, JEAN PHILIPPE

Nouveau | Systême | De Musique | Theorique, | Où l'on découvre le Principe de toutes les Regles | necessaires à la Pratique, | Pour servir d'Introduction au Traité de l'Harmonie; | Par Monsieur Rameau, cy-devant Organiste | de la Cathedrale de Clermont en Auvergne. | De L'Imprimerie | De Jean-Baptiste-Christophe Ballard, | Seul Imprimeur du Roy pour la Musique. A Paris, | Au Mont-Parnasse. | M.DCCXXVI. | Avec Privilege Dv Roy.

4° viij, 114, [6] p., illus., 2 fold. pl., 3 mounted pl., music
Pages [5]–[6] at end: Catalogue | Des autres Livres de Musique Théorique, imprimez en France, | . . .

Signatures of Christian Cannabich and Carl Cannabich on fly-leaf
Hirsch I, no. 485; RISM B VI, 683–684
HOUGHTON (2 copies)

1259   RAMEAU, JEAN PHILIPPE

[Pieces | de Clavecin | Avec Une Table | Pour Les Agrémens | Par Monsieur Rameau | . . . | A Paris. | Chés {Boivin, à la Règle d'Or, rüe Saint Honoré | Le Clair, à la Croix d'Or, rue du Roule | L'auteur, | M.DCC.XXXI.]

obl. 2° *Score:* 1 ℓ., [1], 33 p.
Page 31 incorrectly imposed on the verso of page 28; pages 29, 30 are printed as leaves and hinged to the top of leaves containing pages 28 and 32 respectively
Imperfect: title-page lacking; supplied in manuscript
RISM A I, no. R 184
HOUGHTON

1260   RAMEAU, JEAN PHILIPPE

Nouvelles Suites | De | Pieces De Clavecin | Composées | Par Mr. Rameau. | avec des remarques sur les différens genres de Musique. | Gravées par Mlle. Loüise Roussel. | . . . | A Paris, | Chez {L'Auteur, rüe des deux Boule aux trois Rois. | Le Sr. Boivin, Md. rüe St. honoré à la Régle D'or. | Le Sr. Leclerc, Md. rüe du Roule à la Croix D'or. | Avec Privilége du Roy. [ca. 1734]

obl. 2° *Score:* 1 ℓ., 29 p., 1 ℓ.
Page [1]: Ouvrages De Mr. Rameau
RISM A I, no. R 188
HOUGHTON

1261   RAMEAU, JEAN PHILIPPE

Pigmalion, | Acte De Ballet, | Mis En Musique | Par M. Rameau | Et exécuté pour la premiere fois par l'Académie Royale de | Musique, le 27. Aout 1748. | . . . | A Paris, | Chés {L'Auteur, rüe des bons Enfans. | La Veuve Boivin, rue Saint Honoré, à la Regle d'Or. | M. Leclair, rüe du Roule, à la Croix d'Or. | Avec Approbation et Privilége Du Roi. [ca. 1750]

obl. 4° *Score:* 2 ℓ., 43 p.
Hirsch II, no. 781; RISM A I, no. R 163
HOUGHTON

1262 RAMEAU, JEAN PHILIPPE

Reponse | De | M. Rameau | A Mm. Les Editeurs | de l'Encyclopédie. | Sur | Leur dernier Avertissement. | A Londres, | Et se trouve à Paris, | Chez Sebastien Jorry, Imprimeur | Libraire, Quai des Augustins, près | le Pont S. Michel, aux Cigognes. | M.DCC.LVII.

8° 54 p.
RISM B VI, 685
HOUGHTON

1263 [RAMEAU, JEAN PHILIPPE]

Suite | Des Erreurs | Sur La Musique | Dans L'Encyclopedie. [Paris?, 1756]

8° 39 p., illus.
Page 39: Lû & Approuvé ce 3. Mars 1756. | Trublet.
Caption title
RISM B VI, 683
HOUGHTON

1264 RAMEAU, JEAN PHILIPPE

Traité | De | L'Harmonie | Reduite à ses Principes naturels; | Divisé En Quatre Livres. | Livre I. Du rapport des Raisons & Proportions Har-|moniques. | Livre II. De la nature & de la proprieté des Ac-cords; | Et de tout ce qui peut servir à rendre une | Musique parfaite. | Livre III. Principes de Composition. | Livre IV. Principes d'Accompagnement. | Par Monsieur Rameav, Organiste de la Ca-thedrale | de Clermont en Auvergne. | De L'Imprimerie | De Jean-Baptiste-Chris-tophe Ballard, Seul | Imprimeur du Roy pour la Musique. A Paris, rüe Saint Jean-|de-Beauvais, au Mont-Parnasse. | M.DCC.XXII. | Avec Privilege Du Roy.

4° 4 ℓ., xxiv, 432, 17, [1] p., illus., music
Unnumbered page at end: Catalogue | Des autres Livres de Musique Théorique, imprimez en France, | dont on peut trouver des Exemplaires.
Hirsch I, no. 484; RISM B VI, 685
HOUGHTON (2 copies), MUSIC LIBRARY

1265 RAMEAU, JEAN PHILIPPE

A | Treatise of Music, | Containing The | Principles | Of | Composition. | Wherein | The several Parts thereof are fully ex-plained, and made useful | both to the Professors and Students of that Science. | By Mr. Rameau, | Principal Composer to his Most Christian Majesty, and to the | Opera at Paris. | Translated into English from the Original in the French | Language. | Second Edition. | London, | Printed for J. Murray, No. 32, Fleet-Street; And | Luke White, Dublin. | MDCCLXXIX.

8° 3 ℓ., [3]–180 p., illus., music
RISM B VI, 685
MUSIC LIBRARY

1266 RAMEAU, PIERRE

[Abbrege | De La Nouvelle Methode, Dans | L'Art D'Ecrire Ou De Tracer | Toutes Sortes De | Danses De Ville. | Dedié à Son Altesse Serenissime | Mademoiselle de Baujaulois | et Mise au jour Par le Sr. Rameau Maître | à Danser Or-dinaire de la Maison de | St Majesté Ca-tholique, la Reine seconde | Douairriere d'Espagne. | Et seul privilegié du Roy pour la corection | et augmentation de la Choregraphie | Ouvrage | très utile pour toutes Personnes qui ont scu | ou qui ap-prennent à Danser, puisque par le | se-cour de ce livre, on peut se remettre facile-|ment dans toutes les Danses que l'on a appris. | . . . | A Paris | Chez l'Au-teur fauborg mont marthe | I. Villette à la Croix d'Or rue St. Jacques | Jacque Josse rue St. Jacques à la colombe royal | le Sr. Boivin rue St. Honoré à la regle d'Or | le Sr Des-hayes rue Charlot au marais | Renou sculp. ⟨1725?⟩]

8° 4 ℓ., 60, 51–111 [i. e. 110], [2] p., 1 ℓ., 83 p., illus., 6 pl., music
The second section, which contains dance tunes and choreographic notation, has separate title-page: Seconde Partie | Contenant | Douze des plus belles Danses | de Monsieur Pecour Composi-teur | des Ballets de l'Academie Royalle | de Musique | Et remis en Choregraphie Suivant | la Nouvelle Correction et aug-mentation | du Sr. Rameau Mtre. à Danser Ordinaire | de la Maison de la Reine Seconde doüair|riere d'Espagne Seul Privilegié du | Roy pour l'Art d'ecrire toutes Sortes de | Danses

No. 73 omitted in paging in first sequence; pages 1–83 at end include numbered leaves 9, 44, 57, 64, 71
Imperfect: title-page lacking; title supplied from Beaumont, p. 149–150
RISM B VI, 686
HOUGHTON

RAND, ESTIENNE DU   *See* Durand, Estienne

1267   RATHGEBER, VALENTIN

Decas | Mariano-Musica. | Hoc Est: | X.
Missae | Solennes Diductiores, | Minus-
que | Solennes Breviores | Non Tam Pro |
Festivitatibus | B. V. Mariae, | Quam | Per
Annum Universim Producendis; | à |
Canto, Alto, Tenore, Basso, partim 2.
Violinis, partim | Violino unisono: Item
notandum, Missa nona de 7. doloribus B.
V. | à 2. Alt-Violis s. Bracciis, ultima verò
brevissima à Violino unisono | ad libi-
tum; Clarinis vel Lituis ad 8. Missas, ex
diversis clavibus | ad libitum, exceptâ
primâ solenn. Clarinis obligatis, | & du-
plici Basso Continuo. | Auctore P. Valen-
tino Rathgeber, | Ober-Elsbacensi Fran-
cone Ord. S. Benedicti | in Banth
Professo. | Opus VII. | . . . | Cum Per-
missu Superiorum. | Augustae Vindeli-
corum, | Typis & Sumptibus Joannis Ja-
cobi Lotteri, Anno 1730.

2° 9 pts.: *canto, alto, tenore, basso:* 2
ℓ., 59 [1] p. each; *clarino vel lituo I,
clarino vel lituo II:* 2 *ℓ.,* 27, [1] p. each;
violino I, violino II: 2 *ℓ.,* 70 p. each; *organo:* 4 *ℓ.,* 72 p.
Unnumbered page at end of *canto,
alto, tenore, basso, clarino vel lituo I,
clarino vel lituo II* parts: Verzeichnus der
Musicalischen Büchern, welche bey Jo-
hann Jacob Lotter, | . . . zu haben sind
1730.
RISM A I, no. R 301
HOUGHTON

1268   RATHGEBER, VALENTIN

Harmonia Lugubris | In | Refrigerium
Fidelium | Defunctorum Conscripta |
Continens | Missas | De Requiem VI. | Et |
II. Libera | A | IV. Vocibus ordinariis, In-
strumentis partim necessariis, | partim
pro libitu adhibendis, vel omittendis, |
prout Index Operis docebit, | Denuo Ex-
hibita | Ac | In Lucem Edita | à | P. Valen-
tino Rathgeber, | Ord. S. Benedicti
Monasterii Banthensis in Franconia |
professo, patriâ Ober-Elsbacensi. | Opus
VIII. | . . . | Cum Licentia Superiorum. |
Augustae Vindelicorum, | Typis &
Sumptibus Joannis Jacobi Lotteri,
MDCCXXXI.

2° 1 pt.: *violoncello:* 2 *ℓ.,* 46 p.
RISM A I, no. R 302
HOUGHTON

1269   RATHGEBER, VALENTIN

Harmonia Mariano-Musica, | Sive |
Opus Miscellaneum | Extra-Ordinarium,
| Juxta | Diversitatem Temporum | pro
universis Choris Musicis Catholico-Ro-
manis, | Continens | VI. Litanias | Laure-
tanas | de B. V. Maria, | Cum | XV. Anti-
phonis | Alma Redemptoris III. | Ave
Regina Coelorum III. | Regina Coeli Lae-
tare III. | Salve Regina VI. | Te Deum Lau-
damus II. | Miserere II. | à | IV. Voci-
bus ordinariis C. A. T. B. II. Violinis ne-
cessariis, | II. Tubis vel Lituis ex diversis
Clavibus & Tympano, ad placitum | ad-
hibendis vel omittendis, cum duplici
Basso Continuo. | Praelo publico expo-
sita | â | P. Valentino Rathgeber, Ord. D.
Bened. | Coenobii Banthensis ad SS. Pe-
trum & Dionysium | propè Divos 14.
Auxiliatores in Franconia Professo. |
Opus V. | . . . | Cum Facultate Su-
periorum. | Augustae Vindelicorum, |
Typis & sumptibus Joannis Jacobi Lotteri, Anno MDCCXXVII.

2° 11 pts.: *canto:* 2 *ℓ.,* 40 p.; *alto:* 2 *ℓ.,*
39, [1] p.; *tenore:* 2 *ℓ.,* 32 p.; *basso:* 2 *ℓ.,*
34, [2] p.; *tuba vel lituo I, tuba vel lituo
II:* 2 *ℓ.,* 12 p. each; *tympano:* [1], 3 p.;
violino I, violino II: 2 *ℓ.,* 52 p. each; *violoncello:* 2 *ℓ.,* 58, [2] p.; *organo:* 4 *ℓ.,* 58,
[2] p.
Unnumbered page at end of *alto* part-
book (and elsewhere): Verzeichnus derjenigen Musicalischen Bücher, welche
bey Johann Jacob | Lotter . . . zu haben
sind.
RISM A I, no. R 300
HOUGHTON

1270 RATHGEBER, VALENTIN

Novena | Principalis Constantiniana. | Hoc Est: | Missae Novem | Principales, | Exculto stylo sub modis Musicis concinnatae, & ad ma-|jorem Dei gloriam praelo commissae, | â IV. Vocibus ordinariis. II. Violinis necessariis. II. Clarinis, vel Lituis ex | diversis Clavibus ad libitum producendis, cum duplici Basso cont. | Datae, Dicatae, ac Dedicatae | Reverendissimo, Ac Celsissimo Domino, | Domino | Constantino, | Ex Illustrissima & Antiquissima Familia â Butler, | D. G. Ducalis Ecclesiae Fuldensis Antistiti, | S. R. I. Principi, | Divae Augustae Romanorum Imperatricis | Archi-Cancellario, Per Germaniam Et Galliam Primati, | Anno gloriosissimi Regiminis undecimo, | Quo | De familia Bvtleriana extra nova | Constantini trophaea* | In honore Verae & non Interitvrae gloriae | Labor Magnvs praedicatvr: | Ab Authore | P. Valentino Rathgeber, Ord. Divi Benedicti | ac Monasterij Banthensis in Franconia prope 14. Sanctos Professo. | Opus III. | . . . | Cum Permissu Superiorum. | Augustae Vindelicorum, | Typis ac Sumptibus Joannis Jacobi Lotteri, Anno 1725.

2° 9 pts.: *canto, alto, tenore, basso:* [–]², A–Q² each; *tuba vel lituo I:* [–]², a–g²; *tuba vel lituo II:* [–]², aa–gg²; *violino I, violino II:* [–]², A–U², X1 each; *organo:*)(⁴, A–U²

Includes a part for kettledrum for *Missa II* in eighteenth-century manuscript

Leaf Q2ᵛ in *canto* and *basso* parts: Verzeichnus derjenigen Musicalischen Bůcher, welche bey Verlegern dieses zu haben sind.

RISM A I, no. R 297

HOUGHTON

RAU, GEORG *See* Rhaw, Georg

1271 RAUZZINI, VENANZIO

Six | Favourite Sonatas, | For The | Piano Forte. | Composed By, | Venanzio Rauzzini. | London: | Printed for Harrison, Cluse, & Co. No, 78, Fleet Street. [1799?]

8° *Score:* 81 p. (*The Piano-Forte Magazine,* vol. VIII, no. 6)

Plate nos. 124–127

RISM A I, no. R 435

MUSIC LIBRARY

1272 [RAVENSCROFT, THOMAS, COMP.]

[Pammelia. | Mvsicks | Miscellanie. | Or, | Mixed Varietie Of | Pleasant Roundelayes, and | delightfull Catches, of 3. 4. | 5. 6. 7. 8. 9. 10. Parts | in one. | None so ordinarie as musicall, none so musical, | as not to all, very pleasing and acceptable | London | Printed by William Barley, for | R. B. [i. e. Richard Bonion] and H. W. [i. e. Henry Walley] and are to be sold | at the Spread Eagle at the great | North dore of Paules. | 1609. | Cum Priuilegio.]

4° A², B–G⁴, H²

Gathering F from edition of 1618 inserted after leaf G4

Imperfect: Gathering A, leaf B2, gathering H lacking; title-page and second copy of leaf B1 supplied in negative photostat

RISM A I, no. R 454; RISM B I, no. 1609³¹

HOUGHTON

1273 [RAVENSCROFT, THOMAS, COMP.]

Pammelia. | Mvsickes | Miscellanie: | Or | Mixed Varietie | of plesant Rovndelayes, | and delightfull Catches, | of 3. 4. 5. 6. 7. 8. 9. 10. | Parts in one. | None so ordinary as Musicall, none so Musicall, | as not to all very pleasing and acceptable. | London: | Printed by Thomas Snodham, for | Mathew Lownes and Iohn Browne, 1618. | Cvm Privilegio.

4° A–F⁴

Interleaved copy.

Imperfect: leaf D2 lacking; supplied in manuscript

RISM A I, no. R 455; RISM B I, no. 1618²⁰

HOUGHTON

1274 RAZZI, SERAFINO, COMP.

Libro Primo | Delle Lavdi Spiritvali | Da Diversi Eccell. E Divoti Avtori, | Antichi E Moderni Composte. | Le quali si vsano cantare in Firenze nelle Chiese doppo il Vespro | ò la Compieta à consolatione & trattenimento | de' diuoti serui di Dio. | Con la propria Musica e modo di cantare ciascuna Laude, come si è vsato | da gli antichi, et si vsa in Firenze. | Raccolte dal R. P. Fra Serafino Razzi Fiorentino, dell'ordine | de' Frati Predicatore, à contemplatione delle Monache, | & altre diuote persone. | Nuouamente stampate. | Con Priuilegij della Illustriss. Signoria di Venetia, et del | Duca di Firenze, & di Siena. | In Venetia, ad instantia de' Giunti di Firenze. | M.D.LXIII.

4° 5 ℓ., 147 [i. e. 148] numb. ℓ., [2] p.
Colophon: Stampata in Venetia, per Francesco Rampazetto, | ad instanzia de gli heredi di Bernardo Giunti | di Firenze. 1563.
Number 3 repeated in foliation
RISM B I, no. 1563[6]
HOUGHTON

1275 REBEL, FRANÇOIS

Pirame Et Thisbé | Tragedie. | Mise en Musique | Par Mrs. Rebel Fils, et Francoeur Cadet, | Compositeurs de la Musique de la Chambre du Roy. | Representée pour la premiere fois par l'Academie Royale de | Musique, le 15e. Octobre 1726. | Se Vend à Paris | . . . | Chez | les Srs. {Francoeur Carfourt des quatres Cheminées butte Saint Roch. | Rebel ruë Royal butte Saint Roch. | Boivin Marchand, ruë Saint Honoré à la Regle d'Or. | Et à la porte de l'Opera. | Avec Privilége du Roy. 1726.

obl. 2° *Score:* 4 ℓ., 49, 272 p.
Francoeur's autograph signature on page 272
RISM A I, no. F 1795
MUSIC LIBRARY

1276 REBEL, FRANÇOIS

Le Prince De Noisi, | Ballet-Héroïque, | Représenté, pour la premiere fois, Devant Le Roi | Sur le Théâtre des petits-Appartements à Versailles Le 13. Mars 1749. | Remis Sur le même Théâtre, en présence de Sa Majesté, Le 10. Mars

1750. | Repris, pour la Troisieme fois, sur le Théâtre de Bellevue, aussi en pré-|-sence du Roi, Le 17 Mai 1752. | Représenté, pour la premiere fois, par L'Academie-Royale de Musique, | Le Mardi 16. Septembre 1760. | Mis En Musique Par | Mrs. Rebel Et Francoeur, | Sur-Intendants de la Musique de Sa Majesté, et Directeurs de | L'Académie-Royale de Musique. | Les Paroles Sont de Feu Mr. De la Bruere. | Gravé par Le Sr. Hue | . . . | A Paris | Chés {Les Auteurs, rue St. Nicaize, à L'Academie-Royale de Musique. Le Sr. Bayard, Md. rue St. Honoré à la Regle D'Or. | Le Sr. de la Chevardiere, rue du Roule à la Croix D'Or. Le Sr. Le Claire, Md. rue St. Honoré près la rue Des prouvaires à Ste. Cecile. | Et à la Porte de l'Opera. | Imprimé par Le sr Petitbled, fils | Avec Privilege Du Roi. [1760]

obl. 2° *Score:* 2 ℓ., 167, [1] p.
Francoeur's autograph signature on page 167
RISM A I, no. F 1797
HOUGHTON

1277

Recveil | Des Danses, Ballets, | Allemandes, Brandes, Covrantes, | Sarabandes, &c. | de Diuerses Autheurs A 2. Parties. | . . . | A Anvers, | Chez les Heritiers de Pierre | Phalese au Roy Dauid. | . . . 1642.

obl. 4° 1 pt.: *svperivs:* 1 ℓ., 84, [2] p.
HOUGHTON

1278

Recveil | Des Plvs Beavx | Airs Accompagnes | de Chansons à dancer, Bal-|lets, Chansons folatres, & Ba-|chanales, autrement dites | Vaudeuire, non encores | Imprimes. | TC. | Ausquelles Chansons l'on à mis la Musique de | leur chant, afin que chacun les puisse chanter | et dancer le tout à vne seule voix. | A Caen. | Chez Iaqves Mangeant. | M.DC.XV.

12° 47 numb. ℓ., 1 ℓ.
RISM B I, no. 1615[8]
HOUGHTON

1279

Le | Recveil | Des Plvs Bel-|les Chansons | de dances de ce | temps. | T. C. | A Caen, | Chez Iacqves | Mangent. | 1615.

12° 59 numb. *ℓ.,* 1 *ℓ.*
RISM B I, no. 1615⁹
HOUGHTON

1280

Recveil | Des Plvs Belles | Chansons Des | Comediens François. | En ce comprins les Airs de plusieurs Ballet | qui ont esté faits de nouueau | à la Cour. | Reueu & augmenté de plusieurs | Chansons non encor | veuës. | A Caen, | Chez Iaqves Mangeant [1615?]

12° 94 numb. *ℓ.,* 2 *ℓ.*
RISM B I, no. 1615¹⁰
HOUGHTON

REFLEXIONS D'UN PATRIOTE SUR L'OPÉRA FRANÇOIS *See* Rochemont, de *Reflexions d'un patriote sur l'opéra françois*

1281 REGGIO, PIETRO

Songs set by Signior Pietro Reggio. | . . . [London, 1680]

2° *Score:* 4 *ℓ.,* 42 p., 1 *ℓ.,* 30 p., 1 *ℓ.*
Day no. 52; RISM A I, no. R 724
HOUGHTON

1282 [REICHARDT, JOHANN FRIEDRICH]

Bemerkungen eines Reisenden | über die | zu Berlin | vom | September 1787 bis Ende Januar 1788 | gegebene | öffentliche Musiken, | Kirchenmusik, Oper, Concerte, | und | Königliche Kammermusik | betreffend. | Halle 1788.

8° 79 p.
RISM B VI, 921
MUSIC LIBRARY

1283 REICHARDT, JOHANN FRIEDRICH

Musikalisches | Kunstmagazin | von | Johann Friederich Reichardt. | . . . | Ber-

lin, 1782.[–1791.] | Im Verlage des Verfassers.

4° 2 vols.: *1782:* XII, 214 p., music; *1791:* 2 *ℓ.,* 126, [2] p., music
RISM B VI, 691
MUSIC LIBRARY

1284 REICHARDT, JOHANN FRIEDRICH

Ueber | die Pflichten | des | Ripien-Violinisten, | von | Johann Friedrich Reichardt, | Königl. Preussischen Capellmeister. | Berlin und Leipzig, | bey George Jacob Decker, 1776.

8° 92 p., illus., music
RISM B VI, 692
MUSIC LIBRARY

1285 [REICHARDT, JOHANN FRIEDRICH]

Vertraute Briefe | Über | Frankreich. | Auf Einer Reise | Im Jahr 1792 Geschrieben. | . . . | Berlin, | Bei Johann Friedrich Unger. | 1792.[–1793]

8° 2 vols.: *vol. I:* XIV, 354 p.; *vol. II:* 1 *ℓ.,* 445 p.
RISM B VI, 692
MUSIC LIBRARY

1286 REINHARD, LEONARD

Kurzer und deutlicher | Unterricht | von dem | General-Bass, | in welchem | durch deutliche Regeln und leichte Exempel nach dem neuesten | Musicalischen Stylo gezeiget wird, wie die Anfänger in dieser höchst-nütz-|lichen Wissenschafft zu einer gründlichen Fertigkeit auf die leichteste Art | gelangen können, | verfertiget | von | Leonhard Reinhard, | Litterarum Humaniorum & Musices Cultore. | Augspurg, gedruckt und verlegt von Johann Jacob Lotters seel. Erben. 1750.

obl. 4° 60 p., illus., music
RISM B VI, 693
MUSIC LIBRARY

1287 [REISCH, GREGOR]

Margarita Philosophica. [Strassburg, 1504]

4° [−]⁶, a−c⁶, d−z⁸, aa−pp⁸, qq⁶, rr⁸, ss⁴, tt⁸ (tt8 blank), illus., 3 fold. pl., music
Colophon: Rursus exaratum p[er] uigili, noua, itēq[ue] | secūdaria hac opera Joannis Schotti | Argentineñ. Chalchographi Ciuis: ad | 17. kl'. Apriles Anno gratie. 1504.
RISM B VI, 694; Wolfenbüttel, no. 1276
HOUGHTON

1288 [REISCH, GREGOR]

Margarita Philosophica. [Basel, 1508]

4° a−z⁸, A−N⁸, O−P⁶, Q−R⁸, illus., fold. pl., music
Colophon: Tertio industria complicū Micha|elis Furterij, et Jōanis Scoti | studiosiissime pressa. Ba-|sile[a]e ad. 14 Kal'. Mar|tias. Anno Christi. | 1508
Title-page trimmed and mounted
Imperfect: two plates lacking
RISM B VI, 694
HOUGHTON

1289 REISCH, GREGOR

Margarita | Filosofica | Del Rdo. P. F. Gregorio Reisch, | Nella quale si trattano con bellissimo, & breue metodo | non solo tutte le dottrine comprese nella | Ciclopedia dagli antichi, | Cioè Cerchio, ouer Rotolo delle scienze; | Ma Molte Altre Ancora Aggivntevi | di nouo da Orontio Fineo Matematico Regio. | Tradotta nuouamente dalla lingua Latina nell'Italiana da | Giovan Paolo Gallvcci Salodiano | Accademico Veneto; | E dal medesimo accresciuta di varie, e bellissime cose | come nella Nona Pagina si vede. | Non meno per i curiosi diletteuole, che vtile, e giouueuole per gli Studiosi. | Con Licenza de' Superiori, & Priuilegij. | In Venetia, M.D.XCIX. | Appresso Iacomo Antonio Somascho.

4° 12 ℓ., 1138 p., illus., music
Imperfect: pages 1129, 1130, and plate lacking
RISM B VI, 695−696
HOUGHTON

1290 RELFE, JOHN

Mary's Dream | Or | Sandy's Ghost, | Sung by Miss Chanu | at Hanover Square

Concerts, and at the | Pantheon | Set to Music by | J: Relfe. | . . . | London | Printed by Longman and Broderip No. 26 Cheapside. | and No. 13 Hay Market. | . . . [ca. 1794]

2° *Score:* 5 p.
RISM A I, no. R 1116
MUSIC LIBRARY

REMARQUES CURIEUSES SUR L'ART DE BIEN CHANTER *See* Bacilly, Bénigne de *Remarques curieuses sur l'art de bien chanter*

1291 REUCHLIN, JOHANN

De Accen|tibvs, Et Orthogra|phia, Lingvae Hebrai|cae, à Iohanne Reuchlin Phorcensi | LL. Doctore Libri Tres Car|dinali Adriano dicati. [Hagenau, 1518]

4° LXXXII numb. ℓ., 5 ℓ.
At end: Pentateuchal trope for four voices, in choirbook format
Colophon: Hagenoae in aedibus Thomae Anshelmi Badensis | Anno M.D.XVIII. Mense Februario.
Hirsch I, no. 502
HOUGHTON

1292 REUCHLIN, JOHANN

Joannis Reuchlin Phorcen|sis Sc[a]enica Progymnasmata, Hoc est | Ludicra praeexercitamenta. | . . . [Pforzheim, 1509]

4° a−b⁶, music
Colophon: Phorce in [a]edibus Thom[a]e | Anshelmi. Anno. M.D.IX.
Imperfect: leaf b6 torn, with loss of text
HOUGHTON

1293 RHAW, GEORG

Enchiri-|dion | Vtrivsqve | Mvsicae Practi-|cae a Georgio Rhauo, | ex varijs Musicorum li-|bris, pro pueris in Schola | Vitebergensi | congestum. | [Wittenberg] M.D.XLVI.

8° A−K⁸, L⁴, illus., music
Colophon: Vitebergae | Apvd Georgivm | Rhav.
RISM B VI, 700
HOUGHTON

1294 RICHARDSON, VAUGHAN

A | Collection | Of New | Songs, | For One, Two, and Three | Voices, | Accompany'd vvith Instruments. | Compos'd by Vaughan Richardson Organist of | the Cathedral-Church of Winchester. | Several of the Songs that are not in the Compass, are Transpos'd | for the Flute, at the end of the Book. | London: | Printed by William Pearson, for the Author, and Sold by Mr. Playford | at his Shop in the Temple-Change Fleet-street; Mr. Hare at the Gol-|den Viol in St. Paul's Church-Yard, and at his Shop, in Freeman's | Yard in Cornhill; and all other Musick-Shops in Town 1701.

2° *Score:* 1 ℓ., 32 p.
Day, no. 189; RISM A I, no. R 1314
HOUGHTON

1295 RICHTER, FRANZ XAVER

A | Concerto, | Composed For The | Piano Forte, | By | Richter. | London: | Printed for Harrison & Co. No. 78, Fleet Street. [1798?]

8° *Score:* 11 p. (*The Piano-Forte Magazine*, vol. IV, no. 8)
Plate no. 58
RISM A I, no. R 1346
MUSIC LIBRARY

1296 RIEPEL, JOSEPH

Anfangsgründe | zur | musicalischen | Setzkunst: | Nicht zwar | nach alt-mathematischer Einbildungs-Art | der Zirkel-Harmonisten, | Sondern | durchgehends mit sichtbaren Exempeln | abgefasset. | Erstes Capitel | De | Rhythmopoeïa, | Oder | von der | Tactordnung. | Zu etwa beliebigem Nutzen | herausgegeben | von | Joseph Riepel. | . . . | Regensburg und Wien, im Emerich Felix Baders Buchladen, 1752. | . . .

2° 2 ℓ., 79 p., music
Colophon: Augspurg, gedruckt bey Johann Jacob Lotter. 1752.
Hirsch I, no. 505; RISM B VI, 704
MUSIC LIBRARY

1297 [RINALDO DI CAPUA]

La | Bohemienne | Comedie | En Deux Actes En Vers | Meslée d'Ariettes, | Traduite De La Zingara | Intermede Italien | Par Mr Favart | Representée Pour La Premiere Fois | Par les Comédiens Italiens Ordinaires du Roi | Le 28 Juillet 1755 et à la Cour devant leus Majestés | le 1er Decbre. de la mesme année et le 11. fevrier 1756 | . . . | A Paris | Chez {Mr De la Chevardiere Editeur Successeur de Mr. le Clerc rue du Roule | à la Croix d'Or. Et Aux Adresses Ordinaires de Musique. | à Lyon Mrs. Les Freres Le Goux Place des Cordeliers. | à Marseille. Mr. Jayne le Fils Libraire sur le Port. | . . . | Avec Privilege Du Roi. | Gravé par Melle. Vendome. | Imprimé par Bournelli [1761?]

2° *Score:* 2 ℓ., 95 p.
On recto of preliminary leaf 2: Catalogue | de Musique Vocale et Instrumentale que M. De Lachevardiere Successeur de | M. Le Clerc . . . a fait graver . . . ⟨JohanssonF facs. 47⟩
RISM A I, no. R 1714
MUSIC LIBRARY

1298 [RITSON, JOSEPH, COMP.]

Ancient Songs, | From The Time Of | King Henry The Third, | To The | Revolution. | . . . | London: | Printed for J. Johnson, in St. Pauls Church Yard. | MDCCXC.

8° 2 ℓ., lxxx, 332 p., illus.
Pages i–xxvi: Observations | On The | Ancient English Minstrels
Pages xxvii–lxxvi: Dissertation | On The | Songs, Music, And Vocal And Instru-|mental Performances | Of The | Ancient English.
HOUGHTON

1299 [RITSON, JOSEPH, COMP.]

A | Select | Collection | Of | English Songs. | In Three Volumes. | . . . | London: | Printed for J. Johnson in St. Pauls Church-yard. | MDCCLXXXIII.

8° 3 vols.: *vol. I:* 1 ℓ., xiv, lxxii p., 1 ℓ., 264 p., front., illus.; *vol. II:* 2 ℓ., 342, [32] p., illus.; *vol. III:* [–]1–5, A–K⁸, [2d]A–I⁸
Pages [i]–lxxii in vol. I: A | Historical Essay | On The | Origin and Progress | Of | National Song.
RISM B II, 104
HOUGHTON

1300   [RITSON, JOSEPH, COMP.]

Scotish Song | In Two Volumes. | . . . | London: | Printed for J. Johnson, In St. Pauls Church-|Yard; And J. Egerton, Whitehall. | MDCCXIV. [i. e. MDCCXCIV]

8° 2 vols.: *vol. I:* 1 ℓ., cxix, [1], 289 p., illus.; *vol. II:* 1 ℓ., 262, [4] p., illus.
Pages [xi]–cxix in *vol. I:* A | Historical Essay | On | Scotish Song.
RISM B II, 350
HOUGHTON

1301   [ROCHEMONT, _____ DE]

Reflexions | D'Un Patriote | Sur | L'Opera François, | Et Sur | L'Opera Italien, | Qui présentent le Parallel du goût | des deux Nations dans les beaux Arts. | A Lausanne. | M.DCC.LIV.

8° xij, 137, [1] p.
Hirsch I, no. 509; RISM B VI, 709
HOUGHTON

ROCHETTE DE LAMORLIÈRE, JACQUES *See* Lamorlière, Jacques Rochette de

1302   ROESER, VALENTIN

Twelve | Easy Lessons, | For The | Piano Forte. | Composed By, | V: Roeser. | Opera 6. | London: | Printed for Harrison, Cluse & Co. No. 78, Fleet Street. [1799?]

8° *Score:* 45 p. (*The Piano-Forte Magazine,* vol. IX, no. 2)
Plate nos. 133–134
RISM A I, no. R 1891
MUSIC LIBRARY

RÖSSLER, FRANTIŠEK ANTONIN *See* Rosetti, Anton

1303   ROLLI, PAOLO ANTONIO

Di | Canzonette | E Di | Cantate | Libri Due | Di | Paolo Rolli. | Londra: | Presso Tommaso Edlin. MDCCXXVII.

8° 4 ℓ., 124, XXIIII p.
RISM A I, no. R 2083
MUSIC LIBRARY

ROND D'ALEMBERT, JEAN LE *See* Alembert, Jean Lerond d'

1304   RONSARD, PIERRE DE

Les Amovrs | De P. De Ronsard | Vandomois, Nov-|uellement augmētées par lui, | & commentées par Marc An-|toine de Muret. | Plus quelques Odes de L'auteur, | non encor imprimées. | . . . | Avec Privilege Dv Roy. | A Paris. | Chez la veuue Maurice de la Porte. | 1553.

8° 8 ℓ., 282 [i. e. 262], [2], [63] p.
Pages [2]–[59], second sequence: chansons for four voices in choirbook format by Pierre Certon, Claude Goudimel, Clément Janequin and Marc Antoine de Muret
Unnumbered page [2] after page [262]: Acheué d'imprimer le | xxiij. de May. | 1553.; page [63], second sequence: Acheué d'imprimer le trentieme iour | de septembre, Mil cinq cens | cinquante deux.
Numbers 129–138, 170–179 omitted in paging
RISM B I, no. 1553²¹; Thibault, no. 4
HOUGHTON

ROSE ET COLAS *See* Monsigny, Pierre Alexandre *Rose et Colas*

1305   ROSETTI, ANTON

Three | Favourite | Divertisements | For The | Piano Forte. | Composed By | Sigr. Rosetti. | Op: 2. | London: | Printed for Harrison, Cluse, & Co. No. 78, Fleet Street. [1799?]

8° *Score:* 43 p. (*The Piano-Forte Magazine,* vol. IX, no. 1)
Plate nos. 131–132
RISM A I, no. R 2615
MUSIC LIBRARY

1306   ROSOY, BARANABÉ FARMIAN DE

Dissertation | Sur Le | Drame Lyrique, | Par M. De Rozoi, | Citoyen De Toulouse, | Des Académies, Etc. | Dédiée | A M. le Docteur D. . . . . | A La Haye, | Et se trouve | A Paris, | Chez la veuve Du-

chesne, Libraire, rue St.-Jacques, | au-des-
sous de la Fontaine Saint-Benoît, | au
Temple du Goût. | M.DCC.LXXV.

8° 56 p.
Colophon: De l'Imprimerie de Cl.
Simon, Imprimeur-Libraire, | rue des
Mathurins. 1776.
MUSIC LIBRARY, WIDENER

1307 ROSSETER, PHILIP

[A | Booke Of | Ayres, | Set foorth to be
song | to the Lute, Orpherian, and | Base
Violl, by Philip Rosseter | Lutenist: And
are to be solde | at his house in Fleet-
streete | neere to the Gray-|hound. | At
Lonond [sic] | Printed by Peter Short, by
the assent | of Thomas Morley, | 1601.]

2° A–M²
Imperfect: gatherings A, G lacking;
supplied in facsimile
RISM B I, no. 1601¹⁷
HOUGHTON

1308 ROUSSEAU, JEAN

Traité | De La Viole, | Qui Contient |
Une Dissertation curieuse sur son ori-
gine. | Une Démonstration generale de
son Manche en | quatre Figures, avec
leurs explications. | L'explication de ses
Jeux differents, & particu-|lierement des
Pieces par accords, & de l'ac-|compagne-
ment à fond. | Des Regles certaines, pour
connoître tous les | agrémens qui se peu-
vent pratiquer sur cét | instrument dans
toutes sortes de Pieces de | Musique. | La
veritable maniere de gouverner l'Archet,
& | des Moyens faciles pour transposer
sur toutes | sortes de Tons. | Par Iean
Rovsseav, Maître de | Musique & de
Viole. | Demeurant ruë des Boucheries,
proche le Petit Mar-|ché, devant la Bar-
riere, au Soleil d'Or, chez un | Bonnetier,
Faux-bourg Saint Germain. | A Paris, | Par
Christophe Ballard, seul Imprimeur | du
Roy pour la Musique. | M.DC.LXXXVII. |
Avec Privilege de Sa Majesté.

8° 8 ℓ., 151 p., fold. pl., music
Davidsson II, no. 89; Hirsch I, no. 513;
RISM B VI, 720
HOUGHTON

1309 ROUSSEAU, JEAN JACQUES

The | Favourite Songs | in the Opera
call'd | Le Devin Du Village, | With a
Thorough Bass for the Harpsichord or
Violoncello | Compos'd by | Mr. I. I.
Rousseau. | London, Printed for John
Cox in Sweetings Alley Royal Ex-
change . . . [1755]

obl 2° *Vocal score:* 1 ℓ., 13 p.
RISM A I, no. R 2926
HOUGHTON

1310 ROUSSEAU, JEAN JACQUES

Le Devin | Du Village | Interméde |
Représenté A Fontainebleau | Devant
leurs Majestés | les 18. et 24. Octobre.
1752. | Et A Paris Par | l'Académie Royale
de Musique | le 1er. Mars 1753. | Par | J. J.
Rousseau. | Gravé par Melle. Vandôme,
depuis la 1re. Planche jusqu'à la 50 | . . . |
A Paris | Chez Le Clerc, Ruë St. Honoré,
entre la Ruë des Prouvaires, et | la ruë
Dufour à Sainte Cecile. | Et Aux Adresses
Ordinaires. | Avec Privilege Du Roy.
Jmprimé par Chouin [ca. 1759?]

2° *Score:* 2 ℓ., 95 p.
Hirsch II, no. 821; RISM A I, no. R
2900
HOUGHTON

1311 ROUSSEAU, JEAN JACQUES

Le Devin | Du Village | Interméde |
Représenté A Fontainebleau | Devant
leurs Majestés | les 18. et 24. Octobre.
1752. | Et A Paris Par | l'Académie Royale
de Musique | le 1er. Mars 1753. | Par | J. J.
Rousseau. | . . . | A Paris | Chez M. le
Duc, rue Traversiere St. Honoré, près
l'Hotel de Bayonne | et Aux Adresses Or-
dinaires | A. P. D. R. | G. Magnian Script.
[ca. 1783]

2° *Score:* 2 ℓ., 95 p.
On recto and verso of preliminary leaf
2: [Catalogue] | de Musique Vocale
[–Instrumentale] Appartenant a Monsr.
Le Duc | . . . ⟨A later state of Johans-
sonF facs. 65–66⟩
RISM A I, no. R 2903 ⟨without plate
no.⟩
MUSIC LIBRARY

1312 ROUSSEAU, JEAN JACQUES

A | Dictionary of Music. | Translated from the French of | Mons. J. J. Rousseau. | By William Waring. | London: | Printed for J. French, No. 47, opposite Hatton-|Garden, Holborn. [1779?]

8° 470 p., illus., 2 fold. pl., music
Plates included in paging
Imperfect: pages 117–124 lacking
RISM B VI, 723
WIDENER

1313 ROUSSEAU, JEAN JACQUES

A | Complete Dictionary | Of | Music. | Consisting Of | A copious Explanation of all Words necessary to a true | Knowledge and Understanding of | Music. | Translated from the Original French of | J. J. Rousseau. | By William Waring. | Second Edition. | Dublin, | Printed For Luke White. | MDCCLXXIX.

8° 1 ℓ., 470 p., illus., 2 fold. pl., music
Plates included in paging
RISM B VI, 723
MUSIC LIBRARY

1314 ROUSSEAU, JEAN JACQUES

Dictionnaire | De | Musique, | Par J. J. Rousseau. | . . . | A Paris, | Chez la Veuve Duchesne, Libraire, | rue S. Jacques, au Temple du Goût. | M.DCC.LXVIII. | Avec Approbation Et Privilége du Roi.

8° xiv, [2], 547, [1], 4 p., illus., A–N fold. pl., music
Pages [1]–4 at end: Extrait du Catalogue de Librairie de la Veuve Duchesne.
Hirsch I, no. 521; RISM B VI, 720; Wolfenbüttel, no. 1285
HOUGHTON, MUSIC LIBRARY

1315 ROUSSEAU, JEAN JACQUES

Dictionnaire | De | Musique. | Par J. J. Rousseau. | . . . | A Amsterdam, | Chez Marc Michel Rey, | MDCCLXIX.

12° 2 vols.: *vol. I:* 1 ℓ., XIV, 504 p., illus., fold. pl., music; *vol. II:* 1 ℓ., 372 p., illus., A–N fold. pl. (incl. music)
In his *Oeuvres*, vols. X, XI
RISM B VI, 720–721
HOUGHTON

1316 ROUSSEAU, JEAN JACQUES

Dictionnaire | De | Musique. | Par J. J. Rousseau. | . . . | Geneve. | M.DCC.LXXXI.

4° 1 ℓ., xiv p., 1 ℓ., 772 p., front., illus., A–N pl., music
In his *Oeuvres*, vol. IX
RISM B VI, 721
HOUGHTON

—another copy
Large paper copy
HOUGHTON

1317 ROUSSEAU, JEAN JACQUES

Dictionnaire | De | Musique, | Par | J. J. Rousseau. | . . . | [Paris] Aux Deux-Ponts, | Chez Sanson Et Compagnie. | M.DCC.LXXXII.

12° 2 vols.: *vol. I:* 1 ℓ., 332 p., illus., music; *vol. II:* 3 ℓ., 224 p., illus., music
In his *Oeuvres*, vols. XVII, XVIII
RISM B VI, 722
WIDENER

1318 ROUSSEAU, JEAN JACQUES

Dictionnaire | De | Musique. | . . . [A Paris, | chez {Bélin, Libraire, rue St. Jacques, no. 26. | Caille, rue de la Harpe, no. 150. | Grégoire, rue du Coq St. Honoré. | Volland, quai des Augustins, no. 25. | 1793.]

12° 3 vols.: *vol. I:* 2 ℓ., 375 p., illus., 4 fold. pl. music; *vol. II:* 2 ℓ., 402 p., illus., 4 fold. pl. (incl. music); *vol. III:* 2 ℓ., 300 p., illus., 5 fold. pl. (incl. music)
In his *Oeuvres*, vols. XI–XIII
Half-title; imprint supplied from title-page
RISM B VI, 722
WIDENER

1319 ROUSSEAU, JEAN JACQUES

. . . Dictionnaire De Musique, . . . | A Paris Et A Amsterdam, | Chez J. E. Gabriel Dufour, Successeur de Defer De | Maissoneuve. | De L'Imprimerie De Didot Le Jeune. | An VII. [i.e. 1798/99]

2° 2 vols.: *vol. I:* 494 p., front., illus., music; *vol. II:* 357 p., illus., A–O pl. (1 fold.; incl. music)
In his *Oeuvres*, vols. X, XI
RISM B VI, 723
WIDENER

1320 ROUSSEAU, JEAN JACQUES

Dissertation | Sur | La Musique | Moderne. | Par M. Rousseau. | . . . | A Paris, | Chez G. F. Quillau, Pere, Imprimeur-Juré-Libraire | de l'Université, rue Galande, près la Place-Maubert, | à l'Annonciation. | M.DCC.XLIII. | Avec Approbation & Privilége du Roy.

8° 1 ℓ., xvj, 101, [3] p., illus., fold. pl.
Hirsch I, no. 514; RISM B VI, 723
HOUGHTON

1321 ROUSSEAU, JEAN JACQUES

Dissertation | Sur | La Musique| Moderne. | . . . [A Geneve. | M.DCC.LXXXII.]

4° In his *Oeuvres*, vol. VIII, p. [233]–353, illus., pl.
Half-title; imprint supplied from title-page
RISM B VI, 724
HOUGHTON

—another copy
Large paper copy
HOUGHTON

1322 ROUSSEAU, JEAN JACQUES

Dissertation | Sur La | Musique Moderne. | . . . [A Paris Et A Amsterdam, | Chez J. E. Gabriel Dufour, Successeur de Defer De | Maissonneuve. | De L'Imprimerie De Didot Le Jeune. | An VI. ⟨i. e. 1797/98⟩]

2° In his *Oeuvres*, vol. IX, p. [233]–363, illus., fold. pl.
Half-title; imprint supplied from title-page
WIDENER

1323 ROUSSEAU, JEAN JACQUES

Essai | Sur L'Origine | Des Langues. [A Londrès. ⟨i. e. Paris⟩ | M.DCC.LXXXII.]

24° In his *Mélanges*, vol. V, p. [127]–250
Caption title; imprint supplied from title-page
False imprint; published by Hubert Martin Cazin (see Dufour II, p. 28, no. 4436)
RISM B VI, 725
HOUGHTON (2 copies), WIDENER

1324 ROUSSEAU, JEAN JACQUES

Essai | Sur L'Origine | Des Langues, | Où il est parlé de la Mélodie Et de l'Imitation Musicale. [A Geneve. | M.DCC.LXXXII.]

4° In his *Oeuvres*, vol. VIII, p. [355]–434
Half-title; imprint supplied from title-page
RISM B VI, 725
HOUGHTON

—another copy
Large paper copy
HOUGHTON

1325 ROUSSEAU, JEAN JACQUES

Essai | Sur | L'Origine Des Langues, | Ou Il Est Parlé | De La Mélodie et de l'Imitation Musicale. [A Paris Et A Amsterdam, | Chez J. E. Gabriel Dufour, Successeur de Defer De | Maissonneuve. | De L'Imprimerie De Didot Le Jeune. | An VI. ⟨i. e. 1797/98⟩]

2° In his *Oeuvres*, vol. IX, p. [365]–445
Half-title; imprint supplied from title-page
WIDENER

1326 ROUSSEAU, JEAN JACQUES

Examen | De | Deux Principes | Avancés par M. Rameau, dans sa Brochure intitulée: | Erreurs | Sur | La Musique, | Dans L'Encyclopedie. | . . . [A Geneve. | M.DCC.LXXXII.]

4° In his *Oeuvres*, vol. VIII, p. [513]–539
Half-title; imprint supplied from title-page
RISM B VI, 726
HOUGHTON

—another copy
Large paper copy
HOUGHTON

1327   ROUSSEAU, JEAN JACQUES

Examen | De | Deux Principes | Avancés par Rameau, dans sa | Brochure intitulée: Erreurs sur la | Musique, dans l'Encyclopédie. [A Londres ⟨i. e. Paris⟩ | M.DCC.LXXXII.]

24° In his [*Oeuvres*], vol. [XIX], p. [251]–290
Caption title; imprint supplied from title-page
False imprint; published by Hubert Martin Cazin (see BN CLVII, col. 425)
HOUGHTON (2 copies), WIDENER

1328   ROUSSEAU, JEAN JACQUES

Examen | De | Deux Principes | Avancés Par M. Rameau, | Dans sa Brochure intitulée Erreurs Sur La | Musique, dans l'Encyclopédie. | . . . [A Paris Et A Amsterdam, | Chez J. E. Gabriel Dufour, Successeur de Defer De | Maisonneuve. | De L'Imprimerie De Didot Le Jeune. | An VI. ⟨i. e. 1797/98⟩]

2° In his *Oeuvres*, vol. IX, p. [529]–557
Half-title; imprint supplied from title-page
WIDENER

1329   ROUSSEAU, JEAN JACQUES

Extrait | D'Une Reponse | Du Petit Faiseur | A Son Prête-Nom, | Sur un morceau de l'Orphée de M. le Chevalier Gluck. [A Geneve. | M.DCC.LXXXII.]

4° In his *Oeuvres*, vol VIII, p. [577]–583
Caption title; imprint supplied from title-page
HOUGHTON

—another copy
Large paper copy
HOUGHTON

1330   ROUSSEAU, JEAN JACQUES

Extrait | D'Une Réponse | Du Petit Faiseur | A Son Prête-Nom, | Sur un mor-

ceau de l'Orphée de M. le Chevalier Gluck. [A Paris Et A Amsterdam, | Chez J. E. Gabriel Dufour, Successeur de Defer De | Maisonneuve. | De L'Imprimerie De Didot Le Jeune. | An VI. ⟨i. e. 1797/98⟩]

2° In his *Oeuvres*, vol. IX, p. [596]–602
Caption title; imprint supplied from title-page
WIDENER

ROUSSEAU, JEAN JACQUES Fragmens d'observations sur l'Alceste italien de M. le chevalier Gluck   *See* Rousseau, Jean Jacques *Lettre à M. Burney sur la musique*

1331   ROUSSEAU, JEAN JACQUES

Lettre | A M. Burney | Sur | La Musique, | Avec Fragmens d'Observations sur l'Alceste Italien de M. le | Chevalier Gluck. [A Geneve. | M.DCC.LXXXII.]

4° In his *Oeuvres*, vol. VIII, p. [541]–576, music
Half-title; imprint supplied from title-page
RISM B VI, 731
HOUGHTON

—another copy
Large paper copy
HOUGHTON

1332   ROUSSEAU, JEAN JACQUES

Lettre | A M. Burney | Sur | La Musique, | Avec Fragmens d'Observations sur l'Alceste Italien | de M. le Chevalier Gluck. [A Paris Et A Amsterdam, | Chez J. E. Gabriel Dufour, Successeur de Defer De | Maisonneuve. | De L'Imprimerie De Didot Le Jeune. | An VI. ⟨i. e. 1797/98⟩]

2° In his *Oeuvres*, vol. IX, p. [559]–595, music
Half-title; imprint supplied from title-page
WIDENER

1333   ROUSSEAU, JEAN JACQUES

Lettre | A Monsieur | L'Abbé Raynal, | Au sujet d'un nouveau Mode de Musique, inventé par | M. Blainville. [A Geneve. | M.DCC.LXXXII.]

4° In his *Oeuvres,* vol. VIII, p. [507]–511

Caption title; imprint supplied from title-page

HOUGHTON

—another copy
Large paper copy
HOUGHTON

1334   ROUSSEAU, JEAN JACQUES

Lettre | A Monsieur | L'Abbé Raynal, | Au sujet d'un nouveau Mode de Musique, inventé par | M. Blainville. [A Paris Et A Amsterdam, | Chez J. E. Gabriel Dufour, Successeur de Defer De | Maisonneuve. | De L'Imprimerie De Didot Le Jeune. | An VI. ⟨i. e. 1797/98⟩]

2° In his *Oeuvres,* vol. IX, p. [523]–527
Caption title; imprint supplied from title-page
WIDENER

1335   ROUSSEAU, JEAN JACQUES

Lettre | D'Un Symphoniste | De L'Academie Royale | De Musique, | A Ses Camarades De L'Orchestre. [A Geneve. | M.DCC.LXXXII.]

4° In his *Oeuvres,* vol. VIII, p. [495]–506
Caption title; imprint supplied from title-page
RISM B VI, 733
HOUGHTON

—another copy
Large paper copy
HOUGHTON

1336   ROUSSEAU, JEAN JACQUES

Lettre | D'Un Symphoniste | De l'Académie Royale de Musique, | A Ses Camarades De L'Qrchestre. [A Londres ⟨i. e. Paris⟩ | M.DCC.LXXXII.]

24° In his [*Oeuvres*], vol. [XX], p. [266]–281
Caption title; imprint supplied from title-page
False imprint; published by Hubert Martin Cazin (see BN CLVII, col. 425)
HOUGHTON (2 copies), WIDENER

1337   ROUSSEAU, JEAN JACQUES

Lettre | D'Un | Symphoniste | De l'Académie Royale de Musique, | A Ses Camarades De L'Orchestre. [⟨Paris⟩ Aux Deux-Ponts, | Chez Sanson Et Compagnie. | M.DCC.LXXXII.]

12° In his *Oeuvres,* vol. XV, p. [253]–263
Caption title; imprint supplied from title-page
RISM B VI, 733
WIDENER

1338   ROUSSEAU, JEAN JACQUES

Lettre | D'Un Symphoniste | De L'Académie Royale | De Musique, | A Ses Camarades De L'Orchestre. [A Paris Et A Amsterdam, | Chez J. E. Gabriel Dufour, Successeur de Defer De | Maissoneuve. | De L'Imprimerie De Didot Le Jeune. | An VI. ⟨i. e. 1797/98⟩]

2° In his *Oeuvres,* vol IX, p. [511]–522
Caption title; imprint supplied from title-page
WIDENER

1339   ROUSSEAU, JEAN JACQUES

Lettre | Sur | La Musique | Françoise. | Par J. J. Rousseau. | . . . | [Paris] M.DCC.LIII.

8° 2 ℓ., 92 p.
RISM B VI, 734
HOUGHTON

1340   ROUSSEAU, JEAN JACQUES

Lettre | Sur | La Musique | Françoise, | Par J. J. Rousseau. | . . . | Deuxiéme Édition. | [Paris] M.DCC.LIII.

8° 4 ℓ., 92 p.
RISM B VI, 734
HOUGHTON

1341   ROUSSEAU, JEAN JACQUES

Lettre | Sur La | Musique | Françoise. | Par J. J. Rousseau. [A Amsterdam, | Chez Marc-Michel Rey, | M.DCC.LXIX. | Avec Privilège de nos Seigneurs les Etats de | Hollande & de Westfrise.]

12° In his *Oeuvres,* vol. I, p. [237]–303
Caption title; imprint supplied from
title-page
RISM B VI, 735
HOUGHTON

1342   ROUSSEAU, JEAN JACQUES

Lettre | Sur | La Musique | Françoise. [A
Geneve. | M.DCC.LXXXII.]

4° In his *Oeuvres,* vol. VIII, p. [435]–
494
Half-title; imprint supplied from title-
page
RISM B VI, 735
HOUGHTON

—another copy
Large paper copy
HOUGHTON

1343   ROUSSEAU, JEAN JACQUES

Lettre | Sur | La Musique | Françoise. |
. . . [A Londres. ⟨i. e. Paris⟩ |
M.DCC.LXXXII]

24° In his [*Oeuvres*], vol. [XX],
p. [175]–265
Caption title; imprint supplied from
title-page
False imprint; published by Hubert
Martin Cazin (see BN CLVII, col. 425)
HOUGHTON (2 copies), WIDENER

1344   ROUSSEAU, JEAN JACQUES

Lettre | Sur | La Musique | Françoise. |
. . . [⟨Paris⟩ Aux Deux-Ponts,|
Chez Sanson Et Compagnie. |
M.DCC.LXXXII.]

12° In his *Oeuvres,* vol. XV, p. [199]–
252 [i. e. 260]
Half-title; imprint supplied from title-
page
Numbers 233, 234 omitted, 244–252
repeated in paging
Hirsch I, no. 524
WIDENER

1345   ROUSSEAU, JEAN JACQUES

Lettre | Sur | La Musique Françoise. [A
Paris Et A Amsterdam, | Chez J. E. Ga-
briel Dufour, Successeur de Defer De |

Maisonneuve. | De L'Imprimerie De
Didot Le Jeune. | An VI. ⟨i. e. 1797/98⟩]

2° In his *Oeuvres,* vol. IX, p. [447]–510
Half-title; imprint supplied from title-
page
RISM B VI, 736
WIDENER

1346   ROUSSEAU, JEAN JACQUES

Projet | Concernant | De Nouveaux
Signes | Pour La Musique. | . . . [A Ge-
neve. | M.DCC.LXXXII.]

4° In his *Oeuvres,* vol. VIII, p. [217]–
232
Half-title; imprint supplied from title-
page
RISM B VI, 736
HOUGHTON

—another copy
Large paper copy
HOUGHTON

1347   ROUSSEAU, JEAN JACQUES

Projet | Concernant | De Nouveaux
Signes | Pour | La Musique. [A Paris Et A
Amsterdam, | Chez J. E. Gabriel Dufour,
Successeur de Defer De | Maisonneuve. |
De L'Imprimerie De Didot Le Jeune. | An
VI. ⟨i. e. 1797/98⟩]

2° In his *Oeuvres,* vol. IX, p. [215]–232
Half-title; imprint supplied from title-
page
WIDENER

1348   ROUSSEAU, JEAN JACQUES

Recueil | des | Oeuvres de Musique | de
| J. J. Rousseau | . . . | Ce Recueil est
gravé par Richomme [Paris, 1793]

8° *vol. I:* 1 ℓ., 319 [i. e. 321], VI p.,
front.
In his *Oeuvres,* vol. XXXVII
Number 50 repeated twice in paging
Incomplete: *vol. II* lacking
WIDENER

1349   ROUSSEAU, JEAN JACQUES

Traités | Sur La | Musique. [Geneve. |
M.DCC.LXXXI.]

8° 437 [i. e. 445], [1] p., illus., fold. pl., music

Half-title; imprint supplied from page [3]

Numbers 201–208 repeated in paging

HOUGHTON

1350 ROUSSEAU, JEAN JACQUES

Traités | Sur La | Musique. | . . . [A Paris, | chez {Bélin, Libraire, rue St. Jacques, no. 26. | Caille, rue de la Harpe, no. 150. | Grégoire, rue du Coq St. Honoré. | Volland, quai des Augustins, no. 25. | 1793.]

12° 2 ℓ., 406 p., 1 ℓ., illus., music
In his *Oeuvres,* vol. XXVII
Half-title; imprint supplied from title-page

WIDENER

1351 ROUSSIER, PIERRE JOSEPH

L'Harmonie | Pratique, | Ou | Exemples | Pour Le Traité Des Accords, | Par M. Roussier, Chanoine d'Ecouis. | Mis au jour par M. Bailleux. | A Paris, | Chez L'Éditeur, Marchand de Musique ordinaire | des Menus-Plaisirs du Roi, rue S. Honoré, | à la Régle d'or. | A Lyon, chez M. Castaud. | A Toulouse, chez M. Brunet. | A Bordeaux, à Bruxelles, & à Lille, | Chez les Marchands de Musique. [1775?]

8° xvj, [2], 111 [i. e. 113] p., pl., music
Pages 1–4 of text printed as numbered leaves 1, 2
Page xvj: . . . Vu l'Approbation, permis di'mprimer, [*sic*] ce 1 Nov. 1775. | Albert.
Hirsch I, no. 529; RISM B VI, 737
MUSIC LIBRARY

1352 ROUSSIER, PIERRE JOSEPH

Mémoire | Sur La Musique | Des Anciens, | Où l'on expose le Principe des Proportions | authentiques, dites de Pythagore, & de divers | Systêmes de Musique chez les Grecs, les Chinois | & les Egyptiens. | Avec un Parallèle entre le Systême des Egyptiens | & celui des Modernes. | Par M. l'Abbé Roussier. | . . . | A Paris, | Chez Lacombe, Libraire, rue Christine. | M.DCC.LXX. | Avec Approbation Et Privilége Du Roi.

4° 2 ℓ., xxiv, 252 p., illus., 2 pl., music
Hirsch I, no. 528; RISM B VI, 738
MUSIC LIBRARY

1353 ROUSSIER, PIERRE JOSEPH

Observations | Sur Différens Points | D'Harmonie, | Par M. l'Abbé Roussier. | . . . | A Genève, | Et se trouvent à Paris, | Chez Bailleux, Marchand de Musique des menus | plaisirs du Roi, rue S. Honoré, à la Regle d'Or. | M.DCC.LV. | . . .

8° 4 ℓ., 249 p., illus., pl. (music)
RISM B VI, 738
MUSIC LIBRARY

1354 [ROUSSIER, PIERRE JOSEPH]

Traité | Des | Accords, | Et De Leur Succession; | Selon Le Systéme | De La Basse-Fondamentale; | Pour servir de Principes d'Harmonie à ceux qui étudient | la Composition ou l'Accompagnement du Clavecin; | Avec Une Méthode D'Accompagnement. | . . . | A Paris, | Chez M. Bailleux, Marchand de Musique ordinaire du | Roi, rue S.-Honoré. vis-à-vis celle des Bourdonnois, | à la Regle d'or. | M.D.CC.LXIV. | Avec Approbation, & Privilége du Roi.

8° xxxij, 192 p., illus., 4 pl. (incl. music)
Colophon: De L'Imprimerie de Ballard, Imprimeur du Roi.
RISM B VI, 739
MUSIC LIBRARY

1355 [ROUSSIER, PIERRE JOSEPH]

Traité | Des | Accords, | Et De Leur Succession, | Selon Le Systéme | De La Basse-Fondamentale; | Pour servir de Principes d'Harmonie à ceux qui étudient | la Composition ou l'Accompagnement du Clavecin. | Avec Une Methode D'Accompagnement. | . . . | A Paris, | Chez {Duchesne, Libraire, rue S. Jacques, au-dessous de la | Fontaine S. Benoît, au Temple du Goût. | Dessain junior, libraire, Quai des Augustins, à la | Bonne-Foi. | A Lyon, chez Jean-Marie Bruyset, Imprimeur-Libraire, | Rue S. Dominique. | M.D.CC.LXIV. | Avec Approbation & Privilège du Roi.

8° xxviij, [4], 192 p., illus., 4 pl., (incl. music)
Colophon: De l'Imprimerie de Ballard, Imprimeur du Roi.
RISM B VI, 739
MUSIC LIBRARY

ROY, ADRIAN LE *See* Le Roy, Adrian

LE ROY ET LE FERMIER *See* Monsigny, Pierre Alexandre *Le Roy et le fermier*

RUE, PIERRE DE LA *See* La Rue, Pierre de

S

1356 SABBATINI, LUIGI ANTONIO

La Vera Idea | Delle | Musicali Numeriche | Segnature | Diretta Al Giovane Studioso | Dell'Armonìa | Da F. Luigi Anto. Sabbatini M. C. | Maestro Di Cappella Nella Basilica | Di S. Antonio Di Padova. | Venezia, MDCCXCIX. | Presso Sebastian Valle. | Con Sovrano Permesso.

4° 1 ℓ., IV, CLXXIX, [1] p., pl. (port.), music
Colophon: Si dispensa dal Librajo | Silvestro Gnoato | in Mercerìa a S. Giuliano | . . .
Hirsch I, no. 533; RISM B VI, 743
HOUGHTON (2 copies, 2d imperfect: preliminary leaf and plate lacking), MUSIC LIBRARY (imperfect: plate lacking)

1357 SACCHI, GIOVENALE

Del Nvmero E | Delle Misvre | Delle Corde | Mvsiche E Loro | Corrispondenze | Dissertazione | Del P. D. Giovenale | Sacchi Bernabita | In Milano. MDCCLXI.

8° 126 p., illus.
Colophon: Per Giuseppe Mazzucchelli, successore Malatesta.
Hirsch I, no. 534; RISM B VI, 743–744
MUSIC LIBRARY

1358 SACCHI, GIOVENALE

Della Natura E Perfezione Della | Antica Musica De' Greci E Della | Utilita Che Ci Potremmo Noi Pro|mettere Dalla Nostra Applican|dola Secondo Il Loro Esempio | Alla Educazione De' Giovani | Dissertazioni III | Del P. D. Giovenale | Sacchi Bernabita | In Milano. MDCCLXXVIII.

8° 5 ℓ., 207 p.
Colophon: Per Antonio Mogni nella Stamperìa Malatesta. | Con licenza de' Superiori.
RISM B VI, 744
MUSIC LIBRARY

1359 SACCHINI, ANTONIO MARIA GASPARO

Chimene | ou | Le Cid | Tragédie Lyrique | En trois Actes | Mise en Musique | Par | Sacchini. | . . . | A Paris | Chez Le Duc, au Magazin de Musique et d'Instrumens, Rue neuve des Petits champs, | vis-à-vis la Trésorerie, | et Rue du Roule, á la Croix d'Or, No. 290. | Ecrit par Ribiere. [ca. 1797?]

2° *Score:* 1 ℓ., 274 p.
Plate no. 15
RISM A I, no. S 134
MUSIC LIBRARY

1360 SACCHINI, ANTONIO MARIA GASPARO

La Colonie | Opéra Comique | En Deux Actes | Imité de l'Italien et Parodié sur la Musique | Del Sgr. Sacchini. | Représenté pour la 1re. fois par les Comédiens Italiens | Ordinaires du Roi le 16 Aoust 1775. | Et a Fontainebleau devant leurs Majestés, le 4 Novembre | . . . | A Paris | Chez Mr. d'Enouville . . . | Beaublé Scrip. | Avec Privilége du Roi. Imprimé par Basset. [1776?]

2° *Score:* 1 ℓ., 211 p.
Imprint partially covered by cancel label reading: Chez Melle. Castagnery Privilégiée du Roy, À la Musique Royale, | Rue dés Prouvaires, près la rue St. Honoré.
Hirsch II, no. 829; RISM A I, no. S 169
MUSIC LIBRARY

1361 SACCHINI, ANTONIO MARIA
GASPARO

Dardanus | Tragedie Lyrique | En quatre Actes. | Mise en Musique | Par | Sacchini | . . . | A Paris | Chez Le Duc . . . | Ecrit par Ribiere [1791?]

2° *Score:* 1 ℓ., 269 p.
Plate no. 85 A
Imprint partially covered by cancel label reading: A Paris chez Augte. Le Duc Editeur et Marchand de Musique Rue de la Loi No. 267 | près celle Faydeau. | Jnstruments de Musique a Vendre et a Louer.
Hirsch II, no. 825; RISM A I, no. S 115
MUSIC LIBRARY

1362 SACCHINI, ANTONIO MARIA
GASPARO

Evelina | Opera | En Trois Actes | Paroles De Mr. Guillard. | Musique de Sacchini & son dernier Ouvrage | Représenté pour La premiere fois | sur le Théâtre de l'Académie Rle. de Musique | Le Mardi 29. Avril 1788. | Dédié | A Madame | De La Briche | . . . | A Paris | Chez Imbault; au mont d'or, rue St. Honoré, entre | l'hôtel d'Aligre et la rue des Poulies, No. 627. | . . . [1788]

2° *Score:* 1 ℓ., 329 p.
Plate no. 175
On verso of preliminary leaf: Catalogue | de Musique Vocale & Instrumentale mise au jour par Imbault . . . ⟨JohanssonF facs. 38⟩
Hirsch II, no. 828; RISM A I, no. S 89
MUSIC LIBRARY

1363 SACCHINI, ANTONIO MARIA
GASPARO

Oedipe | A Colone | Opéra en trois Actes | Mis en Musique | Par | A. Sacchini. | . . . | Chez Imbault au mont d'Or rue St honoré entre l'hôtel d'Aligre | et la rue des Poulies, No. 627. | A Paris [1787?]

2° *Score:* 1 ℓ., 235 p.
Plate no. 100
Cancel label at foot of title-page reads: Chez le duc, au Magasin de Musique et d'Instruments à Paris. | Rue neuve des petits Champs No. 1286, vis à vis la Trésorerie | Et Rue du Roulle à la Croix d'Or No. 290. | . . .
RISM A I, no. S 199
MUSIC LIBRARY

1364 SACCHINI, ANTONIO MARIA
GASPARO

[L'Olympiade | Ou | Le Triomphe De L'Amitié | Drame Héroïque | en Trois Actes et en Vers. | Imité de l'Italien | et Parodié sur la Musique du Celebre Sgr. Sacchini. | Dedié | À Madame la Duchesse de Fronsac | Représenté pour la Premiere fois par les Comédiens Italiens | Ordinaires du Roi le 2 Octobre 1777. | et a Fontainebleau devant leurs Majestés le 24 du même mois | . . . | A Paris. | Chez Mr. d'Enouville Receveur de Loteries rue de Vannes près Celle | du Four St. Honoré à la nouvelle Halle | et aux Adresses Ordinaires | A. P. D. R. | Imprimé par Basset ⟨1777?⟩]

2° *Score:* 1 ℓ., 219 [i. e. 217] p.
Numbers 83, 84 omitted in paging
Imperfect: title-page lacking; supplied in positive photostat
Hirsch II, no. 831; RISM A I, no. S 243
MUSIC LIBRARY

1365 SACCHINI, ANTONIO MARIA
GASPARO

Premier Recueil | Des Ariettes | De L'Olympiade | Opera Comique | De Mr. Saccehini | Arrangé | Pour le Clavecin, Forte-piano ou Harpe. | . . . | A Paris | Chez Melle. Girard, Mde. de Musique, Rue du Roule, à la Nouveauté. Aux Adresses Ordinaires. | à Lyon, à Bordeaux, à Toulouse, à Rouen, à Caen, à Dijon, à Geneve, à Strasbourg, et à Lille. | Chez tous les Marchands de Musique. [ca. 1780]

obl. 2° *Vocal score:* 1 ℓ., 21 p.
On verso of preliminary leaf: Catalogue | De toutes sortes de Musique Vocale et Instrumentale, que Melle. Girard, Mde. | de Musique, a fait graver . . .
RISM A I, no. S 251
MUSIC LIBRARY

1366   SACCHINI, ANTONIO MARIA
GASPARO

Renaud | Tragedie Lyrique | en Trois
Actes | Representée pour la premiere fois
par l'Académie | de Musique le Mardi 25.
Fevrier 1783. | Mis en Musique | Par | M.
Sacchini | . . . | A Paris. | Chez Le Duc
Successeur de Mr. de la Chevardiere Rue
du Roule | au Magazin de Musique et
d'Instruments | No. 6 [1791?]

2° *Score:* 1 ℓ., 243 p.
Plate no. 83 A
RISM A I, no. S 63
MUSIC LIBRARY

SADLER, JOHN, PUBL. The Muses Delight *See* The Muses Delight

SAGITTARIUS, HENRICUS   *See* Schütz,
Heinrich

1367   SALIERI, ANTONIO

[Les | Danaïdes, | Tragédie Lirique | en
cinq Actes | Dédiée | A La Reine | par |
Mr. Saliéri | Maitre de la Musique | de sa
Majesté Impériale et Royale | & des Spec-
tacles de la Cour de Vienne | Representée
pour la premiere fois | par l'Académie
Royale de Musique | le Lundi 19 Avril
1784. | . . . | A Paris. | Chez Des Lauriers
Md. de Papiers, rue St. Honoré à côte de
celle des Prouvaires. 1784?]

2° *Score:* 2 ℓ., 274 p.
Imperfect: title-page lacking; supplied
in positive photostat
Hirsch II, no. 835; RISM A I, no. S 491
MUSIC LIBRARY

1368   SALIERI, ANTONIO

Les | Danaïdes, | Tragédie Lirique | en
cinq Actes | Mise En Musique | Par | Sa-
lieri | Eleve | De Gluck. | Representée
pour la premiere fois | par l'Académie
Nationale de Musique | le Lundi 19 Avril
1784. | . . . | A Paris. | Chez Des Lauriers
Md. de Papiers, rue St. Honoré à côte de
celle des Prouvaires. [1784?]

2° *Score:* 2 ℓ., 274 p.
Plate no. 16
RISM A I, no. S 491
HOUGHTON

1369   SALIERI, ANTONIO

Tarare | Opéra | en cinq Actes | avec un
Prologue, | Représenté pour la premiere
fois | Sur Le Théatre | de l'Académie Rle.
de Musique | Le Vendredi 8 Juin 1787. |
Paroles de Mr. De Beaumarchais, Musi-
que de Mr. Salieri, | Maître de Chapelle
de la Chambre de S. M. l'Empereur. | A
Paris, | Chez Imbault, Marchand de Mu-
sique au Mont d'or rue St. Honoré | entre
l'hôtel d'Aligre et la rue des Poulies No.
627. | . . . [1787]

2° *Score:* 2 ℓ., 544 p., 1 ℓ.
Plate no. 127
On recto of leaf at end: Catalogue | de
Musique Vocale & Instrumentale mise
au jour par Imbault, | . . . ⟨JohanssonF
facs. 37⟩
Hirsch II, no. 837; RISM A I, no. S 579
MUSIC LIBRARY

1370   SALINAS, FRANCISCO DE

Francisci Sa-|linae Bvrgensis | Abbatis
Sancti Pancratii | de Rocca Scalegna
in regno Neapolitano, Et in Academia
Salmanticensi | Musicae Professoris, de
Musica libri Septem, in quibus eius
doctrinae | veritas tam quae ad Harmo-
niam, quàm quae ad Rhythmum | per-
tinet, iuxta sensus ac rationis iudicium
osten|ditur, Et demonstratur. | Cvm du-
plici Indice Capitum & Rerum. | Sal-
manticae | Excudebat Mathias Ga-
stius. | M.D.LXXVII. | Esta tassado
en seyscientos marauedis.

2° 9 ℓ., 438 p., 9 ℓ., illus., 2 pl., music
Twenty-six pages of *Additiones* in
contemporary manuscript at end
Plates included in paging
Davidsson II, no. 90; Hirsch I, no. 539;
RISM B VI, 748–749; Wolfenbüttel, no.
1287
HOUGHTON

1371   SALMON, THOMAS

An | Essay | To the Advancement of |
Musick, | By | Casting away the Perplex-
ity of | Different Cliffs. | And Uniting all
sorts of Musick | Lute, | Viol, | Violin, | }
{Organ, | Harpsechord, | Voice, &c. | In
one Universal Character. | By Thomas
Salmon, Master | of Arts of Trinity Col-

lege in Oxford. | . . . | London, | Printed by J. Macock, and are to be Sold by | John Car at the Middle-Temple-Gate. 1672.

8° 8 ℓ., 92, [1] p., front., illus., 5 fold. pl., music
Hirsch I, no. 540; RISM B VI, 749
HOUGHTON

1372

[Item deleted]

**1373   SAMMARTINI, GIOVANNI
        BATTISTA**

Six Sonatas | Or | Duets | For Two | German Flutes or Violins. | Compos'd By Sigr. | Gio. Batista St. Martini | Of Milan. | Opera IV. | London. Printed for I. Walsh in Catharine Street in the Strand. | . . . [ca. 1748]

2° *Score:* 1 ℓ., 26 p.
Walsh II, no. 1307
HOUGHTON

1374   SAMMARTINI, GIUSEPPE

Eight | Overtures | In Eight Parts | For | Violins, Hoboys, French Horns, &c. | with a Through Bass for the | Harpsichord or Violoncello. | And | Six Grand Concertos | For Violins &c. | Compos'd by Sigr. | Giuseppe St. Martini. | London. Printed for I. Walsh in Catharine Street in the Strand. | . . . [1752]

2° 9 pts.: *violino primo:* 1 ℓ., 31 p., 1 ℓ., 19 p.; *violino secondo:* 1 ℓ., 29 p., 1 ℓ., 19 p.; *corno primo, corno secondo:* 7 p. each; *oboe primo* [in part *violino primo ripieno*]: 1 ℓ., 27 p., 1 ℓ., 11 p.; *oboe secondo* [in part *violino secondo ripieno*]: 1 ℓ., 24 p., 1 ℓ., 11 p.; *tympany:* 1 ℓ.; *alto viola:* 1 ℓ., 22 p., 1 ℓ., 13 p.; *violoncello e cembalo:* 1 ℓ., 22 p., 1 ℓ., 19 p.
Concertos have separate title-page: Six | Grand | Concertos | For Violins &c. in | Eight Parts | Compos'd By Sigr. | Giuseppe St. Martini | Opera 8va. | . . .
Imperfect: 2 (*corno?*) parts for concertos lacking
RISM A I, no. S 703; Walsh II, no. 1318
HOUGHTON (2 copies, 2d lacks overtures), MUSIC LIBRARY (lacks concertos)

1375   SAMMARTINI, GIUSEPPE

XII Sonate | A | due Violini, e Violoncello, | e Cembalo, Se piace, | Opera Terza, | Dedicata | All' | Altezza Reale | di | Augusta | Principessa di Vallia | da Giuseppe San Martini | Milanese | MDCCXLIII | Londra.

2° 3 pts.: *violino primo:* 2 ℓ., 36 [i. e. 37] p.; *violino secondo:* 1 ℓ., 36 [i. e. 37] p.; *violoncello:* 2 ℓ., 34 p.
Minuet in Sonata IX omitted in all parts; extra leaf containing minuet hinged to page 28 in the *violino primo* and *violino secondo* parts; slip hinged to page 24 in the *violoncello* part
RISM A I, no. S 720; Walsh II, no. 1328
HOUGHTON

1376   SAMMARTINI, GIUSEPPE

XII Sonate | A | due Violini, e Violoncello, | e Cembalo, Se piace, | Opera Terza, | Dedicata | All' | Altezza Reale | di | Augusta | Principessa di Vallia | da Giuseppe San Martini | London Printed for and Sold by I. Walsh | Musick Printer & Instrument Maker to his Majesty | in Catharine Street in the Strand. [1747]

2° 3 pts.: *violino primo, violino secondo:* 1 ℓ., 36 p. each; *violoncello:* 1 ℓ., 34 p.
RISM A I, no. S 722; Walsh II, no. 1330
HOUGHTON

1377

Sammlung | auserlesener geistlicher | Lieder, | aus | den bessten neuern | Dichtern, | mit | angenehmen und leichten | Melodieen; | vorzüglich | zum Gebrauch der Schulen. | St. Gallen. 1784. | zu finden bey Jacob Huber zur Eintracht.

8° 4 ℓ., 274, [6] p.
MUSIC LIBRARY

SAN MARTINI, GIUSEPPE   *See* Sammartini, Giuseppe

SANTA MARÍA, TOMÁS DE   *See* Tomás de Santa María

1378 SARTI, GIUSEPPE

Les Noces De Dorine | Ou | Helene et Francique | Opera en Quatre Actes | Musique Par | M. Sarti. | Parolles de Mr *** | Réprésente au théatre de Monsieur | . . . | A. Papis [*sic*] | Chez le Sr Sieber Musicien rue St honore entre celles des | Vielles Etuve et celle D'orleans chez l'Apothicaire N.' 92. [ca. 1790]

2° *Score:* 1 *ℓ.*, 275 p.
Plate no. 1161
Hirsch II, no. 839; RISM A I, no. S 933
MUSIC LIBRARY

1379 SAUVEUR, JOSEPH

Application | Des | Sons Harmoniques | A La Composition | Des Jeux D'Orgues. | Tiré des Memoires de 1702. de l'Academie Royale des Sciences. | Par Mr Sauveur, Maître de Mathematiques du Roy d'Es-|pagne, de Monseigneur le Duc de Bourgogne, de Monseigneur | le Duc de Berry: Lecteur & Professeur du Roy pour les Mathe-|matiques; Et de l'Academie Royale des Sciences. [Paris?, 1702?]

4° 23 p., illus., 2 pl.
RISM B VI, 755
MUSIC LIBRARY

1380 SAUVEUR, JOSEPH

Principes | D'Acoustique | Et | De Musique, | Ov | Système General | Des Intervalles Des Sons, | & de son application à tous les Systêmes & à tous les | Instrumens de Musique. | Inseré dans les Memoires de 1701. de l'Academie Royale des Sciences. | Par Mr Sauveur, Maître de Mathematiques du Roy d'Espagne, de | Monseigneur le Duc de Bourgogne, de Monseigneur le Duc de Berry: | Lecteur & Professeur du Roy pour les Mathematiques: Et de l'Academie | Royale des Sciences. [Paris?, 1701?]

4° 1 *ℓ.*, 68, [2] p., illus., 3 pl. (incl. music)
RISM B VI, 755
MUSIC LIBRARY

1381 [SCARLATTI, ALESSANDRO]

Songs | In The New | Opera, | Call'd | Pyrrhus and Demetrius | All ye Singing

Parts being transpos'd into ye G: Cliff & put into such Keys that brings them | into ye Compass of Treble or Tenor Voices. The whole being done from ye Original by that | Compleat writer of Musick Mr. Armstrong. and by him carefully corrected. also he hath made | words to 17 of ye Italian Songs, thus mark'd † | [London] Sold by I: Walsh Musicall Instrument maker in Or-|-dinary to her Majesty, & P. Randall at the Harp and Ho-boy | . . . | and I. Hare Musick Instrument maker at ye Golden Viol and Flute . . . [1709]

2° *Vocal score:* 5 *ℓ.*, 58 numb. *ℓ.*
Imprint covered by cancel label reading: Sold by Mickepher Rawlins against the Globe Tavern in | the Strand near Charing-Cross. London.
RISM A I, no. S 1176; Walsh I, no. 293
MUSIC LIBRARY

1382 SCARLATTI, DOMENICO

Forty two | Suits Of Lessons | For the | Harpsichord | Composed by | Sigr. Domenico Scarlatti | . . . | London Printed for John Johnson at the Harp and Crown in Cheapside | . . . [ca. 1748]

obl. 2° *Score:* 2 vols.: *vol. I:* 2 *ℓ.*, 62 p.; *vol. II:* 1 *ℓ.*, 67 p.
Includes a fugue by Alessandro Scarlatti
RISM A I, no. S 1191
HOUGHTON

SCELLERY, CHARLES EMMANUEL BORJON DE *See* Borjon, Charles Emmanuel

1383 SCHALE, CHRISTIAN FRIEDRICH

Sei Brevi Sonate | per | Cembalo | composto | da | Christiano Federico Schale | Virtuoso di Camera | Di S. M. Il Ré Di Prvssia | parte tertia | alle spese della Vedoua di Balt: Schmid Norimb: | . . . [ca. 1775]

obl. 2° *Score:* 1 *ℓ.*, 21 p.
Plate no. LIV
RISM A I, no. S 1258
HOUGHTON

1384   SCHEIBE, JOHANN ADOLPH

Johann Adolph Scheibens, | Kŏnigl.
Dånis. Capellmeisters, | Critischer | Mu-
sikus. | Neue, | vermehrte und verbes-
serte | Auflage. | Leipzig, | bey Bernhard
Christoph Breitkopf, 1745.

8° 24 ℓ., 1059 [i.e. 1056], [22] p.
Pages [899]–1048: M. Johann Abra-
ham | Birnbaums | Vertheidigung | seiner
| unparteyischen Anmerkungen | ŭber
eine | bedenkliche Stelle in dem sechsten
Stŭcke | des critischen Musikus, | wider |
Johann Adolph Scheibens | Beantwor-
tung derselben. | 1739. | Von dem Ver-
fasser des critischen Musikus aufs neue |
zum Drucke befŏrdert, und mit Anmer-
kungen | erlåutert.
Pages 1055, 1056 misnumbered 1057,
1059 respectively
RISM B VI, 760
MUSIC LIBRARY

1385   SCHEIBE, JOHANN ADOLPH

Tragische | Kantaten | fŭr | eine oder
zwo Singestimmen und das Clavier. |
Nåmlich: | des Herrn von Gerstenbergs |
Ariadne auf Naxos, | und | Johann Elias
Schlegels | Prokris und Cephalus. | In die
Musick gesetzt, | und nebst einem
Sendschreiben, worinnen vom Recitatio
ŭberhaupt und | von diesen Kantaten
insonderheit geredet wird, | herausge-
geben von | Johann Adolph Scheiben, |
Kŏnigl. Dån. Kapellmeister. | Koppenha-
gen und Leipzig | In der Mummischen
Buchhandlung, | 1765.

2° *Score:* 6 ℓ., 80 p.
RISM A I, no. S 1331; RISM B VI, 761
MUSIC LIBRARY

1386   SCHEIDLER, JOHANN DAVID

Sammlung | kleiner Klavierstŭcke, |
fŭr Liebhaber, | dem | Durchlauchtigsten
Erbprinzen | zu Sachsen-Gotha und Al-
tenburg | in Unterthånigkeit zugeeignet |
von | Johann David Scheidler, | Herzog-
lich Såchsisch-Gothaischen Kammer-
musikus. | Gotha, | in Kommission bey
Karl Wilhelm Ettinger. | 1779.

obl. 2° *Score:* 2 ℓ., 32 p.
RISM A I, no. S 1343
MUSIC LIBRARY

1387   SCHETKY, JOHANN GEORG
        CHRISTOFF

Six | Canzonets | For the Voice | with
an Accompanyment | for the | Piano
Forte | Composed by | J. G. C. Schetky. |
The Words by Mr: Woods. | Edinr.
Printed and Sold by N. Stewart & Co.
Music | Sellers No. 37 South Bridge." |
. . . [ca. 1800]

2° *Score:* 19 p.
RISM A I, no. S 1481
MUSIC LIBRARY

1388   SCHMID, BERNHARD, ED.

[Zwey Bŭcher. | Einer Neu-|en Kunstli-
chen Tabu-|latur auff Orgel vnd Instru-
ment. | Deren das Erste ausserlesne Mo-
teten vnd Stuck | zu sechs, fŭnff vnd vier
Stimmen, auss den Kunstreichesten vnd
| Weitherŭmbtesten Musicis vnd Com-
ponisten diser vnser zeit | abgesetzt. Das
ander Allerley schŏne Teutsche, Italie-
nische, | Frantzŏsische, Geistliche vnd
Weltliche Lieder, mit fŭnff | vnd vier
Stimmen, Passamezo, Galliardo | vnd
Tåntze in sich begreifft. | Alles inn ein
richtige bequemliche vnd artliche ord-
|nung, deren dergleichen vormals nie im
Truck aussgangen, | Allen Organisten
vnd angehenden Instrumentisten zu
nutz, | vnd der Hochloblichen Kunst zu
Ehren, auffs | Neue zusamen gebracht,
colloriret | vnd vbersehen. | Durch Bern-
hart Schmid, Bur-|ger vnd Organisten zu
Strassburg. | Getruckt zu Strassburg, bei
Bernhart Jobin. | M.D.LXXvij.]

2° [–]⁴, A–Y⁴, Z⁶, illus. (port.)
Imperfect: gathering [–], leaf Z6 lack-
ing; supplied in positive photostat
Brown, no. 1577₆; RISM B I, no. 1577¹²
HOUGHTON

SCHMIDT, JOHANN CHRISTOPH   *See*
Smith, John Christopher

SCHMIDT, THEODOR   *See* Smith, Theodore

SCHMITT, BERNHARD   *See* Schmid, Bernhard

1389 SCHNELL, JOHANN JACOB

VI. | Missae Neo-Editae | A Vocibus 4.
C. A. T. B. Violinis 2. necessariis. Lituis
2. ex Cla-|vibus diversis pro libitu. Or-
gano. Violoncello ad libitum. | Nec Non |
V. | Inserta in locis debitis Concerta à
Violinis 2. concertantibus. | Violinis 2.
Ripienis. Organo. Violoncello non obli-
gato. | Dedicatae | Reverendissimo, Ac
Celsissimo | Principi, Ac Domino, | D.
Friderico | Carolo | S. R. Imperii Principi,
Et Episcopo | Bambergensi, | Ecclesiae
Cathedralis Herbipolensis, Et Equestris |
Ad Sanctum Albanum Moguntiae | Prae-
posito, &c. &c. | Principi, Ac Do-
mino, Domino Meo Clementissimo. | A
Me Authore | Joanne Jacobo Schnell, Cel-
sissimi Principis Bambergensis | Musico
Aulico Et Camerali. | Opus I. | . . . | Bam-
bergae, | Sumptibus Authoris. | Impressae
apud Georgium Andream Gertner, Re-
verendissimi Capituli, | & Almae Acade-
miae Typographum. 1729.

2° 9 pts.: *canto, alto:* [−]1, A–H², I 1
each; *tenore:* [−]1, A–H²; *basso:* [−]1,
A–G², H1; *lituo I:* [−]1, A–F², G1; *lituo
II:* [−]1, A–F²; *violino I:* [−]1, A–L², M1;
violino II: [−]1, A–I², K1; *organo:* [−]1,
[2d][−]², A–M², N1
RISM A I, no. S 1894
HOUGHTON

SCHNÜFFIS, LAURENTIUS VON *See*
Laurentius von Schnüffis

1390 SCHOBERT, JOHANN

Op. 1

Deux | Sonates | pour le | Clavecin |
avec accompagnement de Violon, | par |
Mr. Schobert | Clavecineste de S. A. Sme.
Monseigneur | Le Prince de Conty. |
Oeuvre I | London. . . . | Printed and sold
by R. Bremner. opposite | Somerset
House in the Strand. | . . . [ca. 1770]

2° 1 pt.: *clavecin:* 15 p.
RISM A I, no. S 1918
MUSIC LIBRARY

1391 SCHOBERT, JOHANN

Op. 1

Two | Sonatas, | For The | Piano Forte; |
Composed By | Mr. Schobert. | London: |

Printed for Harrison, Cluse, & Co. No.
78, Fleet Street. [1798?]

8° *Score:* 24 p. (*The Piano-Forte Maga-
zine,* vol. V, no. 7)
Plate no. 79
RISM A I, no. S 1921 (op. 1)
MUSIC LIBRARY

1392 SCHOBERT, JOHANN

Op. 3

Deux | Sonates, | Pour Le | Piano Forte, |
Par, | Mr. Schobert. | London: | Printed for
Harrison & Co. No. 78, Fleet Street.
[1798?]

8° *Score:* 22 p. (*The Piano-Forte Maga-
zine,* vol. IV, no. 9)
Plate no. 59
RISM A I, no. S 1934 (op. 3)
MUSIC LIBRARY

1393 SCHOBERT, JOHANN

Op. 6

Trois | Sonatas | pour le | Clavecin |
avec accompagnements de Violon et
Basse | ad Libitum | par Mr. Schobert | de
la Musique de Son Altesse Sérénissime
Monseigneur | Le Prince De Conty |
Opera VI. . . . | London Printed and Sold
by R. Bremner. | Opposite Somerset
House | in the Strand. [ca. 1770]

2° 1 pt.: *clavecin:* 19 p.
RISM A I, no. S 1946
MUSIC LIBRARY

1394 SCHOBERT, JOHANN

Op. 9

Trois | Sinfonies | Pour le | Clavecin |
Avec lAccompagnement | d'un Violon |
& deux Cornes de Chasse ad libitum |
Composees par | Sr. Schobert | Oeuvre
[I]X. . . . | London | Printed for Longman
and Broderip No. 26 in Cheapside |
. . . [ca. 1780]

2° 2 pts.: *clavecin:* III, 2-21 p.; *violino:*
7 p.
Page III in *clavecin* part: | Musical Pub-
lications | Printed and Sold by Longman
& Broderip . . .
Imprint in *clavecin* part covered by
cancel label reading: Chez Mr. Boyer,

Rue de Richelieu, à la Clef d'or, | Passage du Caffé de Foy.
RISM A I, no. S 1964
MUSIC LIBRARY

1395 SCHOBERT, JOHANN

Op. 16

IV | Sonates | Pour le | Clavecin | Violon et Basse | par | M Schobert | de la Musique de Son Altesse Serenisime Monseigneur | Le Prince De Conty. | Opera XVI. . . . | London. | Printed and sold by R: Bremner opposite | Somerset House in the Strand. | . . . [1770?]

2° 1 pt.: *clavecin:* 23 p.
RISM A I, no. S 2006
MUSIC LIBRARY

1396 SCHOBERT, JOHANN

Op. 17

IV | Sonates | pour le | Clavecin | avec Accompagnement de | Violon | Par | Mr. Schobert | Claveciniste de S. A. S. Monseigneur | Le Prince de Conty. | Opera XVII | . . . | London | Printed for R. Bremner in the Strand | . . . [ca. 1775]

2° 1 pt.: *clavecin:* 25 p.
RISM A I, no. S 2011
MUSIC LIBRARY

1397 SCHREYER, GREGOR

Sacrificium | Matutinum, | Seu | Missae VI. | Breves | à | Quatuor Vocibus ordinariis, | Violinis duobus obligatis, | Clarinis duobus aut Cornibus ad libitum, | cum duplici Basso, juxta modernum Stylum, | A | R. P. Gregorio Schreyer, | Ordinis SS. P. Benedicti in Exempto Monasterio Montis Sancti Andechs | Professo Capitulari &c. | Compositae. | Opus II. | . . . | Augustae Vindelicorum, | Sumptibus Matthaei Rieger, Bibliopolae. | Anno à Partu Virginis MDCCLXIII.

2° 1 pt.: *organo:* 6 ℓ., 68 p.
HOUGHTON

1398 SCHROETER, JOHANN SAMUEL, SUPPOSED COMPOSER

The | Field of Battle | For the | Piano Forte, | Composed by | Schroeter. | Lon-

don | Printed for Harrison & Co. No. 18, Paternoster Row. [1797]

8° *Score:* 14 p. (*The Piano-Forte Magazine,* vol. I [no. 5])
MUSIC LIBRARY

1399 SCHROETER, JOHANN SAMUEL

Six | Sonatas, | For The | Piano Forte. | Composed By | J. S. Schroeter. | Op: 2d. | London: | Printed for Harrison, Cluse, & Co. No. 78, Fleet Street. [1799?]

8° *Score:* 43 p. (*The Piano-Forte Magazine,* vol. VI, no. 5)
Plate nos. 90–91
MUSIC LIBRARY

1400 SCHROETER, JOHANN SAMUEL

Six | Sonatas, | For The | Piano-Forte; | Composed By, | S. Schroeter. | London: | Printed for Harrison, Cluse, & Co. No. 78, Fleet Street [1799?]

8° *Score:* 28 p. (*The Piano-Forte Magazine,* vol. VII, no. 3)
Plate nos. 98–99
MUSIC LIBRARY

1401 SCHÜTZ, HEINRICH

Psalmen Davids, | Niebevor in deutsche Reime gebracht | Durch | D. Cornelium Beckern, | und nachmals | Mit Eilff alten, und Zwey und Neuntzig neuen Melodeyen | von dem Churf. S. Capellmeister | Heinrich Schützen, | in den Druck gegeben, | ietzund aber, | Auff des Durchlauchtigsten Fürsten und Herrns, | Herrn Johann Georgens | des Andern, | Churfürstens zu Sachsen und Burggra-|fens zu Magdeburg, u. | anderweite gnädigste Anordnung, | Auffs neue übersehen, auch durchaus zu Kirchen und Schulen | Gebrauche, mit so vielen, auf ieglichen Psalm eingerichteten, | eigenen Melodeyen, vermehret, | Nach seiner Contrapuncts-Ahrt, | mit 4. Stimmen gestellet, | Durch | obgemelten Autorem | H. S. | Der Zeit Churf. S. ältern Capellmeistern, | Sammt | Zu Ende angehängten dreyen nützlichen Registern. | Gedruckt zu Dressden in Wolffgang Seyfferts Druckerey | durch Gottfried Seyfferten, | 1661.

2° 5 ℓ., 172 [i. e. 173] numb. ℓ., [8] p.
In choirbook format
Numbers 41, 77 repeated, 171 omitted
in paging
HOUGHTON

SCHULTHEISS, MICHAEL *See* Praetorius,
Michael

1402　SCHULZ, JOHANN ABRAHAM
PETER

Lieder im Volkston, | bey dem Claviere
zu singen, | von | J. A. P. Schulz, | Capell-
meister Sr. Kŏnigl. Hoheit des Prinzen
Heinrich von Preussen. | Erster Theil. |
Zweyte verbesserte Auflage. | Berlin, |
bey George Jacob Decker, Kŏniglichem
Hofbuchdrucker. 1785.

obl. 2° *Score:* 2 ℓ., 47, [1] p.
MUSIC LIBRARY

1403　SCHULZ, JOHANN ABRAHAM
PETER

Lieder im Volkston, | bey dem Claviere
zu singen, | von | J. A. P. Schulz, | Capell-
meister Sr. Kŏn. Hoheit des Prinzen
Heinrich von Preussen. | Zweyter Theil. |
Berlin, 1785. | bey George Jacob Decker,
Kŏnigl. Hofbuchdrucker.

obl. 2° *Score:* 1 ℓ., 49, [1] p.
MUSIC LIBRARY

1404　SCHULZ, JOHANN ABRAHAM
PETER

Lieder im Volkston, | bey dem Claviere
zu singen, | von | J. A. P. Schulz, | Kŏnig-
lich Dănischem Capellmeister. | Dritter
Theil. | Berlin, 1790. | bey Heinrich Au-
gust Rottmann, Kŏniglichem Hof-
buchhăndler.

obl. 2° *Score:* 2 ℓ., 56 p.
Hirsch III, no. 1091
MUSIC LIBRARY

SCHUTZE, MICHAEL *See* Praetorius, Michael

1405　SCHWANENBERGER, JOHANN
GOTTFRIED

Sonate | A | Due Violini | E | Violon-
cello. | Del | Sigr: Giov: Schwanberger, |
Maestro di Cappella in attual | Servizio
di S A. S. il Duca | Regnante di Brunsvic |
Luneburg. | In Brunsvic. | Nella Liberia
della Casa degli | Orfanelli. [pref. 1767]

2° 2 pts. *violino primo:* 2 ℓ., 7 p.; *violino secondo:* 7 p.
HOUGHTON

SCHWARTZENDORF, JOHANN PAUL AE-
GIDIUS *See* Martini, Jean Paul Égide

SCHWIEGER, JACOB Die　Geharnschte
Venus *See* Stieler, Kaspar von *Die geharnschte Venus*

1406　SCHWINDL, FRIEDRICH

Six | Sonatas | For | Two Violins and
Bass. | Dedicated to Monsr. | Le Comte de
Heiden de Reinestein | Gentilhomme de
la Chambre de S. A. S. Monseigr. | Le
Prince d'Orange & Nassau &c. | By | F:
Schwindl | Opa. 5th. . . . | London |
Printed & Sold by J: Longman & Co. No.
26, Cheapside, . . . [1769?]

2° 3 pts.: *violino primo, violino secondo, basso:* 1 ℓ., 13 p. each
MUSIC LIBRARY

1407　SCHWINDL, FRIEDRICH

Quatre | Sonates | Pour | Le Clavecin |
Avec Accompagnement | d'Un Violon &
Violoncelle, | Composees Par | Frederic |
Schwindl | Oeuvre VIII. | . . . | A Paris |
Chez le Sr. Borrelly rue et vis-a-vis la
ferme de l'Abbaye St Victor. | Et aux
Adresses Ordinaires. | En Province | Chez
Mrs. Les Mds. de Musique. | A. P. D. R
[177–?]

2° 1 pt.: *clavecin:* [1], 4–15 p.
MUSIC LIBRARY

SCOTISH SONG *See* Ritson, Joseph,
comp. *Scotish Song*

THE SECOND BOOK OF THE PLEASANT
MUSICAL COMPANION *See* The Pleasant
Musical Companion

1408 SEBASTIANI, CLAUDIUS

Bellvm | Mvsicale, | Inter Plani Et
Mensv-|ralis Cantvs Reges, De | Princi-
patu in Musicae Pro-|uincia obtinendo,
con-|tendentes. | Clavdio Sebastiani
Meten-|si, Organista, Authore. | Habes
Candide Lector, In Hoc Bello Mvsicali, |
non solum omnes controuersias Musi-
corum hinc inde agitatas, uerum etiam |
quicquid ad artificium ipsius Musices
pertinet, opus suis figuris & | Notis illu-
stratum, quale antehac neq; uisum neq;
audi-|tum. Fruaris ergo ut decet Candide.
| Dvlce Bellvm Inexpertis. [Strassburg,
1563]

4°★⁴, A–V⁴, X1–3, 1 ℓ., illus., music
Colophon: Argent. In Officina | Pavli
Machaeropoei, | Anno M.D.LXIII.
RISM B VI, 776–777; Wolfenbüttel,
no. 1300
HOUGHTON

1409

The | Secrets of a Woman's Heart. | An |
Epistle | From A | Friend, | To | Signior
F[arine]lli. | Occasion'd by the Epistle of
Mrs. C[onstantia] | P[hilli]ps, to the An-
gelick Signior F[arine]lli. | . . . | London: |
Printed for E. Cook, in Black-fryars, and
sold at the Pam-|phlet-Shops of London
and Westminster. . . . | M.DCC.XXXV.

2° 15 p.
A reply in verse to *The Happy Courte-
zan*
Foxon, S179
HOUGHTON

A SELECT COLLECTION OF ENGLISH
SONGS *See* Ritson, Joseph, comp. *A Select Collection of English Songs*

SELECT COLLECTION OF THE MOST ES-
TEEMED CATCHES, CANONS, GLEES &
MADRIGALS *See* Longman & Broderip's,
Select Collection of the most Esteemed
Catches, Canons, Glees & Madrigals

1410

A | Select Collection | Of | New Fa-
vourite | And | Popular Songs, | By | the
most Celebrated | Composers. | London. |
Printed for Harrison & Co No. 18, Paternoster Row. [1797?]

8° *Score:* 1 ℓ., 6–128, [4] p. (*The Piano-
Forte Magazine,* vol. II, no. 6)
RISM B II, 105
MUSIC LIBRARY

1411

A | Selection | of the most | Favourite
Scots-Songs | Chiefly Pastoral. | Adapted
for the Harpsichord, | with an Accompa-
niment for a | Violin. | By | Eminent Mas-
ters | Respectfully Inscribed | To Her
Grace | The Duchess of Gordon | . . . |
London | Printed for Willm. Napier,
Music Seller to their Majesties. | No. 49
Great Queen Street Lincoln's Inn Fields. |
Neele sc. 352. Strand. [1790–1794]

2° *Score:* 3 vols.: [*vol. I*]: 1 ℓ., iv, 16, 77
[i. e. 153], [4] p., front.; *vol. II:* 2 ℓ., 101
[i. e. 199], [4] p., front.; [*vol. III*]: 51 [i. e.
100] p.
Vol. II has title: A | Selection | of | Orig-
inal Scots Songs | in | Three Parts | The
Harmony by | Haydn | Dedicated by Per-
mission | to | Her Royal Highness the
Duchess of York | . . .
Extra leaves with additional verses inserted in each vol.
Imperfect: title-page, plate and preliminary material lacking in vol. III
RISM B II, 107
MUSIC LIBRARY

1412 [SENFL, LUDWIG, ED.]

Liber Selectarvm | Cantionvn Qvas |
Vvlgo Mvtetas | Appellant Sex | Qvinqve
Et | Qvator | Vocvm [Augsburg, 1520]

2° 2 ℓ., 272 numb. ℓ., illus. (coat of
arms)
In choirbook format
Colophon: . . . Cum autē cantus &
vocum suauissima infle-|xio atque mo-
dulatio non minima Musicae pars exi-
stat, factū | est, vt peritissimi mei Muni-
cipes Sigismundus Grimmius, | Medicus,
et Marcus Wirsungus, accurata eorū so-

lertia, stu-|dio item exactissimo, labore summo, et etiã impensa nõ medio-|cri, librum hunc iucundissimum & artis plenum, Cantũ exqui-|sitissimorum elegantioribus characteribus, et rarissimis vocũ | notulis exornatũ, ab erudito et exp[er]to Musico Luduuico Sen-|felio Augustano Rauracensi . . . | Ex aedib. nostris. v. Kal's Nouêbris. Anno salutis. M.D.XX.

> Hirsch III, no. 1099; RISM B I, no 1520[4]
> HOUGHTON

1413　SERRE, JEAN ADAM

Essais | Sur | Les Principes | De | L'Harmonie, | Où L'On Traite | De la Théorie de l'Harmonie en général, | Des Droits respectifs de l'Harmonie & de la | Melodie, | De la Basse Fondamentale, | Et de l'Origine du Mode Mineur. | Par Monsieur Serre. | . . . | A Paris, | Chez Prault Fils, Quai de Conty, vis-à-vis la Descente | du Pont-Neuf, à la Charité. | M.DCC.LIII. | Avec Approbation & Privilège du Roi.

> 8° 4 ℓ., 159, [1] p., 2 pl., (incl. music)
> RISM B VI, 780
> MUSIC LIBRARY

1414

The | Session | Of | Musicians. | In Imitation of the | Session of Poets. | . . . | London: | Printed for M. Smith, near the Royal-Exchange, in Corn-|hill. 1724. . . .

> 2° 12 p.
> In verse
> Foxon, S223
> HOUGHTON

1415　SHERARD, JAMES

Sonate | à Tré | doi Violini, e Violone | col Basso per l'Organo | Di | Giacomo Sherard | Filarmonico | Opera prima | A Amsterdam | Chez Estienne Roger Marchand libraire. | . . . [1701]

> 2° 4 pts.: *violino primo:* 2 ℓ., 25 p.: *violino secondo, violoncello, organo:* 1 ℓ., 25 p. each
> MUSIC LIBRARY

1416　SHIELD, WILLIAM

The | Flitch Of Bacon, | A Comic Opera, | Now Performing with Universal Applause | at the | Theatre Royal in the Hay Market, | Part of it Composed and Part Compiled by | W. Shield. | London, Printed for the Author and sold by | William Napier, No. 474, Strand. | Ashby Script. | N. B. Mr. Napier to render this Work more useful to the Public in general has Printed the Second Violin with the Harpsichord Part. [1778?]

> obl. 2° *Short score:* 1 ℓ., 53 p.
> HOUGHTON, MUSIC LIBRARY

1417　SHIELD, WILLIAM

The Highland Reel, | A | Musical Romance, | as it is Performed at the | Theatre Royal Covent Garden | Selected & Composed by | Willm. Shield. | The Words by J. O'Keefe Esqr. | . . . | London | Printed by Longman and Broderip No. 26 Cheapside and No. 13 Hay Market | Music Sellers and musical Instrument makers, to His Royal Highness the Prince of Wales. | . . . [1788?]

> 2° *Short score:* III, 2–48 p.
> Page III: Musical Publications | Printed and Sold by Longman & Broderip . . .
> MUSIC LIBRARY

1418　SHIELD, WILLIAM

Marian, | an Opera, | as perform'd at the | Theatre Royal | Covent Garden, | Compos'd & Selected by | W. Shield, | the Words by | Mrs. Brooke. | . . . | London Printed by Longman & Broderip No. 26, Cheapside & No. 13 Hay Market Music Sellers & Musical Instrument | Makers To His Royal Highness The Prince of Wales . . . [1788?]

> obl. 2° *Short score:* 1 ℓ., 57 p.
> MUSIC LIBRARY

1419　SHIELD, WILLIAM

Robin Hood | or | Sherwood Forest | A Comic Opera, | as Performed with Universal Applause, at the | Theatre-Royal, Covent-Garden; | Selected & Composed by | William Shield. | The Words by Leod.

MacNally Esqr. . . . | London | Printed by John Bland, at his Music Warehouse No. 45, Holborn | . . . [ca. 1785]

obl. 2° *Vocal score:* 1 ℓ., 65 p.
MUSIC LIBRARY

1420   SHIELD, WILLIAM

Rosina, | A | Comic Opera, | as Performed at | The | Theatre Royal, Covent Garden; | Composed and Selected | By | William Shield. | . . . | London: Printed for J. Dale, at his Musical Library, No. 132, Oxford Street. | . . . [ca. 1791]

obl. 2° *Short score:* 1 ℓ., 38 p.
Page [1]: Music Printed at Dale's Musical Library 132 Oxford Street . . .
MUSIC LIBRARY (2 copies)

—Another copy
This copy contains an additional Dale advertisement for musical instruments on the verso of the title-page
Page [1]: Music Printed by J. Dale No. 19 Cornhill & 132 Oxford Street.
Imperfect: pages, 35, 36 lacking
MUSIC LIBRARY

1421   SHIELD, WILLIAM

Rosina, | A | Comic Opera, | As Performed At The | Theatre Royal, | Covent Garden; | Composed & Selected, | By, | William Shield. | London: | Printed for Harrison & Co. No. 18, Paternoster Row. [1798?]

8° *Vocal score:* 1 ℓ., 5–44, [2] p. (*The Piano-Forte Magazine*, vol. IV, no. 1)
Plate nos. 51–52
MUSIC LIBRARY

SIBBALD, JAMES, PUBL. A Collection of Catches, Canons, Glees, Duettos &c *See* A Collection of Catches, Canons, Glees, Duettos &c.

SILVA, MANUEL NUNES DA *See* Nunes da Silva, Manuel

1422   SILVA LEITE, ANTONIO DA

Rezumo | De | Todas As Regras, E Preceitos Da Cantoria, Assim | Da | Musica Metrica, | Como Do | Canto-Chaõ. | Dividido Em Duas Partes. | Composto por | Antonio Da Silva Leite, | Natural da Cidade do Porto. | Para o uso dos seus Discipulos. | Porto: | Na Officina de Antonio Alvarez Ribeiro, | Anno de 1787. | Com Licença da Real Mesa Censoria. | Vende-se na mesma Officina, na rua de S. Miguel | nas casas. No. 260.

4° 4 ℓ., 43, [2] p., illus., fold. pl., music
RISM B VI, 784
HOUGHTON

1423   SIME, DAVID, COMP.

The | Edinburgh | Musical Miscellany: | A | Collection | Of The Most Approved | Scotch, English, And Irish | Songs, | Set To Music. | Selected by D. Sime, Edinburgh. | Edinburgh: | Printed for W. Gordon, T. Brown, N. R. Cheyne, | C. Elliot, Et Silvester Doig, Edinburgh; W. Coke, | Leith; J. Gillies, Glasgow, Et G. Milln, | Et W. Brown, Dundee. | MDCCXCII. [-M,DCC,XCIII.]

8° 2 vols.: [*vol. I*]: 1 ℓ., x, 359, [1] p., front.; *vol. II:* xi, [13]–372 p.
Imprint, vol. II: Edinburgh: | Printed for John Elder, T. Brown, and C. Elliot, | Edinburgh; and W. Coke, Leith. | M,DCC,XCIII.
Unnumbered page at end in vol. I: Books printed for and sold by | Silvester Doig . . .
MUSIC LIBRARY

1424   SIMPSON, CHRISTOPHER

Chelys, | Minuritionum Artificio Exornata: | Sive, | Minuritiones ad Basin, etiam Ex tempore Modulandi Ratio. | In Tres Partes Distributa. | The Division-Viol, | Or, | The Art of Playing Ex tempore upon a Ground. | Divided Into Three Parts. | Pars I. Chelyos tractandae Praecepta. Part I. Of the Viol it self, with | Instructions to Play upon it. | Pars II. Melothesiae Compendium. Part II. Vse of the Concords, or a | Compendium of Descant. | Pars III. Minuritiones ad Basin aptan-|di Methodus. Part III. The Method of ordering | Division to a Ground. | Authore Christophoro Simpson. | Editio Secvnda. | London, | Printed by W. Godbid for Henry Brome at the Gun in Ivy-lane. | M.DC.LXV[II.]

2° 6 ℓ., 67 [i. e. 77] p., front. (port.), illus., pl., music
Numbers 53–62 repeated in paging
"II." added to imprint date in hand stamp
Plate included in paging
Text in English and Latin, in parallel columns
RISM B VI, 786
HOUGHTON

1425 SIMPSON, CHRISTOPHER

A | Compendium | Of | Practical Musick | In Five Parts: | Teaching, by a New, and easie Method, | I. The Rudiments of Song. | 2. The Principles of Composition. | 3. The Vse of Discords. | 4. The Form of Figurate Descant. | 5. The Contrivance of Canon. | By Christopher Simpson. | . . . | London, Printed by William Godbid for Henry Brome | in Little Britain. M.DC.LXVII.

8° 8 ℓ., 176 p., front. (port.), illus., music
Hirsch I, no. 555; RISM B VI, 784
HOUGHTON

1426 SIMPSON, CHRISTOPHER

A | Compendium | Of | Practical Musick | In Five Parts. | Teaching, by a New, and easie Method, | 1. The Rudiments of Song. | 2. The Principles of Composition. | 3. The Use of Discords. | 4. The Form of Figurate Descant. | 5. The Contrivance of Canon. | Together with | Lessons for Viols, &c. | The Third Edition. | By Christopher Simpson. | . . . | London, | Printed by M. C. [i. e. Mary Clark] for Henry Brome, at the | Gun near the West-end of St. Pauls. | MDCLXXVIII.

8° 7 ℓ., 192 p., front. (port.), illus., music
RISM B VI, 784
HOUGHTON

1427 SIMPSON, CHRISTOPHER

A | Compendium: | Or, | Introduction | To | Practical Music. | In Five Parts. | Teaching, by a New and Easy Method. |

I. The Rudiments of Song. | II. The Principles of Composition. | III. The Use of Discords. | IV. The Form of Figurate Descant. | V. The Contrivance of Canon. | By Christopher Sympson. | The Eighth Edition, with Additions: Much | more Correct than any Former, the Examples | being put in the most useful Cliffs. | . . . | London: | Printed by W. Pearson, for Arthur Bettesworth, and | Charles Hitch, in Pater-Noster-Row; Samuel Birt, | in Ave-Mary-Lane; John Clarke, in Duck-Lane; | Thomas Astley, in St. Paul's Church-Yard; and | John Oswald, in Little-Britain. M.DCC.XXXII.

8° 7 ℓ., 144 p., front. (port.), illus., music
RISM B VI, 785
MUSIC LIBRARY

1428 SIMPSON, CHRISTOPHER

A Compendium, or | Introduction to Practical Music, | in five Parts. | Teaching by a new & easy method, 1st. the rudiments of Song. 2d. the principles of Compo-|sition 3d. the use of Discords. 4th. the form of figurate Descants. 5th. ye contrivance of Canons. | By Christopher Sympson. | The Ninth Edition with material Additions corrected from many gross Errors in | the former Editions, the examples being put in the most useful Cliffs. | . . . | London; Printed & sold by Longman, Lukey and Co. | Musical Instrument Makers & Music-Sellers No. 26, Cheapside. [ca. 1775]

obl. 8° 1 ℓ., vi, 90 p., front. (port.), illus., music
RISM B VI, 785
HOUGHTON

1429 SIMPSON, CHRISTOPHER

The Division-Violist: | Or | An Introduction | To the Playing upon a Grovnd: | Divided into Two Parts. | The First, Directing the Hand, with Other Prepa-|rative Instructions. | The Second, Laying open the Manner and Method of | Playing Ex-tempore, or Composing Division | to a Grovnd. | To which, are Added some Divisions made upon Grounds | for the

Practice of Learners. | By Chr. Simpson. | London, | Printed by William Godbid, and sold by John Playford, | at his Shop in the Inner-Temple. 1659.

2° 5 *ℓ.*, 67 p., illus., pl., music
Plate included in paging
Imperfect: frontispiece portrait, pages 3, 4 lacking, supplied in facsimile; pages 51, 52 lacking
Hirsch I, no. 553; RISM B VI, 785
HOUGHTON

SIMPSON, JOHN, PUBL. The Amphion *See* The Amphion

SIMPSON, JOHN, PUBL. Calliope, or English Harmony *See* Calliope, or English Harmony

SIMPSON, JOHN, PUBL. The Compleat Tutor for the Flute *See* The Compleat Tutor for the Flute

SIMPSON, JOHN, PUBL. The Delightful Pocket Companion for the German Flute *See* The Delightful Pocket Companion for the German Flute

1430   SIPRUTINI, EMANUEL

Six | Solos | For a | Violin | With a | Thorough Bass | For the | Harpsichord | Compos'd | By | Sigr. Emanuel Siprutini | Opera Prima | . . . | London Printed for Thompson and Sons in St. Pauls Church Yard | . . . [ca. 1763]

2° *Score:* 1 *ℓ.*, 29 p.
HOUGHTON

1431

Six | Favourite Songs, | For The | Voice and Piano Forte. | Composed By |

Mr: Arne.   Mr: Carter.
Dr: Arnold.   Mr: Hook.
Mr: Battishill.   Mr: Webbe.

The Words By | Mr. Harrison. | London: | Printed for Harrison & Co. No. 18. Paternoster Row. | . . . [1797?]

8° *Score:* 2 *ℓ.*, 4–14 p. (*The Piano-Forte Magazine,* vol. I, no. 8)
RISM B II, 175
MUSIC LIBRARY

1432

Six | Sonatas, | For The | Piano Forte. | Composed By |

Bach,   Wagen[s]eil,
Benda,   Hasse, &
Gzaun, [*sic*]   Kernberger.

London: | Printed for Harrison, Cluse, & Co. No. 78 Fleet Street. [1799?]

8° *Score:* 39 p. (*The Piano-Forte Magazine,* vol. VII, no. 6)
Plate nos. 102–103
MUSIC LIBRARY

1433

Sixteen | Cotillons | or | French Dances | As Perform'd at Court and all polite Assemblies | For the Harpsichord, Violin, German Flute or Hautboy | with proper Directions to each Dance . . . | London | Printed for C. & S. Thompson No. 75 St. Pauls Church Yard | . . . [177–?]

obl. 8° *Score:* 2 *ℓ.*, [33] numb. *ℓ.*
Numbered leaves printed on one side only
Imperfect: numbered leaf 33 lacking
MUSIC LIBRARY

1434   [SMITH, ALEXANDER, COMP.]

The | Musical Miscellany; | a | Select Collection | of the | most approved | Scots, English, & Irish | Songs. | set to Music. | Perth: | Printed by J. Brown. | MDCCLXXXVI.

12° 2 *ℓ.*, xii, 347 p., front.
RISM B II, 247
HOUGHTON

1435   SMITH, JOHN CHRISTOPHER

The | Fairies | An | Opera. | The Words taken from | Shakespear &c. | Set to Music by | Mr. Smith. | . . . | London. Printed for I. Walsh in Catharine Street in the Strand. [1755]

2° *Score:* 2 ℓ., 92 p.

On recto of second preliminary leaf: Musick Compos'd by Mr. Handel, Printed for I. Walsh . . .

Walsh II, no. 1374

MUSIC LIBRARY

1436   SMITH, JOHN CHRISTOPHER

A Collection of | Lessons | For The | Harpsicord | Compos'd By | Mr. Smith | Author of the Opera call'd The Fairies. | Opera IV | London. Printed for I. Walsh in Catharine Street in the Strand. | . . . [1757]

obl. 2° *Score:* 1 ℓ., 42–81 p.

[Vol. II] of a collection, paged continuously; vol. I, which is lacking, contains Smith's Lessons opus III (see Schnapper II, 958)

Walsh II, no. 1379

HOUGHTON

1437   SMITH, JOHN STAFFORD, COMP.

A | Collection of | English Songs, | in Score | for Three and Four Voices | Composed about the Year 1500 | Taken from M.S.S. of the same Age | Revised and Digested by | John Stafford Smith | . . . | London. | Printed for J: Bland No: 45 Holborn | . . . [1779?]

2° *Score:* 3 ℓ., 12, 65 p., illus., pl.

RISM B II, 64

MUSIC LIBRARY

1438   SMITH, ROBERT

Harmonics, | Or | The Philosophy | Of Musical Sounds. | By | Robert Smith, D. D, F. R. S, | And Master of Trinity College | In the University of Cambridge. | . . . | The Second Edition, | Much improved and augmented. | London: | Printed for T. and J. Merrill Booksellers in Cambridge: | Sold by B. Dod, J. Whiston and B. White, | J. Nourse, and M. Cooper in London; | J. Fletcher, and D. Prince in Oxford. | MDCCLIX.

8° xx, 280 p., 7 ℓ., illus., 31 pl. (incl. music)

RISM B VI, 788

MUSIC LIBRARY

1439   SMITH, ROBERT

A | Postscript | To | Dr. Smith's Harmonics, | Upon | The changeable harpsichord: | Which being supplied with all the useful flat | and sharp sounds and tuned in the best man-|ner, is made as harmonious as possible: and | yet the execution of music upon this perfect | instrument is the same as upon the common | harpsichord. | London: | Printed for T. and J. Merrill in Cambridge, and B. Dod | in London: Sold also by J. Whiston and B. White, | J. Nourse, T. Payne, L. Davis and C. Reymers, in | London; J. Fletcher, and D. Prince, in Oxford; R. | and A. Foulis in Glasgow; and A. Kincaid, and A. Do-|naldson, in Edinburgh. | M.DCC.LXII.

8° 12 p., illus., pl. (incl. music)

RISM B VI, 788

MUSIC LIBRARY

1440   SMITH, THEODORE

Three | Favourite Duets, | for two Performers on one | Harpsichord or Piano Forte | Dedicated to the Right Honorable | Lady Ann and Lady Sarah Windsor | Composed by | Theodore Smith. | . . . | London | Printed by Longman & Broderip No. 26, Cheapside, | Music-Sellers to the Royal Family. | . . . [ca. 1780]

2° *Score:* 1 ℓ., 15 p.

MUSIC LIBRARY

1441   SMITH, THEODORE

A Second Set of | Three | Favorite Duets, | For two Performers on one | Harpsichord or Piano Forte, | Dedicated to | Miss Thomson, | and | Miss Lucy Thomson, | Composed by | Theodore Smith. | . . . | London; Engrav'd & Printed, by Longman & Broderip, No. 26, Cheapside, | Music Sellers to the Royal Family. | . . . [1780?]

2° *Score:* 1 ℓ., 16–29 p.

MUSIC LIBRARY

1442   SMITH, THEODORE

A Third Sett of | Three | Favourite Duets | For Two Performers on One | Harpsichord or Piano Forte, | Dedicated to the Honorable | Lady Maria and Lady Ann Bowes; | Composed by | Theodore Smith | . . . | London | Printed & sold by Longman and Broderip No. 26, Cheapside, | . . . [ca. 1780]

2° *Score:* 1 ℓ., 18 p.
Page 2: Engrav'd by T. Straight No. 138 St. Martins Lane.
MUSIC LIBRARY

SOHR, MARTIN *See* Agricola, Martin

1443 SOLANO, FRANCISCO IGNACIO

Nova Instrucção Musical, | Ou | Theorica Pratica | Da | Musica Rythmica, | Com A Qual Se Fo'rma, E Ordena Sobre | os mais solidos fundamentos hum Novo Methodo, e verdadeiro | Systema para constituir hum intelligente Solfista, e destrissimo | Cantor, nomeando as Nótas, ou Figuras da Solfa pelos seus | mais proprios, e improprios nomes, a que chamamos ordi-|narios, e extraordinarios no Canto Natural, e Acciden-|tal, de que procede toda a difficuldade da Musica. | Offerecida | Ao Muito Poderoso, E Fidelissimo Rei | Nosso Senhor | D. Jose' I. | Por seu Author | Francisco Ignacio Solano. | Lisboa, | Na Officina de Miguel Manescal Da Costa, | Impressor do Santo Officio. | Anno CIꓛ.IꓛCC.LXIV. | Com todas as licencas necessarias.

4° 30 ℓ., 340 p., 2 ℓ., 47, [1] p., illus., fold. pl., music
RISM B VI, 790
MUSIC LIBRARY

1444 SOLIÉ, JEAN PIERRE

Propriété de l'Éditeur d'après le Décret du 19 Juillet 1793. | Le Secret | Opera en un Acte | Paroles d'Hoffman | Mises en Musique | Par Solié | Représenté pour la premiere fois au Théâtre Italien | Le premier Floreal An 4. (20 Avril 1796 vieux Stile) | . . . | A Paris | Chez Jmbault Md. de Musique et de Cordes d'Jnstruments Rue Honoré No. 200. | entre la Rue des Poulies et la Maison d'Aligre. | Et Péristile du Théâtre de l'Opera Comique Rue Favart No. 461. | . . . | Gravé par Van Jxem. [1800?]

2° *Score:* 1 ℓ., 117 p.
Plate no. 42
MUSIC LIBRARY

1445 SOLNITZ, ANTON WILHELM

Six | Sonatas | For Two | Violins | with a Thorough Bass for the | Harpsicord or Violoncello | Compos'd by | Antonio Guglielmo Solniz. | London. Printed for I. Walsh, in Catharine Street, in the Strand. | . . . [1750]

2° 2 pts.: *primo:* 1 ℓ., 12 p.; *secondo:* 1 ℓ., 9 p.
Walsh II, no. 1389
HOUGHTON

1446

Some | Observations | On | Dr. Brown's Dissertation | On the Rise, Union, &c. &c. &c. of | Poetry And Musick. | In a Letter to Dr. B*****. | . . . | London: | Printed for W. Johnston, in Ludgate-Street. | MDCCLXIV.

4° 1 ℓ., 59 p.
MUSIC LIBRARY

1447

. . . | Songs and Fancies, | To Three, Four or | Five Parts, | Both apt for Voices and Viols. | With a brief Introduction | to Musick, | As is taught by Thomas | Davidson, in the Musick-|School of Aberdene. | Second Edition, Corrected | and Enlarged. | Aberdene, | Printed by John Forbes, and are to be sold at his shop, | Anno Domini. M.DC.LXVI.

obl. 4° 1 pt.: *cantus:* [−]⁴, ††⁴, A–K⁴, L², illus.
Imperfect: closely cropped; some pages torn, with loss of text and music
RISM B I, no. 1666³
HOUGHTON

1448

. . . | Songs and Fancies, | To Three, Four, or | Five Parts, | Both apt for Voices and Viols | With a brief Intro-|duction to Musick. | As is taught in the Mu-|sick-School of Aberdeen. | The Third Edition, much | Enlarged and Corrected. | Printed in Aberdeen, by Iohn Forbes, | and are to be sold at his Printing-House above the Meal-|Market, at the Sign of the Tovvns-Armes. 1682.

obl. 4° 1 pt.: *cantus:* [–]², A–O⁴, illus.

Leaves L3ʳ–(O3ʳ): Severall of the Choisest | Italian Songs | Composed By | Giovanni Giacomo Castoldi [*sic*] da Carravaggio. | Together also, with some of the Best | new English-Ayres. | Collected from their chiefest Authors, | All in Three Parts, | Viz. Two Trebles and a Bass.

RISM B I, no. 1682⁵

HOUGHTON

SONGS IN THE NEW OPERA CALL'D PYRRHUS AND DEMETRIUS *See* Scarlatti, Alessandro *Songs in the New Opera Call'd Pyrrhus and Demetrius*

SORE, MARTIN *See* Agricola, Martin

SOULIER, JEAN PIERRE *See* Solié, Jean Pierre

1449

Les | Spectacles | De Paris, | Ou Suite Du | Calendrier | Historique | Et Chronologique | Des | Théatres. | . . . | Troisiéme [–Quarante-Deuxieme] Partie. | Qui doit servir pour l'année 1754. [–1793.] | A Paris, | Chez Duchesne, Libraire, rue S. Jacques, | au-dessous de la Fontaine S. Benoît, | au Temple du Goût. | M.DCC.LIV. [–⟨1793⟩] | Avec Approbation & Privilége du Roi.

12° 22 vols.: *pt. 3, 1754:* 5 ℓ., 208, [8] p.; *pt. 5, 1756:* 6 ℓ., 161, [7] p.; *pt. 6, 1757:* 8 ℓ., 147, [5] p.; *pt. 7, 1758:* 8 ℓ., 152 p.; *pt. 8, 1759:* 6 ℓ., iv, 144 p.; *pt. 9, 1760:* 12 ℓ., 140 p.; *pt. 10, 1761:* 12 ℓ., 180 p.; *pt. 11, 1762:* 8 ℓ., 152 p.; *pt. 12, 1763:* 12 ℓ., 155, [1] p.; *pt. 21, 1772:* 23, 181, [3] p.; *pt. 23, 1774:* 24, 210, [6] p.; *pt. 24, 1775:* 12 ℓ., 229, [10] p.; *pt. 25, 1776:* 12 ℓ., 229, [9] p.; *pt. 26, 1777:* 12 ℓ., 238, [2] p.; *pt. 28, 1779:* 8 ℓ., 8, 233, [6] p.; *pt. 29, 1780:* 8 ℓ., 8,238, [2] p.; *pt. 30–35, 1781–1786:* 24, 240 p. each; *pt. 36, 1787:* 24, 239, [1] p.; *pt. 39, 1790:* 12 ℓ., 240 p.; *pt. 40, 1791:* 13 ℓ., 240 p.; *pt. 41,*

1792: 15 ℓ., [27]–263, 82 p., 1 ℓ.; *pt. 42, 1793:* 360 p.

Title varies; parts 41, 42 have title: Les | Spectacles | De Paris, | Et De Toute la France, | . . .

Continuation of *Almanach historique et chronologique de tous les spectacles*

Imperfect: pages [5]–16 lacking in vol. for 1774; pages 145, 146, 167, 168 lacking in vol. for 1785

Grand-Carteret, no. 180

HOUGHTON

1450   SPIESS, MEINRAD

Cithara | Davidis | Noviter Animata. | Hoc Est | Psalmi | Vespertini, | A | 4. Voc. ordinariis. 2. VV. 2. VV. Violone. Organo. & | ad Psalmos intermedios unâ voce principaliter praecinente. | Authore | P. Meinrado Spiess, | Celeberrimi & Imperialis Monasterii B. V. M. Ursinensis | Ord. S. P. Benedicti Professo, & ibidem p. t. Chori | Directore. | Opus II. | Anno | qVI fVIt DoMInICae InCarnatIonIs. | . . . | Constantiae, | Typis, & Sumptibus Leonardi Parcus Episcopalis Typographi, | Anno M.DCC.XVII.

2° 10 pts.: *vox principalis:* [A]², B–F²; *canto:* A–E²; *alto, tenore, basso:* [A]², B–E² each; *violino I, violino II:* [A]², B–H² each; *viola I, viola II:* [A]², B–E² each; *organum:* [–]²,)(1,)()(², A–L²

HOUGHTON

1451   SPIESS, MEINRAD

Hyperdulia Musica. | Hoc Est: | VIII. Lytaniae | Lauretanae | De | B. V. Maria, | Suaviter Ac Graviter Decantandae | à | IV. Vocibus, Canto, Alto, Tenore, Basso, | II. Violinis, II. Violis, Violone, Organo, | & IV. Ripienis: | Quibus ultimô Locô adjunguntur | Lytaniae | De | Venerabili Sacramento, | Singularî prorsus Industriâ, & ex tenerô Devotionis Affectu | Ergà | Superbenedictissimam Dei, Pulchraeque Dilectionis | Matrem, | Compositae ab Ejusdem Gloriosissimae Virginis | Servorum, ac Clientum infimo | P. Meinrado Spiess, | Imperialis B. V. Mariae Monasterii Ursinensis, | Ord S. P. Benedicti Professo, &c. | . . . | Opus VI. | Cvm Licentia Svperiorvm. | Augustae Vindelicorum, Sumptibus Francisci Josephi Eysenbarth, & Josephi Endele Bibliopol. | Typis Joannis Michaëlis Labhart, Reverendiss. ac Sereniss. Principis & Episcopi Augustani Typogr. | Anno M.DCCXXVI.

2° 1 pt.: *basso pro organo:* 1 ℓ., 41 p.
Imperfect: page 41 containing index torn, with loss of text
HOUGHTON

1452 STABILE, ANNIBALE

. . . | Di Annibal Stabile | Il Terzo Libro | De Madrigali A Cinqve Voci. | Nouamente posti in luce. | In Vinegia Appresso l'Herede di Girolamo Scotto. | MDLXXXV.

4° 1 pt.: *tenore:* 24 p.
Vogel, no. 2643
HOUGHTON

1453 STAES, FERDINAND

Three | Sonatas | for the | Harpsichord | or | Piano Forte, | with an Accompanyment for a | Violin & Violoncello, | Composed by | Ferdinand Staes. | Op. [III] . . . | London. | Printed by S. Babb at his Musical Library No 132, Oxford Street, | . . . [ca. 1780]

2° 1 pt.: *violoncello:* 7 p.
"III" added to title-page in manuscript
MUSIC LIBRARY

1454 STANLEY, JOHN

Six | Concertos | Set for the | Harpsicord or Organ | Compos'd by | Mr. John Stanley | Organist of the Temple, and St. Andrews. | N. B. The 1st. & 2d. Repienos, Tenor, & Basso Repieno of | His Violin Concertos, are the Instrumental Parts to the above. | London. Printed for I. Walsh, in Catharine Street, in the Strand. | . . . [ca. 1745]

2° 1 pt.: *harpsicord or organ:* 1 ℓ., 32 p.
Hirsch IV, no. 1660a; Walsh II, no. 1415
HOUGHTON

1455 [STEDMAN, FABIAN]

Campanalogia: | Or The | Art | Of | Ringing | Improved. | With plain and

easie Rules to | guide the Practitioner in the | Ringing all kinds of Changes. | To | Which is added, great variety of | New Peals. | London, | Printed by W. Godbid, for W. S. and are to | be sold by Langley Curtis in Goat-Court | on Ludgate-hill. 1677.

8° 4 ℓ., 231 p., music
The music is in bell-ringer's notation
RISM B VI, 804
HOUGHTON

1456 STEIBELT, DANIEL

Romeo et Juliette | Opera | en trois Actes, en Prose | Représenté pour la premiere fois sur le | Théâtre de la rüe Feydeau le 10 7bre. 1793 (vieux stile) | Mis en Musique | Par D. Steibelt | . . . | A Paris | Chez Boyer, Rue de la Loi, à la Clef d'Or, | Passage de l'ancien Caffé de foy. | . . . [after 1792]

2° *Score:* 1 ℓ., 361 p.
MUSIC LIBRARY

1457 STEIBELT, DANIEL

Trois | Sonates | Pour | Le Forte-Piano la Premiere avec Violon | Obligé, la Seconde avec Violon et Basse | (ad libitum) la troisme. sans Accompagnement | Dediées | A Mademoiselle | L Foäche | Par D. Steibelt | Oeuvre 2me. | . . . | A Paris | Chez M. Boyer, Rue de Richelieu à la Clef d'or, | Passage du Caffé de foy. | Chez Made. Le Menu Rue du Roulle a la Clef d'or, [ca. 1790]

2° 3 pts.: *forte-piano:* 1 ℓ., 33 p.; *violino:* 6 p.; *violoncello:* 3 p.
MUSIC LIBRARY

1458 STEIBELT, DANIEL

Three | Sonatas | for the | Piano Forte | with an Accompaniment for a | Violin Ad Libitum | Composed by and Dedicated to | Miss Isabella Savery | By | D. Steibelt. | Op 35 . . . | London | Printed by Longman Clementi & Compy. | Music Sellers to their Majesties his Royal Highness | Prince of Wales & all the Royal Family | . . . [1799?]

2° Score and 1 pt.: *score:* 1 ℓ., 46 p.; *violino:* 8 p.
MUSIC LIBRARY

1459 STERKEL, JOHANN FRANZ XAVER

Twelve Pieces | for the | Harpsichord | or | Piano Forte. | Composed by | Sigr. Sterkel | of Vienne. | Op. X. . . . | London. | Printed for J. Bland No: 45 Holborn | . . . [ca. 1780]

2° *Score:* 1 ℓ., 16 p.
Page [1]: A Catalogue Of | Vocal and Instrumental Music. Printed | And Sold by J: Bland . . .
MUSIC LIBRARY

1460 STERKEL, JOHANN FRANZ XAVER

Recueil | des 12. Pieces | pour le | Clavecin ou Piano Forte | Composé par | Mr. Sterkel. | Mis au jour par le Sr. Schott Graveur de la Cour à Mayence. | . . . Oeuvre. 22. [178–?]

obl. 4° *Score:* 23 p.
Plate no. 34
HOUGHTON

1461 STEVENS, RICHARD JOHN SAMUEL

Ten Glees | for | Three, Four, Five & Six Voices, | Composed by | R. J. S. Stevens. | Op. V. . . . | London. | Printed for the Author, Charterhouse. | . . . | Simpkins sc. 9, Clements Inn. [ca. 1798]

obl. 2° *Score:* 2 ℓ., 59 p.
Stevens' autograph signature on title-page
MUSIC LIBRARY

1462 STICKL, FRANZ

Psalmi | Vespertini | Pro Toto | Anno. | à | Quatuor Vocibus. Violino Unisono | in duplo necessario. | Cum | Duplici Basso continuo pro Organo, | & Violone &c. concinnati. | à | Francisco Stickl, | Superioris Parochiae ad Speciosam Virgin. Ingolstadij | Academico Organaedo. | Opus I. | . . . | Augustae Vindelicorum. | Sumptibus Matthiae Wolff, Bibliopolae, |

Typis Joannis Jacobi Lotteri, | Anno MDCCXXI.

2° 6 pts.: *canto, alto, tenore:* [−]1, A–K², L1 each; *basso:* [−]1, A–K²; *violino unisono:* [−]1, A–M², N1; *organo:*)(1–3, A–N², O1
HOUGHTON

1463 [STIELER, KASPAR VON]

Die | Geharnschte Venus | oder | Liebes-Lieder im Kriege gedich-|tet mit neuen Gesang-Weisen zu | singen und zu spielen gesezzet | nebenst | ettlichen Sinnreden der | Liebe | Verfertiget | und | Lustigen Gemühtern zu Gefallen | heraus gegeben | von | Filidor dem Dorfferer. | Hamburg, | Gedrukkt bey Michael Pfeif-fern. | In Verlegung Christian Guht, Buchhån-|lers im Tuhm, Im Jahr 1660.

12° A–P¹², front.
Imperfect: leaf K12 torn, with loss of words and music; facsimile leaf inserted
RISM B I, no. 1660³
HOUGHTON

1464 [STILLINGFLEET. BENJAMIN]

Principles | And Power | Of Harmony. | . . . | London: | Printed By J. and H. Hughs: | And Sold By S. Baker And G. Leigh, York-Street; | B. White, Fleet-Street; J. Robson, New Bond-Street; | And J. Walter, Charing-Cross. | MDCCLXXI.

4° vii, [1], 154, [6] p., pl.
RISM B VI, 809
MUSIC LIBRARY

1465 STOESSEL, JOHANN CHRISTOPH

Kurtzgefasstes | Musicalisches | Lexicon, | Worinnen | Eine nützliche Anleitung und grůndlicher | Begriff von der Music enthalten, die Termini | technici erklåret, die Instrumente erlåutert und die | vornehmsten Musici beschrieben sind, | Nebst einer | Historischen Beschreibung | von der Music Nahmen, Eintheilung, | Ursprung, Erfindung, Ver-mehrung und Ver-|besserung, biss sie zu itziger Vortrefflichkeit gelanget, | auch wunderbaren Wůrckung und Gebrauch, | ingleichen ihren vornehmsten Cultoribus, | so von der Welt Anfang biss auf | unsere Zeit gelebet, | Alles aus derer besten und berühmtesten Musico-|rum ihren Schrifften mit Fleiss zusammen gesucht, in | Alphabetische Ordnung gebracht, und denen Liebhabern | musicalischer Wissenschafften zu fernern Nachdencken | wohlmeynend vorgestellet. | Chemnitz, 1737, | bey Johann Christoph und Johann David Stösseln.

8° 8 ℓ., 430 [i. e. 432] p., illus.
Numbers 143, 144 repeated in paging
MUSIC LIBRARY

1466   STORACE, STEPHEN

The Cherokee | an | Opera | in Three Acts, | As Performed at the | Theatre Royal Drury Lane, | the Music | Principally Composed | By | Stephen Storace. | . . . | London, Printed & Sold by J. Dale, No. 19, Cornhill, & No. 132, Oxford Street, opposite Hanover Square. [1791?]

obl. 2° *Vocal score:* 1 ℓ., 83 p.
Page [1]: Opera's &c. Printed by J. Dale . . .
MUSIC LIBRARY

1467   STORACE, STEPHEN

The Haunted Tower | A | Comic Opera | Performed at the | Theatre Royal Drury Lane | Adapted for the | German Flute | Selected and Composed by | Stn. Storace | . . . | London | Printed by Longman and Broderip No. 26 Cheapside and No. 13 Hay Market [ca. 1789]

obl. 8° 1 ℓ., 64 p.
HOUGHTON

1468   STORACE, STEPHEN

The Haunted Tower, | a | Comic Opera | in Three Acts, | As Performed at the | Theatre Royal Drury Lane, | the Music | Selected, Adapted & Composed | By Stephen Storace. | . . . | London. Printed by Longman & Broderip, No. 26, Cheapside, & No. 13, Haymarket. . . . [ca. 1790]

obl. 2° *Vocal score:* 1 ℓ., 72 p.
RISM B II, 199
MUSIC LIBRARY

1469   STORACE, STEPHEN

No Song No Supper | A | Comic Opera | Adapted for the | German Flute | The Music Composed and Compiled by | Stephen Storace | . . . | London | Printed by Longman and Broderip No. 26 Cheapside and No. 13 Hay Market. [after 1782]

obl. 8° 49 p.
HOUGHTON

1470   STORACE, STEPHEN

The Pirates, | an | Opera | in Three Acts, | As Performed at the | Theatre Royal Drury Lane | the Music | Composed | By Stephen Storace. | . . . | London. Printed & Sold by J. Dale, No. 19, Cornhill & No. 132, Oxford Street opposite Hanover Square. [1792?]

obl. 2° *Vocal score:* 1 ℓ., 93 p.
Page [1]: Music Printed by J. Dale . . .
Hirsch IV, no. 1286
MUSIC LIBRARY

1471   STORACE, STEPHEN

The Siege of Belgrade, | an | Opera | in Three Acts, | As Performed at the | Theatre Royal Drury Lane, | the Music | Principally Composed | By Stephen Storace. | . . . | London, Printed & Sold by J. Dale, No. 19 Cornhill; & No. 133 Oxford Street, opposite Hanover Square. | . . . [1791?]

obl. 2° *Vocal score:* 1 ℓ., 82 p.
MUSIC LIBRARY (2 copies)

1472   STUCK, JOHANN BAPTIST, CALLED BATISTIN

Cantates Françoises | A Voix Seule, Avec Symphonies, | Dédiées | A Son Altesse Royale | Monseigneur | Le Duc D'Orleans, | Par Jean-Baptiste Stuck, Florentin. | Livre Premier. | A Paris, | Chez Christophe Ballard, seul Imprimeur du Roy pour la Musique, rüe Saint Jean de Beauvais, | au Mont-Parnasse. | M.D.CCXIII. | Avec Privilege De Sa Majesté.

obl. 2° *Score:* 2 ℓ., 98, [2] p
MUSIC LIBRARY

1473   STUCK, JOHANN BAPTIST,
         CALLED BATISTIN

Cantates | Françoises | A Voix Seule Et
Basse-Continue, | Avec Et Sans Sym-
phonies; | Par Jean-Baptiste Stuck,
Florentin; Ordinaire de la Musique | de S.
A. R. Monseigneur le Duc d'Orleans. | A
Paris, | Chez Christophe Ballard, seul Im-
primeur du Roy pour la Musique, ruë
Saint Jean de Beauvais, | au Mont-Par-
nasse. | M.DCCVIII. | Avec Privilege De
Sa Majesté.

obl. 2° *Score:* 2 ℓ., 70, [2] p.
Page [2] at end: Prix Des Cantates
Françoises
MUSIC LIBRARY

1474   STUCK, JOHANN BAPTIST,
         CALLED BATISTIN

Cantates | Françoises | A I. II. Voix Et
Basse-Continue, | Avec Symphonies; |
Par Jean-Baptiste Stuck, Florentin; Or-
dinaire de la Musique | de Son Altesse
Royale Monseigneur le Duc d'Orleans. |
A Paris, | Chez Christophe Ballard, seul
Imprimeur du Roy pour la Musique, | ruë
Saint Jean de Beauvais, au Mont-Par-
nasse. | M.DCCXI. | Avec Privilege De Sa
Majesté.

obl. 2° *Score:* 2 ℓ., 45, [1] p.
MUSIC LIBRARY

SUEUR, JEAN FRANÇOIS LE   *See* Le Sueur,
Jean François

SUITE DES ERREURS SUR LA MUSIQUE DANS
L'ENCYCLOPEDIE *See* Rameau, Jean Philippe *Suite des erreurs sur la musique
dans l'Encyclopedie*

SUMMER AMUSEMENT   *See* Arnold, Samuel *Summer Amusement*

T

1475   [TABOUROT, JEHAN]

Orchesographie, | Metode, Et Teorie |
En Forme De Discovrs Et Tablatvre |
Povr Apprendre A Dancer, Battre Le |

Tambour en toute sorte & diuersité de
batte-|ries, Iouër du fifre & arigot, tirer
des armes | & escrimer, auec autres hon-
nestes | exercices fort conuenables | à la
Ieunesse. | Affin | D'estre bien venue en
toute Ioyeuse compagnie & y monstrer
sa dexteritè | & agilité de corps. | Par
Thoinot Arbeau demeurant a Lengres. |
. . . | A Lengres, | Par Iehan des Preyz Im-
primeur & Libraire. tenant sa bouti-|que
en la ruë des merciers dicte les Pilliers. |
M.D.XCVI. | Auec Priuilege du Roy.

4° 104 numb. ℓ., illus., music
Brown, no. 1596₁; RISM B VI, 93
HOUGHTON

1476   TAG, CHRISTIAN GOTTHILF

Siebenzig | Veränderungen | über | ein
Andantino fürs Clavier. | meinem
Freunde | dem | Herrn Musikdirector
Hiller | in Leipzig | gewidmet | von |
Christian Gotthilf Tag. | Leipzig und
Dessau, | in der Buchhandlung der Ge-
lehrten. | 1784.

2° *Score:* 2 ℓ., 42, [2] p.
MUSIC LIBRARY

1477   TANS'UR, WILLIAM

Heaven on Earth; | Or, The | Beauty of
Holiness. | In Two Books. | Containing, |
I. The Whole Book of the Proverbs | of
King Solomon, Composed in English
Verse; | And Set to Musick. | II. The Song
of Songs, which is the | Song of Solomon.
| Together, | With various Hymns, An-
thems, and Ca-|nons: With Instructions
to the Musick; | And Expositional Notes
on the Whole. | Composed in Two,
Three, and Four Musical Parts accord-
|ing to the most Authentick Rules, and
set down in Score for Voice or | Instru-
ment. | By William Tans'ur, of Barns, in
Surry. Author of | The Melody of the
Hearts, and The Harmony of Sion. | . . . |
London: | Printed by A. Pearson, for S.
Birt, at the Bible and Ball, in Ave-|Mary
Lane. Also Sold by the Author.
M.DCC.XXXVIII. | . . .

8° *Score:* 3 ℓ., 8, 221, [3] p., front.
(port.)
Some pages torn, with loss of text and
music
MUSIC LIBRARY

1478 TANS'UR, WILLIAM

A | New Musical Grammar: | Or, The | Harmonical Spectator. | Containing | All the useful Theoretical, Practical, and | Technical Parts of | Musick. | Being a New and Correct | Introduction | To | All the Rudiments, Terms, and Characters, | And | Composition in all its Branches. | With | Several Scales for Musical Instruments; | And | Philosophical Demonstrations, | On | The Nature of Sound. | Laid down in so concise and easy a Method, as | to be understood by the meanest Practitioner, | whether Vocal or Instrumental, by Way of | Question and Answer. With variety of Cuts | correctly engraved. | By William Tansur: Musico Theorico. | Author of The Universal Harmony, &c. | Printed for the Author, and sold by him, and in Lon-|don, by Jacob Robinson, Bookseller, in Ludgatestreet, | and by most Booksellers, in Town and Country. | . . . M.DCC.XL.VI.

12° 1 ℓ., iv, [2], 156 [i. e. 160] p., illus., music
Numbers 134, 135, 138 and 139 repeated in paging
RISM B VI, 817
MUSIC LIBRARY

1479 TANS'UR, WILLIAM

A | New Musical Grammar, | And | Dictionary: | Or, | A General Introduction | To The Whole | Art of Musick. | In Four Books. | Teaching, | I. The Rudiments of Tones, Diatonick, and Semitonick; according | to the Gamut.—With Rules for Tuning the Voice, and Beating of | Time; the Nature of Keys, and Transposition; and of all other Characters | used in Musick. | II. Containing such plain and easy Directions as are necessary for | Tuning, and Playing on, the Organ, Harpsichord, Bass-Viol, Violin, Haut-|boy, Flute, Bassoon, &c.—With Songs and Lessons in great Variety; in 2, | 3, and 4 Parts.—With Rules for Tuning of Bells, and Pricking of Chime-|Barrels, &c. And the Structure of an Organ considered, in all its curious | Branches: And a Feeling Scale of Musick for such as are blind. | III. The Theory of Sound, from its Natural Causes: Or, A Philoso-|phical, and Mathematical Dissertation thereon; in a concise and easy Method, | &c. To-

gether with the Principles of Practical Musick: Or, the most Authen-|tick Rules of Composition, either in 2, 3, 4, 5, 6, 7, or 8 Musical Parts: | Shewing the Allowed Passages of all Concords, and Discords; and the | Contrivance of Fuge, or Canon, in great Variety. | IV. The Musicians Historical, and Technical Dictionary; explica-|ting above 550 of the most useful Terms that generally occur in Musick; | as they are taken from the Greek, French, Latin, and Italian Writers. With | an Account of Instruments, and their Inventors, &c. | The Whole is extracted from the best Authors, both Ancient, and Modern; | and methodically digested to every Capacity.—With a Preface prefactory; | and a Table to the Whole. | . . . | The Third Edition, with large Additions. | By William Tans'ur, Senior, Musico-Theorico. | London: Printed by Robert Brown, for James Hodges, near London-|Bridge. Also sold by the Author; and by his Son, late Cho-|rister of Trinity-College, Cambridge. 1756. . . .

8° xii, [4], 176 p., illus., music
Imperfect: some pages torn, with loss of text; pages 49–56, 113–120 lacking
RISM B VI, 817–818
MUSIC LIBRARY

1480 TAPIA, MARTÍN DE

Vergel De Mvsica | spiritual specula-tiua y actiua. del | qual, muchas, diuersas y suaues flores se puedē coger. Dirigi-|do al yllustrissimo y Reuerēdissimo Señor dō Frācisco Tello | de San Doual Obispo de Osma y del Cōsejo de su Magestad | Autor el Bachiller Tapia Numantino. | Tratase lo primero con grāde artificio y profundidad, las | alabanças, las gracias, la dignidad, Las virtudes y prerrogati-|uas dela musica y despues, Las artes de Cantollano, | Organo y Contrapūto, en suma y en Theorica. | . . . | [Osma, 1570]

4° 4 ℓ., cxx numb. ℓ., illus., music
Colophon: . . . fue impresso ēla Incly|ta vniuersidad dela Villa del Burgo de Osma por Diego | Fernandez de Cordoua impressor. Acabose a veynte y ocho | dias del mes de Mayo, Año de nuestra redemp|cion de mil & quiniētos y setenta años.
Hirsch I, no. 570; RISM B VI, 818–819
HOUGHTON

1481 TARTINI, GIUSEPPE

Sonate | A Violino Solo | Col Basso | Da
Signore | Giuseppe Tartini. | Di Padoua |
Opera VII. | Gravées par Melle. Bertin. |
. . . | A Paris | Chez {Madame Boivin,
Mde. rüe St. Honoré à la Regle d'Or. |
Monsieur le Clerc, Md. rüe du Roule à la
Croix d'Or. | Mademoiselle Castagneri,
Mde rue des Prouvaires | A Lyon | Mon-
sieur de Brotonne, [sic] Md. rüe Mer-
ciere. | Avec Privilege Du Roy. [1748]

2° *Score:* 1 ℓ., 27, [1] p.
Brainard, p. xxxvii–xxxviii
MUSIC LIBRARY

1482 [TARTINI, GIUSEPPE]

Trattato | Di | Musica | Secondo La
Vera Scienza | Dell' Armonia. | In Padova,
MDCCLIV. | Nella Stamperia del Semi-
nario. | Appresso Giovanni Manfrè. | Con
Licenza De' Superiori, E Privilegio.

4° 4 ℓ., 175, [1] p., illus., fold. pl.,
music
Hirsch I, no. 571; RISM B VI, 820
HOUGHTON

1483 TESSARINI, CARLO

Nouvelle Methode | Pour Apprendre
Par Theorie | Dans Un Mois De Tems | à |
Jouer Du Violon, | Divisée En Trois
Classes; | Avec Des | Leçons à Deux Vio-
lons | Par Gradation. | Dediée | A Mon-
sieur | De Perceval | Conseiller Receveur
General de Sa Majesté | Imperial Aposto-
lique des Domaines aides & | subsides, &
Lieutenant de la Cour Feudal | de la Ville
& Province de Malines. | Da Carlo Tes-
sarini Da Rimini. | . . . | A Paris, | Se
Vend aux Adresses Ordinaires. | Avec
Privilege du Roy. [17—]

2° 2 ℓ., 4, 3, 4 p., 2 pl. (incl. port.),
music
HOUGHTON

1484 THALESIO, PEDRO

Arte | De Canto Chão, | Com Hvma
Breve | Instrucção, pera os Sacerdotes,
Diaconos, | Subdiaconos, & moços do
Coro, | conforme ao vso Romano. | Com-

posta, & ordenada por o Mestre Pedro
Thalesio, Cathedratico | de Musica na in-
signe Vniuersidade de Coimbra. | Diri-
gida ao Illustrissimo, & Reuerendissimo
Senhor Dō Affonso | Furtado de
Mendoça, Bispo de Coimbra Conde de
Arganil, | do Conselho do Estado de Sua
Magestade, &c. | Em Coimbra, | Com
Licença da Sancta Inquisição, & Ordi-
nario. | Na Impressão de Diego Gomez de
Loureyro. Anno 1618.

4° 6 ℓ., 140 p., illus., music
RISM B VI, 827
MUSIC LIBRARY

1485

The | Theater of Music: | Or, A | Choice
Collection of the newest and best Songs |
Sung at the Court, and Public Theaters. |
The Words composed by the most inge-
nious Wits of the Age, and set to | Music
by the greatest Masters in that Science. |
With | A Theorbo-Bass to each Song for
the Theorbo, or Bass-Viol. | Also | Sym-
phonies and Retornels in 3 Parts to sev-
eral of them for the Violins and Flutes. |
The First Book. | London, | Printed by J.
Playford, for Henry Playford and R.C.
[i. e. Richard Carr] and are to be sold near
the | Temple Church, and at the Middle-
Temple Gate, 1685. ·

2° *Score:* 2 ℓ., 76 p.
Page 76: Mvsic Books Printed for John
Playford . . .
Day, no. 78; RISM B I, no. 1685[5]
HOUGHTON

1486

The | Theater of Music: | Or, A | Choice
Collection of the newest and best Songs |
Sung at the Court, and Public Theaters. |
The Words composed by the most inge-
nious Wits of the Age, and set to | Music
by the greatest Masters in that Science. |
With | A Thorow-Bass to each Song for
the Theorbo, or Bass-Viol. | Also | Sym-
phonies and Retornels in 3 Parts to sev-
eral of them for the Violins and Flutes. |
The Second Book. | London, | Printed by
J. P. [i. e. John Playford the younger] for
Henry Playford and R. C. [i. e. Richard
Carr] and sold by Henry Playford near

O genero diatonico procede em seu diateſſarão por tres interuallos: ſ. por dous tonos compoſtos, & hum ſemitono mayor.

C genero Chromatico, procede por outros tres interuallos:
conuemaſaber por hum ſemitono mayor, outro menor, & tres
ſemitonos incompoſtos, dous mayores, & hum menor em hũ
interuallo.

O genero Enarmonico, procede tambem por tres interuallos: ſ. por dous dieſis compoſtos, & dous tonos incõpoſtos.
Compoſto he, quando procede por interuallo conjunto.
Incompoſto he, quando procede por interuallo ſeparado, co-
mo ſe vè nos exemplos ſeguintes.

Exemplos dos Diateſſaroẽs dos tres generos.

Diateſſarão. Diatonico.   Quarta. Diatonica.

Diateſſarão. Chromatico.   Quarta. Chromatica.

Diateſſarão. Enarmonico.   Quarta. Enarmonica.

O genero Diatonico, he proprio, & natural do Canto chão.

O genero Chromatico, procede por diuiſoẽs, & dieſis de quatro comas.

O genero Enarmonico, procede por dieſis de duas comas, que
he ametade do Semitono menor.

D   Deſtes

Ioſep. Zarl.
Inſtit. har.
li.2.c.16. &
lib.3.c.72.
Idem Zarl.
demõ. har.
lib.4 defin.
3. 4. & 5.
IoãoMaria
Artuſi. na
arte de Cõ-
trapõt. c.7.
Ludo. Zac-
co.li.1.c.50.
Tolom. li.
2.c.15.
N. Burtio.
lib. 1. c. 12.
D.N.Vicẽ-
tin.li.1.c.5.
6. 7. & 8.
Artuſi.li.1.
dialog. da
muſic. fol.
17. & 18.

Montano.
fol 19.
Ioſep.Zarl.
inſtit. har.
lib.2. c. 30.
Boet.lib.1.
c.22.
Bermu.lib.
iiij c.47.
Euclid. in-
ſtit. harm.

1484 THALESIO, *Arte de canto chão*, Coimbra, 1618: page 25 (173 × 122 mm.); heading, initials, and staff lines printed in red

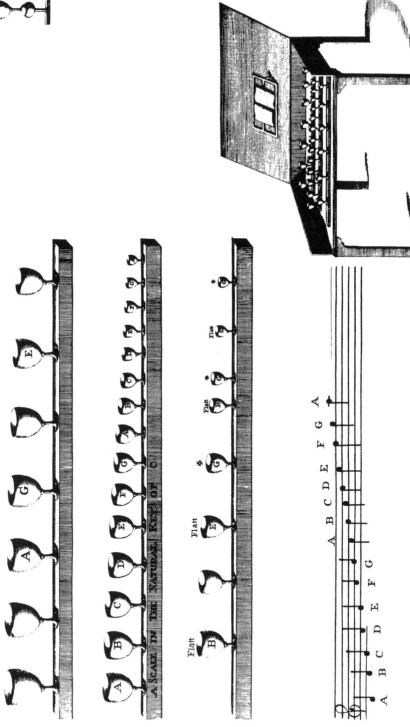

1494 THICKNESSE, *Instructions for Playing on the Musical Glasses*, London?, 1761: frontispiece (281 × 170 mm.)

the | Temple Church, and John Carr at the Middle-Temple Gate, 1685.

2° Score: 2 ℓ., 52 p.
Preliminary leaf 2ʳ: Mvsick Books sold by John Carr . . .
Preliminary leaf 2ᵛ: Mvsick Books sold by John Playford, at his Shop near the Temple Church. | . . . | Other Books lately Printed, and sold at the same Shop by Henry Playford.
Day, no. 79; RISM B I, no. 1685⁶
HOUGHTON

1487

The | Theatre of Music: | Or, A | Choice Collection of the newest and best Songs | Sung at the Court, and Public Theaters. | The Words composed by the most ingenious Wits of the Age, and set to | Music by the greatest Masters in that Science. | With | A Thorow-Bass to each Song for the Theorbo, or Bass-Viol. | Also | Symphonies and Retornels in 3 Parts to several of them, for the Violins and Flutes. | The Third Book. | London, | Printed for Henry Playford and R. C. [i. e. Richard Carr] and sold by Henry Playford near the Temple | Church, and John Carr at the Middle-Temple Gate, 1686.

2° Score: 2 ℓ., 56 p.
Preliminary leaf 2ʳ: Mvsick Books sold by John Carr, at the Middle-Temple Gate.
Preliminary leaf 2ᵛ: Mvsick Books sold by John Playford, at his Shop near the Temple Church. | . . . | Other Books lately Printed, and sold at the same Shop by Henry Playford.
Day, no. 86; RISM B I, no. 1686³
HOUGHTON

1488

The | Theater of Music: | Or, A | Choice Collection of the newest and best Songs | Sung at the Court, and Public Theaters. | The Words composed by the most ingenious Wits of the Age, and set to | Music by the greatest Masters in that Science. | With | A Thorow-Bass to each Song for the Harpsichord, Theorbo, or Bass-Viol. | The Fourth and Last Book. | London, | Printed by B. Motte, for Henry Playford,

at his Shop near the Temple Church, 1687.

2° Score: 2 ℓ., 88 p.
Day, no. 94; RISM B I, no. 1687⁵
HOUGHTON

1489

Thesaurus Musicus: | Being, A | Collection of the Newest Songs | Performed | At Their Majesties Theatres; and at the Consorts in | Viller-street in York-Buildings, and in Charles-street | Covent-Garden. | With A | Thorow-Bass to each Song for the Harpsichord, Theorbo, or Bass-Viol. | To which is Annexed | A Collection of Aires, Composed for two Flutes, by several Masters. | The First Book. | London, | Printed by J. Heptinstall for John Hudgebut. And are to be Sold by John Carr, at | the Middle-Temple Gate in Fleetstreet, and by John Money, Stationer at the Miter | in Miter Court in Fleet-street. And at most Musick-Shops in Town. 1693.

2° Score: 2 ℓ., 38 p.
Day, no. 121; RISM B I, no. 1693⁸
HOUGHTON

1490

Thesaurus Musicus: | Being, A | Collection of the Newest Songs | Performed | At Their Majesties Theatres; and at the Consorts in | Viller-street in York-Buildings, and in Charles-street | Covent-Garden. | With A | Thorow-Bass to each Song, for the Harpsichord, Theorbo, or Bass-Viol. | To which is Annexed, | A Collection of Airs, Composed for two Flutes, by several Masters. | The Second Book. | . . . | London, | Printed by J. Heptinstall for Henry Playford, and are to be sold at his Shop near | the Temple-Church; and John Money, Stationer, at the Mitre in Mitre-Court in | Fleetstreet. And at most Musick-Shops in Town. 1694.

2° Score: 1 ℓ., 42 p.
Day, no. 129, first entry; RISM B I, no. 1694⁷
HOUGHTON

1491

Thesaurus Musicus: | Being, A | Collection of the Newest Songs | Performed | At Their Majesties Theatres; and at the Consorts in | Viller-street in York-Buildings, and in Charles-street | Covent-Garden. | With A | Thorow-Bass to each Song, for the Harpsichord, Theorbo, or Bass-Viol. | To which is Annexed, | A Collection of Airs, Composed for two Flutes, by several Masters. | The Third Book. | . . . | London, | Printed by J. Heptinstall for John Hudgebutt. And are to be sold by John Carr, at his | Shop near the Middle-Temple-Gate in Fleetstreet, and John Money, at the Mitre in | Mitre Court in Fleetstreet, where Masters and Shopkeepers may have them. And at most | Musick-Shops in Town. . . . 1695.

2° *Score:* 1 ℓ., 30 [i. e. 42] p.
Pages 1–4 numbered as leaves 1, 2;
page 40 misnumbered 30
Day, no. 139, first entry; RISM B I, no. 1695[11]
HOUGHTON

1492

Thesaurus Musicus: | Being, A | Collection of the Newest Songs | Performed | At His Majesties Theatres; and at the Consorts in | Viller-street in York-buildings, and in Charles-street | Covent-Garden. Most of the Songs being within the | Composs of the Flute. | With A | Thorow-Bass to each Song, for the Harpsicord, Theorbo, or Bass-Viol. | Composed by most of the Ingenious Masters of the Town. | The Fourth Book. | London, | Printed by J. Heptinstall for John Hudgebutt. And are to be sold by John Carr, at his | Shop near the Middle-Temple-Gate in Fleetstreet, and Daniel Dring at the Harrow and | Crown at the corner of Cliffords-Inn-Lane in Fleetstreet, where Masters and Shopkeepers may have | them. And at most Musick-Shops in Town. . . . 1695.

2° *Score:* 1 ℓ., 34 p.
Day, no. 140 (without illustration on title-page); RISM B I, no. 1695[12]
HOUGHTON

1493

Thesaurus Musicus: | Being, A | Collection of the Newest Songs | Performed | At His Majesties Theatres; and at the Consort in | Viller-street in York-buildings. Most of the Songs | being within the Compass of the Flute. | With A | Thorow-Bass to each Song, for the Harpsicord, Theorbo, or Bass-Viol. | To which is Annexed, | A Collection of Airs, Composed for Two Flutes, by several Masters. | The Fifth Book. | London, | Printed by J. Heptinstall, for John Hudgebutt, and are to be sold by Samuel Scott, at | his Shop near the Middle-Temple-Gate in Fleetstreet, and Daniel Dring at the Har-|row and Crown at the corner of Cliffords-Inn-Lane in Fleetstreet, where Masters and | Shopkeepers may have them. And at most Musick-Shops in Town. 1696. | . . .

2° *Score:* 1 ℓ., 36 p.
Day, no. 154; RISM B I, no. 1696[9]
HOUGHTON

1494   THICKNESSE, ANN (FORD)

By Miss Ford, | Instructions | For Playing On The | Musical Glasses: | So That | Any Person, who has the least Knowledge of | Music, or a Good Ear, may be able to perform | in a few Days, if not in a few Hours. | With Clear and Proper | Directions | How | To provide a compleat Set of Well-Tuned Glasses, at a | very moderate Expence. [London?, 1761]

2° 1 ℓ., 5, 20 p., front.
Imprint date from Grove I, 205
HOUGHTON

THOMPSON, CHARLES & SAMUEL, PUBL. Sixteen Cotillons or French Dances *See* Sixteen Cotillons or French Dances

THOMPSON, ROBERT, PUBL. A Collection of Songs and Ballads Sung by Mr. Lowe and Miss Stevenson *See* A Collection of Songs and Ballads Sung by Mr. Lowe and Miss Stevenson

1495

Thompson's Compleat Collection of 100 Favourite Minuets, perform'd at

Court, Bath, | Tunbridge & all Publick
Assemblies Set for the Harpsichord Vio-
lin or German Flute . . . | Printed for
C. & S. Thompson No. 75 St. Paul's
Church Yard, London. | . . . [ca. 1770]

obl. 8° *Score: vol. I:* 3 ℓ., 100 numb. ℓ.
RISM B II, 389
HOUGHTON

1496   THOMSON, WILLIAM

Orpheus Caledonius | or | a Collection
of the best | Scotch Songs | set to Musick |
by | W. Thomson. | London, Engrav'd &
Printed for the Author at | his house in
Leicester Fields | . . . [1726?]

2° *Score:* 2 ℓ., 4 p., 1 ℓ., 2 p., 58
numb. ℓ.
RISM B II, 274
HOUGHTON

1497   THOMSON, WILLIAM

Orpheus Caledonius: | Or, A | Collec-
tion | Of | Scots Songs. | Set to Musick |
By | W. Thomson. | . . . | The Second Edi-
tion. | London: | Printed for the Author,
at his House in | Leicester-Fields. |
M.DCC.XXXIII.

8° 2 vols.: *vol. I:* 8 ℓ., 114, [2], 6 p., 50
numb. ℓ.; *vol. II:* 2 ℓ., 110, [2], 4 p., 50
numb. ℓ.
RISM B II, 274
HOUGHTON (2 copies)

1498

Three | Celebrated | English | Over-
tures; | Adapted For, The | Piano Forte. |
London: | Printed for Harrison, Cluse, &
Co. No. 78, Fleet Street. [1798?]

8° *Score:* 1 ℓ., 20 p. (*The Piano-Forte
Magazine,* vol. V, no. 3)
Plate no. 70
Contents: overtures to *Royal Shep-
herd* by George Rush, *A Peep Behind the
Curtain* by François Hippolyte Barthéle-
mon, and *Widow of Delphi* by Thomas
Hamley Butler
MUSIC LIBRARY

1499   TIGRINI, ORAZIO

Il | Compendio | Della Mvsica | Nel
Qvale Brevemente Si Tratta | Dell'Arte
del Contrapunto, | Diviso In Qvatro
Libri. | Del R. M. Oratio Tigrini | Cano-
nico Aretino. | Nouamente composto, &
dato in luce. | Con Privileggio. | In Vene-
tia, MDLXXXVIII. | Appresso Ricciardo
Amadino.

4° 6 ℓ., 135, [1] p., music
RISM B VI, 831–832
HOUGHTON

TILLET, ÉVRARD TITON DU   *See* Titon du
Tillet, Évrard

1500   TITON DU TILLET, ÉVRARD

Le | Parnasse | François, | Dedié Au Roi,
| Par M. Titon Du Tillet, Commissaire
Provincial des Guerres, | ci-devant Ca-
pitaine de Dragons, & Maître-d'Hôtel de
feue | Madame La Dauphine, Mere du
Roi. | A Paris, | De l'Imprimerie de Jean-
Baptiste Coignard Fils, | Imprimeur du
Roi. | MDCCXXXII. [–1743] | Avec Ap-
probation Et Privilege Du Roi.

2° 4 ℓ., 832, xciij [i. e. cvij], [3] p., 2
fronts., 25 pl. (ports.)
Pages 661–832: Suite | Du | Parnasse |
François, | Jusqu'en 1743 | . . .
Thirteen unnumbered pages after page
lxxxi; number lxxxj repeated in paging
Hirsch I, no. 579 (variant); RISM B VI,
834
HOUGHTON

1501   TOMÁS DE SANTA MARÍA

Libro llamado | Arte de tañer Fantasia,
assi para Tecla | como para Vihuela, y
todo instrumẽto, en que se pudiere |
tañer a tres, y a quatro vozes, y a mas. Por
el qual en breue tiẽpo, y | con poco tra-
bajo, facilmẽte se podria tañer Fantasia.
Elqual | por mandado del muy alto con-
sejo Real fue examina-|do, y aprouado por
el eminẽte musico de su | Magestad An-
tonio de Cabeçon, y | por Iuan de
Cabeçon, | su hermano. | Compuesto por
elmuy Reuerendo padre Fray Thomas de
Sancta | Maria, dela Orden delos Predica-
dores. Natu-|ral de la villa de Madrid. |

Dirigido al Illustrissimo Señor don Fray Bernardo de Fresneda, | Obispo de Cuenca, Cõmissario general, y Confessor de su Magestad. &c. | Impresso en Valladolid, por Francisco Fernandez de | Cordoua, Impressor de su Magestad. Con licencia, | y priuilegio Real, por diez años. | Eneste año, de 1565. | . . .

4° 4 ℓ., 90, 124 numb. ℓ., illus., music
In this copy the last word of the first line of the dedication on preliminary leaf 2ʳ is "embio,"
Brown, no. 1565₅; RISM B VI, 752–753
HOUGHTON

—another copy
In this copy the last word of the first line of the dedication on preliminary leaf 2ʳ is "Reuerēdissi-|ma", and the recto of leaf 124 is blank
HOUGHTON

1502   TOMLINSON, KELLOM

The | Art | Of | Dancing | Explained by | Reading and Figures; | Whereby the | Manner of Performing the Steps | Is Made Easy | By a New and Familiar Method: | Being the | Original Work | First Design'd in the Year 1724, | And now Published by | Kellom Tomlinson, Dancing-Master. | In Two Books. | . . . | London. | Printed for the Author: | And are to be had of him, at the Red and Gold Flower Pot next Door to Edwards's | Coffee-House, over against the Bull and Gate, in High-Holbourn. | MDCCXXXV.

4° 12 ℓ., [3]–159, [1] p., 37 pl. (incl. music)
The plates include melodies and choreographic notation
RISM B VI, 836
HOUGHTON

LE TONNELIER   *See* Gossec, François Joseph *Le Tonnelier*

TORINO, ILLUMINATO DA, FRATE   *See* Illuminato da Torino, frate

1503   TOSI, PIETRO FRANCESCO

Observations | On The | Florid Song; | Or, | Sentiments | On The | Ancient and Modern Singers. | Written in Italian | By Pier. Francesco Tosi, | Of the Phil-Harmonic Academy at | Bologna. | Translated into English | By Mr. Galliard; | Useful for all Performers, Instrumen-|tal as well as Vocal. | To which are added, | Explanatory Annotations, | and Examples in Musick. | . . . | London: | Printed for J. Wilcox, at Virgil's Head, in | the Strand. 1742.

12° xviii, [2], 184 p., 6 fold. pl. (music)
RISM B VI, 839
HOUGHTON

TOUCHES, ANDRÉ CARDINAL DES   *See* Destouches, André Cardinal

TRAITÉ DE LA MUSETTE   *See* Borjon, Charles Emmanuel *Traité de la musette*

TRAITÉ DES ACCORDS   *See* Roussier, Pierre Joseph *Traité des accords*

TRATTATO DI MUSICA SECONDO LA VERA SCIENZA DELL' ARMONIA   *See* Tartini, Giuseppe *Trattato di musica secondo la vera scienza dell' armonia*

TREIBENREIF, PETER   *See* Tritonius, Petrus

1504   TRITONIUS, PETRUS

Harmonie Petri Tritonii | super odis Horatii Flacci. | . . . [Augsburg, 1507]

4° A⁸, B⁶, C⁸
In choirbook format
Colophon: Denuo impresse per Er|hardum oeglin Augustae | M.D.VII.uicesima se|cunda die Augustit.
Hirsch III, no. 1128
HOUGHTON

THE TRIUMPHES OF ORIANA   *See* Morley, Thomas, comp. *Madrigales: The Triumphes of Oriana*

1505   TSCHORTSCH, JOHANN GEORG

Incensum Mysticum | Ad Aram | Magnae Coelorum Reginae | Adolendum, |

Seu | Offertoria | XIV. | Pro | Festivita-
tibus | Gloriosissimae Semper | Virginis
Mariae | Usurpanda. | Concertantibus 4.
Vocibus, 2. Violinis necessariis, ac du-
|plici Basso continuo: Alto Viola & 2.
Lituis, ac Tympano in ul-|timo Offer-
torio, non nisi ad Libitum | adhibendîs. |
Authore | R. D. Joanne Georgio
Tschortsch, | Sacerdote, & Beneficiato
Fuggeriano Swazii in Tyroli, | Dioecesis
Brixinensis. | Opus Tertium. |. . .| Cum
Permissu Superiorum. | Augustae Vinde-
licorum, | Typis & sumptibus Joannis Ja-
cobi Lotteri, Anno MDCCXXXIII.

2° 1 pt.: *organo:* 3 ℓ., 28 p.
HOUGHTON

1506   TSCHORTSCH, JOHANN GEORG

Sacerdos | Musicus | Concertans, | Seu |
Concinens | Litanias | Decem | Laure-
tano-|Marianas, Concertantibus 4. Vo-
cibus obligatis, 2. Violinis non | quidem
necessariis, valdè tamen utilibus, | cum
Basso Viola, seu Violoncello, | ac duplici
Basso Continuo. | Nec non 4. Ripienis
pro Choro pleno | singulari studio ela-
boratas. | Authore | R. D. Joanne Georgio
Tschortsch, | Sacerdote Tyrolensi â Swa-
zio Dioecesis | Brixinensis. | Opus I. |. . .
| Augustae Vindelicorum, | Sumptibus
Matthiae Wolff, Bibliopolae. | Typis
Joannis Jacobi Lotteri, Anno 1725.

2° 1 pt.: *organo:* 3 ℓ., 31 p.
HOUGHTON

1507   TUBEL, CHRISTIAN GOTTLIEB

Korte Onderrichting | Van De | Mu-
siek, | met daar by gevoegde | LXXVII.
Handstukkies, | voor het Clavier. | Benee-
vens | eene korte Verhandeling van het |
Contrapunct, | door den Heer | C. G.
Tubel, | Agent van zyne Doorluchtige |
Hoogheid, den Regeerende Hartog | van
Brunswyk en Luneburg. | Tot Amster-
dam | by Johannes Cóvens. [1766]

obl. 8° 2 ℓ., 4, 3–123 p., illus., music
Title-page also in German; text in
German and Dutch in parallel columns
RISM B VI, 845–846
MUSIC LIBRARY

1508   TÜRK, DANIEL GOTTLOB

Klavierschule, | oder | Anweisung zum
Klavierspielen | für | Lehrer und Ler-
nende, | mit kritischen Anmerkungen |
von | Daniel Gottlob Türk, | Musikdirek-
tor bey der Universität zu Halle. | Leipzig
und Halle. | Auf Kosten des Verfassers; in
Kommission bey Schwickert in Leipzig, |
und bey Hemmerde und Schwetschke in
Halle. 1789.

4° 4 ℓ., 408, [12], 15 p., illus., music
Page [12], second sequence: Leipzig,
gedruckt bey Joh. Gottlob Immannuel
Breitkopf, 1789.
Pages [1]–15 at end: Zwölf Hand-
stücke | zum Gebrauche beym Unter-
richten.
Hirsch I, no. 585; RISM B VI, 846
MUSIC LIBRARY

1509   TÜRK, DANIEL GOTTLOB

Neue | Klavier-Schule, | oder: | Anwei-
sung zum Klavierspielen | für | Lehrer
und Lernende; | mit kritischen Anmer-
kungen, | von | Daniel Gottlob Türk, |
Musikdirektor bey der Königl. Fried-
richs-Universität zu Halle, und Orga-
nist | an der Stadt-Pfarrkirche zu St.
Moritz daselbst. | (Neueste verbesserte
und in den Violinschlüssel übersetzte
Auflage.) | Wien, 1798. | In Commis-
sion der Hohenleitterschen Buch-und
Kunsthandlung am Kohlmarkte.

4° 3 ℓ., [III]–XL, 374 [i. e. 376], [12], 15
p., illus., music
Pages [1]–15 at end: Zwölf Hand-
stücke, | zum Gebrauch beym Unterrich-
ten.
Two unnumbered pages after page 168
RISM B VI, 846
MUSIC LIBRARY

1510   TÜRK, DANIEL GOTTLOB

Sechs Sonaten | für das Clavier, | von |
Daniel Gottlob Türk. | Leipzig und
Halle, | in Commission bey Bernhard
Christoph Breitkopf und Sohn. | 1776.

2° *Score:* 2 ℓ., 42, [2] p.
MUSIC LIBRARY

1511   Türk, Daniel Gottlob

Sechs Sonaten | für das Clavier, | Dem | Hochgebohrnen Grafen und Herrn, | Herrn | Heinrich den sieben und vierzigsten jüngern Reuss | unterthänig zugeeignet, | von | Daniel Gottlob Türk. | Zweyte Sammlung. | Leipzig und Halle, | in Commission bey Johann Gottlob Immanuel Breitkopf. | 1777

   2° *Score:* 2 ℓ., 48 p.
   MUSIC LIBRARY

1512   Türk, Daniel Gottlob

Von den | wichtigsten Pflichten | eines | Organisten. | Ein Beytrag | zur Verbesserung | der | musikalischen Liturgie | von | D. G. Türk. | Halle, | auf Kosten des Verfassers; | in Kommission bey Schwickert zu Leipzig, | und in der Hemmerdeschen Buchhandlung zu Halle. | 1787.

   8° 240 p., illus., music
   Hirsch IV, no. 1549; RISM B VI, 847
   MUSIC LIBRARY

1513   [Turberville, George]

The Noble Art Of | Venerie or Hvnting. | Wherein is handled and set out the Vertues, Nature, and Pro-|perties of fifteene sundry Chaces, together with the order and | manner how to Hunt and kill euery one of them. | Translated & collected for the pleasure of all Noblemen | and Gentlemen, out of the best approoued Authors, which | haue written any thing concerning the same: And reduced | into such order and proper termes as are vsed here | in this noble Realme of Great Britaine. | At London, | Printed by Thomas Purfoot. | An. Dom. 1611.

   4° 3 ℓ., 200, [4], 201–250 [i. e. 248], [4] p., illus., music
   Pages [1]–[4] at end: hunting calls
   Numbers 205, 206 omitted in paging
   HOUGHTON (2 copies)

1514   Turner, William

Sound Anatomiz'd | In A | Philosophical Essay | On | Musick. | Wherein is explained | The Nature of Sound, both in its Essence | and Regulation, &c. Contrived for the Use | of the Voice in Singing, as well as for those | who Play on Instruments. | Together with | A thorough Explanation of all the different | Moods used in Musick, for regulating Time | in the different Divisions of Measures used | therein. | All render'd plain and easy, to the meanest | Capacities, by familiar Similies. | To which is added, | A Discourse, concerning the Abuse of Musick. | By William Turner. | London, | Printed by William Pearson, over-against | Wright's-Coffee-House, in Aldersgate-street, for the Author, | and Sold by M. Turner, at the Post-House, in Russel-|street, Covent-Garden, and no where else in England. 1724.

   4° 4 ℓ., 80, 7 p., illus., music
   Pages 1–7 at end: On the Abuse | Of | Musick.
   RISM B VI, 847–848
   MUSIC LIBRARY

1515

Two Divine | Hymns: | Being A | Suppliment | To the Second Book of | Harmoniae Sacra. | London: | Printed by W. Pearson, in Red-Cross-Alley in Jewin-Street, | for Henry Playford, at his Shop in the Temple-Change | Fleet-street. . . . | . . . 1700.

   2° *Score:* 8 p.
   RISM B I, no. 1700[1]
   HOUGHTON

U

1516   Ulloa, Pedro de

Musica | Universal, | ô | Principios Universales | De La Musica, | Dispuestos | Por El Padre Maestro Pedro De Ulloa, | de la Compañia de Jesus, Cathedratico de Mathematicas | de los Estudios Reales del Colegio Imperial, | y Cosmographo Maior del Supremo | Consejo de las

Indias. | Dedicados | A El Señor Don Igna-cio De Loyola, | Cavallero del Orden de Santiago, Primogenito | de los Señores Marqueses | de la Olmeda. | Con Privile-gio, en Madrid: En la Imprenta | de Mu-sica, por Bernardo Peralta. | Año de 1717.

4° 6 ℓ., 104 p., illus., 2 pl., music
RISM B VI, 851
MUSIC LIBRARY

1517

Universal Harmony | Or, The | Gentle-man & Ladie's | Social Companion: | Consisting | Of a great Variety of the Best & most Favourite | English & Scots songs, Cantatas &c. &c. | With a Curious Design, | By way of headpiece, | Ex-pressive of the sense of each particulr Song | All neatly Engraved on Quarto Copper Plates, | And set to Music for the Voice, Violin, Hautboy, German & Com-mon | Flute, with a Thorough Basse for the Organ, harpsicho. Spinet, &c. | By the Best Masters. | The whole calculated to keep People in good Spirits, good | health, & good humour, to promote Social Friendship in all Compys. | and Univer-sal Harmony in every Neighbourhood. | London: | Printed for J. Newbery at ye. Bible & Crown, without Temple Bar. 1745. | T. Kitchin sculp.

4° Score: 1 ℓ., 129 numb. ℓ., illus.
RISM B II, 393–394
HOUGHTON

1518   URBANI, PIETRO, ED.

A Favorite Selection | of | Scots Tunes | By | Urbani & Liston | Properly arranged as Duettos for | Two German Flutes or Two Violins | By P. Urbani. | Book 1st. . . . | . . . | Edinr. Printed and Sold by Urbani & Liston No. 10 Princes Street . . . [ca. 1798]

obl. 8° 1 pt.: *secondo:* 2 ℓ., 24 p.
MUSIC LIBRARY

URFEY, THOMAS D'   *See*   D'Urfey, Thomas

V

1519   VALENTINE, ROBERT

Six | Sonata's | of two Parts | for | Two | Violins | Compos'd by | Mr. Valentine | at Rome | Opera Quarta | London Printed for I: Walsh Servt. in Ordinary to his Ma-jesty at the | Harp and Hoboy in Cath-erine Street in the Strand, and I: Hare at the | Viol and Flute in Cornhill near the Royall Exchange. [ca. 1715]

2° 2 pts.: *violino primo, violino se-condo:* 1 ℓ., 12 p. each
Walsh I, no. 480
HOUGHTON

1520   VALENTINE, ROBERT

Six | Sonatas | of two Parts | for two | [Violins] | Compos'd by | Mr Valentine | at Rome | Opera 7ma. | Note all ye Chois-est Works of this author may be had where these are sold | London Printed and sold by Daniel Wright next the Sun Tavern the Corner of Brook | Street in Holbourn. [1721?]

2° 2 pts.: *violino primo, violino se-condo:* 1 ℓ., 6 numb. ℓ. each
Cancel label reading "Violins" covers the word "Flutes" on the title-page of the *violino primo* part
Imperfect: numbered leaf 6 lacking in *violino primo* part
HOUGHTON

1521   VALENZOLA, PIETRO

. . . | Madrigali Di Pietro Valenzola | Spagnolo, | Cantor dignissimo nella Ca-pella della Illustrissima Signoria di Vene-tia in S. Marco, | a cinque voci, con vno a sei, et vno Dialogo a otto, | Nouamente con ogni diligentia stampati, et dati in luce. | Libro Primo | In Venetia Appresso | Angelo Gardano. | 1578

obl. 4° 5 pts.: *canto, alto, tenore, basso, qvinto:* 1 ℓ., 21, [1] p. each
Page 21 misnumbered 20 in *qvinto* part-book
Imperfect: title-leaf, pages 1–6 lacking

in *canto* part-book; title supplied from *alto* part-book

Vogel, no. 2790

HOUGHTON

1522   VALERIUS, ADRIANUS, COMP.

Neder-Landtsche | Gedenck-Clanck. | Kortelick openbarende de voornaemste geschiedenissen van de seventhien Neder-|Landsche Provintien, 't sedert den aenvang der Inlandsche beroerten | ende troublen, tot den Iare 1625. | Verciert met verscheydene aerdige figuerlicke platen, | Ende | Stichtelijcke Rimen ende Liedekens, met aenwijsingen, soo uyt de H. Schriftuere, als uyt de boecken van | geleerde Mannen, tot verklaringe der uytgevallen saecken dienende. | De Liedekens (meest alle nieu zijnde) gestelt op Musyck-noten, ende elck op een | verscheyden Vois, beneffens de Tablatuer vande Luyt ende Cyther. | Alles dienende tot stichtelijck vermaeck ende leeringhe, van | allen Lief-hebbers des Vaderlants. | Door | Adrianum Valerium. | . . . | Tot Haerlem, | Gedruct voor d'Erfgenamen vanden Autheur, woonende ter Veer in Zeeland. 1626. | Met previlegie voor ses Iaren.

obl. 4° 4 *ℓ.*, 295, [3] p. illus.

RISM B I, 1626[14]

HOUGHTON

VALET, NICOLAS *See* Vallet, Nicolas

1523   [VALLE, GUGLIELMO DELLA]

Memorie Storiche | Del | P. M. Giambattista Martini | Minor Conventuale Di Bologna | Celebre Maestro di Cappella. | Napoli MDCCLXXXV. | Nella Stamperia Simoniana. | Con licenze de' Superiori.

8° VIII, 152 p.

MUSIC LIBRARY

1524   VALLET, NICOLAS

Paradisus Musicus Testudinis, in quo | Multae insignes et ante hunc diem inauditae, Gallicae, Germanicae, | Anglicae, Hispanicae, Polonicae, cantiones; | Nec non | Varia Praeludia, Fantasiae, Tripudia cōtinentur: | Praeterea punctis tuṁ suprà

tuṁ ad latus singulis cuiusque tactus literis | adscriptis, eorumque praemissa explicatione, docetur quibus tum dextrae | tum sinistrae manus digitis chorda tangenda pulsandave sit, | Auctore Nicolao Valletto. | Omnia in aes incisa. | Amstelodami. | Apud Joannem Janssonium Bibliopolam. Ao. 1618

obl. 4° 3 *ℓ.*, 94 p., 3 *ℓ.*

HOUGHTON

1525   VALLET, NICOLAS

XXI. Pseavmes | De David, | Accommodés pour chanter & | jouer du Luth ensemble. | Par Nicolas Valet. | A Amsterdam, | Chez Ian Ianssz, demeurant sur Lieu à la Carte Marine. | L'An M.DC.XIX.

obl. 4° *Score:* 1 *ℓ.*, 50 p.

HOUGHTON

1526   VALLET, NICOLAS

Le second Livre | De | Tablature de Luth, | Intitulé | Le Secret Des Mvses: | Contenant plusieurs belles pieces non encor ouyes par ci-devant, fort faciles & utiles | pour tous Amateurs. Ensemble plusieurs autres pieces mises en Tablature selon la mode plus | belle, & plus facile qui se puisse trouver, entr' autres quelques pieces mises: | pour ioüer a quatre Luts differemment accordez. | Par Nicolas Valet. | A Amsterdam, | Chez Ian Ianssz, demeurant sur Leau à la Carte Marine. | L'An CIↃ.IↃ.XIX. [i. e. 1619] | Avec Privilege.

obl. 4° 2 *ℓ.*, 50 p., 1 *ℓ.*

The pieces for four lutes are in *Tafelmusik* format

RISM B I, no. 1619[17]

HOUGHTON

VALLIÈRE, LOUIS CÉSAR DE LA BAUM LE BLANC, DUC DE LA *See* La Vallière, Louis César de la Baume Le Blanc, duc de

VAŇHAL, JAN KŘTITEL *See* Wanhal, Johann Baptist

1527   VANNEO, STEFANO

Recanetvm De Mvsica Avrea | A Ma-
gistro Stephano Vanneo Recinensi | Ere-
mita Avgvstiniano In Ascvlana | Ecclesia
chori Moderatore nuper aeditum, & so-
lerti studio Enucleatum, | Vincentio Ros-
seto Veronensi Interprete. | Romae Apvd
Valerivm Doricvm Brixiensem, | Anno
Virginei Partus M.D.XXXIII. Cum gratia
& Priuilegio | Clemen. VII. Pont. Max.
Ad Decennium.

2° 4 ℓ., 93 numb. ℓ., illus., music
Hirsch I, no. 589; RISM B VI, 857
HOUGHTON

1528   VAUCANSON, JACQUES DE

An | Account | Of The | Mechanism |
Of An | Automaton, | Or | Image playing
on the German-Flute: | As it was pre-
sented in a Memoire, to the Gen-|tlemen
of the Royal-Academy of Sciences | at
Paris. | By M. Vaucanson, Inventor and
Maker | of the said Machine. | Together
With | A Description of an artificial
Duck, eating, | drinking, macerating the
Food, and voiding Excrements; | pluming
her Wings, picking her Feathers, and per-
forming | several Operations in Imitation
of a living Duck: Contrived | by the same
Person. | As Also | That of another Image,
no less wonderful than the first, playing |
on the Tabor and Pipe; as he has given an
Account of them | since the Memoire
was written. | Translated out of the
French Original, by J.T. Desa-|guliers,
L.L.D.F.R.S. Chaplain to his Royal |
Highness the Prince of Wales. | London:
Printed by T. Parker, and sold by Mr. |
Stephen Varillon at the Long Room, at
the Opera House | in the Hay-market,
where these Mechanical Figures are to be
seen at | 1, 2, 5, and 7, o'Clock in the Af-
ternoon. 1742.

4° 24 p., front., (illus.)
RISM B VI, 858
HOUGHTON

1529   VAUCANSON, JACQUES DE

Le | Mécanisme | Du Fluteur | Auto-
mate, | Presenté a Messieurs de
l'Académie Royale | des Sciences. | Par
M. Vaucanson, Auteur de cette Machine.

| Avec | La description d'un Canard Arti-
ficiel, mangeant, beuvant, | digerant & se
vuidant, épluchant ses aîles & ses plu-
|mes, imitant en diverses manieres un
Canard vivant. | Inventé par la mesme. |
Et aussi | Celle d'une autre figure, égale-
ment merveilleuse, jouant du | Tam-
bourin & de la Flute, suivant la relation,
qu'il | en a donnée dépuis son Mémoire
écrit. | A Paris, | Chez Jacques Guerin,
Imprimeur-Libraire, Quai | des Augus-
tins. | Et Se Vend | Dans la Sale de dite
figures Automates. | M.DCC.XXXVIII. |
Avec Permission Du Roi.

4° 11 [i. e. 23] p., front.
Page 23 misnumbered 11
RISM B VI, 858
HOUGHTON

1530   [VEAL, GEORGE]

Musical Travels | Through | England. |
By | Joel Collier, Organist. | . . . | London:
| Printed for G. Kearsly, in Fleet-street. |
M.DCC.LXXIV. | . . .

8° viii, 59, [1] p.
A satire on Dr. Burney's *Musical
Travels*
RISM B VI, 231
MUSIC LIBRARY

1531   [VEAL, GEORGE]

Musical Travels | Through | England. |
By the late Joel Collier, | Licentiate In
Music. | With An | Appendix. | Contain-
ing | An Authentic Account | Of The |
Author's Last Illness And Death. | By |
Nat. Collier, School-Master. | . . . | The
Third Edition. | London: | Printed for G.
Kearsly, in Fleet-street. | M.DCC.LXXV. |
. . .

8° vii, [1], 112, 28 p.
Pages [1]–28 at end: Appendix
RISM B VI, 232
MUSIC LIBRARY

1532   [VEAL, GEORGE]

Musical Travels | Through | England. |
By The Late | Joel Collier, | Licentiate In
Music. | . . . | A New Edition. | . . . |
London: | Printed for G. Kearsley, at
Johnson's   Head,   Fleet-street. |
M.DCC.LXXXV.

1524 VALLET, *Paradisus musicus testudinis*, Amsterdam, 1618: title-page (132 × 202 mm.)

1526 VALLET, *Le Second Livre de tablature de luth*,

1525 VALLET, *XXI Pseaumes de David,*
Amsterdam, 1619: page 29 (detail, 21 ×
18 mm.)

1526 VALLET [Description *below, left*]:
page 36 (detail, 20 × 18 mm.)

Amsterdam, 1619: pages 36–37 (both 122 × 203 mm.)

8° xiv, [2], 126, 32 p.
Pages [1]–32 at end: Appendix
RISM B VI, 232
MUSIC LIBRARY

1533   VECCHI, ORAZIO

. . . | Madrigali | A Cinqve Voci |
Di Horatio Vecchi | Nouamente Stampati. | Libro Primo. | Con Privilegio. | In
Venetia Appresso Angelo Gardano |
M.D.LXXXIX.

4° 5 pt.: *canto:* 1 ℓ., 21 [1] p.; *alto, tenore, basso, qvinto:* 1 ℓ., 22 p. each
Imperfect: pages 7–14 in *canto* partbook, pages 15–22 in *basso* part-book
and pages 17–20 in *qvinto* part-book
lacking
Vogel, no. 2826
HOUGHTON

1534   VECCHI, ORAZIO

. . . | Madrigali | A Sei Voci | D'Horatio
Vecchi | Nouamente stampati. | Libro
Primo. | In Venetia Appresso Angelo Gardano. | MDLXXXIII.

4° 6 pts.: *canto, alto, tenore, basso,
qvinto:* 1 ℓ., 21, [1] p. each; *sesto:* 25,
[1] p.
Imperfect: pages 7–14 lacking in *basso*
part-book
Vogel, no. 2827
HOUGHTON

1535   VECCHI, ORAZIO

. . . | Di Horatio | Vecchi Da | Modena.
| Piu è diversi Madrigali è Canzonette | à
5. 6. 7. 8. 9. Et 10. voci, per avan-|ti
separatamente iti in luce, Et ora in|sieme
raccolti. | In Norimbergo, | Nella Stamperia delli Gerlachii. | M.D.XCIIII.

4° 1 pt.: *qvinto:* Aa–Qq⁴
Bound with a late sixteenth-century
manuscript part-book
Vogel, no. 2830
HOUGHTON

VENOSA, CARLO GESUALDO, PRINCIPE DI
See Gesualdo, Carlo, principe di Venosa

1536   VENTO, MATTIA

A 3d. Book of | Six Sonatas | for the |
Harpsichord | with an Accompanyment
for a | Violin or German Flute | Dedicated
to | His Most Serene Highness | Charles |
Hereditary Prince of Brunswick Lunebourg &c &c | Composed by | Mathias
Vento | London Printed by Welcker in
Gerrard Street St. Ann's Soho | . . .
[1766?]

2° *Score:* 1 ℓ., 33 p.
MUSIC LIBRARY

1537   VENTO, MATTIA

A Fourth Sett | of Six | Sonatas. | for the
| Harpsichord | with an Accompanyment
for a Flute Violin & Violincello | Humbly
Dedicated to | the Right Honble: the Earl
of Plymouth | Composed by | Matthias
Vento | London Printed by Welcker in
Gerrard Street St. Ann's Soho | . . .
[1768?]

2° *Score:* 1 ℓ., 34 p.
MUSIC LIBRARY

**1538   VERACINI, FRANCESCO
        MARIA**

Sonate Accademiche | A Violino Solo e
Basso | Dedicate | Alla Sacra Real Maestà
| Di | Augusto III | Re Di Pollonia &c. &c.
| Et Elettore Di Sassonia &c. &c. | Da |
Francesco Ma: Veracini Fiorentino |
Compositor di Camera della Medesima |
S. R. M. | Opera Seconda | A Londra, e a
Firenze per l'Autore. [1744]

obl. 2° *Score:* 3 ℓ., [1], 91 p., front.
(port.)
HOUGHTON

1539

'T Vermaakelyk | Zang-Prieel | Of |
Vreugdige Byeenkomst Van | Herders | En
| Herderinnen, | Op de Nieuwste en
Keurelykste Marche, | Menuette, Gigaas,
Aartjes, &c. | Te Haarlem, Gedrukt by de
Erfgen: van Iz: van Hulkenroy, | in de
Lange Begynestraat, in de Konings Hulk.
[ca. 1760]

4° *Score:* 2 ℓ., 43, [1] p.

Imprint date supplied from Goovaerts, p. 150

MUSIC LIBRARY

1540

Het Tweede Deel, | Van Het | Vermaakelyk | Zang-Prieel | Of | Vreugdige Byeenkomst Van | Herders | En | Herderinnen. | Op de Nieuwste en Keurelykste Marche, Menuette, | Gigaas, Gavotte, Bourees, Aartjes, &c. | Te Haarlem, Gedrukt by de Erfgen: van Iz: van Hulkenroy, | in de Lange Begynestraat, in de Konings Hulk. [ca. 1760]

4° 27 [i. e. 47], [1] p.
Page 47 misnumbered 27
Imprint date supplied from Goovaerts, p. 150

MUSIC LIBRARY

1541

Het Derde Deel, | Van Het | Vermaakelyk | Zang-Prieel | Of | Vreugdige Byeenkomst Van | Herders | En | Herderinnen. | Op de Nieuwste en Keurelykste Marche, Menuette, | Gigaas, Gavotte, Bourees, Aartjes, &c. | Voor twee Stemmen eerste en tweede Cantus. | Te Haarlem, Gedrukt by de Erfgen: van Iz: van Hulkenroy, | in de Lange Begynestraat, in de Konings Hulk. [ca.1760]

4° 47, [2] p.
Imprint date supplied from Goovaerts, p. 150

MUSIC LIBRARY

1542   VERMOOTEN, WILLEM

Zinspeelende | Liefdens Gezangen. | Verdeeld in Acht-en-twintig Stukken door | Willem Hessen, | En op Muzyk gebragt door | Willem Vermooten, | Voor twee Stemmen | Cantus en Bassus. | . . . | Te Haarlem, Gedrukt by Izaak Van Hulkenroy, | in de Lange Beggynestraat, in de Konings Hulk. [1741?]

4° 1 pt.: *cantus:* 7 ℓ., 59, [1] p., front.
Frontispiece dated 1741
Unnumbered page at end: By de Drukker deezer Sinspeelende Liefdens Gezangen, is mede Gedrukt | en te beko-

men, deeze naavolgende Werkjes, alle voorzien met Muzyk

MUSIC LIBRARY

1543   VEROVIO, SIMONE, PUBL.

Canzonette | A quattro Voci, Composti da diuersi | Eccti. Musici, Con | L'intauolatura del Cimbalo | et del Livto | Raccolto et stampato da Simone Verouio | In Roma 1591 Con Licentia di Supri.

2° 1 ℓ., [40] p.
In choirbook format, with keyboard score and lute tablature at foot of facing pages
Brown, no. 1591$_{11}$; RISM B I, no. 1591[12]

HOUGHTON

VERTRAUTE BRIEFE ÜBER FRANKREICH *See* Reichardt, Johann Friedrich *Vertraute Briefe über Frankreich*

1544   VETTER, DANIEL

Musicalischer | Kirch-und Haus-Ergötzlichkeit/ | Anderer Theil/ | Bestehend | In denen noch zurücke gelassenen gewöhnlichen Geistlichen Liedern/ | wie auch Morgen-Tisch-Abend-und Sterbe-Gesängen | auff eine' gantz angenehme/ | jedoch leichte Manier | in Italiänische Tabulatur gesetzet | und in Kupffer gestochen | so | dass allemahl der Cho-|ral eines jedweden Liedes auff der Orgel | nachgehends eine gebrochene Variation auff dem Spinett oder Clavicordio zu | tractiren | folget | mit sonderbahrem Fleiss auffgesetzet | Von | Daniel Vetter/ | Organisten zu S. Nicolai in Leipzig. | [Leipzig] Zu finden bey dem Autore. | Gedruckt | mit Krügerischen Schrifften. | [ded. 1713]

obl. 2° *Score:* 7 ℓ., [93] p.
Plate no. P. 2
HOUGHTON

VICENTE LUSITANO *See* Lusitano, Vicente

LA VIE DU R. P. MARIN MERSENNE *See* Coste, Hilarion de *La Vie du R. P. Marin Mersenne*

VIENNE, FRANÇOIS DE *See* Devienne, François

VIÉVILLE, JEAN LAURENT LE CERF DE LA *See* Le Cerf de la Viéville, Jean Laurent

LA VILLANELLA RAPITA *See* Bianchi, Francesco *La villanella rapita*

VILLARD, ADRIAN *See* Willaert, Adrian

VIOLINO, CARLO DEL *See* Cesarini, Carlo Francesco

1545   VITALI, FILIPPO

Il Secondo Libro | De Madrigali | A Cinqve Voci | Di Filippo Vitali | Maestro Della Mvsica Nell' Accademia De | Rvgginosi | In firenze appresso Pietro cec-concelli alle stelle Medicee | con licenzia de superiori 1623

4° 1 pt.: *tenore:* 2 ℓ., 18 p., 1 ℓ.
Vogel, no. 2944
HOUGHTON

1546   VIVALDI, ANTONIO

Il Cimento Dell' Armonia | E Dell' Inventione | Concerti | a 4 e 5 | Consacrati | All' Illustrissimo Signore | Il Signor Venceslao Conte di Marzin, Signore Ereditario | di Hohenelbe, Lomniz, Tschista, Krzinetz, Kaunitz, Doubek, | et Sowoluska, Cameriere Attuale, e Consigliere di | S. M. C. C. | Da D. Antonio Vivaldi | Maestro in Italia dell' Illustrismo: Signor Conte Sudetto, | Maestro dè Concerti del Pio Ospitale della Pieta in Venetia, | e Maestro di Capella dà Camera di S. A. S. il Signor | Principé Filippo Langravio d'Hassia Darmistath. | Opera Ottava | Libro Primo | A Amsterdam | Spesa di Michele Carlo Le Cene | Libraro. | . . . [1725]

2° 5 pts.: *violino principale:* 1 ℓ., 4, 25 p.; *violino primo:* 1 ℓ., 19 p.; *violino secondo:* 1 ℓ., 18 p.; *alto viola:* 1 ℓ., 14 p.; *organo e violoncello:* 2 ℓ., 15 p.
No. 520 on title-page
Ryom, p. 57
HOUGHTON

—another copy
1 pt.: *organo e violoncello:* 2 ℓ., 15 p., front. (port.)
HOUGHTON

1547   VIVALDI, ANTONIO

Il Cimento Dell' Armonia | E Dell' Inventione | Concerti | a 4 e 5 | Consacrati | All' Illustrissimo Signore | Il Signor Venceslao Conte di Marzin Signore Ereditario | di Hohenelbe Lomniz, Tschista Krzinetz Kounitz Doubek | et Sowoluska, Cameriere Attuale, e Consigliere di | S. M. C. C. | Da D. Antonio Vivaldi | Maestro in Italia dell' Illustrismo: Signor Conte Sudetto, | Maestro dè Concerti del Pio Ospitale dellà Pieta in Venetia, | e Maestro di Capella dà Camera di S. A. S. il Signor | Principe Filippo Langravio d'Hassia Darmistath. | Opera Ottava | Libro Secondo | A Amsterdam | Spesa di Michele Carlo Le Cene | Libraro | . . . [1725]

2° 5 pts.: *violino principale:* 1 ℓ., 25 p.; *violino primo, violino secondo:* 1 ℓ., 13 p. each; *alto viola:* 1 ℓ., 10 p.; *organo e violoncello:* 1 ℓ., 18 p.
No. 521 on title-page
Ryom, p. 57
HOUGHTON (2 copies of *organo e violoncello* part)

1548   VIVALDI, ANTONIO

Two Celebrated | Concertos | the one Commonly call'd | the | Cuckow | and | the other | Extravaganza | Compos'd | by | Sigr: Antonia Vivaldi | London Printed for and Sold by I: Walsh Servt. to his Majesty at | the Harp and Hoboy in Catherine Street in the Strand: and I: Hare at | the Viol and Flute in Cornhill near the Royall Exchange [1720]

2° 2 pts.: *alto viola:* 1 ℓ., 3 numb. ℓ.; *violoncello:* 1 ℓ., 6 p.
Numbered leaves printed on one side only
Ryom, p. 59; Walsh I, no. 579
HOUGHTON

1549   VIVALDI, ANTONIO

Two Celebrated | Concertos | the one Commonly call'd | the | Cuckow | and |

the other | Extravaganza | Compos'd | by | Sigr: Antonia Vivaldi | . . . | London Printed for and Sold by I: Walsh Servt. to his Majesty at | the Harp and Hoboy in Catherine Street in the Strand: . . . [ca. 1730]

2° 5 pts.: *violino primo concertino:* [1], 8 p.; *violino secondo concertino:* [1], 4 p.; *violino primo concerto grosso:* 4 p.; *alto viola:* [1], 3 p.; *organo:* 6 p.
Number 453 on title-page
I. Hare's name and address erased from plate
Imperfect: title-page lacking in *violino primo concerto grosso* and *organo* parts
Ryom, p. 59; Walsh II, no. 1518
HOUGHTON

1550 VIVALDI, ANTONIO

L'Estro Armonico | Concerti | Consacrati | All'Altezza Reale | Di | Ferdinando III | Gran Prencipe Di Toscana | Da D. Antonio Vivaldi | Musico di Violino e Maestro de Concerti del | Pio Ospidale della Pieta di Venezia | Opera Terza | Libro Primo. | A Amsterdam | Aux depens D'Estienne Roger Marchand Libraire | . . . [after 1716?]

2° 8 pts.: *violino primo:* 3 ℓ., 23 p.; *violino secondo:* 1 ℓ., 15 p.; *violino terzo:* 1 ℓ., 14 p.; *violino quarto:* 1 ℓ., 12 p.; *alto primo, alto secondo:* 1 ℓ., 11 p. each; *violoncello:* 1 ℓ., 13 p.; *violone e cembalo:* 1 ℓ., 14 p.
No. 50 on title-page
Ryom, p. 54
HOUGHTON

1551 VIVALDI, ANTONIO

L'Estro Armonico | Concerti | Consacrati | All'Altezza Reale | Di | Ferdinando III. | Gran Prencipe Di Toscana | Da D. Antonio Vivaldi | Musico di Violino e Maestro de Concerti del | Pio Ospidale della Pieta di Venezia | Opera Terza | Libro Secondo. | A Amsterdam | Aux depens D'Estienne Roger Marchand Libraire | . . . [after 1716?]

2° 8 pts.: *violino primo:* 1 ℓ., 21 p.; *violino secondo:* 1 ℓ., 16 p.; *violino terzo:* 1 ℓ., 14 p.; *violino quarto:* 1 ℓ., 15 p.; *alto primo, alto secondo:* 1 ℓ., 12 p. each; *vio-*

loncello: 1 ℓ., 14 p.; *violone e cembalo:* 1 ℓ., 13 p.
No. 51 on title-page
Ryom, p. 54
HOUGHTON

1552 VIVALDI, ANTONIO

Select Harmony; | being | XII | Concertos | in Six Parts, | for | Violins and other Instruments; | Collected from the Works | of | Antonio Vivaldi, | His 6th. 7th. 8th. and 9th. Operas: | being a well-chosen Collection of his most | Celebrated Concertos. | The whole carefully corected. | . . . | London. Printed for and sold by I: Walsh servant to his Majesty at the Harp | and Hoboy in Catharine street in the Strand. and Ioseph Hare at the Viol & | Hoboy in Cornhill near the Royal Exchange. [1730]

2° 5 pts.: *violino primo principale:* 2 ℓ., 49 p.; *violino primo:* 1 ℓ., 27 p.; *violino secondo:* 1 ℓ., 26 p.; *alto viola:* 1 ℓ., 21 p.; *organo & violoncello* (2 copies): 1 ℓ., 30 p.
Ryom, p. 59; Walsh II, no. 1357
HOUGHTON

1553

The | Vocal Enchantress | Presenting | An Elegant Selection of | the Most Favourite | Hunting, Sea, Love, & Miscellaneous | Songs, | Sung by Edwin, Mrs. Cargill, | Bannister, Mrs. Kennedy, | Webster, Mrs. Wrighten, | &c. &c. &c. | With the Music prefixed to each. | London, | Printed for J. Fielding. No. 23. Pater-noster Row. | . . . [1783?]

12° 5 ℓ., 350, [2] p., front.
Imperfect: pages 349, 350 lacking
RISM B II, 397
HOUGHTON

1554

The | Vocal Magazine. | Containing | A Selection | Of | The Most Esteemed | English, Scots, And Irish Songs, | Antient And Modern: | Adapted For The Harpsichord Or Violin. | . . . | Edinburgh: | Printed by C. Stewart & Co. | 1797. [–1799.] | . . .

8° *Score:* 3 vols.: *1797:* [–]⁴, [2d][–]²,
[A]⁴, B–Z⁴, 2A⁴, Bb–Gg⁴; *1798:* [–]⁴,
A–D⁴, E², F–Z⁴, Aa–Gg⁴; *1799:* [–]⁴,
A–Z⁴, Aa–Gg⁴
RISM B II, 398
HOUGHTON

1555

Vocal Music | Or The | Songsters Com-
panion | containing | a new and choice
Collection | of the greatest variety of |
Songs, Cantatas &c. | with the music pre-
fixt to each, | together with an alphabeti-
cal | Index of the whole. | [London]
Printed | for Robert Horsfield, | at No. 22,
in Ludgate Street | . . . [1770?–1771?]

12° 2 vols.: [vol. I]: 4 ℓ., 280 p.; *vol. II:*
2 ℓ., 284 p.
Capitalization varies on title-page of
vol. II
Imperfect: numerous pages lacking in
vol. I
RISM B II, 398
HOUGHTON (vol. II), MUSIC LIBRARY
(vol. I)

1555a

Vocal Music: | Or The | Songster's
Companion. | Containing | A new and
choice Collection | Of The | Greatest
Variety | Of | Songs, Cantatas, etc. | With
the Music prefixed to each. | Adapted to
the Violin and German-Flute. | Together
with an Alphabetical Index of the |
whole. | Volume The First. | The Second
Edition Improved. | London: | Printed by
Baker and Galabin, in | Cullum-Street, |
For Robert Horsfield, Number 22. | in
Ludgate-Street. | M.DCC.LXXII.

12° 4 ℓ., 280 p.
HOUGHTON

1556

Vocal Music, | or the | Songster's Com-
panion | being a complete Collection | of
Songs, Cantatas, &c, | with the Music
prefix'd to each | adapted for the | Violin
or German Flute, | Selected from the first
& second Vo-|-lumes of a favorite Work
formerly | Published under that Title; |
To which is now added a variety of |

other New & choice Songs &c not insert-
|-ed in any part of ye foregoing Work. |
With an Alphabetical Index | of the
whole. | [London] Printed for J. Bew No.
28 Paternoster Row. [ca. 177?]

12° 4 ℓ., 280 p.
Imperfect: pages 143–144 lacking
RISM B II, 398–399
WIDENER

VOGELGESANG, ANDREAS   *See* Ornithoparchus, Andreas

VOGELHOFER, ANDREAS   *See* Ornithoparchus, Andreas

1557   VOGLER, GEORG JOSEPH

Klaveerudtog | af | Hermann von Unna,
| et Drama i 5 Akter | med | Chor og Bal-
letter | af | Abbe Vogler. | Kiøbenhavn. |
Trykt og forlagt af S. Sønnischsen, | Kon-
gel. privileg. Node- og Bogtrykker.
[1800?]

large obl. 4° *Vocal score:* 1 ℓ., 38 p.
MUSIC LIBRARY

VOLCYR, NICOLAUS   *See* Wollick, Nicolaus

VON   SCHNÜFFIS,   LAURENTIUS   *See*
Laurentius von Schnüffis

VON WINTER, PETER   *See* Winter, Peter
von

VUIGLIART,   ADRIAN   *See*   Willaert,
Adrian

1558   VULTURINUS, PANCRATIUS

Fratris Pancratij Vulturini Slesitae Ere-
mitani de | monte Ceruino Opusculum
Musices. [Venice, ca. 1508]

8° In his *Carminũ Libri duo,* leaves
f4ʳ–g4ʳ
Colophon: Impressum Venetijs per
Bernardinum | Venetum de Vitalibus.
Caption title
RISM B VI, 634
HOUGHTON

W

1559 WAGENSEIL, GEORG
CHRISTOPH

Six | Sonatas | for | Two Violins, | a |
Violoncello, | or | Harpsichord. | Com-
posed by | Christopher Wagenseil. | Op:
3za: | London: | Printed for I. Walsh in
Catharine Street in the Strand. | . . . [ca.
1765]

2° 3 pts.: *violino primo, violino se-
condo:* 1 ℓ., 14 p. each; *basso:* 1 ℓ., 13 p.
Walsh II, no. 1530
HOUGHTON

1560 WAGENSEIL, JOHANN
CHRISTOPH

Joh. Christophori Wagenseilii | De |
Sacri Rom. Imperii Libera | Civitate
Noribergensi | Commentatio. | Accedit, |
De | Germaniae Phonascorvm | Von | Der
Meister-Singer, | Origine, Praestantia,
Vtilitate, | Et Institvtis, | Sermone Ver-
nacvlo Liber. | Altdorfi Noricorvm |
Typis Impensiqve Jodoci Wilhelmi Koh-
lesii. | cIɔIɔc xcvii.

4° 576 [i. e. 583] p., front. (port.), illus.,
15 pl. (4 fold.)
Eleven unnumbered pages of music
after page 554
Numerous errors in paging
Hirsch I, no. 604; RISM B VI, 873
HOUGHTON (2 copies), WIDENER

1561 WAGNER, FREDERICK

Twelve | New English | Songs, | With a
Thorough Bass for the | Harpsichord, |
Compos'd by | Frederick Wagner | Of
Mitcham. | [London] Published by the
Author. to be had at Mr. Thompsons mu-
sick Shop in St Paul's Church | Yard, Mr.
C. Claggett at Mrs. Phillip's musick
Shop in Bedford Court & by Mr. Bride in
Exeter' change [ca. 1770]

obl. 2° *Score:* 1 ℓ., 27 p.
Imperfect: pages 25–27 lacking
MUSIC LIBRARY

WALSH, JOHN, THE ELDER, PUBL. The British Musical Miscellany *See* The British
Musical Miscellany

WALSH, JOHN, THE ELDER, PUBL. The
Merry Musician *See* The Merry Musician

WALSH, JOHN, THE YOUNGER, PUBL. The
British Orpheus *See* The British Orpheus

WALSH, JOHN, THE YOUNGER, PUBL. The
Catch Club *See* The Catch Club

WALSH, JOHN, THE YOUNGER, PUBL. Farinelli's Celebrated Songs *See* Farinelli's
Celebrated Songs

1562 WALTER, THOMAS

The | Grounds and Rules | Of | Musick |
Explained: Or, | An Introduction to the
Art of Singing | by Note. | Fitted to the
meanest Capacities. | By Thomas Walter.
M. A. | Recommended by several Minis-
ters. | . . . | Boston: Printed by J. Frank-
lin, for S. Gerrish, near the Brick Church
in Cornhill. 1721.

obl. 8° 1 ℓ., iii, [1], 24 p., 16 ℓ., illus.,
music
Three leaves of hymns and psalms for
three voices in contemporary manuscript bound in at end
Numbered leaves printed on one side
only
HOUGHTON

1563 WALTER, THOMAS

The | Grounds and Rules | Of | Musick |
Explained: Or, | An Introduction to the
Art of Singing | by Note. | Fitted to the
meanest Capacities. | By Thomas Walter,
M. A. | Recommended by several Minis-
ters. | The Second Edition. | . . . | Boston:
Printed by B. Green, for S. Gerrish, near
the Brick Meeting-House in Cornhill.
1723.

obl. 8° 1 ℓ., iii, [1], 25 [1] p., 16 numb.
ℓ., illus., music

Twenty-six leaves of hymn and psalm tunes in contemporary manuscript bound in at end

Numbered leaves printed on one side only

Imperfect: leaf 16 lacking; supplied in positive photostat

RISM B VI, 876

HOUGHTON

1564   WALTER, THOMAS

The | Grounds and Rules | Of | Musick | Explained: Or, | An Introduction to the Art of | Singing by Note. | Fitted to the meanest Capacities. | By Thomas Walter, M. A. | Recommended by several Ministers. | The Third Edition. | . . . | Boston: | Printed by J. Draper for S. Gerrish. | MDCCXL.

12° 1 ℓ., iii, [1], 40 p., 12 numb. ℓ., illus., music

Front fly leaf contains two psalms for three voices in contemporary manuscript

HOUGHTON

1565   WALTER, THOMAS

The | Grounds and Rules | Of | Musick | Explained: Or, | An Introduction to the Art of Singing | by Note. | Fitted to the meanest Capacities. | By Thomas Walter, M. A. | Recommended by several Ministers. | . . . | Boston: Printed for Samuel Gerrish, 1746.

obl. 8° 1 ℓ., iii, [1], 25 p., 16 numb. ℓ., illus., music

Eleven leaves of hymn tunes and secular tunes in contemporary manuscript bound in at end

Numbered leaves printed on one side only

RISM B VI, 876

HOUGHTON

1566   WALTER, THOMAS

The | Grounds and Rules of | Musick | Explained: Or, | An Introduction to the Art of Singing by Note. | Fitted to the Meanest Capacities. | By Thomas Walter, M. A. | Recommended by several Ministers. | . . . | Boston: Printed and Sold by Benjamin Mecom at | the New Printing-Office near the Town-House. 1760.

obl. 8° 1 ℓ., iii, [1], 25 p., 24 numb. ℓ., illus., music

Nineteen leaves of hymns and psalms for three to four voices in contemporary manuscript bound in at end

Preliminary leaf 1ᵛ: Thoughts on Poetry and Musick: By Dr. Watts.

Numbered leaves printed on one side only

HOUGHTON

1567   WALTER, THOMAS

The | Grounds and Rules of | Musick | Explained: Or, | An Introduction to the Art of Singing by Note. | Fitted to the Meanest Capacities. | By Thomas Walter, M. A. | Recommended by several Ministers. | . . . | Boston: Printed by Benjamin Mecom at the New | Printing-Office near the Town-House, for Thomas Johnston, in Brattle-Street. [1760?]

obl. 8° 1 ℓ., iii, [1], 25 p., 20 numb. ℓ., illus., music

Eight leaves of hymns and psalms for three to four voices in contemporary manuscript bound in at end

Unnumbered page at beginning: Thoughts on Poetry and Musick: By Dr. Watts.

Numbered leaves printed on one side only

HOUGHTON

1568   WALTER, THOMAS

The | Grounds and Rules of | Musick | Explained: Or, | An Introduction to the Art of Singing by Note. | Fitted to the Meanest Capacities. | By Thomas Walter, M. A. | Recommended by several Ministers. | . . . | Boston: Printed for, and Sold by Thomas Johnston, in Brattle-Street, over | against the Rev. Mr. Cooper's Meeting-House. 1764.

obl. 8° 1 ℓ., iii, [1], 25 p., 44 numb. ℓ., illus., music

Unnumbered page at beginning: Thoughts on Poetry and Musick: By Dr. Watts.

Imperfect: numbered leaf 44 lacking; supplied to positive photostat

HOUGHTON

1569   WANHAL, JOHANN BAPTIST

A Favourite | Overture, | For The | Piano Forte | Composed By | Vanhall. | London: | Printed for Harrison & Co. No. 78, Fleet Street. [1798?]

8° *Score:* 12 p. (*The Piano-Forte Magazine,* vol. IV, no. 5)
Plate no. 57
MUSIC LIBRARY

1570   WARD, JOHN

The | First Set | of English | Madrigals | To | 3. 4. 5. and 6. parts: | apt both for Viols | and Voyces. | With a Mourning Song | in memory of Prince | Henry. | Newly Composed by | John Ward. | . . . | [London] Printed by Thomas Snodham. 1613.

4° 1 pt.: *sextvs:* [A]², B⁴, C²
HOUGHTON

1571   WARREN, AMBROSE

The | Tonometer: | Explaining and Demonstrating, by an easie Method, | in Numbers and Proportion, | All the 32 distinct and different | Notes, Adjuncts or Suppliments | Contained in | Each of Four Octaves inclusive, of the Gamut, | or Common Scale of Musick. | With their exact Difference and Distance. | Whereby the Practitioner on any Key'd, or Fretted Instrument, may | easily know how to Tune the same. | And also, with great exactness, how to Transpose any Musick from | one Key to another, Sharp or Flat, Higher or Lower; | With proper Sharps or Flats thereto. | Never before published. | By Ambrose Warren, a Lover of Musick. | [London] At the Westminster Printing-Office, near New Palace-Yard, | Printed by J. Cluer and Alex. Campbell; and sold by B. Creake, at the Bible | in Jermyn-street, St. James's. 1725. | Sold also at the Printing-Office in Bow Church-Yard; at both which Places may be had | the First and Second Pocket Volume of Opera Songs; also the Opera's of Julius Caesar, | Tamerlane and Rodelinda, in Score and for the Flute: Likewise Musical Cards, Etc.

4° 1 ℓ., 24 p. front. (illus.), 3 fold. pl., music
RISM B VI, 878–879
HOUGHTON

1572   WARREN, EDMUND THOMAS, COMP.

A Collection of | Catches Canons and Glees | For | Three, four, five, six and nine Voices | never before published | Selected by | Thomas Warren | John Phillips sculpt. | London Printed for, & sold by the Editor at Mrs. Burgess's in great | Queen Street Lincolns Inn Fields, & at the Music Shops. MDCCLXIII.

obl. 2° *Score:* 3 ℓ., 31 p., 1 ℓ., 31 p.
HOUGHTON, MUSIC LIBRARY (imperfect)

1573   WARREN, EDMUND THOMAS, COMP.

A Second Collection of | Catches Canons and Glees | For | Three, Four, Five and Eight Voices | Most humbly inscrib'd to the | Noblemen and Gentlemen of the Catch-Club | at St. Alban's Tavern | By their much Oblig'd | and Devoted Servant | Thos. Warren. | Caulfield Sculpt. | London Printed for Peter Welcker in Gerrard Street St. Ann's Soho | Where may be had the first Collection. Likewise a Collection of Catches in a Pocket Volume. [ca. 1764]

obl. 2° *Score:* 1 ℓ., 51 p.
HOUGHTON

1574   WARREN, EDMUND THOMAS, COMP.

A Third Collection of | Catches Canons and Glees | For | Three, Four, Five and Eight Voices | Most humbly inscrib'd to the | Noblemen and Gentlemen of the Catch-Club | at St. Alban's Tavern | By their much Oblig'd | and Devoted Servant | Thos. Warren. | Caulfield Sculpt. | London Printed for Peter Welcker in Gerrard Street St. Ann's Soho | Where may be had the first Collection. Likewise a Collection of Catches in a Pocket Volume. [ca. 1765]

obl. 2° *Score:* 2 ℓ., 42 p.
HOUGHTON

1575 WARREN, EDMUND THOMAS,
COMP.

A fourth Collection of | Catches
Canons and Glees | For | Three, Four,
Five and Eight Voices | Most humbly in-
scrib'd to the | Noblemen and Gentle-
men of the Catch-Club at | St. Albans
Tavern | by their much Oblig'd | and De-
voted Servant | Thos. Warren. | Caulfield
Sculpt. | London Printed by Welcker in
Gerrard Street St. Ann's Soho | Where
may be had the 1st. 2d. and 3d. Book of
Catches Canons and Glees . . . [ca.
1766]

obl. 2° *Score:* 2 ℓ., 41 p.
HOUGHTON

1576 WARREN, EDMUND THOMAS,
COMP.

A Fifth Collection of | Catches Canons
and Glees | for three and four | Voices. |
Most humbly inscrib'd to the | Noble-
men and Gentlemen of the Catch Club |
at St. Alban's Tavern | by their much
oblig'd | and Devoted Servant | Thos.
Warren. | London Printed by Welcker in
Gerrard Street St. Ann's Soho | Where
may be had the four preceeding Books of
Catches Canons and Glees . . . [ca.
1767]

obl. 2° *Score:* 2 ℓ., 42 p.
HOUGHTON

1577 WARREN, EDMUND THOMAS,
COMP.

A Sixth Collection of | Catches
Canons and Glees | for three and four |
Voices | Most humbly inscribed to the |
Noblemen and Gentlemen | of the Catch
Club at the | Thatch'd House Tavern St.
James's | by their much oblig'd and De-
voted Servant | Thos. Warren | Engrav'd
by Caulfield | London Printed by
Welcker in Gerrard Street St. Ann's Soho
| Where may be had the five preceeding
Books . . . [ca. 1768]

obl. 2° *Score:* 2 ℓ., 42 p.
HOUGHTON

1578 WARREN, EDMUND THOMAS,
COMP.

A Seventh Collection of | Catches
Canons and Glees | for three and four |
Voices | Most humbly inscribed to the |
Noblemen and Gentlemen | of the Catch
Club at the | Thatch'd House Tavern St.
James's | by their much oblig'd and De-
voted Servant | Thos. Warren | Engrav'd
by Caulfield | London Printed by
Welcker in Gerrard Street St. Ann's Soho
| Where may be had the Six preceeding
Books . . . [ca. 1769]

obl. 2° *Score:* 2 ℓ., 50 p.
HOUGHTON

1579 WARREN, EDMUND THOMAS,
COMP.

An Eighth Collection of | Catches
Canons and Glees | for three, four and
five | Voices | Most humbly inscribed to
the | Noblemen and Gentlemen | of the
Catch Club at the | Thatch'd House Tav-
ern St. James's | by their much oblig'd
and Devoted Servant | Thos. Warren | En-
grav'd by Caulfield | London Printed by
Welcker in Gerrard Street St. Ann's Soho
| Where may be had the preceeding 7
Books of Catches Canons & Glees
. . . [ca. 1770]

obl. 2° *Score:* 2 ℓ., 45 p.
HOUGHTON

1580 WARREN, EDMUND THOMAS,
COMP.

A Ninth Collection of | Catches
Canons and Glees | for three, four and
five | Voices | Most humbly inscribed to
the | Noblemen and Gentlemen | of the
Catch Club at the | Thatch'd House Tav-
ern St. James's | by their much oblig'd
and Devoted Servant | . . . | Thos. War-
ren | Engrav'd by Caulfield | London
Printed by Longman and Broderip No. 26
Cheapside | Where may be had the pre-
ceeding 8 Books of Catches Canons &
Glees . . . [ca. 1771]

obl. 2° *Score:* 2 ℓ., 41 p.
HOUGHTON

1581 WARREN, EDMUND THOMAS, COMP.

A [Tenth] Collection of | Catches, Canons and Glees | For three, four, five and Six | Voices | Most humbly Inscribed | To the Noblemen and Gentlemen of the | Catch Club | at the Thatch'd House Tavern, St. James's | by their much oblig'd | and devoted Servant | Thos. Warren. | London Printed by Welcker in Gerrard Street St. Ann's Soho | Where may be had the ten [*sic*] preceeding Books of Catches Canons and Glees . . . [ca. 1772]

obl. 2° *Score:* 2 ℓ., 44 p.
Series number added in manuscript
HOUGHTON

1582 WARREN, EDMUND THOMAS, COMP.

A[n] [11th] Collection of | Catches, Canons and Glees | For three, four, five and Six | Voices | Most humbly Inscribed | To the Noblemen and Gentlemen of the | Catch Club | at the Thatch'd House Tavern, St. James's | by their much oblig'd | and devoted Servant | Thos. Warren. | London Printed by Welcker in Gerrard Street St. Ann's Soho | Where may be had the ten preceeding Books of Catches Canons and Glees . . . [ca. 1773]

obl. 2° *Score:* 2 ℓ., 46 p.
Series number added in manuscript
HOUGHTON

1583 WARREN, EDMUND THOMAS, COMP.

A [Twelfth] Collection of | Catches Canons and Glees | for three, four and five | Voices | Most humbly inscribed to the | Noblemen and Gentlemen | of the Catch Club at the | Thatch'd House Tavern St. James's | by their much oblig'd and Devoted Servant | Thos. Warren | Engrav'd by Caulfield | London Printed by Welcker in Gerrard Street St. Ann's Soho | Where may be had the preceeded 8 [*sic*] Books of Catches Canons & Glees . . . [ca. 1774]

obl. 2° *Score:* 2 ℓ., 46 p.
Series number added in manuscript
HOUGHTON

1584 WARREN, EDMUND THOMAS, COMP.

A Thirteenth Collection of | Catches, Canons and Glees | for three and four Voices | most humbly inscribed to the | Noblemen and Gentlemen | of the Catch Club at the | Thatch'd House Tavern, St. James's | by their much oblig'd and devoted Servant | Thomas Warren | . . . | London Printed and Sold by Longman and Broderip No. 26 Cheapside | Where may be had the Twelve preceeding Books . . . [ca. 1775]

obl. 2° *Score:* 2 ℓ., 46 p.
HOUGHTON

1585 WARREN, EDMUND THOMAS, COMP.

A Fourteenth Collection of | Catches Canons and Glees | for three, four and five | Voices | Most humbly inscribed to the | Noblemen and Gentlemen | of the Catch Club at the Thatch'd House Tavern, St. James's | by their much obliged and devoted Servant | Thomas Warren . . . | Engrav'd by Caulfield | London Printed and Sold by Longman and Broderip No. 26 Cheapside | Where may be had the Thirteen preceeding Books . . . [ca. 1776]

obl. 2° *Score:* 2 ℓ., 46 p.
HOUGHTON

1586 WARREN, EDMUND THOMAS, COMP.

A Fifteenth Collection of | Catches Canons and Glees | for three, four and five | Voices | Most humbly inscribed to the | Noblemen and Gentlemen | of the Catch Club at the Thatch'd House Tavern, St. James's | by their much obliged and devoted Servant | Thomas Warren . . . | Engrav'd by Caulfield | London Printed and Sold by Longman and Broderip No. 26 Cheapside | Where may be had the Fourteen preceeding Books . . . [ca. 1777]

obl. 2° *Score:* 2 ℓ., 42 p.
HOUGHTON

**1587   WARREN, EDMUND THOMAS,
          COMP.**

A Sixteenth Collection of | Catches, Canons and Glees | For three, four and five | Voices | Most humbly Inscribed | To the Noblemen and Gentlemen of the | Catch Club | at the Thatch'd House Tavern St. James's | by their much obliged and devoted Servant | Thomas Warren | . . . | London Printed by Longman and Broderip No. 26 Cheapside | Music Sellers to the Royal Family | Where may be had all the preceeding Books . . . [ca. 1778]

obl. 2° *Score:* 2 ℓ., 51 p.
HOUGHTON

**1588   WARREN, EDMUND THOMAS,
          COMP.**

A Seventeenth Collection of | Catches, Canons, and Glees, | For Three, Four, and Five | Voices, | Most Humbly Inscrib'd to the | Noblemen and Gentlemen, of the | Catch Club, | At the Thatch'd House Tavern St: James's, | by their much Oblig'd and devoted Servant | Thomas Warren. | London Printed and sold by J. Blundell No. 10 Hay Market | Where may be had the 16 preceeding Books . . . [ca. 1780]

obl. 2° *Score:* 2 ℓ., 60 p.
HOUGHTON

**1589   WARREN, EDMUND THOMAS,
          COMP.**

An Eighteenth Collection of | Catches, Canons and Glees | For three, four and five | Voices | Most humbly Inscribed | To the Noblemen and Gentlemen of the | Catch Club | at the Thatch'd House Tavern St. James's | by their much obliged and devoted Servant | Thomas Warren | London Printed by Longman and Broderip No. 26 Cheapside | Music Sellers to the Royal Family | Where may be had all the preceeding Books . . . [ca. 1780]

obl. 2° *Score:* 2 ℓ., 55 p.
HOUGHTON

**1590   WARREN, EDMUND THOMAS,
          COMP.**

A Nineteenth Collection of | Catches, Canons, and Glees, | For three, four, and five | Voices | Most humbly Inscribed | To the Noblemen and Gentlemen of the | Catch Club | at the Thatch'd House Tavern St. James's, | by their much obliged and devoted Servant | Thomas Warren. | London Printed for the Editor by Longman and Broderip No. 26 Cheapside | Music Sellers to the Royal Family | Where may be had all the preceeding Books . . . [ca. 1781]

obl. 2° *Score:* 2 ℓ., 55 p.
HOUGHTON

**1591   WARREN, EDMUND THOMAS,
          COMP.**

A Twentieth Collection of | Catches Canons and Glees | for three four and five | Voices | Most humbly Inscribed | To the Noblemen and Gentlemen of the | Catch Club | at the Thatch'd House Tavern St. James's | by their much obliged and devoted Servant | Thomas Warren | London Printed for the Editor in Tavistock Street Bedford Square, and may be had at Longman's | Music Shop in Cheapside: Likewise the former Collections at the reduc'd Price. [ca. 1782]

obl. 2° *Score:* 2 ℓ., 54 p.
HOUGHTON

**1592   WARREN, EDMUND THOMAS,
          COMP.**

A Twenty first Collection of | Catches Canons and Glees | for three four and five | Voices | Most humbly Inscribed | To the Noblemen and Gentlemen of the | Catch Club | at the Thatch'd House Tavern St, James's | by their much obliged and devoted Servant | Thomas Warren | London. Printed and Sold by Longman and Broderip No. 26 Cheapside and No. 13 Hay Market | Likewise the former Collections at the reduced Prices. [ca. 1783]

obl. 2° *Score:* 2 ℓ., 54 p.
HOUGHTON

1593 WARREN, EDMUND THOMAS, COMP.

A Twenty second Collection of | Catches Canons and Glees | for three four and five | Voices | Most humbly Inscribed To the Noblemen and Gentlemen of the | Catch Club | at the Thatch'd House Tavern St. James's | by their much Obliged & devoted Servant | Thomas Warren. | London, Printed for the Editor in Tavistock Street Bedford Square, and may be had at Longman's | Music Shop No. 26 Cheapside. likewise the former Collections at the reduced Prices. [ca. 1784]

obl. 2° *Score:* 2 ℓ., 54 p.
HOUGHTON

1594 WARREN, EDMUND THOMAS, COMP.

A Twenty-third Collection of | Catches Canons and Glees | for three four and five | Voices | Most humbly Inscribed | To the Noblemen and Gentlemen of the | Catch Club | at the Thatch'd House Tavern St. James's | by their much Obliged & devoted Servant | Thomas Warren. | London. Printed for the Editor in Tavistock Street Bedford Square, and may be had at Longman's | Music Shop No. 26 Cheapside. likewise the former Collections at the reduced Prices. [ca. 1785]

obl. 2° *Score:* 2 ℓ., 54 p.
HOUGHTON

1595 WATLEN, JOHN

The Celebrated | Circus Tunes | Perform'd at Edinburgh this Season, With | The Addition of Some New | Reels and Strathspeys | Set For The | Piano Forte | Or | Violin And Bass | By John Watlen | . . . | Edinr. Printed for the Author, to be had at his House No. 17 Princes Street | . . . [ca. 1791]

2° *Score:* 3 ℓ., 2–30 p.
MUSIC LIBRARY

1596 WATSON, THOMAS, COMP.

. . . | The first sett, | Of Italian Madrigalls Englished, | not to the sense of the originall dittie, | but after the affection of the | Noate. | By Thomas Watson Gentleman. | There are also heere inserted two excellent | Madrigalls of Master VVilliam | Byrds, composed after the | Italian vaine, at the request | of the sayd Thomas | Watson. | Imprinted at London by Tho-|mas Este, the assigné of William Byrd, | & are to be sold at the house of the sayd T. Este, | being in Aldersgate street, at the signe | of the black Horse. 1590. | Cum priuilegio Regiae Maiestatis.

4° 6 pts.: *svperivs, contratenor, tenor, bassvs:* [A]², B–D⁴, E² each; *medivs:* [A]², B–C⁴, D²; *sextvs:* [A]², B⁴
Gathering B missigned C in *medivs* part-book
Imperfect: gathering B lacking in *tenor* part-book; supplied in facsimile
RISM B I, no. 1590²⁹
HOUGHTON

WATTS, JOHN, PUBL. The Musical Miscellany *See* The Musical Miscellany

1597 [WEBB, DANIEL]

Observations | On The | Correspondence | Between | Poetry and Music. | By the Author of | An Enquiry into the Beauties of | Painting. | . . . | London, | Printed for J. Dodsley, in Pall-mall. | MDCCLXIX.

8° vii, 155 p., 2 ℓ.
RISM B VI, 879
HOUGHTON

1598 WEBBE, SAMUEL

An Eighth Book Of | Glees, Canons, And Catches. | Composed by | Samuel Webbe, | Dedicated to the Revd. Mr. Becher. | Prebendary Of Southwell. | London Printed for the Author, Red Lion Square, Corner of Leigh Street. | and to be had at Blands, Music Warehouse, 45. Holborn. & the other Music Shops. | . . . [ca. 1795]

obl. 2° *Score:* 1 ℓ., 59, [1] p.
MUSIC LIBRARY

1599   WEBBE, SAMUEL

The Ladies | Catch Book | being | A Collection of | Catches, Canons and Glees | The Words of which will not offend the nicest Delicacy | Composed by | Samuel Webbe | London. Printed for S and A Thompson No. 75 St. Pauls Church Yard. | . . . [1778?]

obl. 2° *Score:* 1 ℓ., 30 p.
MUSIC LIBRARY

1600   WEELKES, THOMAS

. . . | Balletts | And | Madrigals | To | fiue voyces, vvith | one to 6. voyces: newly published | By | Thomas Weelkes. | In London | Printed By Thomas Este, | the assigne of William Barley. | 1608.

4° 3 pts.: *cantvs, tenor, bassvs:* [A]², B–D⁴ each
Imperfect: damaged by fire, with loss of text and music
HOUGHTON

1601   WEELKES, THOMAS

. . . | Madrigals | To | 3. 4. 5. & 6. voyces. | Made & newly published | By | Thomas VVeelkes. | At London | Printed by Thomas Este. | 1597.

4° 1 pt.: *sextvs:* [A]², B1–3
HOUGHTON

1602   WEELKES, THOMAS

. . . | Madrigals | Of | 5. and 6. parts, apt for the | Viols and voices. | Made & newly published | By | Thomas Weelkes of the Coledge | at Winchester, | Organist. | At London | Printed by Thomas Este, the assigne | of Thomas Morley. | 1600.

4° 2 pts.: *alto, tenore:* [A]², B⁴, C1 each
HOUGHTON

1603   WEELKES, THOMAS

. . . | Madrigals | Of | 6. parts, apt for the Viols | and voices. | Made & newly published | By | Thomas Weelkes of the Coledge | at Winchester, | Organist. | At London | Printed by Thomas Este, the assigne | of Thomas Morley. | 1600.

4° 5 pts.: *canto, alto, tenore, basso:* C2–4, D⁴ each; *sesto:* C–D⁴
HOUGHTON

WELCKER, PETER, PUBL. A Collection of Catches by the following Masters *See* A Collection of Catches by the following Masters

1604   WERT, GIACHES DE

. . . | Di Giaches De Wert | Il Secondo Libro De Madrigali | A Cinqve Voci, | Nouamente Ristampati. | In Venetia Appresso Angelo Gardano. | M.D.LXXXXVI.

obl. 4° 1 pt.: *alto:* 29 [i. e. 31], [1] p.
Nos. 7, 8 repeated in paging
Vogel, no. 2975
HOUGHTON

1605   WERT, GIACHES DE

. . . | Di Giaches De Wert | L'Ottavo Libro De Madrigali | A Cinqve Voci. | Nouamente Ristampato. | In Venetia Appresso Angelo Gardano. | M.D.LXXXXVI.

obl. 4° 1 pt.: *alto:* 1 ℓ., 25, [1] p.
Vogel, no. 2991
HOUGHTON

1606   WESLEY, SAMUEL

Twelve | Sonatinas | for the | Piano-Forte. | Or | Harpsichord, | with the proper Fingering marked | & Composed by | Samuel Wesley. | . . . Op. 4. . . . | London Printed for the Author, | & sold by Rt. Birchall at his Musical Circulating Library No. 133 New Bond street. [ca. 1799]

2° *Score:* 1 ℓ., 11 p.
MUSIC LIBRARY

WEVER, ARNOLD, PUBL. C. P. E. Bachs, Nichelmanns und Håndels Sonaten und Fugen *See* Bach, Carl Philip Emanuel *C. P. E. Bachs, Nichelmanns und Håndels Sonaten und Fugen*

WHEBLE, JOHN, PUBL. The New Merry Companion *See* The New Merry Companion

THE WHOLE VOLUME COMPLEAT INTI-
TULED THE MONTHLY MASKS OF VOCAL
MUSICK *See* The Monthly Masks of
Vocal Musick

1607 WILBYE, JOHN

. . . | The First Set | Of English | Madri-
gals | To | 3. 4. 5. and 6. voices: | Newly
Composed | By | Iohn Wilbye. | At Lon-
don: | Printed by Thomas Este. | 1598.

4° 6 pts.: *cantvs, altvs, bassvs:* A–D⁴
each; *tenor:* [A]², B–D⁴; *qvintvs:* A–B⁴,
C²; *sextvs:* [A]², B⁴
Hirsch III, no. 1150
HOUGHTON

1608 WILLAERT, ADRIAN

. . . | Tiers Livre De | Chansons A
Trois Parties | Composé par Ad. Vuillart.
| Imprimé en Trois volumes | A Paris. |
M.D.LXXVIII. | Par Adrian le Roy, &
Robert Ballard. | Imprimeurs du Roy. |
Auec priuilege de sa magesté pour dix
ans.

obl. 8° 1 pt.: *svperivs:* 24 numb. ℓ.
Lesure, no. 219 bis; RISM B I, no.
1578¹⁶
HOUGHTON

1609 WILSON, JOHN

Cheerfull Ayres | Or Ballads | First
composed for one single Voice and | since
set for three Voices | By | John Wilson Dr
in Mvsick | Professor of the same in the |
Vniversity of Oxford. | Oxford. | Printed
by W. Hall, for Ric. Davis. | Anno Dom.
MDCLX.

obl 4° 1 pt: *cantus primus:* 4 ℓ., 147 p.
RISM B I, no. 1660⁴
HOUGHTON

1610 WINTER, PETER VON

Die Brüder als Nebenbuhler | (I Fratelli
Rivali) | eine Oper in 2. Aufzügen | von |
Peter Winter. | mit italienisch und deut-
schem Text, | in Klavierauszug übertra-
gen | von Cannabich. | bei N. Simrock | in
Bonn. | . . . [1799]

obl. 2° *Vocal score:* 1 ℓ., 191 p.
Plate no. 80
MUSIC LIBRARY

1611 [WOLLICK, NICOLAUS]

Opus Aureum. | Musice castigatissimū
| de Gregoriana et Figuratiua atq[ue]
con|trapūcto simplici percōmode
tra|ctans oṁib[us] cantu oblectan|tibus
vtile et necessa-|rium ediuersis | excer-
ptum | . . . [Cologne, 1504]

4° A⁶, B⁴, C⁶, D–E⁴, F⁶, G⁴, H1–5, illus.,
music
Colophon: . . . Impressum Colo-|nie
in edibus honesti viri Henrici Quentell.
Anno | domini M.ccccc.iiij.
RISM B VI, 899
HOUGHTON

WOLQUIER, NICOLAUS *See* Wollick,
Nicolaus

1612 WORGAN, JOHN

The | Agreeable Choice. | A | Collec-
tion of Songs | Sung by | Miss Burchell,
Miss Stevenson, and Mr. Lowe | at Vaux-
Hall-Gardens. | Set By | Mr. Worgan. |
London Printed for I. Walsh, in Cath-
arine Street, in the Strand. | . . . [1751]

2° *Score:* 1 ℓ., 20 p.
Walsh II, no. 1555
HOUGHTON

1613 WORGAN, JOHN

A | Trio. | For Three Voices. | With | In-
struments. | Sung by | Miss Burchell Miss
Stevenson & Mr. Lowe. | In Vaux Hall
Gardens. | Set by | Iohn Worgan. M. B. |
London. | Printed for the Author and Sold
at his House in Millman Street facing St.
Iohn's Chapel Bedford Row Holbourn. |
With his Majesty's Royal Licence |
MDCCLV.

2° *Score:* 1 ℓ., 22 p.
Text incipit: "Hence, hence, fly hence
grim Melancholy's train"
HOUGHTON

WRIGHT, DANIEL, PUBL. The American
Musical Miscellany *See* The American
Musical Miscellany

Y

1614   YONGE, NICHOLAS, COMP.

Mvsica Transalpina. | . . . | Madrigales translated of foure, fiue and sixe parts, | chosen out of diuers excellent Authors, vvith the first and | second part of La Verginella, made by Maister Byrd, | vpon two Stanz's of Ariosto and brought | to speake English with | the rest. | Published by N. Yonge, in fauour of such as | take pleasure in Musick of voices. | Imprinted at London by Tho-|mas East, the assignè of William | Byrd. 1588. | Cum Priuilegio Regiae Maiestatis.

4° 6 pts.: *cantvs, altvs:* A², [2d]A⁴, B–H⁴ each; *tenor, bassvs:* A², [2d]A⁴, B–G⁴, H1–3 each; *qvintvs:* A², [2d]A⁴, B–F⁴, G1–3; *sextvs:* A², [2d]A⁴, B⁴, illus. (coat of arms)
RISM B I, no. 1588²⁹
HOUGHTON

1615   YONGE, NICHOLAS, COMP.

Mvsica Transalpina. | . . . | The Second Booke | Of | Madrigalles, to 5. & 6. voices: | translated out of sundrie | Italian Authors | & | Newly Pvblished | By | Nicolas Yonge. | At London | Printed by Thomas Este. | 1597.

4° 6 pts.: *cantvs, altvs, tenor, bassvs, qvintvs:* [A]², B–D⁴ each; *sextvs:* [A]², B⁴; illus. (coat of arms) in each part-book
RISM B I, no. 1597²⁴
HOUGHTON

Z

1616   ZACCONI, LODOVICO

Prattica | Di Mvsica | Vtile Et Necessaria Si Al Composi-|tore per Comporre i Canti suoi regolatamente, si anco al | Cantore per assicurarsi in tutte le cose cantabili. | Divisa In Qvattro Libri. | Ne I Qvali Si Tratta Delle Can-|tilene ordinarie, de Tempi de Prolationi, de Propor-

tioni, de Tuo-|ni, et della conuenienze de tutti gli Istrumenti Musicali. | S'Insegna A Cantar Tvtte Le Compositioni | antiche, Si dichiara tutta la Messa del Palestina titolo Lomè Armè, | con altre cose d'importanza & diletteuole. | Vltimamente s'insegna il modo di fiorir una parte con uaghi et moderni accenti. | Composta Dal R. P. F. Lodovico Zacconi | da Pesaro, del Ordine di Santo Agostino, | Musico del Sereniss. Duca di Bauiera, &c. | Con Privilegio. | In Venetia, MDXCVI. | Appresso Bartolomeo Carampello.

2° 6 *ℓ.*, 218 [i. e. 219] numb. *ℓ.*, illus., music
Number 50 repeated in foliation
RISM B VI, 903–904
HOUGHTON

1617   ZARLINO, GIOSEFFO

Dimostrationi | Harmoniche | Del R. M. Gioseffo Zarlino | Da Chioggia | Maestro Di Capella Della Illvstris. Signoria | Di Venetia. | Nelle quali realmente si trattano le cose della Musica: | & si resoluono molti dubij d'importanza. | Opera molto necessaria à tutti quelli, che desiderano | di far buon profitto in questa nobile | Scienza. | Con la Tauola delle materie notabili contenute nell'opera. | . . . | Con Privilegio. | In Venetia, Per Francesco de i Franceschi Senese. 1571.

2° 4 *ℓ.*, 312, [10] p., 1 *ℓ.*, illus.
Davidsson II, no. 106; Hirsch I, no. 624; RISM B VI, 907
HOUGHTON (2 copies)

1618   ZARLINO, GIOSEFFO

. . . | Le Dimostrationi Harmoniche | Divise In Cinqve Ragionamenti. | Ne I Qvali Si Discorrono Et Dimostrano | le cose della Musica; & si risoluono molti dubij d'importanza à tutti quelli, | che desiderano di far buon profitto nella Intelligentia di cotale Scienza. | Con la Tauola delle materie notabili contenute nell'opera. | In Venetia, MDLXXXIX. | Appresso Francesco de' Franceschi Senese.

2° 8 ℓ., 287 p., illus.
In his *Opere,* vol. II
Hirsch I, no 627; RISM B VI, 906–907;
Wolfenbüttel, no. 1333, 2
HOUGHTON (2 copies)

1619   ZARLINO, GIOSEFFO

Le Istitvtioni | Harmoniche | Di M.
Gioseffo Zarlino Da Chioggia; | Nelle
quali; oltra le materie appartenenti | Alla
Mvsica; | Si trouano dichiarati molti
luoghi | di Poeti, d'Historici, & di Filo-
sofi; | Si come nel leggerle si potrà chiara-
mente vedere. | . . . | Con Priuilegio dell'
Illustriss. Signoria di Venetia, | Per anni
X. | In Venetia MDLVIII.

2° 6 ℓ., 347 p., illus., music
RISM B VI, 907
HOUGHTON

1620   ZARLINO, GIOSEFFO

Le Istitvtioni | Harmoniche | Del Re-
verendo M. Gioseffo Zarlino | Da Chiog-
gia; | Nelle quali; oltra le materie appar-
tenenti | Alla Mvsica; | Si trouano
dichiarati molti luoghi | di Poeti, d'Hi-
storici, & di Filosofi; | Si come nel leg-
gerle si potrà chiaramente vedere. | . . . |
Con Priuilegio dell'Illustriss. Signoria di
Venetia, | per anni X. | In Venetia, | Ap-
presso Francesco Senese, al segno della
Pace. | MDLXII.

2° 6 ℓ., 347 p., illus., music
RISM B VI, 908
HOUGHTON

1621   ZARLINO, GIOSEFFO

. . . | L'Istitvtioni Harmoniche | Divise
In Qvattro Parti; | Nelle Qvali, Oltra Le
Materie Della | Musica, si trouano molti
luoghi de Famosissimi Scrittori di-
chiarati. | Con Dve Tavole, L'Vna Della
Cose Principali; | & l'altra delle più nota-
bili, che nell'Opera si ritrouano. | In Ve-
netia, MDLXXXIX. | Appresso Francesco
de' Franceschi Senese.

2° 16 ℓ., 448 p., illus., music
In his *Opere,* vol. I
Hirsch I, no. 626; RISM B VI, 906–907;
Wolfenbüttel, no. 1333, 1
HOUGHTON (2 copies)

ZÈDE, NICOLAS DE   *See* Dezède, Nicolas

1622   ZEILER, GALLUS

Latria Musica, | Deo Eucharistico
Sacra, | Complectens | XX. | Benedi-
ctiones | Pro Solemni Octava | Corporis
Christi; | Quas inter 16. Tantum ergo, 2.
Ecce Panis Ange-|lorum, I. Ave vivens
Hostia, I. Panis Angelicus: quibus | acce-
dit Hymnus Pange Lingua, in omnibus
Processionibus | Venerabilis hujus Sacra-
menti decantari solitus, | ac breve Te
Deum Laudamus. | à | 4. Vocibus ordi-
nariis, 2. Violinis & Organo necessar. ô |
Violoncello. 2. Clarinis vel Lituis, partim
necessariò, partim pro | libitu, adhi-
bendis: una cum Tympano. | Authore | P.
Gallo Zeiler, | Ord. S. P. Bened. antiquis-
simi Monasterii ad S. Magnum Fûessae |
professo Capitulari. | Opus VI. | Cum li-
centia Superiorum evulgatum. | . . . |
Augustae Vindelicorum, | Typis &
Sumptibus Haeredum Joannis Jacobi Lot-
teri, MDCCXXXIX.

2° 1 pt.: *organo:* 4 ℓ., 12 p.
HOUGHTON

1623   ZIEGLER, JOHANN GOTTFRIED

Menuetten | Fürs Clavier | Durch Alle
Töne, | Von | Johann Gottfried Ziegler, |
ehemaligem Cammermusicus in der
gräfl. Brühlischen Capelle. | Leipzig, | Bey
Bernhard Christoph Breitkopf Und Sohn.
[1770?]

obl. 2° *Score:* 27 p.
HOUGHTON

1624   ZIMMERMANN, ANTON

Andromeda | und | Persevs | Ein Melo-
dram | im | Clavierauszug | von Herrn Ca-
pellmeister A. Zimermann. | . . . | Zu
finden in der Kunsthandlung der Artaria
Compag. in Wien. [1781]

obl. 2° *Vocal score:* 1 ℓ., 50 p.
Plate no. 17
Hirsch IV, no. 1309
MUSIC LIBRARY

1625 ZINGARELLI, NICOLA
ANTONIO

Antigone | Opéra | En Trois Actes |
Représenté pour la premiere fois | par
L'academie Royale de Musique | Le 30
Avril 1790 | Paroles de Mr Marmontel |
Musique de Mr Zingarelli | . . . | A Paris |
Chez Jmbault au Mont d'Or rue St
Honoré | près L'hotel d'Aligre No. 627 |
Gravé par Mme Oricheler [1790?]

2° *Score:* 1 ℓ., 415 p.
Hirsch II, no. 976
MUSIC LIBRARY

1626 ZUMSTEEG, JOHANN RUDOLF

Des | Pfarrers Tochter | von Tauben-
hayn, | eine Ballade | von | G. A. Bürger. |
In Musik gesetzt | von | I. R. Zumsteeg. |
Leipzig, | in der Breitkopfischen Musik-
handlung. | [1797?]

obl. 2° *Score:* 1 ℓ., 26 p.
MUSIC LIBRARY

1627 ZUMSTEEG, JOHANN RUDOLF

Die Geister-Insel. | Ein Singspiel in 3
Akten | von | J. F. [i. e. F. W.] Gotter, in
Musik gesezt von J. R. Zumsteeg. | Im
Klavierauszug. | Bei Breitkopf & Härtel
in Leipzig. [1799]

obl. 2° *Vocal score:* 3 ℓ., 264 p.
Hirsch IV, no. 1311
MUSIC LIBRARY

1628 ZUMSTEEG, JOHANN RUDOLF

Lenore | von | G. A. Buerger in Musik
gesezt von I. R. Zumsteeg | Leipzig | Bey
Breitkopf & Haertel. [ca. 1796]

obl. 2° *Score:* 1 ℓ., 46 p.
MUSIC LIBRARY

Additions and Corrections

Item 142, correct location to: HOUGHTON.

Item 207, correct reference to: RISM A I, no. B 2417.

Item 210, add reference: RISM A I, no. B 2480.

Item 344, add note: Page 10: Books lately Printed for, and Sold by, Henry Playford . . .

Item 403 should properly be entered under the heading: [COFERATI, MATTEO, COMP.],
and moved to follow item 363.

Item 791 should properly be entered under the heading: [PRIXNER, SEBASTIAN], *and
moved to page 211.*

Item 1027, correct date to: MDCLXXXIX.

Items 1042 and 1043, correct both dates to: [1784 or 85].

Item 1494, add reference: RISM B VI, 828.

Items 1530–1532 should properly be entered under the heading: [BICKNELL, JOHN],
and moved to follow item 214.

Bibliography, page 288, add: LONSDALE, ROGER. "Dr. Burney, 'Joel Collier', and Sa-
brina." In *Evidence in Literary Scholarship: Essays in Memory of James Marshall
Osborn,* edited by René Wellek and Alvaro Ribeiro, p. 281–308. Oxford: Clarendon
Press, 1979.

Bibliography, page 289, add: POGUE, SAMUEL F. *Jacques Moderne: Lyons Music Printer
of the Sixteenth Century.* Travaux d'humanisme et renaissance, 101. Geneva: Droz,
1969.

BIBLIOGRAPHY
AND INDEX

BIBLIOGRAPHY

ALDRICH, RICHARD. *A Catalogue of Books Relating to Music in the Library of Richard Aldrich.* New York, 1931.

ANDREWS, HERBERT K. "Printed Sources of William Byrd's *Psalmes, Sonets and Songs,*" *Music & Letters,* 44 (1963) : 5–20.

BEAUMONT, CYRIL W. *A Bibliography of Dancing.* London: The Dancing Times, 1929.

BENTON, RITA. *Ignace Pleyel: A Thematic Catalogue of his Compositions.* New York: Pendragon Press, 1977.

BENZING, JOSEF. *Die Buchdrucker des 16. und 17. Jahrhunderts im deutschen Sprachgebiet.* Beiträge zum Buch- und Bibliothekswesen, 12. Wiesbaden: O. Harrassowitz, 1963.

BERZ, ERNST-LUDWIG. *Die Notendrucker und ihre Verleger in Frankfurt am Main von den Anfängen bis etwa 1630: Eine bibliographische und drucktechnische Studie zur Musikpublikation.* Catalogus musicus, 5. Kassel: Internationale Vereinigung der Musikbibliotheken, Internationale Gesellschaft für Musikwissenschaft, 1970.

BIBLIOTHÈQUE NATIONALE, PARIS. *Catalogue général des livres imprimés de la Bibliothèque nationale: Auteurs.* 227 vols. Paris, 1897–1977. [BN]

BOBILLIER, MARIE [MICHEL BRENET]. "La librairie musicale en France de 1653 à 1790, d'après les Registres de privilèges," *Sammelbände der Internationalen Musikgesellschaft,* 8 (1906–07) : 401–466.

BOWERS, FREDSON. *Principles of Bibliographical Description.* Princeton: Princeton University Press, 1949.

BRAINARD, PAUL. *Le sonate per violino di Giuseppe Tartini: Catalogo tematico.* Studi e recerche dell'Accademia Tartiniana di Padova. Le opere di Giuseppe Tartini, sezione 3: Studi e ricerche di studiosi moderni, 2. Milano: Distribuzione Carisch, 1975.

BRISTOL, ROGER PATTRELL. *Index of Printers, Publishers, and Booksellers Indicated by Charles Evans in his American Bibliography.* Charlottesville: Bibliographical Society of the University of Virginia, 1961.

BRITISH MUSEUM, DEPT. OF PRINTED BOOKS. *Catalogue of Books Printed in the XVth Century now in the British Museum.* 10 vols. London, 1908–71. [BMC]

BRITISH MUSEUM, DEPT. OF PRINTED BOOKS. *General Catalogue of Printed Books.* Photolithographic edition, to 1955. 263 vols. London, 1959–66. [BMGC]

BROWN, HOWARD MAYER. *Instrumental Music Printed before 1600: A Bibliography.* Cambridge, Mass.: Harvard University Press, 1965.

BRUNET, JACQUES-CHARLES. *Manuel du libraire et de l'amateur de livres.* 5th ed. 6 vols. Paris: Firmin Didot, 1860–65.

Cinq catalogues d'éditeurs de musique à Paris (1824–1834): Dufaut et Dubois, Petit, Frère, Delahante-Érard, Pleyel. Avec une introduction de François Lesure. Archives de l'édition musicale française, 2. Geneva: Minkoff Reprint, 1976.

COPINGER, WALTER A. *Supplement to Hain's Repertorium bibliographicum; or, Collections towards a New Edition of that Work.* 2 vols. London: H. Sotheran, 1895–1902.

CUCUEL, GEORGES. "Notes sur quelques musiciens, luthiers, éditeurs et graveurs de musique au XVIIIe siècle. Première série," *Sammelbände der Internationalen Musikgesellschaft,* 14 (1912–13) : 243–252.

CUCUEL, GEORGES. "Quelques documents sur la librairie musicale au XVIIIe siècle," *Sammelbände der Internationalen Musikgesellschaft,* 13 (1911–12) : 385–392.

DAVIDSSON, ÅKE. *Bibliographie zur Geschichte des Musikdrucks.* Acta universitatis Upsaliensis. Studia musicologica Upsaliensia, n.s., 1. Uppsala, 1965.

DAVIDSSON, ÅKE. *Catalogue critique et descriptif des imprimés de musique des XVIe et XVIIe siècles conservés dans les bibliothèques suédoises (excepté la Bibliothèque de l'Université Royale d'Upsala).* Studia musicologica Upsaliensia, 1. Uppsala, 1952.   [Davidsson I]

DAVIDSSON, ÅKE. *Catalogue critique et descriptif des ouvrages théoriques sur la musique imprimés au XVIe et au XVIIe siècles, et conservés dans les bibliothèques suédoises.* Studia musicologica Upsaliensia, 2. Uppsala, 1953.   [Davidsson II]

DAY, CYRUS LAWRENCE, and MURRIE, ELEANORE BOSWELL. *English Song-Books, 1651– 1702: A Bibliography, with a First-Line Index of Songs.* [Bibliographical Society Publication] for 1937. London: The Bibliographical Society, 1940.

DELALAIN, PAUL. *L'imprimerie et la librairie à Paris de 1789 à 1813.* Paris: Delalain frères, 1899.

DEUTSCH, OTTO ERICH. *Musikverlags-Nummern: Eine Auswahl von 40 datierten Listen, 1710–1900.* 2d ed., 1st German ed. Berlin: Verlag Merseburger, 1961.

DEVRIÈS, ANIK. *Édition et commerce de la musique gravée à Paris dans la première moitié du XVIIIe siècle: Les Boivin, les Leclerc.* Archives de l'édition musicale française, 1. Geneva: Minkoff, 1976.

DEVRIÈS, ANIK. "Les éditions musicales Sieber," *Revue de musicologie,* 55 (1969) : 20– 46.

DEVRIÈS, ANIK, and LESURE, FRANÇOIS. *Dictionnaire des éditeurs de musique français, Volume I: Des origines à environs 1820.* Archives de l'édition musicale française, 4. 2 vols. Geneva: Minkoff, 1979.

DUFOUR, THÉOPHILE. *Récherches bibliographiques sur les oeuvres imprimées de J.-J. Rousseau, suivies de l'inventaire des papiers de Rousseau conservés a la Bibliothèque de Neuchâtel.* 2 vols. Paris: L. Giraud-Badin, 1925.

EITNER, ROBERT. *Biographisch-bibliographisches Quellen-Lexikon der Musiker und Musikgelehrten christlicher Zeitrechnung bis Mitte des neunzehnten Jarhunderts.* 2d ed. 11 vols. Graz: Akademische Druck- und Verlagsanstalt, 1959–60.

EITNER, ROBERT. *Buch- und Musikalienhändler, Buch- und Musikaliendrucker nebst Notenstecher, nur die Musik betreffend, nach den Originaldrucken verzeichnet.* Beilage zu den Monatshefte für Musikgeschichte. Leipzig: Breitkopf & Härtel, 1904.

FALCK, MARTIN. *Wilhelm Friedemann Bach.* 2d ed. Studien zur Musikgeschichte, 1. Leipzig: C. F. Kahnt, 1919.   [F.]

FISKE, ROGER. *English Theatre Music in the Eighteenth Century.* London: Oxford University Press, 1973.

FOXON, DAVID F. *English Verse 1701–1750: A Catalogue of Separately Printed Poems with Notes on Contemporary Collected Editions.* 2 vols. Cambridge: Cambridge University Press, 1975.

GÉRARD, YVES. *Thematic, Bibliographical and Critical Catalogue of the Works of Luigi Boccherini.* London: Oxford University Press, 1969.   [G.]

GERICKE, HANNELORE. *Der Wiener Musikalienhandel von 1700 bis 1778.* Wiener musikwissenschaftliche Beiträge, 5. Graz: H. Böhlaus Nachf., 1960.

Gesamtkatalog der Wiegendrucke. 8 vols. (A–Flühe). Leipzig: K. W. Hiersemann; Stuttgart: A. Hiersemann, 1925–.   [GW]

GOFF, FREDERICK R. *Incunabula in American Libraries: A Third Census of Fifteenth-Century Books Recorded in North American Collections.* New York: Bibliographical Society of America, 1964.

GOOVAERTS, ALPHONSE. *Histoire et bibliographie de la typographie musicale dans les Pays Bas.* Mémoires de l'Académie royale de Belgique, Collection in-8°, 29. Antwerp: P. Kockx, 1880.

GRAND-CARTERET, JOHN. *Les almanachs français: Bibliographie-iconographie des almanachs, années, annuaires, calendriers, chansonniers, étrennes, états, heures, listes, livres d'adresses, tableaux, tablettes, et autres publications annuelles éditées à Paris (1600–1895).* Paris: J. Alisie, 1896.

GREGORY, JULIA, *see* LIBRARY OF CONGRESS.

Grove's Dictionary of Music and Musicians. 5th ed., edited by Eric Blom. 9 vols. and supplement. London: Macmillan, 1954–61.

GUIOMAR, PAULE. "J. J. Imbault," *Fontes artis musicae,* 13 (1966) : 43–46.

HAIN, LUDWIG. *Repertorium bibliographicum, in quo libri omnes ab arte typographica inventa usque ad annum MD.* 2 vols. Stuttgart: J. G. Cotta, 1826–28.

HARVARD COLLEGE LIBRARY, DEPT. OF PRINTING AND GRAPHIC ARTS. *Catalogue of Books and Manuscripts, Part I: French 16th Century Books.* Compiled by Ruth Mortimer. 2 vols. Cambridge, Mass.: Harvard University Press, Belknap Press, 1964.
[MortimerF]

HARVARD COLLEGE LIBRARY, DEPT. OF PRINTING AND GRAPHIC ARTS. *Catalogue of Books and Manuscripts, Part II: Italian 16th Century Books.* Compiled by Ruth Mortimer. 2 vols. Cambridge, Mass.: Harvard University Press, Belknap Press, 1974.
[MortimerI]

HATIN, EUGÈNE. *Bibliographie historique et critique de la presse périodique française; ou, Catalogue systématique et raisonné de tous les écrits périodiques de quelque valeur publiés ou ayant circulé en France depuis l'origine du journal jusqu'à nos jours . . .* Paris: Firmin-Didot, 1866.

HERZOG-AUGUST-BIBLIOTHEK. *Musik: Alte Drucke bis etwa 1750.* Beschrieben von Wolfgang Schmieder, Mitarbeit von Gisela Hartwieg. Kataloge der Herzog-August-Bibliothek Wolfenbüttel, 12–13. 2 vols. Frankfurt: V. Klostermann, 1967.

HEUSSNER, HORST. "Nürnberger Musikverlag und Musikalienhandel im 18. Jahrhundert." In *Musik und Verlag: Karl Vötterle zum 65. Geburtstag am 12. April 1968,* p. 319–341. Kassel: Bärenreiter, 1968.

HIGHFILL, PHILIP H.; BURNIM, KALMAN A.; and LANGHANS, EDWARD A. *A Biographical Dictionary of Actors, Actresses, Musicians, Dancers, Managers & other Stage Personnel in London, 1660–1800.* 6 vols. (A–Gyngell). Carbondale: Southern Illinois University Press, 1973–.

HILMAR, ROSEMARY. *Der Musikverlag Artaria & Comp.: Geschichte und Probleme der Druckproduktion.* Publikationen des Instituts für Österreichische Musikdokumentation, 6. Tutzing: H. Schneider, 1977.

HIRSCH, PAUL. *Katalog der Musikbibliothek Paul Hirsch.* Herausgegeben von Kathi Meyer und Paul Hirsch. Publication of the Paul Hirsch Music Library, 2d series: Catalogue of the Library, 1–4. 4 vols. Berlin: M. Breslauer; Frankfurt; Cambridge: At the University Press, 1928–47.

HOBOKEN, ANTHONY VAN. *Joseph Haydn: Thematisch-bibliographisches Werkverzeichnis.* 3 vols. Mainz: B. Schott's Söhne, 1957–78. [H.]

HOPKINSON, CECIL. *A Bibliography of the Works of C. W. von Gluck, 1714–1787.* London, 1959. [HopkinsonG]

HOPKINSON, CECIL. *A Dictionary of Parisian Music Publishers, 1700–1950.* London, 1954.

HUMPHRIES, CHARLES, and SMITH, WILLIAM C. *Music Publishing in the British Isles from the Beginning until the Middle of the Nineteenth Century: A Dictionary of Engravers, Printers, Publishers and Music Sellers, with a Historical Introduction.* 2d ed., with supplement. Oxford: B. Blackwell, 1970.

INTERNATIONAL ASSOCIATION OF MUSIC LIBRARIES, COMMISSION FOR BIBLIOGRAPHICAL RESEARCH. *Guide for Dating Early Published Music: A Manual of Bibliographical Practices.* Compiled by D. W. Krummel. Hackensack, N. J.: J. Boonin, 1974.

JOHANSSON, CARI. *French Music Publishers' Catalogues of the Second Half of the Eighteenth Century.* Publications of the Library of the Royal Swedish Academy of Music, 2. 2 vols. Stockholm, 1955. [JohanssonF]

JOHANNSON, CARI. *J. J. & B. Hummel Music-Publishing and Thematic Catalogues.* Publications of the Library of the Royal Swedish Academy of Music, 3. 2 vols. Stockholm, 1972. [JohanssonH]

KÖCHEL, LUDWIG VON. *Chronologisch-thematisches Verzeichnis sämtlicher Tonwerke Wolfgang Amadé Mozarts, nebst Angabe der verlorengegangenen, angefangenen, von fremder Hand bearbeiteten, zweifelhaften und unterschobenen Kompositionen.* 6th ed., edited by Franz Giegling, Alexander Weinmann and Gerd Sievers. Wiesbaden: Breitkopf & Härtel, 1964. [K.]

KRUMMEL, DONALD W. *English Music Printing, 1553–1700.* Bibliographical Society Publication for the Year 1971. London: The Bibliographical Society, 1975.

KRUMMEL, DONALD W. "Late 18th Century French Music Publishers' Catalogs in the Library of Congress," *Fontes artis musicae,* 7 (1960) : 61–64.

LANG, HELMUT W. *Die Buchdrucker des 15. bis 17. Jahrhunderts in Österreich, mit einer Bibliographie zur Geschichte des österreichischen Buchdrucks bis 1700.* Bibliotheca bibliographica Aureliana, 42. Baden-Baden: Koerner, 1972.

LEPREUX, GEORGES. *Gallia typographica; ou, Répertoire bibliographique et chronologique de tous les imprimeurs de France depuis les origines de l'imprimerie jusqu'à la révolution.* Revue des bibliothèques, supplement 1–3, 5, 7–8, 12. 7 vols. Paris: H. Champion, 1909–14.

LESURE, FRANÇOIS. *Bibliographie des éditions musicales publiées par Estienne Roger et Michel-Charles Le Cène (Amsterdam, 1696–1743).* Publications de la Société française de musicologie, 2d series, 12. Paris: Société française de musicologie, 1969. [LesureR]

LESURE, FRANÇOIS, and THIBAULT, GENEVIÈVE. *Bibliographie des éditions d'Adrian Le Roy et Robert Ballard (1551–1598).* Publications de la Société française de musicologie, 2d series, 9. Paris: Société française de musicologie, 1955. [LesureL]

LIBRARY OF CONGRESS, MUSIC DIVISION. *Catalogue of Early Books on Music (Before 1800).* By Julia Gregory. Washington, D. C.: Government Printing Office, 1913. [Gregory]

LOEWENBERG, ALFRED. *Annals of Opera, 1597–1940: Compiled from the Original Sources.* 3d ed., revised and corrected. Totowa, N.J.: Rowman and Littlefield, 1978.

The London Stage, 1660–1800: A Calendar of Plays, Entertainments & Afterpieces, together with Casts, Box-Receipts and Contemporary Comment, Compiled from the Playbills, Newspapers and Theatrical Diaries of the Period. 5 vols. Carbondale: Southern Illinois University Press, 1960–68.

[LOTTIN, AUGUSTIN MARTIN]. *Catalogue chronologie des libraires et des libraires-imprimeurs de Paris, depuis l'an 1470 . . . jusqu'à présent.* Paris: J. R. Lottin, 1789.

MCKENZIE, DONALD F., ED. *Stationers' Company Apprentices, 1701–1800.* Oxford Bibliographical Society. Publications, n.s., 19. Oxford: Oxford Bibliographical Society, 1978.

MCKERROW, RONALD B. *An Introduction to Bibliography for Literary Students.* Oxford: Clarendon Press, 1927.

MATTHÄUS, WOLFGANG. *Johann André Musikverlag zu Offenbach am Main: Verlagsgeschichte und Bibliographie, 1772–1800.* Tutzing: H. Schneider, 1973.

MILLIOT, SYLVETTE. "Une Couple de marchands de musique au XVIIIᵉ siècle: Les Boivin," *Revue de musicologie,* 54 (1968) : 105–113.

MORTIMER, RUTH, *see* HARVARD COLLEGE LIBRARY

MULLER, JEAN. *Dictionnaire abrégé des imprimeurs/éditeurs français du seizième siècle.* Bibliotheca bibliographica Aureliana, 30. Répertoire bibliographique des livres imprimés en France au seizième siècle, fascicule hors série. Baden-Baden: Heitz, 1970.

Die Musik in Geschichte und Gegenwart: Allgemeine Enzyklopädie der Musik. Unter Mitarbeit zahlreicher Musikforscher des In- und Auslandes herausgegeben von Friedrich Blume. 14 vols. & supplement (2 vols.). Kassel: Bärenreiter, 1949–.
[MGG]

PALLIER, DENIS. *Récherches sur l'imprimerie à Paris pendant la Ligue (1585–1594).* Centre de récherches d'histoire et de philologie de la IVᵉ section de l'Ecole pratique des hautes études, 6. Histoire et civilisation du livre, 9. Geneva: Droz, 1975.

PLOMER, HENRY R. *A Dictionary of the Printers and Booksellers who were at Work in England, Scotland and Ireland from 1668 to 1725.* Oxford: The Bibliographical Society, 1922.

PLOMER, HENRY R. *A Dictionary of the Printers and Booksellers who were at Work in England, Scotland and Ireland from 1726 to 1775.* Those in England by H. R. Plomer, Scotland by G. H. Bushnell, Ireland by E. R. McC. Dix. Oxford: The Bibliographical Society, 1932.

POŠTOLKA, MILAN. *Leopold Koželuh, život a dílo.* Prague: Státní hudební vydavatelství, 1964.
[P.]

Répertoire international des sources musicales. Series A I: *Einzeldrucke vor 1800.* Redaktion Karlheinz Schlager. 7 vols. (A–Schreyer). Kassel: Bärenreiter, 1971–.
[RISM A I]

Répertoire international des sources musicales. Series B I: *Recueils imprimés, XVIᵉ–XVIIᵉ siècles.* Ouvrage publié sous la direction de François Lesure. Munich: G. Henle, 1960.
[RISM B I]

Répertoire international des sources musicales. Series B II: *Recueils imprimés, XVIIIᵉ siècle.* Ouvrage publié sous la direction de François Lesure. Munich: G. Henle, 1964.
[RISM B II]

Répertoire international des sources musicales. Series B IV: *Écrits imprimés concernant la musique.* Ouvrage publié sous la direction de Francois Lesure. 2 vols. Munich: G. Henle, 1971.
[RISM B IV]

RHEINFURTH, HANS. *Der Musikverlag Lotter in Augsburg (ca. 1719–1845).* Musikbibliographische Arbeiten, 3. Tutzing: H. Schneider, 1977.

RYOM, PETER. *Antonio Vivaldi: Table de concordances des oeuvres (RV).* Copenhagen: Engstrøm & Sødring, 1973.

SARTORI, CLAUDIO. *Bibliografia della musica strumentale italiana stampata in Italia fino al 1700.* Biblioteca di bibliografia italiana, 23, 56. 2 vols. Florence: L. S. Olschki, 1952–68.
[SartoriB]

SARTORI, CLAUDIO. *Bibliografia delle opere musicali stampate da Ottaviano Petrucci.* Biblioteca di bibliografia italiana, 18. Florence: L. S. Olschki, 1948.
[SartoriP]

SARTORI, CLAUDIO. *Dizionario degli editori musicali italiani (tipografi, incisori, librai-editori).* Biblioteca di bibliografia italiana, 32. Florence: L. S. Olschki, 1958.
[SartoriD]

SCHNAPPER, EDITH B., ED. *The British Union-Catalogue of Early Music Printed before the Year 1801: A Record of the Holdings of over One Hundred Libraries throughout the British Isles.* 2 vols. London: Butterworths Scientific Publications, 1957.

SMITH, WILLIAM C. *A Bibliography of the Musical Works Published by John Walsh during the Years 1695–1720.* Bibliographical Society Publication for the Year 1941. London: The Bibliographical Society, 1948.   [Walsh I]

SMITH, WILLIAM C. *Handel: A Descriptive Catalogue of the Early Editions.* 2d ed., with supplement. Oxford: B. Blackwell, 1970.   [Smith]

SMITH, WILLIAM C., and HUMPHRIES, CHARLES. *A Bibliography of the Musical Works Published by the Firm of John Walsh during the Years 1721–1766.* Bibliographical Society Publication for the Year 1966. London: The Bibliographical Society, 1968.
                          [Walsh II]

STEELE, ROBERT. *The Earliest English Music Printing: A Description and Bibliography of English Printed Music to the Close of the Sixteenth Century.* Illustrated monographs, 11. London: The Bibliographical Society, 1903. Reprinted photographically with corrections. Meisenheim, Ger.: Hain, 1965.

STELLFELD, JEAN A. *Bibliographie des éditions musicales plantiniennes.* Académie royale de Belgique, Classes des beaux-arts. Mémoires, Collection in-8°, 5, fasc. 3. Brussels: Palais des académies, 1949.

STILLWELL, MARGARET BINGHAM. *Incunabula in American Libraries: A Second Census of Fifteenth-Century Books Owned in the United States, Mexico and Canada.* Monograph series, 1. New York: The Bibliographical Society of America, 1940.

TERRY, CHARLES SANFORD. *John Christian Bach.* London: Oxford University Press, 1929.

THIBAULT, GENEVIÈVE, and PERCEAU, LOUIS. *Bibliographie des poésies de P. de Ronsard mises en musique au XVIᵉ siècle.* Publications de la Société française de musicologie, 2d series, 8. Paris: E. Droz, 1941.

TODD, WILLIAM B. *A Directory of Printers and Others in Allied Trades, London and Vicinity, 1800–1840.* London: Printing Historical Society, 1972.

TYSON, ALAN. *Thematic Catalogue of the Works of Muzio Clementi.* Tutzing: H. Schneider, 1967.

VOGEL, EMIL, et al. *Bibliografia della musica italiana vocale profana pubblicata dal 1500 al 1700.* New ed., edited by François Lesure and Claudio Sartori. 3 vols. Pomezia: Staderini-Minkoff, 1977.

WALSH, *see under* SMITH

WEINMANN, ALEXANDER. *Die Wiener Verlagswerke von Franz Anton Hoffmeister.* Beiträge zur Geschichte des alt-Wiener Musikverlages, series 2, no. 8. Vienna: Universal, 1964.

WOTQUENNE, ALFRED. *Catalogue thématique des oeuvres de Charles Philippe Emmanuel Bach (1714–1788).* Leipzig: Breitkopf & Härtel, 1905.   [W.]

ZIMMERMAN, FRANKLIN B. *Henry Purcell, 1659–1695: An Analytical Catalogue of his Music.* London: Macmillan, 1963.

INDEX

C

E

H

M

N

O

P